WITHDRAWN

REFERENCE

Not to be taken from this room

A to ZOO
Subject Access to Children's Picture Books

A to ZOO
Subject Access to Children's Picture Books

● Carolyn W. Lima

R. R. BOWKER COMPANY
New York & London, 1982

81-1155

To My Husband, John

Published by
R. R. Bowker Company
1180 Avenue of the Americas
New York, N.Y. 10036
Copyright © 1982 by Xerox Corporation
All rights reserved
Printed and bound in the
United States of America

Illustrations by Ruth Karpes

**Library of Congress Cataloging
in Publication Data**

Lima, Carolyn W.
    A to zoo.

    Bibliography: p.
    Includes index.
    1. Picture-books for children—Bibliography.
2. Catalogs, Subject. I. Title.
Z1037.L715   [PN1009.A1]   011'.62   81-18018
ISBN 0-8352-1400-1   AACR2

Epigraph

"A picturebook is text, illustrations, total design; an item of manufacture and a commercial product; a social, cultural, historical document; and, foremost, an experience for a child.

"As an art form it hinges on the interdependence of pictures and words, on the simultaneous display of two facing pages, and on the drama of the turning of the page.

"On its own terms its possibilities are limitless."

Bader, Barbara. *American Picturebooks from Noah's Ark to the Beast Within.* New York: Macmillan, 1976, p. 1

Contents

Preface

The picture book, long a source of delight and learning for young readers, has gained even more importance during the past few years with the increase in emphasis on early childhood education and the growing need for supervised child care for working mothers. Teachers, librarians, and parents are finding the picture book to be an important learning and entertainment tool. But choosing the right book for a particular situation is time-consuming and frustrating without some guidance. The right book is more easily selected when the subject is defined as a specific, rather than simply choosing the first title that appears to treat the subject wanted from among the many thousands of books available.

It is no simple task to select the best book for any particular young reader, and many librarians, teachers, and parents do not have the time or materials to develop an intimate familiarity with the field. Consequently, it is hoped that *A to Zoo: Subject Access to Children's Picture Books*, the first published comprehensive guide of its kind, will provide the necessary help and make the task easier.

The titles in *A to Zoo* are based on the San Diego, California, Public Library's collection of picture books for children. This large and versatile collection is typical of the best and most carefully chosen children's works acquired over a period of time. The picture book, as broadly defined within the scope of this book, is a fiction or nonfiction title that has suitable vocabulary for preschoolers to grade two, with illustrations occupying as much or more space than the text.

How to Use This Book

A to Zoo can be used to obtain information about children's picture books in two principal ways: to learn the titles, authors, and illustrators of books on a particular subject, such as cavemen or magic; or to ascertain the subject (or subjects) when only the title, author and title, or illustrator and title are known. For example, if the title *I Will Not Go to Market Today* is known, this volume will enable the user to discover that *I Will Not Go to Market Today* is written by Harry Allard, illustrated by James Marshall, and published by Dial Press in 1979 and that it also concerns birds (chickens) and shopping.

For ease and convenience of reference use, *A to Zoo* is divided into five sections:

Subject Headings
Subject Guide
Bibliographic Guide
Title Index
Illustrator Index

SUBJECT HEADINGS: This section contains an alphabetical listing of the subjects cataloged in this book with cross-references. To facilitate reference use, and because subjects are requested in a variety of terms, the listing of subject headings contains cross-references. The numerical classification system, from 001 to 204 is *for use with this book only*. It does not replace the classification system in use with children's books in any library or school. Subheadings are arranged alphabetically under each general topic, for example:

008 Animals (general topic)
008.01 Animals—anteaters (subheading)
008.02 Animals—antelopes (subheading)

If the user wants books on the desert, this section will show that Desert is a subject classification having the number 041.

SUBJECT GUIDE: This subject-arranged guide to more than 4,400 picture books for preschool children through second graders is cataloged under 543 subjects. The guide reflects the arrangement in the Subject Headings, alphabetically arranged by subject heading and subheading, with corresponding classification numbers identifying each heading. Titles are listed alphabetically by author within each subject heading. Many books, of course, relate to more than one subject, and this comprehensive listing is meant to provide a means of identifying all those books that may contain information or material on a particular subject.

After finding that the desired subject "Desert" is listed in the Subject Headings section using the classification number 041, a look in the Subject Guide reveals that under 041 Desert are four titles listed by author in alphabetical order.

BIBLIOGRAPHIC GUIDE: This section gives bibliographic information for children's picture books included in this volume. It is arranged alphabetically by author or title when the author is unknown and contains bibliographic information in this order: author, title, illustrator, miscellaneous notes when given, publisher and date of publication, and subjects, listed according to numerical classification in the Subject Headings section. After finding that four titles are listed in the Subject Guide under the desired subject of Desert, this section will show the complete data for each of the four titles, as for example:

Caudill, Rebecca. *Wind, Sand and Sky*. Illus.
by Donald Carrick. New York: Dutton,
1976.
041 Desert; 134 Poetry, rhyme.

In the case of joint authors, the second author is listed in alphabetical order, with "jt. author" designation, title of book, and complete names of the book authors. The user can then locate the first-named author for complete bibliographic information. For example:

Ahlberg, Allan, jt. author. *Burglar Bill*. By
Janet Ahlberg, and Allan Ahlberg.

Bibliographic information for this title will be found in the Bibliographic Guide section under: Ahlberg, Janet, and Ahlberg, Allan.

Titles for an author who is both a single author and a joint author are interfiled alphabetically.

Where the author is not known, the entry is listed alphabetically by title with complete bibliographic information following the same format as given above.

For pseudonyms, bibliographic information is contained under the actual name of the author. For example, the pseudonym Aliki is listed in alphabetical order, but refers the user to Brandenberg, Aliki Liacouras.

TITLE INDEX: This section contains an alphabetical listing of all titles in the book with authors in parentheses, such as:

Wind, Sand and Sky (Rebecca Caudill)

If a title has no author, the name of the illustrator is given if available.

ILLUSTRATOR INDEX: This section contains an alphabetical listing of illustrators with titles and authors, such as:

Carrick, Donald. Wind, Sand and Sky (Rebecca Caudill)

When the author/illustrator is the same person, the name of the author is repeated parenthetically.

Introduction
Genesis of the English-Language Picture Book

Each year increasing numbers of children's books are published, each one touched in some way by those that preceded it. But how or by what path did the unique genre known as children's picture books arrive at this present and prolific state? Certainly, to imagine a time when children's books did not exist takes more than a little effort. Probably the roots of what we know as children's literature lie in the stories and folktales told and retold through the centuries in every civilization since humans first learned to speak. These stories were narrated over and over as a sort of oral history, literature, and education.[1] But they were not intended, either primarily or exclusively, for children. It was only through the passing years, as the children who were at least part of any audience responded with interest and delight to these tales, and as adults found less leisure time to be entertained in an increasingly busy world, that the stories and folktales came to be regarded as belonging to the world of the child.

Book art or book illustration began with manuscripts—handwritten on parchment or other materials, rolled or scrolled, and later loosely bound into books—that were illuminated or "decorated in lively, vigorous and versatile styles."[2] In time, these decorations, some realistic, some intricate, some imaginative, took on the technological advances of other art forms, notably stained glass, and color was introduced to these illustrated texts.[3]

The children's books that existed in the Middle Ages, before the invention of movable type, were rarely intended to amuse the reader. They were, instead, mostly instructional and moralizing. Monastic teachers, writing essentially for the children of wealthy families, usually wrote in Latin and "began the tradition of didacticism that was to dominate children's books for hundreds of years."[4]

Children's books of that day frequently followed either the rhymed format or the question-and-answer form, both attributed to Aldhelm, abbot of Malmesbury.[5] An early encyclopedia, thought to be the work of Anselm (1033–1109), archbishop of Canterbury, addressed such subjects as "manners and customs, natural science, children's duties, morals, and religious precepts."[6] The books were intended for instruction and indoctrination in the principles of moral and religious belief and behavior,[7] an intent that persisted even after the invention of movable type. Indeed, "children were not born to live happy but to die holy, and true education lay in preparing the soul to meet its maker."[8]

Perhaps the first printed book that was truly intended for children, other than elementary Latin grammar texts, was the French *Les Contenances de la Table*, on the courtesies and manners of dining.[9] Printed and illustrated children's books in Europe followed the invention of printing in the fifteenth century.

Those first books were printed in lowercase letters, and "blank spaces were left on the page for initials and marginal decorations to be added in color by hand. In general, the effect was the same as in manuscript."[10] Some well-known and important artists of the time did the illustrations, using woodcuts, engravings, and lithographic processes.[11]

This combination of pictures and printed text, still with the intent of teaching and incorporating the earlier, but persistent dedication to moral and religious education, finally resulted in what is often assumed to be the first real children's picture book, in 1657—the *Orbis Pictus* of John Amos Comenius.[12] The simple idea by this Czechoslovakian author was that a child would learn most quickly by naming and showing the object at the same time, a seventeenth-century ABC! Noted for its many illustrations, the book contained the seeds of future children's publications, softening somewhat the earlier "harshness with which, in the unsympathetic age, the first steps of learning were always associated."[13]

In the English language, children's books followed a parallel pattern. William Caxton is given credit for a legacy to young readers by publishing *Aesops' Fables* (about 1484).[14] His stories, the first for English children in their own language, gave the lessons of The Fox and the Grapes and The Tortoise and the Hare to children of the fifteenth century and all who followed thereafter.

Nearly 200 years later, American authors and books for American children, in English, began to appear. Like English publications before them, these books reflected a basic profile of moral and religious education. American John Cotton's *Spiritual Milk for Boston Babes* (1646) was not an especially easy text for the young minds that had to master its Puritan lessons. Later came similar books such as *Pilgrim's Progress* by John Bunyan (1678), *The New England Primer* with its rhyming alphabet (1691), and *Divine and Moral Songs for Children* by Isaac Watts (1715).

In the early eighteenth century, a significant movement began in English children's books with the publication of *Robinson Crusoe* by Daniel Defoe (1715), a narrative that delighted children as well as adults. This innovation, utilizing children's books to carry more intricate messages, perhaps aimed at adults as well as older children, reflected a growing sophistication of society, and perhaps some shifting of purely religious or moral bases toward political morality. An all-time favorite with young readers, *Gulliver's Travels* by Jonathan Swift, published in 1726, illustrates this dual thrust. This work, embellished with a wit and rather pointed sarcasm that is sure to escape the young, nonetheless delighted children with the inhabitants of mythical lands and has managed to survive through the years. Perhaps the ultimate development of this trend is found in Lewis Carroll's *Alice's Adventures in Wonderland* (1865), which manages to be perfectly palatable and interesting to children, yet contains subtle lessons for adult society. Although based on earlier plays and vignettes that had been written only for the purpose of entertainment and use of imagination, *Alice,* and other books of the time, began to reflect a change in society's view of children and of reading materials suitable for children.

The English translation of *Tales of Mother Goose* by Charles Perrault in 1729 made moral lessons for young readers less didactic, but it was 1744 that "saw the real foundation of something today everywhere taken for granted—the production of books for children's enjoyment."[15] This book from a small bookstall in London was *A Little Pretty Pocket-Book,* "now famous as the first book for children published by John Newbery"[16] and may indeed be the first book recognizing children as people with intelligence and other human needs, notably the need for humor and entertainment.[17]

For the next 20 years or so, Newbery published well-illustrated and inexpensive little books for young readers. Soon other books designed especially for children followed this trend. Pictures became an essential and integral part of the book, somewhat downplaying the soul-saving educational harshness of earlier books and promoting amusement and enlightened education. Thomas Bewick's first book specifically intended for children, *A Pretty Book of Pictures for Little Masters and Misses, or Tommy Trip's History of Beasts and Birds,* was published in 1779; and its particular effort represented major strides in the refinement of woodcuts used for book illustration. Bewick "developed better tools for this work, made effective use of the white line, and carried the woodcut to a new level of beauty."[18] His efforts and those of his brother John not only achieved a high level of artistic achievement for woodcuts, but had a more lasting effect on illustrators and illustrations for children's books. "An interesting by-product of the Bewicks' contribution is that artists of established reputation began to sign their pictures for children's books."[19] Some talented artists lovingly produced children's books with special artistic achievement, although their principal skills may have been directed toward adults. For example, William Blake, an artist and poet of considerable renown, published *Songs of Innocence* in 1789. "The artist wrote the verses, illustrated them, engraved, hand-colored, and bound the book."[20] The garlands and scrolls were lovingly engraved, and "he gave it color and beautifully drawn figures of people, especially children. The pictures are not realistic but delicate fantasies, almost dreamlike in character....But here are color and a tender perception of the artless grace of children."[21]

Such loving dedication did not long enjoy a singular place in publishing history. Before long commercialism entered the scene and, although some very dedicated people in America and England alike continued to develop books for children, some hackwork also appeared. "Publishers, realizing that children formed a new and somewhat undiscriminating market, were quick to take advantage of the fact. Having chosen a suitable title, and having available some spare woodcut blocks that might be sufficiently relevant for a juvenile book, a publisher would commission a story or series of tales to be woven around the illustrations. One of the results was that illustrations of different proportions might be used in the same story, while on other occasions it was clear that the pictures were by different artists. Sometimes the inclusion of a picture was obviously forced, such as the example that occurs in one of the editions of *Goody Two-Shoes,*" attributed to Oliver Goldsmith.[22]

Fortunately, the "hacks" did not totally invade the field of children's picture books. Carefully designed works, crafted with an eye toward the complete and final unit, with special consideration for the means of reproduction, appeared under the guidance of innovative and bold publishers. Beautiful printing became the mark of publishers such as Edmund Evans, printer and artist in his own right, who with his special skill in color engraving published the works of Walter Crane, Randolph Caldecott, and Kate Greenaway. "The work of the three great English picture-book artists of the nineteenth century represents the best to be found in picture books for children in any era; the strength of design and richness of color and detail of Walter Crane's pictures; the eloquence, humor, vitality, and movement of Randolph Caldecott's art; and the tenderness, dignity, and grace of the very personal interpretation of Kate Greenaway's enchanted land of childhood."[23]

These three were indeed great names of the century in the history of children's picture books. The first nursery picture books of Walter Crane, an apprentice wood engraver, were *Sing a Song for Sixpence, The House That Jack Built, Dame Trot and Her Comical Cat,* and *The History of Cock Robin and Jenny Wren,* published by the firm of Warne in 1865 and 1866. Crane was one of the first of the modern illustrators who believed that text and illustrations should be in harmony, forming a complete unit.

Randolph Caldecott, who began drawing at age six, could make animals seemingly come alive on a page. During his short life (1846–1886), he illustrated numerous books for children with fine examples of fun and good humor such as *The Diverting History of John Gilpin, The Babes in the Wood,* and many others from about 1877 until near his death.

Kate Greenaway's simple verses made an appropriate accompaniment to her lovely drawings. *Under the Window* was her first picture book published by Routledge in 1878. Everywhere in her books are the flowers she so loved. She is probably best known for her *Almanacs,* published between 1883 and 1897.

Like Crane, Caldecott, and Greenaway, the works of Beatrix Potter became as well known to American children as to English. Potter, a self-taught artist addicted to pets with charming characteristics, produced a number of tales for young children, the best known being *The Tale of Peter Rabbit* (1901), which presented the illustrations as an integral part of the story and marked a pivotal point in the development of the modern picture book in Europe.

The very excellence of the growing children's book field in England eclipsed the technologically inferior American product, virtually driving American efforts from the marketplace until nearly 15 years after World War I.[24] Meanwhile, the books of English artists such as Leslie Brook, Arthur Rackham, Edmund Dulac, Charles Folkard, and others continued the tradition of excellence through the first three decades of the twentieth century.

Despite the superior English publications, "a self-conscious and systematic concern for children and the books they read had been growing in the United States."[25] Children's libraries and children's librarians appeared around the turn of the century. In 1916, the Bookshop for Boys and Girls was founded in Boston.[26] In 1924 the Bookshop published *The Horn Book Magazine,* "the first journal in the world to be devoted to the critical appraisal of children's books."[27] Another publication, *Junior Libraries,* made its appearance in 1954; this periodical later became *School Library Journal,* published by R. R. Bowker. In this area, the Americans were ten years ahead of Europeans.

Publishers and editors were becoming more and more oriented toward children's literature. In 1919 Macmillan established a Children's Book Department to be separate from its adult publishing line; other publishing houses began to do the same. Children's Book Week was instituted, an idea that started with Franklin K. Mathiews and was supported by Frederic G. Melcher. A landmark in children's book publishing was established in the United States in 1922 when Melcher, then chief editor of *Publishers Weekly,* proposed at the 1921 American Library Association meeting, that a medal be awarded each year for the year's most distinguished contribution to American literature for children written by an American citizen or resident and published in the United States. Named for John Newbery, the medal was first awarded to Hendrik Willem van Loon for his book *The Story of Mankind.*

Melcher, who was always aware of the significance of books in the lives of children, later proposed the establishment of a similar award for picture books, named in honor of Randolph Caldecott whose pictures still delight today's children. Since 1938 the Caldecott Medal has been awarded annually by an awards committee of the American Library Association's Children's Services Division to the illustrator of the most distinguished American picture book for children published in the United States during the preceding year. Again, the recipient must reside in or be a citizen of the United States.

The end of the 1920s marked the newly emerging prominence of the modern children's picture book in America. Mainly imported from Europe until that time, children's picture books now began to be published in America. William Nicholson's *Clever Bill* (1927) was followed the next year by one of the most successful picture books of all time, *Millions of Cats* by Wanda Gág. The perfect marriage of the rhythmic prose and flowing movement of her dramatic black-and-white drawings tell a simple, direct story with a folk flavor. This title is still included in the repertoire of today's storytellers and continues to be taken from the shelves by young readers.

The explosion of children's book publishing became known as "The Golden Thirties."[28] By 1930, many publishers had set up separate editing departments expressly for the purpose of publishing children's materials. The White House Conference on Child Health and Protection was held that year to study the plight of the child.[29] Improved technologies accelerated and economized book production. The stage was set for the modern picture book with its profuse illustration. Until this time there were only a few great children's books, illustrated with pictures that were largely an extension of the text. "Yet in a very few years, in respect to the books for the younger children, the artist has attained a place of equal importance with the writer."[30]

The period between the two world wars brought many foreign authors and illustrators to America to join and collaborate with American authors and artists. Their talents and varied backgrounds have contributed immensely to the changes in the picture book in America, which truly came into its own in this period of lower production costs. The years of the 1930s and into the 1940s produced a spectacular number and variety of profusely illustrated books for young children.[31] The many new authors and illustrators then beginning their careers in this developing field of children's picture books have continued to keep their places in the hearts of children; such familiar names as Marjorie Flack, Maud and Miska Petersham, Ingri and Edgar d'Aulaire, Ludwig Bemelmans, Theodor Geisel (Dr. Seuss), Marcia Brown, Feodor Rojankovsky, James Daugherty, Robert Lawson, Marguerite de Angeli, Virginia Lee Burton, Robert McCloskey, and many, many more.

The war years of the mid-1940s affected the progress of children's picture books with shortages of materials, priorities, poor quality paper, narrow margins, inferior bindings, and less color and illustration. However, the postwar years began a boom in children's publishing, adding to the list of talented authors and illustrators such names as Maurice Sendak, Brian Wildsmith, Trina Schart Hyman, Paul Galdone, Leo Politi, Ezra Jack Keats, Gyo Fujikawa, Arnold Lobel, and so many more.

Through the years, many factors have contributed to the growth, even explosion, of children's picture books—society's changing attitudes toward the child; the development of children's libraries, awards, councils, and studies; increasing interest in children's reading on the part of publishers, educators, and literary critics; changing technologies; and the development of American artists and authors. Today the picture book is a part of growing up, a teaching tool, an entertainment medium, a memory to treasure. Perhaps only imagination and the talent of the artist and author can define its limits.

Professionalism, curiosity on all subjects, and freedom of expression have brought the children's picture book into the 1980s with a bewildering array of materials from which to choose. Imaginary animals of the past and future line the shelves with the cats, dogs, horses, and dolphins of the modern day. Fantasy lands compete with tales of spaceships and astronauts; dreams of the future can be found with the realities of the past; picture books of all kinds for all kinds of children—and adults—to enjoy!

For the teacher, librarian, or parent who wishes to open this fantastic world of color and imagination for the child, some tool is necessary to put oneself in touch with the great number of possibilities for enjoyment in the picture book field of today. *A to Zoo: Subject Access to Children's Picture Books* is designed with just this purpose in mind.

For those interested in exploring more deeply the world of children's publishing and the children's picture book, the following is a list of suggested titles for further reading.

Further Reading

Alderson, Brian. *Looking at Picture Books 1973*. Chicago: Children's Book Council, 1974.

*Arbuthnot, May Hill, and Sutherland, Zena. *Children and Books*, 4th ed. Glenview, Ill.: Scott, Foresman, 1972.

Arbuthnot, May Hill et al., *The Arbuthnot Anthology*, 4th ed. Glenview, Ill.: Scott, Foresman, 1976.

*Bader, Barbara. *American Picturebooks from Noah's Ark to the Beast Within*. New York: Macmillan, 1976.

Barchilon, Jacques, and Pettit, Henry. *The Authentic Mother Goose Fairy Tales and Nursery Rhymes*. Athens, Ohio: Swallow Press, 1960.

Barry, Florence V. *A Century of Children's Books*. London: Methuen, 1922.

Bland, David. *A History of Book Illustration*, 2nd ed. London: Faber & Faber, 1969.

———. *The Illustration of Books*. London: Faber & Faber, 1962.

Bodger, Joan. *How the Heather Looks*. New York: Viking, 1965.

Braun, Saul. "Sendak Raises the Shade on Childhood." *New York Times Magazine*, June 7, 1970, p. 34+.

Cianciola, Patricia. *Illustrations in Children's Books*. Dubuque, Iowa: William C. Brown, 1970.

Comenius, John Amos. *The Orbis Pictus of John Amos Comenius*. Detroit: Singing Tree, 1968.

*Indicates especially recommended titles in this reading list.

Crouch, Marcus. *Treasure Seekers and Borrowers: Children's Books in Britain 1900–1960*. London: Library Association, 1962.

Darling, Richard L. *The Rise of Children's Book Reviewing in America, 1865–1881*. New York: Bowker, 1968.

Darton, F. J. H. *Children's Books in England: Five Centuries of Social Life*, 2nd ed. New York: Cambridge Univ. Press, 1958.

Duvoisin, Roger. "Children's Book Illustration: The Pleasure and Problems." *Top of the News* 22: 30 (Nov. 1965).

Earle, Alice Morse. *Child Life in Colonial Days*. New York: Macmillan, 1899.

Eckenstein, Lina. *Comparative Studies in Nursery Rhymes*. London: Duckworth, 1906; Detroit: Singing Tree, 1968.

Egoff, Sheila; Stubbs, G. T.; and Ashley, L. F., eds. *Only Connect: Readings on Children's Literature*. New York: Oxford Univ. Press, 1969.

Ellis, Alec. *A History of Children's Reading and Literature*. Elmsford, N.Y.: Pergamon Press, 1968.

Eyre, Frank. *British Children's Books in the Twentieth Century*. New York: Dutton, 1973.

———. *Twentieth Century Children's Books*. Cambridge, Mass.: Robert Bentley, 1953.

Field, Louise F. *The Child and His Book: Some Account of the History and Progress of Children's Literature in England*. Detroit: Singing Tree, 1968.

Fisher, Margery Turner. *Intent upon Reading: A Critical Appraisal of Modern Fiction for Children*. Leicester, England: Brockhampton Press, 1961.

Fox, Geoffrey Percival, and others, eds. *Writers, Critics, and Children: Articles from Children's Literature in Education*. New York: Agathon Press, 1976.

*Freeman, Ruth Sunderlin. *Children's Picture Books, Yesterday and Today*. Watkins Glen, N.Y.: Century House, 1967.

Gillespie, Margaret C., and Conner, John W. *Creative Growth Through Literature for Children and Adolescents*. Columbus, Ohio: Merrill, 1975.

Gottlieb, Gerald. *Early Children's Books and Their Illustration*. Boston: Godine, 1975.

Green, Percy B. *A History of Nursery Rhymes*. Detroit: Singing Tree, 1968.

Green, Roger Lancelyn. *Tellers of Tales: British Authors of Children's Books from 1800 to 1964*. New York: Watts, 1965.

*Greenaway, Kate. *The Kate Greenaway Treasury*. Cleveland: World, 1967.

Halsey, Rosalie V. *Forgotten Books of the American Nursery*. Detroit: Singing Tree, 1969.

*Haviland, Virginia. *Children and Literature: Views and Reviews*. New York: Lothrop, 1973.

———. *Children's Literature: A Guide to Reference Sources*. Washington, D.C.: Library of Congress, 1966.

Huber, Miriam Blanton. *Story and Verse for Children*. New York: Macmillan, 1965.

*Hürlimann, Bettina. *Three Centuries of Children's Books in Europe*. Ed. and trans. Brian Alderson. London: Oxford Univ. Press, 1967.

James, Philip. *Children's Books of Yesterday*. Ed. C. Geoffrey Holme. London and New York: Studio, 1933.

Jan, Isabelle. *On Children's Literature*. Ed. Catherine Storr. New York: Schocken Books, 1974.

Kiefer, Monica. *American Children Through Their Books, 1700–1835*. Philadelphia: Univ. of Pennsylvania Press, 1948, 1970.

Klemin, Diana. *The Illustrated Book*. New York: Potter, 1970.

Lanes, Selma G. "The Art of Maurice Sendak: A Diversity of Influences Inform an Art for Children." *Artforum* IX (May 1971): 70–73.

Leif, Irving P. *Children's Literature: A Historical and Contemporary Bibliography*. Troy, N.Y.: Whitston, 1977.

Lewis, John. *Twentieth Century Book: Its Illustration and Design*. New York: Reinhold, 1967.

Lukens, Rebecca J. *A Critical Handbook of Children's Literature*. Glenview, Ill.: Scott, Foresman, 1976.

*MacCann, Donnarae, and Richard, Olga. *The Child's First Books*. New York: Wilson, 1973.

Mahony, Bertha E.; Latimer, Louise P.; and Folmsbee, Beulah, comps. *Illustrators of Children's Books, 1744–1945*. Boston: Horn Book, 1947.

*Meigs, Cornelia; Eaton, Anne; Nesbitt, Elizabeth; and Viguers, Ruth Hill. *A Critical History of Children's Literature.* New York: Macmillan, 1953; rev. ed., 1969.

Moore, Anne Carroll. *My Roads to Childhood.* New York: Doubleday, 1939.

Muir, Percy. *English Children's Books, 1600–1900.* New York: Praeger, 1969.

*Newbery, John. *A Little Pretty Pocket-Book: A Facsimile.* London: Oxford Univ. Press, 1966.

Opie, Iona, and Opie, Peter. *A Family Book of Nursery Rhymes.* New York: Oxford Univ. Press, 1964.

———. *The Oxford Dictionary of Nursery Rhymes.* New York: Oxford Univ. Press, 1951.

The Original Mother Goose's Melody, As First Issued by John Newbery, of London, about A.D. 1760. Reproduced in facsimile from the edition as reprinted by Isaiah Thomas of Worcester, Mass., about A.D. 1785, with introductory notes by William H. Whitmore. Detroit: Singing Tree, 1969.

Pitz, Henry C. *Illustrating Children's Books: History, Techniques, Production.* New York: Watson-Guptill, 1963.

Quayle, Eric. *The Collector's Book of Children's Books.* New York: Potter, 1971.

Richard, Olga. "The Visual Language of the Picture Book." *Wilson Library Bulletin* (Dec. 1969).

Rosenbach, Abraham S. W. *Early American Children's Books with Bibliographical Descriptions of the Books in His Private Collection.* Foreword by A. Edward Newton. Portland, Maine: Southworth Press, 1933.

Sadker, Myra, and Sadker, David Miller. *Now Upon a Time: A Contemporary View of Children's Literature.* New York: Harper, 1977.

Salway, Lance, ed. *A Peculiar Gift.* New York: Penguin, 1976.

Sendak, Maurice. "Mother Goose's Garnishings." *Book Week.* Fall Children's Issue (Oct. 31, 1965): 5, 38–40; also printed in Haviland, *Children and Literature,* pp. 188–195.

Smith, Dora V. *Fifty Years of Children's Books.* Urbana, Ill.: National Council of Teachers of English, 1963.

*Sutherland, Zena, and Arbuthnot, May Hill. *Children and Books,* 5th ed. Glenview, Ill.: Scott, Foresman, 1977.

Targ, William, ed. *Bibliophile in the Nursery.* New York: World, 1969.

Thomas, Katherine Elwes. *The Real Personages of Mother Goose.* New York: Lothrop, 1930.

Thwaite, Mary. *From Primer to Pleasure in Reading,* 2nd ed. London: The Library Association, 1972.

Townsend, John Rowe. *Written for Children: An Outline of English Children's Literature,* rev. ed. New York: Lothrop, 1974.

Viguers, Ruth Hill; Dalphin, Marcia; and Miller, Bertha Mahony, comps. *Illustrators of Children's Books, 1946–1956.* Boston: Horn Book, 1958.

Weitenkampf, Frank. *The Illustrated Book.* Cambridge, Mass.: Harvard Univ. Press, 1938.

Welch, D'Alte. *A Bibliography of American Children's Books Printed Prior to 1821.* Worcester, Mass.: American Antiquarian Society, 1972.

*Whalley, Joyce Irene. *Cobwebs to Catch Flies: Illustrated Books for the Nursery and Schoolroom 1700–1900.* Berkeley: Univ. of California Press, 1975.

White, Dorothy M. Neal. *Books Before Five.* New York: Oxford Univ. Press, 1954.

White, Mary Lou. *Children's Literature: Criticism and Response.* Columbus, Ohio: Merrill, 1976.

*Wilkin, Binnie Tate. *Survival Themes in Fiction for Children and Young People.* Metuchen, N.J.: Scarecrow, 1978.

Notes

1. Caroline M. Hewins, "The History of Children's Books (1888)," in *Children and Literature: Views and Reviews,* ed. Virginia Haviland (New York: Lothrop, 1973), p. 30.

2. Donnarae MacCann and Olga Richard, *The Child's First Books: A Critical Study of Pictures and Texts* (New York: Wilson, 1973), p. 11.

3. Ibid.

4. Zena Sutherland and May Hill Arbuthnot, *Children and Books,* 5th ed. (Glenview, Ill.: Scott, Foresman, 1977), p. 37.

5. Ibid.

6. Ibid.

7. Ibid.

8. Bettina Hürlimann, *Three Centuries of Children's Books in Europe,* trans. and ed. Brian Alderson (London: Oxford Univ. Press, 1967), p. xii.

9. Sutherland and Arbuthnot, *Children and Books,* p. 37.

10. MacCann and Richard, *The Child's First Books,* p. 11.

11. Ibid.

12. Hürlimann, *Three Centuries,* pp. 127–129.

13. Ruth Sunderlin Freeman, *Children's Picture Books, Yesterday and Today* (Watkins Glen, N.Y.: Century House, 1967), p. 12.

14. May Hill Arbuthnot and Zena Sutherland, *Children and Books,* 4th ed. (Glenview, Ill.: Scott, Foresman, 1972), p. 52.

15. John Newbery, *A Little Pretty Pocket-Book: A Facsimile* (London: Oxford Univ. Press, 1966), p. 2.

16. Ibid., p. 3.

17. Ibid., p. 2.

18. Arbuthnot and Sutherland, *Children and Books,* pp. 53–54.

19. Ibid., p. 54.

20. Ibid.

21. Ibid.

22. Joyce Irene Whalley, *Cobwebs to Catch Flies: Illustrated Books for the Nursery and Schoolroom 1700–1900* (Berkeley: Univ. of California Press, 1975), p. 14.

23. Ruth Hill Viguers, "Introduction," in Kate Greenaway, *The Kate Greenaway Treasury* (Cleveland: World, 1967), p. 13.

24. Barbara Bader, *American Picturebooks from Noah's Ark to the Beast Within* (New York: Macmillan, 1976), p. 7.

25. Viguers, "Introduction," p. 39.

26. Ibid.

27. Ibid.

28. Sutherland and Arbuthnot, *Children and Books,* p. 122.

29. Binnie Tate Wilkin, *Survival Themes in Fiction for Children and Young People* (Metuchen, N.J.: Scarecrow, 1978), p. 21.

30. Cornelia Meigs, Anne Eaton, Elizabeth Nesbitt, and Ruth Hill Viguers, *A Critical History of Children's Literature* (New York: Macmillan, 1953), p. 587.

31. Ibid., p. 438.

Subject Headings

In this alphabetical subject list, main headings are boldface, subheads lightface, with a numerical classification system from 001 to 204. Subheads carry number assigned to *main* heading in sequential order, e.g., the number for **Activities** is **002**. Subheadings appear as 002.01 Activities—babysitting; 002.02 Activities—bathing, etc.

001	**ABC Books**
002	**Activities**
002.01	Activities—babysitting
002.02	Activities—bathing
002.03	Activities—cooking
002.04	Activities—dancing
002.05	Activities—flying
002.06	Activities—gardening
002.07	Activities—jumping
002.08	Activities—knitting
002.09	Activities—painting
002.10	Activities—photographing
002.11	Activities—picnicking
002.12	Activities—playing
002.13	Activities—reading
002.14	Activities—swinging
002.15	Activities—trading
002.16	Activities—traveling
002.17	Activities—vacationing
002.18	Activities—walking
002.19	Activities—whistling
002.20	Activities—working
002.21	Activities—writing
003	**Adoption**
	Africa. *See* Foreign Lands—Africa
	Afro-Americans. *See* Ethnic groups in the U.S.—Afro-Americans
	Age, old. *See* Old age
	Airplane pilots. *See* Careers—airplane pilots
004	**Airplanes**
	Albatrosses. *See* Birds—albatrosses
	Alligators. *See* Reptiles—alligators, crocodiles
	Ambition. *See* Character traits—ambition
005	**Amphibians**
006	**Anatomy**
007	**Angels**
	Anger. *See* Emotions—anger
008	**Animals**
008.01	Animals—anteaters
008.02	Animals—antelopes
	Animals—apes. *See* Animals—gorillas; Animals—monkeys
008.03	Animals—armadillos
008.04	Animals—badgers

008.05	Animals—bats
008.06	Animals—bears
008.07	Animals—beavers
	Animals—bulls. *See* Animals—cows, bulls
008.08	Animals—camels
008.09	Animals—cats
008.10	Animals—cats, wild
008.11	Animals—chipmunks
008.12	Animals—cows, bulls
008.13	Animals—deer
008.14	Animals—dogs
008.15	Animals—dolphins
008.16	Animals—donkeys
008.17	Animals—elephants
008.18	Animals—foxes
008.19	Animals—gerbils
008.20	Animals—giraffes
008.21	Animals—goats
008.22	Animals—gorillas
008.23	Animals—groundhogs
008.24	Animals—guinea pigs
008.25	Animals—hamsters
	Animals—hares. *See* Animals—rabbits
008.26	Animals—hedgehogs
008.27	Animals—hippopotami
008.28	Animals—horses
008.29	Animals—hyenas
008.30	Animals—kangaroos
008.31	Animals—kinkajous
008.32	Animals—koala bears
	Animals—leopards. *See* Animals—cats, wild
008.33	Animals—llamas
008.34	Animals—mice
008.35	Animals—moles
008.36	Animals—mongooses
008.37	Animals—monkeys
008.38	Animals—moose
008.39	Animals—muskrats
008.40	Animals—otters
008.41	Animals—pack rats
	Animals—panthers. *See* Animals—cats, wild
008.42	Animals—pigs
008.43	Animals—porcupines

008.44 Animals—possums
008.45 Animals—prairie dogs
008.46 Animals—rabbits
008.47 Animals—raccoons
008.48 Animals—rats. *See also* Animals—
  pack rats
008.49 Animals—rhinoceros
008.50 Animals—sea lions
008.51 Animals—seals
008.52 Animals—sheep
008.53 Animals—skunks
008.54 Animals—sloths
008.55 Animals—snails
008.56 Animals—squirrels
008.57 Animals—tapirs
  Animals—tigers. *See* Animals—cats,
  wild
008.58 Animals—walruses
008.59 Animals—weasels
008.60 Animals—whales
008.61 Animals—wolves
008.62 Animals—worms
  Animals, dislike of. *See* Behavior—
  animals, dislike of
009 **Animals—endangered**
  Anteaters. *See* Animals—anteaters
  Antelopes. *See* Animals—antelopes
  Anti-violence. *See* Violence, anti-
  violence
  Ants. *See* Insects and spiders
  Apes. *See* Animals—gorillas;
  Animals—monkeys
  Appearance. *See* Character traits—
  appearance
  April Fools' Day. *See* Holidays—
  April Fools' Day
010 **Arctic**
  Arguing. *See* Behavior—fighting,
  arguing
  Armadillos. *See* Animals—
  armadillos
011 **Art**
  Artists. *See* Careers—artists
  Australia. *See* Foreign lands—
  Australia
  Austria. *See* Foreign lands—Austria
  Authors—children. *See* Children as
  authors
012 **Automobiles**

013 **Babies**
  Babysitting. *See* Activities—
  babysitting
  Bad day. *See* Behavior—bad day
  Badgers. *See* Animals—badgers
  Bakers. *See* Careers—bakers
  Balloons. *See* Toys—balloons
  Balls. *See* Toys—balls
014 **Barns**
  Barons. *See* Royalty
  Baseball. *See* Sports—baseball

Basketball. *See* Sports—basketball
Bathing. *See* Activities—bathing
Bats. *See* Animals—bats
Beach. *See* Sea and seashore
Bears. *See* Animals—bears
Beavers. *See* Animals—beavers
015 **Bedtime**
Bees. *See* Insects and spiders
016 **Behavior**
016.01 Behavior—animals, dislike of
016.02 Behavior—bad day
016.03 Behavior—boasting
016.04 Behavior—boredom
016.05 Behavior—bullying
016.06 Behavior—carelessness
016.07 Behavior—copying
016.08 Behavior—disbelief
016.09 Behavior—dissatisfaction
016.10 Behavior—fighting, arguing
016.11 Behavior—forgetfulness
016.12 Behavior—gossip
016.13 Behavior—greed
016.14 Behavior—growing up
016.15 Behavior—hiding
016.16 Behavior—hiding things
016.17 Behavior—hurrying
016.18 Behavior—indifference
016.19 Behavior—losing things
016.20 Behavior—lost
016.21 Behavior—lying
016.22 Behavior—misbehavior
016.23 Behavior—mistakes
016.24 Behavior—misunderstanding
016.25 Behavior—nagging
016.26 Behavior—needing someone
016.27 Behavior—running away
016.28 Behavior—saving things
016.29 Behavior—secrets
016.30 Behavior—seeking better things
016.31 Behavior—sharing
016.32 Behavior—sibling rivalry. *See also*
  Emotions—envy, jealousy
016.33 Behavior—solitude
016.34 Behavior—stealing
016.35 Behavior—talking to strangers
016.36 Behavior—trickery
016.37 Behavior—unnoticed, unseen
016.38 Behavior—wishing
016.39 Behavior—worrying
  Being different. *See* Character
  traits—being different
  Bicycling. *See* Sports—bicycling
017 **Birds**
017.01 Birds—albatrosses
017.02 Birds—buzzards
017.03 Birds—canaries
017.04 Birds—chickens
017.05 Birds—cockatoos
017.06 Birds—crows
017.07 Birds—doves
017.08 Birds—ducks
017.09 Birds—eagles

017.10 Birds—flamingos
017.11 Birds—geese
Birds—gulls. *See* Birds—sea gulls
017.12 Birds—hawks
Birds—hens. *See* Birds—chickens
017.13 Birds—ostriches
017.14 Birds—owls
017.15 Birds—parrots, parakeets
017.16 Birds—peacocks, peahens
017.17 Birds—pelicans
017.18 Birds—penguins
017.19 Birds—pigeons
017.20 Birds—robins
Birds—roosters. *See* Birds—chickens
017.21 Birds—sandpipers
017.22 Birds—sea gulls
017.23 Birds—sparrows
017.24 Birds—storks
017.25 Birds—swans
017.26 Birds—turkeys
017.27 Birds—vultures
017.28 Birds—woodpeckers
017.29 Birds—wrens
018 **Birthdays**
Blindness. *See* Handicaps—blindness
Blocks. *See* Toys—blocks
Boasting. *See* Behavior—boasting
019 **Boats, ships**
Boredom. *See* Behavior—boredom
Bravery. *See* Character traits—bravery
020 **Bridges**
Brothers. *See* Behavior—sibling rivalry; Family life
Brownies. *See* Elves and little people
Bugs. *See* Insects and spiders
Bulls. *See* Animals—cows, bulls
Bullying. *See* Behavior—bullying
Burros. *See* Animals—donkeys
021 **Buses**
Butterflies. *See* Insects and spiders
Buzzards. *See* Birds—buzzards

Cab drivers. *See* Careers—taxi drivers
Cabs. *See* Careers—taxi drivers; Taxis
022 **Cable cars**
Camels. *See* Animals—camels
Camping. *See* Sports—camping
Canada. *See* Foreign lands—Canada
Canaries. *See* Birds—canaries
023 **Careers**
023.01 Careers—airplane pilots
023.02 Careers—artists
023.03 Careers—bakers
023.04 Careers—barbers

Careers—cab drivers. *See* Careers—taxi drivers
023.05 Careers—carpenters
023.06 Careers—clockmakers
Careers—cooks. *See* Careers—bakers
023.07 Careers—dentists
023.08 Careers—detectives
023.09 Careers—doctors
023.10 Careers—firefighters
023.11 Careers—fishermen
023.12 Careers—fortune tellers
023.13 Careers—garbage collectors
023.14 Careers—judges
023.15 Careers—maids
023.16 Careers—mail carriers
023.17 Careers—military
023.18 Careers—nuns
023.19 Careers—nurses
023.20 Careers—peddlers
Careers—physicians. *See* Careers—doctors
Careers—pilots. *See* Careers—airplane pilots
023.21 Careers—police officers
023.22 Careers—railroad engineers
023.23 Careers—seamstresses
023.24 Careers—shoemakers
023.25 Careers—tailors
023.26 Careers—taxi drivers
023.27 Careers—teachers
023.28 Careers—telephone operators
023.29 Careers—truck drivers
023.30 Careers—veterinarians
023.31 Careers—window cleaners
Carelessness. *See* Behavior—carelessness
Caribbean Islands. *See* Foreign lands—Caribbean Islands
Carousels. *See* Merry-go-rounds
Carpenters. *See* Careers—carpenters
Cats. *See* Animals—cats
Cats, wild. *See* Animals—cats, wild
024 **Cavemen**
025 **Caves**
026 **Character traits**
026.01 Character traits—ambition
026.02 Character traits—appearance
026.03 Character traits—being different
026.04 Character traits—bravery
026.05 Character traits—cleanliness
026.06 Character traits—cleverness
026.07 Character traits—completing things
026.08 Character traits—compromising
026.09 Character traits—conceit
Character traits—cruelty to animals. *See* Character traits—kindness to animals
026.10 Character traits—curiosity
026.11 Character traits—flattery

026.12 Character traits—freedom
026.13 Character traits—generosity
026.14 Character traits—helpfulness
026.15 Character traits—honesty
026.16 Character traits—individuality
026.17 Character traits—kindness
026.18 Character traits—kindness to animals
026.19 Character traits—laziness
Character traits—littleness. See Character traits—smallness
026.20 Character traits—loyalty
026.21 Character traits—luck
026.22 Character traits—meanness
026.23 Character traits—optimism
Character traits—ostracism. See Character traits—being different
026.24 Character traits—patience
026.25 Character traits—perseverance
026.26 Character traits—practicality
026.27 Character traits—pride
026.28 Character traits—questioning
026.29 Character traits—selfishness
026.30 Character traits—shyness
026.31 Character traits—smallness
Chickens. See Birds—chickens
027 **Children as authors**
China. See Foreign lands—China
Chinese-Americans. See Ethnic groups in the U.S.—Chinese-Americans
Chinese New Year. See Holidays—Chinese New Year
Chipmunks. See Animals—chipmunks
Christmas. See Holidays—Christmas
028 **Circus, clowns.** See also Jesters
029 **City**
Cleanliness. See Character traits—cleanliness
Cleverness. See Character traits—cleverness
Clockmakers. See Careers—clockmakers
030 **Clocks.** See also Time
031 **Clothing**
Clouds. See Weather—clouds
Clowns. See Circus, clowns; Jesters
Clubs. See Gangs, clubs
Cockatoos. See Birds—cockatoos
Codes. See Secret codes
Cold. See Weather—cold
Color. See Concepts—color
Communication. See Language; Letters; Telephone
Computers. See Machines
Completing things. See Character traits—completing things
Compromising. See Character traits—compromising

Conceit. See Character traits—conceit
032 **Concepts**
032.01 Concepts—color
Concepts—counting. See Counting
032.02 Concepts—distance
032.03 Concepts—in and out
032.04 Concepts—left and right
032.05 Concepts—measurement
Concepts—numbers. See Counting
032.06 Concepts—opposites
Concepts—self. See Self-concept
032.07 Concepts—shape
032.08 Concepts—size
032.09 Concepts—speed
032.10 Concepts—up and down
032.11 Concepts—weight
Conservation. See Ecology
Cooking. See Activities—cooking
Cooks. See Careers—bakers
Copying. See Behavior—copying
Coral Islands. See Foreign lands—South Sea Islands
033 **Counting**
034 **Country**
035 **Cowboys**
Cows. See Animals—cows, bulls
Crabs. See Crustacea
Creatures. See Goblins; Monsters
Crickets. See Insects and spiders
036 **Crime**
Crippled. See Handicaps
Crocodiles. See Reptiles—alligators, crocodiles
Crows. See Birds—crows
Cruelty to animals. See Character traits—kindness to animals
037 **Crustacea**
038 **Cumulative tales**
Curiosity. See Character traits—curiosity
Currency. See Money
Cycles. See Motorcycles; Sports—bicycling
Czechoslovakia. See Foreign lands—Czechoslovakia

Dancing. See Activities—dancing
Dark. See Night
Dawn. See Morning
039 **Days of the week, months of the year**
Deafness. See Handicaps—deafness
040 **Death**
Deer. See Animals—deer
Demons. See Devil; Monsters
Denmark. See Foreign lands—Denmark
Dentists. See Careers—dentists
Department stores. See Shopping; Stores

041	**Desert**
	Detective stories. *See* Problem solving
	Detectives. *See* Careers—detectives
042	**Devil**
043	**Dictionaries**
044	**Dinosaurs**
	Disbelief. *See* Behavior—disbelief
	Dissatisfaction. *See* Behavior—dissatisfaction
	Distance. *See* Concepts—distance
	Diving. *See* Sports—skin diving
045	**Divorce**
	Doctors. *See* Careers—doctors
	Dogs. *See* Animals—dogs
	Dolls. *See* Toys—dolls
	Dolphins. *See* Animals—dolphins
	Donkeys. *See* Animals—donkeys
	Doves. *See* Birds—doves
	Down and up. *See* Concepts—up and down
046	**Dragons**
	Dragonflies. *See* Insects and spiders
	Drawing games. *See* Games
047	**Dreams**
	Ducks. *See* Birds—ducks
	Dwarfs. *See* Elves and little people
	Dying. *See* Death
	Eagles. *See* Birds—eagles
	Ears. *See* Anatomy
048	**Earth**
	Easter. *See* Holidays—Easter
	Eating. *See* Food
049	**Ecology**
	Education. *See* School
050	**Eggs**
	Egypt. *See* Foreign lands—Africa; Foreign lands—Egypt
	Elephants. *See* Animals—elephants
051	**Elves and little people.** *See also* Fairies
	Embarrassment. *See* Emotions—embarrassment
	Emergencies. *See* Hospitals
052	**Emotions**
052.01	Emotions—anger
052.02	Emotions—embarrassment
052.03	Emotions—envy, jealousy. *See also* Behavior—sibling rivalry
052.04	Emotions—fear
052.05	Emotions—happiness
052.06	Emotions—hate
	Emotions—jealousy. *See* Emotions—envy, jealousy
052.07	Emotions—loneliness
052.08	Emotions—love
052.09	Emotions—sadness
	Emotions—unhappiness. *See* Emotions—happiness; Emotions—sadness

	Emperors. *See* Royalty
	Endangered animals. *See* Animals—endangered
	England. *See* Foreign lands—England
	Entertainment. *See* Theater
	Envy. *See* Emotions—envy, jealousy
	Eskimos. *See* Ethnic groups in the U.S.—Eskimos
053	**Ethnic groups in the U.S.**
053.01	Ethnic groups in the U.S.—Afro-Americans
053.02	Ethnic groups in the U.S.—Chinese-Americans
053.03	Ethnic groups in the U.S.—Eskimos
053.04	Ethnic groups in the U.S.—Indians
053.05	Ethnic groups in the U.S.—Japanese-Americans
053.06	Ethnic groups in the U.S.—Mexican-Americans
053.07	Ethnic groups in the U.S.—Multi-ethnic
	Ethnic groups in the U.S.—Native Americans. *See* Ethnic groups in the U.S.—Eskimos; Ethnic groups in the U.S.—Indians
053.08	Ethnic groups in the U.S.—Puerto Rican-Americans
054	**Etiquette**
	Evening. *See* Night; Twilight
	Experiments. *See* Science
	Eyes. *See* Anatomy
	Faces. *See* Anatomy
055	**Fairies**
	Fairy tales. *See* Folk and fairy tales
056	**Fairs**
	Fall. *See* Seasons—fall
057	**Family life**
	Family life—brothers. *See* Behavior—sibling rivalry; Family life
057.01	Family life—fathers
057.02	Family life—grandparents; great-grandparents
057.03	Family life—mothers
057.04	Family life—the only child
	Family life—sisters. *See* Behavior—sibling rivalry; Family life
	Family life—stepparents, stepchildren. *See* Divorce
058	**Farms**
	Fathers. *See* Family life—fathers
	Fear. *See* Emotions—fear
	Feelings. *See* Emotions
	Feet. *See* Anatomy
	Fighting. *See* Behavior—fighting, arguing
	Fingers. *See* Anatomy

Finishing things. *See* Character traits—completing things

059 Fire
Fire engines. *See* Careers—firefighters; Trucks
Firefighters. *See* Careers—firefighters
Fireflies. *See* Insects and spiders

060 Fish
Fishermen. *See* Careers—fishermen
Fishing. *See* Careers—fishermen; Sports—fishing
Flamingos. *See* Birds—flamingos
Flattery. *See* Character traits—flattery
Flies. *See* Insects and spiders

061 Flowers. *See also* Plants
Flying. *See* Activities—flying

062 Folk and fairy tales

063 Food
Football. *See* Sports—football
Fog. *See* Weather—fog

064 Foreign lands
064.01 Foreign lands—Africa. *See also* Foreign lands—Egypt
064.02 Foreign lands—Australia
064.03 Foreign lands—Austria
064.04 Foreign lands—Canada
064.05 Foreign lands—Caribbean Islands
064.06 Foreign lands—China
064.07 Foreign lands—Czechoslovakia
064.08 Foreign lands—Denmark
064.09 Foreign lands—Egypt. *See also* Foreign lands—Africa
064.10 Foreign lands—England
064.11 Foreign lands—France
064.12 Foreign lands—Germany
064.13 Foreign lands—Greece
064.14 Foreign lands—Holland
064.15 Foreign lands—Hungary
064.16 Foreign lands—India
064.17 Foreign lands—Ireland
064.18 Foreign lands—Italy
064.19 Foreign lands—Japan
064.20 Foreign lands—Korea
064.21 Foreign lands—Lapland
064.22 Foreign lands—Lithuania
064.23 Foreign lands—Malaysia
064.24 Foreign lands—Mexico
064.25 Foreign lands—Norway
064.26 Foreign lands—Pakistan
064.27 Foreign lands—Poland
064.28 Foreign lands—Portugal
064.29 Foreign lands—Puerto Rico
064.30 Foreign lands—Russia
064.31 Foreign lands—Scotland
Foreign lands—Siam. *See* Foreign lands—Thailand
064.32 Foreign lands—South America
064.33 Foreign lands—South Sea Islands
064.34 Foreign lands—Spain
064.35 Foreign lands—Sweden
064.36 Foreign lands—Switzerland
064.37 Foreign lands—Thailand
064.38 Foreign lands—Turkey
064.39 Foreign lands—Tyrol
064.40 Foreign lands—Ukraine
064.41 Foreign lands—Vatican City

065 Foreign languages
066 Forest, woods
Forgetfulness. *See* Behavior—forgetfulness

067 Format, unusual
Fortune tellers. *See* Careers—fortune tellers
Fourth of July. *See* Holidays—Fourth of July
Foxes. *See* Animals—foxes
France. *See* Foreign lands—France
Freedom. *See* Character traits—freedom

068 Friendship
Frogs. *See* Amphibians

069 Games
070 Gangs, clubs
Garbage collectors. *See* Careers—garbage collectors
Gardening. *See* Activities—gardening
Geese. *See* Birds—geese
Generosity. *See* Character traits—generosity
Gerbils. *See* Animals—gerbils
Germany. *See* Foreign lands—Germany

071 Ghosts
072 Giants
Gilbert Islands. *See* Foreign lands—South Sea Islands
Giraffes. *See* Animals—giraffes

073 Glasses
Goats. *See* Animals—goats

074 Goblins
Gorillas. *See* Animals—gorillas
Gossip. *See* Behavior—gossip
Grandparents. *See* Family life—grandparents; great-grandparents
Grasshoppers. *See* Insects and spiders
Great-grandparents. *See* Family life—grandparents; great-grandparents
Greece. *See* Foreign lands—Greece
Greed. *See* Behavior—greed
Grocery stores. *See* Shopping; Stores
Groundhog Day. *See* Holidays—Groundhog Day
Groundhogs. *See* Animals—groundhogs

Growing up. *See* Behavior—
    growing up
Guinea pigs. *See* Animals—guinea
    pigs
Gulls. *See* Birds—Sea gulls
Guns. *See* Weapons
Gymnastics. *See* Sports—gymnastics
075 Gypsies

076 Hair
Halloween. *See* Holidays—
    Halloween
Hamsters. *See* Animals—hamsters
077   Handicaps
077.01 Handicaps—blindness
077.02 Handicaps—deafness
Hands. *See* Anatomy
Happiness. *See* Emotions—
    happiness
Hares. *See* Animals—rabbits
Hating. *See* Emotions—hating
078 Hawaii
Hawks. *See* Birds—hawks
079 Health
Hearing. *See* Handicaps—deafness;
    Senses
Hedgehogs. *See* Animals—
    hedgehogs
080 Helicopters. *See also*
    Transportation
Helpfulness. *See* Character traits—
    helpfulness
Hens. *See* Birds—chickens
081 Hibernation
Hiding. *See* Behavior—hiding
Hiding things. *See* Behavior—
    hiding things
082 Hieroglyphics
Hippopotami. *See* Animals—
    hippopotami
History, U.S. *See* U.S. history
083 Holidays
083.01 Holidays—April Fools' Day
083.02 Holidays—Chinese New Year
083.03 Holidays—Christmas
083.04 Holidays—Easter
083.05 Holidays—Fourth of July
083.06 Holidays—Groundhog Day
083.07 Holidays—Halloween
083.08 Holidays—New Year's Day
083.09 Holidays—St. Patrick's Day
083.10 Holidays—Thanksgiving
083.11 Holidays—Valentine's Day
083.12 Holidays—Washington's Birthday
Holland. *See* Foreign lands—
    Holland
Homes. *See* Houses
Honesty. *See* Character traits—
    honesty
Honeybees. *See* Insects and spiders
Horses. *See* Animals—horses

Horses, rocking. *See* Toys—rocking
    horses
084 Hospitals
085 Hotels
086 Houses
087 Humor
Hungary. *See* Foreign lands—
    Hungary
Hunting. *See* Sports—hunting
Hurrying. *See* Behavior—hurrying
Hyenas. *See* Animals—hyenas

Ice skating. *See* Sports—ice skating
Iguanas. *See* Reptiles—iguanas
088 Illness
Illusions. *See* Optical illusions;
    Magic
089 Imagination
089.01 Imagination—imaginary friends
In and out. *See* Concepts—in and
    out
India. *See* Foreign lands—India
Indians. *See* Ethnic Groups in the
    U.S.—Indians
Indifference. *See* Behavior—
    indifference
Individuality. *See* Character traits—
    individuality
Indonesian Archipelago. *See*
    Foreign lands—South Sea
    Islands
090 Insects and spiders
Interracial marriage. *See* Marriage,
    interracial
Ireland. *See* Foreign lands—
    Ireland
091 Islands
Italy. *See* Foreign lands—Italy

Japan. *See* Foreign lands—Japan
Japanese-Americans. *See* Ethnic
    groups in the U.S.—Japanese-
    Americans
Jealousy. *See* Emotions—envy,
    jealousy
092 Jesters
093 Jewish culture
Jobs. *See* Careers
Jokes. *See* Riddles
Judges. *See* Careers—judges
Jumping. *See* Activities—jumping

Kangaroos. *See* Animals—
    kangaroos
Kindness. *See* Character traits—
    kindness
Kindness to animals. *See* Character
    traits—kindness to animals
Kings. *See* Royalty

Kinkajous. *See* Animals—kinkajous

094 Kites

095 Knights. *See also* Middle ages

Knitting. *See* Activities—knitting

Koala bears. *See* Animals—koala bears

Korea. *See* Foreign lands—Korea

Ladybugs. *See* Insects and spiders

096 Language

Languages, foreign. *See* Foreign languages

Lapland. *See* Foreign lands—Lapland

097 Laundry

Law. *See* Careers—judges; Crime

Laziness. *See* Character traits—laziness

Left and right. *See* Concepts—left and right

098 Left-handedness

Leopards. *See* Animals—cats, wild

Leprechauns. *See* Elves and little people

099 Letters

100 Libraries

101 Lighthouses

Lions. *See* Animals—cats, wild

Lithuania. *See* Foreign lands—Lithuania

Little people. *See* Elves and little people

Littleness. *See* Character traits—smallness

Lizards. *See* Reptiles—lizards

Llamas. *See* Animals—llamas

Loneliness. *See* Emotions—loneliness

Losing things. *See* Behavior—losing things

Lost. *See* Behavior—lost

Love. *See* Emotions—love

Loyalty. *See* Character traits—loyalty

Luck. *See* Character traits—luck

Lying. *See* Behavior—lying

102 Machines

103 Magic

Maids. *See* Careers—maids

Mail carriers. *See* Careers—mail carriers

Malaysia. *See* Foreign lands—Malaysia

Manners. *See* Etiquette

104 Mardi Gras

Marriage. *See* Weddings

105 Marriage, interracial

Meanness. *See* Character traits—meanness

Measurement. *See* Concepts—measurement

Mermaids. *See* Mythical creatures

106 Merry-go-rounds

Mexican-Americans. *See* Ethnic groups in the U.S.—Mexican-Americans

Mexico. *See* Foreign lands—Mexico

Mice. *See* Animals—mice

107 Middle ages. *See also* Knights

Military. *See* Careers—military

Minorities. *See* Ethnic groups in the U.S.

Misbehavior. *See* Behavior—misbehavior

108 Missions

Mist. *See* Weather—fog; Weather—rain

Mistakes. *See* Behavior—mistakes

Misunderstanding. *See* Behavior—misunderstanding

Moles. *See* Animals—moles

109 Money

Mongooses. *See* Animals—mongooses

Monkeys. *See* Animals—monkeys

110 Monsters

Months of the year. *See* Days of the week, months of the year

111 Moon

Moose. *See* Animals—moose

112 Morning

Mosquitos. *See* Insects and spiders

Mother Goose. *See* Nursery rhymes

Mothers. *See* Family life—mothers

113 Motorcycles

114 Moving

Mules. *See* Animals—donkeys

Multi-ethnic. *See* Ethnic groups in the U.S.—Multi-ethnic

Multiple-birth children. *See* Triplets; Twins

115 Museums

Muskrats. *See* Animals—muskrats

116 Music

Mysteries. *See* Problem solving

117 Mythical creatures

Nagging. *See* Behavior—nagging

118 Names

Native Americans. *See* Ethnic groups in the U.S.—Eskimos; Ethnic groups in the U.S.—Indians

Needing someone. *See* Behavior—needing someone

New Year's Day. *See* Holidays—New Year's Day

119 Night

Nightmares. *See* Bedtime; Goblins; Monsters; Night

No text. *See* Wordless
Noah. *See* Religion—Noah
120 **Noise**
121 **Non-sexist**
Norway. *See* Foreign lands—
    Norway
Noses. *See* Anatomy
Numbers. *See* Counting
Nuns. *See* Careers—nuns
122 **Nursery rhymes**
Nurses. *See* Careers—nurses

123 **Octopod**
124 **Oil**
125 **Old age**
Olympics. *See* Sports—Olympics
Only child. *See* Family life—the
    only child
Opossums. *See* Animals—possums
Opposites. *See* Concepts—opposites
126 **Optical illusions**
Optimism. *See* Character traits—
    optimism
127 **Orphans**
Ostriches. *See* Birds—ostriches
Ostracism. *See* Character traits—
    being different
Otters. *See* Animals—otters
Out and in. *See* Concepts—in and
    out
Owls. *See* Birds—owls

Pack rats. *See* Animals—pack rats
Painters. *See* Activities—painting;
    Careers—artists
Painting. *See* Activities—painting
Pakistan. *See* Foreign lands—
    Pakistan
Panthers. *See* Animals—cats, wild
128 **Parades**
Parakeets. *See* Birds—parrots,
    parakeets
Parrots. *See* Birds—parrots,
    parakeets
129 **Participation**
130 **Parties**
Patience. *See* Character traits—
    patience
Peacocks. *See* Birds—peacocks,
    peahens
Peddlers. *See* Careers—peddlers
Pelicans. *See* Birds—pelicans
Penguins. *See* Birds—penguins
Perseverance. *See* Character
    traits—perseverance
Petroleum. *See* Oil
131 **Pets**
Phoenix. *See* Mythical creatures
Photography. *See* Activities—
    photographing

Physicians. *See* Careers—doctors
Picknicking. *See* Activities—
    picknicking
Pigeons. *See* Birds—pigeons
Pigs. *See* Animals—pigs
Pilots. *See* Careers—airplane pilots
132 **Pirates**
Planes. *See* Airplanes
133 **Plants.** *See also* Flowers; Trees
Playing. *See* Activities—playing
134 **Poetry, rhyme**
Poland. *See* Foreign lands—Poland
Police officers. *See* Careers—police
    officers
Poor. *See* Poverty
Porcupines. *See* Animals—
    porcupines
Porpoise. *See* Animals—dolphins
Portugal. *See* Foreign lands—
    Portugal
Possums. *See* Animals—possums
135 **Poverty**
136 **Power failure**
Practicality. *See* Character traits—
    practicality
Prairie dogs. *See* Animals—prairie
    dogs
Pride. *See* Character traits—pride
Princes. *See* Royalty
Princesses. *See* Royalty
137 **Problem solving**
138 **Progress**
Puerto Rican-Americans. *See*
    Ethnic groups in the U.S.—
    Puerto Rican-Americans
139 **Puppets**

Queens. *See* Royalty
Questioning. *See* Character traits—
    questioning

Rabbits. *See* Animals—rabbits
Raccoons. *See* Animals—raccoons
Racing. *See* Sports—racing
Railroad engineers. *See* Careers—
    railroad engineers
Rain. *See* Weather—rain
Rainbows. *See* Weather—rainbows
Rats. *See* Animals—rats; Animals—
    pack rats
Reading. *See* Activities—reading
140 **Rebuses**
141 **Religion**
141.01 Religion—Noah
Repetitive tales. *See* Cumulative
    tales
142 **Reptiles**
142.01 Reptiles—alligators, crocodiles
142.02 Reptiles—iguanas
142.03 Reptiles—lizards

142.04 Reptiles—snakes
142.05 Reptiles—turtles
Rhinoceros. *See* Animals—
rhinoceros
Rhymes. *See* Nursery rhymes;
Poetry, rhyme
143 Riddles
Right and left. *See* Concepts—left
and right
144 Rivers
Robins. *See* Birds—robins
145 Robots
Rocking horses. *See* Toys—rocking
horses
146 Rocks
Roosters. *See* Birds—chickens
147 Royalty
Running. *See* Sports—racing
Running away. *See* Behavior—
running away
Russia. *See* Foreign lands—Russia

Sadness. *See* Emotions—sadness
148 Safety
Sailors. *See* Careers—military
St. Patrick's Day. *See* Holidays—St.
Patrick's Day
149 Sandman
Sandpipers. *See* Birds—sandpipers
Saving things. *See* Behavior—
saving things
150 Scarecrows
151 School
152 Science
Scotland. *See* Foreign lands—
Scotland
153 Sea and seashore
Sea gulls. *See* Birds—sea gulls
Sea lions. *See* Animals—sea lions
Sea serpents. *See* Mythical
creatures
Seahorses. *See* Crustacea
Seals. *See* Animals—seals
Seamstresses. *See* Careers—
seamstresses
154 Seasons
154.01 Seasons—fall
154.02 Seasons—spring
154.03 Seasons—summer
154.04 Seasons—winter
155 Secret codes
Secrets. *See* Behavior—secrets
Seeing. *See* Handicaps—blindness;
Senses
Seeking better things. *See*
Behavior—seeking better things
156 Self-concept
Selfishness. *See* Character traits—
selfishness
157 Senses
158 Shadows

159 Shakespeare
Shape. *See* Concepts—shape
Sharing. *See* Behavior—sharing
Sheep. *See* Animals—sheep
Ships. *See* Boats, ships
Shoemakers. *See* Careers—
shoemakers
160 Shopping
Shows. *See* Theater
Shyness. *See* Character traits—
shyness
Siam. *See* Foreign lands—Thailand
Sibling rivalry. *See* Behavior—
sibling rivalry; Family life
Sickness. *See* Illness
Sisters. *See* Behavior—sibling
rivalry; Family life
Size. *See* Concepts—size
Skating. *See* Sports—ice skating
Skiing. *See* Sports—skiing
Skin diving. *See* Sports—skin
diving
Skunks. *See* Animals—skunks
161 Sky
162 Sleep
Sloths. *See* Animals—sloths
Smallness. *See* Character traits—
smallness
Smelling. *See* Senses
Snails. *See* Animals—snails
Snakes. *See* Reptiles—snakes
Snow. *See* Weather—snow
163 Snowmen
Snowplows. *See* Machines
Society Islands. *See* Foreign
lands—South Sea Islands
Soldiers. *See* Careers—military
Soldiers, toy. *See* Toys—soldiers
Solitude. *See* Behavior—solitude
164 Songs
Sounds. *See* Noise
South America. *See* Foreign
lands—South America
South Sea Islands. *See* Foreign
lands—South Sea Islands
165 Space and space ships
Spain. *See* Foreign lands—Spain
Sparrows. *See* Birds—sparrows
Spectacles. *See* Glasses
Speed. *See* Concepts—speed
Spelunking. *See* Caves
Spiders. *See* Insects and spiders
Spooks. *See* Ghosts; Goblins
166 Sports
166.01 Sports—baseball
166.02 Sports—basketball
166.03 Sports—bicycling
166.04 Sports—camping
166.05 Sports—fishing
166.06 Sports—football
166.07 Sports—gymnastics
166.08 Sports—hunting

166.09 Sports—ice skating
166.10 Sports—Olympics
166.11 Sports—racing
166.12 Sports—skiing
166.13 Sports—skin diving
166.14 Sports—surfing
166.15 Sports—swimming
166.16 Sports—tennis
Spring. *See* Seasons—spring
Squirrels. *See* Animals—squirrels
167 **Stars**
Stealing. *See* Behavior—stealing;
Crime
Steam shovels. *See* Machines
Steamrollers. *See* Machines
Stepparents, stepchildren. *See*
Divorce
Stones. *See* Rocks
168 **Stores**
Storks. *See* Birds—storks
Streams. *See* Rivers
String. *See* Toys—string
Sullivan Islands. *See* Foreign
lands—South Sea Islands
Summer. *See* Seasons—summer
Surfing. *See* Sports—surfing
Swans. *See* Birds—swans
Sweden. *See* Foreign lands—
Sweden
Swimming. *See* Sports—swimming
Swinging. *See* Activities—swinging
Switzerland. *See* Foreign lands—
Switzerland
169 **Sun**

Tailors. *See* Careers—tailors
Talking to strangers. *See*
Behavior—talking to strangers
Tapirs. *See* Animals—tapirs
Tasting. *See* Senses
Taxi drivers. *See* Careers—taxi
drivers
170 **Taxis.** *See also* Careers—taxi
drivers; Transportation
Teachers. *See* Careers—teachers
Teddy bears. *See* Toys—teddy
bears
171 **Teeth.** *See also* Careers—dentists
172 **Telephone**
Telephone operators. *See*
Careers—telephone operators
Telling time. *See* Clocks; Time
Temper tantrums. *See* Emotions—
anger
Tennis. *See* Sports—tennis
Textless. *See* Wordless
Thailand. *See* Foreign lands—
Thailand
Thanksgiving. *See* Holidays—
Thanksgiving
173 **Theater**

Tigers. *See* Animals—cats, wild
174 **Time.** *See also* Clocks
Toes. *See* Anatomy
175 **Tongue twisters**
176 **Tools**
Tortoises. *See* Reptiles—turtles
Touching. *See* Senses
Towns. *See* City
177 **Toys**
177.01 Toys—balloons
177.02 Toys—balls
Toys—bears. *See* Toys—teddy
bears
177.03 Toys—blocks
177.04 Toys—dolls
177.05 Toys—rocking horses
177.06 Toys—soldiers
177.07 Toys—string
177.08 Toys—teddy bears
177.09 Toys—trains
Tractors. *See* Machines
Trading. *See* Activities—trading
178 **Traffic signs**
179 **Trains**
Trains, toy. *See* Toys—trains
180 **Transportation**
181 **Trees**
Trickery. *See* Behavior—trickery
182 **Triplets**
Trolleys. *See* Cable cars
183 **Trolls.** *See also* Mythical creatures
Truck drivers. *See* Careers—truck
drivers
184 **Trucks**
Turkey. *See* Foreign lands—
Turkey
Turkeys. *See* Birds—turkeys
Turtles. *See* Reptiles—turtles
185 **Twilight**
186 **Twins**

Ukraine. *See* Foreign lands—
Ukraine
187 **Umbrellas**
Unhappiness. *See* Emotions—
happiness; Emotions—sadness
188 **UNICEF**
Unicorns. *See* Mythical creatures
189 **U.S. history**
Unnoticed. *See* Behavior—
unnoticed, unseen
Unseen. *See* Behavior—unnoticed,
unseen
Unusual format. *See* Format,
unusual
Up and down. *See* Concepts—up
and down

Vacationing. *See* Activities—
vacationing

Vacuum cleaners. *See* Machines
Valentine's Day. *See* Holidays—
   Valentine's Day
190 Values
Vampires. *See* Monsters
Vatican City. *See* Foreign lands—
   Vatican City
Veterinarians. *See* Careers—
   veterinarians
191 Violence, anti-violence. *See also*
   War; Weapons
192 Volcanoes
Vultures. *See* Birds—vultures

Walking. *See* Activities—walking
Walruses. *See* Animals—walruses
193 War
Washington's Birthday. *See*
   Holidays—Washington's
   Birthday
194 Weapons
Weasels. *See* Animals—weasels
195 Weather
195.01 Weather—clouds
195.02 Weather—cold
195.03 Weather—floods
195.04 Weather—fog
195.05 Weather—rain
195.06 Weather—rainbows
195.07 Weather—snow
195.08 Weather—wind
196 Weddings

Weekdays. *See* Days of the week,
   months of the year
197 Wheels
Weight. *See* Concepts—weight
Whales. *See* Animals—whales
Whistling. *See* Activities—whistling
Wind. *See* Weather—wind
198 Windmills
Window cleaners. *See* Careers—
   window cleaners
Winter. *See* Seasons—winter
Wishing. *See* Behavior—wishing
199 Witches
200 Wizards
Wolves. *See* Animals—wolves
Woodchucks. *See* Animals—
   groundhogs
Woodpeckers. *See* Birds—
   woodpeckers
Woods. *See* Forest, woods
201 Wordless
Working. *See* Activities—working
202 World. *See also* Earth
Worms. *See* Animals—worms
Worrying. *See* Behavior—worrying
Wrecking machines. *See* Machines
Wrens. *See* Birds—wrens
Writing. *See* Activities—writing
Writing letters. *See* Letters

203 Zodiac
204 Zoos. *See also* Animals

Subject Guide

This is a subject-arranged guide to the picture books. It is arranged alphabetically by subject heading and subheading, with corresponding classification numbers identifying each heading. (Subjects are listed according to the numerical classification in the Subject Headings section.) Titles are listed alphabetically by author within each subject listing.

001 ABC Books

Alexander, Anne. ABC of Cars and Trucks
Anno, Mitsumasa. Anno's Alphabet
Barry, Katharina. A Is for Anything; An ABC Book of Pictures and Rhymes
Baskin, Leonard. Hosie's Alphabet
Berenstain, Stanley, and Berenstain, Janice. The Berenstains' B Book
Bond, Jean Carey. A Is for Africa
Brown, Judith Gwyn. Alphabet Dreams
Brown, Marcia. All Butterflies
Peter Piper's Alphabet
Brown, Margaret Wise. Sleepy ABC
Bruna, Dick. B Is for Bear; An ABC
Budney, Blossom. N Is for Nursery School
Burningham, John Mackintosh. John Burningham's ABC
Carle, Eric. All About Arthur
Chardiet, Bernice. C Is for Circus
Chwast, Seymour, and Moskof, Martin Stephen. Still Another Alphabet Book
Cleary, Beverly. The Hullabaloo ABC
Cohen, Peter Zachary. Authorized Autumn Charts of the Upper Red Canoe River Country
Coletta, Irene, and Coletta, Hallie. From A to Z
Cooney, Barbara. A Garland of Games and Other Diversions
Crews, Donald. We Read: A to Z
Delaunay, Sonia. Sonia Delaunay's Alphabet
Duvoisin, Roger Antoine. A for the Ark
Eichenberg, Fritz. Ape in Cape
Emberley, Edward Randolph. Ed Emberley's ABC
Falls, Charles Buckles. ABC Book
Farber, Norma. As I Was Crossing Boston Common
Feelings, Muriel L. Jambo Means Hello; A Swahili Alphabet Book
Fife, Dale. Adam's ABC
Floyd, Lucy, and Lasky, Kathryn. Agatha's Alphabet, with Her Very Own Dictionary

Freeman, Don. Add-A-Line Alphabet
Fujikawa, Gyo. Gyo Fujikawa's A to Z Picture Book
Gág, Wanda. ABC Bunny
Garten, Jan. The Alphabet Tale
Geisel, Theodor Seuss. Dr. Seuss's ABC
Hooper Humperdink. . . ? Not Him!
Goody Two Shoes' Picture Book
Grant, Sandy. Hey, Look at Me! A City ABC
Greenaway, Kate. A Apple Pie
Gretz, Susanna. Teddybears ABC
Grossbart, Francine B. A Big City
Gunning, Monica. The Two Georges: Los Dos Jorges
Holl, Adelaide. The ABC of Cars, Trucks and Machines
Ilsley, Velma. A Busy Day for Chris
M Is for Moving
Ipcar, Dahlov Zorach. I Love My Anteater with an A
Kuskin, Karla Seidman. ABCDEFGHIJK-LMNOPQRSTUVWXYZ
Lear, Edward. ABC
Nonsense Alphabets
Leisk, David Johnson. Harold's ABC's
Little, Mary E. ABC for the Library
Low, Joseph. Adam's Book of Odd Creatures
McGinley, Phyllis. All Around the Town
McMillan, Bruce. The Alphabet Symphony
Margalit, Avi. The Hebrew Alphabet Book
Mendoza, George. The Alphabet Boat; A Seagoing Alphabet Book
Norman Rockwell's American ABC
Miles, Miska. Apricot ABC
Miller, Edna Anita. Mousekin's ABC
Montresor, Beni. A for Angel
Morse, Samuel French. All in a Suitcase
Moss, Jeffrey; Stiles, Norman; and Wilcox, Daniel. The Sesame Street ABC Storybook
Mother Goose. In a Pumpkin Shell; A Mother Goose ABC
Munari, Bruno. ABC
Newberry, Clare Turlay. The Kittens' ABC
Niland, Deborah. ABC of Monsters

Ogle, Lucille, and Thoburn, Tine. A B See
Oxenbury, Helen. Helen Oxenbury's ABC of Things
A Peaceable Kingdom; The Shaker Abecedarius
Peppé, Rodney. The Alphabet Book
Piatti, Celestino. Celestino Piatti's Animal ABC
Rey, Hans Augusto. Curious George Learns the Alphabet
    Look for the Letters
Rojankovsky, Feodor Stepanovich. ABC, an Alphabet of Many Things
    Animals in the Zoo
Ruben, Patricia. Apples to Zippers
Scarry, Richard McClure. Richard Scarry's ABC Word Book
    Richard Scarry's Great Big Schoolhouse
Sea World Alphabet Book
Seignobosc, Françoise. The Gay ABC
Sendak, Maurice. Alligators All Around
The Sesame Street Book of Letters
Shuttlesworth, Dorothy E. ABC of Buses
Smith, William Jay. Puptents and Pebbles
Steiner, Charlotte. Charlotte Steiner's ABC
Tallon, Robert. Zag, a Search through the Alphabet
Towend, Jack. Railroad ABC
Tudor, Tasha. A Is for Annabelle
Waber, Bernard. An Anteater Named Arthur
Walters, Marguerite. The City-Country ABC
Watson, Nancy Dingman. What Does A Begin With?
Wildsmith, Brian. Brian Wildsmith's ABC
Williams, Garth Montgomery. The Big Golden Animal ABC
Wondriska, William. A Long Piece of String

002 Activities

Crume, Marion W. Let Me See You Try
    Listen!
    What Do You Say?
Gipson, Morrell. Hello, Peter
Hallinan, Patrick K. I'm Glad to Be Me
    Just Being Alone
Holzenthaler, Jean. My Feet Do
    My Hands Can
Maestro, Betsy. Busy Day
Rockwell, Harlow. I Did It
    Look at This
Scarry, Richard McClure. Richard Scarry's Busy Busy World
Simon, Norma. What Do I Do?
Vasiliu, Marcea. What's Happening?

002.01 Activities—babysitting

Byars, Betsy Cromer. Go and Hush the Baby
Carlson, Natalie Savage. Marie Louise's Heyday
Chalmers, Mary Eileen. Be Good, Harry
Cole, William. What's Good for a Three-Year-Old?
Coombs, Patricia. Dorrie and the Goblin
Finfer, Celentha; Wasserberg, Esther; and Weinberg, Florence. Grandmother Dear
Greenberg, Barbara. The Bravest Babysitter
Hughes, Shirley. George the Babysitter
Hurd, Edith Thacher. Hurry Hurry Stop, Stop
Moore, Lilian. Little Raccoon and No Trouble at All
Newberry, Clare Turlay. T-Bone, the Baby-Sitter
Puner, Helen Walker. The Sitter Who Didn't Sit
Rayner, Mary. Mr. and Mrs. Pig's Evening Out
Schick, Eleanor. Peter and Mr. Brandon
Van Den Honert, Dorry. Demi the Baby Sitter
Watson, Jane Werner. My Friend the Babysitter
Watson, Pauline. Curley Cat Baby-Sits
Wells, Rosemary. Stanley and Rhoda
Williams, Barbara. Jeremy Isn't Hungry

002.02 Activities—bathing

Ambrus, Victor G. The Sultan's Bath
Barrett, Judith. I Hate to Take a Bath
Bethell, Jean. Bathtime
Burningham, John Mackintosh. Time to Get Out of the Bath, Shirley
McLeod, Emilie Warren. One Snail and Me
Manushkin, Fran. Bubblebath
Reavin, Sam. Hurray For Captain Jane!
Rudolph, Marguerita. Sharp and Shiny
Yolen, Jane. No Bath Tonight
Zion, Gene. Harry the Dirty Dog

002.03 Activities—cooking

de Paola, Thomas Anthony. Pancakes for Breakfast
    The Popcorn Book
Devlin, Wende, and Devlin, Harry. Old Black Witch
    Old Witch and the Polka-Dot Ribbon
    Old Witch Rescues Halloween
Hitte, Kathryn, and Hayes, William D. Mexicallie Soup
Hoban, Lillian. Arthur's Christmas Cookies

Kahl, Virginia Caroline. The Duchess Bakes a Cake

Kitt, Tamara. Sam and the Impossible Thing

Lasker, Joseph Leon. Lentil Soup

Lindman, Maj Jan. Flicka, Ricka, Dicka Bake a Cake

Petie, Haris. The Seed the Squirrel Dropped

Schwalje, Marjory. Mr. Angelo

Ungerer, Tomi. Zeralda's Ogre

Wiesner, William. Too Many Cooks

Zion, Gene. The Sugar Mouse Cake

002.04 Activities—dancing

de Paola, Thomas Anthony. Oliver Button Is a Sissy

Fern, Eugene. Pepito's Story

Isadora, Rachel. Max

Marshall, James. George and Martha Encore

Mayer, Mercer. The Queen Always Wanted to Dance

Quin-Harkin, Janet. Peter Penny's Dance

Tallon, Robert. Handella

002.05 Activities—flying

Anderson, Lonzo. Mr. Biddle and the Birds

Benchley, Nathaniel. The Flying Lessons of Gerald Pelican

Bradfield, Roger. The Flying Hockey Stick

Brenner, Barbara. The Flying Patchwork Quilt

Coombs, Patricia. Dorrie and the Halloween Plot

Duvoisin, Roger Antoine. Petunia Takes a Trip

Gramatky, Hardie. Loopy

Hays, Hoffman Reynolds, and Hays, Daniel. Charley Sang a Song

Jenny, Anne. The Fantastic Story of King Brioche the First

Kuskin, Karla Seidman. Just Like Everyone Else

Peet, Bill. Merle the High Flying Squirrel

Phleger, Frederick B. Ann Can Fly

Titus, Eve. Anatole Over Paris

Trez, Denise, and Trez, Alain. Maila and the Flying Carpet

Ungerer, Tomi. The Mellops Go Flying

Valens, Evans G. Wingfin and Topple

Watson, Clyde. Midnight Moon

Wende, Philip. Bird Boy

Wolkstein, Diane. The Cool Ride in the Sky

002.06 Activities—gardening

Barrett, Judith. Old MacDonald Had an Apartment House

Berson, Harold. Pop Goes the Turnip

de Paola, Thomas Anthony. Four Stories for Four Seasons

Domanska, Janina. The Best of the Bargain

Hader, Berta Hoerner, and Hader, Elmer Stanley. Mister Billy's Gun

Ichikawa, Satomi. Suzanne and Nicholas in the Garden

Ipcar, Dahlov Zorach. The Land of Flowers

Keeping, Charles William James. Joseph's Yard

Krauss, Ruth. The Carrot Seed

Marino, Dorothy Bronson. Buzzy Bear in the Garden

Morgenstern, Elizabeth. The Little Gardeners

Rockwell, Harlow. The Compost Heap

Shecter, Ben. Partouche Plants a Seed

Taylor, Mark. A Time for Flowers

Trimby, Elisa. Mr. Plum's Paradise

002.07 Activities—jumping

Bright, Robert. My Hopping Bunny

Stephens, Karen. Jumping

002.08 Activities—knitting

Holl, Adelaide. Mrs. McGarrity's Peppermint Sweater

Laurin, Anne. Little Things

002.09 Activities—painting

Adams, Adrienne. The Easter Egg Artists

Becker, Edna. Nine Hundred Buckets of Paint

Duvoisin, Roger Antoine. The House of Four Seasons

Freeman, Don. The Chalk Box Story

Kessler, Leonard P. Mr. Pine's Purple House

Miller, Warren. Pablo Paints a Picture

Pinkwater, Manus. Big Orange Splot

Spier, Peter. Oh, Were They Ever Happy!

Weisgard, Leonard. Mr. Peaceable Paints

002.10 Activities—photographing

Villarejo, Mary. The Tiger Hunt

Watts, Mabel. Weeks and Weeks

Willard, Nancy. Simple Pictures Are Best

002.11 Activities—picnicking

Brandenberg, Franz. A Picnic, Hurrah!
Coombs, Patricia. Dorrie and the Weather-Box
Daugherty, James Henry. The Picnic
Ets, Marie Hall. In the Forest
Freschet, Berniece. The Ants Go Marching
Goodall, John Strickland. The Surprise Picnic
Hurd, Edith Thacher. No Funny Business
Lathrop, Dorothy Pulis. Who Goes There?
Robertson, Lilian. Picnic Woods
Van Stockum, Hilda. Day on Skates
Wood, Joyce. Grandmother Lucy Goes on a Picnic
Yeoman, John. The Bears' Water Picnic

002.12 Activities—playing

Alexander, Martha G. I'll Be the Horse If You'll Play with Me
Baugh, Dolores M., and Pulsifer, Marjorie P. Slides
    Swings
Benet, William Rose. Timothy's Angels
Bonsall, Crosby Newell. And I Mean It, Stanley
    Piggle
Bram, Elizabeth. Saturday Morning Lasts Forever
Breinburg, Petronella. Doctor Shawn
Brown, Myra Berry. First Night Away from Home
Carroll, Ruth Robinson. Where's the Bunny?
Cartlidge, Michelle. Pippin and Pod
Christian, Mary Blount. The Sand Lot
Cole, William. What's Good for a Four-Year-Old?
    What's Good for a Six-Year-Old?
Erickson, Phoebe. Uncle Debunkel or Barely Believable Bear
Ets, Marie Hall. Play with Me
Fitzhugh, Louise, and Scoppetone, Sandra. Bang Bang You're Dead
Gelman, Rita Golden. Dumb Joey
Hillert, Margaret. Play Ball
Jewell, Nancy. Try and Catch Me
Keats, Ezra Jack. Skates
    The Snowy Day
Krahn, Fernando. Robot-Bot-Bot
Lenski, Lois L. Let's Play House
Lipkind, William, and Mordvinoff, Nicolas. Sleepyhead
McNulty, Faith. When a Boy Wakes Up in the Morning
Marino, Dorothy Bronson. Edward and the Boxes
Mayers, Patrick. Just One More Block
Meeks, Esther K. The Hill That Grew
Mitchell, Cynthia. Playtime

Pearson, Susan. That's Enough for One Day!
Raebeck, Lois. Who Am I?
Roberts, Thom. Pirates in the Park
Rudolph, Marguerita. Sharp and Shiny
Russ, Lavinia. Alec's Sand Castle
Sendak, Maurice. The Sign on Rosie's Door
Steiner, Charlotte. Kiki's Play House
    Look What Tracy Found
Udry, Janice May. Mary Ann's Mud Day
Viorst, Judith. Sunday Morning
Waber, Bernard. Ira Sleeps Over
Wahl, Jan. Push Kitty
Winthrop, Elizabeth. That's Mine!
Ziner, Feenie. Counting Carnival
Zolotow, Charlotte Shapiro. The Park Book
    The White Marble

002.13 Activities—reading

Bank Street College of Education. People Read
Black, Irma Simonton. The Little Old Man Who Could Not Read
Cohen, Miriam. When Will I Read?
Duvoisin, Roger Antoine. Petunia
Friskey, Margaret. Mystery of the Gate Sign
Geisel, Theodor Seuss. I Can Read with My Eyes Shut!
Hoban, Lillian. Arthur's Prize Reader
Hurd, Edith Thacher. Johnny Lion's Book
Kuskin, Karla Seidman. Watson, the Smartest Dog in the U.S.A
Lexau, Joan M. Olaf Reads
Ormondroyd, Edward. Broderick
Pearson, Susan. That's Enough for One Day!

002.14 Activities—swinging

Marks, Marcia Bliss. Swing Me, Swing Tree

002.15 Activities—trading

De Regniers, Beatrice Schenk. Was It a Good Trade?
Gill, Bob, and Reid, Alastair. A Balloon for a Blunderbuss
Hirsh, Marilyn Joyce. The Pink Suit
Hughes, Shirley. David and Dog
Langstaff, John Meredith. The Swapping Boy
Stroyer, Poul. It's a Deal
Watts, Mabel. Something for You, Something for Me

002.16 Activities—traveling

Blech, Dietlind. Hello Irina
Bolognese, Donald Alan. A New Day
Brunhoff, Jean de. The Travels of Babar
Carle, Eric. The Rooster Who Set Out to
    See the World
Geisel, Theodor Seuss. I Had Trouble
    Getting to Solla Sollew
Gray, Genevieve. How Far, Felipe?
Greene, Carla. A Motor Holiday
Kessler, Leonard P. Mrs. Pine Takes a
    Trip
Lenski, Lois L. Davy Goes Places
May, Charles Paul. High-Noon Rocket
Steger, Hans-Ulrich. Traveling to Tripiti
Tapio, Pat Decker. The Lady Who Saw the
    Good Side of Everything
Ungerer, Tomi. Adelaide
Wooley, Catherine. Rockets Don't Go to
    Chicago, Andy

002.17 Activities—vacationing

Adams, Adrienne. The Easter Egg Artists
Bemelmans, Ludwig. Hansi
Bond, Michael. Paddington at the Seaside
Briggs, Raymond. Father Christmas Goes
    on Holiday
Bright, Robert. Georgie and the Noisy
    Ghost
Brunhoff, Laurent de. Babar's Cousin,
    That Rascal Arthur
    Babar's Mystery
Carrick, Carol. The Washout
Du Bois, William Pène. Otto and the Magic
    Potatoes
Duvoisin, Roger Antoine. Petunia Takes a
    Trip
Fatio, Louise. The Happy Lion's Vacation
Goodall, John Strickland. Paddy Pork's
    Holiday
Kessler, Leonard P. Are We Lost, Daddy?
Lindman, Maj Jan. Snipp, Snapp, Snurr
    and the Red Shoes
Schick, Eleanor. Summer at the Sea
Stevenson, James. The Sea View Hotel
Thomson, Ruth. Peabody All at Sea
Tobias, Tobi. At the Beach
Wright, Dare. Holiday for Edith and the
    Bears

002.18 Activities—walking

Brown, Margaret Wise. Four Fur Feet
Buckley, Helen Elizabeth. Grandfather and I
Kingman, Lee. Peter's Long Walk
Klein, Leonore. Henri's Walk to Paris
Lenski, Lois L. I Went for a Walk
Showers, Paul. The Listening Walk
Thomas, Ianthe. Walk Home Tired, Billy
    Jenkins

Tworkov, Jack. The Camel Who Took a
    Walk
Viorst, Judith. Try It Again, Sam
Wood, Joyce. Grandmother Lucy Goes on
    a Picnic
Wright, Ethel. Saturday Walk
Zimelman, Nathan. Walls Are to Be
    Walked On
Zolotow, Charlotte Shapiro. One Step, Two
    The Summer Night

002.19 Activities—whistling

Alexander, Anne. I Want to Whistle
Ambrus, Victor G. The Three Poor Tailors
Avery, Kay. Wee Willow Whistle
Bason, Lillian. Pick a Raincoat, Pick a
    Whistle
Keats, Ezra Jack. Whistle for Willie

002.20 Activities—working

Allen, Jeffrey. Mary Alice, Operator
    Number 9
Arkin, Alan. Tony's Hard Work Day
Burton, Virginia Lee. Mike Mulligan and
    His Steam Shovel
Carle, Eric. Walter the Baker
Clark, Ann Nolan. The Little Indian
    Pottery Maker
Gág, Wanda. Gone Is Gone
Harper, Anita. How We Work
Horvath, Betty F. Jasper Makes Music
Krahn, Fernando. Robot-Bot-Bot
Lasker, Joseph Leon. Mothers Can Do
    Anything
Lindman, Maj Jan. Snipp, Snapp, Snurr
    and the Yellow Sled
McGowen, Tom. The Only Glupmaker in
    the U.S. Navy
Merriam, Eve. Mommies at Work
Petrides, Heidrun. Hans and Peter
Puner, Helen Walker. Daddys, What They
    Do All Day
Ross, Jessica. Ms. Klondike
Sandberg, Inger, and Sandberg, Lasse.
    Come On Out, Daddy

002.21 Activities—writing

Felt, Sue. Rosa-Too-Little
Geisel, Theodor Seuss. I Can Write! A
    Book by Me, Myself, with a Little
    Help from Theo. LeSieg
Hoban, Lillian. Arthur's Pen Pal
Johnston, Johanna. That's Right Edie
Joslin, Sesyle. Dear Dragon and Other
    Useful Letter Forms for Young
    Ladies and Gentlemen, Engaged in
    Everyday Correspondence
Krauss, Ruth. I Write It
Martin, Patricia Miles. The Pointed Brush

003 Adoption

Buck, Pearl Sydenstricker. Welcome Child
Bunin, Catherine, and Bunin, Sherry. Is
    That Your Sister?
Caines, Jeannette Franklin. Abby
Chapman, Noralee. The Story of Barbara
Lapsley, Susan. I Am Adopted
Milgram, Mary. Brothers Are All the Same
Rondell, Florence, and Michaels, Ruth.
    The Family That Grew
Stein, Sara Bonnett. The Adopted One
Udry, Janice May. Theodore's Parents
Wasson, Valentine P. The Chosen Baby

004 Airplanes

Firmin, Peter. Basil Brush Goes Flying
Gramatky, Hardie. Loopy
Lenski, Lois L. The Little Airplane
Nolan, Dennis. Wizard McBean and His
    Flying Machine
Olschewski, Alfred. We Fly
Phleger, Frederick B. Ann Can Fly
Scarry, Richard McClure. Richard Scarry's
    Great Big Air Book
Spier, Peter. Bored—Nothing to Do!
Ungerer, Tomi. The Mellops Go Flying
Wheeling, Lynn. When You Fly
Young, Miriam Burt. If I Flew a Plane
Zaffo, George J. The Big Book of Real
    Airplanes
    The Giant Nursery Book of Things
    That Go

005 Amphibians

Alexander, Martha G. No Ducks in Our
    Bathtub
Canfield, Jane White. The Frog Prince
Carrick, Malcolm. Today Is Shrew's Day
Charles, Robert H. The Roundabout Turn
Chenery, Janet. The Toad Hunt
Cortesi, Wendy W. Explore a Spooky
    Swamp
Dauer, Rosamond. Bullfrog Builds a
    House
    Bullfrog Grows Up
Duvoisin, Roger Antoine. Periwinkle
Flack, Marjorie. Tim Tadpole and the
    Great Bullfrog
Freschet, Berniece. The Old Bullfrog
A Frog He Would A-Wooing Go, illus. by
    William Stobbs
Frog Went A-Courtin', illus. by Feodor
    Stepanovich Rojankovsky
Gackenbach, Dick. Crackle, Gluck and the
    Sleeping Toad
Geisel, Theodor Seuss. Would You Rather
    Be a Bullfrog?
Harrison, David Lee. The Case of Og, the
    Missing Frog

Keith, Eros. Rrra-ah
Kellogg, Steven. The Mysterious Tadpole
Kepes, Juliet. Frogs, Merry
Kumin, Maxine W., and Sexton, Anne.
    Eggs of Things
Lane, Carolyn. The Voices of Greenwillow
    Pond
Lionni, Leo. Fish Is Fish
Lobel, Arnold Stark. Days with Frog and
    Toad
    Frog and Toad All Year
    Frog and Toad Are Friends
    Frog and Toad Together
McPhail, David. Captain Toad and the
    Motorbike
Martin, Patricia Miles. Jump Frog Jump
Massie, Diane Redfield. Walter Was a Frog
Mayer, Mercer. A Boy, a Dog, a Frog, and
    a Friend
    A Boy, a Dog and a Frog
    Frog Goes to Dinner
    Frog on His Own
    Frog, Where Are You?
    One Frog Too Many
Pendery, Rosemary. A Home for Hopper
Potter, Beatrix. The Tale of Mr. Jeremy
    Fisher
Pursell, Margaret Sanford. Sprig the Tree
    Frog
Rockwell, Anne F. Big Boss
Rockwell, Anne F., and Rockwell, Harlow.
    Toad
Seeger, Peter. Foolish Frog
Smith, Jim. The Frog Band and
    Durrington Dormouse
    The Frog Band and the Onion Seller
Stevenson, James. Monty
Stratemeyer, Clara Georgeanna, and
    Smith, Henry Lee, Jr. Frog Fun
    Tuggy
Tresselt, Alvin R. The Frog in the Well
Van Woerkom, Dorothy O. Sea Frog, City
    Frog
Wahl, Jan. Doctor Rabbit's Foundling
Yeoman, John. The Bears' Water Picnic
Zakhoder, Boris. Rosachok

006 Anatomy

Bishop, Claire Huchet. The Man Who Lost
    His Head
Brenner, Barbara. Faces, Faces
Castle, Sue. Face Talk, Hand Talk, Body
    Talk
Elkin, Benjamin. Gillespie and the Guards
Geisel, Theodor Seuss. The Foot Book
Holzenthaler, Jean. My Feet Do
    My Hands Can
Krauss, Ruth. Eyes, Nose, Fingers, Toes
Perkins, Al. The Ear Book
    Hand, Hand, Fingers, Thumb
    The Nose Book

Weiss, Leatie. Funny Feet
Yudell, Lynn Deena. Make a Face

007 Angels

Benét, William Rose. Timothy's Angels
Kavanaugh, James. The Crooked Angel
Knight, Hilary. Angels and Berries and
Candy Canes
Krahn, Fernando. A Funny Friend from
Heaven
Lathrop, Dorothy Pulis. An Angel in the
Woods
Martin, Judith, and Charlip, Remy. The
Tree Angel
Ness, Evaline. Marcella's Guardian Angel
Teal, Valentine. Angel Child

008 Animals

Aldridge, Josephine Haskell. The Best of
Friends
Allen, Jeffrey. Mary Alice, Operator
Number 9
Armour, Richard Willard. Animals on the
Ceiling
Aruego, José. Look What I Can Do
Aulaire, Ingri Mortenson d', and Aulaire,
Edgar Parin d'. Animals Everywhere
Baker, Betty. Partners
Bang, Betsy. The Old Woman and the Red
Pumpkin
Bannon, Laura May. The Scary Thing
Barry, Katharina. A Is for Anything; An
ABC Book of Pictures and Rhymes
Battles, Edith. What Does the Rooster Say,
Yoshio?
Baugh, Dolores M., and Pulsifer, Marjorie
P. Let's See the Animals
Baylor, Byrd. We Walk in Sandy Places
Beach, Stewart. Good Morning, Sun's Up
Bernstein, Margery, and Kobrin, Janet.
Coyote Goes Hunting for Fire
Bethell, Jean. Bathtime
Binzen, Bill. Alfred Goes House Hunting
Brooke, Leonard Leslie. Johnny Crow's
Garden
Johnny Crow's New Garden
Johnny Crow's Party
Brown, Marcia. The Blue Jackal
The Bun
Brown, Margaret Wise. Fox Eyes
Wait Till the Moon Is Full
Burningham, John Mackintosh. Mr.
Gumpy's Outing
Byars, Betsy Cromer. The Groober
Calhoun, Mary. Euphonia and the Flood
Carrick, Malcolm. Today Is Shrew's Day
Cathon, Laura E. Tot Botot and His Little
Flute
Chalmers, Audrey. Hundreds and
Hundreds of Pancakes

Chicken Little. Chicken Licken
Henny Penny, illus. by Paul Galdone
Henny Penny, illus. by William Stobbs
Cortesi, Wendy W. Explore a Spooky
Swamp
Dennis, Suzanne E. Answer Me That
De Regniers, Beatrice Schenk. It Does Not
Say Meow!
May I Bring a Friend?
Domanska, Janina. What Do You See?
Du Bois, William Pène. Bear Circus
Bear Party
Duplaix, Georges. Animal Stories
Duvoisin, Roger Antoine. A for the Ark
The Crocodile in the Tree
Jasmine
Our Veronica Goes to Petunia's Farm
Petunia
Petunia and the Song
Petunia, Beware!
Petunia Takes a Trip
Petunia's Treasure
Eckert, Horst. Tonight at Nine
Eichenberg, Fritz. Ape in Cape
Dancing in the Moon
Elkin, Benjamin. Why the Sun Was Late
Emberley, Barbara. One Wide River to
Cross
Ets, Marie Hall. Another Day
Beasts and Nonsense
Elephant in a Well
In the Forest
Just Me
Mister Penny
Mr. Penny's Circus
Mr. Penny's Race Horse
Play with Me
Evans, Eva Knox. Sleepy Time
Farber, Norma. How the Left-Behind
Beasts Built Ararat
Fay, Hermann. My Zoo
Fife, Dale. The Little Park
Fischer, Hans. The Birthday
Fisher, Aileen Lucia. Do Bears Have
Mothers Too?
We Went Looking
Where Does Everyone Go?
Flack, Marjorie. Ask Mr. Bear
Flora, James. The Day the Cow Sneezed
Francis, Frank. The Magic Wallpaper
Freeman, Don. Add-A-Line Alphabet
Frith, Michael K. Some of Us Walk, Some
Fly, Some Swim
Fromm, Lilo. Muffel and Plums
Futamata, Eigoro. How Not to Catch a
Mouse
Garelick, May. Look at the Moon
Garten, Jan. The Alphabet Tale
Gay, Zhenya. Look!
What's Your Name?
Geisel, Theodor Seuss. Mr. Brown Can
Moo, Can You?

Would You Rather Be a Bullfrog?

Gendel, Evelyn. Tortoise and Turtle Abroad

Ginsburg, Mirra. The Fox and the Hare
Mushroom in the Rain

Gobhai, Mehlli. Lakshmi the Water Buffalo Who Wouldn't

Gordon, Shirley. Grandma Zoo

Grabianski, Janusz. Grabianski's Wild Animals

Graham, John. A Crowd of Cows
I Love You, Mouse

Greenwood, Ann. A Pack of Dreams

Grimm, Jakob Ludwig Karl, and Grimm, Wilhelm Karl. The Bremen Town Musicians

Grosvenor, Donna. Zoo Babies

Haley, Gail Diana Einhart. Noah's Ark

Hall, Bill. A Year in the Forest

Hamberger, John F. The Day the Sun Disappeared

Hawkinson, John, and Hawkinson, Lucy Ozone. Robins and Rabbits

Hazen, Barbara Shook. Where Do Bears Sleep?

Henrioud, Charles. Mr. Noah and the Animals. Monsieur Noe et les Animaux

Hoban, Tana. Big Ones, Little Ones

Hoff, Carol. The Four Friends

Hogrogian, Nonny. Billy Goat and His Well-Fed Friends

Holl, Adelaide. The Rain Puddle

Holm, Mayling Mack. A Forest Christmas

Houston, John A. A Room Full of Animals

Hurd, Edith Thacher. Christmas Eve

Hutchins, Pat. The Silver Christmas Tree
Surprise Party

Ipcar, Dahlov Zorach. Animal Hide and Seek
Bright Barnyard
Brown Cow Farm
A Flood of Creatures
I Like Animals
I Love My Anteater with an A
Wild and Tame Animals

Jacobs, Joseph. Hereafterthis

Jaynes, Ruth. Tell Me Please! What's That?

Keats, Ezra Jack. Over in the Meadow
Pet Show!

Kepes, Juliet. Five Little Monkeys

Kessler, Ethel. What's inside the Box?

Kessler, Ethel, and Kessler, Leonard P. Do Baby Bears Sit in Chairs?

Kessler, Leonard P. Kick, Pass and Run
On Your Mark, Get Set, Go!

Kingman, Lee. Peter's Long Walk

Kipling, Rudyard. The Miracle of the Mountain

Kirn, Ann Minette. Beeswax Catches a Thief

Koffler, Camilla, and Gregor, Arthur. Animal Babies

Krahn, Fernando. The Biggest Christmas Tree on Earth

Krüss, James. 3 X 3, Three by Three

Kuskin, Karla Seidman. The Animals and the Ark
James and the Rain
Roar and More

Kwitz, Mary DeBall. When It Rains

Langstaff, John Meredith. Over in the Meadow

Lapp, Eleanor J. The Mice Came in Early This Year

Lathrop, Dorothy Pulis. Who Goes There?

Leisk, David Johnson. We Wonder What Will Walter Be, When He Grows Up?

Lenski, Lois L. Animals for Me
Big Little Davy

Lewis, Stephen. Zoo City

Lionni, Leo. The Biggest House in the World

Lipkind, William, and Mordvinoff, Nicolas. The Boy and the Forest

Lippman, Peter. New at the Zoo

The Little Red Hen, illus. by Janina Domanska

The Little Red Hen, illus. by Paul Galdone

The Little Red Hen, illus. by Mel Pekarsky

Lobel, Arnold Stark. A Holiday for Mister Muster
A Zoo for Mister Muster

Löfgren, Ulf. One-Two-Three

Low, Joseph. Adam's Book of Odd Creatures

McLeod, Emilie Warren. One Snail and Me

McNeer, May Yonge. Little Baptiste

Maestro, Betsy, and Maestro, Giulio. Leopard Is Sick

Maestro, Giulio. One More and One Less

Mann, Peggy. King Laurence the Alarm Clock

Marshall, James. Four Little Troubles
Willis

Martin, Patricia Miles. Sylvester Jones and the Voice in the Forest.

Massie, Diane Redfield. The Baby Beebee Bird

Mayer, Mercer. What Do You Do with a Kangaroo?

Meeks, Esther K. Friendly Farm Animals
Something New at the Zoo

Miles, Miska. Noisy Gander

Miller, Judith R. Nabob and the Geranium

Morrison, Sean. Is That a Happy Hippopotamus?

Morse, Samuel French. All in a Suitcase

Munari, Bruno. Animals for Sale
Bruno Munari's Zoo
The Elephant's Wish
Who's There? Open the Door

Nakano, Hirotaka. Elephant Blue

Nakatani, Chiyoko. The Zoo in My Garden
Old MacDonald Had a Farm, illus. by Mel
    Crawford
Old MacDonald Had a Farm, illus. by
    Abner Graboff
Old MacDonald Had a Farm, illus. by
    Robert Mead Quackenbush
Oxenbury, Helen. The Animal House
Pack, Robert. Then What Did You Do?
Palazzo, Tony. Animal Babies
    Animals 'Round the Mulberry Bush
Palmer, Helen Marion. I Was Kissed by a
    Seal at the Zoo
    Why I Built the Boogle House
Palmer, Mary. The No-Sort-of-Animal
Paterson, Diane. If I Were a Toad
Payne, Josephine Balfour. The Stable That
    Stayed
A Peaceable Kingdom; The Shaker
    Abecedarius
Peet, Bill. The Ant and the Elephant
    Farewell to Shady Glade
    The Gnats of Knotty Pine
Petersham, Maud Fuller, and Petersham,
    Miska. The Box with Red Wheels
Piatti, Celestino. Celestino Piatti's Animal
    ABC
Piers, Helen. A Helen Piers Animal Book
Polushkin, Maria. Who Said Meow?
Potter, Beatrix. Appley Dapply's Nursery
    Rhymes
    Cecily Parsley's Nursery Rhymes
    Ginger and Pickles
    A Treasury of Peter Rabbit and Other
    Stories
Provensen, Alice, and Provensen, Martin.
    Our Animal Friends
    The Year at Maple Hill Farm
Quackenbush, Robert Mead. Calling
    Doctor Quack
    Detective Mole
    Detective Mole and the Secret Clues
    Detective Mole and the Tip-Top
    Mystery
    Pete Pack Rat
Raskin, Ellen. And It Rained
    Who, Said Sue, Said Whoo?
Rey, Hans Augusto. Tit for Tat
    Where's My Baby?
Rey, Margret Elisabeth Waldstein, and Rey,
    Hans Augusto. Billy's Picture
Ricciuti, Edward R. An Animal for Alan
Rice, Eve. Sam Who Never Forgets
Richter, Mischa. Quack?
Robinson, Irene Bowen, and Robinson,
    William Wilcox. Picture Book of
    Animal Babies
Robinson, William Wilcox. On the Farm
Rockwell, Anne F. The Good Llama
    Poor Goose
Rojankovsky, Feodor Stepanovich. Animals
    in the Zoo

Animals on the Farm
The Great Big Animal Book
The Great Big Wild Animal Book
Roscoe, William. The Butterfly's Ball
Roughsey, Dick. The Giant Devil-Dingo
Russell, Solveig Paulson. What Good Is a
    Tail?
Sandberg, Inger. Nicholas' Favorite Pet
Scarry, Richard McClure. Is This the
    House of Mistress Mouse?
    Richard Scarry's Great Big Mystery
    Book
Schatz, Letta. The Extraordinary Tug-of-
    War
Schick, Eleanor. A Surprise in the Forest
Seignobosc, Françoise. The Big Rain
    The Story of Colette
Selsam, Millicent Ellis. All Kinds of Babies
    Benny's Animals and How He Put
    Them in Order
    Hidden Animals
    When an Animal Grows
Sendak, Maurice. Very Far Away
Sharmat, Marjorie Weinman. Walter the
    Wolf
Shecter, Ben. Stone House Stories
Short, Mayo. Andy and the Wild Ducks
Simon, Mina Lewiton, and Simon, Howard.
    If You Were an Eel, How Would
    You Feel?
Singer, Isaac Bashevis. Why Noah Chose
    the Dove
Skaar, Grace Marion. What Do the
    Animals Say?
Skorpen, Liesel Moak. All the Lassies
Slobodkin, Louis. Friendly Animals
    Melvin, the Moose Child
    Our Friendly Friends
Slobodkina, Esphyr. The Wonderful Feast
Snyder, Dick. One Day at the Zoo
    Talk to Me, Tiger
Spier, Peter. Gobble, Growl, Grunt
Spilka, Arnold. Little Birds Don't Cry
Steig, William. Sylvester and the Magic
    Pebble
Stevens, Carla. Hooray for Pig!
    The Pig and the Blue Flag
    Stories from a Snowy Meadow
Stratemeyer, Clara Georgeanna, and
    Smith, Henry Lee, Jr. Pepper
Szekeres, Cyndy. Long Ago
Taylor, Mark. "Lamb," Said the Lion, "I
    Am Here"
Tensen, Ruth Marjorie. Come to the Zoo!
Thomas, Patricia. "Stand Back," Said the
    Elephant, "I'm Going to Sneeze"
Tippett, James Sterling. I Know Some
    Little Animals
Tison, Annette, and Taylor, Talus. Animal
    Hide and Seek
Tresselt, Alvin R. The Little Lost Squirrel
    The Mitten

Wake Up, Farm!

Tworkov, Jack. The Camel Who Took a Walk

Uchida, Yoshiko. The Rooster Who Understood Japanese

Udry, Janice May. Is Susan Here?

Ueno, Noriko. Elephant Buttons

Unteracker, John. The Dreaming Zoo

Vance, Eleanor Graham, comp. From Little to Big; A Parade of Animal Poems

Van Woerkom, Dorothy O. The Rat, the Ox and the Zodiac

Varga, Judy. The Monster Behind Black Rock

Vigna, Judith. Couldn't We Have a Turtle Instead?

Villarejo, Mary. The Tiger Hunt

Vogel, Ilse-Margret. One Is No Fun but 20 Is Plenty

Vorse, Mary Ellen. Skinny Gets Fat
Wakey Goes to Bed

Waber, Bernard. "You Look Ridiculous," Said the Rhinoceros to the Hippopotamus

Wahl, Jan. Pleasant Fieldmouse
The Pleasant Fieldmouse Storybook
Pleasant Fieldmouse's Halloween Party

Walker, Challis. Three and Three

Ward, Nanda Weedon. The Black Sombrero

Ward, Nanda Weedon, and Haynes, Robert. The Elephant That Ga-lumphed

Watson, Jane Werner. The Marvelous Merry-Go-Round

Weil, Ann. Animal Families

Welber, Robert. Goodbye—Hello

Wiese, Kurt. The Thief in the Attic

Wildsmith, Brian. Brian Wildsmith's Wild Animals
Python's Party

Williams, Garth Montgomery. The Big Golden Animal ABC

Wiseman, Bernard. Little New Kangaroo

Wolo (pseud.). The Secret of the Ancient Oak

Wondriska, William. Which Way to the Zoo?

Woodcock, Louise Phinney. Hi Ho! Three in a Row

Wooley, Catherine. Andy and His Fine Friends

Yolen, Jane. An Invitation to the Butterfly Ball; A Counting Rhyme

Zakhoder, Boris. Rosachok

Zalben, Jane Breskin. Basil and Hillary

Zoll, Max Alfred. Animal Babies

008.01 Animals—anteaters

Waber, Bernard. An Anteater Named Arthur

008.02 Animals—antelopes

Wooley, Catherine. A Drink for Little Red Diker

008.03 Animals—armadillos

Simon, Sidney B. The Armadillo Who Had No Shell

008.04 Animals—badgers

Potter, Beatrix. The Tale of Mr. Tod

Tompert, Ann. Badger on His Own

008.05 Animals—bats

Freeman, Don. Hattie the Backstage Bat

Ungerer, Tomi. Rufus

008.06 Animals—bears

Alexander, Martha G. And My Mean Old Mother Will Be Sorry, Blackboard Bear
Blackboard Bear
I Sure Am Glad to See You, Blackboard Bear

Austin, Margot. Growl Bear

Bartoli, Jennifer. Snow on Bear's Nose

Benchley, Nathaniel. Red Fox and His Canoe

Berenstain, Stanley. The Bear Detectives: The Case of the Missing Pumpkin

Berenstain, Stanley, and Berenstain, Janice. Bears in the Night
Bears on Wheels
The Berenstain Bears and the Spooky Old Tree
The Berenstains' B Book
He Bear, She Bear
Inside Outside Upside Down

Bishop, Claire Huchet. Twenty Two Bears

Bond, Michael. Paddington at the Circus
Paddington at the Seaside
Paddington at the Tower
Paddington's Lucky Day

Bonners, Susan. Panda

Bowden, Joan Chase. Bear's Surprise Party

Bright, Robert. Me and the Bears

Brincklae, Julie. Gordon's House

Brustlein, Janice. Little Bear Marches in the St. Patrick's Day Parade
Little Bear's Christmas
Little Bear's New Year's Party
Little Bear's Pancake Party
Little Bear's Thanksgiving

Carleton, Barbee Oliver. Benny and the Bear

Delton, Judy. Brimhall Comes to Stay
Brimhall Turns to Magic

Dennis, Morgan. Burlap

Dorian, Marguerite. When the Snow Is Blue

Evers, Alf. There's No Such Animal

Fatio, Louise. The Happy Lion and the Bear

Flack, Marjorie. Ask Mr. Bear

Foreman, Michael. Moose

Freeman, Don. Bearymore

Ginsburg, Mirra. Two Greedy Bears

Guilfoile, Elizabeth. Nobody Listens to Andrew

Hellsing, Lennart. The Wonderful Pumpkin

Hoff, Sydney. Grizzwold

Jeschke, Susan. Angela and Bear

Koffler, Camilla. Two Little Bears

Koffler, Camilla, and Bonsal, Crosby Newell. Polar Bear Brothers

Kraus, Robert. Milton the Early Riser

Krauss, Ruth. Bears

Kuratomi, Chizuko. Mr. Bear and the Robbers

Lipkind, William. Nubber Bear

McCloskey, Robert John. Blueberries for Sal

Mack, Stanley. Ten Bears in My Bed, a Goodnight Countdown

McPhail, David. The Bear's Toothache
Henry Bear's Park

Marino, Dorothy Bronson. Buzzy Bear and the Rainbow
Buzzy Bear Goes Camping
Buzzy Bear Goes South
Buzzy Bear in the Garden
Buzzy Bear's Busy Day

Marshall, James. What's the Matter with Carruthers?

Mayer, Mercer. Two Moral Tales

Minarik, Else Holmelund. Father Bear Comes Home
A Kiss for Little Bear
Little Bear
Little Bear's Friend
Little Bear's Visit

Monsell, Helen Albee. Paddy's Christmas

Parker, Nancy Winslow. The Ordeal of Byron B. Blackbear

Peet, Bill. Big Bad Bruce

Pinkwater, Manus. The Bear's Picture

Ressner, Phil. August Explains

Rockwell, Anne F. A Bear, a Bobcat and Three Ghosts

Sharmat, Marjorie Weinman. I'm Terrific

Siewert, Margaret, and Savage, Kathleen. Bear Hunt

Sivulich, Sandra Stroner. I'm Going on a Bear Hunt

Skorpen, Liesel Moak. Outside My Window

Steiner, Jörg, and Müller, Jörg. The Bear Who Wanted to Be a Bear

Stevenson, James. The Bear Who Had No Place to Go

Taylor, Mark. Henry the Explorer

The Three Bears. The Story of the Three Bears, illus. by Leonard Leslie Brooke
The Story of the Three Bears, illus. by William Stobbs

The Three Bears, illus. by Paul Galdone

The Three Bears, illus. by Feodor Stepanovich Rojankovsky

The Three Bears, illus. by Irma Wilde

Turkle, Brinton Cassady. Deep in the Forest

Van Woerkom, Dorothy O. Becky and the Bear

Venable, Alan. The Checker Players

Ward, Lynd Kendall. The Biggest Bear

Whitney, Julie. Bears Are Sleeping

Wildsmith, Brian. The Lazy Bear

Winter, Paula. The Bear and the Fly

Yeoman, John. The Bears' Water Picnic

Zimnik, Reiner. The Bear on the Motorcycle

Zirbes, Laura. How Many Bears?

008.07 Animals—beavers

Bowen, Vernon. The Lazy Beaver

Tresselt, Alvin R. The Beaver Pond

008.08 Animals—camels

Goodenow, Earle. The Last Camel

McKee, David. The Day the Tide Went Out and Out and Out

Tworkov, Jack. The Camel Who Took a Walk

008.09 Animals—cats

Aulaire, Ingri Mortenson d', and Aulaire, Edgar Parin d'. Foxie, the Singing Dog

Averill, Esther Holden. The Fire Cat
Jenny's Birthday Book

Berg, Jean Horton. The O'Learys and Friends
The Wee Little Man

Blegvad, Lenore Hochman, ed. Mittens for Kittens, and Other Rhymes about Cats

Boegehold, Betty. Pawpaw's Run
Three to Get Ready

Bonsall, Crosby Newell. The Case of the Cat's Meow
Listen, Listen!

Brandenberg, Franz. No School Today!
A Picnic, Hurrah!

Bright, Robert. Miss Pattie

Brown, Marcia. Felice

Brown, Margaret Wise. A Pussycat's Christmas
When the Wind Blew

Brown, Myra Berry. Benjy's Blanket
Burch, Robert. Joey's Cat
Calhoun, Mary. Cross-Country Cat
    The Witch of Hissing Hill
    Wobble the Witch Cat
Cameron, Polly. The Cat Who Thought
    He Was a Tiger
Carle, Eric. Have You Seen My Cat?
Cass, Joan. The Cats Go to Market
Chalmers, Audrey. A Kitten's Tale
Chalmers, Mary Eileen. Be Good, Harry
    George Appleton
    Merry Christmas, Harry
    Take a Nap, Harry
    Throw a Kiss, Harry
Chenery, Janet. Pickles and Jack
Clymer, Eleanor Lowenton. Horatio
    Horatio Goes to the Country
Cook, Bernadine. Looking for Susie
Cretan, Gladys Yessayan. Lobo and
    Brewster
Damjan, Mischa (pseud.). The Little Prince
    and the Tiger Cat
Daugherty, Charles Michael. Wisher
Davies, Sumiko. Kittymouse
Dennis, Morgan. Skit and Skat
De Regniers, Beatrice Schenk. Cats Cats
    Cats Cats Cats
Diska, Pat. Andy Says Bonjour!
Duvoisin, Roger Antoine. Veronica and the
    Birthday Present
Ets, Marie Hall. Mr. T. W. Anthony Woo
Fatio, Louise, and Duvoisin, Roger
    Antoine. Marc and Pixie and the
    Walls in Mrs. Jones's Garden
Feder, Jane. Beany
Fischer, Hans. Pitschi, the Kitten Who
    Always Wanted to Do Something Else
Flack, Marjorie. Angus and the Cat
    William and His Kitten
Flory, Jane. We'll Have a Friend for Lunch
Gág, Wanda. Millions of Cats
Gantos, John B. Rotten Ralph
Geisel, Theodor Seuss. The Cat in the Hat
    The Cat in the Hat Comes Back!
Goodall, John Strickland. The Surprise
    Picnic
Grabianski, Janusz. Cats
Haley, Gail Diana Einhart. The Post Office
    Cat
Hazen, Barbara Shook. Tight Times
Hillert, Margaret. The Little Runaway
Hoff, Sydney. Katy's Kitty; Three Kitty
    Stories
Holmes, Efner Tudor. The Christmas Cat
Hurd, Edith Thacher. Come and Have
    Fun
    No Funny Business
    The So-So Cat
Hürlimann, Ruth. The Proud White Cat
Ipcar, Dahlov Zorach. The Cat at Night
    The Cat Came Back

Iwamatsu, Tomoe Sasako. Momo's Kitten
Jack Sprat. The Life of Jack Sprat, His
    Wife and His Cat
Keats, Ezra Jack. Hi, Cat!
    Kitten for a Day
    Psst, Doggie
Kent, Jack. The Fat Cat
Knotts, Howard Clayton. The Winter Cat
Koenig, Marion. The Wonderful World of
    Night
Koffler, Camilla. I'll Show You Cats
Krahn, Fernando. Catch That Cat!
Krasilovsky, Phyllis. Scaredy Cat
Lansdown, Brenda. Galumpf
Laskowski, Jerzy. Master of the Royal Cats
Lasson, Robert. Orange Oliver
Lear, Edward. The Owl and the Pussy-Cat,
    illus. by Barbara Cooney
    The Owl and the Pussy-Cat, illus. by
    William Pène Du Bois
    The Owl and the Pussy-Cat, illus. by
    Gwen Fulton
Lexau, Joan M. Come Here, Cat
Lindman, Maj Jan. Flicka, Ricka, Dicka and
    the Three Kittens
Lipkind, William, and Mordvinoff, Nicolas.
    Russet and the Two Reds
    The Two Reds
Livermore, Elaine. Find the Cat
MacArthur-Onslow, Annette. Minnie
Mandry, Kathy. The Cat and the Mouse
    and the Mouse and the Cat
Mayer, Mercer. The Great Cat Chase
Meddaugh, Susan. Too Short Fred
Minarik, Else Holmelund. Cat and Dog
Moskin, Marietta D. Lysbet and the Fire
    Kittens
The Moving Adventures of Old Dame
    Trot and Her Comical Cat
Murphey, Sara. The Animal Hat Shop
Newberry, Clare Turlay. April's Kittens
    The Kittens' ABC
    Marshmallow
    Mittens
    Pandora
    Percy, Polly and Pete
    Smudge
    T-Bone, the Baby-Sitter
    Widget
Nicoll, Helen. Meg and Mog
    Meg at Sea
    Meg on the Moon
    Meg's Eggs
Northrop, Mili. The Watch Cat
Oakley, Graham. The Church Cat Abroad
    The Church Mice Adrift
    The Church Mice and the Moon
    The Church Mice at Bay
    The Church Mice Spread Their Wings
    The Church Mouse
Otto, Margaret Glover. The Little Brown
    Horse

Panek, Dennis. Catastrophe Cat
    Catastrophe Cat at the Zoo
Peet, Bill. Jennifer and Josephine
Peppé, Rodney. Cat and Mouse
Perrault, Charles. Puss in Boots, illus. by
    Marcia Brown
    Puss in Boots, illus. by Hans Fischer
    Puss in Boots, illus. by Paul Galdone
    Puss in Boots, illus. by Julia Noonan
    Puss in Boots, illus. by William Stobbs
    Puss in Boots, illus. by Barry Wilkinson
Politi, Leo. Lito and the Clown
Potter, Beatrix. The Pie and the Patty-Pan
    Rolly-Polly Pudding
    The Sly Old Cat
    The Story of Miss Moppet
Ridlon, Marci. Kittens and More Kittens
Robinson, Thomas Pendleton. Buttons
Ross, George Maxim. When Lucy Went
    Away
Schatz, Letta. Whiskers My Cat
Seidler, Rosalie. Grumpus and the
    Venetian Cat
Seignobosc, Françoise. Minou
Selsam, Millicent Ellis. How Kittens Grow
Shaw, Richard. The Kitten in the Pumpkin
    Patch
Skaar, Grace Marion. Nothing But (Cats)
    and All About (Dogs)
Skaar, Grace Marion, and Woodcock,
    Louise Phinney. The Very Little
    Dog; and The Smart Little Kitty
Sloan, Carolyn. Carter Is a Painter's Cat
Slobodkin, Louis. Colette and the Princess
Slobodkina, Esphyr. Pinky and the
    Petunias
Steiner, Charlotte. Kiki and Muffy
Stratemeyer, Clara Georgeanna, and
    Smith, Henry Lee, Jr. Pepper
Sutton, Eve. My Cat Likes to Hide in
    Boxes
Tapio, Pat Decker. The Lady Who Saw the
    Good Side of Everything
Taylor, Mark. The Case of the Missing
    Kittens
Thompson, Harwood. The Witch's Cat
Titus, Eve. Anatole and the Cat
Turner, Nancy Byrd. When It Rains Cats
    and Dogs
Udry, Janice May. "Oh No, Cat!"
Ungerer, Tomi. No Kiss for Mother
Untermeyer, Louis. The Kitten Who
    Barked
Vacheron, Edith, and Kahl, Virginia
    Caroline. Here Is Henri!
    More about Henri!
Viorst, Judith. The Tenth Good Thing
    about Barney
Waber, Bernard. Good-Bye, Funny
    Dumpy-Lumpy
    Mice on My Mind
    Rich Cat, Poor Cat

Wagner, Jenny. John Brown, Rose and the
    Midnight Cat
Wahl, Jan. Push Kitty
Waldman, Dorothy. Goomer
Walker, David E. Pimpernel and the
    Poodle
Warburg, Sandol Stoddard. My Very Own
    Special Particular Private and
    Personal Cat
Watson, Pauline. Curley Cat Baby-Sits
Weih, Erica. Count the Cats
Wezel, Peter. The Naughty Bird
Whitney, Alma Marshak. Leave Herbert
    Alone
Williams, Gweneira Maureen. Timid
    Timothy, the Kitten Who Learned to
    Be Brave
Wilson, Joyce Lancaster. Tobi
Wooley, Catherine. The Cat That Joined
    the Club
Wright, Dare. The Doll and the Kitten
    The Lonely Doll Learns a Lesson
    Look at a Kitten
Wright, Josephine. Cotton Cat and Martha
    Mouse
Yeoman, John. Mouse Trouble

008.10 Animals—cats, wild

Adams, Richard George. The Tyger
    Voyage
Anderson, Clarence William. Blaze and the
    Mountain Lion
Anderson, Paul S. Red Fox and the
    Hungry Tiger
Bannerman, Helen Brodie Cowan. The
    Story of Little Black Sambo
Bemelmans, Ludwig. Marina
Brown, Marcia. Once a Mouse
Brown, Margaret Wise. The Sleepy Little
    Lion
Daugherty, James Henry. Andy and the
    Lion
    The Picnic
Devlin, Wende, and Devlin, Harry. Aunt
    Agatha, There's a Lion under the
    Couch!
Dines, Glen. A Tiger in the Cherry Tree
Domanska, Janina. Why So Much Noise?
Fatio, Louise. The Happy Lion
    The Happy Lion and the Bear
    The Happy Lion in Africa
    The Happy Lion Roars
    The Happy Lion's Quest
    The Happy Lion's Rabbits
    The Happy Lion's Treasure
    The Happy Lion's Vacation
    The Three Happy Lions
Fenner, Carol Elizabeth. Tigers in the
    Cellar
Foreman, Michael. War and Peas
Freeman, Don. Dandelion

Galdone, Paul. Androcles and the Lion
    The Horse, the Fox, and the Lion
Geisel, Theodor Seuss. I Can Lick 30
    Tigers Today and Other Stories
Grabianski, Janusz. Androcles and the Lion
Hawkins, Mark. A Lion Under Her Bed
Hurd, Edith Thacher. Johnny Lion's Bad
    Day
    Johnny Lion's Book
    Johnny Lion's Rubber Boots
Ipcar, Dahlov Zorach. Stripes and Spots
Kepes, Charles. Run, Little Monkeys, Run,
    Run, Run
Kirn, Ann Minette. Leopard on a String
Kishida, Eriko. The Lion and the Bird's
    Nest
Kraus, Robert. Leo the Late Bloomer
La Fontaine, Jean de. The Lion and the
    Rat
Maestro, Betsy, and Maestro, Giulio.
    Leopard Is Sick
Mahy, Margaret. A Lion in the Meadow
Makower, Sylvia. Samson's Breakfast
Mann, Peggy. King Laurence the Alarm
    Clock
Newberry, Clare Turlay. Herbert the Lion
Peet, Bill. Eli
    Hubert's Hair Raising Adventures
    Randy's Dandy Lions
Prelutsky, Jack. The Terrible Tiger
Rockwell, Anne F. A Bear, a Bobcat and
    Three Ghosts
    Big Boss
Rose, Gerald. The Tiger-Skin Rug
Sargent, Robert. A Trick on a Lion
Siddiqui, Ashraf. Bhombal Dass, the Uncle
    of Lion
Siepmann, Jane. The Lion on Scott Street
Skorpen, Liesel Moak. If I Had a Lion
Skurzynski, Gloria. The Magic Pumpkin
Stephenson, Dorothy. How to Scare a Lion
Stewart, Elizabeth Laing. The Lion Twins
Taylor, Mark. Henry Explores the Jungle
Townsend, Kenneth. Felix the Bald-
    Headed Lion
Tworkov, Jack. The Camel Who Took a
    Walk
Varga, Judy. Miss Lollipop's Lion
Villarejo, Mary. The Tiger Hunt
Wersba, Barbara. Do Tigers Ever Bite
    Kings?
Whitney, Alex. Once a Bright Red Tiger
Williamson, Hamilton. Lion Cub: A Jungle
    Tale
Yurdin, Betty. The Tiger in the Teapot

008.11 Animals—chipmunks

Fatio, Louise, and Duvoisin, Roger
    Antoine. Marc and Pixie and the
    Walls in Mrs. Jones's Garden

Moore, Lilian. Little Raccoon and No
    Trouble at All
Prince, Dorothy E. Speedy Gets Around
Williams, Barbara. Chester Chipmunk's
    Thanksgiving

008.12 Animals—cows, bulls

Carrick, Donald. The Deer in the Pasture
Dennis, Wesley. Flip and the Cows
Ets, Marie Hall. The Cow's Party
Hader, Berta Hoerner, and Hader, Elmer
    Stanley. The Story of Pancho and the
    Bull with the Crooked Tail
Koch, Dorothy Clarke. When the Cows Got
    Out
Krasilovsky, Phyllis. The Cow Who Fell in
    the Canal
Leaf, Munro. The Story of Ferdinand the
    Bull
Lent, Blair. Pistachio
Meeks, Esther K. Curious Cow
Merrill, Jean. Tell about the Cowbarn,
    Daddy
Sewall, Marcia. The Wee, Wee Mannie and
    the Big, Big Coo
Wright, Dare. Look at a Calf

008.13 Animals—deer

Bemelmans, Ludwig. Parsley
Carrick, Donald. The Deer in the Pasture
Lindman, Maj Jan. Snipp, Snapp, Snurr
    and the Reindeer
Schlein, Miriam. Deer in the Snow

008.14 Animals—dogs

Alexander, Martha G. Bobo's Dream
Ambler, Christopher Gifford. Ten Little
    Foxhounds
Annett, Cora. The Dog Who Thought He
    Was a Boy
Ardizzone, Edward Jeffrey Irving. Tim's
    Friend Towser
Aulaire, Ingri Mortenson d', and Aulaire,
    Edgar Parin d'. Foxie, the Singing
    Dog
Barton, Byron. Jack and Fred
    Where's Al?
Batherman, Muriel. Some Things You
    Should Know about My Dog
Battles, Edith. The Terrible Terrier
Bemelmans, Ludwig. Madeline's Rescue
Beresford, Elisabeth. Snuffle to the Rescue
Black, Irma Simonton. Big Puppy and
    Little Puppy
Blegvad, Lenore Hochman, ed. Hark!
    Hark! The Dogs Do Bark, and Other
    Rhymes about Dogs
Bolognese, Elaine, and Bolognese, Donald
    Alan. The Sleepy Watchdog

Bonsall, Crosby Newell. And I Mean It,
  Stanley
  Listen, Listen!
Bontemps, Arna Wendell, and Conroy,
  Jack. The Fast Sooner Hound
Bowden, Joan Chase. Boo and the Flying
  Flews
Bridgman, Elizabeth P. New Dog Next
  Door
Bridwell, Norman. Clifford's Good Deeds
  Clifford's Halloween
Brown, Margaret Wise. Country Noisy
  Book
  Indoor Noisy Book
  The Quiet Noisy Book
  Winter Noisy Book
Brustlein, Janice. Mr. and Mrs. Button's
  Wonderful Watchdogs
Buckley, Helen Elizabeth. Josie's Buttercup
Burningham, John Mackintosh.
  Cannonball Simp
  The Dog
Calhoun, Mary. Houn' Dog
  Mrs. Dog's Own House
Carrick, Carol. The Accident
  The Foundling
Carroll, Ruth Robinson. What Whiskers
  Did
Chalmers, Audrey. Hector and Mr. Murfit
Chenery, Janet. Pickles and Jack
Christian, Mary Blount. No Dogs Allowed,
  Jonathan!
Ciardi, John. Scrappy the Pup
Coontz, Otto. The Quiet House
Dennis, Morgan. Burlap
  The Pup Himself
  Skit and Skat
Du Bois, William Pène. Giant Otto
  Otto and the Magic Potatoes
  Otto at Sea
  Otto in Africa
  Otto in Texas
Dupre, Ramona Dorrel. Too Many Dogs
Duvoisin, Roger Antoine. Day and Night
Eastman, Philip Day. Go, Dog, Go!
Ehrlich, Bettina. Pantaloni
Elkin, Benjamin. The Big Jump and Other
  Stories
Erickson, Phoebe. Just Follow Me
Ets, Marie Hall. Mr. T. W. Anthony Woo
Flack, Marjorie. Angus and the Cat
  Angus and the Ducks
  Angus Lost
Freeman, Don. Ski Pup
Frith, Michael. I'll Teach My Dog 100
  Words
Gackenbach, Dick. Claude and Pepper
  Claude the Dog
  Pepper and All the Legs
Gág, Wanda. Nothing at All
Galdone, Paul. The Horse, the Fox, and
  the Lion

Gannett, Ruth Stiles. Katie and the Sad
  Noise
Goodspeed, Peter. Hugh and Fitzhugh
Grabianski, Janusz. Dogs
Graham, Margaret Bloy. Benjy and the
  Barking Bird
  Benjy's Boat Trip
  Benjy's Dog House
Hamberger, John F. Hazel Was an Only
  Pet
  The Lazy Dog
Hoban, Russell Conwell. The Stone Doll of
  Sister Brute
Hoff, Sydney. Barkley
  Lengthy
  Pete's Pup; Three Puppy Stories
Holt, Margaret. David McCheever's
  Twenty-Nine Dogs
Hurd, Edith Thacher. Little Dog,
  Dreaming
Ipcar, Dahlov Zorach. Black and White
Iwasaki, Chihiro. What's Fun Without a
  Friend?
Kahl, Virginia Caroline. Away Went
  Wolfgang
  Maxie
Keats, Ezra Jack. Kitten for a Day
  My Dog Is Lost!
  Psst, Doggie
  Skates
  Whistle for Willie
Kopczynski, Anna. Jerry and Ami
Kuskin, Karla Seidman. Watson, the
  Smartest Dog in the U.S.A
Laskowski, Jerzy. Master of the Royal Cats
Lathrop, Dorothy Pulis. Puppies for Keeps
Leaf, Munro. Noodle
Leichman, Seymour. Shaggy Dogs and
  Spotty Dogs and Shaggy and Spotty
  Dogs
Leisk, David Johnson. The Blue Ribbon
  Puppies
  Terrible Terrifying Toby
Lenski, Lois L. Davy and His Dog
  Debbie and Her Dolls
  A Dog Came to School
Levy, Elizabeth. Something Queer Is Going
  On
Lexau, Joan M. Go Away, Dog
Lindman, Maj Jan. Flicka, Ricka, Dicka and
  a Little Dog
  Flicka, Ricka, Dicka and Their New
  Skates
  Snipp, Snapp, Snurr and the Seven
  Dogs
Lipkind, William, and Mordvinoff, Nicolas.
  Finders Keepers
Lopshire, Robert Martin. Put Me in the
  Zoo
Machetanz, Sara, and Machetanz, Fred. A
  Puppy Named Gia

Marshall, James. Miss Dog's Christmas
Treat
Speedboat
Martin, Patricia Miles. Show and Tell
Martin, Sarah Catherine. The Comic
Adventures of Old Mother Hubbard
and Her Dog
Old Mother Hubbard and Her Dog,
illus. by Paul Galdone
Old Mother Hubbard and Her Dog,
illus. by Evaline Ness
Mayer, Mercer. A Boy, a Dog, a Frog, and
a Friend
A Boy, a Dog and a Frog
Miles, Miska. Somebody's Dog
Minarik, Else Holmelund. Cat and Dog
Modell, Frank. Tooley! Tooley!
Nakatani, Chiyoko. The Day Chiro Was
Lost
Newberry, Clare Turlay. Barkis
Overbeck, Cynthia. Rusty the Irish Setter
Peet, Bill. The Whingdingdilly
Perkins, Al. The Digging-est Dog
Politi, Leo. Emmet
The Nicest Gift
Potter, Beatrix. The Pie and the Patty-Pan.
Prather, Ray. Double Dog Dare
Rey, Margret Elisabeth Waldstein. Pretzel
Pretzel and the Puppies
Rice, Eve. Papa's Lemonade and Other
Stories
Rockwell, Anne F. Willy Runs Away
Rose, Mitchel. Norman
Rowand, Phyllis. George
George Goes to Town
Sandberg, Inger. Nicholas' Favorite Pet
Saxon, Charles D. Don't Worry about
Poopsie
Scott, Sally. Little Wiener
There Was Timmy!
Selsam, Millicent Ellis. How Puppies Grow
Sewell, Helen Moore. Birthdays for Robin
Ming and Mehitable
Shortall, Leonard W. Andy, the Dog
Walker
Singer, Marilyn. The Dog Who Insisted He
Wasn't
Skaar, Grace Marion. Nothing But (Cats)
and All About (Dogs)
Skaar, Grace Marion, and Woodcock,
Louise Phinney. The Very Little
Dog; and The Smart Little Kitty
Skorpen, Liesel Moak. All the Lassies
Old Arthur
Steig, William. Caleb and Kate
Steiner, Charlotte. Lulu
Pete and Peter
Stratemeyer, Clara Georgeanna, and
Smith, Henry Lee, Jr. Tuggy
Sugita, Yutaka. My Friend Little John and
Me
Surany, Anico. Kati and Kormos

Taylor, Mark. The Case of the Missing
Kittens
Old Blue, You Good Dog You
Taylor, Sydney. The Dog Who Came to
Dinner
Tippett, James Sterling. Shadow and the
Stocking
Titus, Eve. Anatole and the Poodle
Turkle, Brinton Cassady. The Sky Dog
Turner, Nancy Byrd. When It Rains Cats
and Dogs
Udry, Janice May. Alfred
What Mary Jo Wanted
Untermeyer, Louis. The Kitten Who
Barked
Van Den Honert, Dorry. Demi the Baby
Sitter
Wagner, Jenny. John Brown, Rose and the
Midnight Cat
Wahl, Jan. Frankenstein's Dog
Walker, David E. Pimpernel and the
Poodle
Ward, Lynd Kendall. Nic of the Woods
Weil, Lisl. Bitzli and the Big Bad Wolf
Pudding's Wonderful Bone
Weiss, Harvey. The Sooner Hound
Wiese, Kurt. The Dog, the Fox and the
Fleas
Williamson, Stan. The No-Bark Dog
Wold, Jo Anne. Well! Why Didn't You Say
So?
Wooley, Catherine. Part-Time Dog
The Puppy Who Wanted a Boy
Wright, Lula Esther. Little Lost Dog
Zion, Gene. Harry and the Lady Next
Door
Harry by the Sea
Harry the Dirty Dog
No Roses for Harry!
Zolotow, Charlotte Shapiro. The Poodle
Who Barked at the Wind

008.15 Animals—dolphins

Benchley, Nathaniel. The Several Tricks of
Edgar Dolphin
Morris, Robert A. Dolphin
Nakatani, Chiyoko. Fumio and the
Dolphins

008.16 Animals—donkeys

Aesopus. The Miller, His Son, and Their
Donkey
Brown, Marcia. Tamarindo
Calhoun, Mary. Old Man Whickutt's
Donkey
Duvoisin, Roger Antoine. Donkey-Donkey
Ehrlich, Bettina. Cocolo Comes to America
Cocolo's Home
Piccolo
Evans, Katherine. The Man, the Boy, and
the Donkey

Gramatky, Hardie. Bolivar
Gray, Genevieve. How Far, Felipe?
La Fontaine, Jean de. The Miller, the Boy
  and the Donkey
McCrea, James, and McCrea, Ruth. The
  King's Procession
Maiorano, Robert. Francisco
Palazzo, Tony. Bianco and the New World
Seignobosc, Françoise. Chouchou
Showalter, Jean B. The Donkey Ride
Steig, William. Farmer Palmer's Wagon
  Ride
  Sylvester and the Magic Pebble
Van Woerkom, Dorothy O. Donkey Ysabel

008.17 Animals—elephants

Brunhoff, Jean de. Babar and Father
  Christmas
  Babar and His Children
  Babar and Zephir
  Babar the King
  The Story of Babar, the Little Elephant
  The Travels of Babar
Brunhoff, Laurent de. Babar and the
  Willy-Wully
  Babar Comes to America
  Babar Loses His Crown
  Babar Visits Another Planet
  Babar's Birthday Surprise
  Babar's Castle
  Babar's Cousin, That Rascal Arthur
  Babar's Fair Will Be Opened Next
    Sunday
  Babar's Mystery
Delton, Judy. Penny Wise, Fun Foolish
Domanska, Janina. Why So Much Noise?
Ets, Marie Hall. Elephant in a Well
Foulds, Elfrida Vipont. The Elephant and
  the Bad Baby
Geisel, Theodor Seuss. Horton Hatches the
  Egg
  Horton Hears a Who
Hoff, Sydney. Oliver
Hogan, Inez. About Nono, the Baby
  Elephant
Joslin, Sesyle. Baby Elephant and the
  Secret Wishes
  Baby Elephant Goes to China
  Baby Elephant's Trunk
  Brave Baby Elephant
  Senor Baby Elephant, the Pirate
Klein, Suzanne. An Elephant in My Bed
Koffler, Camilla. The Little Elephant
Kraus, Robert. Boris Bad Enough
Lawrence, John D. Pope Leo's Elephant
Lipkind, William, and Mordvinoff, Nicolas.
  Chaga
Löfgren, Ulf. The Traffic Stopper That
  Became a Grandmother Visitor
McKee, David. Elmer, the Story of a
  Patchwork Elephant

Martin, William Ivan, and Martin, Bernard
  Herman. Smoky Poky
Mayer, Mercer. Ah-choo
Nakàno, Hirotaka. Elephant Blue
Patz, Nancy. Pumpernickel Tickle and
  Mean Green Cheese
Peet, Bill. The Ant and the Elephant
  Ella
Perkins, Al. Tubby and the Lantern
  Tubby and the Poo-Bah
Petersham, Maud Fuller, and Petersham,
  Miska. The Circus Baby
Platt, Kin. Big Max
Quigley, Lillian. The Blind Men and the
  Elephant
Rosenberg, Ethel Clifford. Why Is an
  Elephant Called an Elephant?
Saxe, John Godfrey. The Blind Men and
  the Elephant
Schlein, Miriam. Elephant Herd
Simont, Marc. How Come Elephants?
Slobodkina, Esphyr. Pezzo the Peddler and
  the Circus Elephant
Steig, William. An Eye for Elephants
Tresselt, Alvin R. The Smallest Elephant in
  the World
Wahl, Jan. Hello, Elephant
Ward, Nanda Weedon, and Haynes,
  Robert. The Elephant That Ga-
  lumphed
Weisgard, Leonard. Silly Willy Nilly
Wells, Herbert George. The Adventures of
  Tommy
Williamson, Hamilton. Little Elephant
Young, Miriam Burt. If I Rode an
  Elephant

008.18 Animals—foxes

Aesopus. Three Fox Fables
Ambrus, Victor G. A Country Wedding
Anderson, Paul S. Red Fox and the
  Hungry Tiger
Bemelmans, Ludwig. Welcome Home
Berson, Harold. Henry Possum
Brown, Marcia. The Bun
  The Neighbors
Brown, Margaret Wise. Fox Eyes
Burningham, John Mackintosh. Harquin,
  the Fox Who Went Down to the
  Valley
Calhoun, Mary. Houn' Dog
Carroll, Ruth Robinson. What Whiskers
  Did
Chaucer, Geoffrey. Chanticleer and the
  Fox
Domanska, Janina. The Best of the
  Bargain
Fatio, Louise. The Red Bantam
Firmin, Peter. Basil Brush and a Dragon
  Basil Brush Builds a House
  Basil Brush Finds Treasure

Basil Brush Gets a Medal
Basil Brush Goes Flying
The Fox Went Out on a Chilly Night
Galdone, Paul. The Horse, the Fox, and
the Lion
Ginsburg, Mirra. The Fox and the Hare
Mushroom in the Rain
Two Greedy Bears
Hogrogian, Nonny. One Fine Day
Hutchins, Pat. Rosie's Walk
Lifton, Betty Jean. The Many Lives of
Chio and Goro
Lindgren, Astrid Ericsson. The Tomten
and the Fox
Lionni, Leo. In the Rabbitgarden
Lipkind, William, and Mordvinoff, Nicolas.
The Christmas Bunny
The Little Tiny Rooster
Miles, Miska. The Fox and the Fire
Potter, Beatrix. The Tale of Mr. Tod
Preston, Edna Mitchell. Squawk to the
Moon, Little Goose
Rockwell, Anne F. Big Boss
Schlein, Miriam. The Four Little Foxes
Steig, William. Roland the Minstrel Pig
Tompert, Ann. Little Fox Goes to the End
of the World
Varga, Judy. The Mare's Egg
Watson, Clyde. Tom Fox and the Apple
Pie
Wells, Rosemary. Don't Spill It Again,
James
Wiese, Kurt. The Dog, the Fox and the
Fleas

008.19 Animals—gerbils

Tobias, Tobi. Petey

008.20 Animals—giraffes

Duvoisin, Roger Antoine. Periwinkle
Rey, Hans Augusto. Cecily G and the Nine
Monkeys
Wynants, Miche. The Giraffe of King
Charles X

008.21 Animals—goats

Ambrus, Victor G. The Three Poor Tailors
Asbjørnsen, Peter Christen. The Three
Billy Goats Gruff, illus. by Paul
Galdone
The Three Billy Goats Gruff, illus. by
William Stobbs
Asbjørnsen, Peter Christen, and Moe,
Jørgen Engebretsen. The Three Billy
Goats Gruff
Berson, Harold. Balarin's Goat
Blood, Charles L., and Link, Martin. The
Goat in the Rug
Chandoha, Walter. A Baby Goat for You

Damjan, Mischa (pseud.). The Wolf and
the Kid
Daudet, Alphonse. The Brave Little Goat
of Monsieur Seguin
Dunn, Judy. The Little Goat
Hillert, Margaret. The Three Goats
Hogrogian, Nonny. Billy Goat and His
Well-Fed Friends
Leaf, Munro. Gordon, the Goat
Lipkind, William, and Mordvinoff, Nicolas.
Billy the Kid
Miller, Albert. The Hungry Goat
Seignobosc, Françoise. Biquette, the White
Goat
Springtime for Jeanne-Marie
Siddiqui, Ashraf. Bhombal Dass, the Uncle
of Lion
Slobodkin, Louis. The Polka-Dot Goat
Up High and Down Low
Tudor, Tasha. Corgiville Fair
Watson, Nancy Dingman. The Birthday
Goat

008.22 Animals—gorillas

Hazen, Barbara Shook. The Gorilla Did It!
Hoff, Sydney. Julius
Krahn, Fernando. The Great Ape
Schertle, Alice. The Gorilla in the Hall

008.23 Animals—groundhogs

Cohen, Carol L. Wake Up Groundhog!
Coombs, Patricia. Tilabel
Hamberger, John F. This Is the Day
Kesselman, Wendy Ann. Time for Jody
Leisk, David Johnson. Will Spring Be
Early?
McNulty, Faith. Woodchuck
Palazzo, Tony. Waldo the Woodchuck
Watson, Wendy. Has Winter Come?

008.24 Animals—guinea pigs

Meshover, Leonard, and Feistel, Sally. The
Guinea Pigs That Went to School
Potter, Beatrix. The Tale of Tuppenny
Pursell, Margaret Sanford. Polly the
Guinea Pig

008.25 Animals—hamsters

Claude-Lafontaine, Pascale. Monsieur
Bussy, the Celebrated Hamster

008.26 Animals—hedgehogs

Brook, Judy. Tim Mouse Goes
Downstream
Tim Mouse Visits the Farm
Domanska, Janina. The Best of the
Bargain

Holden, Edith B. The Hedgehog Feast
Myller, Lois. No! No!
Potter, Beatrix. The Tale of Mrs. Tiggy-
    Winkle
Ruck-Pauguet, Gina. Little Hedgehog
Yeoman, John. The Bears' Water Picnic

008.27 Animals—hippopotami

Allen, Frances. Little Hippo
Bennett, Rainey. The Secret Hiding Place
Boynton, Sandra. Hester in the Wild
Brown, Marcia. How, Hippo!
Croswell, Volney. How to Hide a
    Hippopotamus
Duvoisin, Roger Antoine. Lonely Veronica
    Our Veronica Goes to Petunia's Farm
    Veronica
    Veronica and the Birthday Present
    Veronica's Smile
Kishida, Eriko. The Hippo Boat
Lasher, Faith B. Hubert Hippo's World
Mahy, Margaret. The Boy Who Was
    Followed Home
Marshall, James. George and Martha
    George and Martha Encore
    George and Martha One Fine Day
    George and Martha Rise and Shine
Mayer, Mercer. Hiccup
    Oops
Parker, Nancy Winslow. Love from Uncle
    Clyde
Scarry, Richard McClure. The Adventures
    of Tinker and Tanker
Slobodkin, Louis. Hustle and Bustle
Sugita, Yutaka. Helena the Unhappy
    Hippopotamus
Thaler, Mike. There's a Hippopotamus
    under My Bed
Waber, Bernard. "You Look Ridiculous,"
    Said the Rhinoceros to the
    Hippopotamus
Young, Miriam Burt. Please Don't Feed
    Horace

008.28 Animals—horses

Anderson, Clarence William. Billy and
    Blaze
    Blaze and the Forest Fire
    Blaze and the Gray Spotted Pony
    Blaze and the Gypsies
    Blaze and the Indian Cave
    Blaze and the Lost Quarry
    Blaze and the Mountain Lion
    Blaze and Thunderbolt
    Blaze Finds Forgotten Roads
    Blaze Finds the Trail
    Blaze Shows the Way
    The Crooked Colt
    Lonesome Little Colt
    A Pony for Linda

A Pony for Three
    Rumble Seat Pony
Arundel, Jocelyn. Shoes for Punch
Baker, Betty. Three Fools and a Horse
Beatty, Hetty Burlingame. Bucking Horse
Bemelmans, Ludwig. Madeline in London
Blech, Dietlind. Hello Irina
Bowden, Joan Chase. A New Home for
    Snow Ball
Burton, Virginia Lee. Calico the Wonder
    Horse, or The Saga of Stewy Slinker
Chandler, Edna Walker. Pony Rider
Cretien, Paul D., Jr. Sir Henry and the
    Dragon
Dennis, Wesley. Flip
    Flip and the Cows
    Flip and the Morning
    Tumble, the Story of a Mustang
Ets, Marie Hall. Mr. Penny's Race Horse
Farley, Walter. Little Black, a Pony
    Little Black Goes to the Circus
Fatio, Louise. Anna, the Horse
Felton, Harold W. Pecos Bill and the
    Mustang
Galdone, Paul. The Horse, the Fox, and
    the Lion
Gaston, Susan. New Boots for Salvador
Gay, Zhenya. Wonderful Things
Goble, Paul. The Girl Who Loved Wild
    Horses
Grabianski, Janusz. Horses
Heilbroner, Joan. Robert the Rose Horse
Hoff, Sydney. Chester
    The Horse in Harry's Room
    Thunderhoff
Ipcar, Dahlov Zorach. One Horse Farm
    World Full of Horses
Jeffers, Susan. All the Pretty Horses
Keeping, Charles William James. Molly o'
    the Moors, the Story of a Pony
Kraus, Robert. Springfellow
Krauss, Ruth. Charlotte and the White
    Horse
Krum, Gertrude. The Four Riders
Lasell, Fen. Michael Grows a Wish
Lipkind, William, and Mordvinoff, Nicolas.
    Even Steven
Lobel, Arnold Stark. Lucille
McGinley, Phyllis. The Horse Who Lived
    Upstairs
Martin, Patricia Miles. Friend of Miguel
Meeks, Esther K. Playland Pony
Miller, Jane. Birth of a Foal
Otto, Margaret Glover. The Little Brown
    Horse
Paterson, Andrew Barton. Mulga Bill's
    Bicycle
Peet, Bill. Cowardly Clyde
Pender, Lydia. Barnaby and the Horses
Rabinowitz, Sandy. What's Happening to
    Daisy?
Richards, Jane. A Horse Grows Up

Rounds, Glen H. Once We Had a Horse
   The Strawberry Roan
Sewell, Helen Moore. Peggy and the Pony
Slobodkina, Esphyr. The Wonderful Feast
Thompson, Vivian Laubach. The Horse
   That Liked Sandwiches
Ward, Lynd Kendall. The Silver Pony
Wooley, Catherine. Andy and the Runaway
   Horse
   The Horse with the Easter Bonnet
Wright, Dare. Look at a Colt
Young, Miriam Burt. If I Rode a Horse
Zimnik, Reiner. The Proud Circus Horse

008.29 Animals—hyenas

Newberry, Clare Turlay. Lambert's
   Bargain
Prelutsky, Jack. The Mean Old Mean
   Hyena

008.30 Animals—kangaroos

Braun, Kathy. Kangaroo and Kangaroo
Leisk, David Johnson. Upside Down
Payne, Emmy. Katy No-Pocket
Ungerer, Tomi. Adelaide
Wiseman, Bernard. Little New Kangaroo

008.31 Animals—kinkajous

Vandivert, Rita. Barnaby

008.32 Animals—koala bears

Leavens, George. Kippy the Koala
Snyder, Dick. One Day at the Zoo

008.33 Animals—llamas

Rockwell, Anne F. The Good Llama

008.34 Animals—mice

Angelo, Nancy Carolyn Harris. Camembert
Bell-Zano, Gina. The Wee Moose
Belpré, Pura. Perez and Martina
Berson, Harold. A Moose Is Not a Moose
Boegehold, Betty. Pippa Mouse
   Pippa Pops Out!
Boegehold, Bettty, and Szekeres, Cyndy.
   Here's Pippa Again!
Brandenberg, Franz. Nice New Neighbors
   What Can You Make of It?
Brook, Judy. Tim Mouse Goes
   Downstream
   Tim Mouse Visits the Farm
Brown, Marcia. Once a Mouse
Brown, Palmer. Cheerful
   Something for Christmas
Carle, Eric. Do You Want to Be My
   Friend?
Cartlidge, Michelle. Pippin and Pod
Coombs, Patricia. Mouse Cafe
Cressey, James. Max the Mouse

Dauer, Rosamond. Bullfrog Grows Up
Daugherty, James Henry. The Picnic
Davies, Sumiko. Kittymouse
de Paola, Thomas Anthony. Charlie Needs
   a Cloak
Doty, Roy. Old One Eye Meets His Match
Emberley, Edward Randolph. A Birthday
   Wish
Ets, Marie Hall. Mr. T. W. Anthony Woo
Fisher, Aileen Lucia. Sing Little Mouse
Freeman, Don. The Guard Mouse
   Norman the Doorman
Freeman, Don, and Freeman, Lydia. Pet of
   the Met
Freschet, Berniece. Bear Mouse
Futamata, Eigoro. How Not to Catch a
   Mouse
Gág, Wanda. Snippy and Snappy
Galdone, Paul. The Town Mouse and the
   Country Mouse
Goodall, John Strickland. Creepy Castle
Gurney, Nancy, and Gurney, Eric. The
   King, the Mice and the Cheese
Harris, Leon A. The Great Picture
   Robbery
Hawkinson, John. The Old Stump
Heathers, Anne, and Frances, Esteban.
   The Thread Soldiers
Hoban, Lillian. The Sugar Snow Spring
Hoff, Carol. The Four Friends
Houston, John A. A Mouse in My House
Hurd, Edith Thacher. Come and Have
   Fun
Hürlimann, Ruth. The Mouse with the
   Daisy Hat
Ivimey, John William. The Complete
   Version of Ye Three Blind Mice
Keenan, Martha. The Mannerly
   Adventures of Little Mouse
Kellogg, Steven. The Island of the Skog
Kraus, Robert. I, Mouse
   Whose Mouse Are You?
Kumin, Maxine W., and Sexton, Anne.
   Joey and the Birthday Present
Kuskin, Karla Seidman. What Did You
   Bring Me?
Kwitz, Mary DeBall. Mouse at Home
Linch, Elizabeth Johanna. Samson
Lionni, Leo. Alexander and the Wind-Up
   Mouse
   Frederick
   Geraldine, the Music Mouse
   The Greentail Mouse
   In the Rabbitgarden
Little, Mary E. Ricardo and the Puppets
Lobel, Arnold Stark. Martha the Movie
   Mouse
   Mouse Soup
   Mouse Tales
Low, Joseph. The Christmas Grump
McNulty, Faith. Mouse and Tim

Mandry, Kathy. The Cat and the Mouse
and the Mouse and the Cat
Miles, Miska. Mouse Six and the Happy
Birthday
Miller, Edna Anita. Mousekin Finds a
Friend
Mousekin's ABC
Mousekin's Christmas Eve
Mousekin's Close Call
Mousekin's Family
Mousekin's Golden House
Oakley, Graham. The Church Cat Abroad
The Church Mice Adrift
The Church Mice and the Moon
The Church Mice at Bay
The Church Mice Spread Their Wings
The Church Mouse
Ormondroyd, Edward. Broderick
Peppé, Rodney. Cat and Mouse
Piers, Helen. The Mouse Book
Polushkin, Maria. Mother, Mother, I Want
Another
Potter, Beatrix. The Tailor of Gloucester
The Tale of Johnny Town-Mouse
The Tale of Mrs. Tittlemouse
The Tale of Two Bad Mice
Potter, Russell. The Little Red Ferry Boat
Roach, Marilynne K. Two Roman Mice
Schermer, Judith. Mouse in House
Schlein, Miriam. Home, the Tale of a
Mouse
Schoenherr, John Carl. The Barn
Seidler, Rosalie. Grumpus and the
Venetian Cat
Seignobosc, Françoise. Small-Trot
Simon, Sidney B. Henry the Uncatchable
Mouse
Smith, Jim. The Frog Band and
Durrington Dormouse
Steig, William. Amos and Boris
Stevenson, James. The Sea View Hotel
Stone, Bernard. Emergency Mouse
Thompson, George Selden. The Mice, the
Monks and the Christmas Tree
Titus, Eve. Anatole
Anatole and the Cat
Anatole and the Piano
Anatole and the Pied Piper
Anatole and the Poodle
Anatole and the Robot
Anatole and the Thirty Thieves
Anatole and the Toyshop
Anatole in Italy
Anatole Over Paris
Vinson, Pauline. Willie Goes to School
Willie Goes to the Seashore
Vreeken, Elizabeth. Henry
Waber, Bernard. Mice on My Mind
Wahl, Jan. Pleasant Fieldmouse
The Pleasant Fieldmouse Storybook
Pleasant Fieldmouse's Halloween Party
Wells, Rosemary. Noisy Nora

Stanley and Rhoda
Wenning, Elizabeth. The Christmas Mouse
Wright, Josephine. Cotton Cat and Martha
Mouse
Yeoman, John. Mouse Trouble
Zion, Gene. The Sugar Mouse Cake

008.35 Animals—moles

Firmin, Peter. Basil Brush and a Dragon
Basil Brush Builds a House
Basil Brush Finds Treasure
Basil Brush Gets a Medal
Basil Brush Goes Flying
Hoban, Russell Conwell. The Mole Family's
Christmas
Johnston, Tony. The Adventures of Mole
and Troll
Murschetz, Luis. Mister Mole
Quackenbush, Robert Mead. Detective
Mole
Detective Mole and the Secret Clues
Detective Mole and the Tip-Top
Mystery

008.36 Animals—mongooses

Carlson, Natalie Savage. Marie Louise's
Heyday
Runaway Marie Louise

008.37 Animals—monkeys

Brunhoff, Jean de. Babar and Zephir
Bulette, Sara. The Splendid Belt of Mr.
Big
Carle, Eric. All About Arthur
Elkin, Benjamin. Such Is the Way of the
World
Galdone, Paul. The Monkey and the
Crocodile
Gelman, Rita Golden. Professor Coconut
and the Thief
Goodall, John Strickland. Jacko
Hoban, Lillian. Arthur's Christmas Cookies
Arthur's Honey Bear
Arthur's Pen Pal
Arthur's Prize Reader
Hurd, Edith Thacher. Last One Home Is a
Green Pig
Kaye, Geraldine. The Sea Monkey
Kepes, Charles. Run, Little Monkeys, Run,
Run, Run
Kepes, Juliet. Five Little Monkeys
Knight, Hilary. Where's Wallace?
Mathieson, Egon. Oswald, the Monkey
Meshover, Leonard, and Feistel, Sally. The
Monkey That Went to School
Olds, Helen Diehl. Miss Hattie and the
Monkey

Parish, Peggy. Jumper Goes to School
Preston, Edna Mitchell. Monkey in the
  Jungle
Rey, Hans Augusto. Cecily G and the Nine
  Monkeys
  Curious George
  Curious George Gets a Medal
  Curious George Learns the Alphabet
  Curious George Rides a Bike
  Curious George Takes a Job
Rey, Margret Elisabeth Waldstein. Curious
  George Flies a Kite
  Curious George Goes to the Hospital
Rietveld, Jane. Monkey Island
Rockwell, Anne F. The Stolen Necklace
Slobodkina, Esphyr. Caps for Sale
Suba, Susanne. The Monkeys and the
  Pedlar
Williamson, Hamilton. Monkey Tale
Wolkstein, Diane. The Cool Ride in the
  Sky
Wolo (pseud.). Tweedles Be Brave!

008.38 Animals—moose

Foreman, Michael. Moose
Geisel, Theodor Seuss. Thidwick, the Big
  Hearted Moose
Hoff, Sydney. Santa's Moose
McNeer, May Yonge. My Friend Mac
Marshall, James. The Guest
Platt, Kin. Big Max in the Mystery of the
  Missing Moose
Slobodkin, Louis. Melvin, the Moose Child

008.39 Animals—muskrats

Hoban, Russell Conwell. Harvey's Hideout

008.40 Animals—otters

Benchley, Nathaniel. Oscar Otter
Hoban, Russell Conwell. Emmet Otter's
  Jug-Band Christmas
Sheehan, Angela. The Otter
Tompert, Ann. Little Otter Remembers
  and Other Stories
Wisbeski, Dorothy. Picaro, a Pet Otter

008.41 Animals—pack rats

Miller, Edna Anita. Pebbles, a Pack Rat
Quackenbush, Robert Mead. Pete Pack Rat

008.42 Animals—pigs

Augarde, Stephen Andre. Pig
Bishop, Claire Huchet. The Truffle Pig
Boynton, Sandra. Hester in the Wild
Brand, Millen. This Little Pig Named
  Curly

Brooks, Ron. This Little Pig Went to
  Market
Brown, Judith Gwyn. Max and the Truffle
  Pig
Dyke, John. Pigwig
Gackenbach, Dick. The Pig Who Saw
  Everything
Goodall, John Strickland. The Adventures
  of Paddy Pork
  The Ballooning Adventures of Paddy
  Pork
  Paddy Pork's Holiday
  Paddy's Evening Out
Hoban, Lillian. Mr. Pig and Sonny Too
Lobel, Arnold Stark. Small Pig
  A Treeful of Pigs
Marshall, James. Portly McSwine
  Yummers!
Peck, Robert Newton. Hamilton
Peet, Bill. Chester the Worldly Pig
Pomerantz, Charlotte. The Piggy in the
  Puddle
Potter, Beatrix. The Tale of Little Pig
  Robinson
  The Tale of Pigling Bland
Rayner, Mary. Garth Pig and the Ice
  Cream Lady
  Mr. and Mrs. Pig's Evening Out
Shecter, Ben. Partouche Plants a Seed
Steig, William. The Amazing Bone
  Farmer Palmer's Wagon Ride
  Roland the Minstrel Pig
Stevens, Carla. Hooray for Pig!
  The Pig and the Blue Flag
Stolz, Mary Slattery. Emmett's Pig
Three Little Pigs. The Story of the Three
  Little Pigs, illus. by Leonard Leslie
  Brooke
  The Story of the Three Little Pigs, illus.
  by William Stobbs
  The Three Little Pigs, illus. by William
  Pène Du Bois
  The Three Little Pigs, illus. by Paul
  Galdone
  The Three Little Pigs, illus. by Irma Wilde
Tripp, Wallace. The Tale of a Pig
Ungerer, Tomi. Christmas Eve at the
  Mellops'
  The Mellops Go Diving for Treasure
  The Mellops Go Flying
  The Mellops Go Spelunking
  The Mellops Strike Oil
Varga, Judy. Pig in the Parlor
Walker, Barbara K. Pigs and Pirates
Watson, Pauline. Wriggles, the Little
  Wishing Pig
Weisgard, Leonard. The Clean Pig
Wild, Robin, and Wild, Jocelyn. Little Pig
  and the Big Bad Wolf
Wondriska, William. Mr. Brown and Mr.
  Gray
Yeoman, John. The Bears' Water Picnic

Zakhoder, Boris. How a Piglet Crashed the
    Christmas Party
Zalben, Jane Breskin. Basil and Hillary

008.43 Animals—porcupines

Annett, Cora. When the Porcupine Moved
    In
Conford, Ellen. Eugene the Brave
Massie, Diane Redfield. Tiny Pin
Scarry, Patricia M. Little Richard and
    Prickles

008.44 Animals—possums

Berson, Harold. Henry Possum
Burch, Robert. Joey's Cat
Carlson, Natalie Savage. Marie Louise's
    Heyday
Conford, Ellen. Impossible Possum
    Just the Thing for Geraldine
Hoban, Russell Conwell. Nothing to Do
Sharmat, Marjorie Weinman. Burton and
    Dudley
Taylor, Mark. Old Blue, You Good Dog
    You
Winthrop, Elizabeth. Potbellied Possums

008.45 Animals—prairie dogs

Schweitzer, Byrd Baylor. Amigo

008.46 Animals—rabbits

Adams, Adrienne. The Christmas Party
    The Easter Egg Artists
Anderson, Lonzo, and Adams, Adrienne.
    Two Hundred Rabbits
Annett, Cora. When the Porcupine Moved
    In
Balian, Lorna. Humbug Rabbit
Bartoli, Jennifer. In a Meadow, Two Hares
    Hide
Bate, Lucy. Little Rabbit's Loose Tooth
Becker, John L. Seven Little Rabbits
Berson, Harold. Pop Goes the Turnip
Bornstein, Ruth. Indian Bunny
Bright, Robert. My Hopping Bunny
Brown, Marcia. The Neighbors
Brown, Margaret Wise. The Golden Egg
    Book
    Goodnight, Moon
    Little Chicken
    The Runaway Bunny
Bruna, Dick. Miffy
    Miffy at the Seaside
    Miffy at the Zoo
    Miffy in the Hospital
    Miffy in the Snow
Carrick, Carol. A Rabbit for Easter
Carroll, Ruth Robinson. What Whiskers
    Did

Where's the Bunny?
Chalmers, Mary Eileen. Kevin
Chandoha, Walter. A Baby Bunny for You
Delton, Judy. Brimhall Turns to Magic
    Three Friends Find Spring
Dorsky, Blanche. Harry, a True Story
Fatio, Louise. The Happy Lion's Rabbits
Friskey, Margaret. Mystery of the Gate
    Sign
Gackenbach, Dick. Hattie Be Quiet, Hattie
    Be Good
    Hattie Rabbit
    Mother Rabbit's Son Tom
Gág, Wanda. ABC Bunny
Gay, Zhenya. Small One
Ginsburg, Mirra. The Fox and the Hare
Green, Adam. The Funny Bunny Factory
Heyward, Dubose. The Country Bunny
    and the Little Gold Shoes
Hoban, Tana. Where Is It?
Hogrogian, Nonny. Carrot Cake
Jameson, Cynthia. A Day with Whisker
    Wickles
Jewell, Nancy. The Snuggle Bunny
Kahl, Virginia Caroline. The Habits of
    Rabbits
Kirn, Ann Minette. The Tale of a
    Crocodile
Kraus, Robert. Big Brother
    Daddy Long Ears
    The Littlest Rabbit
Kraus, Robert, and Bodecker, Nils Mogens.
    Good Night Richard Rabbit
Kuratomi, Chizuko. Mr. Bear and the
    Robbers
La Fontaine, Jean de. The Hare and the
    Tortoise
Lifton, Betty Jean. The Rice-Cake Rabbit
Lipkind, William, and Mordvinoff, Nicolas.
    The Christmas Bunny
Littlefield, William. The Whiskers of Ho
    Ho
Low, Joseph. Benny Rabbit and the Owl
Maril, Lee. Mr. Bunny Paints the Eggs
Mathews, Louise. Bunches and Bunches of
    Bunnies
Miles, Miska. Rabbit Garden
    Small Rabbit
Moreman, Grace E. No, No, Natalie
Newberry, Clare Turlay. Marshmallow
Parish, Peggy. Too Many Rabbits
Parry, Marian. King of the Fish
Peet, Bill. Huge Harold
Potter, Beatrix. The Story of a Fierce Bad
    Rabbit
    The Tale of Benjamin Bunny
    The Tale of Mr. Tod
    The Tale of Peter Rabbit
    The Tale of the Flopsy Bunnies
Rey, Margret Elisabeth Waldstein. Spotty
Sargent, Robert. A Trick on a Lion

Scarry, Patricia M. Little Richard and Prickles
Scarry, Richard McClure. The Adventures of Tinker and Tanker
Schlein, Miriam. Little Rabbit, the High Jumper
Schweninger, Ann. The Hunt for Rabbit's Galosh
Steiner, Charlotte. My Bunny Feels Soft
Steiner, Jörg. Rabbit Island
Stevenson, James. Monty
Tresselt, Alvin R. The Rabbit Story
Trez, Denise, and Trez, Alain. Rabbit Country
Tripp, Wallace. My Uncle Podger
Van Woerkom, Dorothy O. Harry and Shellburt
Wahl, Jan. Carrot Nose
    Doctor Rabbit's Foundling
    The Five in the Forest
Watson, Wendy. Lollipop
Weil, Lisl. The Candy Egg Bunny
Wells, Rosemary. Morris's Disappearing Bag; A Christmas Story
Wiese, Kurt. Happy Easter
    Rabbit Brothers Circus One Night Only
    The Rabbit's Revenge
Williams, Garth Montgomery. The Rabbits' Wedding
Wolf, Ann. The Rabbit and the Turtle
Zolotow, Charlotte Shapiro. The Bunny Who Found Easter
    Mr. Rabbit and the Lovely Present

008.47 Animals—raccoons

Bemelmans, Ludwig. Marina
Brown, Margaret Wise. Wait Till the Moon Is Full
Duvoisin, Roger Antoine. Petunia, I Love You!
Hoban, Lillian. Here Come Raccoons
Martin, Patricia Miles. The Raccoon and Mrs. McGinnis
Miklowitz, Gloria D. Save That Raccoon!
Moore, Lilian. Little Raccoon and No Trouble at All
    Little Raccoon and the Outside World
    Little Raccoon and the Thing in the Pool
Wells, Rosemary. Benjamin and Tulip

008.48 Animals—rats

Berson, Harold. The Rats Who Lived in the Delicatessen
Cressey, James. Fourteen Rats and a Rat-Catcher
Doty, Roy. Old One Eye Meets His Match
Kouts, Anne. Kenny's Rat
La Fontaine, Jean de. The Lion and the Rat

Miles, Miska. Wharf Rat
Oakley, Graham. The Church Mice Adrift
Potter, Beatrix. The Sly Old Cat
Ross, Tony, reteller. The Pied Piper of Hamelin
Schiller, Barbara. The White Rat's Tale
Sharmat, Marjorie Weinman. Mooch the Messy
Stevenson, James. Wilfred the Rat
Van Woerkom, Dorothy O. The Rat, the Ox and the Zodiac

008.49 Animals—rhinoceros

Standon, Anna. The Singing Rhinoceros

008.50 Animals—sea lions

Olds, Elizabeth. Plop, Plop, Ploppie

008.51 Animals—seals

Freeman, Don. The Seal and the Slick
Hoff, Sydney. Sammy the Seal

008.52 Animals—sheep

Beskow, Elsa Maartman. Pelle's New Suit
Brown, Margaret Wise. Little Lost Lamb
de Paola, Thomas Anthony. Charlie Needs a Cloak
Dunn, Judy. The Little Lamb
Ginsburg, Mirra. The Strongest One of All
Ipcar, Dahlov Zorach. The Land of Flowers
Peet, Bill. Buford, the Little Bighorn
Russell, Betty. Run Sheep Run
Slobodkin, Louis. Up High and Down Low
Steiner, Charlotte. Red Ridinghood's Little Lamb

008.53 Animals—skunks

Kitt, Tamara. A Special Birthday Party for Someone Very Special
Schoenherr, John Carl. The Barn

008.54 Animals—sloths

Knight, Hilary. Sylvia the Sloth

008.55 Animals—snails

Marshall, James. The Guest
Rockwell, Anne F. The Story Snail
Ungerer, Tomi. Snail Where Are You?

008.56 Animals—squirrels

Palazzo, Tony. Federico, the Flying Squirrel
Peet, Bill. Merle the High Flying Squirrel

Potter, Beatrix. The Tale of Squirrel
Nutkin
The Tale of Timmy Tiptoes
Pratten, Albra. Winkie, the Grey Squirrel
Sharmat, Marjorie Weinman. Sophie and
Gussie
The Trip
Tresselt, Alvin R. The Little Lost Squirrel
Wildsmith, Brian. Squirrels
Yeoman, John. The Bears' Water Picnic
Young, Miriam Burt. Miss Suzy's Easter
Surprise
Zion, Gene. The Meanest Squirrel I Ever
Met
Zweifel, Frances W. Bony

008.57 Animals—tapirs

Maestro, Giulio. The Tortoise's Tug of
War

008.58 Animals—walruses

Bonsall, Crosby Newell. What Spot?
Hoff, Sydney. Walpole
Stevenson, James. Winston, Newton, Elton,
and Ed

008.59 Animals—weasels

Lobel, Arnold Stark. Mouse Soup

008.60 Animals—whales

Applebaum, Neil. Is There a Hole in Your
Head?
Benchley, Nathaniel. The Deep Dives of
Stanley Whale
Duvoisin, Roger Antoine. The Christmas
Whale
Haiz, Danah. Jonah's Journey
Hurd, Edith Thacher. What Whale?
Where?
King, Patricia. Mabel the Whale
Lent, Blair. John Tabor's Ride
McCloskey, Robert John. Burt Dow, Deep
Water Man
Maestro, Giulio. The Tortoise's Tug of
War
Phleger, Frederick B. The Whales Go By
Postgate, Oliver, and Firmin, Peter. Noggin
and the Whale
Roy, Ronald. A Thousand Pails of Water
Steig, William. Amos and Boris

008.61 Animals—wolves

Ambrus, Victor G. A Country Wedding
Damjan, Mischa (pseud.). The Wolf and
the Kid

Daudet, Alphonse. The Brave Little Goat
of Monsieur Seguin
De Regniers, Beatrice Schenk. Red Riding
Hood
Evans, Katherine. The Boy Who Cried
Wolf
Friskey, Margaret. Indian Two Feet and
the Wolf Cubs
Goble, Paul. The Friendly Wolf
Gunthrop, Karen. Adam and the Wolf
Harper, Wilhelmina, reteller. The
Gunniwolf
Little Red Riding Hood, illus. by Paul
Galdone
Little Red Riding Hood, illus. by
Bernadette Watts
Parish, Peggy. Granny, the Baby and the
Big Gray Thing
Peck, Robert Newton. Hamilton
Prokofiev, Sergei Sergeievitch. Peter and
the Wolf, illus. by Warren Chappell
Peter and the Wolf, illus. by Frans
Haacken
Peter and the Wolf, illus. by Alan
Howard
Peter and the Wolf, illus. by Kozo
Shimizu
Rayner, Mary. Garth Pig and the Ice
Cream Lady
Mr. and Mrs. Pig's Evening Out
Rockwell, Anne F. The Wolf Who Had a
Wonderful Dream
Schick, Alice, and Schick, Joel. Just This
Once
Sharmat, Marjorie Weinman. Walter the
Wolf
Skurzynski, Gloria. The Magic Pumpkin
Three Little Pigs. The Story of the Three
Little Pigs, illus. by Leonard Leslie
Brooke
The Story of the Three Little Pigs, illus.
by William Stobbs
The Three Little Pigs, illus. by William
Pène Du Bois
The Three Little Pigs, illus. by Paul
Galdone
The Three Little Pigs, illus. by Irma Wilde
Wild, Robin, and Wild, Jocelyn. Little Pig
and the Big Bad Wolf

008.62 Animals—worms

Wong, Herbert H., and Vassel, Matthew F.
Our Earthworms
Wooley, Catherine. Andy and the Wild
Worm

009 Animals—endangered

Cromie, William J. Steven and the Green
Turtle

010 Arctic

Bonsall, Crosby Newell. What Spot?

011 Art

Angelo, Nancy Carolyn Harris. Camembert
Brandenberg, Franz. What Can You Make
of It?
Fifield, Flora. Pictures for the Palace
Freeman, Don. Norman the Doorman
Harris, Leon A. The Great Picture
Robbery
Hurd, Edith Thacher. Wilson's World
Leisk, David Johnson. Harold and the
Purple Crayon
A Picture for Harold's Room
Pinkwater, Manus. The Bear's Picture
Rey, Margret Elisabeth Waldstein, and Rey,
Hans Augusto. Billy's Picture
Sharon, Mary Bruce. Scenes from
Childhood
Sloan, Carolyn. Carter Is a Painter's Cat
Villarejo, Mary. The Art Fair

012 Automobiles

Alexander, Anne. ABC of Cars and Trucks
Baugh, Dolores M., and Pulsifer, Marjorie
P. Trucks and Cars to Ride
Biro, Val. Gumdrop, the Adventures of a
Vintage Car
Bridwell, Norman. Clifford's Good Deeds
Burningham, John Mackintosh. Mr.
Gumpy's Motor Car
Cummings, W. T. Miss Esta Maude's Secret
Eckert, Horst. The Magic Auto
Ets, Marie Hall. Little Old Automobile
Holl, Adelaide. The ABC of Cars, Trucks
and Machines
Lenski, Lois L. The Little Auto
Löfgren, Ulf. The Traffic Stopper That
Became a Grandmother Visitor
Peet, Bill. Jennifer and Josephine
Scarry, Richard McClure. The Great Big
Car and Truck Book
Richard Scarry's Cars and Trucks and
Things That Go
Wooley, Catherine. Charley and the New
Car
Young, Miriam Burt. If I Drove a Car

013 Babies

Ahlberg, Janet, and Ahlberg, Allan.
Burglar Bill
Alexander, Martha G. Nobody Asked Me
If I Wanted a Baby Sister
Andry, Andrew C., and Kratka, Suzanne
C. Hi, New Baby
Arnstein, Helen S. Billy and Our New
Baby
Bolognese, Donald Alan. A New Day

Byars, Betsy Cromer. Go and Hush the
Baby
Chaffin, Lillie D. Tommy's Big Problem
Clifton, Lucille B. Everett Anderson's Nine
Months Long
Dragonwagon, Crescent. Wind Rose
Flack, Marjorie. The New Pet
Foulds, Elfrida Vipont. The Elephant and
the Bad Baby
Gill, Joan. Hush, Jon!
Gray, Genevieve. Keep an Eye on Kevin:
Safety Begins at Home
Greenberg, Barbara. The Bravest
Babysitter
Greenfield, Eloise. She Come Bringing Me
That Little Baby Girl
Hanson, Joan. I Don't Like Timmy
Hazen, Barbara Shook. Why Couldn't I Be
an Only Kid Like You, Wigger?
Hirsh, Marilyn Joyce. Where Is Yonkela?
Hirsh, Marilyn Joyce, and Narayan, Maya.
Leela and the Watermelon
Hoban, Russell Conwell. A Baby Sister for
Frances
Holland, Viki. We Are Having a Baby
Hush Little Baby
Jarrell, Mary. Knee Baby
Keats, Ezra Jack. Peter's Chair
Krasilovsky, Phyllis. The Very Little Boy
The Very Little Girl
Kraus, Robert. Big Brother
Langstaff, Nancy. A Tiny Baby for You
Lexau, Joan M. Finders Keepers, Losers
Weepers
Manushkin, Fran. Baby
Newberry, Clare Turlay. Cousin Toby
T-Bone, the Baby-Sitter
Parish, Peggy. Granny, the Baby and the
Big Gray Thing
Petersham, Maud Fuller, and Petersham,
Miska. The Box with Red Wheels
Politi, Leo. Rosa
Pursell, Margaret Sanford. A Look at Birth
Rice, Eve. What Sadie Sang
Schick, Eleanor. Peggy's New Brother
Schlein, Miriam. Laurie's New Brother
Selsam, Millicent Ellis. All Kinds of Babies
Shapp, Martha; Shapp, Charles; and
Shepard, Sylvia. Let's Find Out about
Babies
Sheffield, Margaret. Where Do Babies
Come From?
Showers, Paul. A Baby Starts to Grow
Before You Were a Baby
Stein, Sara Bonnett. Making Babies
That New Baby
Vigna, Judith. Couldn't We Have a Turtle
Instead?
Warburg, Sandol Stoddard. Curl Up Small
Watts, Bernadette. David's Waiting Day
Williams, Barbara. Jeremy Isn't Hungry
Wolde, Gunilla. Betsy's Baby Brother

Wooley, Catherine. Gus and the Baby
Ghost
Zolotow, Charlotte Shapiro. Do You Know
What I'll Do?

014 Barns

Carrick, Carol. The Old Barn
Martin, Patricia Miles. The Raccoon and
Mrs. McGinnis
Merrill, Jean. Tell about the Cowbarn,
Daddy
Schoenherr, John Carl. The Barn
Sewell, Helen Moore. Blue Barns

015 Bedtime

Bang, Molly G. Wiley and the Hairy Man
Beckman, Kaj. Lisa Cannot Sleep
Berenstain, Stanley, and Berenstain, Janice.
Bears in the Night
Brown, Margaret Wise. A Child's Good-
Night Book
Goodnight, Moon
Coatsworth, Elizabeth Jane. Good Night
Cole, William. Frances Face-Maker
de Paola, Thomas Anthony. Fight the
Night
Ginsburg, Mirra. Which Is the Best Place?
Goffstein, Marilyn Brooks. Sleepy People
Hawkins, Mark. A Lion Under Her Bed
Hoban, Russell Conwell. Bedtime for
Frances
Goodnight
Jeffers, Susan. All the Pretty Horses
Johnston, Johanna. Edie Changes Her
Mind
Joslin, Sesyle. Brave Baby Elephant
Kraus, Robert, and Bodecker, Nils Mogens.
Good Night Little One
Good Night Richard Rabbit
Krauss, Ruth. The Bundle Book
Kuskin, Karla Seidman. A Space Story
Leaf, Munro. Boo, Who Used to Be Scared
of the Dark
Levine, Joan. A Bedtime Story
Lifton, Betty Jean. Goodnight Orange
Monster
Lippman, Peter. New at the Zoo
Low, Joseph. Benny Rabbit and the Owl
Mack, Stanley. Ten Bears in My Bed, a
Goodnight Countdown
Marcin, Marietta. A Zoo in Her Bed
Marshall, James. What's the Matter with
Carruthers?
Marzollo, Jean. Close Your Eyes
Mayer, Mercer. There's a Nightmare in My
Closet
Oberhansli, Gertrud. Sleep, Baby, Sleep
Petersham, Maud Fuller, and Petersham,
Miska. Off to Bed
Plath, Sylvia. The Bed Book

Polushkin, Maria. Mother, Mother, I Want
Another
Preston, Edna Mitchell. Monkey in the
Jungle
Schneider, Nina. While Susie Sleeps
Sharmat, Marjorie Weinman. Goodnight,
Andrew. Goodnight, Craig
Skorpen, Liesel Moak. Outside My Window
Smith, Robert Paul. Nothingatall,
Nothingatall, Nothingatall
Steiner, Charlotte. The Sleepy Quilt
Storm, Theodor. Little John
Strahl, Rudi. Sandman in the Lighthouse
Sugita, Yutaka. Good Night 1, 2, 3
Tobias, Tobi. Chasing the Goblins Away
Trez, Denise, and Trez, Alain. Good
Night, Veronica
Viorst, Judith. My Mama Says There
Aren't Any: Zombies, Ghosts,
Vampires, Creatures, Demons,
Monsters, Fiends, Goblins, or Things
Vorse, Mary Ellen. Wakey Goes to Bed
Waber, Bernard. Ira Sleeps Over
Warburg, Sandol Stoddard. Curl Up Small
Watson, Clyde. Midnight Moon
Watson, Wendy. Fisherman Lullabies
Wilder, Alec. Lullabies and Night Songs
Winthrop, Elizabeth. Bunk Beds
Zolotow, Charlotte Shapiro. The Sleepy
Book
The Summer Night
Wake Up and Good Night
When the Wind Stops

016 Behavior

Babbitt, Lorraine. Pink Like the Geranium
Beim, Jerrold. The Swimming Hole
Benchley, Nathaniel. Oscar Otter
Boegehold, Betty. Three to Get Ready
Carle, Eric. The Grouchy Ladybug
Caudill, Rebecca, and Ayars, James.
Contrary Jenkins
Ets, Marie Hall. Bad Boy, Good Boy
Play with Me
Gackenbach, Dick. Hattie Be Quiet, Hattie
Be Good
Gaeddert, Lou Ann Bigge. Noisy Nancy
Nora
Hoban, Russell Conwell. Dinner at
Alberta's
Hogrogian, Nonny. Carrot Cake
Horvath, Betty F. Be Nice to Josephine
Myller, Lois. No! No!
Paterson, Diane. Wretched Rachel
Sharmat, Marjorie Weinman. Scarlet
Monster Lives Here
Stover, Jo Ann. If Everybody Did
Supraner, Robyn. Would You Rather Be a
Tiger?
Wittels, Harriet, and Greisman, Joan.
Things I Hate!

016.01 Behavior—animals, dislike of

Bemelmans, Ludwig. Madeline and the Bad Hat
Goldfrank, Helen Colodny. An Egg Is for Wishing
Udry, Janice May. Alfred

016.02 Behavior—bad day

Andrews, Frank Emerson. Nobody Comes to Dinner
Edwards, Dorothy, and Williams, Jenny. A Wet Monday
Hoban, Russell Conwell. The Sorely Trying Day
Keenen, George. The Preposterous Week
Keith, Eros. Bedita's Bad Day
Lexau, Joan M. I Should Have Stayed in Bed
Viorst, Judith. Alexander and the Terrible, Horrible, No Good, Very Bad Day
Vreeken, Elizabeth. One Day Everything Went Wrong
Wells, Rosemary. Unfortunately Harriet

016.03 Behavior—boasting

Bonsall, Crosby Newell. Mine's the Best
Duvoisin, Roger Antoine. See What I Am
Ellentuck, Shan. A Sunflower as Big as the Sun
Lopshire, Robert Martin. I Am Better Than You!
Lund, Doris Herold. You Ought to See Herbert's House
Miller, Warren. The Goings On at Little Wishful

016.04 Behavior—boredom

Alexander, Martha G. We Never Get to Do Anything
Delton, Judy. My Mom Hates Me in January
Duvoisin, Roger Antoine. Veronica's Smile
Hoban, Russell Conwell. Nothing to Do
Krauss, Ruth. A Good Man and His Good Wife
Raskin, Ellen. Nothing Ever Happens on My Block
Reit, Seymour. The King Who Learned to Smile
Spier, Peter. Bored—Nothing to Do!
Wooley, Catherine. Mr. Turtle's Magic Glasses

016.05 Behavior—bullying

Alexander, Martha G. I Sure Am Glad to See You, Blackboard Bear
Christopher, Matthew F. Johnny No Hit

Cohen, Miriam. Tough Jim
Keats, Ezra Jack. Goggles
Kessler, Leonard P. Last One in Is a Rotten Egg
Peet, Bill. Big Bad Bruce

016.06 Behavior—carelessness

Brandenberg, Aliki Liacouras. Keep Your Mouth Closed, Dear
Carrick, Carol. A Rabbit for Easter
de Paola, Thomas Anthony. The Quicksand Book
Ilsley, Velma. The Pink Hat
Mayer, Mercer. Oops
Panek, Dennis. Catastrophe Cat
Pender, Lydia. Barnaby and the Horses

016.07 Behavior—copying

Aruego, José. Look What I Can Do

016.08 Behavior—disbelief

Gunthrop, Karen. Adam and the Wolf

016.09 Behavior—dissatisfaction

Byars, Betsy Cromer. The Groober
Duvoisin, Roger Antoine. Petunia, Beware!
Ets, Marie Hall. The Cow's Party
Fischer, Hans. Pitschi, the Kitten Who Always Wanted to Do Something Else
Gackenbach, Dick. Mother Rabbit's Son Tom
Hille-Brandts, Lene. The Little Black Hen
Hoban, Lillian. Stick-in-the-Mud Turtle
Keats, Ezra Jack. Jennie's Hat
McDermott, Gerald. The Stonecutter; A Japanese Folk Tale
McGinley, Phyllis. The Horse Who Lived Upstairs
Massie, Diane Redfield. Walter Was a Frog
Palmer, Mary. The No-Sort-of-Animal
Peet, Bill. The Caboose Who Got Loose
The Whingdingdilly
Price, Roger. The Last Little Dragon
Walker, Challis. Three and Three
Wiesner, William. Turnabout
Zakhoder, Boris. Rosachok
Zolotow, Charlotte Shapiro. It's Not Fair

016.10 Behavior—fighting, arguing

Alexander, Martha G. I'll Be the Horse If You'll Play with Me
Beim, Lorraine Levy, and Beim, Jerrold. Two Is a Team
Bonsall, Crosby Newell. Who's a Pest?
Burningham, John Mackintosh. Mr. Gumpy's Outing
Christian, Mary Blount. The Sand Lot

Dayton, Mona. Earth and Sky
Gilchrist, Theo E. Halfway up the
    Mountain
Hoban, Russell Conwell. Harvey's Hideout
    The Sorely Trying Day
Minarik, Else Holmelund. No Fighting, No
    Biting!
Sharmat, Marjorie Weinman. I'm Not
    Oscar's Friend Any More
Slobodkin, Louis. Hustle and Bustle
Steadman, Ralph. The Bridge
Udry, Janice May. Let's Be Enemies
Venable, Alan. The Checker Players
Wells, Rosemary. Benjamin and Tulip
Winthrop, Elizabeth. That's Mine!
Zolotow, Charlotte Shapiro. The
    Quarreling Book
    The Unfriendly Book

016.11 Behavior—forgetfulness

Copp, Jim. Martha Matilda O'Toole
de Paola, Thomas Anthony. Strega Nona
Dines, Glen. A Tiger in the Cherry Tree
Galdone, Joanna. Gertrude, the Goose
    Who Forgot
Galdone, Paul. The Magic Porridge Pot
Hutchins, Pat. Don't Forget the Bacon!
MacGregor, Ellen. Theodor Turtle
Miles, Miska. Chicken Forgets
Patz, Nancy. Pumpernickel Tickle and
    Mean Green Cheese
Schweninger, Ann. The Hunt for Rabbit's
    Galosh
Weisgard, Leonard. Silly Willy Nilly

016.12 Behavior—gossip

Berson, Harold. The Thief Who Hugged a
    Moonbeam
Chicken Little. Chicken Licken
    Henny Penny, illus. by Paul Galdone
    Henny Penny, illus. by William Stobbs
Holl, Adelaide. The Runaway Giant
Hutchins, Pat. Surprise Party
Varga, Judy. The Monster Behind Black
    Rock
Zolotow, Charlotte Shapiro. The Hating
    Book

016.13 Behavior—greed

Andersen, Hans Christian. The Woman
    with the Eggs
Aulaire, Ingri Mortenson d', and Aulaire,
    Edgar Parin d'. Don't Count Your
    Chicks
Battles, Edith. The Terrible Terrier
    The Terrible Trick or Treat
Berson, Harold. The Rats Who Lived in
    the Delicatessen
Bolliger, Max. The Golden Apple

Bonsall, Crosby Newell. It's Mine! A
    Greedy Book
Brown, Marcia. The Bun
de Paola, Thomas Anthony. Andy (That's
    My Name)
Evans, Katherine. The Maid and Her Pail
    of Milk
Ginsburg, Mirra. Two Greedy Bears
Kuskin, Karla Seidman. What Did You
    Bring Me?
La Fontaine, Jean de. The Rich Man and
    the Shoemaker
Lionni, Leo. The Biggest House in the
    World
Mahy, Margaret. Rooms for Rent
Matsutani, Miyoko. How the Withered
    Trees Blossomed
Peet, Bill. Kermit the Hermit
Perkins, Al. King Midas and the Golden
    Touch
Watts, Bernadette, reteller. Mother Holly
Winthrop, Elizabeth. That's Mine!

016.14 Behavior—growing up

Aitken, Amy. Ruby!
Brown, Myra Berry. Benjy's Blanket
Bruna, Dick. I Can Dress Myself
Chaffin, Lillie D. Tommy's Big Problem
Ciardi, John. Scrappy the Pup
Corey, Dorothy. Tomorrow You Can
Dauer, Rosamond. Bullfrog Grows Up
Delton, Judy, and Knox-Wagner, Elaine.
    The Best Mom in the World
Fassler, Joan. Don't Worry Dear
    The Man of the House
Felt, Sue. Rosa-Too-Little
Fribourg, Marjorie G. Ching-Ting and the
    Ducks
Hanson, Joan. I Won't Be Afraid
Krasilovsky, Phyllis. The Very Little Boy
    The Very Little Girl
Kraus, Robert. Leo the Late Bloomer
Krauss, Ruth. The Growing Story
Leisk, David Johnson. We Wonder What
    Will Walter Be, When He Grows Up?
Massie, Diane Redfield. Tiny Pin
Mordvinoff, Nicolas. Coral Island
Newberry, Clare Turlay. Percy, Polly and
    Pete
Schlein, Miriam. Billy, the Littlest One
    Herman McGregor's World
    When Will the World Be Mine?
Smith, Robert Paul. When I Am Big
Turkle, Brinton Cassady. Obadiah the
    Bold
Welber, Robert. Goodbye—Hello
Wittman, Sally Christensen. A Special
    Trade
Wooley, Catherine. A Drink for Little Red
    Diker
Zagone, Theresa. No Nap for Me

Zolotow, Charlotte Shapiro. May I Visit?
  Someone New
  When I Have a Little Girl
  When I Have a Son

016.15 Behavior—hiding

Matus, Greta. Where Are You, Jason?
Zion, Gene. Hide and Seek Day

016.16 Behavior—hiding things

Croswell, Volney. How to Hide a
  Hippopotamus

016.17 Behavior—hurrying

Hurd, Edith Thacher. Hurry Hurry
Lexau, Joan M. Olaf Is Late
Steiner, Charlotte. What's the Hurry,
  Harry?

016.18 Behavior—indifference

Hogrogian, Nonny. The Hermit and Harry
  and Me
Roy, Ronald. Three Ducks Went
  Wandering
Sendak, Maurice. Pierre, a Cautionary Tale
  in Five Chapters and a Prologue
Sharmat, Marjorie Weinman. I Don't Care
Watts, Mabel. The Day It Rained
  Watermelons

016.19 Behavior—losing things

Ardizzone, Edward Jeffrey Irving, and
  Ardizzone, Aingelda. The Little Girl
  and the Tiny Doll
Ayer, Jacqueline Brandford. Nu Dang and
  His Kite
Bowden, Joan Chase. Who Took the Top
  Hat Trick?
Brunhoff, Laurent de. Babar Loses His
  Crown
Burningham, John Mackintosh. The
  Blanket
Carrick, Carol. A Rabbit for Easter
Chorao, Kay. Molly's Lies
  Molly's Moe
Coombs, Patricia. The Lost Playground
Freeman, Don. Corduroy
Goldfrank, Helen Colodny. One Mitten
  Lewis
Kellogg, Steven. The Mystery of the Magic
  Green Ball
  The Mystery of the Missing Red Mitten
Lexau, Joan M. Finders Keepers, Losers
  Weepers
Livermore, Elaine. Lost and Found
McGinley, Phyllis. Lucy McLockett

McNeely, Jeannette. Where's Izzy?
Munari, Bruno. Jimmy Has Lost His Cap
Sharmat, Marjorie Weinman. The Trip
White, Florence M. How to Lose Your
  Lunch Money

016.20 Behavior—lost

Anderson, Clarence William. Blaze Finds
  Forgotten Roads
  Blaze Finds the Trail
Ayer, Jacqueline Brandford. Little Silk
Barton, Byron. Where's Al?
Bemelmans, Ludwig. Madeline and the
  Gypsies
Berson, Harold. Henry Possum
Boegehold, Betty. Pawpaw's Run
Bolliger, Max. Sandy at the Children's Zoo
Bornstein, Ruth. Annabelle
Brown, Judith Gwyn. Max and the Truffle
  Pig
Brown, Marcia. Tamarindo
Brown, Margaret Wise. Little Lost Lamb
Carle, Eric. Have You Seen My Cat?
Carrick, Carol, and Carrick, Donald. The
  Highest Balloon on the Common
Cartlidge, Michelle. Pippin and Pod
Cohen, Miriam. Lost in the Museum
Erickson, Phoebe. Just Follow Me
Farber, Norma. Where's Gomer?
Flack, Marjorie. Angus Lost
Francis, Frank. The Magic Wallpaper
Gay, Zhenya. Small One
Goble, Paul. The Friendly Wolf
Guilfoile, Elizabeth. Have You Seen My
  Brother?
Hader, Berta Hoerner, and Hader, Elmer
  Stanley. Lost in the Zoo
Hirsh, Marilyn Joyce. Where Is Yonkela?
Keats, Ezra Jack. My Dog Is Lost!
Kessler, Leonard P. Are We Lost, Daddy?
Koffler, Camilla. Two Little Bears
Lisker, Sonia O. Lost
Lubell, Winifred Milius, and Lubell, Cicil.
  Rosalie, the Bird Market Turtle
McCloskey, Robert John. Blueberries for
  Sal
Nakatani, Chiyoko. The Day Chiro Was
  Lost
Olsen, Ib Spang. Cat Alley
Peet, Bill. Ella
Politi, Leo. The Nicest Gift
Rey, Margret Elisabeth Waldstein. Curious
  George Goes to the Hospital
Sauer, Julia Lina. Mike's House
Saxon, Charles D. Don't Worry about
  Poopsie
Seignobosc, Françoise. Minou
  Springtime for Jeanne-Marie
Shortall, Leonard W. Andy, the Dog
  Walker
Slobodkin, Louis. Yasu and the Strangers

Sotomayor, Antonio. Khasa Goes to the
Fiesta
Standon, Anna, and Standon, Edward
Cyril. Little Duck Lost
Taylor, Mark. The Case of the Missing
Kittens
Henry the Castaway
Henry the Explorer
Tresselt, Alvin R. The Little Lost Squirrel
Vreeken, Elizabeth. The Boy Who Would
Not Say His Name
Wold, Jo Anne. Well! Why Didn't You Say
So?
Wright, Lula Esther. Little Lost Dog
Young, Evelyn. Tale of Tai

016.21 Behavior—lying

Chorao, Kay. Molly's Lies
Christopher, Matthew F. Jackrabbit Goalie
Evans, Katherine. The Boy Who Cried
Wolf
Gackenbach, Dick. Crackle, Gluck and the
Sleeping Toad
Helena, Ann. The Lie
Lexau, Joan M. Finders Keepers, Losers
Weepers
Sharmat, Marjorie Weinman. A Big Fat
Enormous Lie
Turkle, Brinton Cassady. The Adventures
of Obadiah

016.22 Behavior—misbehavior

Allard, Harry, and Marshall, James. Miss
Nelson Is Missing!
Brunhoff, Laurent de. Babar's Cousin,
That Rascal Arthur
Cartlidge, Michelle. Pippin and Pod
Cole, William. That Pest Jonathan
Flack, Marjorie, and Wiese, Kurt. The
Story about Ping
Gackenbach, Dick. Pepper and All the Legs
Gantos, John B. Rotten Ralph
Goodall, John Strickland. Naughty Nancy
Harper, Wilhelmina, reteller. The
Gunniwolf
Hazen, Barbara Shook, and Ungerer,
Tomi. The Sorcerer's Apprentice
Hoban, Russell Conwell. How Tom Beat
Captain Najork and His Hired
Sportsmen
Hogan, Inez. About Nono, the Baby
Elephant
Jameson, Cynthia. The Clay Pot Boy
Jeffers, Susan. Wild Robin
Koenig, Marion. The Wonderful World of
Night
Leaf, Munro. A Flock of Watchbirds
Lipkind, William. Nubber Bear
Lobel, Arnold Stark. Prince Bertram the
Bad

Moreman, Grace E. No, No, Natalie
Myller, Lois. No! No!
Potter, Beatrix. The Tale of Benjamin
Bunny
The Tale of Peter Rabbit
The Tale of Two Bad Mice
Preston, Edna Mitchell. Horrible Hepzibah
Squawk to the Moon, Little Goose
Sendak, Maurice. Where the Wild Things
Are
Watson, Wendy. Lollipop
White, Florence M. How to Lose Your
Lunch Money
Williams, Barbara. Whatever Happened to
Beverly Bigler's Birthday?

016.23 Behavior—mistakes

Bonsall, Crosby Newell. The Case of the
Dumb Bells
Brandenberg, Franz. No School Today!
Bridwell, Norman. Clifford's Good Deeds
Coombs, Patricia. Dorrie's Play
Firmin, Peter. Basil Brush Goes Flying
Gág, Wanda. Gone Is Gone
Galdone, Paul. Obedient Jack
Jacobs, Joseph. Hereafterthis
Lexau, Joan M. It All Began with a Drip,
Drip, Drip
Waber, Bernard. Nobody Is Perfick

016.24 Behavior—misunderstanding

Berg, Jean Horton. The O'Learys and
Friends
Bryant, Sara Cone. Epaminondas and His
Auntie
Carrick, Carol. Old Mother Witch
Eastman, Philip Day. Are You My Mother?
Hopkins, Lee Bennett. I Loved Rose Ann
Jacobs, Joseph. Master of All Masters
Kraus, Robert. Ladybug! Ladybug!
Lionni, Leo. Fish Is Fish
McClintock, Marshall. A Fly Went By
Parish, Peggy. Amelia Bedelia
Amelia Bedelia and the Surprise Shower
Amelia Bedelia Helps Out
Come Back, Amelia Bedelia
Good Work, Amelia Bedelia
Play Ball, Amelia Bedelia
Teach Us, Amelia Bedelia
Thank You, Amelia Bedelia
Polushkin, Maria. Mother, Mother, I Want
Another
Wold, Jo Anne. Well! Why Didn't You Say
So?

016.25 Behavior—nagging

Mahy, Margaret. Mrs. Discombobulous
Stalder, Valerie. Even the Devil Is Afraid
of a Shrew

016.26 Behavior—needing someone

Guilfoile, Elizabeth. Nobody Listens to Andrew
Kent, Jack. There's No Such Thing as a Dragon
Lobel, Anita. A Birthday for the Princess
Oppenheim, Joanne. On the Other Side of the River
Scott, Ann Herbert. On Mother's Lap Sam
Sendak, Maurice. Very Far Away
Singer, Marilyn. The Pickle Plan
Sugita, Yutaka. Helena the Unhappy Hippopotamus
Wells, Rosemary. Noisy Nora
Wolde, Gunilla. Betsy and the Chicken Pox
Wooley, Catherine. Part-Time Dog

016.27 Behavior—running away

Adoff, Arnold. Where Wild Willie?
Alexander, Martha G. And My Mean Old Mother Will Be Sorry, Blackboard Bear
Brown, Margaret Wise. The Runaway Bunny
Brunhoff, Jean de. The Story of Babar, the Little Elephant
Burton, Virginia Lee. Choo Choo, the Story of a Little Engine Who Ran Away
Carlson, Natalie Savage. Runaway Marie Louise
Carroll, Ruth Robinson. What Whiskers Did
Clifton, Lucille B. My Brother Fine with Me
Coombs, Patricia. Lisa and the Grompet
Freeman, Don. Beady Bear
Gackenbach, Dick. Claude and Pepper
The Gingerbread Boy, illus. by Paul Galdone
The Gingerbread Boy, illus. by William Curtis Holdsworth
The Gingerbread Man, illus. by Gerald Rose
Goodall, John Strickland. The Adventures of Paddy Pork
Greene, Graham. The Little Train
Hillert, Margaret. The Little Runaway
Hoban, Russell Conwell. A Baby Sister for Frances
Hogrogian, Nonny. Billy Goat and His Well-Fed Friends
Knight, Hilary. Where's Wallace?
LaFarge, Phyllis. Joanna Runs Away
Lobel, Arnold Stark. Small Pig
Rockwell, Anne F. Willy Runs Away
Seligman, Dorothy Halle. Run Away Home
Sendak, Maurice. Very Far Away
Sharmat, Marjorie Weinman. Rex
Wright, Dare. Edith and Mr. Bear

Zimnik, Reiner. The Bear on the Motorcycle
The Proud Circus Horse
Zion, Gene. Harry the Dirty Dog
Zolotow, Charlotte Shapiro. Big Sister and Little Sister

016.28 Behavior—saving things

Brandenberg, Franz. What Can You Make of It?
Braun, Kathy. Kangaroo and Kangaroo
Calhoun, Mary. The Traveling Ball of String
Delton, Judy. Penny Wise, Fun Foolish
Foster, Doris Van Liew. A Pocketful of Seasons

016.29 Behavior—secrets

Auerbach, Marjorie. King Lavra and the Barber
Brandenberg, Franz. A Secret for Grandmother's Birthday
Cummings, W. T. Miss Esta Maude's Secret
Lifton, Betty Jean. The Secret Seller

016.30 Behavior—seeking better things

Rose, Anne K. As Right as Right Can Be

016.31 Behavior—sharing

Albert, Burton. Mine, Yours, Ours
Azaad, Meyer. Half for You
Beim, Jerrold. The Smallest Boy in Class
Caudill, Rebecca. A Pocketful of Cricket
Devlin, Wende, and Devlin, Harry. Cranberry Christmas
Ets, Marie Hall. The Cow's Party
Flory, Jane. The Unexpected Grandchild
Gackenbach, Dick. Claude the Dog
Galdone, Paul. The Magic Porridge Pot
Houston, John A. The Bright Yellow Rope
Keats, Ezra Jack. Peter's Chair
Politi, Leo. Mr. Fong's Toy Shop
Schulman, Janet. Jack the Bum and the Halloween Handout
Sharmat, Marjorie Weinman. The Trip
Sherman, Ivan. I Do Not Like It When My Friend Comes to Visit
Turkle, Brinton Cassady. Rachel and Obadiah
Watson, Clyde. Tom Fox and the Apple Pie
Watts, Mabel. Something for You, Something for Me
Weil, Lisl. Pudding's Wonderful Bone
Wezel, Peter. The Good Bird
Wilson, Christopher B. Hobnob
Winthrop, Elizabeth. That's Mine!

Wright, Josephine. Cotton Cat and Martha Mouse

016.32 Behavior—sibling rivalry

Alexander, Martha G. I'll Be the Horse If You'll Play with Me
   Nobody Asked Me If I Wanted a Baby Sister
Amoss, Berthe. It's Not Your Birthday
   Tom in the Middle
Arnstein, Helen S. Billy and Our New Baby
Bonsall, Crosby Newell. Mine's the Best
Brothers and Sisters Are Like That!
Bulla, Clyde Robert. Keep Running, Allen!
Caines, Jeannette Franklin. Abby
Chenery, Janet. Wolfie
Clifton, Lucille B. My Brother Fine with Me
Conaway, Judith. I'll Get Even
Ginsburg, Mirra. Two Greedy Bears
Gray, Genevieve. Keep an Eye on Kevin: Safety Begins at Home
Greenfield, Eloise. She Come Bringing Me That Little Baby Girl
Hazen, Barbara Shook. Why Couldn't I Be an Only Kid Like You, Wigger?
Hoban, Lillian. Arthur's Pen Pal
Hoban, Russell Conwell. A Baby Sister for Frances
Hoban, Russell Conwell, and Hoban, Lillian. Some Snow Said Hello
Keats, Ezra Jack. Peter's Chair
Lexau, Joan M. The Homework Caper
Lobel, Anita. The Seamstress of Salzburg
Low, Alice. The Witch Who Was Afraid of Witches
Mallett, Anne. Here Comes Tagalong
Mayers, Patrick. Just One More Block
Milgram, Mary. Brothers Are All the Same
Ormondroyd, Edward. Theodore's Rival
Politi, Leo. Rosa
Postma, Lidia. The Stolen Mirror
Schick, Eleanor. Peggy's New Brother
Schlein, Miriam. Laurie's New Brother
Scott, Ann Herbert. On Mother's Lap
Sewell, Helen Moore. Jimmy and Jemima
Stevenson, James. Winston, Newton, Elton, and Ed
Turkle, Brinton Cassady. Rachel and Obadiah
Viorst, Judith. I'll Fix Anthony!
Wells, Rosemary. Benjamin and Tulip
   Stanley and Rhoda
Winthrop, Elizabeth. That's Mine!
Wolde, Gunilla. Betsy and the Chicken Pox
   Betsy's Baby Brother
Zolotow, Charlotte Shapiro. Big Brothers
   If It Weren't for You

016.33 Behavior—solitude

Bennett, Rainey. The Secret Hiding Place
Bulla, Clyde Robert. Keep Running, Allen!
Carrick, Carol. Sleep Out
Ehrlich, Amy. The Everyday Train
Hallinan, Patrick K. Just Being Alone
Hayes, Geoffrey. Bear by Himself
Tresselt, Alvin R. I Saw the Sea Come In
Yezback, Steven. Pumpkinseeds

016.34 Behavior—stealing

Cole, Joanna. The Secret Box
Dyke, John. Pigwig
Foulds, Elfrida Vipont. The Elephant and the Bad Baby

016.35 Behavior—talking to strangers

De Regniers, Beatrice Schenk. Red Riding Hood
Joyce, Irma. Never Talk to Strangers
Little Red Riding Hood, illus. by Paul Galdone
Little Red Riding Hood, illus. by Bernadette Watts
Potter, Beatrix. The Tale of Little Pig Robinson
Weil, Lisl. Bitzli and the Big Bad Wolf

016.36 Behavior—trickery

Aesopus. Three Fox Fables
Annett, Cora. When the Porcupine Moved In
Brown, Marcia. The Blue Jackal
Chicken Little. Chicken Licken
   Henny Penny, illus. by Paul Galdone
   Henny Penny, illus. by William Stobbs
Dines, Glen. Gilly and the Wicharoo
Domanska, Janina. The Best of the Bargain
Duvoisin, Roger Antoine. Petunia, I Love You!
Elkin, Benjamin. Gillespie and the Guards
Evans, Katherine. The Boy Who Cried Wolf
Galdone, Paul. The Horse, the Fox, and the Lion
Potter, Beatrix. The Pie and the Patty-Pan
   The Story of Miss Moppet
Rockwell, Anne F. The Gollywhopper Egg
Ungerer, Tomi. The Beast of Monsieur Racine
Varga, Judy. The Mare's Egg
Wildsmith, Brian. Python's Party
Zemach, Harve. The Tricks of Master Dabble

016.37 Behavior—unnoticed, unseen

Bishop, Bonnie. No One Noticed Ralph
Kroll, Steven. The Candy Witch
Udry, Janice May. How I Faded Away

016.38 Behavior—wishing

Ayer, Jacqueline Brandford. A Wish for
Little Sister
Brandenberg, Franz. I Wish I Was Sick,
Too!
Bright, Robert. Me and the Bears
Chapman, Carol. Barney Bipple's Magic
Dandelions
Clifton, Lucille B. Three Wishes
Daugherty, Charles Michael. Wisher
Emberley, Edward Randolph. A Birthday
Wish
Fuchshuber, Annegert. The Wishing Hat
Gackenbach, Dick. Hattie Rabbit
Geisel, Theodor Seuss. I Wish That I Had
Duck Feet
    Please Try to Remember the First of
    Octember!
Goldfrank, Helen Colodny. An Egg Is for
Wishing
Haas, Irene. The Maggie B
Iwasaki, Chihiro. The Birthday Wish
Jaffe, Rona. Last of the Wizards
Krauss, Ruth. Mama, I Wish I Was Snow.
Child, You'd Be Very Cold
Lasell, Fen. Michael Grows a Wish
Munari, Bruno. The Elephant's Wish
Paterson, Diane. If I Were a Toad
Perkins, Al. King Midas and the Golden
Touch
Reed, Kit. When We Dream
Seignobosc, Françoise. Jeanne-Marie
Counts Her Sheep
Sewell, Helen Moore. Peggy and the Pony
Shimin, Symeon. I Wish There Were Two
of Me
Tobias, Tobi. Jane, Wishing
Unteracker, John. The Dreaming Zoo
Varga, Judy. Janko's Wish
Walker, Challis. Three and Three
Watson, Pauline. Wriggles, the Little
Wishing Pig
Weisgard, Leonard. Who Dreams of
Cheese?
Williams, Barbara. Someday, Said Mitchell
Zimelman, Nathan. To Sing a Song as Big
as Ireland
Zolotow, Charlotte Shapiro. Someday

016.39 Behavior—worrying

Marshall, James. Portly McSwine
Sharmat, Marjorie Weinman. Thornton the
Worrier

017 Birds

Alexander, Martha G. Out! Out! Out!
Anderson, Lonzo. Mr. Biddle and the
Birds
Ayer, Jacqueline Brandford. A Wish for
Little Sister
Azaad, Meyer. Half for You
Baskin, Tobias. Hosie's Aviary
Baum, Willi. Birds of a Feather
Brock, Emma Lillian. The Birds' Christmas
Tree
Bruna, Dick. Little Bird Tweet
Chönz, Selina. Florina and the Wild Bird
Cortesi, Wendy W. Explore a Spooky
Swamp
Daniels, Guy, translator. The Peasant's Pea
Patch
Delton, Judy. Penny Wise, Fun Foolish
Duff, Maggie. Rum Pum Pum
Eastman, Philip Day. Are You My Mother?
Flap Your Wings
Fender, Kay. Odette, a Bird in Paris
Fisher, Aileen Lucia. We Went Looking
Freeman, Don. Fly High, Fly Low
French, Fiona Mary. The Blue Bird
Fujita, Tamao. The Boy and the Bird
Geisel, Theodor Seuss. Horton Hatches the
Egg
    Thidwick, the Big Hearted Moose
Hader, Berta Hoerner, and Hader, Elmer
Stanley. Mister Billy's Gun
Holl, Adelaide. The Remarkable Egg
Ipcar, Dahlov Zorach. Bright Barnyard
    The Song of the Day Birds and the
    Night Birds
Kantrowitz, Mildred. When Violet Died
Kishida, Eriko. The Lion and the Bird's
Nest
Krauss, Ruth. The Happy Egg
Kumin, Maxine W. Mittens in May
Lifton, Betty Jean. Joji and the Amanojaku
    Joji and the Dragon
    Joji and the Fog
Lionni, Leo. Inch by Inch
    Tico and the Golden Wings
Lubell, Winifred Milius, and Lubell, Cicil.
Rosalie, the Bird Market Turtle
McKee, David. Two Can Toucan
Massie, Diane Redfield. The Baby Beebee
Bird
Mayer, Mercer. Two Moral Tales
Mendoza, George. The Scribbler
Munari, Bruno. Bruno Munari's Zoo
    Tic, Tac and Toc
Ness, Evaline. Pavo and the Princess
Olds, Elizabeth. Feather Mountain
Peet, Bill. Eli
    The Pinkish, Purplish, Bluish Egg
Postgate, Oliver, and Firmin, Peter. Noggin
the King

Seidler, Rosalie. Grumpus and the
Venetian Cat
Selsam, Millicent Ellis. Tony's Birds
Stone, A. Harris. The Last Free Bird
Taylor, Sydney. Mr. Barney's Beard
Valentine, Ursula, translator. Herr
Minkipatt and His Friends
Varley, Dimitry. The Whirly Bird
Velthuijs, Max. The Painter and the Bird
Wells, Rosemary. A Song to Sing, O!
Wezel, Peter. The Good Bird
The Naughty Bird
Wildsmith, Brian. Brian Wildsmith's Birds
Wolo (pseud.). The Secret of the Ancient
Oak

017.01 Birds—albatrosses

Hoff, Sydney. Albert the Albatross

017.02 Birds—buzzards

Sandburg, Helga. Anna and the Baby
Buzzard
Wolkstein, Diane. The Cool Ride in the
Sky

017.03 Birds—canaries

Freeman, Don. Quiet! There's a Canary in
the Library
Tudor, Tasha. Thistly B

017.04 Birds—chickens

Allard, Harry. I Will Not Go to Market
Today
Andersen, Hans Christian. The Ugly
Duckling, illus. by Adrienne Adams
The Ugly Duckling, illus. by Johannes
Larsen
The Ugly Duckling, illus. by Will
Nickless
The Ugly Duckling, illus. by Josef
Palecek
Aulaire, Ingri Mortenson d', and Aulaire,
Edgar Parin d'. Don't Count Your
Chicks
Foxie, the Singing Dog
Benchley, Nathaniel. The Strange
Disappearance of Arthur Cluck
Bourke, Linda. Ethel's Exceptional Egg
Brothers, Aileen. Jiffy, Miss Boo and Mr.
Roo
Brown, Margaret Wise. Little Chicken
Carle, Eric. The Rooster Who Set Out to
See the World
Chaucer, Geoffrey. Chanticleer and the
Fox
Chicken Little. Chicken Licken
Henny Penny, illus. by Paul Galdone
Henny Penny, illus. by William Stobbs

Ehrhardt, Reinhold. Kikeri or The Proud
Red Rooster
Fatio, Louise. The Red Bantam
Fox, Robin. Le Poulet, the Rooster Who
Laid Eggs
Ginsburg, Mirra. The Chick and the
Duckling
The Golden Goose
Groves-Raines, Antony. The Tidy Hen
Hader, Berta Hoerner, and Hader, Elmer
Stanley. Cock-A-Doodle-Do; The
Story of a Little Red Rooster
Hartelius, Margaret A. The Chicken's
Child
Hewett, Anita. The Little White Hen
Hille-Brandts, Lene. The Little Black Hen
Hutchins, Pat. Rosie's Walk
Jackson, Jacqueline. Chicken Ten
Thousand
Jaynes, Ruth. Three Baby Chicks
Kwitz, Mary DeBall. Little Chick's Story
Lexau, Joan M. Crocodile and Hen
Lifton, Betty Jean. The Many Lives of
Chio and Goro
Lindman, Maj Jan. Flicka, Ricka, Dicka and
the Big Red Hen
Lipkind, William, and Mordvinoff, Nicolas.
The Little Tiny Rooster
The Little Red Hen, illus. by Janina
Domanska
The Little Red Hen, illus. by Paul Galdone
The Little Red Hen, illus. by Mel Pekarsky
Little Tuppen: An Old Tale
Littlefield, William. The Whiskers of Ho
Ho
Lobel, Anita. King Rooster, Queen Hen
Lobel, Arnold Stark. How the Rooster
Saved the Day
Miles, Miska. Chicken Forgets
Murphey, Sara. The Animal Hat Shop
O'Neill, Mary. Big Red Hen
Otto, Margaret Glover. The Little Brown
Horse
Polushkin, Maria. The Little Hen and the
Giant
Provensen, Alice, and Provensen, Martin.
My Little Hen
Pursell, Margaret Sanford. Jessie the
Chicken
Rockwell, Anne F. The Wonderful Eggs of
Furicchia
Scarry, Richard McClure. Egg in the Hole
Book
Selsam, Millicent Ellis. Egg to Chick
Sherman, Nancy. Gwendolyn and the
Weathercock
Gwendolyn the Miracle Hen
Sondergaard, Arensa, and Reed, Mary M.
Biddy and the Ducks
Uchida, Yoshiko. The Rooster Who
Understood Japanese
Van Horn, Grace. Little Red Rooster

Waber, Bernard. How to Go about Laying an Egg

Williams, Garth Montgomery. The Chicken Book

Zemach, Harve. The Speckled Hen; A Russian Nursery Rhyme

017.05 Birds—cockatoos

Wolo (pseud.). Tweedles Be Brave!

017.06 Birds—crows

Hazelton, Elizabeth Baldwin. Sammy, the Crow Who Remembered

017.07 Birds—doves

Freeman, Don. The Turtle and the Dove

Peet, Bill. The Pinkish, Purplish, Bluish Egg

Potter, Beatrix. The Tale of the Faithful Dove

Singer, Isaac Bashevis. Why Noah Chose the Dove

017.08 Birds—ducks

Allen, Jeffrey. Mary Alice, Operator Number 9

Brown, Margaret Wise. The Golden Egg Book

Conover, Chris. Six Little Ducks

Delton, Judy. Three Friends Find Spring

Dunn, Judy. The Little Duck

Duvoisin, Roger Antoine. Two Lonely Ducks

Flack, Marjorie. Angus and the Ducks

Flack, Marjorie, and Wiese, Kurt. The Story about Ping

Fribourg, Marjorie G. Ching-Ting and the Ducks

Friskey, Margaret. Seven Diving Ducks

Georgiady, Nicholas P. Gertie the Duck

Ginsburg, Mirra. The Chick and the Duckling

Hader, Berta Hoerner, and Hader, Elmer Stanley. Cock-A-Doodle-Do; The Story of a Little Red Rooster

Hillert, Margaret. The Funny Baby

Hurd, Edith Thacher. Last One Home Is a Green Pig

McCloskey, Robert John. Make Way for Ducklings

Miles, Miska. Noisy Gander

Potter, Beatrix. The Tale of Jemima Puddle-Duck

Richter, Mischa. Eric and Matilda Quack?

Roy, Ronald. Three Ducks Went Wandering

Seignobosc, Françoise. Springtime for Jeanne-Marie

Sewell, Helen Moore. Blue Barns

Shaw, Evelyn S. A Nest of Wood Ducks

Sheehan, Angela. The Duck

Sondergaard, Arensa, and Reed, Mary M. Biddy and the Ducks

Standon, Anna, and Standon, Edward Cyril. Little Duck Lost

Stevenson, James. Monty

Tudor, Bethany. Samuel's Tree House Skiddycock Pond

Tudor, Tasha. The White Goose

Turska, Krystvna. The Woodcutter's Duck

Unwin, Nora Spicer. Poquito, the Little Mexican Duck

Wildsmith, Brian. The Little Wood Duck

Woods, Ruth Maurine. Little Quack

017.09 Birds—eagles

Foreman, Michael. Moose

017.10 Birds—flamingos

Rossetti, Christina Georgina. What Is Pink?

017.11 Birds—geese

Burningham, John Mackintosh. Borka, the Adventures of a Goose with No Feathers

Chandoha, Walter. A Baby Goose for You

Duvoisin, Roger Antoine. Petunia
  Petunia and the Song
  Petunia, Beware!
  Petunia, I Love You!
  Petunia Takes a Trip
  Petunia's Christmas
  Petunia's Treasure

Freeman, Don. Will's Quill

Galdone, Joanna. Gertrude, the Goose Who Forgot

Holmes, Efner Tudor. Amy's Goose

Koch, Dorothy Clarke. Gone Is My Goose

Low, Joseph. Boo to a Goose

Preston, Edna Mitchell. Squawk to the Moon, Little Goose

Rockwell, Anne F. Poor Goose

Sewell, Helen Moore. Blue Barns

Zijlstra, Tjerk. Benny and His Geese

017.12 Birds—hawks

Baylor, Byrd. Hawk, I'm Your Brother

017.13 Birds—ostriches

Koffler, Camilla, and Bonsall, Crosby Newell. Look Who's Talking

017.14 Birds—owls

Benchley, Nathaniel. The Strange
    Disappearance of Arthur Cluck
Bennett, Rainey. After the Sun Goes Down
Duvoisin, Roger Antoine. Day and Night
Eastman, Philip Day. Sam and the Firefly
Flower, Phyllis. Barn Owl
Foster, Doris Van Liew. Tell Me, Mr. Owl
Goodenow, Earle. The Owl Who Hated the
    Dark
Kirn, Ann Minette. I Spy
Kraus, Robert. Owliver
Lear, Edward. The Owl and the Pussy-Cat,
    illus. by Barbara Cooney
    The Owl and the Pussy-Cat, illus. by
      William Pène Du Bois
    The Owl and the Pussy-Cat, illus. by
      Gwen Fulton
Lobel, Arnold Stark. Owl at Home
Nicoll, Helen. Meg at Sea
    Meg's Eggs
Piatti, Celestino. The Happy Owls
Potter, Beatrix. The Tale of Squirrel
    Nutkin
Scarry, Patricia M. Little Richard and
    Prickles
Scharen, Beatrix. Tillo
Schoenherr, John Carl. The Barn
Slobodkin, Louis. The Wide-Awake Owl
Wildsmith, Brian. The Owl and the
    Woodpecker
Zimnik, Reiner. Little Owl

017.15 Birds—parrots, parakeets

Bishop, Bonnie. No One Noticed Ralph
Graham, Margaret Bloy. Benjy and the
    Barking Bird
Holman, Felice. Victoria's Castle
Potter, Stephen. Squawky, the Adventures
    of a Clasperchoice
Zacharis, Boris. But Where Is the Green
    Parrot?

017.16 Birds—peacocks, peahens

Alan, Sandy. The Plaid Peacock
Hamberger, John F. The Peacock Who
    Lost His Tail
Kepes, Juliet. The Seed That Peacock
    Planted
Peet, Bill. The Spooky Tail of Prewitt
    Peacock
Wittman, Sally Christensen. Pelly and Peak

017.17 Birds—pelicans

Benchley, Nathaniel. The Flying Lessons of
    Gerald Pelican
Fatio, Louise. Hector and Christiana
Freeman, Don. Come Again, Pelican

Lear, Edward. The Pelican Chorus
Wise, William. Nanette the Hungry Pelican
Wittman, Sally Christensen. Pelly and Peak

017.18 Birds—penguins

Fatio, Louise. Hector Penguin
Stevenson, James. Winston, Newton, Elton,
    and Ed
Weiss, Leatie. Funny Feet

017.19 Birds—pigeons

Peet, Bill. Fly, Homer, Fly
Shulman, Milton. Preep, the Little Pigeon
    of Trafalgar Square

017.20 Birds—robins

Cock Robin. The Courtship, Merry
    Marriage, and Feast of Cock Robin
    and Jenny Wren, to Which Is Added
    the Doleful Death of Cock Robin
Flack, Marjorie. The Restless Robin
Hawkinson, John, and Hawkinson, Lucy
    Ozone. Robins and Rabbits
Stern, Elsie-Jean. Wee Robin's Christmas
    Song

017.26 Birds—turkeys

Hurd, Edith Thacher. Sandpipers

017.22 Birds—sea gulls

Ness, Evaline. Do You Have the Time,
    Lydia?
Pursell, Margaret Sanford. Shelley the Sea
    Gull
Turkle, Brinton Cassady. Thy Friend,
    Obadiah

017.23 Birds—sparrows

Thompson, George Selden. Sparrow Socks

017.24 Birds—storks

Brown, Margaret Wise, and Gergely,
    Tibor. Wheel on the Chimney

017.25 Birds—swans

Andersen, Hans Christian. The Ugly
    Duckling, illus. by Adrienne Adams
    The Ugly Duckling, illus. by Johannes
      Larsen
    The Ugly Duckling, illus. by Will
      Nickless
    The Ugly Duckling, illus. by Joseph
      Palecek
Canfield, Jane White. Swan Cove

017.26 Birds—turkeys

Balian, Lorna. Sometimes It's Turkey—
Sometimes It's Feathers

017.27 Birds—vultures

Duvoisin, Roger Antoine. Petunia, I Love
You!
Ungerer, Tomi. Orlando the Brave
Vulture
Wolkstein, Diane. The Cool Ride in the
Sky

017.28 Birds—woodpeckers

Wildsmith, Brian. The Owl and the
Woodpecker

017.29 Birds—wrens

Cock Robin. The Courtship, Merry
Marriage, and Feast of Cock Robin
and Jenny Wren, to Which Is Added
the Doleful Death of Cock Robin

018 Birthdays

Amoss, Berthe. It's Not Your Birthday
Anderson, Clarence William. Billy and
Blaze
Annett, Cora. The Dog Who Thought He
Was a Boy
Averill, Esther Holden. Jenny's Birthday
Book
Ayer, Jacqueline Brandford. A Wish for
Little Sister
Bannon, Laura May. Manuela's Birthday in
Old Mexico
Barrett, Judith. Benjamin's 365 Birthdays
Bell, Norman. Linda's Air Mail Letter
Bemelmans, Ludwig. Madeline in London
Beskow, Elsa Maartman. Peter's
Adventures in Blueberry Land
Bible, Charles. Jennifer's New Chair
Brandenberg, Aliki Liacouras. June 7!
Brandenberg, Franz. A Secret for
Grandmother's Birthday
Brunhoff, Laurent de. Babar's Birthday
Surprise
Carle, Eric. Secret Birthday Message
Chalmers, Audrey. A Birthday for Obash
Chalmers, Mary Eileen. A Hat for Amy
Jean
Clifton, Lucille B. Don't You Remember?
Coombs, Patricia. Dorrie and the Birthday
Eggs
Daly, Maureen. Patrick Visits the Library
Duvoisin, Roger Antoine. Veronica and the
Birthday Present
Elkin, Benjamin. The Loudest Noise in the
World

Emberley, Edward Randolph. A Birthday
Wish
Fern, Eugene. Birthday Presents
Fischer, Hans. The Birthday
Flack, Marjorie. Ask Mr. Bear
Freeman, Don. The Guard Mouse
Mop Top
Geisel, Theodor Seuss. Happy Birthday to
You
Hooper Humperdink . . . ? Not Him!
Goodall, John Strickland. Shrewbettina's
Birthday
Hillert, Margaret. The Birthday Car
Hoban, Russell Conwell. A Birthday for
Frances
Hutchins, Pat. The Best Train Set Ever
Happy Birthday, Sam
Iwamatsu, Jun. Umbrella
Iwasaki, Chihiro. The Birthday Wish
Jaynes, Ruth. What Is a Birthday Child?
Keats, Ezra Jack. A Letter to Amy
Kitt, Tamara. A Special Birthday Party for
Someone Very Special
Kumin, Maxine W., and Sexton, Anne.
Joey and the Birthday Present
Lasell, Fen. Michael Grows a Wish
Lenski, Lois L. A Surprise for Davy
Lexau, Joan M. Go Away, Dog
Me Day
Lindman, Maj Jan. Flicka, Ricka, Dicka
Bake a Cake
Snipp, Snapp, Snurr and the Red Shoes
Lobel, Anita. A Birthday for the Princess
Lowrey, Janette Sebring. Six Silver Spoons
McNeill, Janet. The Giant's Birthday
Miklowitz, Gloria D. Barefoot Boy
Miles, Miska. Mouse Six and the Happy
Birthday
Minarik, Else Holmelund. Little Bear
Moon, Grace. One Little Indian
Munari, Bruno. The Birthday Present
Myller, Rolf. How Big Is a Foot?
Myrick, Jean Lockwood. Ninety-Nine
Pockets
Ness, Evaline. Josefina February
Oleson, Claire. For Pepita, an Orange Tree
Parish, Peggy. Snapping Turtle's All
Wrong Day
Parker, Nancy Winslow. Love from Uncle
Clyde
Perkins, Al. Tubby and the Lantern
Prager, Annabelle. The Surprise Party
Sandberg, Inger. Nicholas' Favorite Pet
Sewell, Helen Moore. Birthdays for Robin
Shimin, Symeon. A Special Birthday
Steiner, Charlotte. Birthdays Are for
Everyone
Steptoe, John. Birthday
Stolz, Mary Slattery. Emmett's Pig

Uchida, Yoshiko. Sumi's Special
    Happening
Waber, Bernard. Lyle and the Birthday
    Party
Watson, Nancy Dingman. Annie's
    Spending Spree
    The Birthday Goat
    Tommy's Mommy's Fish
Williams, Barbara. Whatever Happened to
    Beverly Bigler's Birthday?
Zimelman, Nathan. Once When I Was Five
Zolotow, Charlotte Shapiro. Mr. Rabbit and
    the Lovely Present

019 Boats, ships

Ardizzone, Edward Jeffrey Irving. Little
    Tim and the Brave Sea Captain
    Ship's Cook Ginger
    Tim All Alone
    Tim and Charlotte
    Tim and Ginger
    Tim and Lucy Go to Sea
    Tim in Danger
    Tim to the Rescue
    Tim's Friend Towser
    Tim's Last Voyage
Benchley, Nathaniel. Red Fox and His
    Canoe
Brook, Judy. Tim Mouse Goes
    Downstream
Brown, Judith Gwyn. The Happy Voyage
Burn, Doris. The Summerfolk
Burningham, John Mackintosh. Mr.
    Gumpy's Outing
Calhoun, Mary. Euphonia and the Flood
Carrick, Carol. The Washout
Cohen, Peter Zachary. Authorized Autumn
    Charts of the Upper Red Canoe
    River Country
de Paola, Thomas Anthony. Four Stories
    for Four Seasons
Devlin, Harry. The Walloping Window
    Blind
Domanska, Janina. I Saw a Ship A-Sailing
Du Bois, William Pène. Otto at Sea
Flack, Marjorie. The Boats on the River
Fry, Christopher. The Boat That Mooed
Graham, Lorenz. Song of the Boat
Graham, Margaret Bloy. Benjy's Boat Trip
Gramatky, Hardie. Little Toot
    Little Toot on the Thames
    Little Toot through the Golden Gate
Haas, Irene. The Maggie B
Haley, Gail Diana Einhart. Noah's Ark
Hillert, Margaret. The Yellow Boat
Hurd, Edith Thacher. What Whale?
    Where?
Kellogg, Steven. The Island of the Skog
Kuskin, Karla Seidman. The Animals and
    the Ark
Lenski, Lois L. The Little Sail Boat

Mr. and Mrs. Noah
Lindman, Maj Jan. Sailboat Time
McCloskey, Robert John. Burt Dow, Deep
    Water Man
Mahy, Margaret. Sailor Jack and the
    Twenty Orphans
Marshall, James. Speedboat
Martin, Patricia Miles. No, No, Rosina
Massie, Diane Redfield. The Komodo
    Dragon's Jewels
Mendoza, George. The Alphabet Boat; A
    Seagoing Alphabet Book
Mother Goose. Hurrah, We're Outward
    Bound!
Perkins, Al. Tubby and the Poo-Bah
Potter, Beatrix. The Tale of Little Pig
    Robinson
Potter, Russell. The Little Red Ferry Boat
Reavin, Sam. Hurray for Captain Jane!
Reesink, Maryke. The Golden Treasure
Shecter, Ben. If I Had a Ship
Shortall, Leonard W. Tod on the Tugboat
Spier, Peter. Noah's Ark
Surany, Anico. Ride the Cold Wind
Swift, Hildegarde Hoyt, and Ward, Lynd
    Kendall. The Little Red Lighthouse
    and the Great Gray Bridge
Taylor, Mark. Henry the Castaway
Thomson, Ruth. Peabody All at Sea
Tudor, Bethany. Skiddycock Pond
Venable, Alan. The Checker Players
Vinton, Iris. Look Out for Pirates!
Young, Miriam Burt. If I Sailed a Boat
Zaffo, George J. The Giant Nursery Book
    of Things That Go

020 Bridges

Lobel, Anita. Sven's Bridge
Oppenheim, Joanne. On the Other Side of
    the River
Steadman, Ralph. The Bridge
Swift, Hildegarde Hoyt, and Ward, Lynd
    Kendall. The Little Red Lighthouse
    and the Great Gray Bridge

021 Buses

Jewell, Nancy. Bus Ride
Shuttlesworth, Dorothy E. ABC of Buses
Young, Miriam Burt. If I Drove a Bus

022 Cable cars

Burton, Virginia Lee. Maybelle, the Cable
    Car
Gramatky, Hardie. Sparky
MacCabe, Naomi, and MacCabe, Lorin.
    Cable Car Joey
Taniuchi, Kota. Trolley

023 Careers

Azaad, Meyer. Half for You
Bank Street College of Education. People
  Read
Burnett, Carol. What I Want to Be When I
  Grow Up
Harper, Anita. How We Work
Klein, Norma. Girls Can Be Anything
Kraus, Robert. Owliver
Lasker, Joseph Leon. Mothers Can Do
  Anything
Merriam, Eve. Mommies at Work
Morrison, Bill. Louis James Hates School
Oppenheim, Joanne. On the Other Side of
  the River
Puner, Helen Walker. Daddys, What They
  Do All Day
Rowe, Jeanne A. City Workers
Sandberg, Inger, and Sandberg, Lasse.
  Come On Out, Daddy
Scarry, Richard McClure. Richard Scarry's
  Busiest People Ever
  What Do People Do All Day?
Seignobosc, Françoise. What Do You Want
  to Be?
Stewart, Robert. The Daddy Book
Weil, Lisl. Mimi
Winn, Marie. The Man Who Made Fine
  Tops

023.01 Careers—airplane pilots

Greene, Carla. Railroad Engineers and
  Airplane Pilots: What Do They Do?

023.02 Careers—artists

Angelo, Nancy Carolyn Harris. Camembert
Miller, Warren. Pablo Paints a Picture
Payne, Josephine Balfour. The Stable That
  Stayed
Pinkwater, Manus. The Bear's Picture
Sloan, Carolyn. Carter Is a Painter's Cat
Velthuijs, Max. The Painter and the Bird
Ventura, Piero, and Ventura, Marisa. The
  Painter's Trick
Weisgard, Leonard. Mr. Peaceable Paints

023.03 Careers—bakers

Carle, Eric. Walter the Baker
Kessler, Leonard P. Soup for the King
Zion, Gene. The Sugar Mouse Cake

023.04 Careers—barbers

Auerbach, Marjorie. King Lavra and the
  Barber
Barry, Robert E. Next Please
Freeman, Don. Mop Top

Kunhardt, Dorothy. Billy the Barber
Peet, Bill. Hubert's Hair Raising
  Adventures

023.05 Careers—carpenters

Greene, Carla. I Want to Be a Carpenter

023.06 Careers—clockmakers

Ardizzone, Edward Jeffrey Irving. Johnny
  the Clock Maker

023.07 Careers—dentists

Duvoisin, Roger Antoine. Crocus
Lapp, Carolyn. The Dentists' Tools
Richter, Alice, and Numeroff, Laura Joffe.
  You Can't Put Braces on Spaces
Rockwell, Harlow. My Dentist

023.08 Careers—detectives

Berenstain, Stanley. The Bear Detectives:
  The Case of the Missing Pumpkin
Bonsall, Crosby Newell. The Case of the
  Hungry Stranger
Lawrence, James D. Binky Brothers and
  the Fearless Four
  Binky Brothers, Detectives
Platt, Kin. Big Max
  Big Max in the Mystery of the Missing
  Moose
Quackenbush, Robert Mead. Detective
  Mole
  Detective Mole and the Secret Clues
  Detective Mole and the Tip-Top
  Mystery
Sharmat, Marjorie Weinman. Nate the
  Great
  Nate the Great and the Lost List
  Nate the Great and the Phony Clue
  Nate the Great Goes Undercover
Thomson, Ruth. Peabody All at Sea
  Peabody's First Case

023.09 Careers—doctors

Breinburg, Petronella. Doctor Shawn
Charlip, Remy, and Supree, Burton.
  "Mother, Mother I Feel Sick"
Gilbert, Helen Earle. Dr. Trotter and His
  Big Gold Watch
Goodsell, Jane. Katie's Magic Glasses
Greene, Carla. Doctors and Nurses: What
  Do They Do?
Lerner, Marguerite Rush. Doctors' Tools

Rockwell, Harlow. My Doctor
Thompson, Frances B. Doctor John
Viorst, Judith. The Tenth Good Thing
    about Barney
Wahl, Jan. Doctor Rabbit's Foundling
Wolde, Gunilla. Betsy and the Doctor

023.10 Careers—firefighters

Averill, Esther Holden. The Fire Cat
Bridwell, Norman. Clifford's Good Deeds
Brown, Margaret Wise. The Little Fireman
Chalmers, Mary Eileen. Throw a Kiss,
    Harry
Gramatky, Hardie. Hercules
Lenski, Lois L. The Little Fire Engine
Rey, Hans Augusto. Curious George
Spiegel, Doris. Danny and Company 92
Weiss, Harvey. The Sooner Hound
Zaffo, George J. The Big Book of Real
    Fire Engines

023.11 Careers—fishermen

Aldridge, Josephine Haskell. Fisherman's
    Luck
Gramatky, Hardie. Nikos and the Sea God
Martin, Patricia Miles. No, No, Rosina
Matsutani, Miyoko. The Fisherman under
    the Sea
Napoli, Guillier. Adventure at Mont St.
    Michael
Parker, Dorothy D. Liam's Catch

023.12 Careers—fortune tellers

Coombs, Patricia. Dorrie and the Fortune
    Teller
Jeschke, Susan. Firerose

023.13 Careers—garbage collectors

Zion, Gene. Dear Garbage Man

023.14 Careers—judges

Zemach, Harve. The Judge

023.15 Careers—maids

Parish, Peggy. Amelia Bedelia
    Amelia Bedelia and the Surprise Shower
    Amelia Bedelia Helps Out
    Come Back, Amelia Bedelia
    Good Work, Amelia Bedelia
    Play Ball, Amelia Bedelia
    Teach Us, Amelia Bedelia
    Thank You, Amelia Bedelia

023.16 Careers—mail carriers

Bell, Norman. Linda's Air Mail Letter
Drummond, Violet H. The Flying Postman
Haley, Gail Diana Einhart. The Post Office
    Cat
Keats, Ezra Jack. A Letter to Amy
Maury, Inez. My Mother the Mail Carrier:
    Mi Mama la Cartera
Scarry, Richard McClure. Richard Scarry's
    Postman Pig and His Busy Neighbors

023.17 Careers—military

Ambrus, Victor G. Brave Soldier Janosch
Emberley, Barbara. Drummer Hoff
Greene, Carla. Soldiers and Sailors: What
    Do They Do?
Langstaff, John Meredith. Soldier, Soldier,
    Won't You Marry Me?
McGowen, Tom. The Only Glupmaker in
    the U.S. Navy
Mahy, Margaret. Sailor Jack and the
    Twenty Orphans

023.18 Careers—nuns

Routh, Jonathan. The Nuns Go to Africa

023.19 Careers—nurses

Greene, Carla. Doctors and Nurses: What
    Do They Do?
Kraus, Robert. Rebecca Hatpin
Whitney, Alma Marshak. Just Awful

023.20 Careers—peddlers

Jacobs, Joseph. The Crock of Gold, Being
    "The Pedlar of Swaffham"
Rockwell, Anne F. A Bear, a Bobcat and
    Three Ghosts
Slobodkina, Esphyr. Caps for Sale
    Pezzo the Peddler and the Circus
    Elephant
    Pezzo the Peddler and the Thirteen Silly
    Thieves
Suba, Susanne. The Monkeys and the
    Pedlar

023.21 Careers—police officers

Chapin, Cynthia. Squad Car 55
Guilfoile, Elizabeth. Have You Seen My
    Brother?
Keats, Ezra Jack. My Dog Is Lost!
Lattin, Anne. Peter's Policeman
Lenski, Lois L. Policeman Small
McCloskey, Robert John. Make Way for
    Ducklings
Schlein, Miriam. The Amazing Mr.
    Pelgrew

Vreeken, Elizabeth. The Boy Who Would
Not Say His Name
Weil, Lisl. Mimi

023.22 Careers—railroad engineers

Greene, Carla. Railroad Engineers and
Airplane Pilots: What Do They Do?
Lenski, Lois L. The Little Train

023.23 Careers—seamstresses

Lobel, Anita. The Seamstress of Salzburg
Olds, Helen Diehl. Miss Hattie and the
Monkey

023.24 Careers—shoemakers

Gilbert, Helen Earle. Mr. Plum and the
Little Green Tree
La Fontaine, Jean de. The Rich Man and
the Shoemaker

023.25 Careers—tailors

Ambrus, Victor G. The Three Poor Tailors
Potter, Beatrix. The Tailor of Gloucester

023.26 Careers—taxi drivers

Moore, Lilian. Papa Albert
Ross, Jessica. Ms. Klondike

023.27 Careers—teachers

Allard, Harry, and Marshall, James. Miss
Nelson Is Missing!
Cummings, W. T. Miss Esta Maude's Secret
Feder, Paula Kurzband. Where Does the
Teacher Live?

023.28 Careers—telephone operators

Allen, Jeffrey. Mary Alice, Operator
Number 9

023.29 Careers—truck drivers

Greene, Carla. Truck Drivers: What Do
They Do?

023.30 Careers—veterinarians

Greene, Carla. Animal Doctors: What Do
They Do?

023.31 Careers—window cleaners

Rey, Hans Augusto. Curious George Takes
a Job

024 Cavemen

Hoff, Sydney. Stanley
Seyton, Marion. The Hole in the Hill
Slobodkin, Louis. Dinny and Danny

025 Caves

Ungerer, Tomi. The Mellops Go
Spelunking

026 Character traits

Leisk, David Johnson. The Emperor's Gift
Seignobosc, Françoise. Jeanne-Marie in
Gay Paris

026.01 Character traits—ambition

Aitken, Amy. Ruby!
Balet, Jan B. Joanjo; A Portuguese Tale
Claude-Lafontaine, Pascale. Monsieur
Bussy, the Celebrated Hamster
Graham, Al. Timothy Turtle
Gramatky, Hardie. Little Toot
Hochman, Sandra. The Magic Convention
Holl, Adelaide. My Father and I
Kumin, Maxine W. Speedy Digs Downside
Up
Seignobosc, Françoise. What Do You Want
to Be?
Shecter, Ben. Hester the Jester
Turska, Krystyna. The Magician of Cracow
Uchida, Yoshiko. Sumi's Prize

026.02 Character traits—appearance

Andersen, Hans Christian. The Ugly
Duckling, illus. by Adrienne Adams
The Ugly Duckling, illus. by Johannes
Larsen
The Ugly Duckling, illus. by Will
Nickless
The Ugly Duckling, illus. by Joseph
Palecek
Bonsall, Crosby Newell. Listen, Listen!
de Paola, Thomas Anthony. Big Anthony
and the Magic Ring
Fatio, Louise. The Happy Lion and the
Bear
Freeman, Don. Dandelion
McDermott, Gerald. The Magic Tree; A
Tale from the Congo
Ness, Evaline. The Girl and the Goatherd
Numeroff, Laura Joffe. Amy for Short
Ormondroyd, Edward. Theodore
Scott, Natalie. Firebrand, Push Your Hair
Out of Your Eyes

026.03 Character traits—being different

Andersen, Hans Christian. The Ugly
    Duckling, illus. by Adrienne Adams
    The Ugly Duckling, illus. by Johannes
    Larsen
    The Ugly Duckling, illus. by Will
    Nickless
    The Ugly Duckling, illus. by Joseph
    Palecek
Aulaire, Ingri Mortenson d', and Aulaire,
    Edgar Parin d'. Nils
Blue, Rose. I Am Here: Yo Estoy Aqui
Brightman, Alan. Like Me
Burningham, John Mackintosh. Borka, the
    Adventures of a Goose with No
    Feathers
Carle, Eric. The Mixed-Up Chameleon
Coombs, Patricia. The Lost Playground
Duvoisin, Roger Antoine. Our Veronica
    Goes to Petunia's Farm
    Veronica
Emberley, Edward Randolph. Rosebud
Fern, Eugene. Pepito's Story
Krasilovsky, Phyllis. The Very Tall Little
    Girl
Lerner, Marguerite Rush. Lefty: The Story
    of Left-Handedness
Levine, Rhoda. Harrison Loved His
    Umbrella
Peet, Bill. The Spooky Tail of Prewitt
    Peacock
Rey, Margret Elisabeth Waldstein. Spotty
Simon, Norma. Why Am I Different?
Simon, Sidney B. The Armadillo Who Had
    No Shell
Wildsmith, Brian. The Little Wood Duck

026.04 Character traits—bravery

Anglund, Joan Walsh. The Brave Cowboy
Ardizzone, Edward Jeffrey Irving. Little
    Tim and the Brave Sea Captain
    Peter the Wanderer
    Tim and Charlotte
    Tim to the Rescue
Benchley, Nathaniel. The Deep Dives of
    Stanley Whale
Burgert, Hans-Joachim. Samulo and the
    Giant
Carleton, Barbee Oliver. Benny and the
    Bear
Conford, Ellen. Eugene the Brave
Coombs, Patricia. Molly Mullett
Coville, Bruce, and Coville, Katherine. The
    Foolish Giant
Dreifus, Miriam W. Brave Betsy
Dyke, John. Pigwig
Fatio, Louise. The Red Bantam
Ginsburg, Mirra. The Strongest One of All
Holl, Adelaide. Sir Kevin of Devon

Horvath, Betty F. Jasper and the Hero
    Business
Lexau, Joan M. It All Began with a Drip,
    Drip, Drip
Low, Joseph. Boo to a Goose
Matsutani, Miyoko. The Witch's Magic
    Cloth
Mayer, Mercer. Liza Lou and the Yeller
    Belly Swamp
Peet, Bill. Cowardly Clyde
Polushkin, Maria. The Little Hen and the
    Giant
Schertle, Alice. The Gorilla in the Hall
Sewell, Helen Moore. Jimmy and Jemima
Taylor, Mark. Henry Explores the Jungle
    Henry Explores the Mountains
    Henry the Castaway
    Henry the Explorer
Titus, Eve. Anatole and the Cat
Van Woerkom, Dorothy O. Becky and the
    Bear
Wells, Herbert George. The Adventures of
    Tommy
Williams, Gweneira Maureen. Timid
    Timothy, the Kitten Who Learned to
    Be Brave

026.05 Character traits—cleanliness

Groves-Raines, Antony. The Tidy Hen
Howells, Mildred. The Woman Who Lived
    in Holland
Hurd, Edith Thacher. Stop, Stop
Krasilovsky, Phyllis. The Man Who Did
    Not Wash His Dishes
Potter, Beatrix. The Tale of Mrs.
    Tittlemouse
Rudolph, Marguerita. Sharp and Shiny
Sharmat, Marjorie Weinman. Mooch the
    Messy
Weisgard, Leonard. The Clean Pig

026.06 Character traits—cleverness

Anderson, Paul S. Red Fox and the
    Hungry Tiger
Ardizzone, Edward Jeffrey Irving. Peter
    the Wanderer
Asbjørnsen, Peter Christen. The Three
    Billy Goats Gruff, illus. by Paul
    Galdone
    The Three Billy Goats Gruff, illus. by
    William Stobbs
Asbjørnsen, Peter Christen, and Moe,
    Jørgen Engebretsen. The Three Billy
    Goats Gruff
Baker, Betty. Partners
Bang, Betsy. The Old Woman and the Red
    Pumpkin
Bang, Molly G. Wiley and the Hairy Man
Bannerman, Helen Brodie Cowan. The
    Story of Little Black Sambo

Bemelmans, Ludwig. Welcome Home
Benchley, Nathaniel. The Several Tricks of
     Edgar Dolphin
Bishop, Claire Huchet, and Wiese, Kurt.
     The Five Chinese Brothers
Boegehold, Betty. Pawpaw's Run
Brown, Marcia. The Bun
Burningham, John Mackintosh. Harquin,
     the Fox Who Went Down to the
     Valley
Burton, Virginia Lee. Calico the Wonder
     Horse, or The Saga of Stewy Slinker
Byfield, Barbara Ninde. The Haunted
     Churchbell
Coombs, Patricia. The Magic Pot
Damjan, Mischa (pseud.). The Wolf and
     the Kid
Dines, Glen. Gilly and the Wicharoo
Domanska, Janina. The Best of the
     Bargain
     King Krakus and the Dragon
     Why So Much Noise?
Elkin, Benjamin. Gillespie and the Guards
     Lucky and the Giant
Galdone, Paul. The Monkey and the
     Crocodile
Hirsh, Marilyn Joyce. The Rabbi and the
     Twenty-Nine Witches
Jaffe, Rona. Last of the Wizards
Kennedy, Richard. The Contests at
     Cowlick
Lobel, Arnold Stark. How the Rooster
     Saved the Day
     Mouse Soup
Parish, Peggy. Zed and the Monsters
Parry, Marian. King of the Fish
Perrault, Charles. Puss in Boots, illus. by
     Marcia Brown
     Puss in Boots, illus. by Hans Fischer
     Puss in Boots, illus. by Paul Galdone
     Puss in Boots, illus. by Julia Noonan
     Puss in Boots, illus. by William Stobbs
     Puss in Boots, illus. by Barry Wilkinson
Potter, Beatrix. The Sly Old Cat
     The Tale of the Flopsy Bunnies
Prokofiev, Sergei Sergeievitch. Peter and
     the Wolf, illus. by Warren Chappell
     Peter and the Wolf, illus. by Frans
     Haacken
     Peter and the Wolf, illus. by Alan
     Howard
     Peter and the Wolf, illus. by Kozo
     Shimizu
Rockwell, Anne F. Big Boss
     The Stolen Necklace
Schatz, Letta. The Extraordinary Tug-of-
     War
Schulman, Janet. Jack the Bum and the
     UFO
Siddiqui, Ashraf. Bhombal Dass, the Uncle
     of Lion

Simon, Sidney B. Henry the Uncatchable
     Mouse
Skurzynski, Gloria. The Magic Pumpkin
Three Little Pigs. The Story of the Three
     Little Pigs, illus. by Leonard Leslie
     Brooke
     The Story of the Three Little Pigs, illus.
     by William Stobbs
     The Three Little Pigs, illus. by William
     Pène Du Bois
     The Three Little Pigs, illus. by Paul
     Galdone
     The Three Little Pigs, illus. by Irma Wilde
Van Woerkom, Dorothy O. The Rat, the
     Ox and the Zodiac
Walker, Barbara K. Teeny-Tiny and the
     Witch-Woman
Wild, Robin, and Wild, Jocelyn. Little Pig
     and the Big Bad Wolf
Williams, Jay. School for Sillies
Wolkstein, Diane. The Cool Ride in the
     Sky
Zemach, Harve. Nail Soup

026.07 Character traits—completing things

Flack, Marjorie. Angus and the Cat
Ness, Evaline. Do You Have the Time,
     Lydia?
Petrides, Heidrun. Hans and Peter

026.08 Character traits—compromising

Hogrogian, Nonny. Carrot Cake
Wildsmith, Brian. The Owl and the
     Woodpecker

026.09 Character traits—conceit

Flack, Marjorie. Angus and the Ducks
Peet, Bill. Ella
Sharmat, Marjorie Weinman. I'm Terrific

026.10 Character traits—curiosity

Coombs, Patricia. Dorrie and the
     Dreamyard Monsters
Flack, Marjorie. Angus and the Cat
     Angus and the Ducks
Gackenbach, Dick. The Pig Who Saw
     Everything
Meeks, Esther K. Curious Cow
Napoli, Guillier. Adventure at Mont St.
     Michael
Rey, Hans Augusto. Curious George
     Curious George Gets a Medal
     Curious George Learns the Alphabet
     Curious George Rides a Bike
     Curious George Takes a Job
Rey, Margret Elisabeth Waldstein. Curious
     George Flies a Kite

Curious George Goes to the Hospital
Waber, Bernard. Lorenzo

026.11 Character traits—flattery

Aesopus. Three Fox Fables
Chaucer, Geoffrey. Chanticleer and the
Fox

026.12 Character traits—freedom

Baylor, Byrd. Hawk, I'm Your Brother
Dennis, Wesley. Tumble, the Story of a
Mustang
Fujita, Tamao. The Boy and the Bird
Hawkinson, John. Where the Wild Apples
Grow
Steiner, Jörg. Rabbit Island

026.13 Character traits—generosity

Anglund, Joan Walsh. Christmas Is a Time
of Giving
Brown, Palmer. Something for Christmas
Brustlein, Janice. Little Bear's Christmas
Chalmers, Mary Eileen. A Hat for Amy
Jean
Farjeon, Eleanor. Mrs. Malone
Hoban, Russell Conwell. Emmet Otter's
Jug-Band Christmas
The Mole Family's Christmas
Houston, John A. The Bright Yellow Rope
Hush Little Baby
Leisk, David Johnson. The Emperor's Gift
Lexau, Joan M. A House So Big
Lindman, Maj Jan. Snipp, Snapp, Snurr
and the Red Shoes
Snipp, Snapp, Snurr and the Yellow
Sled
Lionni, Leo. Tico and the Golden Wings
Ness, Evaline. Josefina February
Rockwell, Anne F. Gogo's Pay Day
Shecter, Ben. If I Had a Ship
Silverstein, Shel. The Giving Tree

026.14 Character traits—helpfulness

Adshead, Gladys L. Brownies—Hush!
Bonsall, Crosby Newell. Who's a Pest?
Bridwell, Norman. Clifford's Good Deeds
Calhoun, Mary. Euphonia and the Flood
Cole, William. Aunt Bella's Umbrella
Davis, Alice V. Timothy Turtle
Devlin, Wende, and Devlin, Harry.
Cranberry Christmas
Du Bois, William Pène. Bear Circus
Ets, Marie Hall. Elephant in a Well
Grabianski, Janusz. Androcles and the Lion
Graham, Al. Timothy Turtle
Gray, Genevieve. Send Wendell
Green, Norma B. The Hole in the Dike
Hill, Elizabeth Starr. Evan's Corner

Holmes, Efner Tudor. Amy's Goose
Houston, John A. The Bright Yellow Rope
Kishida, Eriko. The Lion and the Bird's
Nest
Kraus, Robert. Herman the Helper
Rebecca Hatpin
La Fontaine, Jean de. The Lion and the
Rat
Lindman, Maj Jan. Flicka, Ricka, Dicka and
the New Dotted Dress
Snipp, Snapp, Snurr and the Red Shoes
Marshall, James. What's the Matter with
Carruthers?
Mayer, Mercer. Just for You
Nakàno, Hirotaka. Elephant Blue
Ness, Evaline. Pavo and the Princess
Peet, Bill. The Ant and the Elephant
Cyrus the Unsinkable Sea Serpent
Potter, Beatrix. The Tailor of Gloucester
Rockwell, Anne F. The Bump in the Night
Simon, Norma. What Do I Do?
Slobodkin, Louis. Dinny and Danny
Steig, William. Amos and Boris
Udry, Janice May. Is Susan Here?
Waber, Bernard. Lyle, Lyle Crocodile
Watts, Bernadette, reteller. Mother Holly
Williams, Barbara. Someday, Said Mitchell
Wolde, Gunilla. Betsy's Fixing Day
Zemach, Margot. To Hilda for Helping

026.15 Character traits—honesty

Matsuno, Masako. A Pair of Red Clogs
Taro and the Tofu
Turkle, Brinton Cassady. The Adventures
of Obadiah
Wilson, Julia. Becky

026.16 Character traits—individuality

Anglund, Joan Walsh. Look out the
Window
Conford, Ellen. Impossible Possum
Delaney, Ned. One Dragon to Another
de Paola, Thomas Anthony. Oliver Button
Is a Sissy
Duvoisin, Roger Antoine. Jasmine
Fatio, Louise. Hector Penguin
Gramatky, Hardie. Little Toot through the
Golden Gate
Horvath, Betty F. Will the Real Tommy
Wilson Please Stand Up?
Iwamatsu, Jun. Umbrella
Jaynes, Ruth. What Is a Birthday Child?
Kuskin, Karla Seidman. Which Horse Is
William?
Leaf, Munro. The Story of Ferdinand the
Bull
Levine, Rhoda. Harrison Loved His
Umbrella
Lexau, Joan M. Benjie on His Own
Lionni, Leo. A Color of His Own

Pezzettino
Tico and the Golden Wings
Lystad, Mary. That New Boy
McKee, David. Elmer, the Story of a
Patchwork Elephant
Peet, Bill. Buford, the Little Bighorn
The Spooky Tail of Prewitt Peacock
Pinkwater, Manus. Big Orange Splot
Reeves, James. Rhyming Will
Sendak, Maurice. Pierre, a Cautionary Tale
in Five Chapters and a Prologue
Silverstein, Shel. The Missing Piece
Simon, Norma. I Know What I Like
Why Am I Different?
Singer, Marilyn. The Dog Who Insisted He
Wasn't
The Pickle Plan
Slobodkin, Louis. Millions and Millions and
Millions!
Viorst, Judith. Try It Again, Sam
Waber, Bernard. "You Look Ridiculous,"
Said the Rhinoceros to the
Hippopotamus

026.17 Character traits—kindness

Coville, Bruce, and Coville, Katherine. The
Foolish Giant
Fatio, Louise. The Happy Lion's Rabbits
Gannett, Ruth Stiles. Katie and the Sad
Noise
Geisel, Theodor Seuss. Horton Hatches the
Egg
Horton Hears a Who
Heyward, Dubose. The Country Bunny
and the Little Gold Shoes
Kent, Jack. Clotilda
Lipkind, William, and Mordvinoff, Nicolas.
The Magic Feather Duster
Mizumura, Kazue. If I Built a Village
Ormondroyd, Edward. Theodore
Peterson, Hans. Erik and the Christmas
Horse
Postgate, Oliver, and Firmin, Peter. Noggin
the King
Stevens, Carla. Stories from a Snowy
Meadow
Taylor, Mark. A Time for Flowers
Ungerer, Tomi. Zeralda's Ogre
Wells, Herbert George. The Adventures of
Tommy

026.18 Character traits—kindness to animals

Anderson, Clarence William. Lonesome
Little Colt
Rumble Seat Pony
Brock, Emma Lillian. The Birds' Christmas
Tree
Burch, Robert. The Hunting Trip

Daugherty, James Henry. Andy and the
Lion
Dunn, Judy. The Little Lamb
Duvoisin, Roger Antoine. Happy Hunter
Freeman, Don. The Seal and the Slick
Galdone, Paul. Androcles and the Lion
Georgiady, Nicholas P. Gertie the Duck
Grabianski, Janusz. Androcles and the Lion
Hader, Berta Hoerner, and Hader, Elmer
Stanley. Mister Billy's Gun
Harrison, David Lee. Little Turtle's Big
Adventure
Holmes, Efner Tudor. Amy's Goose
Keats, Ezra Jack. Jennie's Hat
Kumin, Maxine W. Mittens in May
Lathrop, Dorothy Pulis. Who Goes There?
Lipkind, William, and Mordvinoff, Nicolas.
The Boy and the Forest
McNulty, Faith. Mouse and Tim
McPhail, David. The Bear's Toothache
Miklowitz, Gloria D. Save That Raccoon!
Nakatani, Chiyoko. Fumio and the
Dolphins
Newberry, Clare Turlay. Percy, Polly and
Pete
Peet, Bill. Huge Harold
Roy, Ronald. A Thousand Pails of Water
Sandburg, Helga. Anna and the Baby
Buzzard
Turkle, Brinton Cassady. Thy Friend,
Obadiah
Varley, Dimitry. The Whirly Bird
Ward, Lynd Kendall. The Biggest Bear
Wersba, Barbara. Do Tigers Ever Bite
Kings?
Whitney, Alma Marshak. Leave Herbert
Alone

026.19 Character traits—laziness

Baker, Betty. Partners
Bolognese, Elaine, and Bolognese, Donald
Alan. The Sleepy Watchdog
Bowen, Vernon. The Lazy Beaver
Bright, Robert. Gregory, the Noisiest and
Strongest Boy in Grangers Grove
Du Bois, William Pène. Lazy Tommy
Pumpkinhead
Holding, James. The Lazy Little Zulu
Jacobs, Joseph. Lazy Jack
Krasilovsky, Phyllis. The Man Who Did
Not Wash His Dishes
The Little Red Hen, illus. by Janina
Domanska
The Little Red Hen, illus. by Paul Galdone
The Little Red Hen, illus. by Mel Pekarsky
Lobel, Arnold Stark. A Treeful of Pigs
Pack, Robert. How to Catch a Crocodile
Papas, William. Taresh the Tea Planter
Schmidt, Eric von. The Young Man Who
Wouldn't Hoe Corn

Sharmat, Marjorie Weinman. Burton and Dudley
Watts, Bernadette, reteller. Mother Holly
Werth, Kurt. Lazy Jack
Wildsmith, Brian. The Lazy Bear

026.20 Character traits—loyalty

Ardizzone, Edward Jeffrey Irving. Tim to the Rescue
Lasker, Joseph Leon. He's My Brother
McCrea, James, and McCrea, Ruth. The King's Procession
Potter, Beatrix. The Tale of the Faithful Dove

026.21 Character traits—luck

Aldridge, Josephine Haskell. Fisherman's Luck
Bond, Michael. Paddington's Lucky Day
Brown, Margaret Wise, and Gergely, Tibor. Wheel on the Chimney
Brown, Myra Berry. Best of Luck
Delton, Judy. It Happened on Thursday
Geisel, Theodor Seuss. Did I Ever Tell You How Lucky You Are?
Grimm, Jakob Ludwig Karl, and Grimm, Wilhelm Karl. Hans in Luck
Russell, Betty. Big Store, Funny Door
Stafford, Kay. Ling Tang and the Lucky Cricket

026.22 Character traits—meanness

Burningham, John Mackintosh. Borka, the Adventures of a Goose with No Feathers
Carrick, Carol. Old Mother Witch
Freeman, Don. Tilly Witch
Geisel, Theodor Seuss. How the Grinch Stole Christmas
Hoban, Russell Conwell. The Little Brute Family
McCrea, James, and McCrea, Ruth. The Magic Tree
Mahy, Margaret. The Boy with Two Shadows
Prelutsky, Jack. The Mean Old Mean Hyena
Price, Michelle. Mean Melissa
Udry, Janice May. The Mean Mouse and Other Mean Stories
Zion, Gene. The Meanest Squirrel I Ever Met

026.23 Character traits—optimism

Alexander, Sue. Marc the Magnificent
Ayer, Jacqueline Brandford. The Paper Flower Tree
Chalmers, Audrey. A Kitten's Tale

Geisel, Theodor Seuss. Would You Rather Be a Bullfrog?
Hoff, Sydney. Oliver
Krauss, Ruth. The Carrot Seed
Peet, Bill. The Whingdingdilly
Piatti, Celestino. The Happy Owls
Rice, Inez. A Long Long Time
Stevenson, James. "Could Be Worse"
Tapio, Pat Decker. The Lady Who Saw the Good Side of Everything
Wiesner, William. Happy-Go-Lucky
Zakhoder, Boris. Rosachok

026.24 Character traits—patience

Laurin, Anne. Little Things
Steiner, Charlotte. What's the Hurry, Harry?

026.25 Character traits—perseverance

Aesopus. The Miller, His Son, and Their Donkey
Brenner, Barbara. Wagon Wheels
Calhoun, Mary. Old Man Whickutt's Donkey
Conford, Ellen. Just the Thing for Geraldine
Gray, Genevieve. How Far, Felipe?
Hoff, Sydney. Slugger Sal's Slump
Jensen, Virginia Allen. Sara and the Door
Kahl, Virginia Caroline. Maxie
Keats, Ezra Jack. John Henry
Lane, Carolyn. The Voices of Greenwillow Pond
Piper, Watty. The Little Engine That Could
Skorpen, Liesel Moak. All the Lassies
Ungerer, Tomi. The Mellops Go Spelunking

026.26 Character traits—practicality

Evans, Katherine. The Man, the Boy, and the Donkey
Gág, Wanda. Millions of Cats
La Fontaine, Jean de. The Miller, the Boy and the Donkey
Schlein, Miriam. The Pile of Junk
Williams, Jay. The Practical Princess

026.27 Character traits—pride

Andersen, Hans Christian. The Emperor's New Clothes, illus. by Erik Blegvad
The Emperor's New Clothes, illus. by Virginia Lee Burton
The Emperor's New Clothes, illus. by Jack Delano and Irene Delano
The Emperor's New Clothes, illus. by Monika Laimgruber

Clifton, Lucille B. All Us Come Across the Water
Duvoisin, Roger Antoine. Crocus Petunia
Ehrhardt, Reinhold. Kikeri or The Proud Red Rooster
Hamberger, John F. The Peacock Who Lost His Tail
Hürlimann, Ruth. The Proud White Cat
Keats, Ezra Jack. John Henry
Politi, Leo. Mieko
Whitney, Alex. Once a Bright Red Tiger
Zimnik, Reiner. The Proud Circus Horse

026.28 Character traits—questioning

Adler, David A. A Little at a Time
Allard, Harry. May I Stay?
Brown, Margaret Wise. Wait Till the Moon Is Full
Deveaux, Alexis. Na-Ni
Lionni, Leo. Tico and the Golden Wings
Simont, Marc. How Come Elephants?
Stover, Jo Ann. Why? Because
Vance, Eleanor Graham. Jonathan
Williams, Barbara. If He's My Brother

026.29 Character traits—selfishness

Elkin, Benjamin. Lucky and the Giant
Kahl, Virginia Caroline. The Perfect Pancake
Kraus, Robert. Rebecca Hatpin
Lipkind, William, and Mordvinoff, Nicolas. Finders Keepers
Peet, Bill. The Ant and the Elephant
Reesink, Maryke. The Golden Treasure
Rudolph, Marguerita. I Am Your Misfortune

026.30 Character traits—shyness

Dines, Glen. A Tiger in the Cherry Tree
Hogrogian, Nonny. Carrot Cake
Iwamatsu, Jun. The Youngest One
Keats, Ezra Jack. Louie
Keller, Beverly. Fiona's Bee
Krasilovsky, Phyllis. The Shy Little Girl
Lexau, Joan M. Benjie
Udry, Janice May. What Mary Jo Shared
Zolotow, Charlotte Shapiro. A Tiger Called Thomas

026.31 Character traits—smallness

Andersen, Hans Christian. Thumbelina
Beim, Jerrold. The Smallest Boy in Class
de Paola, Thomas Anthony. Andy (That's My Name)
Hoff, Sydney. The Littlest Leaguer
Horvath, Betty F. Hooray for Jasper
Johnston, Johanna. Sugarplum
Kraus, Robert. The Littlest Rabbit

Kumin, Maxine W. Sebastian and the Dragon
Lipkind, William, and Mordvinoff, Nicolas. The Little Tiny Rooster
Martin, Patricia Miles. No, No, Rosina
Meddaugh, Susan. Too Short Fred
Orgel, Doris. On the Sand Dune
Priolo, Pauline. Piccolina and the Easter Bells
Schlein, Miriam. Billy, the Littlest One
Stanley, John. It's Nice to Be Little
Tresselt, Alvin R. The Smallest Elephant in the World
Williams, Barbara. Someday, Said Mitchell
Yolen, Jane. The Emperor and the Kite

027 Children as authors

Krauss, Ruth. Somebody Else's Nut Tree, and Other Tales from Children

028 Circus, clowns

Allen, Jeffrey. Bonzini! The Tattooed Man
Anno, Mitsumasa. Dr. Anno's Magical Midnight Circus
Austin, Margot. Barney's Adventure
Banigan, Sharon Stearns. Circus Magic
Bond, Michael. Paddington at the Circus
Bowden, Joan Chase. Boo and the Flying Flews
Burningham, John Mackintosh. Cannonball Simp
Cameron, Polly. The Cat Who Thought He Was a Tiger
Chardiet, Bernice. C Is for Circus
Coontz, Otto. A Real Class Clown
Du Bois, William Pène. Bear Circus
Ets, Marie Hall. Mr. Penny's Circus
Farley, Walter. Little Black Goes to the Circus
Flack, Marjorie. Wait for William
Freeman, Don. Bearymore
Geisel, Theodor Seuss. If I Ran the Circus
Goodall, John Strickland. The Adventures of Paddy Pork
Gramatky, Hardie. Homer and the Circus Train
Herrmann, Frank. The Giant Alexander and the Circus
Hoff, Sydney. Barkley Oliver
Holl, Adelaide. Mrs. McGarrity's Peppermint Sweater
Krahn, Fernando. A Funny Friend from Heaven
Leisk, David Johnson. Harold's Circus
Lent, Blair. Pistachio
Lipkind, William, and Mordvinoff, Nicolas. Circus Rucus
Lopshire, Robert Martin. Put Me in the Zoo

Maestro, Betsy. Busy Day
Maestro, Betsy, and Maestro, Giulio.
    Harriet Goes to the Circus
Maley, Anne. Have You Seen My Mother?
Marceau, Marcel. The Story of Bip
Marokvia, Merelle. A French School for
    Paul
Mendoza, George. The Marcel Marceau
    Counting Book
Munari, Bruno. The Circus in the Mist
Olds, Elizabeth. Plop, Plop, Ploppie
Palazzo, Tony. Bianco and the New World
Peet, Bill. Chester the Worldly Pig
    Ella
    Randy's Dandy Lions
Peppé, Rodney. Circus Numbers
Petersham, Maud Fuller, and Petersham,
    Miska. The Circus Baby
Politi, Leo. Lito and the Clown
Prelutsky, Jack. Circus
Quackenbush, Robert Mead. The Man on
    the Flying Trapeze
Rey, Hans Augusto. Curious George Rides
    a Bike
    See the Circus
Rockwell, Anne F. Gogo's Pay Day
Rounds, Glen H. The Day the Circus
    Came to Lone Tree
Schreiber, Georges. Bambino Goes Home
    Bambino the Clown
Seignobosc, Françoise. Small-Trot
Slobodkina, Esphyr. Pezzo the Peddler and
    the Circus Elephant
Slocum, Rosalie. Breakfast with the Clowns
Taylor, Mark. Henry Explores the Jungle
Tresselt, Alvin R. The Smallest
    Elephant in the World
Varga, Judy. Circus Cannonball
    Miss Lollipop's Lion
Wiese, Kurt. Rabbit Brothers Circus One
    Night Only
Wildsmith, Brian. Brian Wildsmith's Circus
Zimnik, Reiner. The Bear on the
    Motorcycle
    The Proud Circus Horse

029 City

Adoff, Arnold. Where Wild Willie?
Bank Street College of Education. Around
    the City
    Green Light, Go
    In the City
    My City
    Uptown, Downtown
Barrett, Judith. Old MacDonald Had an
    Apartment House
Bergere, Thea. Paris in the Rain with Jean
    and Jacqueline
Blue, Rose. How Many Blocks Is the
    World?

Bourne, Miriam Anne. Emilio's Summer
    Day
Bright, Robert. Georgie to the Rescue
Brown, Marcia. The Little Carousel
Burton, Virginia Lee. Katy and the Big
    Snow
    The Little House
    Maybelle, the Cable Car
Chalmers, Mary Eileen. Kevin
Clifton, Lucille B. The Boy Who Didn't
    Believe in Spring
    Everett Anderson's Christmas Coming
Colman, Hila. Peter's Brownstone House
Deveaux, Alexis. Na-Ni
Duvoisin, Roger Antoine. Lonely Veronica
    Veronica
Fife, Dale. Adam's ABC
Fraser, Kathleen, and Levy, Miriam F.
    Adam's World, San Francisco
Freeman, Don. Fly High, Fly Low
    The Guard Mouse
Gelman, Rita Golden. Dumb Joey
Gramatky, Hardie. Little Toot through the
    Golden Gate
Grant, Sandy. Hey, Look at Me! A City
    ABC
Grifalconi, Ann. City Rhythms
Grossbart, Francine B. A Big City
Guilfoile, Elizabeth. Have You Seen My
    Brother?
Himler, Ronald Norbert. The Girl on the
    Yellow Giraffe
Hoban, Tana. Is It Red? Is It Yellow? Is It
    Blue?
Hopkins, Lee Bennett, comp. I Think I
    Saw a Snail
Keats, Ezra Jack. Apartment 3
    Goggles
    Hi, Cat!
Keeping, Charles William James. Alfie
    Finds the Other Side of the World
    Through the Window
Lenski, Lois L. Policeman Small
Lewis, Stephen. Zoo City
Lexau, Joan M. Benjie on His Own
    Come Here, Cat
    Me Day
Low, Alice. David's Windows
McCloskey, Robert John. Make Way for
    Ducklings
McGinley, Phyllis. All Around the Town
Martin, Patricia Miles. No, No, Rosina
    Rolling the Cheese
Mizumura, Kazue. If I Built a Village
Olds, Elizabeth. Little Una
Olsen, Ib Spang. Cat Alley
Peet, Bill. Fly, Homer, Fly
Perera, Lydia. Frisky
Pitt, Valerie. Let's Find Out about the City
Raskin, Ellen. Franklin Stein
    Nothing Ever Happens on My Block

Ressner, Phil. Dudley Pippin
Roach, Marilynne K. Two Roman Mice
Rowe, Jeanne A. City Workers
Sauer, Julia Lina. Mike's House
Schick, Eleanor. City in the Winter
   One Summer Night
Scott, Ann Herbert. Let's Catch a Monster
Shecter, Ben. Emily, Girl Witch of New
   York
Simon, Norma. What Do I Do?
Sonneborn, Ruth A. Friday Night Is Papa
   Night
   I Love Gram
   Lollipop's Party
Steptoe, John. Uptown
Thomas, Ianthe. Walk Home Tired, Billy
   Jenkins
Tresselt, Alvin R. It's Time Now!
   A Thousand Lights and Fireflies
   Wake Up, City!
Trimby, Elisa. Mr. Plum's Paradise
Vasiliu, Marcea. What's Happening?
Walters, Marguerite. The City-Country
   ABC
Williamson, Mel, and Ford, George. Walk
   On!
Wold, Jo Anne. Well! Why Didn't You Say
   So?
Wright, Ethel. Saturday Walk
Yezback, Steven. Pumpkinseeds
Zion, Gene. Dear Garbage Man
   Hide and Seek Day
Zolotow, Charlotte Shapiro. One Step, Two
   The Park Book

030 Clocks

Ardizzone, Edward Jeffrey Irving. Johnny
   the Clock Maker
Cohen, Carol L. Wake Up Groundhog!
Gilbert, Helen Earle. Dr. Trotter and His
   Big Gold Watch
Hutchins, Pat. Clocks and More Clocks
Slobodkin, Louis. The Late Cuckoo

031 Clothing

Andersen, Hans Christian. The Emperor's
   New Clothes, illus. by Erik Blegvad
   The Emperor's New Clothes, illus. by
     Virginia Lee Burton
   The Emperor's New Clothes, illus. by
     Jack Delano and Irene Delano
   The Emperor's New Clothes, illus. by
     Monika Laimgruber
Asch, Frank. Yellow Yellow
Azaad, Meyer. Half for You
Babbitt, Lorraine. Pink Like the Geranium
Barrett, Judith. Peter's Pocket
Beskow, Elsa Maartman. Pelle's New Suit
Bowden, Joan Chase. A Hat for the Queen

Bulette, Sara. The Splendid Belt of Mr.
   Big
Chalmers, Mary Eileen. A Hat for Amy
   Jean
Credle, Ellis. Down, Down the Mountain
de Paola, Thomas Anthony. Charlie Needs
   a Cloak
Duvoisin, Roger Antoine. Jasmine
Freeman, Don. Corduroy
   A Pocket for Corduroy
Hoberman, Mary Ann. I Like Old Clothes
Hürlimann, Ruth. The Mouse with the
   Daisy Hat
Jaynes, Ruth. Benny's Four Hats
Jensen, Virginia Allen. Sara and the Door
Keats, Ezra Jack. Jennie's Hat
Krasilovsky, Phyllis. The Girl Who Was a
   Cowboy
Kumin, Maxine W. Mittens in May
Lear, Edward. The Quangle Wangle's Hat
Lexau, Joan M. Who Took the Farmer's
   Hat?
Lobel, Anita. The Seamstress of Salzburg
McClintock, Marshall. What Have I Got?
Matsuno, Masako. A Pair of Red Clogs
Mayer, Mercer. Two Moral Tales
Miklowitz, Gloria D. Barefoot Boy
Murphey, Sara. The Animal Hat Shop
Myrick, Jean Lockwood. Ninety-Nine
   Pockets
Payne, Emmy. Katy No-Pocket
Politi, Leo. Little Leo
Potter, Beatrix. The Tale of Mrs. Tiggy-
   Winkle
Rice, Eve. New Blue Shoes
Rice, Inez. The March Wind
Scott, Ann Herbert. Big Cowboy Western
Sharmat, Marjorie Weinman. The Trip
Shearer, John. The Case of the Sneaker
   Snatcher
Slobodkina, Esphyr. Caps for Sale
   Pezzo the Peddler and the Circus
     Elephant
   Pezzo the Peddler and the Thirteen Silly
     Thieves
Taback, Simms. Joseph Had a Little
   Overcoat
Thompson, George Selden. Sparrow Socks
Townsend, Kenneth. Felix the Bald-
   Headed Lion
Ungerer, Tomi. The Hat
Ushinsky, Konstantin. How a Shirt Grew in
   the Field
Ward, Nanda Weedon. The Black
   Sombrero
Watts, Mabel. A Little from Here, a Little
   from There
Weiss, Harvey. My Closet Full of Hats
Weiss, Leatie. Funny Feet
Westerberg, Christine. The Cap That
   Mother Made

Wooley, Catherine. Gus Was a Gorgeous
     Ghost
   The Horse with the Easter Bonnet
Zion, Gene. No Roses for Harry!

032 Concepts

Albert, Burton. Mine, Yours, Ours
Berenstain, Stanley, and Berenstain, Janice.
     Inside Outside Upside Down
Browner, Richard. Look Again!
Crews, Donald. We Read: A to Z
Emberley, Edward Randolph. Ed
     Emberley's Amazing Look Through
     Book
Freudberg, Judy. Some, More, Most
Green, Mary McBurney. Is It Hard? Is It
     Easy?
Kuskin, Karla Seidman. All Sizes of Noises
Mayer, Mercer. Mine!
Peppé, Rodney. Odd One Out
     Rodney Peppé's Puzzle Book
Ruben, Patricia. True or False?
Scarry, Richard McClure. Richard Scarry's
     Best First Book Ever
   Richard Scarry's Great Big Schoolhouse
The Sesame Street Book of People and
     Things

032.01 Concepts—color

Abisch, Roslyn Kroop. Open Your Eyes
Asch, Frank. Yellow Yellow
Bright, Robert. I Like Red
Brown, Margaret Wise. Red Light, Green
     Light
Carle, Eric. The Mixed-Up Chameleon
Charlip, Remy, and Supree, Burton.
     Harlequin and the Gift of Many
     Colors
Crews, Donald. Freight Train
Dines, Glen. Pitidoe the Color Maker
Duvoisin, Roger Antoine. The House of
     Four Seasons
   See What I Am
Emberley, Edward Randolph. Green Says
     Go
Freeman, Don. The Chalk Box Story
   A Rainbow of My Own
Haskins, Ilma. Color Seems
Hoban, Tana. Is It Red? Is It Yellow? Is It
     Blue?
Kessler, Leonard P. Mr. Pine's Purple
     House
Lionni, Leo. A Color of His Own
   Little Blue and Little Yellow
Lobel, Arnold Stark. The Great Blueness
     and Other Predicaments
Löfgren, Ulf. The Color Trumpet
Lopshire, Robert Martin. Put Me in the
     Zoo

Maril, Lee. Mr. Bunny Paints the Eggs
Pienkowski, Jan. Colors
Pinkwater, Manus. The Bear's Picture
   Big Orange Splot
Podendorf, Illa. Color
Reiss, John J. Colors
Rossetti, Christina Georgina. What Is Pink?
Scott, Rochelle. Colors, Colors All Around
Shub, Elizabeth. Dragon Franz
Spier, Peter. Oh, Were They Ever Happy!
Steiner, Charlotte. My Slippers Are Red
Tison, Annette, and Taylor, Talus. The
     Adventures of the Three Colors
Wolff, Robert Jay. Feeling Blue
   Hello Yellow!
   Seeing Red
Youldon, Gillian. Colors
Zacharis, Boris. But Where Is the Green
     Parrot?
Zolotow, Charlotte Shapiro. Mr. Rabbit and
     the Lovely Present

032.02 Concepts—distance

Tresselt, Alvin R. How Far Is Far?

032.03 Concepts—in and out

Banchek, Linda. Snake In, Snake Out
Ueno, Noriko. Elephant Buttons

032.04 Concepts—left and right

Stanek, Muriel. Left, Right, Left, Right

032.05 Concepts—measurement

Lionni, Leo. Inch by Inch
Myller, Rolf. How Big Is a Foot?

032.06 Concepts—opposites

Banchek, Linda. Snake In, Snake Out
Hoban, Tana. Push-Pull, Empty-Full
Mendoza, George. Sesame Street Book of
     Opposites with Zero Mostel
Provensen, Alice, and Provensen, Martin.
     Karen's Opposites
Spier, Peter. Fast—Slow, High—Low
Wildsmith, Brian. What the Moon Saw
Wolde, Gunilla. This Is Betsy

032.07 Concepts—shape

Atwood, Ann. The Little Circle
Budney, Blossom. A Kiss Is Round
Craig, M. Jean. Boxes
Crews, Donald. Ten Black Dots
Emberley, Edward Randolph. Wing on a
     Flea

Friskey, Margaret. Three Sides and the
Round One
Geisel, Theodor Seuss. The Shape of Me
and Other Stuff
Hefter, Richard. The Strawberry Book of
Shapes
Hoban, Tana. Circles, Triangles, and
Squares
Shapes and Things
Hughes, Peter. The Emperor's Oblong
Pancake
Lionni, Leo. Pezzettino
Martin, Janet. Round and Square
Pienkowski, Jan. Shapes
Podendorf, Illa. Shapes, Sides, Curves, and
Corners
Reiss, John J. Shapes
Reit, Seymour. Round Things Everywhere
Roberts, Cliff. The Dot
Start with a Dot
Salazar, Violet. Squares Are Not Bad
Schlein, Miriam. Shapes
The Sesame Street Book of Shapes
Shaw, Charles Green. It Looked Like Spilt
Milk
Silverstein, Shel. The Missing Piece
Youldon, Gillian. Shapes

032.08 Concepts—size

Anno, Mitsumasa. The King's Flower
Aulaire, Ingri Mortenson d', and Aulaire,
Edgar Parin d'. Too Big
Black, Irma Simonton. Big Puppy and
Little Puppy
Blue, Rose. How Many Blocks Is the
World?
Brown, Marcia. Once a Mouse
Brown, Margaret Wise. The Little Farmer
Bulette, Sara. The Splendid Belt of Mr.
Big
Chalmers, Audrey. Hector and Mr. Murfit
Craig, M. Jean. Boxes
Croswell, Volney. How to Hide a
Hippopotamus
Hoban, Tana. Big Ones, Little Ones
Hutchins, Pat. Titch
Ipcar, Dahlov Zorach. The Biggest Fish in
the Sea
The Land of Flowers
Kalan, Robert. Blue Sea
Kraus, Robert. The Little Giant
Krauss, Ruth. A Bouquet of Littles
Lipkind, William, and Mordvinoff, Nicolas.
Chaga
Peet, Bill. Huge Harold
Pienkowski, Jan. Sizes
Shapp, Charles, and Shapp, Martha. Let's
Find Out What's Big and What's
Small
Ueno, Noriko. Elephant Buttons
Youldon, Gillian. Sizes

032.09 Concepts—speed

Schlein, Miriam. Fast Is Not a Ladybug
Spier, Peter. Fast—Slow, High—Low

032.10 Concepts—up and down

Geisel, Theodor Seuss. A Great Day for
Up
Knight, Hilary. Sylvia the Sloth
Leisk, David Johnson. Upside Down
Slobodkin, Louis. Up High and Down Low
Walters, Marguerite. Up and Down and All
Around
Zion, Gene. All Falling Down

032.11 Concepts—weight

Schlein, Miriam. Heavy Is a Hippopotamus

033 Counting

Allen, Robert. Numbers; A First Counting
Book
Ambler, Christopher Gifford. Ten Little
Foxhounds
Anno, Mitsumasa. Anno's Counting Book
Baum, Arline, and Baum, Joseph. One
Bright Monday Morning
Bayley, Nicola. One Old Oxford Ox
Becker, John L. Seven Little Rabbits
Berenstain, Stanley, and Berenstain, Janice.
Bears on Wheels
The Berenstain Bears' Counting Book
Bishop, Claire Huchet. Twenty Two Bears
Blegvad, Lenore Hochman, and Blegvad,
Erik. One Is for the Sun
Bright, Robert. My Red Umbrella
Carle, Eric. One, Two, Three to the Zoo
The Rooster Who Set Out to See the
World
Charlip, Remy, and Joyner, Jerry. Thirteen
Chwast, Seymour, and Moskof, Martin
Stephen. Still Another Number Book
Cole, Joanna. Fun on Wheels
Conover, Chris. Six Little Ducks
Counting Rhymes
Cretan, Gladys Yessayan. Ten Brothers
with Camels
Crews, Donald. Ten Black Dots
De Caprio, Annie. One, Two
Dodd, Lynley. The Nickle Nackle Tree
Eichenberg, Fritz. Dancing in the Moon
Elkin, Benjamin. Six Foolish Fishermen
Feelings, Muriel L. Monjo Means One; A
Swahili Counting Book
Freschet, Berniece. The Ants Go Marching
Friskey, Margaret. Chicken Little Count-
To-Ten

Seven Diving Ducks

Geisel, Theodor Seuss. Ten Apples Up on Top!

Grayson, Marion F., comp. Let's Count and Count Out

Gregor, Arthur. One, Two, Three, Four, Five

Gretz, Susanna. Teddybears ABC
Teddybears One to Ten

Hay, Dean. Now I Can Count

Hoban, Tana. Count and See

Holt, Margaret. David McCheever's Twenty-Nine Dogs

Ipcar, Dahlov Zorach. Brown Cow Farm
Ten Big Farms

Keats, Ezra Jack. Over in the Meadow

Kraus, Robert, and Bodecker, Nils Mogens. Good Night Richard Rabbit

Krüss, James. 3 X 3, Three by Three

Langstaff, John Meredith. Over in the Meadow

Lasker, Joseph Leon. Lentil Soup

Livermore, Elaine. One to Ten Count Again

Löfgren, Ulf. One-Two-Three

Mack, Stanley. Ten Bears in My Bed, a Goodnight Countdown

McLeod, Emilie Warren. One Snail and Me

Maestro, Betsy, and Maestro, Giulio. Harriet Goes to the Circus

Maestro, Giulio. One More and One Less

Mathews, Louise. Bunches and Bunches of Bunnies

Meeks, Esther K. One Is the Engine, illus. by Ernie King
One Is the Engine, illus. by Joe Rogers

Mendoza, George. The Marcel Marceau Counting Book

Merrill, Jean, and Scott, Frances Gruse. How Many Kids Are Hiding on My Block?

Morse, Samuel French. Sea Sums

Mother Goose. One, Two, Buckle My Shoe

Oxenbury, Helen. Numbers of Things

Peppé, Rodney. Circus Numbers

Petie, Haris. Billions of Bugs

Pienkowski, Jan. Numbers

Price, Christine. One Is God; Two Old Counting Songs

Rand, Ann, and Rand, Paul. Little 1

Reiss, John J. Numbers

Rockwell, Norman. Counting Book

Sazer, Nina. What Do You Think I Saw?

Scarry, Richard McClure. Richard Scarry's Best Counting Book Ever
Richard Scarry's Great Big Schoolhouse

Seignobosc, Françoise. Jeanne-Marie Counts Her Sheep

Sendak, Maurice. One Was Johnny
Seven Little Monsters

The Sesame Street Book of Numbers

Smith, Donald. Farm Numbers 1, 2, 3

Stanek, Muriel. One, Two, Three for Fun

Steiner, Charlotte. Five Little Finger Playmates

Sugita, Yutaka. Good Night 1, 2, 3

Taborin, Gloria. Norman Rockwell's Counting Book

True, Louise. Number Men

Tudor, Tasha. 1 Is One

Vogel, Ilse-Margret. One Is No Fun but 20 Is Plenty

Watson, Nancy Dingman. What Is One?

Weih, Erica. Count the Cats

Wildsmith, Brian. Brian Wildsmith's 1, 2, 3's

Williams, Garth Montgomery. The Chicken Book

Wooley, Catherine. The Little House; A New Math Story-Game

Wright, Betty Ren. Teddy Bear's Book of 1, 2, 3

Yolen, Jane. An Invitation to the Butterfly Ball; A Counting Rhyme

Youldon, Gillian. Numbers

Ziner, Feenie. Counting Carnival

Zirbes, Laura. How Many Bears?

Zolotow, Charlotte Shapiro. One Step, Two

034 Country

Brown, Margaret Wise. Country Noisy Book

Burton, Virginia Lee. The Little House

Caudill, Rebecca, and Ayars, James. Contrary Jenkins

Kingman, Lee. Peter's Long Walk

Payne, Josephine Balfour. The Stable That Stayed

Pender, Lydia. Barnaby and the Horses

Roach, Marilynne K. Two Roman Mice

Teal, Valentine. The Little Woman Wanted Noise

Tresselt, Alvin R. A Thousand Lights and Fireflies

Walters, Marguerite. The City-Country ABC

035 Cowboys

Anderson, Clarence William. Blaze and the Indian Cave
Blaze and the Lost Quarry
Blaze and the Mountain Lion
Blaze and Thunderbolt
Blaze Finds Forgotten Roads
Blaze Finds the Trail

Anglund, Joan Walsh. The Brave Cowboy
Cowboy and His Friend
The Cowboy's Christmas
Cowboy's Secret Life

Aulaire, Ingri Mortenson d', and Aulaire, Edgar Parin d'. Nils
Beatty, Hetty Burlingame. Bucking Horse
Bright, Robert. Georgie Goes West
Burton, Virginia Lee. Calico the Wonder Horse, or The Saga of Stewy Slinker
Chandler, Edna Walker. Cattle Drive
  Cowboy Andy
  Pony Rider
  Secret Tunnel
Felton, Harold W. Pecos Bill and the Mustang
Fitzhugh, Louise, and Scoppetone, Sandra. Bang Bang You're Dead
Greene, Carla. Cowboys: What Do They Do?
Hoff, Sydney. Thunderhoff
Kennedy, Richard. The Contests at Cowlick
Lenski, Lois L. Cowboy Small
Lipkind, William, and Mordvinoff, Nicolas. Even Steven
Quackenbush, Robert Mead. Pete Pack Rat
Scott, Ann Herbert. Big Cowboy Western
Ward, Nanda Weedon. The Black Sombrero
Wise, William. The Cowboy Surprise
Wood, Nancy. Little Wrangler

036 Crime

Ahlberg, Janet, and Ahlberg, Allan. Burglar Bill
Allard, Harry. It's So Nice to Have a Wolf Around the House
Anderson, Clarence William. Blaze and the Gypsies
Berson, Harold. The Thief Who Hugged a Moonbeam
Blake, Quentin. Snuff
Bright, Robert. Georgie and the Robbers
Brunhoff, Laurent de. Babar's Mystery
Brustlein, Janice. Mr. and Mrs. Button's Wonderful Watchdogs
Burton, Virginia Lee. Calico the Wonder Horse, or The Saga of Stewy Slinker
Coombs, Patricia. Dorrie and the Haunted House
Daly, Niki. Vim the Rag Mouse
Duvoisin, Roger Antoine. Petunia and the Song
Gage, Wilson. Down in the Boondocks
Harris, Leon A. The Great Picture Robbery
Heller, George. Hiroshi's Wonderful Kite
Heymans, Margriet. Pippin and Robber Grumblecroak's Big Baby
Jacobs, Joseph. Hereafterthis
Kirn, Ann Minette. I Spy
Lobel, Arnold Stark. How the Rooster Saved the Day
McKee, David. 123456789 Benn

Martin, Patricia Miles. The Raccoon and Mrs. McGinnis
Parish, Peggy. Granny and the Desperadoes
Partch, Virgil Franklin. The Christmas Cookie Sprinkle Snitcher
Politi, Leo. Emmet
Reidel, Marlene. Jacob and the Robbers
Rose, Gerald. The Tiger-Skin Rug
Scarry, Richard McClure. Richard Scarry's Great Big Mystery Book
Schulman, Janet. Jack the Bum and the Haunted House
Slobodkina, Esphyr. Pezzo the Peddler and the Thirteen Silly Thieves
Thomson, Ruth. Peabody All at Sea
  Peabody's First Case
Titus, Eve. Anatole and the Thirty Thieves
Ungerer, Tomi. The Three Robbers
Watson, Nancy Dingman. The Birthday Goat

037 Crustacea

Morris, Robert A. Seahorse
Peet, Bill. Kermit the Hermit
Yamaguchi, Marianne Illenberger. Two Crabs and the Moonlight

038 Cumulative tales

Alger, Leclaire. Always Room for One More
Asbjørnsen, Peter Christen. The Three Billy Goats Gruff, illus. by Paul Galdone
  The Three Billy Goats Gruff, illus. by William Stobbs
Asbjørnsen, Peter Christen, and Moe, Jørgen Engebretsen. The Three Billy Goats Gruff
Baker, Betty. Little Runner of the Longhouse
Barton, Byron. Buzz, Buzz, Buzz
Berson, Harold. The Boy, the Baker, the Miller and More
Bishop, Claire Huchet. Twenty Two Bears
Blegvad, Erik. Burnie's Hill
Bonne, Rose. I Know an Old Lady
Bowden, Joan Chase. The Bean Boy
Brand, Oscar. When I First Came to This Land
Brandenberg, Aliki Liacouras. June 7!
Brown, Marcia. The Bun
  The Neighbors
Burningham, John Mackintosh. Mr. Gumpy's Outing
Burton, Virginia Lee. Katy and the Big Snow
Carle, Eric. Pancakes, Pancakes
Chicken Little. Chicken Licken
  Henny Penny, illus. by Paul Galdone
  Henny Penny, illus. by William Stobbs

Christian, Mary Blount. Nothing Much
	Happened Today
Chwast, Seymour. The House That Jack
	Built
Delaney, A. The Butterfly
Elkin, Benjamin. The King Who Could
	Not Sleep
	Such Is the Way of the World
	Why the Sun Was Late
Emberley, Barbara. Drummer Hoff
Ets, Marie Hall. Elephant in a Well
Evans, Eva Knox. Sleepy Time
Fenton, Edward. The Big Yellow Balloon
Firmin, Peter. Basil Brush Gets a Medal
Flora, James. The Day the Cow Sneezed
	Sherwood Walks Home
Foulds, Elfrida Vipont. The Elephant and
	the Bad Baby
Gág, Wanda. Millions of Cats
Galdone, Paul. The Table, the Donkey and
	the Stick
Garrison, Christian. Little Pieces of the
	West Wind
Geisel, Theodor Seuss. Because a Little
	Bug Went Ka-choo!
	Green Eggs and Ham
The Gingerbread Boy, illus. by Paul
	Galdone
The Gingerbread Boy, illus. by William
	Curtis Holdsworth
The Gingerbread Man, illus. by Gerald
	Rose
The Golden Goose
Heilbroner, Joan. This Is the House
	Where Jack Lives
Hewett, Anita. The Little White Hen
	The Tale of the Turnip
Hoffmann, Felix. A Boy Went Out to
	Gather Pears
Hogrogian, Nonny. One Fine Day
The House That Jack Built, illus. by Paul
	Galdone
The House That Jack Built, illus. by
	Rodney Peppé
The House That Jack Built. La Maison que
	Jacques a Batie
Houston, John A. A Mouse in My House
Hush Little Baby
Hutchins, Pat. Don't Forget the Bacon!
	Good-Night Owl
	Titch
Jacobs, Joseph. Johnny-Cake, illus. by
	Emma Lillian Brock
	Johnny-Cake, illus. by William Stobbs
	Lazy Jack
Jameson, Cynthia. The Clay Pot Boy
Kent, Jack. The Fat Cat
Krahn, Fernando. The Mystery of the
	Giant Footprints
Kroll, Steven. The Tyrannosaurus Game
Lear, Edward. Whizz!
Lenski, Lois L. Susie Mariar

Lexau, Joan M. Crocodile and Hen
Lindman, Maj Jan. Snipp, Snapp, Snurr
	and the Buttered Bread
The Little Red Hen, illus. by Janina
	Domanska
The Little Red Hen, illus. by Paul Galdone
The Little Red Hen, illus. by Mel Pekarsky
Little Tuppen: An Old Tale
Lobel, Anita. The Pancake
McClintock, Marshall. A Fly Went By
Murphey, Sara. The Roly Poly Cookie
Nolan, Dennis. Wizard McBean and His
	Flying Machine
Old MacDonald Had a Farm, illus. by Mel
	Crawford
Old MacDonald Had a Farm, illus. by
	Abner Graboff
Old MacDonald Had a Farm, illus. by
	Robert Mead Quackenbush
The Old Woman and Her Pig
Pack, Robert. Then What Did You Do?
Patrick, Gloria. This Is...
Peet, Bill. The Ant and the Elephant
Petie, Haris. The Seed the Squirrel
	Dropped
Prelutsky, Jack. The Terrible Tiger
Preston, Edna Mitchell. One Dark Night
Raskin, Ellen. Ghost in a Four-Room
	Apartment
Rockwell, Anne F. Poor Goose
Rosenberg, Ethel Clifford. Why Is an
	Elephant Called an Elephant?
Sawyer, Ruth. Journey Cake, Ho!
Scott, William Rufus, adapter. This Is the
	Milk That Jack Drank
Segal, Lore Groszmann. All the Way Home
Seymour, Dorothy Z. The Tent
Silverstein, Shel. A Giraffe and a Half
Skorpen, Liesel Moak. All the Lassies
Steger, Hans-Ulrich. Traveling to Tripiti
Suhl, Yuri. Simon Boom Gives a Wedding
Sutton, Eve. My Cat Likes to Hide in
	Boxes
Talbot, Toby. A Bucketful of Moon
Thoreau, Henry David. What Befell at
	Mrs. Brook's
Tolstoy, Alekesi Nikolaevich. The Great
	Big Enormous Turnip
Tresselt, Alvin R. Rain Drop Splash
Twelve Days of Christmas (English folk
	song). Brian Wildsmith's The Twelve
	Days of Christmas
	Jack Kent's Twelve Days of Christmas
	The Twelve Days of Christmas
Tworkov, Jack. The Camel Who Took a
	Walk
Ueno, Noriko. Elephant Buttons
Varga, Judy. The Monster Behind Black
	Rock
Wahl, Jan. Follow Me Cried Bee
Werth, Kurt. Lazy Jack
Wiesner, William. Happy-Go-Lucky

Zemach, Harve. Mommy Buy Me a China Doll
The Speckled Hen; A Russian Nursery Rhyme
Zemach, Margot. Hush, Little Baby
Ziner, Feenie. Counting Carnival
Zolotow, Charlotte Shapiro. The Quarreling Book

039 Days of the week, months of the year

Carle, Eric. The Very Hungry Caterpillar
Clifton, Lucille B. Some of the Days of Everett Anderson
De Regniers, Beatrice Schenk. Little Sister and the Month Brothers
Lasker, Joseph Leon. Lentil Soup
Lord, Beman. The Days of the Week
Provensen, Alice, and Provensen, Martin. The Year at Maple Hill Farm
Scarry, Richard McClure. Richard Scarry's Best First Book Ever
Richard Scarry's Great Big Schoolhouse
Sendak, Maurice. Chicken Soup with Rice
Shulevitz, Uri. One Monday Morning
Tudor, Tasha. Around the Year
Yolen, Jane. No Bath Tonight

040 Death

Bartoli, Jennifer. Nonna
Beim, Jerrold. With Dad Alone
Bernstein, Joanne, and Gullo, Steven V. When People Die
Brown, Margaret Wise. The Dead Bird
Carrick, Carol. The Accident
Cock Robin. The Courtship, Merry Marriage, and Feast of Cock Robin and Jenny Wren, to Which Is Added the Doleful Death of Cock Robin
de Paola, Thomas Anthony. Nana Upstairs and Nana Downstairs
Fassler, Joan. My Grandpa Died Today
Kantrowitz, Mildred. When Violet Died
Stein, Sara Bonnett. About Dying
Stevens, Carla. Stories from a Snowy Meadow
Tobias, Tobi. Petey
Viorst, Judith. The Tenth Good Thing about Barney
Zolotow, Charlotte Shapiro. My Grandson Lew

041 Desert

Caudill, Rebecca. Wind, Sand and Sky
McKee, David. The Day the Tide Went Out and Out and Out
Ungerer, Tomi. Orlando the Brave Vulture
Wondriska, William. The Stop

042 Devil

Alger, Leclaire. Kellyburn Braes
Coombs, Patricia. The Magic Pot
Galdone, Joanna. Amber Day
Grimm, Jakob Ludwig Karl, and Grimm, Wilhelm Karl. The Bearskinner
Jeschke, Susan. The Devil Did It
Stalder, Valerie. Even the Devil Is Afraid of a Shrew
Turska, Krystyna. The Magician of Cracow
Zemach, Harve. Duffy and the Devil

043 Dictionaries

Floyd, Lucy, and Lasky, Kathryn. Agatha's Alphabet, with Her Very Own Dictionary
Geisel, Theodor Seuss. The Cat in the Hat Beginner Book Dictionary
MacBean, Dilla Wittemore. Picture Book Dictionary
McIntire, Alta. Follett Beginning to Read Picture Dictionary
Rand McNally Picturebook Dictionary
Scarry, Richard McClure. Richard Scarry's Best Word Book Ever

044 Dinosaurs

Corbett, Scott. The Foolish Dinosaur Fiasco
Dinosaurs
Hoff, Sydney. Danny and the Dinosaur
Dinosaur Do's and Don'ts
Hurd, Edith Thacher. Dinosaur, My Darling
Kroll, Steven. The Tyrannosaurus Game
Most, Bernard. If the Dinosaurs Came Back
Nicoll, Helen. Meg's Eggs
Parish, Peggy. Dinosaur Time
Sharmat, Marjorie Weinman. Mitchell Is Moving
Slobodkin, Louis. Dinny and Danny
Sundgaard, Arnold. Jethro's Difficult Dinosaur
Wooley, Catherine. Quiet on Account of Dinosaur
Young, Miriam Burt. If I Rode a Dinosaur
Zallinger, Peter. Dinosaurs

045 Divorce

Caines, Jeannette Franklin. Daddy
Goff, Beth. Where's Daddy?
Hazen, Barbara Shook. Two Homes to Live In
Lexau, Joan M. Me Day
Lisker, Sonia O., and Dean, Leigh. Two Special Cards
Perry, Patricia, and Lynch, Marietta. Mommy and Daddy Are Divorced
Pursell, Margaret Sanford. A Look at Divorce

Rogers, Helen S. Morris and His Brave Lion
Simon, Norma. The Daddy Days
Stein, Sara Bonnett. On Divorce
Thomas, Ianthe. Eliza's Daddy
Tresselt, Alvin R. A Day with Daddy
Zolotow, Charlotte Shapiro. A Father Like That

046 Dragons

Aruego, José. The King and His Friends
Bradfield, Roger. A Good Knight for Dragons
Chalmers, Mary Eileen. George Appleton
Craig, M. Jean. The Dragon in the Clock Box
Cretien, Paul D., Jr. Sir Henry and the Dragon
Davis, Reda. Martin's Dinosaur
Delaney, Ned. One Dragon to Another
de Paola, Thomas Anthony. The Wonderful Dragon of Timlin
Domanska, Janina. King Krakus and the Dragon
Eckert, Horst. Just One Apple
Emberley, Edward Randolph. Klippity Klop
Fassler, Joan. The Man of the House
Firmin, Peter. Basil Brush and a Dragon
Gág, Wanda. The Funny Thing
Garrison, Christian. The Dream Eater
Ivanko and the Dragon
Jeschke, Susan. Firerose
Joslin, Sesyle. Dear Dragon and Other Useful Letter Forms for Young Ladies and Gentlemen, Engaged in Everyday Correspondence
Kent, Jack. There's No Such Thing as a Dragon
Kimmel, Margaret Mary. Magic in the Mist
Kumin, Maxine W. Sebastian and the Dragon
Lifton, Betty Jean. Joji and the Dragon
Lobel, Arnold Stark. Prince Bertram the Bad
McCrea, James, and McCrea, Ruth. The Story of Olaf
Mahood, Kenneth. The Laughing Dragon
Mahy, Margaret. The Dragon of an Ordinary Family
A Lion in the Meadow
Massie, Diane Redfield. The Komodo Dragon's Jewels
Nash, Ogden. Custard the Dragon and the Wicked Knight
Oksner, Robert M. The Incompetent Wizard
Peet, Bill. How Droofus the Dragon Lost His Head
Price, Roger. The Last Little Dragon

Sherman, Nancy. Gwendolyn the Miracle Hen
Shub, Elizabeth. Dragon Franz
Trez, Denise, and Trez, Alain. The Little Knight's Dragon
Varga, Judy. The Dragon Who Liked to Spit Fire
Williams, Jay. Everyone Knows What a Dragon Looks Like
Wooley, Catherine. The Popcorn Dragon

047 Dreams

Alexander, Martha G. Bobo's Dream
Balet, Jan B. Joanjo; A Portuguese Tale
Chwast, Seymour, and Moskof, Martin Stephen. Still Another Children's Book
Coombs, Patricia. Dorrie and the Dreamyard Monsters
Daugherty, Charles Michael. Wisher
Dennis, Wesley. Flip
Donaldson, Lois. Karl's Wooden Horse
Francis, Frank. The Magic Wallpaper
Garrison, Christian. The Dream Eater
Graham, Lorenz. Song of the Boat
Greenfield, Eloise. Africa Dream
Greenwood, Ann. A Pack of Dreams
Hurd, Edith Thacher. Little Dog, Dreaming
Jacobs, Joseph. The Crock of Gold, Being "The Pedlar of Swaffham"
Keats, Ezra Jack. Dreams
Keith, Eros. Nancy's Backyard
Knotts, Howard Clayton. The Lost Christmas
Krahn, Fernando. Sebastian and the Mushroom
McPhail, David. Mistletoe
The Train
Moeschlin, Elsa. Red Horse
Reed, Kit. When We Dream
Rockwell, Anne F. The Wolf Who Had a Wonderful Dream
Scharen, Beatrix. Gigin and Till
Sendak, Maurice. In the Night Kitchen
Storm, Theodor. Little John
Trez, Denise, and Trez, Alain. Good Night, Veronica
Unteracker, John. The Dreaming Zoo
Ward, Lynd Kendall. The Silver Pony
Weisgard, Leonard. Who Dreams of Cheese?
Wende, Philip. Bird Boy
Zolotow, Charlotte Shapiro. Someday

048 Earth

Asimov, Isaac. The Best New Thing
Bernstein, Margery, and Kobrin, Janet. Earth Namer

Dayton, Mona. Earth and Sky
Lewis, Claudia I. When I Go to the Moon

049 Ecology

Arneson, D. J. Secret Places
Burton, Virginia Lee. The Little House
Carrick, Carol, and Carrick, Donald. A
  Clearing in the Forest
de Paola, Thomas Anthony. Michael Bird-
  Boy
Duvoisin, Roger Antoine. Happy Hunter
Fife, Dale. The Little Park
Freeman, Don. The Seal and the Slick
Geisel, Theodor Seuss. The Lorax
Hader, Berta Hoerner, and Hader, Elmer
  Stanley. The Mighty Hunter
Haley, Gail Diana Einhart. Noah's Ark
Hamberger, John F. The Day the Sun
  Disappeared
Hoff, Sydney. Grizzwold
Hurd, Edith Thacher. Wilson's World
Ichikawa, Satomi. Suzanne and Nicholas in
  the Garden
Jewell, Nancy. Try and Catch Me
Keenen, George. The Preposterous Week
Meyer, Louis A. The Clean Air and
  Peaceful Contentment Dirigible
  Airline
Miles, Miska. Rabbit Garden
Mizumura, Kazue. If I Built a Village
Murschetz, Luis. Mister Mole
Parnall, Peter. The Great Fish
Peet, Bill. The Caboose Who Got Loose
  Farewell to Shady Glade
  Fly, Homer, Fly
  The Gnats of Knotty Pine
  The Wump World
Quackenbush, Robert Mead. Calling
  Doctor Quack
Ricciuti, Edward R. Donald and the Fish
  That Walked
Short, Mayo. Andy and the Wild Ducks
Shortall, Leonard W. Just-in-Time-Joey
Stone, A. Harris. The Last Free Bird
Tresselt, Alvin R. The Dead Tree
Wright, Dare. Edith and Little Bear Lend a
  Hand

050 Eggs

Bourke, Linda. Ethel's Exceptional Egg
Brown, Margaret Wise. The Golden Egg
  Book
Coombs, Patricia. Dorrie and the Birthday
  Eggs
Coontz, Otto. The Quiet House
Eastman, Philip Day. Flap Your Wings
Eggs
Geisel, Theodor Seuss. Horton Hatches the
  Egg
Goldfrank, Helen Colodny. An Egg Is for
  Wishing

Kent, Jack. The Egg Book
Krauss, Ruth. The Happy Egg
Kumin, Maxine W., and Sexton, Anne.
  Eggs of Things
Kwitz, Mary DeBall. Little Chick's Story
Maril, Lee. Mr. Bunny Paints the Eggs
Nicoll, Helen. Meg's Eggs
O'Neill, Mary. Big Red Hen
Peet, Bill. The Pinkish, Purplish, Bluish
  Egg
Potter, Beatrix. The Tale of Jemima
  Puddle-Duck
Pursell, Margaret Sanford. Jessie the
  Chicken
  Sprig the Tree Frog
Rockwell, Anne F. The Gollywhopper Egg
  The Wonderful Eggs of Furicchia
Scarry, Richard McClure. Egg in the Hole
  Book
Schick, Eleanor. A Surprise in the Forest
Selsam, Millicent Ellis. The Bug That Laid
  the Golden Eggs
  Egg to Chick
Standon, Anna, and Standon, Edward
  Cyril. Little Duck Lost
Sundgaard, Arnold. Jethro's Difficult
  Dinosaur
Tresselt, Alvin R. The World in the Candy
  Egg
Waber, Bernard. How to Go about Laying
  an Egg
Wahl, Jan. The Five in the Forest
Zemach, Harve. The Speckled Hen; A
  Russian Nursery Rhyme

051 Elves and little people

Adshead, Gladys L. Brownies—Hush!
  Brownies—It's Christmas
Berg, Jean Horton. The Wee Little Man
Beskow, Elsa Maartman. Peter's
  Adventures in Blueberry Land
Bulette, Sara. The Elf in the Singing Tree
Calhoun, Mary. The Hungry Leprechaun
De Regniers, Beatrice Schenk, and Bileck,
  Marvin. Penny
Fish, Helen Dean. When the Root Children
  Wake Up
Funai, Mamoru R. Moke and Poki in the
  Rain Forest
Kennedy, Richard. The Leprechaun's Story
Madden, Don. Lemonade Serenade or the
  Thing in the Garden
Minarik, Else Holmelund. The Little Giant
  Girl and the Elf Boy
Smith, Mary, and Smith, Robert Alan.
  Long Ago Elf
Steiner, Charlotte. Red Ridinghood's Little
  Lamb
Tom Thumb. Grimm Tom Thumb
Tom Thumb, illus. by Leonard Leslie
  Brooke

Tom Thumb, illus. by Felix Hoffmann
Tom Thumb, illus. by William Wiesner
Wooley, Catherine. The Blueberry Pie Elf
Zimelman, Nathan. To Sing a Song as Big as Ireland

052 Emotions

Ancona, George. I Feel; A Picture Book of Emotions
Bach, Alice. The Day After Christmas
Berger, Terry. I Have Feelings
Brenner, Barbara. Faces, Faces
Castle, Sue. Face Talk, Hand Talk, Body Talk
Cole, William. Frances Face-Maker
Conta, Marcia Maher, and Reardon, Maureen. Feelings Between Brothers and Sisters
  Feelings Between Friends
  Feelings Between Kids and Grownups
  Feelings Between Kids and Parents
Edwards, Dorothy, and Williams, Jenny. A Wet Monday
Hazen, Barbara Shook. Happy, Sad, Silly, Mad: A Beginning Book about Emotions
  Two Homes to Live In
Helena, Ann. The Lie
Hoban, Russell Conwell. The Stone Doll of Sister Brute
Hopkins, Lee Bennett. I Loved Rose Ann
Horvath, Betty F. Will the Real Tommy Wilson Please Stand Up?
Krauss, Ruth. The Bundle Book
McCrea, James, and McCrea, Ruth. The Magic Tree
McGovern, Ann. Feeling Mad, Feeling Sad, Feeling Bad, Feeling Glad
Mayer, Mercer. Mine!
Mayers, Patrick. Just One More Block
Ness, Evaline. Pavo and the Princess
Parsons, Ellen. Rainy Day Together
Pursell, Margaret Sanford. A Look at Divorce
Simon, Norma. How Do I Feel?
Tobias, Tobi. Moving Day
  Petey
Tresselt, Alvin R. What Did You Leave Behind?
Wittels, Harriet, and Greisman, Joan. Things I Hate!
Wolde, Gunilla. This Is Betsy
Yudell, Lynn Deena. Make a Face

052.01 Emotions—anger

Alexander, Martha G. And My Mean Old Mother Will Be Sorry, Blackboard Bear
Andrews, Frank Emerson. Nobody Comes to Dinner

Du Bois, William Pène. Bear Party
Hapgood, Miranda. Martha's Mad Day
Sharmat, Marjorie Weinman. I'm Not Oscar's Friend Any More
Simon, Norma. I Was So Mad!
Watson, Jane Werner. Sometimes I Get Angry
Zolotow, Charlotte Shapiro. The Quarreling Book

052.02 Emotions—embarrassment

Alexander, Martha G. Sabrina
Freeman, Don. Quiet! There's a Canary in the Library
Hirsh, Marilyn Joyce. The Pink Suit
Lexau, Joan M. I Should Have Stayed in Bed
Stanek, Muriel. Left, Right, Left, Right
Townsend, Kenneth. Felix the Bald-Headed Lion
Udry, Janice May. How I Faded Away

052.03 Emotions—envy, jealousy

Alexander, Martha G. Nobody Asked Me If I Wanted a Baby Sister
Conford, Ellen. Why Can't I Be William?
Cretan, Gladys Yessayan. Lobo and Brewster
Gill, Joan. Hush, Jon!
Graham, Margaret Bloy. Benjy and the Barking Bird
Greenfield, Eloise. She Come Bringing Me That Little Baby Girl
Hazen, Barbara Shook. Why Couldn't I Be an Only Kid Like You, Wigger?
Hoban, Russell Conwell. A Baby Sister for Frances
  A Birthday for Frances
Lionni, Leo. Alexander and the Wind-Up Mouse
Mayer, Mercer. One Frog Too Many
Miller, Warren. The Goings On at Little Wishful
Ormondroyd, Edward. Theodore's Rival
Schick, Eleanor. Peggy's New Brother
Vigna, Judith. Couldn't We Have a Turtle Instead?
Waber, Bernard. Lyle and the Birthday Party
Wolde, Gunilla. Betsy's Baby Brother
Zemach, Margot. To Hilda for Helping
Zolotow, Charlotte Shapiro. It's Not Fair

052.04 Emotions—fear

Alexander, Anne. Noise in the Night
Alexander, Martha G. I'll Protect You from the Jungle Beasts
Babbitt, Natalie. The Something

Bannon, Laura May. Little People of the
    Night
    The Scary Thing
Byfield, Barbara Ninde. The Haunted
    Churchbell
Chorao, Kay. Lester's Overnight
Clifton, Lucille B. Amifika
Conford, Ellen. Eugene the Brave
Crowe, Robert L. Clyde Monster
Devlin, Wende, and Devlin, Harry. Aunt
    Agatha, There's a Lion under the
    Couch!
Gackenbach, Dick. Harry and the Terrible
    Whatzit ·
Gay, Zhenya. Who's Afraid?
Geisel, Theodor Seuss. The Sneetches and
    Other Stories
Goodenow, Earle. The Owl Who Hated the
    Dark
Greenberg, Barbara. The Bravest
    Babysitter
Hanlon, Emily. What If a Lion Eats Me
    and I Fall into a Hippopotamus' Mud
    Hole?
Hanson, Joan. I Won't Be Afraid
Hoban, Russell Conwell. Goodnight
Kraus, Robert. Noel the Coward
Leaf, Munro. Boo, Who Used to Be Scared
    of the Dark
Lifton, Betty Jean. Goodnight Orange
    Monster
Low, Joseph. Benny Rabbit and the Owl
    Boo to a Goose
Mayer, Mercer. There's a Nightmare in My
    Closet
    You're the Scaredy Cat
Moore, Lilian. Little Raccoon and the
    Thing in the Pool
Nash, Ogden. The Adventures of Isabel
Schertle, Alice. The Gorilla in the Hall
Shortall, Leonard W. Tony's First Dive
Trez, Denise, and Trez, Alain. The Royal
    Hiccups
Turkle, Brinton Cassady. It's Only Arnold
Udry, Janice May. Alfred
Viorst, Judith. My Mama Says There
    Aren't Any: Zombies, Ghosts,
    Vampires, Creatures, Demons,
    Monsters, Fiends, Goblins, or Things
Vogel, Ilse-Margret. The Don't Be Scared
    Book
Watson, Jane Werner. Sometimes I'm
    Afraid
Williams, Gweneira Maureen. Timid
    Timothy, the Kitten Who Learned to
    Be Brave
Winthrop, Elizabeth. Potbellied Possums
Wondriska, William. The Stop
Zolotow, Charlotte Shapiro. The Storm
    Book

052.05 Emotions—happiness

Low, Joseph. The Christmas Grump
McCrea, James, and McCrea, Ruth. The
    Magic Tree
Piatti, Celestino. The Happy Owls
Rice, Eve. What Sadie Sang
Tapio, Pat Decker. The Lady Who Saw the
    Good Side of Everything
Tobias, Tobi. Jane, Wishing
Tripp, Paul. The Strawman Who Smiled
    by Mistake
Williams, Barbara. Someday, Said Mitchell
Wondriska, William. Mr. Brown and Mr.
    Gray
Yabuki, Seiji. I Love the Morning

052.06 Emotions—hate

Udry, Janice May. Let's Be Enemies
Zolotow, Charlotte Shapiro. The Hating
    Book

052.07 Emotions—loneliness

Austin, Margot. Growl Bear
Battles, Edith. One to Teeter-Totter
Brown, Marcia. The Little Carousel
Conaway, Judith. I'll Get Even
Coontz, Otto. The Quiet House
Duvoisin, Roger Antoine. Periwinkle
Fatio, Louise. The Happy Lion Roars
Gág, Wanda. Nothing at All
Goffstein, Marilyn Brooks. Goldie the
    Dollmaker
Iwamatsu, Jun. Crow Boy
Iwasaki, Chihiro. Staying Home Alone on a
    Rainy Day
McNeer, May Yonge. My Friend Mac
Norton, Natalie. A Little Old Man
Seignobosc, Françoise. The Story of Colette
Sonneborn, Ruth A. Lollipop's Party
Spang, Gunter. Clelia and the Little
    Mermaid
Stevenson, James. The Bear Who Had No
    Place to Go
Sugita, Yutaka. Helena the Unhappy
    Hippopotamus
Surany, Anico. Kati and Kormos
Whitehead, Roberta. Peter Opens the Door
Zindel, Paul. I Love My Mother
Zolotow, Charlotte Shapiro. Janey
    The Three Funny Friends
    A Tiger Called Thomas

052.08 Emotions—love

Anglund, Joan Walsh. Love Is a Special
    Way of Feeling
Boegehold, Betty. Pawpaw's Run
Brown, Palmer. Something for Christmas
de Paola, Thomas Anthony. Helga's Dowry
Dragonwagon, Crescent. Wind Rose

Dyke, John. Pigwig
Estes, Eleanor. A Little Oven
Fatio, Louise. The Happy Lion's Treasure
Flack, Marjorie. Ask Mr. Bear
Freeman, Don. Corduroy
Jewell, Nancy. The Snuggle Bunny
Lasky, Kathryn. I Have Four Names for
    My Grandfather
Lexau, Joan M. A House So Big
Mayer, Mercer. Just for You
Miles, Betty. Around and Around...Love
Mizumura, Kazue. If I Were a Cricket...
Paterson, Diane. Wretched Rachel
Rowand, Phyllis. Every Day in the Year
Scott, Ann Herbert. On Mother's Lap
Shecter, Ben. If I Had a Ship
Stewart, Robert. The Daddy Book
Watts, Bernadette. Brigitte and Ferdinand,
    a Love Story
Zindel, Paul. I Love My Mother
Zolotow, Charlotte Shapiro. Do You Know
    What I'll Do?
    May I Visit?
    A Rose, a Bridge and a Wild Black
        Horse
    The Sky Was Blue

052.09 Emotions—sadness

Allen, Frances. Little Hippo
Bartoli, Jennifer. Nonna
de Paola, Thomas Anthony. Nana Upstairs
    and Nana Downstairs
Deveaux, Alexis. Na-Ni
Low, Joseph. The Christmas Grump
Sharmat, Marjorie Weinman. I Don't Care
Sugita, Yutaka. Helena the Unhappy
    Hippopotamus

053.01 Ethnic groups in the U.S.—
Afro-Americans

Adoff, Arnold. Big Sister Tells Me That
    I'm Black
    Where Wild Willie?
Alexander, Martha G. Bobo's Dream
    The Story Grandmother Told
Bang, Molly G. Wiley and the Hairy Man
Beim, Jerrold. The Swimming Hole
Beim, Lorraine Levy, and Beim, Jerrold.
    Two Is a Team
Blue, Rose. Black, Black, Beautiful Black
    How Many Blocks Is the World?
Bonsall, Crosby Newell. The Case of the
    Cat's Meow
    The Case of the Hungry Stranger
Breinburg, Petronella. Doctor Shawn
    Shawn Goes to School
    Shawn's Red Bike
Brenner, Barbara. Wagon Wheels
Burch, Robert. Joey's Cat
Caines, Jeannette Franklin. Abby
    Daddy

Calloway, Northern J. Northern J.
    Calloway Presents Super-Vroomer!
Clifton, Lucille B. All Us Come Across the
    Water
    Amifika
    The Boy Who Didn't Believe in Spring
    Don't You Remember?
    Everett Anderson's Christmas Coming
    Everett Anderson's Friend
    Everett Anderson's Nine Months Long
    Everett Anderson's 1,2,3
    Everett Anderson's Year
    My Brother Fine with Me
    Some of the Days of Everett Anderson
    Three Wishes
Clymer, Eleanor Lowenton. Horatio
Fassler, Joan. Don't Worry Dear
Fife, Dale. Adam's ABC
Fraser, Kathleen, and Levy, Miriam F.
    Adam's World, San Francisco
Freeman, Don. Corduroy
    A Pocket for Corduroy
George, Jean Craighead. The Wentletrap
    Trap
Gill, Joan. Hush, Jon!
Gray, Genevieve. Send Wendell
Greenberg, Polly. O Lord, I Wish I Was a
    Buzzard
Greenfield, Eloise. First Pink Light
    Me and Nessie
    She Come Bringing Me That Little
        Baby Girl
Grifalconi, Ann. City Rhythms
Hill, Elizabeth Starr. Evan's Corner
Hoffman, Phyllis. Steffie and Me
Hopkins, Lee Bennett, comp. I Think I
    Saw a Snail
Horvath, Betty F. Hooray for Jasper
    Jasper and the Hero Business
    Jasper Makes Music
Jensen, Virginia Allen. Sara and the Door
Keats, Ezra Jack. Apartment 3
    Dreams
    Goggles
    Hi, Cat!
    John Henry
    A Letter to Amy
    Louie
    Pet Show!
    Peter's Chair
    Skates
    The Snowy Day
    The Trip
    Whistle for Willie
Kirn, Ann Minette. Beeswax Catches a
    Thief
Lansdown, Brenda. Galumpf
Lexau, Joan M. Benjie
    Benjie on His Own
    I Should Have Stayed in Bed
    Me Day

The Rooftop Mystery
Lipkind, William, and Mordvinoff, Nicolas. Four-Leaf Clover
McGovern, Ann. Black Is Beautiful
Mayer, Mercer. Liza Lou and the Yeller Belly Swamp
Merriam, Eve. Epaminondas
Monjo, Ferdinand N. The Drinking Gourd
Nolan, Madeena Spray. My Daddy Don't Go to Work
Scott, Ann Herbert. Big Cowboy Western
  Let's Catch a Monster
  Sam
Selsam, Millicent Ellis. Tony's Birds
Sharmat, Marjorie Weinman. I Don't Care
Showers, Paul. Look at Your Eyes
  Your Skin and Mine
Sonneborn, Ruth A. I Love Gram
Steptoe, John. Birthday
  My Special Best Words
  Stevie
  Uptown
Taylor, Sydney. The Dog Who Came to Dinner
Thomas, Ianthe. Eliza's Daddy
  Lordy, Aunt Hattie
  Walk Home Tired, Billy Jenkins
Udry, Janice May. Mary Ann's Mud Day
  Mary Jo's Grandmother
  What Mary Jo Shared
  What Mary Jo Wanted
Williamson, Mel, and Ford, George. Walk On!
Williamson, Stan. The No-Bark Dog
Wilson, Julia. Becky
Yezback, Steven. Pumpkinseeds
Ziner, Feenie. Counting Carnival

053.02 Ethnic groups in the U.S.—Chinese-Americans

Behrens, June York. Soo Ling Finds a Way
Politi, Leo. Moy Moy
  Mr. Fong's Toy Shop

053.03 Ethnic groups in the U.S.—Eskimos

Beim, Lorraine Levy, and Beim, Jerrold. Little Igloo
Hopkins, Marjorie. Three Visitors
Machetanz, Sara, and Machetanz, Fred. A Puppy Named Gia
Morrow, Suzanne Stark. Inatuck's Friend
Parish, Peggy. Ootah's Lucky Day
Scott, Ann Herbert. On Mother's Lap

Wiesenthal, Eleanor, and Wiesenthal, Ted. Let's Find Out about Eskimos

053.04 Ethnic groups in the U.S.—Indians

Baker, Betty. Little Runner of the Longhouse
  Three Fools and a Horse
Baylor, Byrd. Hawk, I'm Your Brother
Beatty, Hetty Burlingame. Little Owl Indian
Benchley, Nathaniel. Red Fox and His Canoe
  Small Wolf
Bernstein, Margery, and Kobrin, Janet. Coyote Goes Hunting for Fire
  Earth Namer
Bornstein, Ruth. Indian Bunny
Brock, Emma Lillian. One Little Indian Boy
Clark, Ann Nolan. The Little Indian Basket Maker
  The Little Indian Pottery Maker
Ehrlich, Amy. Zeek Silver Moon
Foster, Marian Curtis. Doki, the Lonely Papoose
Friskey, Margaret. Indian Two Feet and His Eagle Feather
  Indian Two Feet and His Horse
  Indian Two Feet and the Wolf Cubs
Goble, Paul. The Friendly Wolf
  The Girl Who Loved Wild Horses
Hader, Berta Hoerner, and Hader, Elmer Stanley. The Mighty Hunter
Hays, Wilma Pitchford. Little Yellow Fur
Hood, Flora. Living in Navajoland
Jones, Hettie, comp. The Trees Stand Shining; Poetry of the North American Indians
McDermott, Gerald. Arrow to the Sun; A Pueblo Indian Tale
Martin, William Ivan, and Martin, Bernard Herman. Brave Little Indian
Monjo, Ferdinand N. The Drinking Gourd
  Indian Summer
Moon, Grace. One Little Indian
Parish, Peggy. Good Hunting, Little Indian
  Granny and the Indians
  Granny, the Baby and the Big Gray Thing
  Little Indian
  Snapping Turtle's All Wrong Day
Parnall, Peter. The Great Fish
Perrine, Mary. Salt Boy
Rose, Anne K. Spider in the Sky
Wondriska, William. The Stop

053.05 Ethnic groups in the U.S.—Japanese-Americans

Copeland, Helen. Meet Miki Takino
Hawkinson, Lucy Ozone. Dance, Dance, Amy-Chan!

Iwamatsu, Jun. Umbrella
    The Youngest One
Iwamatsu, Tomoe Sasako. Momo's Kitten
Politi, Leo. Mieko
Taylor, Mark. A Time for Flowers

053.06 Ethnic groups in the U.S.—Mexican-Americans

Adams, Ruth Joyce. Fidelia
Bolognese, Donald Alan. A New Day
Ets, Marie Hall. Bad Boy, Good Boy
    Gilberto and the Wind
    Nine Days to Christmas
Felt, Sue. Rosa-Too-Little
Fraser, James Howard. Los Posadas, a
    Christmas Story
Garrett, Helen. Angelo the Naughty One
Hitte, Kathryn, and Hayes, William D.
    Mexicallie Soup
Jaynes, Ruth. Melinda's Christmas Stocking
    Tell Me Please! What's That?
    What Is a Birthday Child?
Ormsby, Virginia H. Twenty-One Children
    Plus Ten
Politi, Leo. A Boat for Peppe
    Juanita
    The Mission Bell
    Pedro, the Angel of Olvera Street
    Song of the Swallows
Schweitzer, Byrd Baylor. Amigo
Serfozo, Mary. Welcome Roberto!
    Bienvenido, Roberto!

053.07 Ethnic groups in the U.S.—Multi-ethnic

Behrens, June. Who Am I?
Belpré, Pura. Santiago
Bettinger, Craig. Follow Me, Everybody
Blue, Rose. I Am Here: Yo Estoy Aqui
Brenner, Barbara. Faces, Faces
Cohen, Miriam. Will I Have a Friend?
Crume, Marion W. Listen!
Greene, Roberta. Two and Me Makes
    Three
Jaynes, Ruth. Benny's Four Hats
    Friends, Friends, Friends
    Tell Me Please! What's That?
    That's What It Is!
    What Is a Birthday Child?
Keats, Ezra Jack. My Dog Is Lost!
Kesselman, Wendy Ann. Angelita
Klein, Leonore. Just Like You
Lansdown, Brenda. Galumpf
May, Julian. Why People Are Different
    Colors
Merrill, Jean, and Scott, Frances Gruse.
    How Many Kids Are Hiding on My
    Block?

Reit, Seymour. Round Things Everywhere
Rosenberg, Ethel Clifford, and Rosenberg,
    David. Your Face Is a Picture
Simon, Norma. What Do I Say?
Solbert, Romaine G., ed. I Wrote My
    Name on the Wall: Sidewalk Songs
Stanek, Muriel. One, Two, Three for Fun
Udry, Janice May. What Mary Jo Shared

053.08 Ethnic groups in the U.S.—Puerto Rican-Americans

Belpré, Pura. Santiago
Blue, Rose. I Am Here: Yo Estoy Aqui
Bourne, Miriam Anne. Emilio's Summer
    Day
Keats, Ezra Jack. My Dog Is Lost!
Kesselman, Wendy Ann. Angelita
Simon, Norma. What Do I Do?
    What Do I Say?
Sonneborn, Ruth A. Friday Night Is Papa
    Night
    Lollipop's Party
    Seven in a Bed

054 Etiquette

Duvoisin, Roger Antoine. Periwinkle
Hoban, Russell Conwell. Dinner at
    Alberta's
    The Little Brute Family
Hoff, Sydney. Dinosaur Do's and Don'ts
Joslin, Sesyle. Dear Dragon and Other
    Useful Letter Forms for Young
    Ladies and Gentlemen, Engaged in
    Everyday Correspondence
    What Do You Do, Dear?
    What Do You Say, Dear?
Keenan, Martha. The Mannerly
    Adventures of Little Mouse
Keller, John G. Krispin's Fair
Leaf, Munro. A Flock of Watchbirds
    How to Behave and Why
    Manners Can Be Fun
Lexau, Joan M. Cathy Is Company
Myller, Lois. No! No!
Parish, Peggy. Mind Your Manners
Petersham, Maud Fuller, and Petersham,
    Miska. The Circus Baby
Potter, Beatrix. The Sly Old Cat
Scarry, Richard McClure. Richard Scarry's
    Please and Thank You Book
Seignobosc, Françoise. The Thank-You
    Book
Sherman, Ivan. I Do Not Like It When My
    Friend Comes to Visit
Slobodkin, Louis. Thank You—You're
    Welcome
Smaridge, Norah Antoinette. You Know
    Better Than That
Stover, Jo Ann. If Everybody Did
Yurdin, Betty. The Tiger in the Teapot

055 Fairies

Anderson, Lonzo, and Adams, Adrienne. Two Hundred Rabbits
Coombs, Patricia. Lisa and the Grompet
Jeschke, Susan. Mia, Grandma and the Genie
Kent, Jack. Clotilda
Mahy, Margaret. Pillycock's Shop

056 Fairs

Bourke, Linda. Ethel's Exceptional Egg
Brunhoff, Laurent de. Babar's Fair Will Be Opened Next Sunday
Carrick, Carol, and Carrick, Donald. The Highest Balloon on the Common
Delton, Judy. Penny Wise, Fun Foolish
Devlin, Wende, and Devlin, Harry. Old Witch and the Polka-Dot Ribbon
Ets, Marie Hall. Mr. Penny's Race Horse
Martin, Patricia Miles. Jump Frog Jump
Seignobosc, Françoise. Jeanne-Marie at the Fair
Tudor, Tasha. Corgiville Fair
Watson, Clyde. Tom Fox and the Apple Pie
Watson, Nancy Dingman. The Birthday Goat
Widdecombe Fair; An Old English Folk Song

057 Family life

Adoff, Arnold. Big Sister Tells Me That I'm Black
   Black Is Brown Is Tan
   Ma nDa La
Alexander, Martha G. I'll Be the Horse If You'll Play with Me
Amoss, Berthe. Tom in the Middle
Anderson, Clarence William. Billy and Blaze
Arkin, Alan. Tony's Hard Work Day
Aulaire, Ingri Mortenson d', and Aulaire, Edgar Parin d'. Nils
Avery, Kay. Wee Willow Whistle
Ayer, Jacqueline Brandford. A Wish for Little Sister
Babbitt, Lorraine. Pink Like the Geranium
Baker, Betty. Little Runner of the Longhouse
Balet, Jan B. The Fence
Bartoli, Jennifer. Nonna
Battles, Edith. One to Teeter-Totter
Beckman, Kaj. Lisa Cannot Sleep
Benton, Robert. Little Brother, No More
Bible, Charles. Jennifer's New Chair
Bishop, Claire Huchet, and Wiese, Kurt. The Five Chinese Brothers
Blaine, Marge. The Terrible Thing That Happened at Our House

Blue, Rose. How Many Blocks Is the World?
Bolliger, Max. The Fireflies
   The Golden Apple
Bolognese, Donald Alan. A New Day
Brandenberg, Aliki Liacouras. June 7!
   Keep Your Mouth Closed, Dear
Bright, Robert. Georgie
Brothers and Sisters Are Like That!
Brown, Jeff. Flat Stanley
Brown, Myra Berry. Pip Camps Out
   Pip Moves Away
Bruna, Dick. Miffy
Bunin, Catherine, and Bunin, Sherry. Is That Your Sister?
Burch, Robert. The Hunting Trip
   Joey's Cat
Byars, Betsy Cromer. Go and Hush the Baby
Caines, Jeannette Franklin. Abby
Cameron, Polly. "I Can't," Said the Ant
Chaffin, Lillie D. Tommy's Big Problem
Chalmers, Mary Eileen. Take a Nap, Harry
Chorao, Kay. Lester's Overnight
Clifton, Lucille B. Amifika
   Don't You Remember?
   Everett Anderson's Nine Months Long
   My Brother Fine with Me
   Some of the Days of Everett Anderson
Cole, William. Frances Face-Maker
   That Pest Jonathan
Conford, Ellen. Why Can't I Be William?
Cook, Bernadine. Looking for Susie
Coombs, Patricia. Lisa and the Grompet
Craig, M. Jean. The Dragon in the Clock Box
Credle, Ellis. Down, Down the Mountain
Cressey, James. Fourteen Rats and a Rat-Catcher
Curry, Nancy. The Littlest House
Delton, Judy. Brimhall Comes to Stay
   It Happened on Thursday
De Regniers, Beatrice Schenk. The Giant Story
   A Little House of Your Own
Edwards, Dorothy, and Williams, Jenny. A Wet Monday
Ehrlich, Amy. Zeek Silver Moon
Ehrlich, Bettina. Of Uncles and Aunts
Ets, Marie Hall. Bad Boy, Good Boy
Fassler, Joan. One Little Girl
Felt, Sue. Rosa-Too-Little
Fenton, Edward. Fierce John
Flack, Marjorie. The New Pet
   Wait for William
Fleisher, Robbin. Quilts in the Attic
Fraser, Kathleen, and Levy, Miriam F. Adam's World, San Francisco
Galdone, Paul. Obedient Jack
Gill, Joan. Hush, Jon!

Goudey, Alice E. The Day We Saw the Sun Come Up

Gray, Genevieve. Send Wendell

Greenberg, Polly. O Lord, I Wish I Was a Buzzard

Greenfield, Eloise. Me and Nessie

Harris, Robie H. Don't Forget to Come Back

Hautzig, Esther. At Home; A Visit in Four Languages

Hazelton, Elizabeth Baldwin. Sammy, the Crow Who Remembered

Hazen, Barbara Shook. Tight Times

Heide, Florence Parry. The Shrinking of Treehorn

Hill, Elizabeth Starr. Evan's Corner

Hirsh, Marilyn Joyce. The Pink Suit

Hitte, Kathryn, and Hayes, William D. Mexicallie Soup

Hoban, Lillian. Arthur's Prize Reader

Hoban, Russell Conwell. A Baby Sister for Frances
    Harvey's Hideout

Hoff, Sydney. My Aunt Rosie

Hoffman, Phyllis. Steffie and Me

Hoke, Helen L. The Biggest Family in the Town

Holland, Viki. We Are Having a Baby
    Homes

Horvath, Betty F. Be Nice to Josephine

Hughes, Shirley. David and Dog

Hutchins, Pat. Titch

Iwasaki, Chihiro. Staying Home Alone on a Rainy Day

Jack Sprat. The Life of Jack Sprat, His Wife and His Cat

Jarrell, Mary. Knee Baby

Keats, Ezra Jack. Apartment 3
    Peter's Chair

Kellogg, Steven. Can I Keep Him?

Kessler, Leonard P. Are We Lost, Daddy?

Koch, Dorothy Clarke. I Play at the Beach

Krasilovsky, Phyllis. The Very Little Boy
    The Very Little Girl
    The Very Tall Little Girl

Kraus, Robert. Big Brother

Krauss, Ruth. The Backward Day

Lapsley, Susan. I Am Adopted

Lasker, Joseph Leon. He's My Brother

Lenski, Lois L. At Our House
    Debbie and Her Family
    The Little Family
    Papa Small

Lexau, Joan M. Benjie
    Every Day a Dragon
    Finders Keepers, Losers Weepers
    Me Day

Lindman, Maj Jan. Flicka, Ricka, Dicka and a Little Dog
    Flicka, Ricka, Dicka and the Big Red Hen

Flicka, Ricka, Dicka and the New Dotted Dress

Flicka, Ricka, Dicka and the Three Kittens

Flicka, Ricka, Dicka and Their New Skates

Flicka, Ricka, Dicka Bake a Cake

Snipp, Snapp, Snurr and the Buttered Bread

Snipp, Snapp, Snurr and the Gingerbread

Snipp, Snapp, Snurr and the Magic Horse

Snipp, Snapp, Snurr and the Red Shoes

Snipp, Snapp, Snurr and the Reindeer

Snipp, Snapp, Snurr and the Seven Dogs

Snipp, Snapp, Snurr and the Yellow Sled

Lisker, Sonia O., and Dean, Leigh. Two Special Cards

McCloskey, Robert John. Blueberries for Sal
    One Morning in Maine

McGinley, Phyllis. Lucy McLockett

Mahy, Margaret. Mrs. Discombobulous

Mallett, Anne. Here Comes Tagalong

Martel, Cruz. Yagua Days

Merrill, Jean, and Solbert, Romaine G. Emily Emerson's Moon

Milgram, Mary. Brothers Are All the Same

Monjo, Ferdinand N. Rudi and the Distelfink

Moore, Lilian. Papa Albert

Myller, Lois. No! No!

Ness, Evaline. Exactly Alike

Nolan, Madeena Spray. My Daddy Don't Go to Work

Parsons, Ellen. Rainy Day Together

Paterson, Diane. Wretched Rachel

Pitt, Valerie. Let's Find Out about the Family

Politi, Leo. Little Leo

Pomerantz, Charlotte. The Mango Tooth

Raskin, Ellen. Ghost in a Four-Room Apartment

Rice, Eve. Ebbie
    Papa's Lemonade and Other Stories

Rider, Alex. Chez nous. At Our House

Schermer, Judith. Mouse in House

Schick, Eleanor. Peggy's New Brother

Schlein, Miriam. Billy, the Littlest One
    Laurie's New Brother
    My Family
    My House

Scott, Ann Herbert. On Mother's Lap
    Sam

Segal, Lore Groszmann. Tell Me a Mitzi
    Tell Me a Trudy

Seligman, Dorothy Halle. Run Away Home

Seyton, Marion. The Hole in the Hill
Sharmat, Marjorie Weinman. Goodnight,
    Andrew. Goodnight, Craig
Simon, Norma. All Kinds of Families
    What Do I Say?
Slobodkin, Louis. Clear the Track
    Magic Michael
Sonneborn, Ruth A. Seven in a Bed
Steig, William. Sylvester and the Magic
    Pebble
Stein, Sara Bonnett. The Adopted One
    Making Babies
    On Divorce
    That New Baby
Steiner, Charlotte. Daddy Comes Home
Steptoe, John. My Special Best Words
Stevenson, James. "Could Be Worse"
Thomas, Ianthe. Eliza's Daddy
Tobias, Tobi. At the Beach
    Jane, Wishing
Tresselt, Alvin R. A Day with Daddy
Udry, Janice May. Theodore's Parents
    What Mary Jo Wanted
Vigna, Judith. Couldn't We Have a Turtle
    Instead?
Viorst, Judith. Alexander and the Terrible,
    Horrible, No Good, Very Bad Day
    I'll Fix Anthony!
    Sunday Morning
Waber, Bernard. Good-Bye, Funny
    Dumpy-Lumpy
Warburg, Sandol Stoddard. The Thinking
    Book
Watson, Clyde. Catch Me and Kiss Me and
    Say It Again
Watson, Pauline. Days with Daddy
Watts, Bernadette. David's Waiting Day
Williams, Barbara. If He's My Brother
Winthrop, Elizabeth. Bunk Beds
Wolde, Gunilla. Betsy and Peter Are
    Different
    Betsy and the Vacuum Cleaner
    Betsy's Baby Brother
    Betsy's Fixing Day
    This Is Betsy
Wooster, Mae. My Busy Day
Wyse, Lois. Two Guppies, a Turtle, and
    Aunt Edna
Young, Evelyn. Wu and Lu and Li
Zemach, Margot. To Hilda for Helping
Zolotow, Charlotte Shapiro. Big Brothers
    Big Sister and Little Sister
    Do You Know What I'll Do?
    A Father Like That
    It's Not Fair
    May I Visit?
    My Grandson Lew
    The Sky Was Blue
    Someone New
    The Summer Night

When I Have a Little Girl
When I Have a Son
William's Doll

057.01 Family life—fathers

Beim, Jerrold. With Dad Alone
Caines, Jeannette Franklin. Daddy
Clifton, Lucille B. Amifika
    Everett Anderson's 1, 2, 3
Fassler, Joan. All Alone with Daddy
Greenfield, Eloise. First Pink Light
Holl, Adelaide. My Father and I
Kauffman, Lois. What's That Noise?
Kessler, Leonard P. Are We Lost, Daddy?
Lenski, Lois L. Papa Small
Lexau, Joan M. Every Day a Dragon
    Me Day
Lubell, Winifred Milius. Here Comes
        Daddy; A Book for Twos and Threes
Marzollo, Jean. Close Your Eyes
Minarik, Else Holmelund. Father Bear
    Comes Home
Monjo, Ferdinand N. The One Bad Thing
    About Father
Nolan, Madeena Spray. My Daddy Don't
    Go to Work
Puner, Helen Walker. Daddys, What They
    Do All Day
Sandberg, Inger, and Sandberg, Lasse.
    Come On Out, Daddy
Simon, Norma. The Daddy Days
Steiner, Charlotte. Daddy Comes Home
Stewart, Robert. The Daddy Book
Thomas, Ianthe. Eliza's Daddy
Tresselt, Alvin R. A Day with Daddy
Udry, Janice May. What Mary Jo Shared
Watson, Pauline. Days with Daddy
Wright, Ethel. Saturday Walk
Zolotow, Charlotte Shapiro. A Father Like
    That
    The Summer Night

057.02 Family life—grandparents; great-grandparents

Adler, David A. A Little at a Time
Alexander, Martha G. The Story
    Grandmother Told
Balian, Lorna. Humbug Rabbit
Bartoli, Jennifer. Nonna
Behrens, June York. Soo Ling Finds a Way
Bible, Charles. Jennifer's New Chair
Brandenberg, Franz. A Secret for
    Grandmother's Birthday
Brooks, Ron. Timothy and Gramps
Buckley, Helen Elizabeth. Grandfather
    and I
Child, Lydia Maria. Over the River and
    Through the Wood
Copeland, Helen. Meet Miki Takino

de Paola, Thomas Anthony. Nana Upstairs and Nana Downstairs
Fassler, Joan. My Grandpa Died Today
Finfer, Celentha; Wasserberg, Esther; and Weinberg, Florence. Grandmother Dear
Flora, James. Grandpa's Farm
Flory, Jane. The Unexpected Grandchild
Goffstein, Marilyn Brooks. Fish for Supper
Goldman, Susan. Grandma Is Somebody Special
Gordon, Shirley. Grandma Zoo
Hawes, Judy. Fireflies in the Night
Hutchins, Pat. Happy Birthday, Sam
Jeschke, Susan. The Devil Did It
  Mia, Grandma and the Genie
Kirk, Barbara. Grandpa, Me and Our House in the Tree
Kraus, Robert. Rebecca Hatpin
Kroll, Steven. If I Could Be My Grandmother
Lapp, Eleanor J. In the Morning Mist
Lasky, Kathryn. I Have Four Names for My Grandfather
Lenski, Lois L. Debbie and Her Grandma
Lexau, Joan M. Benjie
  Benjie on His Own
Low, Alice. David's Windows
Minarik, Else Holmelund. Little Bear's Visit
Parish, Peggy. Granny and the Desperadoes
  Granny and the Indians
  Granny, the Baby and the Big Gray Thing
Peck, Richard. Monster Night at Grandma's House
Raynor, Dorka. Grandparents around the World
Schlein, Miriam. Go with the Sun
Shulevitz, Uri. Dawn
Sonneborn, Ruth A. I Love Gram
Steiner, Charlotte. Kiki and Muffy
Stevenson, James. "Could Be Worse"
Swayne, Samuel F., and Swayne, Zoa. Great-Grandfather in the Honey Tree
Taylor, Mark. A Time for Flowers
Turkle, Brinton Cassady. It's Only Arnold
Udry, Janice May. Mary Jo's Grandmother
Vigna, Judith. Everyone Goes as a Pumpkin
Wahl, Jan. The Fishermen
Williams, Barbara. Kevin's Grandma
Wood, Joyce. Grandmother Lucy Goes on a Picnic
  Grandmother Lucy in Her Garden
Yolen, Jane. No Bath Tonight
Zolotow, Charlotte Shapiro. My Grandson Lew
  William's Doll

057.03 Family life—mothers

Blaine, Marge. The Terrible Thing That Happened at Our House
Delton, Judy, and Knox-Wagner, Elaine. The Best Mom in the World
Eastman, Philip Day. Are You My Mother?
Fassler, Joan. The Man of the House
Fisher, Aileen Lucia. Do Bears Have Mothers Too?
  My Mother and I
Flack, Marjorie. Ask Mr. Bear
Krauss, Ruth. The Bundle Book
Lasker, Joseph Leon. Mothers Can Do Anything
Lexau, Joan M. A House So Big
Mayer, Mercer. Just for You
Merriam, Eve. Mommies at Work
Mizumura, Kazue. If I Were a Mother
Polushkin, Maria. Mother, Mother, I Want Another
Rice, Eve. New Blue Shoes
Scott, Ann Herbert. On Mother's Lap
Standon, Anna, and Standon, Edward Cyril. Little Duck Lost
Tompert, Ann. Little Otter Remembers and Other Stories
Udry, Janice May. Is Susan Here?
Vigna, Judith. Couldn't We Have a Turtle Instead?
Viorst, Judith. My Mama Says There Aren't Any: Zombies, Ghosts, Vampires, Creatures, Demons, Monsters, Fiends, Goblins, or Things
Waber, Bernard. Lyle Finds His Mother
Watson, Nancy Dingman. Tommy's Mommy's Fish
Zindel, Paul. I Love My Mother
Zolotow, Charlotte Shapiro. Mr. Rabbit and the Lovely Present

057.04 Family life—the only child

Conford, Ellen. Why Can't I Be William?
Hallinan, Patrick K. I'm Glad to Be Me
  Just Being Alone
Hamberger, John F. Hazel Was an Only Pet
Hazen, Barbara Shook. Tight Times
  Why Couldn't I Be an Only Kid Like You, Wigger?
Iwasaki, Chihiro. Staying Home Alone on a Rainy Day
Parsons, Ellen. Rainy Day Together
Schick, Eleanor. City in the Winter
  Summer at the Sea
Sharmat, Marjorie Weinman. I Want Mama
Skorpen, Liesel Moak. All the Lassies
Zolotow, Charlotte Shapiro. If It Weren't for You

058 Farms

Augarde, Stephen Andre. Pig
Barrett, Judith. Old MacDonald Had an
Apartment House
Bell-Zano, Gina. The Wee Moose
Benchley, Nathaniel. The Strange
Disappearance of Arthur Cluck
Brand, Millen. This Little Pig Named
Curly
Brenner, Barbara. Wagon Wheels
Bright, Robert. Georgie
Brook, Judy. Tim Mouse Goes
Downstream
Tim Mouse Visits the Farm
Brown, Margaret Wise. The Little Farmer
Summer Noisy Book
Bruna, Dick. Little Bird Tweet
Bunting, Eve. Winter's Coming
Carrick, Donald. The Deer in the Pasture
Caudill, Rebecca. A Pocketful of Cricket
Chaucer, Geoffrey. Chanticleer and the
Fox
Child, Lydia Maria. Over the River and
Through the Wood
Cleary, Beverly. The Hullabaloo ABC
Collier, Ethel. I Know a Farm
Cook, Bernadine. Looking for Susie
Dalgliesh, Alice. The Little Wooden
Farmer
Dennis, Wesley. Flip
Flip and the Cows
Dunn, Judy. The Little Lamb
Duvoisin, Roger Antoine. The Crocodile in
the Tree
Crocus
Jasmine
Our Veronica Goes to Petunia's Farm
Petunia
Petunia and the Song
Petunia, Beware!
Petunia, I Love You!
Petunia's Treasure
Two Lonely Ducks
Veronica
Veronica and the Birthday Present
Ets, Marie Hall. Mister Penny
Mr. Penny's Race Horse
Fatio, Louise. The Red Bantam
Flora, James. Grandpa's Farm
Fox, Robin. Le Poulet, the Rooster Who
Laid Eggs
Gackenbach, Dick. Crackle, Gluck and the
Sleeping Toad
The Pig Who Saw Everything
Green, Mary McBurney. Everybody Has a
House and Everybody Eats
Greenberg, Polly. O Lord, I Wish I Was a
Buzzard
Hader, Berta Hoerner, and Hader, Elmer
Stanley. Cock-A-Doodle-Do; The
Story of a Little Red Rooster

Hawes, Judy. Fireflies in the Night
Hutchins, Pat. Rosie's Walk
Ipcar, Dahlov Zorach. Bright Barnyard
Brown Cow Farm
Hard Scrabble Harvest
One Horse Farm
Ten Big Farms
Israel, Marion Louise. The Tractor on the
Farm
Jacobs, Joseph. Hereafterthis
Koch, Dorothy Clarke. When the Cows Got
Out
Lapp, Eleanor J. The Mice Came in Early
This Year
Lasson, Robert. Orange Oliver
Lenski, Lois L. The Little Farm
Lexau, Joan M. Who Took the Farmer's
Hat?
Lindgren, Astrid Ericsson. The Tomten
Lindman, Maj Jan. Snipp, Snapp, Snurr
and the Buttered Bread
The Little Red Hen, illus. by Janina
Domanska
The Little Red Hen, illus. by Paul Galdone
The Little Red Hen, illus. by Mel Pekarsky
Lobel, Arnold Stark. Small Pig
A Treeful of Pigs
Low, Joseph. Boo to a Goose
McNeer, May Yonge. Little Baptiste
Meeks, Esther K. Friendly Farm Animals
Merrill, Jean. Tell about the Cowbarn,
Daddy
Miles, Miska. Noisy Gander
Mother Goose. To Market! To Market!
Nakatani, Chiyoko. My Day on the Farm
Old MacDonald Had a Farm, illus. by Mel
Crawford
Old MacDonald Had a Farm, illus. by
Abner Graboff
Old MacDonald Had a Farm, illus. by
Robert Mead Quackenbush
Peck, Robert Newton. Hamilton
Petersham, Maud Fuller, and Petersham,
Miska. The Box with Red Wheels
Provensen, Alice, and Provensen, Martin.
Our Animal Friends
The Year at Maple Hill Farm
Rider, Alex. A la Ferme. At the Farm
Robinson, William Wilcox. On the Farm
Rockwell, Anne F. The Gollywhopper Egg
Rojankovsky, Feodor Stepanovich. Animals
on the Farm
The Great Big Animal Book
Schlein, Miriam. Something for Now,
Something for Later
Schmidt, Eric von. The Young Man Who
Wouldn't Hoe Corn
Schoenherr, John Carl. The Barn
Seignobosc, Françoise. The Big Rain
Selsam, Millicent Ellis. More Potatoes!
Sewell, Helen Moore. Blue Barns

Sherman, Nancy. Gwendolyn and the
    Weathercock
Short, Mayo. Andy and the Wild Ducks
Slobodkina, Esphyr. The Wonderful Feast
Smith, Donald. Farm Numbers 1, 2, 3
Stevenson, James. "Could Be Worse"
Stolz, Mary Slattery. Emmett's Pig
Teal, Valentine. The Little Woman
    Wanted Noise
Tolstoy, Alekesi Nikolaevich. The Great
    Big Enormous Turnip
Tresselt, Alvin R. Sun Up
    Wake Up, Farm!
Tripp, Paul. The Strawman Who Smiled
    by Mistake
Van Horn, Grace. Little Red Rooster
Watson, Nancy Dingman. What Does A
    Begin With?
    What Is One?
Wiesner, William. Happy-Go-Lucky
Wright, Dare. Look at a Calf
    Look at a Colt
Yolen, Jane. The Giants' Farm
Zalben, Jane Breskin. Basil and Hillary

059 Fire

Anderson, Clarence William. Blaze and the
    Forest Fire
Augarde, Stephen Andre. Pig
Bernstein, Margery, and Kobrin, Janet.
    Coyote Goes Hunting for Fire
Bible, Charles. Jennifer's New Chair
Brown, Margaret Wise. The Little Fireman
Du Bois, William Pène. Otto and the Magic
    Potatoes
Fire
Gramatky, Hardie. Hercules
Greene, Graham. The Little Fire Engine
Kirn, Ann Minette. The Tale of a
    Crocodile
Lawrence, John D. Pope Leo's Elephant
Mahood, Kenneth. The Laughing Dragon
Miklowitz, Gloria D. Save That Raccoon!
Miles, Miska. The Fox and the Fire
Quackenbush, Robert Mead. There'll Be a
    Hot Time in the Old Town Tonight
Spiegel, Doris. Danny and Company 92
Taylor, Mark. Henry Explores the
    Mountains
Ungerer, Tomi. Adelaide
    The Mellops Strike Oil

060 Fish

Aruego, Jóse. Pilyo the Piranha
Balet, Jan B. Joanjo; A Portuguese Tale
Bruna, Dick. The Fish
Cook, Bernadine. The Little Fish That Got
    Away
Cooper, Elizabeth K. The Fish from Japan
Geisel, Theodor Seuss. McElligot's Pool

One Fish, Two Fish, Red Fish, Blue Fish
Hall, Bill. Fish Tale
Ipcar, Dahlov Zorach. The Biggest Fish in
    the Sea
Kalan, Robert. Blue Sea
Lionni, Leo. Fish Is Fish
    Swimmy
Palmer, Helen Marion. A Fish Out of
    Water
Parnall, Peter. The Great Fish
Parry, Marian. King of the Fish
Phleger, Frederick B. Red Tag Comes
    Back
Ricciuti, Edward R. Donald and the Fish
    That Walked
Selsam, Millicent Ellis. Plenty of Fish
Shaw, Evelyn S. Fish Out of School
Valens, Evans G. Wingfin and Topple
Waber, Bernard. Lorenzo
Wezel, Peter. The Good Bird
Wildsmith, Brian. Brian Wildsmith's Fishes
Wong, Herbert H., and Vassel, Matthew F.
    My Goldfish
Wyse, Lois. Two Guppies, a Turtle, and
    Aunt Edna

061 Flowers

Anno, Mitsumasa. The King's Flower
Chapman, Carol. Barney Bipple's Magic
    Dandelions
Ellentuck, Shan. A Sunflower as Big as the
    Sun
Fisher, Aileen Lucia. And a Sunflower
    Grew
    Petals Yellow and Petals Red
Harper, Wilhelmina, reteller. The
    Gunniwolf
Heilbroner, Joan. Robert the Rose Horse
Ipcar, Dahlov Zorach. The Land of
    Flowers
Slobodkina, Esphyr. Pinky and the
    Petunias
Sugita, Yutaka. The Flower Family
Waber, Bernard. A Rose for Mr. Bloom

062 Folk and fairy tales

Aardema, Verna, reteller. Why Mosquitoes
    Buzz in People's Ears
Abisch, Roslyn Kroop. The Clever Turtle
    The Pumpkin Heads
Adshead, Gladys L. Brownies—Hush!
Aesopus. The Miller, His Son, and Their
    Donkey
    Three Fox Fables
Alger, Leclaire. All in the Morning Early
    Always Room for One More
Allard, Harry. May I Stay?
Ambrus, Victor G. The Sultan's Bath
    The Three Poor Tailors

Andersen, Hans Christian. The Emperor's New Clothes, illus. by Erik Blegvad
 The Emperor's New Clothes, illus. by Virginia Lee Burton
 The Emperor's New Clothes, illus. by Jack Delano and Irene Delano
 The Emperor's New Clothes, illus. by Monika Laimgruber
 The Little Match Girl
 The Princess and the Pea
 Thumbelina
 The Ugly Duckling, illus. by Adrienne Adams
 The Ugly Duckling, illus. by Johannes Larsen
 The Ugly Duckling, illus. by Will Nickless
 The Ugly Duckling, illus. by Joseph Palacek
 The Woman with the Eggs
Aruego, José. Juan and the Asuangs
Asbjørnsen, Peter Christen. The Squire's Bride
 The Three Billy Goats Gruff, illus. by Paul Galdone
 The Three Billy Goats Gruff, illus. by William Stobbs
Asbjørnsen, Peter Christen, and Moe, Jørgen Engebretsen. The Three Billy Goats Gruff
Aulaire, Ingri Mortenson d', and Aulaire, Edgar Parin d'. Don't Count Your Chicks
Bang, Molly G. Wiley and the Hairy Man
Belpré, Pura. Perez and Martina
Bernstein, Margery, and Kobrin, Janet. Coyote Goes Hunting for Fire
 Earth Namer
Berson, Harold. Balarin's Goat
 The Boy, the Baker, the Miller and More
Billy Boy
Bishop, Claire Huchet, and Wiese, Kurt. The Five Chinese Brothers
Blood, Charles L., and Link, Martin. The Goat in the Rug
Bolliger, Max. The Fireflies
Bonne, Rose. I Know an Old Lady
Bowden, Joan Chase. The Bean Boy
Brand, Oscar. When I First Came to This Land
Brooke, Leonard Leslie. The Golden Goose Book
Brown, Marcia. The Blue Jackal
 The Bun
 Once a Mouse
Bryant, Sara Cone. Epaminondas and His Auntie
Calhoun, Mary. Old Man Whickutt's Donkey
Carrick, Malcolm. Happy Jack
Chapman, Gaynor. The Luck Child

Charlip, Remy, and Supree, Burton. Harlequin and the Gift of Many Colors
Chaucer, Geoffrey. Chanticleer and the Fox
Chicken Little. Chicken Licken
 Henny Penny, illus. by Paul Galdone
 Henny Penny, illus. by William Stobbs
Daniels, Guy, translator. The Peasant's Pea Patch
Dayrell, Elphinstone. Why the Sun and the Moon Live in the Sky
De Regniers, Beatrice Schenk. Little Sister and the Month Brothers
 Red Riding Hood
Domanska, Janina. The Best of the Bargain
 King Krakus and the Dragon
 The Tortoise and the Tree
 Why So Much Noise?
Duff, Maggie. Rum Pum Pum
Dukas, Paul Abraham. The Sorcerer's Apprentice
Elkin, Benjamin. The Big Jump and Other Stories
 The King's Wish and Other Stories
 Six Foolish Fishermen
 Such Is the Way of the World
 Why the Sun Was Late
Evans, Katherine. The Boy Who Cried Wolf
 The Maid and Her Pail of Milk
 The Man, the Boy, and the Donkey
Felton, Harold W. Pecos Bill and the Mustang
The Fox Went Out on a Chilly Night
Francis, Frank. Natasha's New Doll
Galdone, Joanna. Amber Day
Galdone, Paul. Androcles and the Lion
 The Horse, the Fox, and the Lion
 The Magic Porridge Pot
 The Monkey and the Crocodile
 Obedient Jack
 The Table, the Donkey and the Stick
 The Town Mouse and the Country Mouse
The Gingerbread Boy, illus. by Paul Galdone
The Gingerbread Boy, illus. by William Curtis Holdsworth
The Gingerbread Man, illus. by Gerald Rose
Ginsburg, Mirra. The Fox and the Hare
Go Tell Aunt Rhody, illus. by Aliki Liacouras Brandenberg
The Golden Goose
Goody Two Shoes' Picture Book
Grabianski, Janusz. Androcles and the Lion
Gramatky, Hardie. Nikos and the Sea God
Greene, Ellin, reteller. Princess Rosetta and the Popcorn Man

Grieg, Edvard Hagerup. E. H. Grieg's Peer Gynt

Grimm, Jakob Ludwig Karl, and Grimm, Wilhelm Karl. The Bearskinner
The Bremen Town Musicians
Hans in Luck

Haley, Gail Diana Einhart. A Story, a Story

Hewett, Anita. The Little White Hen

Hillert, Margaret. The Funny Baby
The Magic Beans
The Three Goats

Hirawa, Yasuko, comp. Song of the Sour Plum and Other Japanese Children's Songs

Hirsh, Marilyn Joyce. Captain Jeri and Rabbi Jacob

The History of Mother Twaddle and the Marvelous Achievements of Her Son Jack

Hürlimann, Ruth. The Proud White Cat

Hush Little Baby

Ivanko and the Dragon

Iwamatsu, Jun. Seashore Story

Jacobs, Joseph. The Crock of Gold, Being "The Pedlar of Swaffham"
Hereafterthis
Johnny-Cake, illus. by Emma Lillian Brock
Johnny-Cake, illus. by William Stobbs
Lazy Jack
Master of All Masters

Jameson, Cynthia. The Clay Pot Boy

Keats, Ezra Jack. John Henry
Over in the Meadow

Kirn, Ann Minette. The Tale of a Crocodile

La Fontaine, Jean de. The Hare and the Tortoise
The Lion and the Rat
The Miller, the Boy and the Donkey
The North Wind and the Sun
The Rich Man and the Shoemaker

Langstaff, John Meredith. Ol' Dan Tucker
Over in theMeadow
The Swapping Boy
The Two Magicians

Langstaff, John Meredith, and Groves-Raines, Antony. On Christmas Day in the Morning!

Leisk, David Johnson. Harold's Fairy Tale

Lenski, Lois L. Susie Mariar

Lent, Blair. John Tabor's Ride

Lexau, Joan M. Crocodile and Hen
It All Began with a Drip, Drip, Drip

Lipkind, William, and Mordvinoff, Nicolas. The Magic Feather Duster

The Little Red Hen, illus. by Janina Domanska

The Little Red Hen, illus. by Paul Galdone

The Little Red Hen, illus. by Mel Pekarsky

Little Red Riding Hood, illus. by Paul Galdone

Little Red Riding Hood, illus. by Bernadette Watts

Little Tuppen: An Old Tale

MacBeth, George. Jonah and the Lord

McDermott, Beverly Brodsky. The Golem, a Jewish Legend

McDermott, Gerald. Anansi the Spider
Arrow to the Sun; A Pueblo Indian Tale
The Stonecutter; A Japanese Folk Tale

McKee, David. The Man Who Was Going to Mind the House

Maestro, Giulio. The Tortoise's Tug of War

Merriam, Eve. Epaminondas

Morel, Eve, comp. Fairy Tales and Fables

Mother Goose. London Bridge Is Falling Down, illus. by Edward Randolph Emberley
London Bridge Is Falling Down!, illus. by Peter Spier

Ness, Evaline. Tom Tit Tot

The Old Woman and Her Pig

Parnall, Peter. The Great Fish

Parry, Marian. King of the Fish

Perrault, Charles. Puss in Boots, illus. by Marcia Brown
Puss in Boots, illus. by Hans Fischer
Puss in Boots, illus. by Paul Galdone
Puss in Boots, illus. by Julia Noonan
Puss in Boots, illus. by William Stobbs
Puss in Boots, illus. by Barry Wilkinson

Polushkin, Maria. The Little Hen and the Giant

Prokofiev, Sergei Sergeievitch. Peter and the Wolf, illus. by Warren Chappell
Peter and the Wolf, illus. by Frans Haacken
Peter and the Wolf, illus. by Alan Howard
Peter and the Wolf, illus. by Kozo Shimizu

Quackenbush, Robert Mead. Clementine

Quigley, Lillian. The Blind Men and the Elephant

Reesink, Maryke. The Golden Treasure

Robbins, Ruth. Baboushka and the Three Kings

Robinson, Adjai. Femi and Old Grandaddie

Rockwell, Anne F. Poor Goose
The Three Bears and Fifteen Other Stories
The Wolf Who Had a Wonderful Dream
The Wonderful Eggs of Furicchia

Rose, Anne K. Spider in the Sky

Ross, Tony, reteller. The Pied Piper of Hamelin

Roughsey, Dick. The Giant Devil-Dingo
Rounds, Glen H. The Boll Weevil
   Casey Jones
   Sweet Betsy from Pike
Rudolph, Marguerita. I Am Your
   Misfortune
Sawyer, Ruth. Journey Cake, Ho!
Say, Allen, reteller. Once under the Cherry
   Blossom Tree
Schatz, Letta. The Extraordinary Tug-of-
   War
Schiller, Barbara. The White Rat's Tale
Seeger, Peter. Foolish Frog
Seuling, Barbara. The Teeny Tiny Woman
Sewall, Marcia. The Wee, Wee Mannie and
   the Big, Big Coo
Showalter, Jean B. The Donkey Ride
Shub, Elizabeth. Clever Kate
Shulevitz, Uri. The Treasure
Siddiqui, Ashraf. Bhombal Dass, the Uncle
   of Lion
Skurzynski, Gloria. The Magic Pumpkin
Spier, Peter. The Erie Canal
   The Legend of New Amsterdam
Stalder, Valerie. Even the Devil Is Afraid
   of a Shrew
The Tall Book of Nursery Rhymes
Taylor, Mark. The Bold Fisherman
   Old Blue, You Good Dog You
Thompson, Harwood. The Witch's Cat
The Three Bears. The Story of the Three
   Bears, illus. by Leonard Leslie
   Brooke
   The Story of the Three Bears, illus. by
   William Stobbs
The Three Bears, illus. by Paul Galdone
The Three Bears, illus. by Feodor
   Stepanovich Rojankovsky
The Three Bears, illus. by Irma Wilde
Three Little Pigs. The Story of the Three
   Little Pigs, illus. by Leonard Leslie
   Brooke
   The Story of the Three Little Pigs, illus.
   by William Stobbs
The Three Little Pigs, illus. by William
   Pène Du Bois
The Three Little Pigs, illus. by Paul
   Galdone
The Three Little Pigs, illus. by Irma Wilde
Tolstoy, Alekesi Nikolaevich. The Great
   Big Enormous Turnip
Tom Thumb. Grimm Tom Thumb
Tom Thumb, illus. by Leonard Leslie
   Brooke
Tom Thumb, illus. by Felix Hoffmann
Tom Thumb, illus. by William Wiesner
Tresselt, Alvin R. The Mitten
Tripp, Wallace. The Tale of a Pig
Turkle, Brinton Cassady. Deep in the
   Forest
Turska, Krystyna. The Magician of Cracow
   The Woodcutter's Duck

Van Woerkom, Dorothy O. The Queen
   Who Couldn't Bake Gingerbread
   The Rat, the Ox and the Zodiac
   Sea Frog, City Frog
   Tit for Tat
Varga, Judy. The Mare's Egg
Watts, Bernadette, reteller. Mother Holly
Weiss, Harvey. The Sooner Hound
Werth, Kurt. Lazy Jack
Westerberg, Christine. The Cap That
   Mother Made
Widdecombe Fair; An Old English Folk
   Song
Wildsmith, Brian. The True Cross
Williams, Jay. Petronella
   The Practical Princess
Wolf, Ann. The Rabbit and the Turtle
Wolkstein, Diane, and Young, Ed. The
   White Wave: A Chinese Tale
Yolen, Jane. Greyling; A Picture Story for
   the Islands of Shetland
Zemach, Harve. Duffy and the Devil
   Nail Soup
Zemach, Margot. It Could Always Be
   Worse
   The Little Tiny Woman
Zijlstra, Tjerk. Benny and His Geese

063 Food

Ambrus, Victor G. A Country Wedding
Asch, Frank. Good Lemonade
Barrett, Judith. An Apple a Day
Berson, Harold. Pop Goes the Turnip
   The Rats Who Lived in the Delicatessen
Beskow, Elsa Maartman. Peter's
   Adventures in Blueberry Land
Black, Irma Simonton. Is This My Dinner?
Bolliger, Max. The Giants' Feast
   The Golden Apple
Brandenberg, Franz. Fresh Cider and
   Apple Pie
Bright, Robert. Gregory, the Noisiest and
   Strongest Boy in Grangers Grove
Bruna, Dick. The Fish
Brustlein, Janice. Little Bear's Pancake
   Party
Burch, Robert. The Hunting Trip
Burgess, Anthony. The Land Where the
   Ice Cream Grows
Burningham, John Mackintosh. The
   Cupboard
Calhoun, Mary. The Hungry Leprechaun
Carle, Eric. Pancakes, Pancakes
   The Very Hungry Caterpillar
   Walter the Baker
Cauley, Lorinda Bryan. Pease Porridge
   Hot: A Mother Goose Cookbook

Chalmers, Audrey. Hundreds and
Hundreds of Pancakes
de Paola, Thomas Anthony. Pancakes for
Breakfast
The Popcorn Book
Devlin, Wende, and Devlin, Harry. Old
Witch and the Polka-Dot Ribbon
Emberley, Edward Randolph. A Birthday
Wish
Flory, Jane. We'll Have a Friend for Lunch
Foreman, Michael. War and Peas
Gackenbach, Dick. Mother Rabbit's Son
Tom
Gág, Wanda. The Funny Thing
Galdone, Paul. The Magic Porridge Pot
Geisel, Theodor Seuss. Green Eggs and
Ham
Scrambled Eggs Super!
Ten Apples Up on Top!
The Gingerbread Boy, illus. by Paul
Galdone
The Gingerbread Boy, illus. by William
Curtis Holdsworth
The Gingerbread Man, illus. by Gerald
Rose
Goodall, John Strickland. The Surprise
Picnic
Greene, Ellin. The Pumpkin Giant
Gunthrop, Karen. Adam and the Wolf
Gurney, Nancy, and Gurney, Eric. The
King, the Mice and the Cheese
Hellsing, Lennart. The Wonderful
Pumpkin
Hirsh, Marilyn Joyce, and Narayan, Maya.
Leela and the Watermelon
Hitte, Kathryn, and Hayes, William D.
Mexicallie Soup
Hoban, Russell Conwell. Bread and Jam
for Frances
Dinner at Alberta's
Holden, Edith B. The Hedgehog Feast
Hughes, Peter. The Emperor's Oblong
Pancake
Hutchins, Pat. Don't Forget the Bacon!
Jack Sprat. The Life of Jack Sprat, His
Wife and His Cat
Jacobs, Joseph. Johnny-Cake, illus. by
Emma Lillian Brock
Johnny-Cake, illus. by William Stobbs
Kahl, Virginia Caroline. The Duchess
Bakes a Cake
The Perfect Pancake
Plum Pudding for Christmas
Kantor, MacKinlay. Angleworms on Toast
Kessler, Leonard P. Soup for the King
Kitt, Tamara. Sam and the Impossible
Thing
Lasker, Joseph Leon. Lentil Soup
Lobel, Anita. The Pancake
McCloskey, Robert John. Blueberries for
Sal

Marshall, James. Miss Dog's Christmas
Treat
Yummers!
Mayer, Mercer. Frog Goes to Dinner
Murphey, Sara. The Roly Poly Cookie
Paterson, Diane. Eat
Petie, Haris. The Seed the Squirrel
Dropped
Retan, Walter. The Steam Shovel That
Wouldn't Eat Dirt
Rice, Eve. Sam Who Never Forgets
Rockwell, Anne F. The Wolf Who Had a
Wonderful Dream
Schwalje, Marjory. Mr. Angelo
Sharmat, Marjorie Weinman. Nate the
Great
Nate the Great and the Lost List
Nate the Great and the Phony Clue
Nate the Great Goes Undercover
Slobodkina, Esphyr. The Wonderful Feast
Slocum, Rosalie. Breakfast with the Clowns
Stamaty, Mark Alan. Minnie Maloney and
Macaroni
Thompson, Vivian Laubach. The Horse
That Liked Sandwiches
Vorse, Mary Ellen. Skinny Gets Fat
Wallner, Alexandra. Munch
Watson, Clyde. Tom Fox and the Apple
Pie
Watson, Nancy Dingman. Sugar on Snow
Winthrop, Elizabeth. Potbellied Possums
Wooley, Catherine. The Blueberry Pie Elf
The Popcorn Dragon
Zion, Gene. The Sugar Mouse Cake

064 Foreign lands

De Regniers, Beatrice Schenk. Little Sister
and the Month Brothers
Geisel, Theodor Seuss. Come Over to My
House

064.01 Foreign lands—Africa

Aardema, Verna, reteller. Why Mosquitoes
Buzz in People's Ears
Abisch, Roslyn Kroop. The Clever Turtle
Adoff, Arnold. Ma nDa La
Bang, Betsy. The Old Woman and the Red
Pumpkin
Bond, Jean Carey. A Is for Africa
Dayrell, Elphinstone. Why the Sun and the
Moon Live in the Sky
de Paola, Thomas Anthony. Bill and Pete
Domanska, Janina. The Tortoise and the
Tree
Du Bois, William Pène. Otto in Africa
Economakis, Olga. Oasis of the Stars
Elkin, Benjamin. Such Is the Way of the
World
Fatio, Louise. The Happy Lion in Africa

Feelings, Muriel L. Jambo Means Hello; A Swahili Alphabet Book
   Monjo Means One; A Swahili Counting Book
Graham, Lorenz. Song of the Boat
Greenfield, Eloise. Africa Dream
Haley, Gail Diana Einhart. A Story, a Story
Holding, James. The Lazy Little Zulu
Kirn, Ann Minette. The Tale of a Crocodile
Laskowski, Jerzy. Master of the Royal Cats
Lexau, Joan M. Crocodile and Hen
McDermott, Gerald. Anansi the Spider
Robinson, Adjai. Femi and Old Grandaddie
Routh, Jonathan. The Nuns Go to Africa
Schatz, Letta. The Extraordinary Tug-of-War
Sonneborn, Ruth A. Friday Night Is Papa Night
Ward, Leila. I Am Eyes; Ni Macho

064.02 Foreign lands—Australia

Paterson, Andrew Barton. Mulga Bill's Bicycle
   Waltzing Matilda
Roughsey, Dick. The Giant Devil-Dingo
Wagner, Jenny. The Bunyip of Berkeley's Creek

064.03 Foreign lands—Austria

Kahl, Virginia Caroline. Away Went Wolfgang

064.04 Foreign lands—Canada

Ward, Lynd Kendall. The Biggest Bear
   Nic of the Woods

064.05 Foreign lands—Caribbean Islands

Anderson, Lonzo. Izzard
Belpré, Pura. Perez and Martina
Dobrin, Arnold Jack. Josephine's 'magination
George, Jean Craighead. The Wentletrap Trap
Ness, Evaline. Josefina February

064.06 Foreign lands—China

Behrens, June York. Soo Ling Finds a Way
Bishop, Claire Huchet, and Wiese, Kurt. The Five Chinese Brothers
Flack, Marjorie, and Wiese, Kurt. The Story about Ping
Fribourg, Marjorie G. Ching-Ting and the Ducks
Handforth, Thomas Scofield. Mei Li
Martin, Patricia Miles. The Pointed Brush

Mosel, Arlene. Tikki Tikki Tembo
Perkins, Al. Tubby and the Lantern
Skipper, Mervyn. The Fooling of King Alexander
Slobodkin, Louis. Moon Blossom and the Golden Penny
Stafford, Kay. Ling Tang and the Lucky Cricket
Van Woerkom, Dorothy O. The Rat, the Ox and the Zodiac
Wiese, Kurt. Fish in the Air
Williams, Jay. Everyone Knows What a Dragon Looks Like
Wolkstein, Diane, and Young, Ed. The White Wave: A Chinese Tale
Yolen, Jane. The Emperor and the Kite
   The Seeing Stick
Young, Evelyn. Tale of Tai
   Wu and Lu and Li

064.07 Foreign lands—Czechoslovakia

Bolliger, Max. The Fireflies

064.08 Foreign lands—Denmark

Bodecker, Nils Mogens, translator. "It's Raining," Said John Twaining
Brande, Marlie. Sleepy Nicholas
Kent, Jack. Hoddy Doddy

064.09 Foreign lands—Egypt

Goodenow, Earle. The Last Camel
Laskowski, Jerzy. Master of the Royal Cats
Van Woerkom, Dorothy O. Abu Ali

064.10 Foreign lands—England

Ambler, Christopher Gifford. Ten Little Foxhounds
Bemelmans, Ludwig. Madeline in London
Bond, Michael. Paddington at the Circus
   Paddington at the Seaside
   Paddington at the Tower
   Paddington's Lucky Day
Burningham, John Mackintosh. Borka, the Adventures of a Goose with No Feathers
Davis, Reda. Martin's Dinosaur
Dines, Glen. Gilly and the Wicharoo
Drummond, Violet H. The Flying Postman
Freeman, Don. The Guard Mouse
   Will's Quill
Goodall, John Strickland. An Edwardian Christmas
   An Edwardian Summer
   The Story of an English Village
Goody Two Shoes' Picture Book
Gramatky, Hardie. Little Toot on the Thames

Haley, Gail Diana Einhart. The Post Office
Cat
Herrmann, Frank. The Giant Alexander
The Giant Alexander and the Circus
Jacobs, Joseph. The Crock of Gold, Being
"The Pedlar of Swaffham"
Keeping, Charles William James. Alfie
Finds the Other Side of the World
Through the Window
Lawrence, John D. The Giant of Grabbist
Mother Goose. London Bridge Is Falling
Down, illus. by Edward Randolph
Emberley
London Bridge Is Falling Down! illus.
by Peter Spier
Oakley, Graham. The Church Cat Abroad
The Church Mice Adrift
The Church Mice and the Moon
The Church Mice at Bay
The Church Mice Spread Their Wings
The Church Mouse
O'Hare, Colette. What Do You Feed Your
Donkey On?
Oxenbury, Helen. The Queen and Rosie
Randall
Ross, Diana. The Story of the Little Red
Engine
Ross, Tony, reteller. The Pied Piper of
Hamelin
Seuling, Barbara. The Teeny Tiny Woman
Shulman, Milton. Preep, the Little Pigeon
of Trafalgar Square
Thompson, Harwood. The Witch's Cat
Widdecombe Fair; An Old English Folk
Song
Willard, Barbara. To London! To London!
Wood, Joyce. Grandmother Lucy in Her
Garden
Zemach, Harve. Duffy and the Devil
Zemach, Margot. Hush, Little Baby

064.11 Foreign lands—France

Abisch, Roslyn Kroop. 'Twas in the Moon
of Wintertime
Angelo, Nancy Carolyn Harris. Camembert
Bemelmans, Ludwig. Madeline
Madeline and the Bad Hat
Madeline and the Gypsies
Madeline's Rescue
Bergere, Thea. Paris in the Rain with Jean
and Jacqueline
Bishop, Claire Huchet. The Truffle Pig
Bring a Torch, Jeannette, Isabella
Brown, Judith Gwyn. Max and the Truffle
Pig
Brunhoff, Jean de. The Story of Babar,
the Little Elephant
Charlip, Remy, and Supree, Burton.
Harlequin and the Gift of Many
Colors

Daudet, Alphonse. The Brave Little Goat
of Monsieur Seguin
Diska, Pat. Andy Says Bonjour!
Fatio, Louise. The Happy Lion
The Happy Lion and the Bear
The Happy Lion in Africa
The Happy Lion Roars
The Happy Lion's Quest
The Happy Lion's Rabbits
The Happy Lion's Treasure
The Three Happy Lions
Fender, Kay. Odette, a Bird in Paris
Fox, Robin. Le Poulet, the Rooster Who
Laid Eggs
Harris, Leon A. The Great Picture
Robbery
Hautzig, Esther. At Home; A Visit in Four
Languages
In the Park; An Excursion in Four
Languages
Ichikawa, Satomi. Suzanne and Nicholas at
the Market
Joslin, Sesyle. Baby Elephant's Trunk
Klein, Leonore. Henri's Walk to Paris
Lubell, Winifred Milius, and Lubell, Cicil.
Rosalie, the Bird Market Turtle
Marokvia, Merelle. A French School for
Paul
Moore, Lilian. Papa Albert
Napoli, Guillier. Adventure at Mont St.
Michael
Rider, Alex. A la Ferme. At the Farm
Chez nous. At Our House
Rockwell, Anne F. Poor Goose
The Wolf Who Had a Wonderful
Dream
Schiller, Barbara. The White Rat's Tale
Seignobosc, Françoise. The Big Rain
Biquette, the White Goat
Chouchou
Jeanne-Marie at the Fair
Jeanne-Marie Counts Her Sheep
Jeanne-Marie in Gay Paris
Minou
Noel for Jeanne-Marie
Springtime for Jeanne-Marie
Shecter, Ben. Partouche Plants a Seed
Slobodkin, Louis. Colette and the Princess
Titus, Eve. Anatole
Anatole and the Cat
Anatole and the Piano
Anatole and the Pied Piper
Anatole and the Poodle
Anatole and the Robot
Anatole and the Thirty Thieves
Anatole and the Toyshop
Anatole Over Paris
Ungerer, Tomi. Adelaide
The Beast of Monsieur Racine
Vacheron, Edith, and Kahl, Virginia
Caroline. Here Is Henri!
More about Henri!

Weelen, Guy. The Little Red Train
Wynants, Miche. The Giraffe of King
    Charles X

064.12 Foreign lands—Germany

Allard, Harry. May I Stay?
Attenberger, Walburga. The Little Man in
    Winter
    Who Knows the Little Man?
Harper, Wilhelmina, reteller. The
    Gunniwolf
Hürlimann, Ruth. The Proud White Cat
Kahl, Virginia Caroline. Droopsi
    Maxie
Morgenstern, Elizabeth. The Little
    Gardeners
Spang, Gunter. Clelia and the Little
    Mermaid
Van Woerkom, Dorothy O. The Queen
    Who Couldn't Bake Gingerbread

064.13 Foreign lands—Greece

Brown, Marcia. Tamarindo
Walker, Barbara K. Pigs and Pirates

064.14 Foreign lands—Holland

Chasek, Judith. Have You Seen
    Wilhelmina Krumpf?
Green, Norma B. The Hole in the Dike
Howells, Mildred. The Woman Who Lived
    in Holland
Krasilovsky, Phyllis. The Cow Who Fell in
    the Canal
Reesink, Maryke. The Golden Treasure
Van Stockum, Hilda. Day on Skates

064.15 Foreign lands—Hungary

Ambrus, Victor G. Brave Soldier Janosch
    The Three Poor Tailors
Brown, Margaret Wise, and Gergely,
    Tibor. Wheel on the Chimney
Ginsburg, Mirra. Two Greedy Bears
Hirsh, Marilyn Joyce. Deborah the
    Dybbuk, a Ghost Story
Surany, Anico. Kati and Kormos
Varga, Judy. Janko's Wish

064.16 Foreign lands—India

Alan, Sandy. The Plaid Peacock
Ambrus, Victor G. The Sultan's Bath
Bannerman, Helen Brodie Cowan. The
    Story of Little Black Sambo
Brown, Marcia. The Blue Jackal
    Once a Mouse
Cassedy, Sylvia, and Thampi, Parvathi.
    Moon-Uncle, Moon-Uncle
Cathon, Laura E. Tot Botot and His Little
    Flute
Domanska, Janina. Why So Much Noise?

Duff, Maggie. Rum Pum Pum
Gobhai, Mehlli. Lakshmi the Water Buffalo
    Who Wouldn't
Hirsh, Marilyn Joyce, and Narayan, Maya.
    Leela and the Watermelon
Kipling, Rudyard. The Miracle of the
    Mountain
Lexau, Joan M. It All Began with a Drip,
    Drip, Drip
Papas, William. Taresh the Tea Planter
Quigley, Lillian. The Blind Men and the
    Elephant
Rockwell, Anne F. The Stolen Necklace
Skurzynski, Gloria. The Magic Pumpkin
Slobodkin, Louis. The Polka-Dot Goat
Trez, Denise, and Trez, Alain. Maila and
    the Flying Carpet
Van Woerkom, Dorothy O. Abu Ali
    The Friends of Abu Ali
Ward, Nanda Weedon, and Haynes,
    Robert. The Elephant That Ga-
    lumphed

064.17 Foreign lands—Ireland

Calhoun, Mary. The Hungry Leprechaun
Kennedy, Richard. The Leprechaun's Story
Parker, Dorothy D. Liam's Catch
Watts, Mabel. The Boy Who Listened to
    Everyone
Zimelman, Nathan. To Sing a Song as Big
    as Ireland

064.18 Foreign lands—Italy

Brown, Marcia. Felice
de Paola, Thomas Anthony. The Clown of
    God
Ehrlich, Bettina. Pantaloni
Galdone, Paul. Androcles and the Lion
Grabianski, Janusz. Androcles and the Lion
Politi, Leo. Little Leo
Priolo, Pauline. Piccolina and the Easter
    Bells
Rockwell, Anne F. The Wonderful Eggs of
    Furicchia
Seidler, Rosalie. Grumpus and the
    Venetian Cat
Titus, Eve. Anatole in Italy
Ungerer, Tomi. The Hat

064.19 Foreign lands—Japan

Bartoli, Jennifer. Snow on Bear's Nose
Battles, Edith. What Does the Rooster Say,
    Yoshio?
Damjan, Mischa (pseud.). The Little Prince
    and the Tiger Cat
DeForest, Charlotte B. The Prancing Pony
Dines, Glen. A Tiger in the Cherry Tree
Fifield, Flora. Pictures for the Palace
Fujita, Tamao. The Boy and the Bird
Garrison, Christian. The Dream Eater

Heller, George. Hiroshi's Wonderful Kite

Hirawa, Yasuko, comp. Song of the Sour Plum and Other Japanese Children's Songs

Iwamatsu, Jun. Crow Boy
Seashore Story
Umbrella
The Village Tree

Iwamatsu, Tomoe Sasako. Plenty to Watch

Lifton, Betty Jean. Joji and the Amanojaku
Joji and the Dragon
The Many Lives of Chio and Goro
The Rice-Cake Rabbit

McDermott, Gerald. The Stonecutter; A Japanese Folk Tale

Matsuno, Masako. A Pair of Red Clogs
Taro and the Bamboo Shoot
Taro and the Tofu

Matsutani, Miyoko. The Fisherman under the Sea
How the Withered Trees Blossomed
The Witch's Magic Cloth

Mosel, Arlene. The Funny Little Woman

Nakatani, Chiyoko. Fumio and the Dolphins

Roy, Ronald. A Thousand Pails of Water

Sasaki, Jeannie, and Uyeda, Frances. Chocho Is for Butterfly

Say, Allen, reteller. Once under the Cherry Blossom Tree

Slobodkin, Louis. Yasu and the Strangers

Uchida, Yoshiko. Sumi's Prize
Sumi's Special Happening

Van Woerkom, Dorothy O. Sea Frog, City Frog

064.20 Foreign lands—Korea

Parry, Marian. King of the Fish

064.21 Foreign lands—Lapland

Lindman, Maj Jan. Snipp, Snapp, Snurr and the Red Shoes

Stalder, Valerie. Even the Devil Is Afraid of a Shrew

064.22 Foreign lands—Lithuania

Rudolph, Marguerita. I Am Your Misfortune

064.23 Foreign lands—Malaysia

Kaye, Geraldine. The Sea Monkey

064.24 Foreign lands—Mexico

Balet, Jan B. The Fence

Bannon, Laura May. Manuela's Birthday in Old Mexico

Ets, Marie Hall. Nine Days to Christmas

Fraser, James Howard. Los Posadas, a Christmas Story

Grifalconi, Ann. The Toy Trumpet

Hader, Berta Hoerner, and Hader, Elmer Stanley. The Story of Pancho and the Bull with the Crooked Tail

Hitte, Kathryn, and Hayes, William D. Mexicallie Soup

Kent, Jack. The Christmas Pinata

Lewis, Thomas. Hill of Fire

Martin, Patricia Miles. Friend of Miguel

Martin, William Ivan. My Days Are Made of Butterflies

Morrow, Elizabeth Reeve Cutter. The Painted Pig

Politi, Leo. Lito and the Clown
Rosa

Unwin, Nora Spicer. Poquito, the Little Mexican Duck

064.25 Foreign lands—Norway

Allard, Harry. May I Stay?

Asbjørnsen, Peter Christen. The Squire's Bride

Aulaire, Ingri Mortenson d', and Aulaire, Edgar Parin d'. Ola
The Terrible Troll-Bird

Benchley, Nathaniel. Snorri and the Strangers

Grieg, Edvard Hagerup. E. H. Grieg's Peer Gynt

Wiesner, William. Happy-Go-Lucky Turnabout

064.26 Foreign lands—Pakistan

Siddiqui, Ashraf. Bhombal Dass, the Uncle of Lion

064.27 Foreign lands—Poland

Domanska, Janina. The Best of the Bargain
Din Dan Don, It's Christmas
King Krakus and the Dragon

Turska, Krystyna. The Magician of Cracow
The Woodcutter's Duck

064.28 Foreign lands—Portugal

Balet, Jan B. The Gift; A Portuguese Christmas Tale
Joanjo; A Portuguese Tale

064.29 Foreign lands—Puerto Rico

Martel, Cruz. Yagua Days

064.30 Foreign lands—Russia

Brown, Marcia. The Bun
  The Neighbors
Campbell, M. Rudolph, adapter. The
  Talking Crocodile
Daniels, Guy, translator. The Peasant's Pea
  Patch
Francis, Frank. Natasha's New Doll
Ginsburg, Mirra. The Fox and the Hare
  The Strongest One of All
  Which Is the Best Place?
Hautzig, Esther. At Home; A Visit in Four
  Languages
  In the Park; An Excursion in Four
  Languages
Jameson, Cynthia. The Clay Pot Boy
Polushkin, Maria. The Little Hen and the
  Giant
Prokofiev, Sergei Sergeievitch. Peter and
  the Wolf, illus. by Warren Chappell
  Peter and the Wolf, illus. by Frans
  Haacken
  Peter and the Wolf, illus. by Alan
  Howard
  Peter and the Wolf, illus. by Kozo
  Shimizu
Robbins, Ruth. Baboushka and the Three
  Kings
Slobodkina, Esphyr. Boris and His
  Balalaika
Tolstoy, Alekesi Nikolaevich. The Great
  Big Enormous Turnip
Varga, Judy. The Mare's Egg
Wiseman, Bernard. Little New Kangaroo
Zemach, Harve. The Speckled Hen; A
  Russian Nursery Rhyme
Zimmerman, Andrea Griffin. Yetta the
  Trickster

064.31 Foreign lands—Scotland

Alger, Leclaire. All in the Morning Early
  Always Room for One More
  Kellyburn Braes
Blegvad, Erik. Burnie's Hill
Jeffers, Susan. Wild Robin
Leaf, Munro. Wee Gillis
Sewall, Marcia. The Wee, Wee Mannie and
  the Big, Big Coo
Yolen, Jane. Greyling; A Picture Story for
  the Islands of Shetland

064.32 Foreign lands—South America

Aruego, José. Pilyo the Piranha
Gramatky, Hardie. Bolivar
Maestro, Giulio. The Tortoise's Tug of
  War
Maiorano, Robert. Francisco
Rockwell, Anne F. The Good Llama

Sotomayor, Antonio. Khasa Goes to the
  Fiesta
Surany, Anico. Ride the Cold Wind

064.33 Foreign lands—South Sea Islands

Aruego, José. Juan and the Asuangs
  Look What I Can Do
Mordvinoff, Nicolas. Coral Island

064.34 Foreign lands—Spain

Garcia Lorca, Federico. The Lieutenant
  Colonel and the Gypsy
Hautzig, Esther. At Home; A Visit in Four
  Languages
  In the Park; An Excursion in Four
  Languages
Leaf, Munro. The Story of Ferdinand the
  Bull
Oleson, Claire. For Pepita, an Orange Tree

064.35 Foreign lands—Sweden

Beskow, Elsa Maartman. Children of the
  Forest
  Pelle's New Suit
  Peter's Adventures in Blueberry Land
Lindgren, Astrid Ericsson. Christmas in the
  Stable
  The Tomten
  The Tomten and the Fox
Lindgren, Astrid Ericsson, and Wikland,
  Ilon. Christmas in Noisy Village
Lindman, Maj Jan. Flicka, Ricka, Dicka and
  a Little Dog
  Flicka, Ricka, Dicka and the New Dotted
  Dress
  Flicka, Ricka, Dicka and Their New
  Skates
  Flicka, Ricka, Dicka Bake a Cake
  Sailboat Time
  Snipp, Snapp, Snurr and the Buttered
  Bread
  Snipp, Snapp, Snurr and the Magic
  Horse
  Snipp, Snapp, Snurr and the Reindeer
  Snipp, Snapp, Snurr and the Seven
  Dogs
  Snipp, Snapp, Snurr and the Yellow
  Sled
Peterson, Hans. Erik and the Christmas
  Horse
Westerberg, Christine. The Cap That
  Mother Made
Zemach, Harve. Nail Soup

064.36 Foreign lands—Switzerland

Carigiet, Alois. The Pear Tree, the Birch
  Tree and the Barberry Bush
Chönz, Selina. A Bell for Ursli

Florina and the Wild Bird
The Snowstorm
Freeman, Don. Ski Pup
Weil, Lisl. Bitzli and the Big Bad Wolf

064.37 Foreign lands—Thailand

Ayer, Jacqueline Brandford. Nu Dang and
His Kite
The Paper Flower Tree
A Wish for Little Sister
Northrop, Mili. The Watch Cat

064.38 Foreign lands—Turkey

Walker, Barbara K. Teeny-Tiny and the
Witch-Woman

064.39 Foreign lands—Tyrol

Bemelmans, Ludwig. Hansi

064.40 Foreign lands—Ukraine

Goldfrank, Helen Colodny. An Egg Is for
Wishing
Lisowski, Gabriel. How Tevye Became a
Milkman
Tresselt, Alvin R. The Mitten
Ushinsky, Konstantin. How a Shirt Grew in
the Field

064.41 Foreign lands—Vatican City

Lawrence, John D. Pope Leo's Elephant

065 Foreign languages

Alger, Leclaire. Kellyburn Braes
Blue, Rose. I Am Here: Yo Estoy Aqui
Diska, Pat. Andy Says Bonjour!
Feelings, Muriel L. Jambo Means Hello; A
Swahili Alphabet Book
Monjo Means One; A Swahili Counting
Book
Frasconi, Antonio. See Again, Say Again
See and Say
Gunning, Monica. The Two Georges: Los
Dos Jorges
Hautzig, Esther. At Home; A Visit in Four
Languages
In the Park; An Excursion in Four
Languages
Henrioud, Charles. Mr. Noah and the
Animals. Monsieur Noe et les
Animaux
The House That Jack Built. La Maison que
Jacques a Batie
Jaynes, Ruth. Tell Me Please! What's That?
Joslin, Sesyle. Baby Elephant Goes to
China
Baby Elephant's Trunk

Senor Baby Elephant, the Pirate
Keats, Ezra Jack. My Dog Is Lost!
Matsutani, Miyoko. How the Withered
Trees Blossomed
Maury, Inez. My Mother the Mail Carrier:
Mi Mama la Cartera
Moore, Lilian. Papa Albert
Mother Goose. Mother Goose in French;
Poesies de la vraie Mere Oie
Mother Goose in Spanish. Poesias de la
Madre Oca
Rimes de la Mere Oie
Rider, Alex. A la Ferme. At the Farm
Chez nous. At Our House
Sasaki, Jeannie, and Uyeda, Frances.
Chocho Is for Butterfly
Serfozo, Mary. Welcome Roberto!
Bienvenido, Roberto!
Simon, Norma. What Do I Say?
Steiner, Charlotte. A Friend Is "Amie"
Uchida, Yoshiko. The Rooster Who
Understood Japanese
Vacheron, Edith, and Kahl, Virginia
Caroline. Here Is Henri!
More about Henri!
Ward, Leila. I Am Eyes; Ni Macho

066 Forest, woods

Arneson, D. J. Secret Places
Beskow, Elsa Maartman. Children of the
Forest
Carrick, Carol, and Carrick, Donald. A
Clearing in the Forest
Ets, Marie Hall. Another Day
In the Forest
Leister, Mary. The Silent Concert
Lipkind, William, and Mordvinoff, Nicolas.
The Boy and the Forest
Martin, Patricia Miles. Sylvester Jones and
the Voice in the Forest
Miklowitz, Gloria D. Save That Raccoon!
Miles, Miska. The Fox and the Fire
Peet, Bill. Big Bad Bruce
Schick, Eleanor. A Surprise in the Forest
Slobodkin, Louis. Melvin, the Moose Child
Tresselt, Alvin R. The Little Lost Squirrel
Wahl, Jan. The Five in the Forest

067 Format, unusual

Carle, Eric. Secret Birthday Message
The Very Hungry Caterpillar
Watch Out! A Giant!
Chwast, Seymour. The House That Jack
Built
Emberley, Edward Randolph. Ed
Emberley's Amazing Look Through
Book
Goodall, John Strickland. The Adventures
of Paddy Pork

The Ballooning Adventures of Paddy
Pork
Creepy Castle
An Edwardian Christmas
An Edwardian Summer
Jacko
The Midnight Adventures of Kelly, Dot
and Esmeralda
Naughty Nancy
Paddy Pork's Holiday
Paddy's Evening Out
Shrewbettina's Birthday
The Story of an English Village
The Surprise Picnic
Lewis, Stephen. Zoo City
Munari, Bruno. The Circus in the Mist
The Elephant's Wish
Jimmy Has Lost His Cap
Tic, Tac and Toc
Who's There? Open the Door
Newell, Peter. Topsys and Turvys
Rey, Hans Augusto. Anybody at Home?
How Do You Get There?
See the Circus
Where's My Baby?
Scarry, Richard McClure. Egg in the Hole
Book
Steiner, Charlotte, and Burlingham, Mary.
The Climbing Book
Taback, Simms. Joseph Had a Little
Overcoat
Tison, Annette, and Taylor, Talus. The
Adventures of the Three Colors
Animal Hide and Seek
Inside and Outside
Waber, Bernard. The Snake, a Very Long
Story
Walters, Marguerite. The City-Country
ABC
Wilkin, Eloise Burns. Ladybug, Ladybug
and Other Nursery Rhymes
Youldon, Gillian. Colors
Numbers
Shapes
Sizes

068 Friendship

Aldridge, Josephine Haskell. The Best of
Friends
Anderson, Paul S. Red Fox and the
Hungry Tiger
Anglund, Joan Walsh. Cowboy and His
Friend
A Friend Is Someone Who Likes You
Ardizzone, Edward Jeffrey Irving. Tim
and Lucy Go to Sea
Aruego, José. The King and His Friends
Baker, Betty. Partners
Battles, Edith. One to Teeter-Totter
Baylor, Byrd. Guess Who My Favorite
Person Is

Beim, Jerrold. The Swimming Hole
Beim, Lorraine Levy, and Beim, Jerrold.
Two Is a Team
Bell, Norman. Linda's Air Mail Letter
Bonsall, Crosby Newell. It's Mine! A
Greedy Book
Piggle
Brandenberg, Franz. Nice New Neighbors
Breinburg, Petronella. Shawn Goes to
School
Briggs, Raymond. The Snowman
Brown, Myra Berry. Best Friends
First Night Away from Home
Burningham, John Mackintosh. The
Friend
Carle, Eric. Do You Want to Be My
Friend?
Carrick, Malcolm. Today Is Shrew's Day
Chorao, Kay. Molly's Lies
Clifton, Lucille B. Everett Anderson's
Friend
Three Wishes
Cohen, Miriam. Best Friends
Will I Have a Friend?
Conford, Ellen. Why Can't I Be William?
Conta, Marcia Maher, and Reardon,
Maureen. Feelings Between Friends
Coontz, Otto. The Quiet House
Coville, Bruce, and Coville, Katherine. The
Foolish Giant
Dauer, Rosamond. Bullfrog Builds a
House
Delton, Judy. Three Friends Find Spring
de Paola, Thomas Anthony. Andy (That's
My Name)
De Regniers, Beatrice Schenk. May I Bring
a Friend?
Drdek, Richard E. Horace the Friendly
Octopus
Duvoisin, Roger Antoine. The Crocodile in
the Tree
Periwinkle
Petunia
Petunia and the Song
Petunia, I Love You!
Fassler, Joan. Boy with a Problem
Fatio, Louise. The Happy Lion
Flory, Jane. We'll Have a Friend for Lunch
Gelman, Rita Golden. Dumb Joey
Ginsburg, Mirra. The Fox and the Hare
Gordon, Shirley. Crystal Is My Friend
Crystal Is the New Girl
Graham, Al. Timothy Turtle
Hallinan, Patrick K. That's What a Friend
Is
Hanson, Joan. I Don't Like Timmy
Helena, Ann. The Lie
Hickman, Martha Whitmore. My Friend
William Moved Away
Hoban, Russell Conwell. A Bargain for
Frances
Best Friends for Frances

Hoff, Sydney. A Walk Past Ellen's House
  Who Will Be My Friends?
Hoffman, Phyllis. Steffie and Me
Hogrogian, Nonny. The Hermit and Harry
  and Me
Horvath, Betty F. Will the Real Tommy
  Wilson Please Stand Up?
Iwamatsu, Jun. The Youngest One
Iwasaki, Chihiro. Will You Be My Friend?
Jaynes, Ruth. Friends, Friends, Friends
Jewell, Nancy. Try and Catch Me
Kantrowitz, Mildred. I Wonder If Herbie's
  Home Yet
Keats, Ezra Jack. A Letter to Amy
  Peter's Chair
Kingman, Lee. Peter's Long Walk
Kishida, Eriko. The Lion and the Bird's
  Nest
Kopczynski, Anna. Jerry and Ami
Kotzwinkle, William. The Day the Gang
  Got Rich
  Up the Alley with Jack and Joe
Krahn, Fernando. The Great Ape
Krasilovsky, Phyllis. The Shy Little Girl
Kraus, Robert. The Three Friends
  The Trouble with Spider
Krauss, Ruth. A Good Man and His Good
  Wife
  A Hole Is to Dig
  I'll Be You and You Be Me
Lexau, Joan M. Cathy Is Company
Lionni, Leo. Alexander and the Wind-Up
  Mouse
  Fish Is Fish
  Little Blue and Little Yellow
Lipkind, William, and Mordvinoff, Nicolas.
  The Two Reds
Lobel, Arnold Stark. Days with Frog and
  Toad
  Frog and Toad All Year
  Frog and Toad Are Friends
  Frog and Toad Together
Lund, Doris Herold. You Ought to See
  Herbert's House
Lystad, Mary. That New Boy
MacGregor, Ellen. Mr. Pingle and Mr.
  Buttonhouse
Mallett, Anne. Here Comes Tagalong
Mandry, Kathy. The Cat and the Mouse
  and the Mouse and the Cat
Marshall, James. George and Martha
  George and Martha Encore
  George and Martha One Fine Day
  George and Martha Rise and Shine
  The Guest
  Speedboat
Mayer, Mercer. A Boy, a Dog, a Frog, and
  a Friend
  A Boy, a Dog and a Frog
  Frog, Where Are You?
Miles, Betty. Having a Friend

Miller, Edna Anita. Mousekin Finds a
  Friend
Minarik, Else Holmelund. Little Bear's
  Friend
Morrow, Suzanne Stark. Inatuck's Friend
Numeroff, Laura Joffe. Amy for Short
Pearson, Susan. Everybody Knows That!
Peet, Bill. Eli
Politi, Leo. Mr. Fong's Toy Shop
Raskin, Ellen. A & The, or William T. C.
  Baumgarten Comes to Town
Rubin, Jeff, and Rael, Rick. Baseball
  Brothers
Schreiber, Georges. Bambino Goes Home
Schulman, Janet. The Big Hello
Sharmat, Marjorie Weinman. Burton and
  Dudley
  Gladys Told Me to Meet Her Here
  I'm Not Oscar's Friend Any More
  Mitchell Is Moving
  Scarlet Monster Lives Here
Sherman, Ivan. I Do Not Like It When My
  Friend Comes to Visit
Slobodkin, Louis. Dinny and Danny
  One Is Good, but Two Are Better
Smaridge, Norah Antoinette. Peter's Tent
Spang, Gunter. Clelia and the Little
  Mermaid
Steadman, Ralph. The Bridge
Steig, William. Amos and Boris
Steiner, Charlotte. A Friend Is "Amie"
Steptoe, John. Stevie
Stevens, Carla. Stories from a Snowy
  Meadow
Stevenson, James. Wilfred the Rat
  The Worst Person in the World
Sugita, Yutaka. Helena the Unhappy
  Hippopotamus
Taylor, Mark. Old Blue, You Good Dog
  You
Tripp, Paul. The Strawman Who Smiled
  by Mistake
Udry, Janice May. Let's Be Enemies
Venable, Alan. The Checker Players
Viorst, Judith. Rosie and Michael
Waber, Bernard. The House on 88th
  Street
  Ira Sleeps Over
  Lovable Lyle
Wiesner, William. Tops
Wildsmith, Brian. The Lazy Bear
Williams, Barbara. Kevin's Grandma
Wittman, Sally Christensen. Pelly and Peak
  A Special Trade
Wooley, Catherine. Gus Was a Friendly
  Ghost
  The Popcorn Dragon
Yeoman, John. Mouse Trouble
Zion, Gene. The Meanest Squirrel I Ever
  Met
Zolotow, Charlotte Shapiro. The Hating
  Book

Hold My Hand
Janey
My Friend John
The Three Funny Friends
The Unfriendly Book
The White Marble

069 Games

Agostinelli, Maria Enrica. I Know
   Something You Don't Know
Ahlberg, Janet, and Ahlberg, Allan. Each
   Peach Pear Plum; An "I Spy" Story
Alexander, Martha G. We Never Get to Do
   Anything
Anglund, Joan Walsh. The Brave Cowboy
   Cowboy's Secret Life
Applebaum, Neil. Is There a Hole in Your
   Head?
Aruego, José. Look What I Can Do
Battles, Edith. One to Teeter-Totter
Baylor, Byrd. Guess Who My Favorite
   Person Is
Beach, Stewart. Good Morning, Sun's Up
Behrens, June York. Can.You Walk the
   Plank?
Bonsall, Crosby Newell. The Day I Had to
   Play with My Sister
   Piggle
Brown, Margaret Wise. Indoor Noisy Book
Byars, Betsy Cromer. Go and Hush the
   Baby
Carroll, Ruth Robinson. Where's the
   Bunny?
Charlip, Remy. Where Is Everybody?
Cohen, Peter Zachary. Authorized Autumn
   Charts of the Upper Red Canoe
   River Country
Cooney, Barbara. A Garland of Games and
   Other Diversions
Craig, M. Jean. Boxes
Delaney, Ned. One Dragon to Another
de Paola, Thomas Anthony. Andy (That's
   My Name)
De Regniers, Beatrice Schenk. What Can
   You Do with a Shoe?
Emberley, Edward Randolph. Klippity
   Klop
Erickson, Phoebe. Uncle Debunkel or
   Barely Believable Bear
The Farmer in the Dell
Fleisher, Robbin. Quilts in the Attic
Fox, Dorothea Warren. Follow Me the
   Leader
French, Fiona Mary. Hunt the Thimble
Glovach, Linda. The Little Witch's Black
   Magic Book of Games
Go Tell Aunt Rhody, illus. by Aliki
   Liacouras Brandenberg
Go Tell Aunt Rhody, illus. by Robert Mead
   Quackenbush
Hahn, Hannelore. Take a Giant Step

Hillert, Margaret. Play Ball
Hoban, Russell Conwell. How Tom Beat
   Captain Najork and His Hired
   Sportsmen
Hoff, Sydney. The Littlest Leaguer
Hurd, Edith Thacher. Last One Home Is a
   Green Pig
Jameson, Cynthia. A Day with Whisker
   Wickles
Johnson, Elizabeth. All in Free but Janey
Kahn, Joan. Seesaw
Keeshan, Robert. She Loves Me, She Loves
   Me Not
Koch, Dorothy Clarke. I Play at the Beach
Krauss, Ruth. The Bundle Book
   Mama, I Wish I Was Snow. Child,
   You'd Be Very Cold
Kroll, Steven. The Tyrannosaurus Game
Lexau, Joan M. Every Day a Dragon
Lipkind, William, and Mordvinoff, Nicolas.
   Sleepyhead
Livermore, Elaine. Find the Cat
   Lost and Found
   One to Ten Count Again
Maestro, Giulio. The Tortoise's Tug of
   War
Martin, Patricia Miles. Rolling the Cheese
Merrill, Jean, and Scott, Frances Gruse.
   How Many Kids Are Hiding on My
   Block?
Montgomerie, Norah Mary, comp. This
   Little Pig Went to Market; Play
   Rhymes
Mother Goose. London Bridge Is Falling
   Down, illus. by Edward Randolph
   Emberley
   London Bridge Is Falling Down!, illus.
   by Peter Spier
   Mother Goose in Hieroglyphics
Munari, Bruno. The Birthday Present
Oxenbury, Helen. The Queen and Rosie
   Randall
Peppé, Rodney. Odd One Out
   Rodney Peppé's Puzzle Book
Raebeck, Lois. Who Am I?
Rockwell, Norman. Counting Book
Sandberg, Inger, and Sandberg, Lasse.
   What Little Anna Saved
Selsam, Millicent Ellis. Is This a Baby
   Dinosaur? And Other Science Picture
   Puzzles
Shaw, Charles Green. The Blue Guess
   Book
   The Guess Book
   It Looked Like Spilt Milk
Siewert, Margaret, and Savage, Kathleen.
   Bear Hunt
Sivulich, Sandra Stroner. I'm Going on a
   Bear Hunt
Steig, William. The Bad Speller
Steiner, Charlotte. Five Little Finger
   Playmates

Red Ridinghood's Little Lamb
Taylor, Mark. Old Blue, You Good Dog You
Thwaite, Ann. The Day with the Duke
Tison, Annette, and Taylor, Talus. Animal Hide and Seek
Ueno, Noriko. Elephant Buttons
Ungerer, Tomi. One, Two, Where's My Shoe?
  Snail Where Are You?
Venable, Alan. The Checker Players
Wildsmith, Brian. Brian Wildsmith's Puzzles
Withers, Carl. Tale of a Black Cat
Withers, Carl, adapter. The Wild Ducks and the Goose
Woodcock, Louise Phinney. Guess Who Lives Here
  Hi Ho! Three in a Row
Wooley, Catherine. The Little House; A New Math Story-Game
Yudell, Lynn Deena. Make a Face
Zacharis, Boris. But Where Is the Green Parrot?
Zion, Gene. Hide and Seek Day
  Jeffie's Party

070 Gangs, clubs

Alexander, Sue. Seymour the Prince
Kotzwinkle, William. The Day the Gang Got Rich
Myrick, Mildred. The Secret Three

071 Ghosts

Alexander, Sue. More Witch, Goblin and Ghost Stories
Aruego, José. Juan and the Asuangs
Benchley, Nathaniel. A Ghost Named Fred
Bright, Robert. Georgie
  Georgie and the Noisy Ghost
  Georgie and the Robbers
  Georgie Goes West
  Georgie to the Rescue
  Georgie's Christmas Carol
  Georgie's Halloween
Coombs, Patricia. Dorrie and the Screebit Ghost
Friedrich, Priscilla, and Friedrich, Otto. The Marshmallow Ghosts
Galdone, Joanna. The Tailypo, a Ghost Story
Hirsh, Marilyn Joyce. Deborah the Dybbuk, a Ghost Story
Johnston, Tony. Four Scary Stories
Lexau, Joan M. Millicent's Ghost
Raskin, Ellen. Ghost in a Four-Room Apartment
Rockwell, Anne F. A Bear, a Bobcat and Three Ghosts

The Bump in the Night
Sandberg, Inger, and Sandberg, Lasse. Little Ghost Godfry
Schulman, Janet. Jack the Bum and the Haunted House
Seuling, Barbara. The Teeny Tiny Woman
Wooley, Catherine. Gus and the Baby Ghost
  Gus Was a Christmas Ghost
  Gus Was a Friendly Ghost
  Gus Was a Gorgeous Ghost
  What's a Ghost Going to Do?
Zemach, Margot. The Little Tiny Woman

072 Giants

Bodwell, Gaile. The Long Day of the Giants
Bolliger, Max. The Giants' Feast
Bradfield, Roger. Giants Come in Different Sizes
Carle, Eric. Watch Out! A Giant!
Coville, Bruce, and Coville, Katherine. The Foolish Giant
De Regniers, Beatrice Schenk. The Giant Story
Du Bois, William Pène. Giant Otto
  Otto and the Magic Potatoes
  Otto at Sea
  Otto in Africa
  Otto in Texas
Elkin, Benjamin. Lucky and the Giant
Greene, Ellin. The Pumpkin Giant
Herrmann, Frank. The Giant Alexander
  The Giant Alexander and the Circus
Hillert, Margaret. The Magic Beans
The History of Mother Twaddle and the Marvelous Achievements of Her Son Jack
Kahl, Virginia Caroline. Giants, Indeed!
Kraus, Robert. The Little Giant
Lawrence, John D. The Giant of Grabbist
Lobel, Arnold Stark. Giant John
McNeill, Janet. The Giant's Birthday
Minarik, Else Holmelund. The Little Giant Girl and the Elf Boy
Polushkin, Maria. The Little Hen and the Giant
Sherman, Ivan. I Am a Giant
Ungerer, Tomi. Zeralda's Ogre
Wiesner, William. Tops
Yolen, Jane. The Giants' Farm

073 Glasses

Brown, Marc Tolon. Arthur's Eyes
Goodsell, Jane. Katie's Magic Glasses
Kessler, Leonard P. Mr. Pine's Mixed-Up Signs
Lasson, Robert. Orange Oliver
Raskin, Ellen. Spectacles
Wise, William. The Cowboy Surprise

Wooley, Catherine. Mr. Turtle's Magic Glasses

074 Goblins

Alexander, Sue. More Witch, Goblin and Ghost Stories
Coombs, Patricia. Dorrie and the Goblin
Haley, Gail Diana Einhart. Go Away, Stay Away
Johnston, Tony. Four Scary Stories
Lifton, Betty Jean. Joji and the Amanojaku
Tobias, Tobi. Chasing the Goblins Away

075 Gypsies

Anderson, Clarence William. Blaze and the Gypsies
Bemelmans, Ludwig. Madeline and the Gypsies
Garcia Lorca, Federico. The Lieutenant Colonel and the Gypsy
Kellogg, Steven. The Mystery of the Magic Green Ball
Mahy, Margaret. Mrs. Discombobulous

076 Hair

Abisch, Roslyn Kroop. The Pumpkin Heads
Bright, Robert. I Like Red
Freeman, Don. Mop Top
Hair
Kunhardt, Dorothy. Billy the Barber
Scott, Natalie. Firebrand, Push Your Hair Out of Your Eyes
Taylor, Sydney. Mr. Barney's Beard
Townsend, Kenneth. Felix the Bald-Headed Lion

077 Handicaps

Brightman, Alan. Like Me
Fanshawe, Elizabeth. Rachel
Fassler, Joan. Howie Helps Himself One Little Girl
Gage, Wilson. Down in the Boondocks
Lasker, Joseph Leon. He's My Brother
Sobol, Harriet L. My Brother Steven Is Retarded
Stein, Sara Bonnett. About Handicaps
White, Paul. Janet at School
Wolf, Bernard. Don't Feel Sorry for Paul

077.01 Handicaps—blindness

Keats, Ezra Jack. Apartment 3
Litchfield, Ada Bassett. A Cane in Her Hand
Quigley, Lillian. The Blind Men and the Elephant

Saxe, John Godfrey. The Blind Men and the Elephant
Yolen, Jane. The Seeing Stick

077.02 Handicaps—deafness

Litchfield, Ada Bassett. A Button in Her Ear
Mother Goose. Nursery Rhymes from Mother Goose in Signed English
Wahl, Jan. Jamie's Tiger
Wolf, Bernard. Anna's Silent World

078 Hawaii

Funai, Mamoru R. Moke and Poki in the Rain Forest

079 Health

Leaf, Munro. Health Can Be Fun
Radlauer, Ruth Shaw. Of Course, You're a Horse!
Wilson, Charles Christopher, and others. Our Good Health

080 Helicopters

Drummond, Violet H. The Flying Postman
Firmin, Peter. Basil Brush Goes Flying
Taylor, Mark. Henry Explores the Mountains
Zaffo, George J. The Big Book of Real Airplanes

081 Hibernation

Bartoli, Jennifer. Snow on Bear's Nose
Brustlein, Janice. Little Bear's Christmas
Cohen, Carol L. Wake Up Groundhog!
de Paola, Thomas Anthony. Four Stories for Four Seasons
Evans, Eva Knox. Sleepy Time
Fisher, Aileen Lucia. Where Does Everyone Go?
Freeman, Don. Bearymore
Kepes, Juliet. Frogs, Merry
Kesselman, Wendy Ann. Time for Jody
Krauss, Ruth. The Happy Day
Marino, Dorothy Bronson. Buzzy Bear Goes South
Marshall, James. What's the Matter with Carruthers?
Miller, Edna Anita. Mousekin's Golden House
Parker, Nancy Winslow. The Ordeal of Byron B. Blackbear
Piers, Helen. Grasshopper and Butterfly
Watson, Wendy. Has Winter Come?
Whitney, Julie. Bears Are Sleeping

082 Hieroglyphics

Mother Goose. Mother Goose in
    Hieroglyphics

083 Holidays

Glovach, Linda. The Little Witch's Black
    Magic Book of Disguises
Kumin, Maxine W. Follow the Fall
Meyer, Elizabeth. The Blue China Pitcher
Sotomayor, Antonio. Khasa Goes to the
    Fiesta
Zolotow, Charlotte Shapiro. Over and Over

083.01 Holidays—April Fools' Day

Krahn, Fernando. April Fools

083.02 Holidays—Chinese New Year

Cheng, Hou-Tien. Chinese New Year
Handforth, Thomas Scofield. Mei Li
Politi, Leo. Moy Moy
Young, Evelyn. Tale of Tai

083.03 Holidays—Christmas

Abisch, Roslyn Kroop. 'Twas in the Moon
    of Wintertime
Adams, Adrienne. The Christmas Party
Adshead, Gladys L. Brownies—It's
    Christmas
Andersen, Hans Christian. The Little
    Match Girl
Anglund, Joan Walsh. Christmas Is a Time
    of Giving
    The Cowboy's Christmas
Ardizzone, Aingelda. The Night Ride
Armour, Richard Willard. The Year Santa
    Went Modern
Bach, Alice. The Day After Christmas
Balet, Jan B. The Gift; A Portuguese
    Christmas Tale
Balian, Lorna. Bah! Humbug?
Barry, Robert E. Mr. Willowby's Christmas
    Tree
Bemelmans, Ludwig. Hansi
Bolognese, Donald Alan. A New Day
Bonsall, Crosby Newell. Twelve Bells for
    Santa
Briggs, Raymond. Father Christmas
    Father Christmas Goes on Holiday
Bright, Robert. Georgie's Christmas Carol
Bring a Torch, Jeannette, Isabella
Brock, Emma Lillian. The Birds' Christmas
    Tree
Brown, Margaret Wise. The Little Fir Tree
    On Christmas Eve
    A Pussycat's Christmas
    The Steamroller
Brown, Palmer. Something for Christmas

Bruna, Dick. Christmas
    The Christmas Book
Brunhoff, Jean de. Babar and Father
    Christmas
Brustlein, Janice. Little Bear's Christmas
Chalmers, Mary Eileen. A Christmas Story
    Merry Christmas, Harry
Clifton, Lucille B. Everett Anderson's
    Christmas Coming
de Paola, Thomas Anthony. The Christmas
    Pageant
    The Clown of God
Devlin, Wende, and Devlin, Harry.
    Cranberry Christmas
Domanska, Janina. Din Dan Don, It's
    Christmas
    I Saw a Ship A-Sailing
Donaldson, Lois. Karl's Wooden Horse
Duvoisin, Roger Antoine. The Christmas
    Whale
    .One Thousand Christmas Beards
    Petunia's Christmas
Erickson, Russell E. Warton's Christmas
    Eve Adventure
Ets, Marie Hall. Nine Days to Christmas
Fatio, Louise. Anna, the Horse
Fenner, Carol Elizabeth. Christmas Tree
    on the Mountain
Foster, Marian Curtis. The Journey of
    Bangwell Putt
Fraser, James Howard. Los Posadas, a
    Christmas Story
Freeman, Jean Todd. Cynthia and the
    Unicorn
The Friendly Beasts and A Partridge in a
    Pear Tree
Gackenbach, Dick. Claude the Dog
Gannett, Ruth Stiles. Katie and the Sad
    Noise
Geisel, Theodor Seuss. How the Grinch
    Stole Christmas
Glovach, Linda. The Little Witch's
    Christmas Book
Goodall, John Strickland. An Edwardian
    Christmas
Haywood, Carolyn. A Christmas Fantasy
Hoban, Lillian. Arthur's Christmas Cookies
Hoban, Russell Conwell. Emmet Otter's
    Jug-Band Christmas
    The Mole Family's Christmas
Hoff, Sydney. Santa's Moose
    Where's Prancer?
Holm, Mayling Mack. A Forest Christmas
Holmes, Efner Tudor. The Christmas Cat
Hurd, Edith Thacher. Christmas Eve
Hutchins, Pat. The Best Train Set Ever
    The Silver Christmas Tree
Jaynes, Ruth. Melinda's Christmas Stocking
Joslin, Sesyle. Baby Elephant and the
    Secret Wishes
Jüchen, Aurel von. The Holy Night, the
    Story of the First Christmas

Kahl, Virginia Caroline. Gunhilde's
Christmas Booke
Plum Pudding for Christmas
Keats, Ezra Jack. The Little Drummer Boy
Kent, Jack. The Christmas Pinata
Kerr, Judith. Mog's Christmas
Knight, Hilary. Angels and Berries and
Candy Canes
Knotts, Howard Clayton. The Lost
Christmas
Krahn, Fernando. The Biggest Christmas
Tree on Earth
How Santa Claus Had a Long and
Difficult Journey Delivering His
Presents
Kroll, Steven. Santa's Crash-Bang
Christmas
Langstaff, John Meredith, and Groves-
Raines, Antony. On Christmas Day in
the Morning!
Lathrop, Dorothy Pulis. An Angel in the
Woods
Leisk, David Johnson. Harold at the North
Pole
Linch, Elizabeth Johanna. Samson
Lindgren, Astrid Ericsson. Christmas in the
Stable
Lindgren, Astrid Ericsson, and Wikland,
Ilon. Christmas in Noisy Village
Lipkind, William, and Mordvinoff, Nicolas.
The Christmas Bunny
Low, Joseph. The Christmas Grump
McGinley, Phyllis. How Mrs. Santa Claus
Saved Christmas
McPhail, David. Mistletoe
Marshall, James. Miss Dog's Christmas
Treat
Martin, Judith, and Charlip, Remy. The
Tree Angel
Miller, Edna Anita. Mousekin's Christmas
Eve
Moeschlin, Elsa. Red Horse
Monsell, Helen Albee. Paddy's Christmas
Moore, Clement Clarke. The Night Before
Christmas, illus. by Gyo Fujikawa
The Night Before Christmas, illus. by
Gustaf Tenggren
The Night Before Christmas, illus. by
Tasha Tudor
A Visit from St. Nicholas; 'Twas the
Night Before Christmas
Nussbaumer, Mares, and Nussbaumer,
Paul. Away in a Manger
Partch, Virgil Franklin. The Christmas
Cookie Sprinkle Snitcher
Peet, Bill. Countdown to Christmas
Peterson, Hans. Erik and the Christmas
Horse
Politi, Leo. The Nicest Gift
Robbins, Ruth. Baboushka and the Three
Kings
Rowand, Phyllis. Every Day in the Year

Schenk, Esther M. Christmas Time
Schick, Alice, and Schick, Joel. Santaberry
and the Snard
Seignobosc, Françoise. Noel for Jeanne-
Marie
Steiner, Charlotte, and Burlingham, Mary.
The Climbing Book
Stephenson, Dorothy. The Night It Rained
Toys
Stern, Elsie-Jean. Wee Robin's Christmas
Song
Thompson, George Selden. The Mice, the
Monks and the Christmas Tree
Tippett, James Sterling. Counting the Days
Shadow and the Stocking
Trent, Robbie. The First Christmas
Tudor, Tasha. The Doll's Christmas
Snow Before Christmas
Tutt, Kay Cunningham. And Now We Call
Him Santa Claus
Twelve Days of Christmas (English folk
song). Brian Wildsmith's The Twelve
Days of Christmas
Jack Kent's Twelve Days of Christmas
The Twelve Days of Christmas
Ungerer, Tomi. Christmas Eve at the
Mellops'
Wahl, Jan. The Muffletumps' Christmas
Party
Wells, Rosemary. Morris's Disappearing
Bag; A Christmas Story
Wenning, Elizabeth. The Christmas Mouse
Wild, Robin, and Wild, Jocelyn. Little Pig
and the Big Bad Wolf
Wooley, Catherine. Gus Was a Christmas
Ghost
The Puppy Who Wanted a Boy
Zakhoder, Boris. How a Piglet Crashed the
Christmas Party
Zolotow, Charlotte Shapiro. The Beautiful
Christmas Tree

083.04 Holidays—Easter

Adams, Adrienne. The Easter Egg Artists
Armour, Richard Willard. The Adventures
of Egbert the Easter Egg
Balian, Lorna. Humbug Rabbit
Benchley, Nathaniel. The Strange
Disappearance of Arthur Cluck
Brown, Margaret Wise. The Golden Egg
Book
The Runaway Bunny
Duvoisin, Roger Antoine. Easter Treat
Friedrich, Priscilla, and Friedrich, Otto.
The Easter Bunny That Overslept
Goldfrank, Helen Colodny. An Egg Is for
Wishing
Green, Adam. The Funny Bunny Factory
Heyward, Dubose. The Country Bunny
and the Little Gold Shoes
Kraus, Robert. Daddy Long Ears

Littlefield, William. The Whiskers of Ho Ho

Maril, Lee. Mr. Bunny Paints the Eggs

Priolo, Pauline. Piccolina and the Easter Bells

Tresselt, Alvin R. The World in the Candy Egg

Tudor, Tasha. A Tale for Easter

Wahl, Jan. The Five in the Forest

Weil, Lisl. The Candy Egg Bunny

Wiese, Kurt. Happy Easter

Wooley, Catherine. The Horse with the Easter Bonnet

Young, Miriam Burt. Miss Suzy's Easter Surprise

Zolotow, Charlotte Shapiro. The Bunny Who Found Easter
  Mr. Rabbit and the Lovely Present

083.05 Holidays—Fourth of July

Shortall, Leonard W. One Way; A Trip with Traffic Signs

Zion, Gene. The Summer Snowman

083.06 Holidays—Groundhog Day

Cohen, Carol L. Wake Up Groundhog!

Coombs, Patricia. Tilabel

Hamberger, John F. This Is the Day

Kesselman, Wendy Ann. Time for Jody

Leisk, David Johnson. Will Spring Be Early?

Palazzo, Tony. Waldo the Woodchuck

083.07 Holidays—Halloween

Adams, Adrienne. A Woggle of Witches

Anderson, Lonzo. Halloween Party

Balian, Lorna. Humbug Witch

Battles, Edith. The Terrible Trick or Treat

Beim, Jerrold. Sir Halloween

Benarde, Anita. The Pumpkin Smasher

Bridwell, Norman. Clifford's Halloween

Bright, Robert. Georgie's Halloween

Calhoun, Mary. The Witch of Hissing Hill
  Wobble the Witch Cat

Carrick, Carol. Old Mother Witch

Coombs, Patricia. Dorrie and the Halloween Plot

Devlin, Wende, and Devlin, Harry. Old Witch Rescues Halloween

Embry, Margaret. The Blue-Nosed Witch

Foster, Doris Van Liew. Tell Me, Mr. Owl

Freeman, Don. Space Witch
  Tilly Witch

Friedrich, Priscilla, and Friedrich, Otto. The Marshmallow Ghosts

Glovach, Linda. The Little Witch's Halloween Book

Greene, Ellin. The Pumpkin Giant

Hellsing, Lennart. The Wonderful Pumpkin

Hurd, Edith Thacher. The So-So Cat

Hutchins, Pat. The Best Train Set Ever

Kahl, Virginia Caroline. Gunhilde and the Halloween Spell

Kroll, Steven. The Candy Witch

Low, Alice. The Witch Who Was Afraid of Witches
  Witch's Holiday

Massey, Jeanne. The Littlest Witch

Miller, Edna Anita. Mousekin's Golden House

Mooser, Stephen. The Ghost with the Halloween Hiccups

Nicoll, Helen. Meg and Mog

Ott, John, and Coley, Pete. Peter Pumpkin

Prelutsky, Jack. It's Halloween

Preston, Edna Mitchell. One Dark Night

Rockwell, Anne F. A Bear, a Bobcat and Three Ghosts

Schulman, Janet. Jack the Bum and the Halloween Handout

Scott, Ann Herbert. Let's Catch a Monster

Shaw, Richard. The Kitten in the Pumpkin Patch

Slobodkin, Louis. Trick or Treat

Vigna, Judith. Everyone Goes as a Pumpkin

Von Hippel, Ursula. The Craziest Halloween

Wahl, Jan. The Muffletumps' Halloween Scare
  Pleasant Fieldmouse's Halloween Party

Watson, Jane Werner. Which Is the Witch?

Wooley, Catherine. Gus Was a Gorgeous Ghost

Young, Miriam Burt. The Witch Mobile

Zolotow, Charlotte Shapiro. A Tiger Called Thomas

083.08 Holidays—New Year's Day

Brustlein, Janice. Little Bear's New Year's Party

083.09 Holidays—St. Patrick's Day

Brustlein, Janice. Little Bear Marches in the St. Patrick's Day Parade

Calhoun, Mary. The Hungry Leprechaun

Zimelman, Nathan. To Sing a Song as Big as Ireland

083.10 Holidays—Thanksgiving

Balian, Lorna. Sometimes It's Turkey—Sometimes It's Feathers

Brustlein, Janice. Little Bear's Thanksgiving

Child, Lydia Maria. Over the River and Through the Wood

Dalgliesh, Alice. The Thanksgiving Story
Devlin, Wende. Cranberry Thanksgiving
Glovach, Linda. The Little Witch's
    Thanksgiving Book
Ipcar, Dahlov Zorach. Hard Scrabble
    Harvest
Lowitz, Sadyebeth, and Lowitz, Anson. The
    Pilgrims' Party
Ott, John, and Coley, Pete. Peter Pumpkin
Tresselt, Alvin R. Autumn Harvest
Williams, Barbara. Chester Chipmunk's
    Thanksgiving

083.11 Holidays—Valentine's Day

Cohen, Miriam. Bee My Valentine!
Keeshan, Robert. She Loves Me, She Loves
    Me Not
Krahn, Fernando. Little Love Story
Schweninger, Ann. The Hunt for Rabbit's
    Galosh

083.12 Holidays—Washington's Birthday

Bulla, Clyde Robert. Washington's
    Birthday

084 Hospitals

Bemelmans, Ludwig. Madeline
Bruna, Dick. Miffy in the Hospital
Collier, James Lincoln. Danny Goes to the
    Hospital
Marino, Barbara Pavis. Eric Needs Stitches
Pope, Billy N., and Emmons, Ramona
    Ware. Your World: Let's Visit the
    Hospital
Rey, Margret Elisabeth Waldstein. Curious
    George Goes to the Hospital
Shay, Arthur. What Happens When You
    Go to the Hospital
Sobol, Harriet L. Jeff's Hospital Book
Sonneborn, Ruth A. I Love Gram
Stein, Sara Bonnett. A Hospital Story
Stone, Bernard. Emergency Mouse
Tamburine, Jean. I Think I Will Go to the
    Hospital
Waber, Bernard. Lyle and the Birthday
    Party
Weber, Alfons. Elizabeth Gets Well
Wolde, Gunilla. Betsy and the Doctor

085 Hotels

Greene, Carla. A Hotel Holiday
Mahy, Margaret. Rooms for Rent
Parkin, Rex. The Red Carpet
Stevenson, James. The Sea View Hotel

086 Houses

Adler, David A. The House on the Roof
Alger, Leclaire. Always Room for One
    More
Arkin, Alan. Tony's Hard Work Day
Becker, Edna. Nine Hundred Buckets of
    Paint
Binzen, Bill. Alfred Goes House Hunting
Brown, Marcia. The Neighbors
Burton, Virginia Lee. The Little House
Calhoun, Mary. Mrs. Dog's Own House
Clymer, Eleanor Lowenton. The Tiny
    Little House
Colman, Hila. Peter's Brownstone House
Curry, Nancy. The Littlest House
Dauer, Rosamond. Bullfrog Builds a
    House
De Regniers, Beatrice Schenk. A Little
    House of Your Own
Erickson, Phoebe. Just Follow Me
Feder, Paula Kurzband. Where Does the
    Teacher Live?
Firmin, Peter. Basil Brush Builds a House
Fisher, Aileen Lucia. Best Little House
Geisel, Theodor Seuss. Come Over to My
    House
    In a People House
Green, Mary McBurney. Everybody Has a
    House and Everybody Eats
Hoberman, Mary Ann. A House Is a
    House for Me
Hoff, Sydney. Stanley
Homes
Jaynes, Ruth. The Biggest House
Kaune, Merriman B. My Own Little House
Kirk, Barbara. Grandpa, Me and Our
    House in the Tree
Krauss, Ruth. A Very Special House
Lent, Blair. From King Boggen's Hall to
    Nothing at All
Low, Alice. David's Windows
Miles, Betty. A House for Everyone
Mizumura, Kazue. If I Built a Village
Palmer, Helen Marion. Why I Built the
    Boogle House
Pinkwater, Manus. Big Orange Splot
Rey, Hans Augusto. Anybody at Home?
Scarry, Richard McClure. Is This the
    House of Mistress Mouse?
Schlein, Miriam. My House
Schulman, Janet. Jack the Bum and the
    Haunted House
Shapp, Martha, and Shapp, Charles. Let's
    Find Out about Houses
Shecter, Ben. Emily, Girl Witch of New
    York
Tison, Annette, and Taylor, Talus. Inside
    and Outside
Tudor, Bethany. Samuel's Tree House
Wooley, Catherine. What's a Ghost Going
    to Do?

087 Humor

Aesopus. The Miller, His Son, and Their Donkey
Allard, Harry. The Stupids Step Out
Allard, Harry, and Marshall, James. The Stupids Have a Ball
Andersen, Hans Christian. The Emperor's New Clothes, illus. by Erik Blegvad
    The Emperor's New Clothes, illus. by Virginia Lee Burton
    The Emperor's New Clothes, illus. by Jack Delano and Irene Delano
    The Emperor's New Clothes, illus. by Monika Laimgruber
Anno, Mitsumasa. Dr. Anno's Magical Midnight Circus
    Topsy-Turvies
    Upside-Downers
Armour, Richard Willard. Animals on the Ceiling
Aulaire, Ingri Mortenson d', and Aulaire, Edgar Parin d'. Don't Count Your Chicks
Baker, Betty. Three Fools and a Horse
Behn, Harry. What a Beautiful Noise
Bishop, Claire Huchet. The Man Who Lost His Head
Bodecker, Nils Mogens, translator. "It's Raining," Said John Twaining
Bonne, Rose. I Know an Old Lady
Borten, Helen. Do You Go Where I Go?
Bossom, Naomi. A Scale Full of Fish and Other Turnabouts
Bowden, Joan Chase. The Bean Boy
Bradfield, Roger. The Flying Hockey Stick
Brecht, Bertolt. Uncle Eddie's Moustache
Brooke, Leonard Leslie. Johnny Crow's Garden
    Johnny Crow's New Garden
    Johnny Crow's Party
Brown, Jeff. Flat Stanley
Bryant, Sara Cone. Epaminondas and His Auntie
Burroway, Janet. The Truck on the Track
Byfield, Barbara Ninde. The Haunted Churchbell
Calhoun, Mary. Old Man Whickutt's Donkey
    The Traveling Ball of String
Cameron, Polly. A Child's Book of Nonsense
Caudill, Rebecca, and Ayars, James. Contrary Jenkins
Cerf, Bennett Alfred. Bennett Cerf's Book of Animal Riddles
    Bennett Cerf's Book of Laughs
    Bennett Cerf's Book of Riddles
    More Riddles
Chalmers, Audrey. Hundreds and Hundreds of Pancakes
Charlip, Remy. Arm in Arm

    Fortunately
Charlip, Remy, and Joyner, Jerry. Thirteen
Charlip, Remy, and Supree, Burton. "Mother, Mother I Feel Sick"
Christian, Mary Blount. Nothing Much Happened Today
Ciardi, John. I Met a Man
Copp, Jim. Martha Matilda O'Toole
Daugherty, James Henry. Andy and the Lion
Dennis, Suzanne E. Answer Me That
de Paola, Thomas Anthony. Bill and Pete
    Strega Nona
De Regniers, Beatrice Schenk. May I Bring a Friend?
Dodgson, Charles Lutwidge. Jabberwocky
Duvoisin, Roger Antoine. Petunia's Christmas
Ellentuck, Shan. Did You See What I Said? A Sunflower as Big as the Sun
Emmett, Fredrick Rowland. New World for Nellie
Erickson, Phoebe. Uncle Debunkel or Barely Believable Bear
Ets, Marie Hall. Beasts and Nonsense
    Mister Penny
Evans, Katherine. The Maid and Her Pail of Milk
    The Man, the Boy, and the Donkey
Farber, Norma. There Once Was a Woman Who Married a Man
Fenton, Edward. The Big Yellow Balloon
Flora, James. The Day the Cow Sneezed
    Grandpa's Farm
    My Friend Charlie
Freeman, Don. Forever Laughter
Frith, Michael K. I'll Teach My Dog 100 Words
A Frog He Would A-Wooing Go
Frog Went A-Courtin'
Fuchshuber, Annegert. The Wishing Hat
Gackenbach, Dick. The Pig Who Saw Everything
Geisel, Theodor Seuss. And to Think That I Saw It on Mulberry Street
    Bartholomew and the Oobleck
    Because a Little Bug Went Ka-choo!
    The Cat in the Hat
    The Cat in the Hat Beginner Book Dictionary
    The Cat in the Hat Comes Back!
    The Cat's Quizzer
    Come Over to My House
    Did I Ever Tell You How Lucky You Are?
    Dr. Seuss's ABC
    Dr. Seuss's Sleep Book
    The Foot Book
    Fox in Socks
    A Great Day for Up
    Green Eggs and Ham
    Happy Birthday to You

Hooper Humperdink...? Not Him!
Hop on Pop
Horton Hatches the Egg
Horton Hears a Who
How the Grinch Stole Christmas
I Can Lick 30 Tigers Today and Other
    Stories
I Can Read with My Eyes Shut!
I Can Write! A Book by Me, Myself,
    with a Little Help from Theo. LeSieg
I Had Trouble Getting to Solla Sollew
I Wish That I Had Duck Feet
If I Ran the Circus
If I Ran the Zoo
In a People House
The King's Stilts
The Lorax
McElligot's Pool
Marvin K. Mooney, Will You Please Go
    Now!
Mr. Brown Can Moo, Can You?
Oh Say Can You Say?
Oh, the Thinks You Can Think!
On Beyond Zebra
One Fish, Two Fish, Red Fish, Blue Fish
Please Try to Remember the First of
    Octember!
Scrambled Eggs Super!
The Shape of Me and Other Stuff
The Sneetches and Other Stories
Ten Apples Up on Top!
There's a Wocket in My Pocket!
Thidwick, the Big Hearted Moose
Wacky Wednesday
Gelman, Rita Golden. Hey, Kid
The Golden Goose
Hall, Donald. Andrew the Lion Farmer
Hart, Jeanne McGahey. Scareboy
Heide, Florence Parry. The Shrinking of
    Treehorn
Heilbroner, Joan. Robert the Rose Horse
Hirsh, Marilyn Joyce. Could Anything Be
    Worse?
Hoban, Russell Conwell. A Near Thing for
    Captain Najork
Holman, Felice. Victoria's Castle
Hutchins, Pat. Clocks and More Clocks
    Don't Forget the Bacon!
    Rosie's Walk
Jeschke, Susan. Firerose
Joslin, Sesyle. Dear Dragon and Other
    Useful Letter Forms for Young
    Ladies and Gentlemen, Engaged in
    Everyday Correspondence
    What Do You Do, Dear?
    What Do You Say, Dear?
Joyce, Irma. Never Talk to Strangers
Keats, Ezra Jack. Skates
Keenen, George. The Preposterous Week
Kent, Jack. Hoddy Doddy
Krahn, Fernando. April Fools
Krauss, Ruth. I'll Be You and You Be Me

This Thumbprint
Kumin, Maxine W. Speedy Digs Downside
    Up
La Fontaine, Jean de. The Miller, the Boy
    and the Donkey
Laurin, Anne. Little Things
Lear, Edward. The Dong with the
    Luminous Nose
    Edward Lear's Nonsense Book
    Lear's Nonsense Verses
    The Nutcrackers and the Sugar-Tongs
    The Pelican Chorus
    The Pobble Who Has No Toes
    The Quangle Wangle's Hat
    Whizz!
Leisk, David Johnson. Harold and the
    Purple Crayon
    Harold's Circus
    Upside Down
Lent, Blair. From King Boggen's Hall to
    Nothing at All
    John Tabor's Ride
Lobel, Arnold Stark. Lucille
    Mouse Tales
    A Treeful of Pigs
McGovern, Ann. Too Much Noise
McPhail, David. The Cereal Box
Maestro, Giulio. The Remarkable Plant in
    Apartment 4
Mahood, Kenneth. The Laughing Dragon
Mahy, Margaret. The Boy Who Was
    Followed Home
Marsh, Jeri. Hurrah for Alexander
Mayer, Mercer. The Queen Always
    Wanted to Dance
    What Do You Do with a Kangaroo?
Miles, Miska. Chicken Forgets
Miller, Albert. The Hungry Goat
Milne, Alan Alexander. Pooh's Quiz Book
Modell, Frank. Tooley! Tooley!
Moffett, Martha. A Flower Pot Is Not a
    Hat
Morrison, Sean. Is That a Happy
    Hippopotamus?
Myller, Rolf. How Big Is a Foot?
Nash, Ogden. The Adventures of Isabel
    The Animal Garden
    A Boy Is a Boy
Newell, Peter. Topsys and Turvys
Pack, Robert. Then What Did You Do?
Palmer, Helen Marion. A Fish Out of
    Water
    I Was Kissed by a Seal at the Zoo
Parish, Peggy. Amelia Bedelia
    Amelia Bedelia and the Surprise Shower
    Amelia Bedelia Helps Out
    Come Back, Amelia Bedelia
    Good Work, Amelia Bedelia
    Granny and the Desperadoes
    Granny and the Indians
    Granny, the Baby and the Big Gray
    Thing

Viorst, Judith. Sunday Morning
Waber, Bernard. How to Go about Laying
    an Egg
    Nobody Is Perfick
    A Rose for Mr. Bloom
    "You Look Ridiculous," Said the
        Rhinoceros to the Hippopotamus
Wahl, Jan. Cabbage Moon
Wiese, Kurt. Fish in the Air
Wiesner, William. Happy-Go-Lucky
    Too Many Cooks
    Turnabout
Willard, Nancy. Simple Pictures Are Best
Williams, Barbara. Jeremy Isn't Hungry
Williams, Jay. School for Sillies
Zemach, Harve. A Penny a Look
    The Tricks of Master Dabble
Zemach, Margot. Hush, Little Baby
    It Could Always Be Worse
Zimmerman, Andrea Griffin. Yetta the
    Trickster

088 Illness

Barrett, Judith. An Apple a Day
Brandenberg, Franz. I Wish I Was Sick,
    Too!
Brown, Margaret Wise. The Little Fir Tree
    When the Wind Blew
Carrick, Carol. Old Mother Witch
Charlip, Remy, and Supree, Burton.
    "Mother, Mother I Feel Sick"
Coombs, Patricia. Dorrie and the Witch
    Doctor
de Groat, Diane. Alligator's Toothache
Delton, Judy. It Happened on Thursday
Duvoisin, Roger Antoine. The Christmas
    Whale
Fern, Eugene. Pepito's Story
Fleischman, Albert Sidney. Kate's Secret
    Riddle
Gackenbach, Dick. Hattie Be Quiet, Hattie
    Be Good
Galbraith, Kathryn Osebold. Sports Are
    Special
Hurd, Edith Thacher. Johnny Lion's Bad
    Day
Hutchins, Pat. The Best Train Set Ever
Knotts, Howard Clayton. The Lost
    Christmas
Lerner, Marguerite Rush. Dear Little
    Mumps Child
    Michael Gets the Measles
    Peter Gets the Chickenpox
Lexau, Joan M. Benjie on His Own
Lobel, Arnold Stark. A Holiday for Mister
    Muster
McPhail, David. The Bear's Toothache
Maestro, Betsy, and Maestro, Giulio.
    Leopard Is Sick
Mann, Peggy. King Laurence the Alarm
    Clock

Marshall, James. Yummers!
Mayer, Mercer. Ah-choo
    Hiccup
Nourse, Alan Edward. Lumps, Bumps and
    Rashes; A Look at Kids' Diseases
Numeroff, Laura Joffe. Phoebe Dexter
    Has Harriet Peterson's Sniffles
Quackenbush, Robert Mead. Calling
    Doctor Quack
Seignobosc, Françoise. Biquette, the White
    Goat
Sharmat, Marjorie Weinman. I Want
    Mama
Shay, Arthur. What Happens When You
    Go to the Hospital
Sonneborn, Ruth A. I Love Gram
Stein, Sara Bonnett. A Hospital Story
Stephenson, Dorothy. How to Scare a Lion
Thurber, James. Many Moons
Tobias, Tobi. A Day Off
Trez, Denise, and Trez, Alain. The Royal
    Hiccups
Udry, Janice May. Mary Jo's Grandmother
Wahl, Jan. Jamie's Tiger
Weber, Alfons. Elizabeth Gets Well
Whitney, Alma Marshak. Just Awful
Williams, Barbara. Albert's Toothache
Wolde, Gunilla. Betsy and the Chicken Pox
    Betsy and the Doctor

089 Imagination

Abisch, Roslyn Kroop. Open Your Eyes
Alexander, Martha G. Bobo's Dream
Andersen, Hans Christian. The Emperor's
    New Clothes, illus. by Erik Blegvad
    The Emperor's New Clothes, illus. by
        Virginia Lee Burton
    The Emperor's New Clothes, illus. by
        Jack Delano and Irene Delano
    The Emperor's New Clothes, illus. by
        Monika Laimgruber
Anno, Mitsumasa. Anno's Alphabet
    Anno's Counting Book
    Anno's Journey
    Dr. Anno's Magical Midnight Circus
    Topsy-Turvies
    Upside-Downers
Armour, Richard Willard. Animals on the
    Ceiling
Behrens, June York. Can You Walk the
    Plank?
Bulette, Sara. The Elf in the Singing Tree
Burgess, Anthony. The Land Where the
    Ice Cream Grows
Burningham, John Mackintosh. Time to
    Get Out of the Bath, Shirley
    Would You Rather...
Chorao, Kay. Lester's Overnight
Cooper, Elizabeth K. The Fish from Japan

Craig, M. Jean. The Dragon in the Clock Box

De Regniers, Beatrice Schenk. Laura's Story
A Little House of Your Own
What Can You Do with a Shoe?

Devlin, Wende, and Devlin, Harry. Aunt Agatha, There's a Lion under the Couch!

Dobrin, Arnold Jack. Josephine's 'magination

Dorian, Marguerite. When the Snow Is Blue

Ets, Marie Hall. In the Forest

Fenner, Carol Elizabeth. Tigers in the Cellar

Fenton, Edward. Fierce John

Firmin, Peter. Basil Brush and a Dragon

Francis, Frank. The Magic Wallpaper

Freeman, Don. The Paper Party
Quiet! There's a Canary in the Library

Gackenbach, Dick. Harry and the Terrible Whatzit

Galbraith, Kathryn Osebold. Sports Are Special

Geisel, Theodor Seuss. And to Think That I Saw It on Mulberry Street
McElligot's Pool
Oh, the Thinks You Can Think!

Hanlon, Emily. What If a Lion Eats Me and I Fall into a Hippopotamus' Mud Hole?

Himler, Ronald Norbert. The Girl on the Yellow Giraffe

Hoban, Russell Conwell. Goodnight

Holl, Adelaide. My Father and I

Holman, Felice. Victoria's Castle

Hurd, Edith Thacher. The White Horse

Jewell, Nancy. Try and Catch Me

Johnson, Elizabeth. All in Free but Janey

Keats, Ezra Jack. Dreams
The Trip

Krauss, Ruth. A Moon or a Button
Open House for Butterflies
Somebody Else's Nut Tree, and Other Tales from Children
This Thumbprint
A Very Special House

Kroll, Steven. The Tyrannosaurus Game

Kumin, Maxine W. Follow the Fall

Kuskin, Karla Seidman. Which Horse Is William?

Leisk, David Johnson. Ellen's Lion
Harold and the Purple Crayon
Harold at the North Pole
Harold's Circus
Harold's Fairy Tale
Harold's Trip to the Sky
A Picture for Harold's Room

Lewis, Stephen. Zoo City

Lexau, Joan M. A House So Big

Lifton, Betty Jean. The Secret Seller

Löfgren, Ulf. The Wonderful Tree

Low, Joseph. Benny Rabbit and the Owl

McClintock, Marshall. What Have I Got?

McPhail, David. The Cereal Box
Mistletoe
The Train

Marceau, Marcel. The Story of Bip

Matus, Greta. Where Are You, Jason?

Mayer, Mercer. I Am a Hunter
Terrible Troll

Most, Bernard. If the Dinosaurs Came Back

Ness, Evaline. Sam, Bangs and Moonshine

Pack, Robert. How to Catch a Crocodile

Postma, Lidia. The Stolen Mirror

Radlauer, Ruth Shaw. Of Course, You're a Horse!

Raskin, Ellen. Franklin Stein
Spectacles

Reavin, Sam. Hurray for Captain Jane!

Reid, Alastair. Supposing

Ressner, Phil. Dudley Pippin

Rice, Inez. A Long Long Time
The March Wind

Roberts, Thom. Pirates in the Park

Russ, Lavinia. Alec's Sand Castle

Scharen, Beatrix. Gigin and Till

Scott, Ann Herbert. Big Cowboy Western

Sendak, Maurice. In the Night Kitchen
The Sign on Rosie's Door
Where the Wild Things Are

Shecter, Ben. Conrad's Castle
If I Had a Ship

Sherman, Ivan. I Am a Giant

Shulevitz, Uri. One Monday Morning

Sicotte, Virginia. A Riot of Quiet

Siepmann, Jane. The Lion on Scott Street

Skorpen, Liesel Moak. If I Had a Lion

Slobodkin, Louis. Clear the Track
Magic Michael

Steiner, Charlotte. Look What Tracy Found

Taniuchi, Kota. Trolley
Up on a Hilltop

Thomas, Ianthe. Walk Home Tired, Billy Jenkins

Tompert, Ann. Little Fox Goes to the End of the World

Udry, Janice May. Is Susan Here?

Velthuijs, Max. The Painter and the Bird

Viorst, Judith. My Mama Says There Aren't Any: Zombies, Ghosts, Vampires, Creatures, Demons, Monsters, Fiends, Goblins, or Things

Vogel, Ilse-Margret. The Don't Be Scared Book

Vreeken, Elizabeth. The Boy Who Would Not Say His Name

Warburg, Sandol Stoddard. The Thinking Book

Watson, Clyde. Midnight Moon
Watson, Jane Werner. The Tall Book of
    Make-Believe
Winthrop, Elizabeth. Bunk Beds
Wooley, Catherine. Andy and the Wild
    Worm
    Rockets Don't Go to Chicago, Andy
Young, Miriam Burt. Jellybeans for
    Breakfast
Zimelman, Nathan. Once When I Was Five
Zolotow, Charlotte Shapiro. A Father Like
    That
    When I Have a Little Girl
    When I Have a Son

089.01 Imagination—imaginary friends

Alexander, Martha G. And My Mean Old
    Mother Will Be Sorry, Blackboard
    Bear
    Blackboard Bear
    I Sure Am Glad to See You, Blackboard
    Bear
    I'll Protect You from the Jungle Beasts
Andrews, Frank Emerson. Nobody Comes
    to Dinner
Greenfield, Eloise. Me and Nessie
Hazen, Barbara Shook. The Gorilla Did It!
Hoff, Sydney. The Horse in Harry's Room
Jeschke, Susan. Angela and Bear
    The Devil Did It
Steiner, Charlotte. Lulu
Wooley, Catherine. Andy and His Fine
    Friends
Zolotow, Charlotte Shapiro. The Three
    Funny Friends

090 Insects and spiders

Aardema, Verna, reteller. Why Mosquitoes
    Buzz in People's Ears
Adelson, Leone. Please Pass the Grass
Barton, Byron. Buzz, Buzz, Buzz
Bees
Belpré, Pura. Perez and Martina
Bolliger, Max. The Fireflies
Brandenberg, Franz. Fresh Cider and
    Apple Pie
Cameron, Polly. "I Can't," Said the Ant
Carle, Eric. The Grouchy Ladybug
    The Very Hungry Caterpillar
Caudill, Rebecca. A Pocketful of Cricket
Chenery, Janet. Wolfie
Conklin, Gladys Plemon. Lucky Ladybugs
Delaney, A. The Butterfly
Delaney, Ned. One Dragon to Another
Du Bois, William Pène. Bear Circus
Eastman, Philip Day. Sam and the Firefly
Elkin, Benjamin. Why the Sun Was Late
Farber, Norma. Never Say Ugh to a Bug

Fisher, Aileen Lucia. We Went Looking
Freschet, Berniece. The Ants Go Marching
    The Web in the Grass
Galdone, Joanna. Honeybee's Party
Garelick, May. Where Does the Butterfly
    Go When It Rains?
Geisel, Theodor Seuss. Because a Little
    Bug Went Ka-choo!
George, Jean Craighead. All Upon a Stone
Graham, Margaret Bloy. Be Nice to
    Spiders
Hawes, Judy. Fireflies in the Night
Ipcar, Dahlov Zorach. Bug City
Jaynes, Ruth. That's What It Is!
Keller, Beverly. Fiona's Bee
Kepes, Juliet. Lady Bird, Quickly
Kimmel, Eric. Why Worry?
Knight, Hilary. A Firefly in a Fir Tree
Kraus, Robert. Ladybug! Ladybug!
    The Trouble with Spider
Lionni, Leo. Inch by Inch
Lobel, Arnold Stark. Grasshopper on the
    Road
McClintock, Marshall. A Fly Went By
McDermott, Gerald. Anansi the Spider
Mizumura, Kazue. If I Were a Cricket...
Myrick, Mildred. Ants Are Fun
Newbolt, Sir Henry John. Rilloby-Rill
Peet, Bill. The Ant and the Elephant
    The Gnats of Knotty Pine
Petie, Haris. Billions of Bugs
Piers, Helen. Grasshopper and Butterfly
Roscoe, William. The Butterfly's Ball
Rounds, Glen H. The Boll Weevil
Ryder, Joanne. Fireflies
Sargent, Robert. A Trick on a Lion
Schlein, Miriam. Fast Is Not a Ladybug
Selsam, Millicent Ellis. The Bug That Laid
    the Golden Eggs
    Terry and the Caterpillars
Terry, James Sterling. I Know Some
    Little Animals
Tippett, James Sterling. I Know Some
    Little Animals
Tison, Annette, and Taylor, Talus. Animal
    Hide and Seek
Waber, Bernard. A Firefly Named Torchy
Wagner, Jenny. Aranea
Wahl, Jan. Follow Me Cried Bee
Wiese, Kurt. The Dog, the Fox and the
    Fleas
Winter, Paula. The Bear and the Fly
Wong, Herbert H., and Vassel, Matthew F.
    My Ladybug
    Our Caterpillars

091 Islands

Brown, Margaret Wise. The Little Island
Burn, Doris. The Summerfolk
Kellogg, Steven. The Island of the Skog
McCloskey, Robert John. Time of Wonder
Mordvinoff, Nicolas. Coral Island

092 Jesters

Freeman, Don. Forever Laughter
Shecter, Ben. Hester the Jester
Thurber, James. Many Moons

093 Jewish culture

Adler, David A. The House on the Roof
Fassler, Joan. My Grandpa Died Today
Goffstein, Marilyn Brooks. Goldie the
  Dollmaker
Hirsh, Marilyn Joyce. Captain Jeri and
  Rabbi Jacob
  Could Anything Be Worse?
  Deborah the Dybbuk, a Ghost Story
  The Pink Suit
  The Rabbi and the Twenty-Nine
  Witches
  Where Is Yonkela?
Levy, Sara G. Mother Goose Rhymes for
  Jewish Children
Lisowski, Gabriel. How Tevye Became a
  Milkman
McDermott, Beverly Brodsky. The Golem,
  a Jewish Legend
Margalit, Avi. The Hebrew Alphabet Book
Segal, Lore Groszmann. Tell Me a Mitzi
  Tell Me a Trudy
Shulevitz, Uri. The Magician
Suhl, Yuri. Simon Boom Gives a Wedding
Zemach, Margot. It Could Always Be
  Worse

094 Kites

Ayer, Jacqueline Brandford. Nu Dang and
  His Kite
Brown, Marcia. The Little Carousel
Cooper, Elizabeth K. The Fish from Japan
Heller, George. Hiroshi's Wonderful Kite
Peet, Bill. Merle the High Flying Squirrel
Rey, Margret Elisabeth Waldstein. Curious
  George Flies a Kite
Titus, Eve. Anatole Over Paris
Uchida, Yoshiko. Sumi's Prize
Wiese, Kurt. Fish in the Air
Yolen, Jane. The Emperor and the Kite

095 Knights

Blake, Quentin. Snuff
Bradfield, Roger. A Good Knight for
  Dragons
Cretien, Paul D., Jr. Sir Henry and the
  Dragon
de Paola, Thomas Anthony. The
  Wonderful Dragon of Timlin
Emberley, Edward Randolph. Klippity
  Klop
Goodall, John Strickland. Creepy Castle
Holl, Adelaide. Sir Kevin of Devon

Ipcar, Dahlov Zorach. Sir Addlepate and
  the Unicorn
McCrea, James, and McCrea, Ruth. The
  Story of Olaf
Mayer, Mercer. Terrible Troll
Peet, Bill. Cowardly Clyde
  How Droofus the Dragon Lost His
  Head
Trez, Denise, and Trez, Alain. The Little
  Knight's Dragon

096 Language

Battles, Edith. What Does the Rooster Say,
  Yoshio?
Berson, Harold. A Moose Is Not a Moose
Bossom, Naomi. A Scale Full of Fish and
  Other Turnabouts
Ellentuck, Shan. Did You See What I Said?
Goodspeed, Peter. Hugh and Fitzhugh
Hunt, Bernice Kohn. Your Ant Is a Which,
  Fun with Homophones
Johnston, Johanna. Speak Up, Edie
Leaf, Munro. Grammar Can Be Fun
Merriam, Eve. A Gaggle of Geese
Parish, Peggy. Amelia Bedelia
  Amelia Bedelia and the Surprise Shower
  Amelia Bedelia Helps Out
  Come Back, Amelia Bedelia
  Good Work, Amelia Bedelia
  Play Ball, Amelia Bedelia
  Teach Us, Amelia Bedelia
Rand, Ann, and Rand, Paul. Sparkle and
  Spin
Richardson, Jack E., Jr. and others. Six in
  a Mix
Sage, Michael. If You Talked to a Boar
Sattler, Helen Roney. Train Whistles; A
  Language in Code
Scarry, Richard McClure. Richard Scarry's
  Best Story Book Ever
Steig, William. The Bad Speller
Steptoe, John. My Special Best Words
Wiesner, William. The Tower of Babel

097 Laundry

Behrens, June York. Soo Ling Finds a Way
Freeman, Don. A Pocket for Corduroy
Ormondroyd, Edward. Theodore

098 Left-handedness

Lerner, Marguerite Rush. Lefty: The Story
  of Left-Handedness

099 Letters

Bell, Norman. Linda's Air Mail Letter
Geisel, Theodor Seuss. On Beyond Zebra
Joslin, Sesyle. Dear Dragon and Other
  Useful Letter Forms for Young

Ladies and Gentlemen, Engaged in
Everyday Correspondence
Keats, Ezra Jack. A Letter to Amy

100 Libraries

Baugh, Dolores M., and Pulsifer, Marjorie
P. Let's Take a Trip
Bonsall, Crosby Newell. Tell Me Some
More
Daly, Maureen. Patrick Visits the Library
Daugherty, James Henry. Andy and the
Lion
Felt, Sue. Rosa-Too-Little
Freeman, Don. Quiet! There's a Canary in
the Library
Gay, Zhenya. Look!
Little, Mary E. ABC for the Library
Ricardo and the Puppets
Rockwell, Anne F. I Like the Library
Sauer, Julia Lina. Mike's House

101 Lighthouses

Myrick, Mildred. The Secret Three
Strahl, Rudi. Sandman in the Lighthouse
Swift, Hildegarde Hoyt, and Ward, Lynd
Kendall. The Little Red Lighthouse
and the Great Gray Bridge

102 Machines

Bate, Norman. Who Built the Bridge?
Who Built the Highway?
Baugh, Dolores M., and Pulsifer, Marjorie
P. Let's Take a Trip
Behn, Harry. All Kinds of Time
Bradfield, Roger. The Flying Hockey Stick
Brown, Margaret Wise. The Steamroller
Burton, Virginia Lee. Katy and the Big
Snow
Mike Mulligan and His Steam Shovel
Du Bois, William Pène. Lazy Tommy
Pumpkinhead
Hoban, Tana. Dig, Drill, Dump, Fill
Holl, Adelaide. The ABC of Cars, Trucks
and Machines
Ipcar, Dahlov Zorach. One Horse Farm
Israel, Marion Louise. The Tractor on the
Farm
Löfgren, Ulf. The Traffic Stopper That
Became a Grandmother Visitor
Retan, Walter. The Snowplow That Tried
to Go South
The Steam Shovel That Wouldn't Eat
Dirt
Rockwell, Anne F., and Rockwell, Harlow.
Machines
Steadman, Ralph. The Little Red
Computer
Wolde, Gunilla. Betsy and the Vacuum
Cleaner

Young, Miriam Burt. If I Drove a Tractor
Zaffo, George J. The Big Book of Real
Building and Wrecking Machines

103 Magic

Alexander, Sue. Marc the Magnificent
Anderson, Lonzo, and Adams, Adrienne.
Two Hundred Rabbits
Babbitt, Samuel F. The Forty-Ninth
Magician
Banigan, Sharon Stearns. Circus Magic
Berson, Harold. The Thief Who Hugged a
Moonbeam
Beskow, Elsa Maartman. Peter's
Adventures in Blueberry Land
Bowden, Joan Chase. Who Took the Top
Hat Trick?
Brenner, Barbara. The Flying Patchwork
Quilt
Brown, Marcia. Once a Mouse
Chapman, Carol. Barney Bipple's Magic
Dandelions
Coombs, Patricia. Dorrie and the Amazing
Magic Elixir
Dorrie and the Blue Witch
Dorrie and the Dreamyard Monsters
Dorrie and the Weather-Box
Dorrie and the Witch's Imp
Dorrie and the Wizard's Spell
Dorrie's Magic
The Magic Pot
Corbett, Scott. Dr. Merlin's Magic Shop
The Foolish Dinosaur Fiasco
The Great Custard Pie Panic
Coville, Bruce, and Coville, Katherine. The
Foolish Giant
Delton, Judy. Brimhall Turns to Magic
de Paola, Thomas Anthony. Big Anthony
and the Magic Ring
Strega Nona
Dines, Glen. A Tiger in the Cherry Tree
Dukas, Paul Abraham. The Sorcerer's
Apprentice
Eckert, Horst. Joshua and the Magic Fiddle
The Magic Auto
Fuchshuber, Annegert. The Wishing Hat
Gackenbach, Dick. Ida Fanfanny
Gág, Wanda. Nothing at All
Galdone, Paul. The Magic Porridge Pot
Hazen, Barbara Shook, and Ungerer,
Tomi. The Sorcerer's Apprentice
Hochman, Sandra. The Magic Convention
Jeschke, Susan. Angela and Bear
Firerose
Rima and Zeppo
Kennedy, Richard. The Porcelain Man
Kepes, Juliet. The Seed That Peacock
Planted
Kimmel, Margaret Mary. Magic in the Mist
Kroll, Steven. The Candy Witch
Fat Magic

Kumin, Maxine W. The Wizard's Tears
Langstaff, John Meredith. The Two
  Magicians
Leichman, Seymour. The Wicked Wizard
  and the Wicked Witch
Lindman, Maj Jan. Snipp, Snapp, Snurr
  and the Magic Horse
Lipkind, William, and Mordvinoff, Nicolas.
  The Boy and the Forest
  The Magic Feather Duster
Lobel, Anita. The Troll Music
Lopshire, Robert Martin. It's Magic?
McDermott, Gerald. The Magic Tree; A
  Tale from the Congo
Mayer, Mercer. Mrs. Beggs and the Wizard
  A Special Trick
Ness, Evaline. Tom Tit Tot
Nicoll, Helen. Meg and Mog
  Meg at Sea
  Meg on the Moon
  Meg's Eggs
Nolan, Dennis. Wizard McBean and His
  Flying Machine
Oksner, Robert M. The Incompetent
  Wizard
Peet, Bill. Countdown to Christmas
Rockwell, Anne F. The Story Snail
  The Wonderful Eggs of Furicchia
Sargent, Robert. A Trick on a Lion
Shecter, Ben. Emily, Girl Witch of New
  York
Shulevitz, Uri. The Magician
Slobodkin, Louis. Magic Michael
Steig, William. The Amazing Bone
  Caleb and Kate
  Sylvester and the Magic Pebble
Thaler, Mike. Madge's Magic Show
Tresselt, Alvin R. The World in the Candy
  Egg
Trez, Denise, and Trez, Alain. Maila and
  the Flying Carpet
Turkle, Brinton Cassady. The Magic of
  Millicent Musgrave
Turska, Krystyna. The Magician of Cracow
Ungerer, Tomi. The Hat
Varga, Judy. Janko's Wish
Wooley, Catherine. Mr. Turtle's Magic
  Glasses
Wyler, Rose. Spooky Tricks

104 Mardi Gras

Lionni, Leo. The Greentail Mouse

105 Marriage, interracial

Adoff, Arnold. Black Is Brown Is Tan

106 Merry-go-rounds

Brown, Marcia. The Little Carousel
Charles, Robert H. The Roundabout Turn

Perera, Lydia. Frisky
Watson, Jane Werner. The Marvelous
  Merry-Go-Round

107 Middle ages

Kahl, Virginia Caroline. The Baron's Booty
  The Duchess Bakes a Cake
  Gunhilde and the Halloween Spell
  Gunhilde's Christmas Booke
  The Habits of Rabbits

108 Missions

Politi, Leo. Song of the Swallows

110 Monsters

Brown, Marcia. The Little Carousel
Rockwell, Anne F. Gogo's Pay Day
Rose, Anne K. As Right as Right Can Be
Slobodkin, Louis. Moon Blossom and the
  Golden Penny
Turkle, Brinton Cassady. Rachel and
  Obadiah
Viorst, Judith. Alexander, Who Used to Be
  Rich Last Sunday
Watson, Nancy Dingman. Annie's
  Spending Spree
Watts, Mabel. The Boy Who Listened to
  Everyone
Wondriska, William. Mr. Brown and Mr.
  Gray

110 Monsters

Aruego, José. Juan and the Asuangs
Babbitt, Natalie. The Something
Bang, Molly G. Wiley and the Hairy Man
Coombs, Patricia. Dorrie and the
  Dreamyard Monsters
  Molly Mullett
Crowe, Robert L. Clyde Monster
Fassler, Joan. The Man of the House
Flora, James. Leopold, the See-Through
  Crumbpicker
Gackenbach, Dick. Harry and the Terrible
  Whatzit
Gág, Wanda. The Funny Thing
Goodall, John Strickland. Creepy Castle
Johnston, Tony. Four Scary Stories
Kahl, Virginia Caroline. Giants, Indeed!
  How Do You Hide a Monster?
Kellogg, Steven. The Island of the Skog
  The Mysterious Tadpole
Kitt, Tamara. Sam and the Impossible
  Thing
Krahn, Fernando. The Mystery of the
  Giant Footprints
Lifton, Betty Jean. Goodnight Orange
  Monster

Mayer, Mercer. Liza Lou and the Yeller
    Belly Swamp
    Mrs. Beggs and the Wizard
    A Special Trick
    Terrible Troll
    There's a Nightmare in My Closet
Memling, Carl. What's in the Dark?
Mosel, Arlene. The Funny Little Woman
Niland, Deborah. ABC of Monsters
Parish, Peggy. Zed and the Monsters
Peck, Richard. Monster Night at
    Grandma's House
Peet, Bill. Cyrus the Unsinkable Sea
    Serpent
Rudolph, Marguerita. I Am Your
    Misfortune
Schroder, William. Pea Soup and Serpents
Sendak, Maurice. Seven Little Monsters
    Where the Wild Things Are
Sharmat, Marjorie Weinman. Scarlet
    Monster Lives Here
Stevenson, James. "Could Be Worse"
Tallon, Robert. The Thing in Dolores'
    Piano
Ungerer, Tomi. The Beast of Monsieur
    Racine
    Zeralda's Ogre
Viorst, Judith. My Mama Says There
    Aren't Any: Zombies, Ghosts,
    Vampires, Creatures, Demons,
    Monsters, Fiends, Goblins, or Things
Wagner, Jenny. The Bunyip of Berkeley's
    Creek
Wahl, Jan. Frankenstein's Dog
Wallace, Daisy. Monster Poems
Watson, Pauline. Wriggles, the Little
    Wishing Pig
Zemach, Harve. The Judge

111 Moon

Balet, Jan B. Amos and the Moon
Brown, Margaret Wise. Goodnight, Moon
    Wait Till the Moon Is Full
Dayrell, Elphinstone. Why the Sun and the
    Moon Live in the Sky
Eckert, Horst. Joshua and the Magic Fiddle
Freeman, Mae, and Freeman, Ira. You Will
    Go to the Moon
Fuchs, Eric. Journey to the Moon
Garelick, May. Look at the Moon
Lewis, Claudia I. When I Go to the Moon
Lifton, Betty Jean. The Rice-Cake Rabbit
McDermott, Gerald. Anansi the Spider
Merrill, Jean, and Solbert, Romaine G.
    Emily Emerson's Moon
Nicoll, Helen. Meg on the Moon
Olsen, Ib Spang. The Boy in the Moon
Preston, Edna Mitchell. Squawk to the
    Moon, Little Goose
Talbot, Toby. A Bucketful of Moon
Thurber, James. Many Moons

Turska, Krystyna. The Magician of Cracow
Udry, Janice May. The Moon Jumpers
Ungerer, Tomi. Moon Man
Wahl, Jan. Cabbage Moon
Watson, Clyde. Midnight Moon
Wildsmith, Brian. What the Moon Saw
Yamaguchi, Marianne Illenberger. Two
    Crabs and the Moonlight
Ziegler, Ursina. Squaps the Moonling

112 Morning

Beach, Stewart. Good Morning, Sun's Up
Brown, Margaret Wise. The Quiet Noisy
    Book
Craig, M. Jean. Spring Is Like the Morning
    What Did You Dream?
Dennis, Wesley. Flip and the Morning
Lapp, Eleanor J. In the Morning Mist
McNulty, Faith. When a Boy Wakes Up in
    the Morning
Mann, Peggy. King Laurence the Alarm
    Clock
Shulevitz, Uri. Dawn
Tresselt, Alvin R. Wake Up, City!
    Wake Up, Farm!
Tworkov, Jack. The Camel Who Took a
    Walk
Yabuki, Seiji. I Love the Morning
Zolotow, Charlotte Shapiro. Wake Up and
    Good Night

113 Motorcycles

McPhail, David. Captain Toad and the
    Motorbike
Zimnik, Reiner. The Bear on the
    Motorcycle

114 Moving

Becker, Edna. Nine Hundred Buckets of
    Paint
Berg, Jean Horton. The O'Learys and
    Friends
Brandenberg, Franz. Nice New Neighbors
    What Can You Make of It?
Brown, Myra Berry. Pip Moves Away
Fisher, Aileen Lucia. Best Little House
Hickman, Martha Whitmore. My Friend
    William Moved Away
Hoff, Sydney. Who Will Be My Friends?
Ilsley, Velma. M Is for Moving
Isadora, Rachel. The Potters' Kitchen
Lexau, Joan M. The Rooftop Mystery
Lystad, Mary. That New Boy
Schlein, Miriam. My House
Schulman, Janet. The Big Hello
Sharmat, Marjorie Weinman. Mitchell Is
    Moving
Tobias, Tobi. Moving Day

Watson, Wendy. Moving
Zolotow, Charlotte Shapiro. Janey

115 Museums

Cohen, Miriam. Lost in the Museum
Freeman, Don. Norman the Doorman
Gramatky, Hardie. Hercules
Hoff, Sydney. Danny and the Dinosaur
Wooley, Catherine. Gus and the Baby
    Ghost
    Gus Was a Christmas Ghost

116 Music

Abisch, Roslyn Kroop. 'Twas in the Moon
    of Wintertime
Alexander, Cecil Frances. All Things
    Bright and Beautiful
Alger, Leclaire. Always Room for One
    More
    Kellyburn Braes
Behn, Harry. What a Beautiful Noise
Bonne, Rose. I Know an Old Lady
Bring a Torch, Jeannette, Isabella
Carle, Eric. I See a Song
Cathon, Laura E. Tot Botot and His Little
    Flute
Conover, Chris. Six Little Ducks
Eckert, Horst. Joshua and the Magic Fiddle
    Tonight at Nine
The Farmer in the Dell
The Fox Went Out on a Chilly Night
Freeman, Don, and Freeman, Lydia. Pet of
    the Met
The Friendly Beasts and A Partridge in a
    Pear Tree
Go Tell Aunt Rhody, illus. by Robert Mead
    Quackenbush
Goffstein, Marilyn Brooks. A Little
    Schubert
Grifalconi, Ann. The Toy Trumpet
Hoban, Russell Conwell. Emmet Otter's
    Jug-Band Christmas
Horvath, Betty F. Jasper Makes Music
Ipcar, Dahlov Zorach. The Cat Came Back
Ivimey, John William. The Complete
    Version of Ye Three Blind Mice
Kahl, Virginia Caroline. Droopsi
    Gunhilde's Christmas Booke
Keats, Ezra Jack. Apartment 3
Kepes, Juliet. The Seed That Peacock
    Planted
Kimmel, Eric. Why Worry?
Langstaff, John Meredith. Oh, A-Hunting
    We Will Go
    Ol' Dan Tucker
    Soldier, Soldier, Won't You Marry Me?
    The Swapping Boy
    The Two Magicians

Langstaff, John Meredith, and Groves-
    Raines, Antony. On Christmas Day in
    the Morning!
Lear, Edward. Edward Lear's Nonsense
    Book
    The Pelican Chorus
Lenski, Lois L. At Our House
    Davy and His Dog
    Davy Goes Places
    Debbie and Her Grandma
    A Dog Came to School
    I Like Winter
    I Went for a Walk
Lionni, Leo. Geraldine, the Music Mouse
Lobel, Anita. The Troll Music
Löfgren, Ulf. The Flying Orchestra
McCloskey, Robert John. Lentil
McMillan, Bruce. The Alphabet Symphony
Maril, Lee. Mr. Bunny Paints the Eggs
Miller, Albert. The Hungry Goat
Mother Goose. Mother Goose's Rhymes
    and Melodies
    Songs from Mother Goose
Newbolt, Sir Henry John. Rilloby-Rill
Nussbaumer, Mares, and Nussbaumer,
    Paul. Away in a Manger
Oberhansli, Gertrud. Sleep, Baby, Sleep
Old MacDonald Had a Farm, illus. by Mel
    Crawford
Old MacDonald Had a Farm, illus. by
    Abner Graboff
Old MacDonald Had a Farm, illus. by
    Robert Mead Quackenbush
Poston, Elizabeth. Baby's Song Book
Prokofiev, Sergei Sergeievitch. Peter and
    the Wolf, illus. by Warren Chappell
    Peter and the Wolf, illus. by Frans
        Haacken
    Peter and the Wolf, illus. by Alan
        Howard
    Peter and the Wolf, illus. by Kozo
        Shimizu
Quackenbush, Robert Mead. Clementine
    The Man on the Flying Trapeze
    Pop! Goes the Weasel and Yankee
        Doodle
    She'll Be Comin' 'Round the Mountain
    Skip to My Lou
    There'll Be a Hot Time in the Old
        Town Tonight
Rey, Hans Augusto. Humpty Dumpty and
    Other Mother Goose Songs
Robbins, Ruth. Baboushka and the Three
    Kings
Rounds, Glen H. The Boll Weevil
    Casey Jones
    The Strawberry Roan
    Sweet Betsy from Pike
Schackburg, Richard. Yankee Doodle
Schick, Eleanor. One Summer Night
Seeger, Peter. Foolish Frog
The Sesame Street Song Book

Slobodkin, Louis. The Wide-Awake Owl
Spier, Peter. The Erie Canal
Steig, William. Roland the Minstrel Pig
Stern, Elsie-Jean. Wee Robin's Christmas Song
Tabor, Troy E. Mother Goose in Hawaii
Tallon, Robert. The Thing in Dolores' Piano
Taylor, Mark. The Bold Fisherman
    Old Blue, You Good Dog You
Titus, Eve. Anatole and the Piano
    Anatole and the Pied Piper
Twelve Days of Christmas (English folk song). Brian Wildsmith's The Twelve Days of Christmas
    Jack Kent's Twelve Days of Christmas
    The Twelve Days of Christmas
Watson, Wendy. Fisherman Lullabies
Watts, Bernadette. Brigitte and Ferdinand, a Love Story
Wells, Rosemary. A Song to Sing, O!
Wenning, Elizabeth. The Christmas Mouse
Wheeler, Opal. Sing Mother Goose
Whitney, Julie. Bears Are Sleeping
Widdecombe Fair; An Old English Folk Song
Wilder, Alec. Lullabies and Night Songs
Zemach, Harve. Mommy Buy Me a China Doll
Zemach, Margot. Hush, Little Baby
Zimelman, Nathan. To Sing a Song as Big as Ireland

117 Mythical creatures

Aruego, José. The King and His Friends
Asbjørnsen, Peter Christen. The Three Billy Goats Gruff, illus. by Paul Galdone
    The Three Billy Goats Gruff, illus. by William Stobbs
Asbjørnsen, Peter Christen, and Moe, Jørgen Engebretsen. The Three Billy Goats Gruff
Aulaire, Ingri Mortenson d', and Aulaire, Edgar Parin d'. The Terrible Troll-Bird
Freeman, Jean Todd. Cynthia and the Unicorn
Gramatky, Hardie. Nikos and the Sea God
Hillert, Margaret. The Three Goats
Ipcar, Dahlov Zorach. Sir Addlepate and the Unicorn
Keeshan, Robert. She Loves Me, She Loves Me Not
Mayer, Mercer. Terrible Troll
Peet, Bill. Cyrus the Unsinkable Sea Serpent
    The Pinkish, Purplish, Bluish Egg
Schroder, William. Pea Soup and Serpents
Spang, Gunter. Clelia and the Little Mermaid

Todaro, John, and Ellen, Barbara. Phillip the Flower-Eating Phoenix
Wagner, Jenny. The Bunyip of Berkeley's Creek

118 Names

Alexander, Martha G. Sabrina
Beim, Jerrold. The Smallest Boy in Class
Benton, Robert. Little Brother, No More
Denney, Diana. The Little Red Engine Gets a Name
de Paola, Thomas Anthony. Andy (That's My Name)
Dragonwagon, Crescent. Wind Rose
Hogan, Inez. About Nono, the Baby Elephant
Low, Joseph. Adam's Book of Odd Creatures
McKee, David. Two Can Toucan
Mosel, Arlene. Tikki Tikki Tembo
Ness, Evaline. Tom Tit Tot
Parish, Peggy. Little Indian
Raskin, Ellen. A & The, or William T. C. Baumgarten Comes to Town
Rice, Eve. Ebbie
Vreeken, Elizabeth. The Boy Who Would Not Say His Name
Waber, Bernard. But Names Will Never Hurt Me
Weil, Ann. The Very First Day
Williams, Jay, and Lubell, Winifred Milius. I Wish I Had Another Name
Wold, Jo Anne. Tell Them My Name Is Amanda

119 Night

Alexander, Anne. Noise in the Night
Ardizzone, Aingelda. The Night Ride
Babbitt, Natalie. The Something
Bannon, Laura May. Little People of the Night
Bennett, Rainey. After the Sun Goes Down
Berenstain, Stanley, and Berenstain, Janice. Bears in the Night
Berg, Jean Horton. The Wee Little Man
Bradbury, Ray. Switch on the Night
Brown, Margaret Wise. Wait Till the Moon Is Full
Brown, Myra Berry. Pip Camps Out
Budney, Blossom. After Dark
Conford, Ellen. Eugene the Brave
Crowe, Robert L. Clyde Monster
Donaldson, Lois. Karl's Wooden Horse
Emberley, Barbara, and Emberley, Edward Randolph. Night's Nice
Fenner, Carol Elizabeth. Tigers in the Cellar
Freeman, Don. The Night the Lights Went Out
Garelick, May. Sounds of a Summer Night

Goodenow, Earle. The Owl Who Hated the Dark

Horwitz, Elinor. When the Sky Is Like Lace

Hurd, Thacher. The Quiet Evening

Ipcar, Dahlov Zorach. The Cat at Night
    The Song of the Day Birds and the Night Birds

Kauffman, Lois. What's That Noise?

Keats, Ezra Jack. Dreams

Koenig, Marion. The Wonderful World of Night

Kraus, Robert, and Bodecker, Nils Mogens. Good Night Little One
    Good Night Richard Rabbit

Leaf, Munro. Boo, Who Used to Be Scared of the Dark

Lexau, Joan M. Millicent's Ghost

Lifton, Betty Jean. Goodnight Orange Monster

Matus, Greta. Where Are You, Jason?

Mayer, Mercer. You're the Scaredy Cat

Memling, Carl. What's in the Dark?

Moeschlin, Elsa. Red Horse

Peck, Richard. Monster Night at Grandma's House

Preston, Edna Mitchell. Monkey in the Jungle

Reidel, Marlene. Jacob and the Robbers

Rowand, Phyllis. It Is Night

Ryan, Cheli Duran. Hildilid's Night

Scharen, Beatrix. Gigin and Till

Schlein, Miriam. Here Comes Night

Schneider, Nina. While Susie Sleeps

Tobias, Tobi. Chasing the Goblins Away

Winthrop, Elizabeth. Potbellied Possums

Zolotow, Charlotte Shapiro. Wake Up and Good Night
    When the Wind Stops
    The White Marble

120 Noise

Alexander, Anne. Noise in the Night

Behn, Harry. What a Beautiful Noise

Berenstain, Stanley, and Berenstain, Janice. Bears in the Night

Berg, Jean Horton. The Wee Little Man

Bright, Robert. Georgie and the Noisy Ghost
    Gregory, the Noisiest and Strongest Boy in Grangers Grove

Brown, Margaret Wise. Country Noisy Book
    Indoor Noisy Book
    Noisy Book
    The Quiet Noisy Book
    SHHhhh......Bang: A Whispering Book
    Summer Noisy Book
    Winter Noisy Book

Cleary, Beverly. The Hullabaloo ABC

Domanska, Janina. Why So Much Noise?

Duvoisin, Roger Antoine. Petunia and the Song

Elkin, Benjamin. The Loudest Noise in the World

Farber, Norma. There Once Was a Woman Who Married a Man

Gaeddert, Lou Ann Bigge. Noisy Nancy Nora

Gage, Wilson. Down in the Boondocks

Garelick, May. Sounds of a Summer Night

Graham, John. A Crowd of Cows

Horvath, Betty F. The Cheerful Quiet

Hutchins, Pat. Good-Night Owl

Kauffman, Lois. What's That Noise?

Kuskin, Karla Seidman. All Sizes of Noises
    Roar and More

Leister, Mary. The Silent Concert

McCloskey, Robert John. Lentil

McGovern, Ann. Too Much Noise

McNulty, Faith. When a Boy Wakes Up in the Morning

Madden, Don. Lemonade Serenade or the Thing in the Garden

Massie, Diane Redfield. The Baby Beebee Bird

Morrison, Sean. Is That a Happy Hippopotamus?

Ogle, Lucille, and Thoburn, Tine. I Hear

Pickett, Carla. Calvin Crocodile and the Terrible Noise

Polushkin, Maria. Who Said Meow?

Raskin, Ellen. Who, Said Sue, Said Whoo?

Richter, Mischa. Quack?

Sicotte, Virginia. A Riot of Quiet

Slobodkin, Louis. Colette and the Princess

Spier, Peter. Crash! Bang! Boom!
    Gobble, Growl, Grunt

Steiner, Charlotte. Listen to My Seashell

Teal, Valentine. The Little Woman Wanted Noise

Tripp, Edward. The Tin Fiddle

Wooley, Catherine. Quiet on Account of Dinosaur

Zion, Gene. Harry and the Lady Next Door

Zolotow, Charlotte Shapiro. The Poodle Who Barked at the Wind
    The Quiet Mother and the Noisy Little Boy

121 Non-sexist

Adoff, Arnold. Black Is Brown Is Tan

Berenstain, Stanley, and Berenstain, Janice. He Bear, She Bear

Berson, Harold. Balarin's Goat

Bonsall, Crosby Newell. The Case of the Scaredy Cats

Brown, Margaret Wise. The Steamroller

Byars, Betsy Cromer. Go and Hush the Baby

Carle, Eric. Do You Want to Be My Friend?
Clifton, Lucille B. The Boy Who Didn't Believe in Spring
Everett Anderson's Friend
Conford, Ellen. Impossible Possum
Coombs, Patricia. Molly Mullett
de Paola, Thomas Anthony. Charlie Needs a Cloak
Oliver Button Is a Sissy
The Farmer in the Dell
Floyd, Lucy, and Lasky, Kathryn. Agatha's Alphabet, with Her Very Own Dictionary
Gág, Wanda. Gone Is Gone
Gordon, Shirley. Crystal Is the New Girl
Grant, Anne. Danbury's Burning! The Story of Sybil Ludington's Ride
Hoberman, Mary Ann. I Like Old Clothes
Horvath, Betty F. Be Nice to Josephine
Hughes, Shirley. George the Babysitter
Isadora, Rachel. Max
Klein, Norma. Girls Can Be Anything
Lasker, Joseph Leon. Mothers Can Do Anything
Levy, Elizabeth. Nice Little Girls
McCloskey, Robert John. One Morning in Maine
Martin, Patricia Miles. Rolling the Cheese
Maury, Inez. My Mother the Mail Carrier: Mi Mama la Cartera
Mayer, Mercer. Liza Lou and the Yeller Belly Swamp
What Do You Do with a Kangaroo?
Merriam, Eve. Boys and Girls, Girls and Boys
Mommies at Work
Ness, Evaline. Do You Have the Time, Lydia?
Pearson, Susan. Everybody Knows That!
Perkins, Al. Don and Donna Go to Bat
Preston, Edna Mitchell. Horrible Hepzibah
Pop Corn and Ma Goodness
Reavin, Sam. Hurray for Captain Jane!
Ross, Jessica. Ms. Klondike
Rounds, Glen H. The Day the Circus Came to Lone Tree
Schick, Eleanor. City in the Winter
Schulman, Janet. Camp Kee Wee's Secret Weapon
Jenny and the Tennis Nut
Shecter, Ben. Hester the Jester
Stewart, Robert. The Daddy Book
Udry, Janice May. Mary Jo's Grandmother
Van Woerkom, Dorothy O. Becky and the Bear
The Queen Who Couldn't Bake Gingerbread
Williams, Jay. Petronella
The Practical Princess
Wolde, Gunilla. Betsy and Peter Are Different

Betsy and the Chicken Pox
Young, Miriam Burt. Jellybeans for Breakfast
Zolotow, Charlotte Shapiro. William's Doll

122 Nursery rhymes

Alderson, Brian. Cakes and Custard
Anglund, Joan Walsh. A Child's Book of Old Nursery Rhymes
Barchilon, Jacques, and Pettit, Henry. The Authentic Mother Goose Fairy Tales and Nursery Rhymes
Baum, Lyman Frank. Mother Goose in Prose
Bayley, Nicola. Nicola Bayley's Book of Nursery Rhymes
Blegvad, Lenore Hochman, ed. Hark! Hark! The Dogs Do Bark, and Other Rhymes about Dogs
Mittens for Kittens, and Other Rhymes about Cats
Bodecker, Nils Mogens, translator. "It's Raining," Said John Twaining
Briggs, Raymond. Fee Fi Fo Fum
Ring-A-Ring O' Roses
The White Land
Brock, Emma Lillian. To Market! To Market!
Brooke, Leonard Leslie. Oranges and Lemons
Brooks, Ron. This Little Pig Went to Market
Brown, Marcia. Peter Piper's Alphabet
Caldecott, Randolph. The Diverting History of John Gilpin
Hey Diddle Diddle, and Baby Bunting
Hey Diddle Diddle Picture Book
Panjandrum Picture Book
The Queen of Hearts
Randolph Caldecott's John Gilpin and Other Stories
Randolph Caldecott's Picture Book, No. 1
Randolph Caldecott's Picture Book, No. 2
Sing a Song for Sixpence
The Three Jovial Huntsmen
Cassedy, Sylvia, and Thampi, Parvathi. Moon-Uncle, Moon-Uncle
Cauley, Lorinda Bryan. Pease Porridge Hot: A Mother Goose Cookbook
Chorao, Kay. The Baby's Lap Book
Chwast, Seymour. The House That Jack Built
Cock Robin. The Courtship, Merry Marriage, and Feast of Cock Robin and Jenny Wren, to Which Is Added the Doleful Death of Cock Robin
De Angeli, Marguerite Lofft. The Book of Nursery and Mother Goose Rhymes
DeForest, Charlotte B. The Prancing Pony

Domanska, Janina. I Saw a Ship A-Sailing
  If All the Seas Were One Sea
Emberley, Barbara. Simon's Song
The House That Jack Built, illus. by Paul
  Galdone
The House That Jack Built. La Maison que
  Jacques a Batie
Ivimey, John William. The Complete
  Version of Ye Three Blind Mice
Jack Sprat. The Life of Jack Sprat, His
  Wife and His Cat
Kepes, Juliet. Lady Bird, Quickly
Lent, Blair. From King Boggen's Hall to
  Nothing at All
Levy, Sara G. Mother Goose Rhymes for
  Jewish Children
Little Tom Tucker
Lobel, Arnold Stark. Gregory Griggs and
  Other Nursery Rhyme People
Martin, Sarah Catherine. The Comic
  Adventures of Old Mother Hubbard
  and Her Dog
  Old Mother Hubbard and Her Dog,
    illus. by Evaline Ness
  Old Mother Hubbard and Her Dog,
    illus. by Paul Galdone
Montgomerie, Norah Mary, comp. This
  Little Pig Went to Market; Play
  Rhymes
Mother Goose. The Annotated Mother
  Goose
  Blessed Mother Goose; Favorite Nursery
    Rhymes for Today's Children
  Brian Wildsmith's Mother Goose
  Carolyn Wells Edition of Mother Goose
  The Charles Addams Mother Goose
  The City and Country Mother Goose
  Frank Baber's Mother Goose Nursery
    Rhymes
  The Gay Mother Goose
  Grafa' Grig Had a Pig, and Other
    Rhymes without Reason from Mother
    Goose
  Hurrah, We're Outward Bound!
  In a Pumpkin Shell; A Mother Goose
    ABC
  Jack Horner and Song of Sixpence
  James Marshall's Mother Goose
  The Little Mother Goose
  London Bridge Is Falling Down, illus.
    by Edward Randolph Emberley
  London Bridge Is Falling Down!, illus.
    by Peter Spier
  Mother Goose, illus. by Roger Antoine
    Duvoisin
  Mother Goose, illus. by Miss Elliott
    (pseud.)
  Mother Goose, illus. by Charles Buckles
    Falls
  Mother Goose, illus. by Gyo Fujikawa
  Mother Goose, illus. by Frederick
    Richardson, 1915

Mother Goose, illus. by Frederick
  Richardson, 1971
Mother Goose, illus. by Frederick
  Richardson, 1971, 1976
Mother Goose, illus. by Gustaf
  Tenggren
Mother Goose, illustrated
Mother Goose and Nursery Rhymes
Mother Goose as Told by Kellogg's
  Singing Lady
The Mother Goose Book, illus. by Alice
  Provensen and Martin Provensen
The Mother Goose Book, illus. by Sonia
  Roetter
Mother Goose in French; Poesies de la
  vraie Mere Oie
Mother Goose in Hieroglyphics
Mother Goose in Spanish. Poesias de la
  Madre Oca
Mother Goose Melodies
Mother Goose Nursery Rhymes, illus. by
  Arthur Rackham, 1969
Mother Goose Nursery Rhymes, illus. by
  Arthur Rackham, 1975
Mother Goose; Or, The Old Nursery
  Rhymes
Mother Goose Rhymes
Mother Goose; Seventy-Seven Verses
Mother Goose, Sixty-Seven Favorite
  Rhymes
Mother Goose; The Old Nursery
  Rhymes
The Mother Goose Treasury
Mother Goose's Melodies; Or, Songs for
  the Nursery
Mother Goose's Melody; Or, Sonnets for
  the Cradle
Mother Goose's Rhymes and Melodies
Nursery Rhyme Book
Nursery Rhymes from Mother Goose in
  Signed English
One I Love, Two I Love, and Other
  Loving Mother Goose Rhymes
One Misty Moisty Morning; Rhymes
  from Mother Goose
One, Two, Buckle My Shoe
The Only True Mother Goose Melodies
The Piper's Son
A Pocket Full of Posies
The Rainbow Mother Goose
The Real Mother Goose
Richard Scarry's Best Mother Goose
  Ever
Richard Scarry's Favorite Mother Goose
  Rhymes
Rimes de la Mere Oie
Ring O' Roses
Songs from Mother Goose
The Tall Book of Mother Goose
The Three Jovial Huntsmen
To Market! To Market!
Tom Tom the Piper's Son

Twenty Nursery Rhymes
Willy Pogany's Mother Goose
The Moving Adventures of Old Dame
   Trot and Her Comical Cat
Nursery Rhymes
Opie, Iona Archibald, comp., and Opie,
   Peter, comp. A Family Book of
   Nursery Rhymes
The Oxford Nursery Rhyme Book
The Puffin Book of Nursery Rhymes
Palazzo, Tony. Animals 'Round the
   Mulberry Bush
Peppé, Rodney. Cat and Mouse
   Hey Riddle Diddle
Petersham, Maud Fuller, and Petersham,
   Miska. The Rooster Crows
Potter, Beatrix. Appley Dapply's Nursery
   Rhymes
   Cecily Parsley's Nursery Rhymes
Rey, Hans Augusto. Humpty Dumpty and
   Other Mother Goose Songs
Robbins, Ruth. The Harlequin and Mother
   Goose; Or, The Magic Stick
Ruskin, John. Dame Wiggins of Lee and
   Her Seven Wonderful Cats
Sendak, Maurice. Hector Protector and As
   I Went over the Water; Two Nursery
   Rhymes
Simple Simon. The History of Simple
   Simon
   Simple Simon
Stearns, Monroe, adapter. Ring-A-Ling
Tabor, Troy E. Mother Goose in Hawaii
Thomas, Katherine Elwes. The Real
   Personages of Mother Goose
Tucker, Nicholas, comp. Mother Goose
   Abroad
   Mother Goose Lost; Nursery Rhymes
Watson, Clyde. Father Fox's Pennyrhymes
Wheeler, Opal. Sing Mother Goose
Wilkin, Eloise Burns. Ladybug, Ladybug
   and Other Nursery Rhymes
Wood, Ray. The American Mother Goose
   Fun in American Folk Rhymes
Zemach, Harve. The Speckled Hen; A
   Russian Nursery Rhyme

123 Octopod

Drdek, Richard E. Horace the Friendly
   Octopus
Kraus, Robert. Herman the Helper
Shaw, Evelyn S. Octopus
Ungerer, Tomi. Emile
Waber, Bernard. I Was All Thumbs

124 Oil

Freeman, Don. The Seal and the Slick
Ungerer, Tomi. The Mellops Strike Oil

125 Old age

Allard, Harry. It's So Nice to Have a Wolf
   Around the House
Farber, Norma. How Does It Feel to Be
   Old?
Fassler, Joan. My Grandpa Died Today
Fender, Kay. Odette, a Bird in Paris
Galdone, Paul. The Horse, the Fox, and
   the Lion
Goffstein, Marilyn Brooks. Fish for Supper
Grimm, Jakob Ludwig Karl, and Grimm,
   Wilhelm Karl. The Bremen Town
   Musicians
Hoff, Sydney. Barkley
Kahl, Virginia Caroline. Maxie
Keeping, Charles William James. Molly o'
   the Moors, the Story of a Pony
Kunhardt, Dorothy. Billy the Barber
Peet, Bill. Smokey
Skorpen, Liesel Moak. Old Arthur
Sonneborn, Ruth A. I Love Gram
Taylor, Mark. Old Blue, You Good Dog
   You
Uchida, Yoshiko. Sumi's Special
   Happening
Wittman, Sally Christensen. A Special
   Trade

126 Optical illusions

Anno, Mitsumasa. Anno's Alphabet
   Anno's Counting Book
   Anno's Journey
   Dr. Anno's Magical Midnight Circus
   Topsy-Turvies
   Upside-Downers
Emberley, Edward Randolph. The Wizard
   of Op

127 Orphans

Bemelmans, Ludwig. Madeline
   Madeline and the Bad Hat
   Madeline and the Gypsies
   Madeline in London
   Madeline's Rescue
Goffstein, Marilyn Brooks. Goldie the
   Dollmaker
Mahy, Margaret. Sailor Jack and the
   Twenty Orphans
Ungerer, Tomi. The Three Robbers

128 Parades

Anderson, Clarence William. Rumble Seat
   Pony
Bright, Robert. Hurrah for Freddie!
Brustlein, Janice. Little Bear Marches in
   the St. Patrick's Day Parade
Emberley, Edward Randolph. The Parade
   Book

Ets, Marie Hall. Another Day
In the Forest
Holt, Margaret. David McCheever's
Twenty-Nine Dogs
Richter, Mischa. Eric and Matilda
Slobodkina, Esphyr. Pezzo the Peddler and
the Circus Elephant
Spier, Peter. Crash! Bang! Boom!
Ziner, Feenie. Counting Carnival

129 Participation

Agostinelli, Maria Enrica. I Know
Something You Don't Know
Black, Irma Simonton. Is This My Dinner?
Brown, Margaret Wise. Country Noisy
Book
Indoor Noisy Book
Noisy Book
The Quiet Noisy Book
The Seashore Noisy Book
Summer Noisy Book
Winter Noisy Book
Cameron, Polly. "I Can't," Said the Ant
Carroll, Ruth Robinson. Where's the
Bunny?
Charlip, Remy. Fortunately
Chwast, Seymour. The House That Jack
Built
Cole, William. Frances Face-Maker
Craig, M. Jean. Boxes
Crume, Marion W. Let Me See You Try
Listen!
What Do You Say?
De Regniers, Beatrice Schenk. It Does Not
Say Meow!
Emberley, Edward Randolph. Ed
Emberley's Amazing Look Through
Book
Klippity Klop
Ets, Marie Hall. Just Me
Talking Without Words; I Can. Can
You?
French, Fiona Mary. Hunt the Thimble
Garten, Jan. The Alphabet Tale
Geisel, Theodor Seuss. Mr. Brown Can
Moo, Can You?
Wacky Wednesday
Heilbroner, Joan. This Is the House
Where Jack Lives
Hewett, Anita. The Tale of the Turnip
Hoban, Tana. Look Again
Hutchins, Pat. Good-Night Owl
Jaynes, Ruth. Benny's Four Hats
Johnson, Ryerson. Let's Walk up the Wall
Kepes, Charles. Run, Little Monkeys, Run,
Run, Run
Kuskin, Karla Seidman. Roar and More
Löfgren, Ulf. One-Two-Three
MacGregor, Ellen. Theodor Turtle
Martin, William Ivan, and Martin, Bernard
Herman. Brave Little Indian

Montgomerie, Norah Mary, comp. This
Little Pig Went to Market; Play
Rhymes
Ogle, Lucille, and Thoburn, Tine. I Hear
Paterson, Diane. If I Were a Toad
Patrick, Gloria. This Is...
Seignobosc, Françoise. The Things I Like
Shaw, Charles Green. It Looked Like Spilt
Milk
Siewert, Margaret, and Savage, Kathleen.
Bear Hunt
Simon, Norma. What Do I Say?
Sivulich, Sandra Stroner. I'm Going on a
Bear Hunt
Skaar, Grace Marion. What Do the
Animals Say?
Skorpen, Liesel Moak. All the Lassies
Slobodkina, Esphyr. Caps for Sale
Pezzo the Peddler and the Circus
Elephant
Pezzo the Peddler and the Thirteen Silly
Thieves
Spier, Peter. Crash! Bang! Boom!
Gobble, Growl, Grunt
Sutton, Eve. My Cat Likes to Hide in
Boxes
Ueno, Noriko. Elephant Buttons
Yudell, Lynn Deena. Make a Face

130 Parties

Adams, Adrienne. The Christmas Party
Allard, Harry, and Marshall, James. The
Stupids Have a Ball
Anderson, Lonzo. Halloween Party
Averill, Esther Holden. Jenny's Birthday
Book
Bible, Charles. Jennifer's New Chair
Bonsall, Crosby Newell. Twelve Bells for
Santa
Bowden, Joan Chase. Bear's Surprise Party
Brooke, Leonard Leslie. Johnny Crow's
Party
Brustlein, Janice. Little Bear's New Year's
Party
Little Bear's Pancake Party
Cohen, Miriam. Tough Jim
Du Bois, William Pène. Bear Party
Ets, Marie Hall. The Cow's Party
Freeman, Don. Dandelion
The Paper Party
Galdone, Joanna. Honeybee's Party
Geisel, Theodor Seuss. Hooper
Humperdink...? Not Him!
Gendel, Evelyn. Tortoise and Turtle
Abroad
Hutchins, Pat. Surprise Party
Keats, Ezra Jack. A Letter to Amy
Lenski, Lois L. A Surprise for Davy
Lipkind, William, and Mordvinoff, Nicolas.
The Christmas Bunny
Meyer, Elizabeth. The Blue China Pitcher

Oxenbury, Helen. The Queen and Rosie Randall

Parish, Peggy. Amelia Bedelia and the Surprise Shower

Potter, Beatrix. The Sly Old Cat

Prager, Annabelle. The Surprise Party

Zion, Gene. Jeffie's Party

131 Pets

Alexander, Martha G. No Ducks in Our Bathtub

Allard, Harry. It's So Nice to Have a Wolf Around the House

Barton, Byron. Jack and Fred

Bishop, Claire Huchet. The Truffle Pig

Boegehold, Betty. Pawpaw's Run

Brothers, Aileen. Jiffy, Miss Boo and Mr. Roo

Brunhoff, Laurent de. Babar and the Willy-Wully

Carrick, Carol. The Accident
    The Foundling

Carrick, Carol, and Carrick, Donald. A Clearing in the Forest

Carroll, Ruth Robinson, and Carroll, Latrobe. Pet Tale

Chenery, Janet. Pickles and Jack

Christian, Mary Blount. Devin and Goliath

Cooper, Elizabeth K. The Fish from Japan

Dunn, Judy. The Little Goat

Fox, Robin. Le Poulet, the Rooster Who Laid Eggs

Fujita, Tamao. The Boy and the Bird

Gackenbach, Dick. Mother Rabbit's Son Tom

Hamberger, John F. Hazel Was an Only Pet

Hoff, Sydney. Katy's Kitty; Three Kitty Stories
    Pete's Pup; Three Puppy Stories

Kahl, Virginia Caroline. The Habits of Rabbits

Keats, Ezra Jack. Pet Show!

Keith, Eros. Rrra-ah

Kellogg, Steven. Can I Keep Him?

Kouts, Anne. Kenny's Rat

Lansdown, Brenda. Galumpf

Lathrop, Dorothy Pulis. Puppies for Keeps

McNulty, Faith. Mouse and Tim

Martin, Patricia Miles. The Rice Bowl Pet

Newberry, Clare Turlay. April's Kittens
    Barkis
    Herbert the Lion
    Percy, Polly and Pete

Newfield, Marcia. Iggy

Palmer, Helen Marion. Why I Built the Boogle House

Politi, Leo. Lito and the Clown

Pratten, Albra. Winkie, the Grey Squirrel

Pursell, Margaret Sanford. Polly the Guinea Pig

    Shelley the Sea Gull

Ricciuti, Edward R. An Animal for Alan

Ridlon, Marci. Kittens and More Kittens

Ross, George Maxim. When Lucy Went Away

Sandberg, Inger. Nicholas' Favorite Pet

Schick, Alice, and Schick, Joel. Just This Once

Schweitzer, Byrd Baylor. Amigo

Seignobosc, Françoise. The Story of Colette

Selsam, Millicent Ellis. Let's Get Turtles Plenty of Fish

Skorpen, Liesel Moak. All the Lassies

Steiner, Charlotte. Polka Dot

Tobias, Tobi. Petey

Vandivert, Rita. Barnaby

Varga, Judy. Miss Lollipop's Lion
    Pig in the Parlor

Viorst, Judith. The Tenth Good Thing about Barney

Vreeken, Elizabeth. Henry

Warburg, Sandol Stoddard. My Very Own Special Particular Private and Personal Cat

Ward, Lynd Kendall. The Biggest Bear

Wisbeski, Dorothy. Picaro, a Pet Otter

Wong, Herbert H., and Vassel, Matthew F. My Goldfish
    My Plant

Wright, Dare. The Lonely Doll Learns a Lesson

Zolotow, Charlotte Shapiro. The Poodle Who Barked at the Wind

Zweifel, Frances W. Bony

132 Pirates

Devlin, Harry. The Walloping Window Blind

Graham, Mary Stuart Campbell. The Pirates' Bridge

Joslin, Sesyle. Senor Baby Elephant, the Pirate

Mahy, Margaret. Sailor Jack and the Twenty Orphans

Perkins, Al. Tubby and the Lantern

Roberts, Thom. Pirates in the Park

Vinton, Iris. Look Out for Pirates!

Walker, Barbara K. Pigs and Pirates

133 Plants

Adelson, Leone. Please Pass the Grass

Ayer, Jacqueline Brandford. The Paper Flower Tree

Berson, Harold. Pop Goes the Turnip

Carle, Eric. The Tiny Seed

Chapman, Carol. Barney Bipple's Magic Dandelions

Credle, Ellis. Down, Down the Mountain

Ellentuck, Shan. A Sunflower as Big as the Sun

Fisher, Aileen Lucia. And a Sunflower
Grew
As the Leaves Fall Down
Mysteries in the Garden
Now That Spring Is Here
Plant Magic
Prize Performance
Seeds on the Go
Swords and Daggers
We Went Looking
Ginsburg, Mirra. Mushroom in the Rain
The Green Grass Grows All Around
Greenberg, Polly. O Lord, I Wish I Was a
Buzzard
Hewett, Anita. The Tale of the Turnip
Hogrogian, Nonny. Apples
Hutchins, Pat. Titch
Ipcar, Dahlov Zorach. Hard Scrabble
Harvest
Kepes, Juliet. The Seed That Peacock
Planted
Krauss, Ruth. The Carrot Seed
The Little Red Hen, illus. by Janina
Domanska
The Little Red Hen, illus. by Paul Galdone
The Little Red Hen, illus. by Mel Pekarsky
Maestro, Giulio. The Remarkable Plant in
Apartment 4
Miller, Judith R. Nabob and the Geranium
Nash, Ogden. The Animal Garden
Oleson, Claire. For Pepita, an Orange Tree
Petie, Haris. The Seed the Squirrel
Dropped
Rey, Hans Augusto. Elizabite, Adventures
of a Carnivorous Plant
Ringi, Kjell. The Sun and the Cloud
Rockwell, Harlow. The Compost Heap
Selsam, Millicent Ellis. More Potatoes!
Seeds and More Seeds
Shecter, Ben. Partouche Plants a Seed
Sugita, Yutaka. The Flower Family
Taylor, Mark. A Time for Flowers
Tolstoy, Alekesi Nikolaevich. The Great
Big Enormous Turnip
Ushinsky, Konstantin. How a Shirt Grew in
the Field
Wondriska, William. The Tomato Patch
Wong, Herbert H., and Vassel, Matthew F.
Our Terrariums
Zion, Gene. The Plant Sitter
Zolotow, Charlotte Shapiro. In My Garden

134 Poetry, rhyme

Adams, Richard George. The Tyger
Voyage
Adelson, Leone. Please Pass the Grass
Adoff, Arnold. Big Sister Tells Me That
I'm Black
Where Wild Willie?
Ahlberg, Janet, and Ahlberg, Allan. Each
Peach Pear Plum; An "I Spy" Story

Alexander, Anne. I Want to Whistle
Alger, Leclaire. All in the Morning Early
Kellyburn Braes
Anglund, Joan Walsh. The Joan Walsh
Anglund Storybook
Armour, Richard Willard. The Adventures
of Egbert the Easter Egg
Animals on the Ceiling
The Year Santa Went Modern
Attenberger, Walburga. The Little Man in
Winter
Who Knows the Little Man?
Atwood, Ann. The Little Circle
Barry, Robert E. Mr. Willowby's Christmas
Tree
Bemelmans, Ludwig. Madeline
Madeline and the Bad Hat
Madeline and the Gypsies
Madeline in London
Madeline's Rescue
Welcome Home
Benét, William Rose. Timothy's Angels
Berenstain, Stanley. The Bear Detectives:
The Case of the Missing Pumpkin
Berenstain, Stanley, and Berenstain, Janice.
The Berenstain Bears and the
Spooky Old Tree
Berg, Jean Horton. The Wee Little Man
Beskow, Elsa Maartman. Children of the
Forest
Peter's Adventures in Blueberry Land
Billy Boy
Black, Irma Simonton. Is This My Dinner?
Blegvad, Erik. Burnie's Hill
Borten, Helen. Do You Go Where I Go?
Do You Know What I Know?
Braun, Kathy. Kangaroo and Kangaroo
Brecht, Bertolt. Uncle Eddie's Moustache
Bright, Robert. My Hopping Bunny
Brooke, Leonard Leslie. Johnny Crow's
Garden
Johnny Crow's New Garden
Brown, Margaret Wise. Four Fur Feet
Sleepy ABC
Whistle for the Train
Brown, Myra Berry. Best Friends
Best of Luck
Bruna, Dick. The Fish
Little Bird Tweet
Buckley, Helen Elizabeth. Josie and the
Snow
Josie's Buttercup
Budney, Blossom. A Kiss Is Round
Burroway, Janet. The Truck on the Track
Cameron, Polly. A Child's Book of
Nonsense
"I Can't," Said the Ant
Caudill, Rebecca. Wind, Sand and Sky
Chardiet, Bernice. C Is for Circus
Charles, Robert H. The Roundabout Turn
Chönz, Selina. A Bell for Ursli
Florina and the Wild Bird

The Snowstorm
Chukovsky, Kornei. The Telephone
Ciardi, John. I Met a Man
Clifton, Lucille B. Everett Anderson's
    Friend
    Everett Anderson's Nine Months Long
    Everett Anderson's 1,2,3
    Everett Anderson's Year
    Some of the Days of Everett Anderson
Clithero, Sally. Beginning-To-Read Poetry
Cole, William. Frances Face-Maker
    That Pest Jonathan
    What's Good for a Four-Year-Old?
    What's Good for a Six-Year-Old?
    What's Good for a Three-Year-Old?
Coletta, Irene, and Coletta, Hallie. From A
    to Z
Conover, Chris. Six Little Ducks
Copp, Jim. Martha Matilda O'Toole
Counting Rhymes
Craft, Ruth. The Winter Bear
Delaunay, Sonia. Sonia Delaunay's
    Alphabet
Dennis, Suzanne E. Answer Me That
de Paola, Thomas Anthony. Songs of the
    Fog Maiden
De Regniers, Beatrice Schenk. Cats Cats
    Cats Cats Cats
    It Does Not Say Meow!
    May I Bring a Friend?
    Red Riding Hood
    Was It a Good Trade?
Dodd, Lynley. The Nickle Nackle Tree
Dodgson, Charles Lutwidge. Jabberwocky
Domanska, Janina. What Do You See?
Eckert, Horst. Tonight at Nine
Elkin, Benjamin. The King Who Could
    Not Sleep
Emberley, Barbara. Drummer Hoff
Emberley, Barbara, and Emberley, Edward
    Randolph. Night's Nice
Emberley, Edward Randolph. Wing on a
    Flea
Ets, Marie Hall. Beasts and Nonsense
Farber, Norma. As I Was Crossing Boston
    Common
    How the Left-Behind Beasts Built
    Ararat
    Never Say Ugh to a Bug
    There Once Was a Woman Who
    Married a Man
    Where's Gomer?
Farjeon, Eleanor. Mrs. Malone
Field, Eugene. Wynken, Blynken and Nod
Finfer, Celentha; Wasserberg, Esther; and
    Weinberg, Florence. Grandmother
    Dear
First Graces
First Prayers
Fisher, Aileen Lucia. And a Sunflower
    Grew
    Best Little House

Do Bears Have Mothers Too?
Going Barefoot
Like Nothing at All
My Mother and I
Mysteries in the Garden
Now That Spring Is Here
Petals Yellow and Petals Red
Plant Magic
Prize Performance
Seeds on the Go
Sing Little Mouse
Swords and Daggers
A Tree with a Thousand Uses
We Went Looking
Where Does Everyone Go?
Freeman, Don. Mop Top
Freeman, Jean Todd. Cynthia and the
    Unicorn
Freschet, Berniece. The Ants Go Marching
Frith, Michael K. I'll Teach My Dog 100
    Words
Gág, Wanda. ABC Bunny
Gage, Wilson. Down in the Boondocks
Galdone, Joanna. Gertrude, the Goose
    Who Forgot
    The Tailypo, a Ghost Story
Garcia Lorca, Federico. The Lieutenant
    Colonel and the Gypsy
Garelick, May. Look at the Moon
    Where Does the Butterfly Go When It
    Rains?
Garten, Jan. The Alphabet Tale
Gay, Zhenya. Look!
    What's Your Name?
Geisel, Theodor Seuss. And to Think That
    I Saw It on Mulberry Street
    Because a Little Bug Went Ka-choo!
    The Cat in the Hat
    The Cat in the Hat Comes Back!
    The Cat's Quizzer
    Come Over to My House
    Did I Ever Tell You How Lucky You
    Are?
    Dr. Seuss's ABC
    Dr. Seuss's Sleep Book
    The Foot Book
    Fox in Socks
    A Great Day for Up
    Green Eggs and Ham
    Happy Birthday to You
    Hooper Humperdink...? Not Him!
    Hop on Pop
    Horton Hatches the Egg
    Horton Hears a Who
    How the Grinch Stole Christmas
    I Can Lick 30 Tigers Today and Other
    Stories
    I Can Read with My Eyes Shut!
    I Can Write! A Book by Me, Myself,
    with a Little Help from Theo. LeSieg
    I Had Trouble Getting to Solla Sollew
    I Wish That I Had Duck Feet

If I Ran the Circus
If I Ran the Zoo
In a People House
The King's Stilts
The Lorax
McElligot's Pool
Marvin K. Mooney, Will You Please Go
   Now!
Mr. Brown Can Moo, Can You?
Oh, the Thinks You Can Think!
On Beyond Zebra
One Fish, Two Fish, Red Fish, Blue Fish
Please Try to Remember the First of
   Octember!
Scrambled Eggs Super!
The Shape of Me and Other Stuff
The Sneetches and Other Stories
Ten Apples Up on Top!
There's a Wocket in My Pocket!
Thidwick, the Big Hearted Moose
Wacky Wednesday
Gelman, Rita Golden. Hey, Kid
Gibson, Myra Tomback. What Is Your
   Favorite Thing to Touch?
Gilchrist, Theo E. Halfway up the
   Mountain
The Gingerbread Boy, illus. by Paul
   Galdone
Graham, Lorenz. Song of the Boat
Grayson, Marion F., comp. Let's Count and
   Count Out
The Green Grass Grows All Around
Greenaway, Kate. Marigold Garden
   Under the Window
Greenwood, Ann. A Pack of Dreams
Gunning, Monica. The Two Georges: Los
   Dos Jorges
Haas, Irene. The Maggie B
Hallinan, Patrick K. That's What a Friend
   Is
Harrison, David Lee. The Case of Og, the
   Missing Frog
Hazen, Barbara Shook. Where Do Bears
   Sleep?
The History of Mother Twaddle and the
   Marvelous Achievements of Her Son
   Jack
Hoban, Russell Conwell. Goodnight
Hoban, Tana. Where Is It?
Hoberman, Mary Ann. A House Is a
   House for Me
   I Like Old Clothes
Holl, Adelaide. Mrs. McGarrity's
   Peppermint Sweater
   Sir Kevin of Devon
Holland, Marion. A Big Ball of String
Hopkins, Lee Bennett, comp. I Think I
   Saw a Snail
Howells, Mildred. The Woman Who Lived
   in Holland
Hunt, Bernice Kohn. Your Ant Is a Which,
   Fun with Homophones

Hurd, Edith Thacher. Caboose
   Come and Have Fun
Hutchins, Pat. The Wind Blew
Hymes, Lucia, and Hymes, James L.
   Oodles of Noodles and Other
   Rhymes
Ilsley, Velma. A Busy Day for Chris
   The Pink Hat
Ipcar, Dahlov Zorach. Black and White
   The Cat Came Back
   Hard Scrabble Harvest
Jerome, Judson. I Never Saw
Jones, Hettie, comp. The Trees Stand
   Shining; Poetry of the North
   American Indians
Jones, Jessie Mae Orton, comp. Small Rain
Kahl, Virginia Caroline. The Baron's Booty
   The Duchess Bakes a Cake
   Gunhilde and the Halloween Spell
   Gunhilde's Christmas Booke
   The Habits of Rabbits
   How Do You Hide a Monster?
   The Perfect Pancake
   Plum Pudding for Christmas
Kavanaugh, James. The Crooked Angel
Keats, Ezra Jack. Over in the Meadow
Kessler, Ethel, and Kessler, Leonard P. Do
   Baby Bears Sit in Chairs?
Kitt, Tamara. Sam and the Impossible
   Thing
Klimowicz, Barbara. The Strawberry
   Thumb
Krauss, Ruth. Bears
   A Bouquet of Littles
Krüss, James. 3 X 3, Three by Three
Kumin, Maxine W. Follow the Fall
   Sebastian and the Dragon
   Speedy Digs Downside Up
   Spring Things
   A Winter Friend
Kuskin, Karla Seidman. All Sizes of Noises
   The Animals and the Ark
   In the Flaky Frosty Morning
   James and the Rain
   Roar and More
   Sand and Snow
Kwitz, Mary DeBall. When It Rains
Lear, Edward. ABC
   The Dong with the Luminous Nose
   Edward Lear's Nonsense Book
   Lear's Nonsense Verses
   Nonsense Alphabets
   The Nutcrackers and the Sugar-Tongs
   The Owl and the Pussy-Cat, illus. by
      Barbara Cooney
   The Owl and the Pussy-Cat, illus. by
      William Pène Du Bois
   The Owl and the Pussy-Cat, illus. by
      Gwen Fulton
   The Pelican Chorus
   The Pobble Who Has No Toes
   The Quangle Wangle's Hat

Whizz!
Leavens, George. Kippy the Koala
Leichman, Seymour. Shaggy Dogs and
    Spotty Dogs and Shaggy and Spotty
    Dogs
  The Wicked Wizard and the Wicked
    Witch
Lenski, Lois L. I Like Winter
  Now It's Fall
  On a Summer Day
  Spring Is Here
  Susie Mariar
Lerner, Marguerite Rush. Dear Little
    Mumps Child
Lewis, Richard, ed. In a Spring Garden
Lipkind, William, and Mordvinoff, Nicolas.
    Sleepyhead
Lobel, Arnold Stark. Martha the Movie
    Mouse
  On the Day Peter Stuyvesant Sailed into
    Town
Lord, Beman. The Days of the Week
Low, Alice. Witch's Holiday
Low, Joseph. Adam's Book of Odd
    Creatures
Lund, Doris Herold. The Paint-Box Sea
McClintock, Marshall. What Have I Got?
McGinley, Phyllis. All Around the Town
  How Mrs. Santa Claus Saved Christmas
  Lucy McLockett
McGovern, Ann. Feeling Mad, Feeling Sad,
    Feeling Bad, Feeling Glad
McKie, Roy, and Eastman, Philip Day.
    Snow
Maestro, Betsy. Fat Polka-Dot Cat and
    Other Haiku
Marcin, Marietta. A Zoo in Her Bed
Marks, Marcia Bliss. Swing Me, Swing Tree
Marzollo, Jean. Close Your Eyes
Massie, Diane Redfield. Tiny Pin
Mathews, Louise. Bunches and Bunches of
    Bunnies
Mendoza, George. The Scribbler
Miles, Betty. Around and Around...Love
Miles, Miska. Apricot ABC
Miller, Edna Anita. Mousekin's ABC
Mitchell, Cynthia. Playtime
The Moon's the North Wind's Cookie
Moore, Clement Clarke. The Night Before
    Christmas, illus. by Gyo Fujikawa
  The Night Before Christmas, illus. by
    Gustaf Tenggren
  The Night Before Christmas, illus. by
    Tasha Tudor
  A Visit from St. Nicholas; 'Twas the
    Night Before Christmas
Morse, Samuel French. Sea Sums
Nash, Ogden. The Adventures of Isabel
  The Animal Garden
  A Boy Is a Boy
  Custard the Dragon and the Wicked
    Knight

Newberry, Clare Turlay. The Kittens' ABC
Nolan, Dennis. Wizard McBean and His
    Flying Machine
O'Hare, Colette. What Do You Feed Your
    Donkey On?
O'Neill, Mary. Big Red Hen
Oppenheim, Joanne. Have You Seen
    Roads?
  Have You Seen Trees?
Pack, Robert. How to Catch a Crocodile
Paterson, Andrew Barton. Mulga Bill's
    Bicycle
Patrick, Gloria. This Is...
A Peaceable Kingdom; The Shaker
    Abecedarius
Peck, Robert Newton. Hamilton
Peet, Bill. Ella
  Hubert's Hair Raising Adventures
  Huge Harold
  Kermit the Hermit
  The Pinkish, Purplish, Bluish Egg
  Randy's Dandy Lions
  Smokey
Peppé, Rodney. Cat and Mouse
  Hey Riddle Diddle
Perkins, Al. The Digging-est Dog
  The Ear Book
  Hand, Hand, Fingers, Thumb
  The Nose Book
Petie, Haris. The Seed the Squirrel
    Dropped
Piatti, Celestino. Celestino Piatti's Animal
    ABC
Plath, Sylvia. The Bed Book
Pomerantz, Charlotte. The Piggy in the
    Puddle
Prelutsky, Jack. Circus
  It's Halloween
  The Mean Old Mean Hyena
  The Terrible Tiger
Preston, Edna Mitchell. Pop Corn and Ma
    Goodness
Provensen, Alice, and Provensen, Martin.
    Karen's Opposites
Puner, Helen Walker. Daddys, What They
    Do All Day
  The Sitter Who Didn't Sit
Quackenbush, Robert Mead. Pop! Goes the
    Weasel and Yankee Doodle
Raskin, Ellen. Ghost in a Four-Room
    Apartment
  Who, Said Sue, Said Whoo?
Reeves, James. Rhyming Will
Rey, Hans Augusto. Elizabite, Adventures
    of a Carnivorous Plant
  Feed the Animals
  See the Circus
  Where's My Baby?
Robbins, Ruth. Baboushka and the Three
    Kings
Roberts, Cliff. Start with a Dot
Roscoe, William. The Butterfly's Ball

Rose, Anne K. How Does the Czar Eat Potatoes?

Rossetti, Christina Georgina. What Is Pink?

Sage, Michael, and Spilka, Arnold. Dippy Dos and Don'ts

Saleh, Harold. Even Tiny Ants Must Sleep

Sazer, Nina. What Do You Think I Saw?

Schweitzer, Byrd Baylor. Amigo

Sendak, Maurice. Pierre, a Cautionary Tale in Five Chapters and a Prologue
Seven Little Monsters

Serraillier, Ian. Suppose You Met a Witch

Sexton, Gwain. There Once Was a King

Sherman, Nancy. Gwendolyn and the Weathercock
Gwendolyn the Miracle Hen

Shortall, Leonard W. One Way; A Trip with Traffic Signs

Shulevitz, Uri. Rain Rain Rivers

Silverstein, Shel. A Giraffe and a Half

Simon, Mina Lewiton. Is Anyone Here?

Slobodkin, Louis. Clear the Track
Friendly Animals
Millions and Millions and Millions!
One Is Good, but Two Are Better
The Seaweed Hat
Up High and Down Low

Smaridge, Norah Antoinette. You Know Better Than That

Smith, William Jay. Puptents and Pebbles
Typewriter Town

Spier, Peter. Noah's Ark

Spilka, Arnold. And the Frog Went "Blah!"
A Lion I Can Do Without
Little Birds Don't Cry
A Rumbudgin of Nonsense

Steig, William. An Eye for Elephants

Stephenson, Dorothy. The Night It Rained Toys

Stevenson, Robert Louis. A Child's Garden of Verses, illus by Erik Blegvad
A Child's Garden of Verses, illus. by Pelagie Doane
A Child's Garden of Verses, illus. by Toni Frissell
A Child's Garden of Verses, illus. by Gyo Fujikawa
A Child's Garden of Verses, illus. by Alice Provensen and Martin Provensen
A Child's Garden of Verses, illus. by Tasha Tudor
A Child's Garden of Verses, illus. by Brian Wildsmith

Stover, Jo Ann. If Everybody Did

Sundgaard, Arnold. Jethro's Difficult Dinosaur

Supraner, Robyn. Would You Rather Be a Tiger?

Sutton, Eve. My Cat Likes to Hide in Boxes

Svendsen, Carol. Hulda

Thomas, Patricia. "Stand Back," Said the Elephant, "I'm Going to Sneeze"

Tippett, James Sterling. Counting the Days
I Know Some Little Animals

Towend, Jack. Railroad ABC

Trent, Robbie. The First Christmas

Tresselt, Alvin R. Follow the Road
Follow the Wind

Tripp, Wallace. A Great Big Ugly Man Came Up and Tied His Horse to Me

True, Louise. Number Men

Tudor, Tasha. Around the Year

Turner, Nancy Byrd. When It Rains Cats and Dogs

Udry, Janice May. A Tree Is Nice

Vance, Eleanor Graham, comp. From Little to Big; A Parade of Animal Poems

Vance, Eleanor Graham. Jonathan

Vogel, Ilse-Margret. The Don't Be Scared Book
One Is No Fun but 20 Is Plenty

Wahl, Jan. Follow Me Cried Bee

Wallace, Daisy. Monster Poems

Wallner, Alexandra. Munch

Walters, Marguerite. Up and Down and All Around

Warburg, Sandol Stoddard. Curl Up Small
My Very Own Special Particular Private and Personal Cat

Watson, Clyde. Catch Me and Kiss Me and Say It Again

Watson, Jane Werner. The Tall Book of Make-Believe

Wells, Rosemary. Don't Spill It Again, James
Noisy Nora

Wersba, Barbara. Do Tigers Ever Bite Kings?

Wheeling, Lynn. When You Fly

Wild, Robin, and Wild, Jocelyn. Little Pig and the Big Bad Wolf

Williams, Garth Montgomery. The Chicken Book

Williams, Jay, and Lubell, Winifred Milius. I Wish I Had Another Name

Wise, William. Nanette the Hungry Pelican

Wiseman, Bernard. Little New Kangaroo

Wittels, Harriet, and Greisman, Joan. Things I Hate!

Wooster, Mae. My Busy Day

Wright, Josephine. Cotton Cat and Martha Mouse

Yolen, Jane. An Invitation to the Butterfly Ball; A Counting Rhyme

Zemach, Harve. The Judge

Ziner, Feenie. Counting Carnival

135 Poverty

Alexander, Lloyd. The King's Fountain
Ambrus, Victor G. The Three Poor Tailors

Andersen, Hans Christian. The Little
 Match Girl
Balet, Jan B. The Fence
Brand, Oscar. When I First Came to This
 Land
Coombs, Patricia. The Magic Pot
de Paola, Thomas Anthony. Helga's Dowry
Deveaux, Alexis. Na-Ni
Ehrlich, Bettina. Pantaloni
Hazen, Barbara Shook. Tight Times
Hoban, Lillian. Stick-in-the-Mud Turtle
Keeping, Charles William James. Joseph's
 Yard
La Fontaine, Jean de. The Rich Man and
 the Shoemaker
McCrea, James, and McCrea, Ruth. The
 King's Procession
Maiorano, Robert. Francisco
Nolan, Madeena Spray. My Daddy Don't
 Go to Work
Rose, Anne K. How Does the Czar Eat
 Potatoes?
Sawyer, Ruth. Journey Cake, Ho!
Sonneborn, Ruth A. Friday Night Is Papa
 Night
Steptoe, John. Uptown

136 Power failure

Rockwell, Anne F., and Rockwell, Harlow.
 Blackout

137 Problem solving

Alexander, Martha G. I'll Protect You
 from the Jungle Beasts
 Out! Out! Out!
 We Never Get To Do Anything
Balet, Jan B. The Fence
Beim, Lorraine Levy, and Beim, Jerrold.
 Two Is a Team
Benarde, Anita. The Pumpkin Smasher
Benchley, Nathaniel. A Ghost Named Fred
Berenstain, Stanley. The Bear Detectives:
 The Case of the Missing Pumpkin
Berg, Jean Horton. The O'Learys and
 Friends
Blaine, Marge. The Terrible Thing That
 Happened at Our House
Bonsall, Crosby Newell. The Case of the
 Cat's Meow
 The Case of the Dumb Bells
 The Case of the Hungry Stranger
 The Case of the Scaredy Cats
Brandenberg, Franz. A Picnic, Hurrah!
Brown, Jeff. Flat Stanley
Bulette, Sara. The Splendid Belt of Mr.
 Big
Chaffin, Lillie D. Tommy's Big Problem
Cressey, James. Fourteen Rats and a Rat-
 Catcher

de Paola, Thomas Anthony. Charlie Needs
 a Cloak
Economakis, Olga. Oasis of the Stars
Elkin, Benjamin. Such Is the Way of the
 World
Emberley, Edward Randolph. Rosebud
Farber, Norma. How the Left-Behind
 Beasts Built Ararat
Fassler, Joan. Boy with a Problem
Feder, Paula Kurzband. Where Does the
 Teacher Live?
Geisel, Theodor Seuss. Did I Ever Tell
 You How Lucky You Are?
Gelman, Rita Golden. Professor Coconut
 and the Thief
Heide, Florence Parry. The Shrinking of
 Treehorn
Horvath, Betty F. The Cheerful Quiet
Houston, John A. The Bright Yellow Rope
 A Mouse in My House
Johnston, Johanna. Edie Changes Her
 Mind
Keats, Ezra Jack. Goggles
 Whistle for Willie
Kellogg, Steven. The Mystery of the
 Missing Red Mitten
Klimowicz, Barbara. The Strawberry
 Thumb
Levy, Elizabeth. Something Queer Is Going
 On
Lexau, Joan M. Benjie
 Benjie on His Own
Lobel, Arnold Stark. On the Day Peter
 Stuyvesant Sailed into Town
McCloskey, Robert John. Lentil
McKee, David. 123456789 Benn
Maiorano, Robert. Francisco
Marshall, James. Four Little Troubles
Mayer, Mercer. What Do You Do with a
 Kangaroo?
Myrick, Jean Lockwood. Ninety-Nine
 Pockets
Ness, Evaline. Do You Have the Time,
 Lydia?
Piers, Helen. A Helen Piers Animal Book
Platt, Kin. Big Max
 Big Max in the Mystery of the Missing
 Moose
Quackenbush, Robert Mead. Detective
 Mole
 Detective Mole and the Secret Clues
 Detective Mole and the Tip-Top
 Mystery
Schermer, Judith. Mouse in House
Schurr, Cathleen. The Long and the Short
 of It
Sharmat, Marjorie Weinman. Nate the
 Great
 Nate the Great and the Lost List
 Nate the Great and the Phony Clue
 Nate the Great Goes Undercover

Shearer, John. The Case of the Sneaker
    Snatcher
Tallon, Robert. Handella
Thompson, Vivian Laubach. Camp-in-the-
    Yard
Thomson, Ruth. Peabody All at Sea
    Peabody's First Case
Titus, Eve. Anatole and the Cat
    Anatole and the Pied Piper
    Anatole and the Poodle
    Anatole and the Robot
    Anatole and the Thirty Thieves
    Anatole and the Toyshop
    Anatole in Italy
Tolstoy, Alekesi Nikolaevich. The Great
    Big Enormous Turnip
Watson, Jane Werner. The Marvelous
    Merry-Go-Round
Wold, Jo Anne. Tell Them My Name Is
    Amanda
Wooley, Catherine. The Blueberry Pie Elf
    What's a Ghost Going to Do?
Wyse, Lois. Two Guppies, a Turtle, and
    Aunt Edna
Zemach, Margot. It Could Always Be
    Worse
Zion, Gene. Harry and the Lady Next
    Door

138 Progress

Barton, Byron. Wheels
Burton, Virginia Lee. The Little House
Coombs, Patricia. Dorrie and the Fortune
    Teller
Duvoisin, Roger Antoine. Lonely Veronica
Fife, Dale. The Little Park
Goodall, John Strickland. The Story of an
    English Village
Greene, Graham. The Little Fire Engine
Harrison, David Lee. Little Turtle's Big
    Adventure
Hoban, Russell Conwell. Arthur's New
    Power
Ipcar, Dahlov Zorach. One Horse Farm
Murschetz, Luis. Mister Mole
Peet, Bill. Countdown to Christmas
    Farewell to Shady Glade
    The Wump World
Schulman, Janet. Jack the Bum and the
    UFO
Shecter, Ben. Emily, Girl Witch of New
    York

139 Puppets

Freeman, Don. The Paper Party
Heymans, Margriet. Pippin and Robber
    Grumblecroak's Big Baby
Keats, Ezra Jack. Louie
Klimowicz, Barbara. The Strawberry
    Thumb

Little, Mary E. Ricardo and the Puppets
Politi, Leo. Mr. Fong's Toy Shop
Steiner, Charlotte. Pete's Puppets

140 Rebuses

Coletta, Irene, and Coletta, Hallie. From A
    to Z
Mother Goose. Mother Goose in
    Hieroglyphics
Partch, Virgil Franklin. The Christmas
    Cookie Sprinkle Snitcher

141 Religion

Alexander, Cecil Frances. All Things
    Bright and Beautiful
Balet, Jan B. The Gift; A Portuguese
    Christmas Tale
Bible. The First Seven Days
    Shadrach, Meshack, and Abednego
Brown, Margaret Wise. On Christmas Eve
Cooney, Barbara. A Little Prayer
de Paola, Thomas Anthony. The Clown of
    God
De Regniers, Beatrice Schenk. David and
    Goliath
Domanska, Janina. Din Dan Don, It's
    Christmas
Field, Rachel Lyman. Prayer for a Child
First Graces
First Prayers
Fitch, Florence Mary. A Book about God
Fraser, James Howard. Los Posadas, a
    Christmas Story
The Friendly Beasts and A Partridge in a
    Pear Tree
Goddard, Carrie Lou. Isn't It a Wonder!
Grabianski, Janusz. Androcles and the Lion
Graham, Lorenz. David He No Fear
    Every Man Heart Lay Down
    Hongry Catch the Foolish Boy
    A Road Down in the Sea
Gramatky, Hardie. Nikos and the Sea God
Haiz, Danah. Jonah's Journey
Hamil, Thomas A. Brother Alonzo
Jones, Jessie Mae Orton, comp. A Little
    Child
    Small Rain
    This Is the Way
Jüchen, Aurel von. The Holy Night, the
    Story of the First Christmas
Keats, Ezra Jack. God Is in the Mountain
    The Little Drummer Boy
Kipling, Rudyard. The Miracle of the
    Mountain
Lindgren, Astrid Ericsson. Christmas in the
    Stable
The Lord's Prayer
MacBeth, George. Jonah and the Lord
McDermott, Beverly Brodsky. Jonah, an
    Old Testament Story

Miyoshi, Sekiya. Singing David
Nussbaumer, Mares, and Nussbaumer, Paul. Away in a Manger
Price, Christine. One Is God; Two Old Counting Songs
Seignobosc, Françoise. The Thank-You Book
Shulevitz, Uri. The Magician
Taylor, Mark. "Lamb," Said the Lion, "I Am Here"
Trent, Robbie. The First Christmas
Vasiliu, Marcea. Everything Is Somewhere
Waddell, Helen Jane. The Story of Saul the King
Weil, Lisl. The Very First Story Ever Told
Wiesner, William. The Tower of Babel

141.01 Religion—Noah

Duvoisin, Roger Antoine. A for the Ark
Farber, Norma. How the Left-Behind Beasts Built Ararat
Where's Gomer?
Goffstein, Marilyn Brooks. My Noah's Ark
Graham, Lorenz. God Wash the World and Start Again
Haley, Gail Diana Einhart. Noah's Ark
Henrioud, Charles. Mr. Noah and the Animals. Monsieur Noe et les Animaux
Kuskin, Karla Seidman. The Animals and the Ark
Lenski, Lois L. Mr. and Mrs. Noah
Lorimer, Lawrence T. Noah's Ark
Palazzo, Tony. Noah's Ark
Singer, Isaac Bashevis. Why Noah Chose the Dove
Smith, Elmer Boyd. The Story of Noah's Ark
Spier, Peter. Noah's Ark
Watson, Jane Werner. Noah's Ark
Webb, Clifford Cyril. The Story of Noah
Wiesner, William. Noah's Ark

142 Reptiles

Cortesi, Wendy W. Explore a Spooky Swamp

142.01 Reptiles—alligators, crocodiles

Brandenberg, Aliki Liacouras. Keep Your Mouth Closed, Dear
Campbell, M. Rudolph, adapter. The Talking Crocodile
de Groat, Diane. Alligator's Toothache
de Paola, Thomas Anthony. Bill and Pete
Duvoisin, Roger Antoine. The Crocodile in the Tree
Crocus
Eastman, Philip Day. Flap Your Wings

Galdone, Paul. The Monkey and the Crocodile
Hartelius, Margaret A. The Chicken's Child
Hoban, Russell Conwell. Arthur's New Power
Dinner at Alberta's
Kirn, Ann Minette. The Tale of a Crocodile
Lexau, Joan M. Crocodile and Hen
Minarik, Else Holmelund. No Fighting, No Biting!
Pack, Robert. How to Catch a Crocodile
Pickett, Carla. Calvin Crocodile and the Terrible Noise
Sendak, Maurice. Alligators All Around
Shaw, Evelyn S. Alligator
Stevenson, James. Monty
Venable, Alan. The Checker Players
Waber, Bernard. The House on 88th Street
Lovable Lyle
Lyle and the Birthday Party
Lyle Finds His Mother
Lyle, Lyle Crocodile

142.02 Reptiles—iguanas

Newfield, Marcia. Iggy

142.03 Reptiles—lizards

Anderson, Lonzo. Izzard
Carle, Eric. The Mixed-Up Chameleon
Lionni, Leo. A Color of His Own
Lopshire, Robert Martin. I Am Better Than You!
McNeely, Jeannette. Where's Izzy?
Massie, Diane Redfield. The Komodo Dragon's Jewels

142.04 Reptiles—snakes

Banchek, Linda. Snake In, Snake Out
Hoff, Sydney. Slithers
Lionni, Leo. In the Rabbitgarden
Ungerer, Tomi. Crictor
Waber, Bernard. The Snake, a Very Long Story
Wildsmith, Brian. Python's Party
Wolo (pseud.). Amanda

142.05 Reptiles—turtles

Abisch, Roslyn Kroop. The Clever Turtle
Christian, Mary Blount. Devin and Goliath
Cromie, William J. Steven and the Green Turtle
Davis, Alice V. Timothy Turtle
Domanska, Janina. The Tortoise and the Tree
Emberley, Edward Randolph. Rosebud

Freeman, Don. The Turtle and the Dove
Freschet, Berniece. Turtle Pond
Gendel, Evelyn. Tortoise and Turtle Abroad
Graham, Al. Timothy Turtle
Harrison, David Lee. Little Turtle's Big Adventure
Hoban, Lillian. Stick-in-the-Mud Turtle Turtle Spring
Iwamatsu, Jun. Seashore Story
La Fontaine, Jean de. The Hare and the Tortoise
Lubell, Winifred Milius, and Lubell, Cicil. Rosalie, the Bird Market Turtle
MacGregor, Ellen. Theodor Turtle
Maestro, Giulio. The Tortoise's Tug of War
Matsutani, Miyoko. The Fisherman under the Sea
Murdocca, Salvatore. Tuttle's Shell
Parry, Marian. King of the Fish
Selsam, Millicent Ellis. Let's Get Turtles
Van Woerkom, Dorothy O. Harry and Shellburt
Wiese, Kurt. The Cunning Turtle
Williams, Barbara. Albert's Toothache
Wolf, Ann. The Rabbit and the Turtle
Wooley, Catherine. Mr. Turtle's Magic Glasses
Wyse, Lois. Two Guppies, a Turtle, and Aunt Edna

143 Riddles

Cerf, Bennett Alfred. Bennett Cerf's Book of Animal Riddles
   Bennett Cerf's Book of Laughs
   Bennett Cerf's Book of Riddles
   More Riddles
De Regniers, Beatrice Schenk. It Does Not Say Meow!
Fleischman, Albert Sidney. Kate's Secret Riddle
Gay, Zhenya. What's Your Name?
Geisel, Theodor Seuss. The Cat's Quizzer
Peppé, Rodney. Hey Riddle Diddle
Potter, Beatrix. The Tale of Squirrel Nutkin

144 Rivers

Brook, Judy. Tim Mouse Goes Downstream
Flack, Marjorie. The Boats on the River
Keeping, Charles William James. Alfie Finds the Other Side of the World

145 Robots

Krahn, Fernando. Robot-Bot-Bot
Titus, Eve. Anatole and the Robot

146 Rocks

Baylor, Byrd. Everybody Needs a Rock
Lionni, Leo. On My Beach There Are Many Pebbles

147 Royalty

Alexander, Lloyd. The King's Fountain
Ambrus, Victor G. The Sultan's Bath
Andersen, Hans Christian. The Emperor's New Clothes, illus. by Erik Blegvad
   The Emperor's New Clothes, illus. by Virginia Lee Burton
   The Emperor's New Clothes, illus. by Jack Delano and Irene Delano
   The Emperor's New Clothes, illus. by Monika Laimgruber
   The Princess and the Pea
Anderson, Lonzo, and Adams, Adrienne. Two Hundred Rabbits
Anno, Mitsumasa. The King's Flower
Aruego, José. The King and His Friends
Auerbach, Marjorie. King Lavra and the Barber
Babbitt, Samuel F. The Forty-Ninth Magician
Balet, Jan B. The King and the Broom Maker
Berson, Harold. The Thief Who Hugged a Moonbeam
Bowden, Joan Chase. A Hat for the Queen
   A New Home for Snow Ball
Bright, Robert. Hurrah for Freddie!
Burningham, John Mackintosh. Time to Get Out of the Bath, Shirley
Chapman, Gaynor. The Luck Child
Coombs, Patricia. Tilabel
Cretien, Paul D., Jr. Sir Henry and the Dragon
Damjan, Mischa (pseud.). The Little Prince and the Tiger Cat
de Paola, Thomas Anthony. The Wonderful Dragon of Timlin
De Regniers, Beatrice Schenk. May I Bring a Friend?
Domanska, Janina. King Krakus and the Dragon
Elkin, Benjamin. The Big Jump and Other Stories
   Gillespie and the Guards
   The King Who Could Not Sleep
   The King's Wish and Other Stories
   The Loudest Noise in the World
Espenscheid, Gertrude E. The Oh Ball
Fern, Eugene. The King Who Was Too Busy
Fleischman, Albert Sidney. Longbeard the Wizard
Foreman, Michael. War and Peas
Freeman, Don. Forever Laughter

Geisel, Theodor Seuss. Bartholomew and the Oobleck
  The King's Stilts
The Golden Goose
Greene, Ellin, reteller. Princess Rosetta and the Popcorn Man
Gurney, Nancy, and Gurney, Eric. The King, the Mice and the Cheese
Hughes, Peter. The Emperor's Oblong Pancake
Kahl, Virginia Caroline. The Baron's Booty
  The Duchess Bakes a Cake
  Gunhilde and the Halloween Spell
  Gunhilde's Christmas Booke
  The Habits of Rabbits
  Plum Pudding for Christmas
Kessler, Leonard P. Soup for the King
Kroll, Steven. Fat Magic
Laskowski, Jerzy. Master of the Royal Cats
Leisk, David Johnson. The Emperor's Gift
  The Frowning Prince
Lobel, Anita. A Birthday for the Princess
  The Seamstress of Salzburg
  Sven's Bridge
Lobel, Arnold Stark. Prince Bertram the Bad
McCrea, James, and McCrea, Ruth. The King's Procession
  The Magic Tree
Mahood, Kenneth. The Laughing Dragon
Matsutani, Miyoko. The Fisherman under the Sea
Mayer, Mercer. The Queen Always Wanted to Dance
Myller, Rolf. How Big Is a Foot?
  Rolling Round
Ness, Evaline. Pavo and the Princess
Oxenbury, Helen. The Queen and Rosie Randall
Peet, Bill. How Droofus the Dragon Lost His Head
Perkins, Al. King Midas and the Golden Touch
Perrault, Charles. Puss in Boots, illus by Marcia Brown
  Puss in Boots, illus. by Hans Fischer
  Puss in Boots, illus. by Paul Galdone
  Puss in Boots, illus. by Julia Noonan
  Puss in Boots, illus. by William Stobbs
  Puss in Boots, illus. by Barry Wilkinson
Postgate, Oliver, and Firmin, Peter. Noggin the King
Reeves, James. Rhyming Will
Reit, Seymour. The King Who Learned to Smile
Rose, Anne K. How Does the Czar Eat Potatoes?
Rosenberg, Ethel Clifford. Why Is an Elephant Called an Elephant?
Schiller, Barbara. The White Rat's Tale
Sexton, Gwain. There Once Was a King
Shulevitz, Uri. One Monday Morning

Skipper, Mervyn. The Fooling of King Alexander
Slobodkin, Louis. Colette and the Princess
Steig, William. Roland the Minstrel Pig
Stephenson, Dorothy. The Night It Rained Toys
Thurber, James. Many Moons
Trez, Denise, and Trez, Alain. Maila and the Flying Carpet
  The Royal Hiccups
Van Woerkom, Dorothy O. The Queen Who Couldn't Bake Gingerbread
Varga, Judy. The Dragon Who Liked to Spit Fire
Wahl, Jan. Cabbage Moon
Wersba, Barbara. Do Tigers Ever Bite Kings?
Williams, Jay. The Practical Princess
  School for Sillies
Wynants, Miche. The Giraffe of King Charles X
Yolen, Jane. The Emperor and the Kite
  The Seeing Stick
Zemach, Harve. The Tricks of Master Dabble
Zion, Gene. The Sugar Mouse Cake

148 Safety

Brown, Margaret Wise. Red Light, Green Light
Glovach, Linda. The Little Witch's Black Magic Book of Games
Gray, Genevieve. Keep an Eye on Kevin: Safety Begins at Home
Joyce, Irma. Never Talk to Strangers
Leaf, Munro. Safety Can Be Fun
McLeod, Emilie Warren. The Bear's Bicycle
Myller, Lois. No! No!
Shortall, Leonard W. One Way; A Trip with Traffic Signs
Smaridge, Norah Antoinette. Watch Out!
Viorst, Judith. Try It Again, Sam
Young, Miriam Burt. Beware the Polar Bear! Safety on Ice

149 Sandman

Strahl, Rudi. Sandman in the Lighthouse

150 Scarecrows

Bolliger, Max. The Wooden Man
Hart, Jeanne McGahey. Scareboy
Lifton, Betty Jean. Joji and the Amanojaku
  Joji and the Dragon
  Joji and the Fog
Miller, Edna Anita. Pebbles, a Pack Rat
Tripp, Paul. The Strawman Who Smiled by Mistake

151 School

Adelson, Leone. All Ready for School
Alexander, Martha G. Sabrina
Allard, Harry, and Marshall, James. Miss Nelson Is Missing!
  The Stupids Have a Ball
Annett, Cora. The Dog Who Thought He Was a Boy
Aulaire, Ingri Mortenson d', and Aulaire, Edgar Parin d'. Nils
Babbitt, Lorraine. Pink Like the Geranium
Bemelmans, Ludwig. Madeline
Blue, Rose. How Many Blocks Is the World?
  I Am Here: Yo Estoy Aqui
Bram, Elizabeth. I Don't Want to Go to School
Brandenberg, Franz. No School Today!
Breinburg, Petronella. Shawn Goes to School
Brooks, Ron. Timothy and Gramps
Budney, Blossom. N Is for Nursery School
Carrick, Carol. A Rabbit for Easter
Caudill, Rebecca. A Pocketful of Cricket
Chorao, Kay. Molly's Lies
Clifton, Lucille B. All Us Come Across the Water
Cohen, Miriam. Bee My Valentine!
  Best Friends
  Lost in the Museum
  The New Teacher
  Tough Jim
  When Will I Read?
  Will I Have a Friend?
Coker, Gylbert. Naptime
Coontz, Otto. A Real Class Clown
Copp, Jim. Martha Matilda O'Toole
Delton, Judy. The New Girl at School
de Paola, Thomas Anthony. Bill and Pete
Dorsky, Blanche. Harry, a True Story
Dreifus, Miriam W. Brave Betsy
Ets, Marie Hall. Bad Boy, Good Boy
Fanshawe, Elizabeth. Rachel
Feder, Paula Kurzband. Where Does the Teacher Live?
Gordon, Shirley. Crystal Is My Friend
  Crystal Is the New Girl
Hader, Berta Hoerner, and Hader, Elmer Stanley. The Mighty Hunter
Hoban, Russell Conwell. Bread and Jam for Frances
Hoffman, Phyllis. Steffie and Me
Isadora, Rachel. Willaby
Iwamatsu, Jun. Crow Boy
Jaynes, Ruth. Friends, Friends, Friends
  Three Baby Chicks
Jenny, Anne. The Fantastic Story of King Brioche the First
Kantrowitz, Mildred. Willy Bear
Leaf, Munro. Robert Francis Weatherbee

Lenski, Lois L. Debbie Goes to Nursery School
  A Dog Came to School
Levy, Elizabeth. Nice Little Girls
Lexau, Joan M. Olaf Is Late
Marokvia, Merelle. A French School for Paul
Martin, Patricia Miles. Show and Tell
Meshover, Leonard, and Feistel, Sally. The Guinea Pigs That Went to School
  The Monkey That Went to School
Moreman, Grace E. No, No, Natalie
Morrison, Bill. Louis James Hates School
Ormsby, Virginia H. Twenty-One Children Plus Ten
Parish, Peggy. Jumper Goes to School
  Teach Us, Amelia Bedelia
Pearson, Susan. Everybody Knows That!
Price, Michelle. Mean Melissa
Rockwell, Harlow. My Nursery School
Rowe, Jeanne A. A Trip Through a School
Scarry, Richard McClure. Richard Scarry's Great Big Schoolhouse
Schick, Eleanor. The Little School at Cottonwood Corners
Selsam, Millicent Ellis. More Potatoes!
Simon, Norma. What Do I Do?
  What Do I Say?
Stein, Sara Bonnett. A Child Goes to School
Udry, Janice May. What Mary Jo Shared
Vinson, Pauline. Willie Goes to School
Weil, Ann. The Very First Day
Welber, Robert. Goodbye—Hello
White, Florence M. How to Lose Your Lunch Money
White, Paul. Janet at School
Whitney, Alma Marshak. Just Awful
Wolde, Gunilla. Betsy's First Day at Nursery School
Wolf, Bernard. Adam Smith Goes to School

152 Science

Asimov, Isaac. The Best New Thing
Bees
Bonners, Susan. Panda
Conklin, Gladys Plemon. Lucky Ladybugs
Cromie, William J. Steven and the Green Turtle
Fisher, Aileen Lucia. And a Sunflower Grew
  As the Leaves Fall Down
  Like Nothing at All
  Mysteries in the Garden
  Now That Spring Is Here
  Petals Yellow and Petals Red
  Plant Magic
  Prize Performance
  Seeds on the Go
  Swords and Daggers

A Tree with a Thousand Uses
Flower, Phyllis. Barn Owl
Freschet, Berniece. Bear Mouse
Frith, Michael K. Some of Us Walk, Some
    Fly, Some Swim
George, Jean Craighead. All Upon a Stone
Hamberger, John F. The Day the Sun
    Disappeared
Hawes, Judy. Fireflies in the Night
Hurd, Edith Thacher. Sandpipers
Jackson, Jacqueline. Chicken Ten
    Thousand
Kumin, Maxine W., and Sexton, Anne.
    Eggs of Things
McNulty, Faith. Woodchuck
May, Charles Paul. High-Noon Rocket
Meshover, Leonard, and Feistel, Sally. The
    Guinea Pigs That Went to School
The Monkey That Went to School
Morris, Robert A. Dolphin
Seahorse
Myrick, Mildred. Ants Are Fun
Parker, Nancy Winslow. The Ordeal of
    Byron B. Blackbear
Phleger, Frederick B. Red Tag Comes
    Back
The Whales Go By
Phleger, Frederick B., and Phleger,
    Marjorie. You Will Live under the
    Sea
Pursell, Margaret Sanford. Jessie the
    Chicken
A Look at Birth
Polly the Guinea Pig
Shelley the Sea Gull
Sprig the Tree Frog
Rabinowitz, Sandy. What's Happening to
    Daisy?
Ricciuti, Edward R. An Animal for Alan
Donald and the Fish That Walked
Richards, Jane. A Horse Grows Up
Russell, Solveig Paulson. What Good Is a
    Tail?
Ryder, Joanne. Fireflies
Scarry, Richard McClure. Richard Scarry's
    Great Big Air Book
Schneider, Herman, and Schneider, Nina.
    Follow the Sunset
Selsam, Millicent Ellis. Benny's Animals
    and How He Put Them in Order
The Bug That Laid the Golden Eggs
Egg to Chick
Greg's Microscope
How Kittens Grow
How Puppies Grow
Is This a Baby Dinosaur? And Other
    Science Picture Puzzles
Let's Get Turtles
More Potatoes!
Plenty of Fish
Seeds and More Seeds
Terry and the Caterpillars

Tony's Birds
When an Animal Grows
You and the World Around You
Shapp, Martha; Shapp, Charles; and
    Shepard, Sylvia. Let's Find Out about
    Babies
Shaw, Evelyn S. Alligator
Fish Out of School
A Nest of Wood Ducks
Octopus
Sheehan, Angela. The Duck
The Otter
Sheffield, Margaret. Where Do Babies
    Come From?
Showers, Paul. A Baby Starts to Grow
Before You Were a Baby
Sugita, Yutaka. The Flower Family
Tresselt, Alvin R. Rain Drop Splash
Wong, Herbert H., and Vassel, Matthew F.
    My Goldfish
My Ladybug
My Plant
Our Caterpillars
Our Earthworms
Our Terrariums
Our Tree
Zallinger, Peter. Dinosaurs

153 Sea and seashore

Ardizzone, Edward Jeffrey Irving. Little
    Tim and the Brave Sea Captain
Peter the Wanderer
Ship's Cook Ginger
Tim All Alone
Tim and Charlotte
Tim and Ginger
Tim and Lucy Go to Sea
Tim in Danger
Tim to the Rescue
Tim's Friend Towser
Tim's Last Voyage
Bond, Michael. Paddington at the Seaside
Bonsall, Crosby Newell. Mine's the Best
Bright, Robert. Georgie and the Noisy
    Ghost
Brown, Margaret Wise. The Seashore
    Noisy Book
Bruna, Dick. Miffy at the Seaside
Burningham, John Mackintosh. Come
    Away from the Water, Shirley
Domanska, Janina. If All the Seas Were
    One Sea
Field, Eugene. Wynken, Blynken and Nod
Freeman, Don. Come Again, Pelican
Garelick, May. Down to the Beach
George, Jean Craighead. The Wentletrap
    Trap
Haas, Irene. The Maggie B
Hoff, Sydney. Albert the Albatross
Iwamatsu, Jun. Seashore Story

Iwasaki, Chihiro. What's Fun Without a
    Friend?
Joslin, Sesyle. Baby Elephant Goes to
    China
Koch, Dorothy Clarke. I Play at the Beach
Kraus, Robert. Herman the Helper
Kumin, Maxine W. The Beach Before
    Breakfast
Kuskin, Karla Seidman. Sand and Snow
Lionni, Leo. On My Beach There Are
    Many Pebbles
    Swimmy
Lund, Doris Herold. The Paint-Box Sea
McCloskey, Robert John. Burt Dow, Deep
    Water Man
    One Morning in Maine
    Time of Wonder
McKee, David. The Day the Tide Went
    Out and Out and Out
Mahy, Margaret. Sailor Jack and the
    Twenty Orphans
Matsutani, Miyoko. The Fisherman under
    the Sea
Mendoza, George. The Scribbler
Morse, Samuel French. Sea Sums
Nakatani, Chiyoko. Fumio and the
    Dolphins
Napoli, Guillier. Adventure at Mont St.
    Michael
Nicoll, Helen. Meg at Sea
Orgel, Doris. On the Sand Dune
Peet, Bill. Cyrus the Unsinkable Sea
    Serpent
    Kermit the Hermit
Phleger, Frederick B., and Phleger,
    Marjorie. You Will Live under the
    Sea
Russ, Lavinia. Alec's Sand Castle
Ryder, Joanne. A Wet and Sandy Day
Schick, Eleanor. Summer at the Sea
Schlein, Miriam. The Sun, the Wind, the
    Sea and the Rain
Sea World Alphabet Book
Shaw, Evelyn S. Fish Out of School
    Octopus
Simon, Mina Lewiton. Is Anyone Here?
Slobodkin, Louis. The Seaweed Hat
Smith, Ray, and Smith, Catriona. The
    Long Dive
Smith, Theresa Kalab. The Fog Is Secret
Steiner, Charlotte. Listen to My Seashell
Strahl, Rudi. Sandman in the Lighthouse
Straker, Joan Ann. Animals That Live in
    the Sea
Taylor, Mark. The Bold Fisherman
Tobias, Tobi. At the Beach
Tresselt, Alvin R. Hide and Seek Fog
    I Saw the Sea Come In
Turkle, Brinton Cassady. Obadiah the
    Bold
    The Sky Dog

Ungerer, Tomi. The Mellops Go Diving
    for Treasure
Vasiliu, Marcea. A Day at the Beach
Vinson, Pauline. Willie Goes to the
    Seashore
Waber, Bernard. I Was All Thumbs
Watson, Nancy Dingman. When Is
    Tomorrow?
Wegen, Ronald. Sand Castle
Wright, Dare. Holiday for Edith and the
    Bears
Zion, Gene. Harry by the Sea

154 Seasons

Beskow, Elsa Maartman. Children of the
    Forest
Blegvad, Erik. Burnie's Hill
Brown, Margaret Wise. The Little Island
Burningham, John Mackintosh. Seasons
Carrick, Carol. The Old Barn
Clifton, Lucille B. Everett Anderson's Year
de Paola, Thomas Anthony. Four Stories
    for Four Seasons
Duvoisin, Roger Antoine. The House of
    Four Seasons
Fisher, Aileen Lucia. As the Leaves Fall
    Down
    Going Barefoot
    Like Nothing at All
Foster, Doris Van Liew. A Pocketful of
    Seasons
Gackenbach, Dick. Ida Fanfanny
Haley, Gail Diana Einhart. Go Away, Stay
    Away
Hall, Bill. A Year in the Forest
Hurd, Edith Thacher. The Day the Sun
    Danced
Kwitz, Mary DeBall. Mouse at Home
Lobel, Arnold Stark. Frog and Toad All
    Year
Oppenheim, Joanne. Have You Seen
    Trees?
Provensen, Alice, and Provensen, Martin.
    A Book of Seasons
    The Year at Maple Hill Farm
Tresselt, Alvin R. It's Time Now!
    Johnny Maple-Leaf
Tudor, Tasha. Around the Year
Udry, Janice May. A Tree Is Nice
Welber, Robert. Song of the Seasons
Welles, Winifred. The Park That Spring
    Forgot
Wellington, Anne. Apple Pie
Wood, Joyce. Grandmother Lucy in Her
    Garden
Zolotow, Charlotte Shapiro. In My Garden

154.01 Seasons—fall

Adelson, Leone. All Ready for School
Bartoli, Jennifer. Snow on Bear's Nose

Bunting, Eve. Winter's Coming
Cohen, Peter Zachary. Authorized Autumn
  Charts of the Upper Red Canoe
  River Country
Kumin, Maxine W. Follow the Fall
Lapp, Eleanor J. The Mice Came in Early
  This Year
Lenski, Lois L. Now It's Fall
Ott, John, and Coley, Pete. Peter Pumpkin
Potter, Beatrix. The Tale of Squirrel
  Nutkin
Taylor, Mark. Henry Explores the
  Mountains
Tresselt, Alvin R. Autumn Harvest
  Johnny Maple-Leaf
Udry, Janice May. Emily's Autumn
Weygant, Noemi. It's Autumn!

154.02 Seasons—spring

Baum, Arline, and Baum, Joseph. One
  Bright Monday Morning
Beer, Kathleen Costello. What Happens in
  the Spring
Belting, Natalie Maree. Summer's Coming
  In
Brustlein, Janice. Little Bear's Pancake
  Party
Chönz, Selina. A Bell for Ursli
Clifton, Lucille B. The Boy Who Didn't
  Believe in Spring
Cohen, Carol L. Wake Up Groundhog!
Craig, M. Jean. Spring Is Like the Morning
Delton, Judy. Three Friends Find Spring
Fish, Helen Dean. When the Root Children
  Wake Up
Fisher, Aileen Lucia. My Mother and I
  Now That Spring Is Here
Hoban, Lillian. The Sugar Snow Spring
  Turtle Spring
Hurd, Edith Thacher. The Day the Sun
  Danced
Kesselman, Wendy Ann. Time for Jody
Krauss, Ruth. The Happy Day
Kumin, Maxine W. Spring Things
Leavens, George. Kippy the Koala
Leisk, David Johnson. Time for Spring
  Will Spring Be Early?
Lenski, Lois L. Spring Is Here
Schlein, Miriam. Little Red Nose
Seignobosc, Françoise. Springtime for
  Jeanne-Marie
Taylor, Mark. Henry the Castaway
Tresselt, Alvin R. Hi, Mr. Robin
Weygant, Noemi. It's Spring!
Wood, Joyce. Grandmother Lucy in Her
  Garden
Zion, Gene. Really Spring

154.03 Seasons—summer

Adelson, Leone. All Ready for Summer
Beim, Jerrold. The Swimming Hole
Bourne, Miriam Anne. Emilio's Summer
  Day
Brown, Margaret Wise. Summer Noisy
  Book
Burn, Doris. The Summerfolk
Chönz, Selina. Florina and the Wild Bird
Chwast, Seymour, and Moskof, Martin
  Stephen. Still Another Children's
  Book
Firmin, Peter. Basil Brush Finds Treasure
Garelick, May. Down to the Beach
Goodall, John Strickland. An Edwardian
  Summer
Kuskin, Karla Seidman. Sand and Snow
Lenski, Lois L. On a Summer Day
Lund, Doris Herold. The Paint-Box Sea
McCloskey, Robert John. Time of Wonder
Schick, Eleanor. One Summer Night
  Summer at the Sea
Taylor, Mark. Henry Explores the Jungle
Thomas, Ianthe. Lordy, Aunt Hattie
Weygant, Noemi. It's Summer!
Yolen, Jane. Milkweed Days
Zion, Gene. Harry by the Sea
  The Summer Snowman

154.04 Seasons—winter

Abisch, Roslyn Kroop. 'Twas in the Moon
  of Wintertime
Adelson, Leone. All Ready for Winter
Attenberger, Walburga. The Little Man in
  Winter
Bartoli, Jennifer. In a Meadow, Two Hares
  Hide
  Snow on Bear's Nose
Brown, Margaret Wise. Winter Noisy Book
Bruna, Dick. Miffy in the Snow
Buckley, Helen Elizabeth. Josie and the
  Snow
Bunting, Eve. Winter's Coming
Burton, Virginia Lee. Katy and the Big
  Snow
Chönz, Selina. The Snowstorm
Craft, Ruth. The Winter Bear
Delton, Judy. My Mom Hates Me in
  January
  Three Friends Find Spring
Eckert, Horst. Dear Snowman
Fisher, Aileen Lucia. Where Does
  Everyone Go?
Flack, Marjorie. Angus Lost
Hoban, Russell Conwell, and Hoban,
  Lillian. Some Snow Said Hello
Hoff, Sydney. When Will It Snow?
Keats, Ezra Jack. The Snowy Day
Knotts, Howard Clayton. The Winter Cat
Krauss, Ruth. The Happy Day

161 Sky

Dayrell, Elphinstone. Why the Sun and the Moon Live in the Sky
Dayton, Mona. Earth and Sky
Shaw, Charles Green. It Looked Like Spilt Milk

162 Sleep

Alexander, Martha G. I'll Protect You from the Jungle Beasts
Beckman, Kaj. Lisa Cannot Sleep
Brande, Marlie. Sleepy Nicholas
Bright, Robert. Me and the Bears
Brown, Margaret Wise. A Child's Good-Night Book
Sleepy ABC
The Sleepy Little Lion
Brown, Myra Berry. First Night Away from Home
Chalmers, Mary Eileen. Take a Nap, Harry
Chorao, Kay. Lester's Overnight
Ciardi, John. Scrappy the Pup
Coker, Gylbert. Naptime
de Paola, Thomas Anthony. Fight the Night
When Everyone Was Fast Asleep
Elkin, Benjamin. The King Who Could Not Sleep
Evans, Eva Knox. Sleepy Time
Field, Eugene. Wynken, Blynken and Nod
Geisel, Theodor Seuss. Dr. Seuss's Sleep Book
Hazen, Barbara Shook. Where Do Bears Sleep?
Hutchins, Pat. Good-Night Owl
Jeffers, Susan. All the Pretty Horses
Kantrowitz, Mildred. Willy Bear
Keats, Ezra Jack. Dreams
Kraus, Robert. Milton the Early Riser
Kraus, Robert, and Bodecker, Nils Mogens. Good Night Little One
Good Night Richard Rabbit
Marino, Dorothy Bronson. Edward and the Boxes
Massie, Diane Redfield. The Baby Beebee Bird
Plath, Sylvia. The Bed Book
Preston, Edna Mitchell. Monkey in the Jungle
Reidel, Marlene. Jacob and the Robbers
Rowand, Phyllis. It Is Night
Saleh, Harold. Even Tiny Ants Must Sleep
Schneider, Nina. While Susie Sleeps
Slobodkin, Louis. The Wide-Awake Owl
Sonneborn, Ruth A. Seven in a Bed
Sugita, Yutaka. Good Night 1, 2, 3
Tobias, Tobi. Chasing the Goblins Away
Trez, Denise, and Trez, Alain. Good Night, Veronica
Vorse, Mary Ellen. Wakey Goes to Bed

Waber, Bernard. Ira Sleeps Over
Weisgard, Leonard. Who Dreams of Cheese?
Whitney, Julie. Bears Are Sleeping
Zagone, Theresa. No Nap for Me
Zolotow, Charlotte Shapiro. The Sleepy Book

163 Snowmen

Briggs, Raymond. The Snowman
Eckert, Horst. Dear Snowman
Erskine, Jim. The Snowman
Holl, Adelaide. The Runaway Giant
Kellogg, Steven. The Mystery of the Missing Red Mitten
Kuskin, Karla Seidman. In the Flaky Frosty Morning
Leisk, David Johnson. Time for Spring
Zion, Gene. The Summer Snowman

164 Songs

Abisch, Roslyn Kroop. 'Twas in the Moon of Wintertime
Alexander, Cecil Frances. All Things Bright and Beautiful
Alger, Leclaire. All in the Morning Early
Always Room for One More
Kellyburn Braes
Bangs, Edward. Yankee Doodle
Billy Boy
Bonne, Rose. I Know an Old Lady
Brand, Oscar. When I First Came to This Land
Briggs, Raymond. The White Land
Bring a Torch, Jeannette, Isabella
Child, Lydia Maria. Over the River and Through the Wood
Conover, Chris. Six Little Ducks
De Regniers, Beatrice Schenk. Was It a Good Trade?
Devlin, Harry. The Walloping Window Blind
Domanska, Janina. Din Dan Don, It's Christmas
Duvoisin, Roger Antoine. Petunia and the Song
Emberley, Barbara. One Wide River to Cross
Simon's Song
The Farmer in the Dell
Fern, Eugene. Birthday Presents
The Fox Went Out on a Chilly Night
The Friendly Beasts and A Partridge in a Pear Tree
A Frog He Would A-Wooing Go
Frog Went A-Courtin'
Go Tell Aunt Rhody, illus. by Aliki Liacouras Brandenberg
Go Tell Aunt Rhody, illus. by Robert Mead Quackenbush

Gordon, Margaret. A Paper of Pins
The Green Grass Grows All Around
Hirawa, Yasuko, comp. Song of the Sour
  Plum and Other Japanese Children's
  Songs
Houston, John A. The Bright Yellow Rope
A Mouse in My House
A Room Full of Animals
Hush Little Baby
Ipcar, Dahlov Zorach. The Cat Came Back
  The Song of the Day Birds and the
  Night Birds
Ivimey, John William. The Complete
  Version of Ye Three Blind Mice
Keats, Ezra Jack. The Little Drummer Boy
  Over in the Meadow
Key, Francis Scott. The Star-Spangled
  Banner, illus. by Paul Galdone
  The Star-Spangled Banner, illus. by
  Peter Spier
Kimmel, Eric. Why Worry?
Langstaff, John Meredith. Oh, A-Hunting
  We Will Go
  Ol' Dan Tucker
  Over in the Meadow
  Soldier, Soldier, Won't You Marry Me?
  The Swapping Boy
  The Two Magicians
Langstaff, John Meredith, and Groves-
  Raines, Antony. On Christmas Day in
  the Morning!
Lear, Edward. The Pelican Chorus
Lenski, Lois L. At Our House
  Davy and His Dog
  Davy Goes Places
  Debbie and Her Grandma
  A Dog Came to School
  I Like Winter
  I Went for a Walk
Lord, Beman. The Days of the Week
Mack, Stanley. Ten Bears in My Bed, a
  Goodnight Countdown
Maril, Lee. Mr. Bunny Paints the Eggs
Miller, Albert. The Hungry Goat
Mother Goose. London Bridge Is Falling
  Down, illus. by Edward Randolph
  Emberley
  London Bridge Is Falling Down!, illus
  by Peter Spier
  Mother Goose's Melodies; Or, Songs for
  the Nursery
  Songs from Mother Goose
Newbolt, Sir Henry John. Rilloby-Rill
Oberhansli, Gertrud. Sleep, Baby, Sleep
Old MacDonald Had a Farm, illus. by Mel
  Crawford
Old MacDonald Had a Farm, illus. by
  Abner Graboff
Old MacDonald Had a Farm, illus. by
  Robert Mead Quakenbush
Paterson, Andrew Barton. Waltzing
  Matilda

Poston, Elizabeth. Baby's Song Book
Preston, Edna Mitchell. Pop Corn and Ma
  Goodness
Price, Christine. One Is God; Two Old
  Counting Songs
Quackenbush, Robert Mead. Clementine
  The Man on the Flying Trapeze
  Pop! Goes the Weasel and Yankee
  Doodle
  She'll Be Comin' 'Round the Mountain
  Skip to My Lou
  There'll Be a Hot Time in the Old
  Town Tonight
Raebeck, Lois. Who Am I?
Rey, Hans Augusto. Humpty Dumpty and
  Other Mother Goose Songs
Robbins, Ruth. Baboushka and the Three
  Kings
Rounds, Glen H. The Boll Weevil
  Casey Jones
  The Strawberry Roan
  Sweet Betsy from Pike
Schackburg, Richard. Yankee Doodle
Seeger, Peter. Foolish Frog
The Sesame Street Song Book
Slobodkin, Louis. The Wide-Awake Owl
Spier, Peter. The Erie Canal
Stern, Elsie-Jean. Wee Robin's Christmas
  Song
Tabor, Troy E. Mother Goose in Hawaii
Taylor, Mark. The Bold Fisherman
  Old Blue, You Good Dog You
Twelve Days of Christmas (English folk
  song). Brian Wildsmith's The Twelve
  Days of Christmas
  Jack Kent's Twelve Days of Christmas
  The Twelve Days of Christmas
Watson, Wendy. Fisherman Lullabies
Wells, Rosemary. A Song to Sing, O!
Wenning, Elizabeth. The Christmas Mouse
Whitney, Julie. Bears Are Sleeping
Widdecombe Fair; An Old English Folk
  Song
Wilder, Alec. Lullabies and Night Songs
Zemach, Harve. Mommy Buy Me a China
  Doll
Zemach, Margot. Hush, Little Baby

165 Space and space ships

Asimov, Isaac. The Best New Thing
Brunhoff, Laurent de. Babar Visits
  Another Planet
Freeman, Don. Space Witch
Freeman, Mae, and Freeman, Ira. You Will
  Go to the Moon
Fuchs, Eric. Journey to the Moon
Kuskin, Karla Seidman. A Space Story
Leisk, David Johnson. Harold's Trip to the
  Sky
May, Charles Paul. High-Noon Rocket
Peet, Bill. The Wump World

Rey, Hans Augusto. Curious George Gets a Medal
Robison, Nancy. UFO Kidnap
Schulman, Janet. Jack the Bum and the UFO
Steadman, Ralph. The Little Red Computer
Ungerer, Tomi. Moon Man
Wooley, Catherine. Rockets Don't Go to Chicago, Andy
Zaffo, George J. The Giant Book of Things in Space
Ziegler, Ursina. Squaps the Moonling

166 Sports

Christopher, Matthew F. Jackrabbit Goalie

166.01 Sports—baseball

Christian, Mary Blount. The Sand Lot
Christopher, Matthew F. Johnny No Hit
Hillert, Margaret. Play Ball
Hoff, Sydney. The Littlest Leaguer
Isadora, Rachel. Max
Kessler, Leonard P. Here Comes the Strikeout
Parish, Peggy. Play Ball, Amelia Bedelia
Perkins, Al. Don and Donna Go to Bat
Rubin, Jeff, and Rael, Rick. Baseball Brothers
Rudolph, Marguerita. I Am Your Misfortune
Sachs, Marilyn. Matt's Mitt
Schulman, Janet. Camp Kee Wee's Secret Weapon

166.02 Sports—basketball

Shearer, John. The Case of the Sneaker Snatcher

166.03 Sports—bicycling

Baugh, Dolores M., and Pulsifer, Marjorie P. Bikes
Breinburg, Petronella. Shawn's Red Bike
McLeod, Emilie Warren. The Bear's Bicycle
Paterson, Andrew Barton. Mulga Bill's Bicycle
Phleger, Frederick B., and Phleger, Marjorie. Off to the Races
Rey, Hans Augusto. Curious George Rides a Bike
Taniuchi, Kota. Up on a Hilltop

166.04 Sports—camping

Boynton, Sandra. Hester in the Wild
Brown, Myra Berry. Pip Camps Out
Carrick, Carol. Sleep Out

Marino, Dorothy Bronson. Buzzy Bear Goes Camping
Mayer, Mercer. You're the Scaredy Cat
Prince, Dorothy E. Speedy Gets Around
Schulman, Janet. Camp Kee Wee's Secret Weapon
Shulevitz, Uri. Dawn
Thompson, Vivian Laubach. Camp-in-the-Yard

166.05 Sports—fishing

Aldridge, Josephine Haskell. Fisherman's Luck
  A Peony and a Periwinkle
Cook, Bernadine. The Little Fish That Got Away
Ehrlich, Bettina. Pantaloni
Elkin, Benjamin. Six Foolish Fishermen
Gelman, Rita Golden. Uncle Hugh, a Fishing Story
Goffstein, Marilyn Brooks. Fish for Supper
Hall, Bill. Fish Tale
Ipcar, Dahlov Zorach. The Biggest Fish in the Sea
Martin, Patricia Miles. No, No, Rosina
Mayer, Mercer. A Boy, a Dog, a Frog, and a Friend
Ness, Evaline. Sam, Bangs and Moonshine
Parker, Dorothy D. Liam's Catch
Potter, Beatrix. The Tale of Mr. Jeremy Fisher
Rey, Margret Elisabeth Waldstein. Curious George Flies a Kite
Surany, Anico. Ride the Cold Wind
Taylor, Mark. The Bold Fisherman
Wahl, Jan. The Fishermen
Watson, Nancy Dingman. Tommy's Mommy's Fish

166.06 Sports—football

Hoff, Sydney. Slugger Sal's Slump
Kessler, Leonard P. Kick, Pass and Run

166.07 Sports—gymnastics

Schulman, Janet. Jenny and the Tennis Nut
Stevens, Carla. The Pig and the Blue Flag

166.08 Sports—hunting

Bemelmans, Ludwig. Parsley
Burch, Robert. The Hunting Trip
Burningham, John Mackintosh. Harquin, the Fox Who Went Down to the Valley
Calhoun, Mary. Houn' Dog
Carrick, Donald. The Deer in the Pasture
Duvoisin, Roger Antoine. Happy Hunter

Hader, Berta Hoerner, and Hader, Elmer Stanley. The Mighty Hunter
Kahl, Virginia Caroline. How Do You Hide a Monster?
Langstaff, John Meredith. Oh, A-Hunting We Will Go
Peet, Bill. Buford, the Little Bighorn
   The Gnats of Knotty Pine
Steiner, Charlotte. Pete and Peter

166.09 Sports—ice skating

Hoban, Lillian. Mr. Pig and Sonny Too
Lindman, Maj Jan. Flicka, Ricka, Dicka and Their New Skates
Van Stockum, Hilda. Day on Skates
Young, Miriam Burt. Beware the Polar Bear! Safety on Ice

166.10 Sports—Olympics

Kessler, Leonard P. On Your Mark, Get Set, Go!

166.11 Sports—racing

Calloway, Northern J. Northern J. Calloway Presents Super-Vroomer!
Hurd, Edith Thacher. Last One Home Is a Green Pig
La Fontaine, Jean de. The Hare and the Tortoise
Phleger, Frederick B., and Phleger, Marjorie. Off to the Races
Van Woerkom, Dorothy O. Harry and Shellburt

166.12 Sports—skiing

Calhoun, Mary. Cross-Country Cat
Freeman, Don. Ski Pup
Lindman, Maj Jan. Snipp, Snapp, Snurr and the Red Shoes
Peet, Bill. Buford, the Little Bighorn

166.13 Sports—skin diving

Ungerer, Tomi. The Mellops Go Diving for Treasure

166.14 Sports—surfing

Ormondroyd, Edward. Broderick

166.15 Sports—swimming

Alexander, Martha G. We Never Get To Do Anything
Beim, Jerrold. The Swimming Hole
Ginsburg, Mirra. The Chick and the Duckling

Kessler, Leonard P. Last One in Is a Rotten Egg
Shortall, Leonard W. Tony's First Dive
Stevens, Carla. Hooray for Pig!

166.16 Sports—tennis

Schulman, Janet. Jenny and the Tennis Nut

167 Stars

Coatsworth, Elizabeth Jane. Good Night
Kuskin, Karla Seidman. A Space Story

168 Stores

Baugh, Dolores M., and Pulsifer, Marjorie P. Let's Go Supermarket
Cooper, Lettice Ulpha. The Bear Who Was Too Big
Freeman, Don. Corduroy
Hastings, Evelyn Belmont. The Department Store
Miller, Alice P. The Little Store on the Corner
Potter, Beatrix. Ginger and Pickles
Rockwell, Anne F., and Rockwell, Harlow. The Supermarket
Scarry, Richard McClure. Richard Scarry's Great Big Mystery Book
Steiner, Jörg, and Müller, Jörg. The Bear Who Wanted to Be a Bear

169 Sun

Dayrell, Elphinstone. Why the Sun and the Moon Live in the Sky
De Regniers, Beatrice Schenk, and Pierce, Leona. Who Likes the Sun?
Elkin, Benjamin. Why the Sun Was Late
Goudey, Alice E. The Day We Saw the Sun Come Up
Hamberger, John F. The Day the Sun Disappeared
Hurd, Edith Thacher. The Day the Sun Danced
La Fontaine, Jean de. The North Wind and the Sun
Ringi, Kjell. The Sun and the Cloud
Schlein, Miriam. The Sun Looks Down
   The Sun, the Wind, the Sea and the Rain
Schneider, Herman, and Schneider, Nina. Follow the Sunset
Shulevitz, Uri. Dawn
Tresselt, Alvin R. Sun Up
Wildsmith, Brian. What the Moon Saw

170 Taxis

Moore, Lilian. Papa Albert
Ross, Jessica. Ms. Klondike

171 Teeth

Bate, Lucy. Little Rabbit's Loose Tooth
de Groat, Diane. Alligator's Toothache
Duvoisin, Roger Antoine. Crocus
McCloskey, Robert John. One Morning in
    Maine
McGinley, Phyllis. Lucy McLockett
Pomerantz, Charlotte. The Mango Tooth
Richter, Alice, and Numeroff, Laura Joffe.
    You Can't Put Braces on Spaces
Teeth
Williams, Barbara. Albert's Toothache

172 Telephone

Allen, Jeffrey. Mary Alice, Operator
    Number 9
Bonsall, Crosby Newell. The Case of the
    Dumb Bells
Chukovsky, Kornei. The Telephone
Telephones
Wyse, Lois. Two Guppies, a Turtle, and
    Aunt Edna

173 Theater

Alexander, Sue. Seymour the Prince
Coombs, Patricia. Dorrie's Play
de Paola, Thomas Anthony. The Christmas
    Pageant
Ets, Marie Hall. Another Day
Freeman, Don. Hattie the Backstage Bat
    Will's Quill
Freeman, Don, and Freeman, Lydia. Pet of
    the Met
Goodall, John Strickland. Paddy's Evening
    Out
Johnston, Johanna. Speak Up, Edie
Lobel, Arnold Stark. Martha the Movie
    Mouse
Maiorano, Robert. Backstage
Martin, Judith, and Charlip, Remy. The
    Tree Angel
Rose, Mitchel. Norman
Steiner, Charlotte. Kiki Is an Actress
Tallon, Robert. Handella

174 Time

Abisch, Roslyn Kroop. Do You Know What
    Time It Is?
Allen, Jeffrey. Mary Alice, Operator
    Number 9
Behn, Harry. All Kinds of Time
Bodwell, Gaile. The Long Day of the
    Giants

Carle, Eric. The Grouchy Ladybug
Hay, Dean. Now I Can Count
Hutchins, Pat. Clocks and More Clocks
May, Charles Paul. High-Noon Rocket
Ness, Evaline. Do You Have the Time,
    Lydia?
Scarry, Richard McClure. Richard Scarry's
    Great Big Schoolhouse
Schlein, Miriam. It's About Time
Seignobosc, Françoise. What Time Is It,
    Jeanne-Marie?
Slobodkin, Louis. The Late Cuckoo
Watson, Nancy Dingman. When Is
    Tomorrow?
Ziner, Feenie, and Thompson, Elizabeth.
    The True Book of Time
Zolotow, Charlotte Shapiro. Over and Over

175 Tongue twisters

Brown, Marcia. Peter Piper's Alphabet
Carle, Eric. All About Arthur
Geisel, Theodor Seuss. Oh Say Can You
    Say?
Patz, Nancy. Pumpernickel Tickle and
    Mean Green Cheese
Pomerantz, Charlotte. The Piggy in the
    Puddle
Smith, Robert Paul. Jack Mack
Wallace, Daisy. Monster Poems

176 Tools

Lerner, Marguerite Rush. Doctors' Tools
Rockwell, Anne F., and Rockwell, Harlow.
    The Toolbox
Thomas, Anthony. Things We Cut
Zaffo, George J. The Giant Nursery Book
    of Things That Work

177 Toys

Alexander, Martha G. The Story
    Grandmother Told
Ardizzone, Aingelda. The Night Ride
Avery, Kay. Wee Willow Whistle
Ayer, Jacqueline Brandford. Nu Dang and
    His Kite
Beckman, Kaj. Lisa Cannot Sleep
Binzen, Bill. Alfred Goes House Hunting
Bornstein, Ruth. Annabelle
Bright, Robert. Hurrah for Freddie!
Chorao, Kay. Molly's Moe
Coombs, Patricia. The Lost Playground
Craig, M. Jean. Boxes
Daly, Niki. Vim the Rag Mouse
Dobrin, Arnold Jack. Josephine's
    'magination
Flora, James. Sherwood Walks Home
Geisel, Theodor Seuss. The King's Stilts
Grifalconi, Ann. The Toy Trumpet
Hillert, Margaret. The Birthday Car

Hughes, Shirley. David and Dog
Jones, Harold. There and Back Again
Kahn, Joan. Seesaw
Leisk, David Johnson. Ellen's Lion
Lionni, Leo. Alexander and the Wind-Up
    Mouse
McPhail, David. Mistletoe
Marcin, Marietta. A Zoo in Her Bed
Politi, Leo. Mr. Fong's Toy Shop
Potter, Beatrix. The Tale of Two Bad Mice
Sandburg, Carl. The Wedding Procession
    of the Rag Doll and the Broom
    Handle and Who Was in It
Scharen, Beatrix. Gigin and Till
Smith, Ray, and Smith, Catriona. The
    Long Dive
   The Long Slide
Steger, Hans-Ulrich. Traveling to Tripiti
Stephenson, Dorothy. The Night It Rained
    Toys
Thelen, Gerda. The Toy Maker
Titus, Eve. Anatole and the Toyshop
Tudor, Bethany. Samuel's Tree House
Tudor, Tasha. Thistly B
Wahl, Jan. Jamie's Tiger

177.01 Toys—balloons

Bonsall, Crosby Newell. Mine's the Best
Carrick, Carol, and Carrick, Donald. The
    Highest Balloon on the Common
Mari, Iela. The Magic Balloon
Sharmat, Marjorie Weinman. I Don't Care

177.02 Toys—balls

Espenscheid, Gertrude E. The Oh Ball
Hamberger, John F. The Lazy Dog
Holl, Adelaide. The Remarkable Egg
Kellogg, Steven. The Mystery of the Magic
    Green Ball
Krahn, Fernando. The Biggest Christmas
    Tree on Earth
McClintock, Marshall. Stop That Ball
Maley, Anne. Have You Seen My Mother?

177.03 Toys—blocks

Hutchins, Pat. Changes, Changes
Mayers, Patrick. Just One More Block
Winthrop, Elizabeth. That's Mine!

177.04 Toys—dolls

Ardizzone, Aingelda. The Night Ride
Ardizzone, Edward Jeffrey Irving, and
    Ardizzone, Aingelda. The Little Girl
    and the Tiny Doll
Ayer, Jacqueline Brandford. Little Silk
Bannon, Laura May. Manuela's Birthday in
    Old Mexico
Dreifus, Miriam W. Brave Betsy

Fatio, Louise. A Doll for Marie
Foster, Marian Curtis. The Journey of
    Bangwell Putt
Francis, Frank. Natasha's New Doll
Goffstein, Marilyn Brooks. Goldie the
    Dollmaker
   Me and My Captain
Hoban, Russell Conwell. The Stone Doll of
    Sister Brute
Johnston, Johanna. Sugarplum
Lenski, Lois L. Debbie and Her Dolls
   Let's Play House
Lexau, Joan M. The Rooftop Mystery
Pincus, Harriet. Minna and Pippin
Politi, Leo. Rosa
Sandburg, Carl. The Wedding Procession
    of the Rag Doll and the Broom
    Handle and Who Was in It
Schulman, Janet. The Big Hello
Shecter, Ben. The Stocking Child
Skorpen, Liesel Moak. Elizabeth
Tudor, Tasha. A Is for Annabelle
   The Doll's Christmas
Udry, Janice May. Emily's Autumn
Wahl, Jan. The Muffletump Storybook
   The Muffletumps
   The Muffletumps' Christmas Party
   The Muffletumps' Halloween Scare
Wilson, Julia. Becky
Wright, Dare. The Doll and the Kitten
   Edith and Big Bad Bill
   Edith and Little Bear Lend a Hand
   Edith and Midnight
   Edith and Mr. Bear
   A Gift from the Lonely Doll
   Holiday for Edith and the Bears
   The Little One
   The Lonely Doll
   The Lonely Doll Learns a Lesson
Zemach, Harve. Mommy Buy Me a China
    Doll
Zolotow, Charlotte Shapiro. William's Doll

177.05 Toys—rocking horses

Donaldson, Lois. Karl's Wooden Horse
Lindman, Maj Jan. Snipp, Snapp, Snurr
    and the Magic Horse
Moeschlin, Elsa. Red Horse
Robertson, Lilian. Runaway Rocking Horse

177.06 Toys—soldiers

Heathers, Anne, and Frances, Esteban.
    The Thread Soldiers
Nicholson, William. Clever Bill

177.07 Toys—string

Calhoun, Mary. The Traveling Ball of
    String

Heathers, Anne, and Frances, Esteban.
The Thread Soldiers
Holland, Marion. A Big Ball of String
Wondriska, William. A Long Piece of
String

177.08 Toys—teddy bears

Alexander, Martha G. I'll Protect You
from the Jungle Beasts
Ardizzone, Aingelda. The Night Ride
Brown, Myra Berry. First Night Away
from Home
Cooper, Lettice Ulpha. The Bear Who Was
Too Big
Craft, Ruth. The Winter Bear
Flora, James. Sherwood Walks Home
Freeman, Don. Beady Bear
Corduroy
A Pocket for Corduroy
Gretz, Susanna. Teddybears ABC
Teddybears One to Ten
Hayes, Geoffrey. Bear by Himself
Hoban, Lillian. Arthur's Honey Bear
Kantrowitz, Mildred. Willy Bear
McLeod, Emilie Warren. The Bear's
Bicycle
Milne, Alan Alexander. Pooh's Quiz Book
Nakatani, Chiyoko. My Teddy Bear
Ormondroyd, Edward. Theodore
Theodore's Rival
Romanek, Enid Warner. Teddy
Siewert, Margaret, and Savage, Kathleen.
Bear Hunt
Skorpen, Liesel Moak. Charles
Steger, Hans-Ulrich. Traveling to Tripiti
Tobias, Tobi. Moving Day
Waber, Bernard. Ira Sleeps Over
Wright, Betty Ren. Teddy Bear's Book of
1, 2, 3
Wright, Dare. The Doll and the Kitten
Edith and Big Bad Bill
Edith and Little Bear Lend a Hand
Edith and Midnight
Edith and Mr. Bear
A Gift from the Lonely Doll
Holiday for Edith and the Bears
The Little One
The Lonely Doll
The Lonely Doll Learns a Lesson

177.09 Toys—trains

McPhail, David. The Train
Wells, Peter. Mr. Tootwhistle's Invention

178 Traffic signs

Bank Street College of Education. Green
Light, Go
Baugh, Dolores M., and Pulsifer, Marjorie
P. Bikes

Brown, Margaret Wise. Red Light, Green
Light
Shortall, Leonard W. One Way; A Trip
with Traffic Signs
Wooley, Catherine. Andy and the Runaway
Horse

179 Trains

Bontemps, Arna Wendell, and Conroy,
Jack. The Fast Sooner Hound
Brown, Margaret Wise. Whistle for the
Train
Burton, Virginia Lee. Choo Choo, the
Story of a Little Engine Who Ran
Away
Crews, Donald. Freight Train
Denney, Diana. The Little Red Engine
Gets a Name
Ehrlich, Amy. The Everyday Train
Emmett, Fredrick Rowland. New World
for Nellie
Gramatky, Hardie. Homer and the Circus
Train
Greene, Graham. The Little Train
Hurd, Edith Thacher. Caboose
Engine, Engine Number 9
Kessler, Ethel, and Kessler, Leonard P. All
Aboard the Train
Lenski, Lois L. The Little Train
McPhail, David. The Train
Martin, William Ivan, and Martin, Bernard
Herman. Smoky Poky
Meeks, Esther K. One Is the Engine, illus.
by Ernie King
One Is the Engine, illus. by Joe Rogers
Peet, Bill. The Caboose Who Got Loose
Smokey
Piper, Watty. The Little Engine That
Could
Ross, Diana. The Story of the Little Red
Engine
Sattler, Helen Roney. Train Whistles; A
Language in Code
Slobodkin, Louis. Clear the Track
Taniuchi, Kota. Up on a Hilltop
Towend, Jack. Railroad ABC
Weelen, Guy. The Little Red Train
Wells, Rosemary. Don't Spill It Again,
James
Wondriska, William. Puff
Wooley, Catherine. I Like Trains
Rockets Don't Go to Chicago, Andy
Young, Miriam Burt. If I Drove a Train

180 Transportation

Burton, Virginia Lee. Maybelle, the Cable
Car
Gramatky, Hardie. Sparky
Hoberman, Mary Ann, and Hoberman,
Norman. How Do I Go?

Koren, Edward. Behind the Wheel
Lenski, Lois L. Davy Goes Places
Oppenheim, Joanne. Have You Seen
    Roads?
Potter, Russell. The Little Red Ferry Boat
Rey, Hans Augusto. How Do You Get
    There?
Zaffo, George J. The Giant Nursery Book
    of Things That Go
    The Giant Nursery Book of Things
    That Work

181 Trees

Bason, Lillian. Pick a Raincoat, Pick a
    Whistle
Bemelmans, Ludwig. Parsley
Brown, Margaret Wise. The Little Fir Tree
Carigiet, Alois. The Pear Tree, the Birch
    Tree and the Barberry Bush
Cleary, Beverly. The Real Hole
Fisher, Aileen Lucia. As the Leaves Fall
    Down
    A Tree with a Thousand Uses
Gilbert, Helen Earle. Mr. Plum and the
    Little Green Tree
Hawkinson, John. The Old Stump
Hutchins, Pat. The Silver Christmas Tree
Iwamatsu, Jun. The Village Tree
Kirk, Barbara. Grandpa, Me and Our
    House in the Tree
Krahn, Fernando. The Biggest Christmas
    Tree on Earth
Löfgren, Ulf. The Wonderful Tree
Miles, Miska. Apricot ABC
Oppenheim, Joanne. Have You Seen
    Trees?
Peet, Bill. Merle the High Flying Squirrel
Petie, Haris. The Seed the Squirrel
    Dropped
Silverstein, Shel. The Giving Tree
Thelen, Gerda. The Toy Maker
Tresselt, Alvin R. The Dead Tree
    Johnny Maple-Leaf
Tudor, Bethany. Samuel's Tree House
Udry, Janice May. A Tree Is Nice
Wiese, Kurt. The Thief in the Attic
Wolo (pseud.). The Secret of the Ancient
    Oak
Wong, Herbert H., and Vassel, Matthew F.
    Our Tree
Zolotow, Charlotte Shapiro. The Beautiful
    Christmas Tree

182 Triplets

Brunhoff, Jean de. Babar and His
    Children
Lindman, Maj Jan. Flicka, Ricka, Dicka and
    the Big Red Hen
    Flicka, Ricka, Dicka and the New Dotted
    Dress

Flicka, Ricka, Dicka and the Three
    Kittens
Flicka, Ricka, Dicka and Their New
    Skates
Flicka, Ricka, Dicka Bake a Cake
Snipp, Snapp, Snurr and the Buttered
    Bread
Snipp, Snapp, Snurr and the
    Gingerbread
Snipp, Snapp, Snurr and the Magic
    Horse
Snipp, Snapp, Snurr and the Red Shoes
Snipp, Snapp, Snurr and the Reindeer
Snipp, Snapp, Snurr and the Seven
    Dogs
Snipp, Snapp, Snurr and the Yellow
    Sled

183 Trolls

Asbjørnsen, Peter Christen. The Three
    Billy Goats Gruff, illus. by Paul
    Galdone
    The Three Billy Goats Gruff, illus. by
    William Stobbs
Asbjørnsen, Peter Christen, and Moe,
    Jørgen Engebretsen. The Three Billy
    Goats Gruff
Aulaire, Ingri Mortenson d', and Aulaire,
    Edgar Parin d'. The Terrible Troll-
    Bird
de Paola, Thomas Anthony. Helga's Dowry
Hillert, Margaret. The Three Goats
Johnston, Tony. The Adventures of Mole
    and Troll
Lindgren, Astrid Ericsson. The Tomten
    The Tomten and the Fox
Lobel, Anita. The Troll Music
Mayer, Mercer. Terrible Troll
Svendsen, Carol. Hulda
Tudor, Tasha. Corgiville Fair

184 Trucks

Alexander, Anne. ABC of Cars and Trucks
Baugh, Dolores M., and Pulsifer, Marjorie
    P. Trucks and Cars to Ride
Burroway, Janet. The Truck on the Track
Gramatky, Hardie. Hercules
Greene, Carla. Truck Drivers: What Do
    They Do?
Holl, Adelaide. The ABC of Cars, Trucks
    and Machines
Scarry, Richard McClure. The Great Big
    Car and Truck Book
    Richard Scarry's Cars and Trucks and
    Things That Go
Young, Miriam Burt. If I Drove a Truck
Zaffo, George J. The Big Book of Real
    Trucks
    The Giant Nursery Book of Things
    That Go

185 Twilight

Udry, Janice May. The Moon Jumpers

186 Twins

Cleary, Beverly. The Real Hole
    Two Dog Biscuits
Clymer, Eleanor Lowenton. Horatio Goes
    to the Country
Hoban, Lillian. Here Come Raccoons
Lawrence, James D. Binky Brothers and
    the Fearless Four
McDermott, Gerald. The Magic Tree; A
    Tale from the Congo
Moore, Lilian. Little Raccoon and No
    Trouble at All
Perkins, Al. Don and Donna Go to Bat
Simon, Norma. How Do I Feel?
Stewart, Elizabeth Laing. The Lion Twins
Thompson, Vivian Laubach. Camp-in-the-
    Yard

187 Umbrellas

Bright, Robert. My Red Umbrella
Cole, William. Aunt Bella's Umbrella
Iwamatsu, Jun. Umbrella
Levine, Rhoda. Harrison Loved His
    Umbrella
Lipkind, William, and Schreiber, Georges.
    Professor Bull's Umbrella

188 UNICEF

Schulman, Janet. Jack the Bum and the
    Halloween Handout

189 U.S. history

Abisch, Roslyn Kroop. The Pumpkin
    Heads
Baker, Betty. The Pig War
Bangs, Edward. Yankee Doodle
Benchley, Nathaniel. George the Drummer
    Boy
    Sam the Minuteman
    Small Wolf
    Snorri and the Strangers
Brenner, Barbara. Wagon Wheels
Bulla, Clyde Robert. Washington's
    Birthday
Cooney, Barbara. A Garland of Games and
    Other Diversions
Dalgliesh, Alice. The Thanksgiving Story
Grant, Anne. Danbury's Burning! The
    Story of Sybil Ludington's Ride
Haley, Gail Diana Einhart. Jack Jouett's
    Ride
Key, Francis Scott. The Star-Spangled
    Banner, illus. by Paul Galdone

The Star-Spangled Banner, illus. by
    Peter Spier
Lobel, Arnold Stark. On the Day Peter
    Stuyvesant Sailed into Town
Lowitz, Sadyebeth, and Lowitz, Anson. The
    Pilgrims' Party
Lowrey, Janette Sebring. Six Silver Spoons
Monjo, Ferdinand N. The Drinking Gourd
    Indian Summer
    The One Bad Thing About Father
    Poor Richard in France
Moskin, Marietta D. Lysbet and the Fire
    Kittens
Quackenbush, Robert Mead. Clementine
    Pop! Goes the Weasel and Yankee
    Doodle
    There'll Be a Hot Time in the Old
    Town Tonight
Schackburg, Richard. Yankee Doodle
Schick, Alice, and Allen, Marjorie N. The
    Remarkable Ride of Israel Bissell As
    Related by Molly the Crow
Spier, Peter. The Erie Canal
    The Legend of New Amsterdam
Szekeres, Cyndy. Long Ago
Turkle, Brinton Cassady. The Adventures
    of Obadiah
    Obadiah the Bold
    Thy Friend, Obadiah
Van Woerkom, Dorothy O. Becky and the
    Bear
Waber, Bernard. Just Like Abraham
    Lincoln

190 Values

Mahy, Margaret. Pillycock's Shop
Schlein, Miriam. The Pile of Junk

191 Violence, anti-violence

Charters, Janet, and Foreman, Michael.
    The General
Duvoisin, Roger Antoine. Happy Hunter
Fitzhugh, Louise, and Scoppetone, Sandra.
    Bang Bang You're Dead
Foreman, Michael. Moose
Hader, Berta Hoerner, and Hader, Elmer
    Stanley. Mister Billy's Gun
Leaf, Munro. The Story of Ferdinand the
    Bull
Lobel, Anita. Potatoes, Potatoes
Peet, Bill. The Pinkish, Purplish, Bluish
    Egg
Sharmat, Marjorie Weinman. Walter the
    Wolf
Wiesner, William. Tops
Wondriska, William. The Tomato Patch

192 Volcanoes

Lewis, Thomas. Hill of Fire

193 War

Ambrus, Victor G. Brave Soldier Janosch
Benchley, Nathaniel. George the Drummer
   Boy
   Sam the Minuteman
Fitzhugh, Louise, and Scoppetone, Sandra.
   Bang Bang You're Dead
Foreman, Michael. War and Peas
Schick, Alice, and Allen, Marjorie N. The
   Remarkable Ride of Israel Bissell As
   Related by Molly the Crow

194 Weapons

Bolliger, Max. The Wooden Man
Duvoisin, Roger Antoine. Happy Hunter
Emberley, Barbara. Drummer Hoff
Fitzhugh, Louise, and Scoppetone, Sandra.
   Bang Bang You're Dead
Hader, Berta Hoerner, and Hader, Elmer
   Stanley. Mister Billy's Gun
Wondriska, William. The Tomato Patch

195 Weather

Ardizzone, Edward Jeffrey Irving. Tim to
   the Rescue
Baum, Arline, and Baum, Joseph. One
   Bright Monday Morning
Bell, Norman. Linda's Air Mail Letter
Bolliger, Max. The Wooden Man
Burgert, Hans-Joachim. Samulo and the
   Giant
Coombs, Patricia. Dorrie and the Weather-
   Box
Gackenbach, Dick. Ida Fanfanny
Greenberg, Barbara. The Bravest
   Babysitter
Jaynes, Ruth. Benny's Four Hats
McCloskey, Robert John. Time of Wonder
Rockwell, Anne F., and Rockwell, Harlow.
   Blackout
Schlein, Miriam. The Sun, the Wind, the
   Sea and the Rain
Tresselt, Alvin R. Sun Up
Vance, Eleanor Graham. Jonathan
Zolotow, Charlotte Shapiro. The Storm
   Book

195.01 Weather—clouds

Ringi, Kjell. The Sun and the Cloud
Shaw, Charles Green. It Looked Like Spilt
   Milk
Turkle, Brinton Cassady. The Sky Dog

195.02 Weather—cold

Hoban, Lillian. The Sugar Snow Spring
Young, Miriam Burt. Beware the Polar
   Bear! Safety on Ice

195.03 Weather—floods

Ipcar, Dahlov Zorach. A Flood of
   Creatures
Tapio, Pat Decker. The Lady Who Saw the
   Good Side of Everything

195.04 Weather—fog

Fry, Christopher. The Boat That Mooed
Keeping, Charles William James. Alfie
   Finds the Other Side of the World
Lifton, Betty Jean. Joji and the Fog
Morse, Samuel French. Sea Sums
Munari, Bruno. The Circus in the Mist
Schroder, William. Pea Soup and Serpents
Smith, Theresa Kalab. The Fog Is Secret
Tresselt, Alvin R. Hide and Seek Fog

195.05 Weather—rain

Aldridge, Josephine Haskell. Fisherman's
   Luck
Bergere, Thea. Paris in the Rain with Jean
   and Jacqueline
Brandenberg, Franz. A Picnic, Hurrah!
Bright, Robert. My Red Umbrella
Burningham, John Mackintosh. Mr.
   Gumpy's Motor Car
Calhoun, Mary. Euphonia and the Flood
Carrick, Carol. Sleep Out
   The Washout
Charlip, Remy. Where Is Everybody?
Cole, William. Aunt Bella's Umbrella
Edwards, Dorothy, and Williams, Jenny. A
   Wet Monday
Freeman, Don. Dandelion
Garelick, May. Where Does the Butterfly
   Go When It Rains?
Ginsburg, Mirra. Mushroom in the Rain
Goudey, Alice E. The Good Rain
Holl, Adelaide. The Rain Puddle
Hurd, Edith Thacher. Johnny Lion's
   Rubber Boots
Iwamatsu, Jun. Umbrella
Iwasaki, Chihiro. Staying Home Alone on a
   Rainy Day
Kalan, Robert. Rain
Keats, Ezra Jack. A Letter to Amy
Keith, Eros. Nancy's Backyard
Kishida, Eriko. The Hippo Boat
Kuskin, Karla Seidman. James and the
   Rain
Kwitz, Mary DeBall. When It Rains
Marino, Dorothy Bronson. Good-Bye
   Thunderstorm
Parsons, Ellen. Rainy Day Together
Preston, Edna Mitchell. Pop Corn and Ma
   Goodness
Raskin, Ellen. And It Rained
Ryder, Joanne. A Wet and Sandy Day
Scheer, Julian. Rain Makes Applesauce

Schlein, Miriam. The Sun, the Wind, the Sea and the Rain
Seignobosc, Françoise. The Big Rain
Sherman, Nancy. Gwendolyn and the Weathercock
Shulevitz, Uri. Rain Rain Rivers
Simon, Norma. The Wet World
Tapio, Pat Decker. The Lady Who Saw the Good Side of Everything
Taylor, Mark. Henry the Castaway
Tresselt, Alvin R. Rain Drop Splash
Turner, Nancy Byrd. When It Rains Cats and Dogs
Wagner, Jenny. Aranea
Wahl, Jan. Follow Me Cried Bee
Wells, Rosemary. Don't Spill It Again, James
Zolotow, Charlotte Shapiro. The Storm Book

195.06 Weather—rainbows

Freeman, Don. A Rainbow of My Own
Kwitz, Mary DeBall. When It Rains
Marino, Dorothy Bronson. Buzzy Bear and the Rainbow
Zolotow, Charlotte Shapiro. The Storm Book

195.07 Weather—snow

Brown, Margaret Wise. Winter Noisy Book
Bruna, Dick. Miffy in the Snow
Buckley, Helen Elizabeth. Josie and the Snow
Burton, Virginia Lee. Katy and the Big Snow
Chönz, Selina. The Snowstorm
Dorian, Marguerite. When the Snow Is Blue
Eckert, Horst. Dear Snowman
Hader, Berta Hoerner, and Hader, Elmer Stanley. The Big Snow
Hoban, Lillian. The Sugar Snow Spring
Hoban, Russell Conwell, and Hoban, Lillian. Some Snow Said Hello
Hoff, Sydney. When Will It Snow?
Iwasaki, Chihiro. The Birthday Wish
Keats, Ezra Jack. The Snowy Day
Krauss, Ruth. The Happy Day
Kuskin, Karla Seidman. In the Flaky Frosty Morning
McKie, Roy, and Eastman, Philip Day. Snow
Retan, Walter. The Snowplow That Tried to Go South
Sauer, Julia Lina. Mike's House
Schick, Eleanor. City in the Winter
Schlein, Miriam. Deer in the Snow
Tresselt, Alvin R. White Snow, Bright Snow
Tudor, Tasha. Snow Before Christmas

Udry, Janice May. Mary Jo's Grandmother
Watson, Nancy Dingman. Sugar on Snow
Zion, Gene. The Summer Snowman
Zolotow, Charlotte Shapiro. Hold My Hand

195.08 Weather—wind

Ardizzone, Edward Jeffrey Irving. Tim's Last Voyage
Brown, Margaret Wise. When the Wind Blew
Ets, Marie Hall. Gilberto and the Wind
Garrison, Christian. Little Pieces of the West Wind
Hutchins, Pat. The Wind Blew
Keats, Ezra Jack. A Letter to Amy
La Fontaine, Jean de. The North Wind and the Sun
Lexau, Joan M. Who Took the Farmer's Hat?
Rice, Inez. The March Wind
Schick, Eleanor. City in the Winter
Schlein, Miriam. The Sun, the Wind, the Sea and the Rain
Thompson, Brenda, and Overbeck, Cynthia. The Winds That Blow
Tresselt, Alvin R. Follow the Wind
  The Wind and Peter
Ungerer, Tomi. The Hat
Zolotow, Charlotte Shapiro. When the Wind Stops

196 Weddings

Ambrus, Victor G. A Country Wedding
Asbjørnsen, Peter Christen. The Squire's Bride
Cock Robin. The Courtship, Merry Marriage, and Feast of Cock Robin and Jenny Wren, to Which Is Added the Doleful Death of Cock Robin
Coombs, Patricia. Mouse Cafe
de Paola, Thomas Anthony. Helga's Dowry
Goodall, John Strickland. Naughty Nancy
Hoban, Lillian. Mr. Pig and Sonny Too
Hogrogian, Nonny. Carrot Cake
Hürlimann, Ruth. The Mouse with the Daisy Hat
Quin-Harkin, Janet. Peter Penny's Dance
Sandburg, Carl. The Wedding Procession of the Rag Doll and the Broom Handle and Who Was in It
Suhl, Yuri. Simon Boom Gives a Wedding
Varga, Judy. Janko's Wish
Williams, Barbara. Whatever Happened to Beverly Bigler's Birthday?
Williams, Garth Montgomery. The Rabbits' Wedding

197 Wheels

Barton, Byron. Wheels
Berenstain, Stanley, and Berenstain, Janice. Bears on Wheels
Myller, Rolf. Rolling Round
Olschewski, Alfred. The Wheel Rolls Over

198 Windmills

Yeoman, John. Mouse Trouble

199 Witches

Adams, Adrienne. A Woggle of Witches
Alexander, Sue. More Witch, Goblin and Ghost Stories
Balian, Lorna. Humbug Witch
Benarde, Anita. The Pumpkin Smasher
Bridwell, Norman. The Witch Next Door
Calhoun, Mary. The Witch of Hissing Hill
Coombs, Patricia. Dorrie and the Amazing Magic Elixir
   Dorrie and the Birthday Eggs
   Dorrie and the Blue Witch
   Dorrie and the Dreamyard Monsters
   Dorrie and the Fortune Teller
   Dorrie and the Goblin
   Dorrie and the Halloween Plot
   Dorrie and the Haunted House
   Dorrie and the Screebit Ghost
   Dorrie and the Weather-Box
   Dorrie and the Witch Doctor
   Dorrie and the Witch's Imp
   Dorrie and the Wizard's Spell
   Dorrie's Magic
   Dorrie's Play
Cretien, Paul D., Jr. Sir Henry and the Dragon
de Paola, Thomas Anthony. Strega Nona
Devlin, Wende, and Devlin, Harry. Old Black Witch
   Old Witch and the Polka-Dot Ribbon
   Old Witch Rescues Halloween
Embry, Margaret. The Blue-Nosed Witch
Francis, Frank. Natasha's New Doll
Freeman, Don. Space Witch
   Tilly Witch
Hirsh, Marilyn Joyce. The Rabbi and the Twenty-Nine Witches
Hurd, Edith Thacher. The So-So Cat
Jeschke, Susan. Rima and Zeppo
Kahl, Virginia Caroline. Gunhilde and the Halloween Spell
Keith, Eros. Bedita's Bad Day
Kroll, Steven. The Candy Witch
Kuskin, Karla Seidman. What Did You Bring Me?
Langstaff, John Meredith. The Two Magicians
Leichman, Seymour. The Wicked Wizard and the Wicked Witch

Lobel, Arnold Stark. Prince Bertram the Bad
Low, Alice. The Witch Who Was Afraid of Witches
   Witch's Holiday
Mahy, Margaret. The Boy Who Was Followed Home
   The Boy with Two Shadows
Massey, Jeanne. The Littlest Witch
Matsutani, Miyoko. The Witch's Magic Cloth
Nicoll, Helen. Meg and Mog
   Meg at Sea
   Meg on the Moon
   Meg's Eggs
Peet, Bill. Big Bad Bruce
   The Whingdingdilly
Serraillier, Ian. Suppose You Met a Witch
Shaw, Richard. The Kitten in the Pumpkin Patch
Shecter, Ben. Emily, Girl Witch of New York
Steig, William. Caleb and Kate
Thompson, Harwood. The Witch's Cat
Walker, Barbara K. Teeny-Tiny and the Witch-Woman
Watson, Jane Werner. Which Is the Witch?
Weil, Lisl. The Candy Egg Bunny
Young, Miriam Burt. The Witch Mobile

200 Wizards

Bradfield, Roger. Giants Come in Different Sizes
Coombs, Patricia. Dorrie and the Amazing Magic Elixir
   Dorrie and the Wizard's Spell
Coville, Bruce, and Coville, Katherine. The Foolish Giant
Dines, Glen. Pitidoe the Color Maker
Emberley, Edward Randolph. The Wizard of Op
Fleischman, Albert Sidney. Longbeard the Wizard
Jaffe, Rona. Last of the Wizards
Kimmel, Margaret Mary. Magic in the Mist
Kumin, Maxine W. The Wizard's Tears
Leichman, Seymour. The Wicked Wizard and the Wicked Witch
Lobel, Arnold Stark. The Great Blueness and Other Predicaments
McCrea, James, and McCrea, Ruth. The Story of Olaf
Mayer, Mercer. Mrs. Beggs and the Wizard
Nolan, Dennis. Wizard McBean and His Flying Machine
Oksner, Robert M. The Incompetent Wizard
Zijlstra, Tjerk. Benny and His Geese

201 Wordless

Alexander, Martha G. Bobo's Dream
  Out! Out! Out!
Anno, Mitsumasa. Anno's Journey
  Dr. Anno's Magical Midnight Circus
  Topsy-Turvies
  Upside-Downers
Banchek, Linda. Snake In, Snake Out
Barton, Byron. Where's Al?
Baum, Willi. Birds of a Feather
Briggs, Raymond. Father Christmas
  Father Christmas Goes on Holiday
  The Snowman
Bruna, Dick. Another Story to Tell
Carle, Eric. Do You Want to Be My
  Friend?
  I See a Song
Carroll, Ruth Robinson. What Whiskers
  Did
  Where's the Bunny?
Charlot, Martin. Sunnyside Up
Coker, Gylbert. Naptime
de Groat, Diane. Alligator's Toothache
de Paola, Thomas Anthony. Pancakes for
  Breakfast
Emberley, Edward Randolph. A Birthday
  Wish
Freeman, Don. Forever Laughter
Fromm, Lilo. Muffel and Plums
Fuchs, Eric. Journey to the Moon
Goodall, John Strickland. The Adventures
  of Paddy Pork
  The Ballooning Adventures of Paddy
  Pork
  Creepy Castle
  An Edwardian Christmas
  An Edwardian Summer
  Jacko
  The Midnight Adventures of Kelly, Dot
  and Esmeralda
  Naughty Nancy
  Paddy Pork's Holiday
  Paddy's Evening Out
  Shrewbettina's Birthday
  The Story of an English Village
  The Surprise Picnic
Hamberger, John F. The Lazy Dog
Hartelius, Margaret A. The Chicken's
  Child
Hoban, Tana. Big Ones, Little Ones
  Circles, Triangles, and Squares
  Dig, Drill, Dump, Fill
  Is It Red? Is It Yellow? Is It Blue?
  Look Again
  Shapes and Things
Hogrogian, Nonny. Apples
Hutchins, Pat. Changes, Changes
Keats, Ezra Jack. Kitten for a Day
  Psst, Doggie
  Skates
Kent, Jack. The Egg Book

Krahn, Fernando. April Fools
  The Biggest Christmas Tree on Earth
  Catch That Cat!
  A Funny Friend from Heaven
  The Great Ape
  How Santa Claus Had a Long and
    Difficult Journey Delivering His
    Presents
  Little Love Story
  The Mystery of the Giant Footprints
  Robot-Bot-Bot
  Sebastian and the Mushroom
  Who's Seen the Scissors?
Lemke, Horst. Places and Faces
Lewis, Stephen. Zoo City
Lisker, Sonia O. Lost
Mari, Iela. The Magic Balloon
Mayer, Mercer. Ah-choo
  A Boy, a Dog, a Frog, and a Friend
  A Boy, A Dog and a Frog
  Bubble, Bubble
  Frog Goes to Dinner
  Frog on His Own
  Frog, Where Are You?
  The Great Cat Chase
  Hiccup
  One Frog Too Many
  Oops
  Two Moral Tales
Ogle, Lucille. I Spy with My Little Eye
Panek, Dennis. Catastrophe Cat at the Zoo
Ringi, Kjell. The Winner
Rojankovsky, Feodor Stepanovich. Animals
  on the Farm
Shimin, Symeon. A Special Birthday
Spier, Peter. Noah's Ark
Sugita, Yutaka. My Friend Little John and
  Me
Turkle, Brinton Cassady. Deep in the
  Forest
Ueno, Noriko. Elephant Buttons
Ungerer, Tomi. One, Two, Where's My
  Shoe?
  Snail Where Are You?
Ward, Lynd Kendall. The Silver Pony
Wezel, Peter. The Good Bird
  The Naughty Bird
Winter, Paula. The Bear and the Fly
Wondriska, William. A Long Piece of
  String

202 World

Brown, Margaret Wise. Four Fur Feet
Domanska, Janina. What Do You See?
Leisk, David Johnson. Upside Down
Peet, Bill. Chester the Worldly Pig
Quin-Harkin, Janet. Peter Penny's Dance
Schlein, Miriam. Herman McGregor's
  World
Schneider, Herman, and Schneider, Nina.
  Follow the Sunset

203 Zodiac

Van Woerkom, Dorothy O. The Rat, the Ox and the Zodiac

204 Zoos

Barry, Robert E. Next Please
Blue, Rose. Black, Black, Beautiful Black
Bolliger, Max. Sandy at the Children's Zoo
Bright, Robert. Me and the Bears
Bruna, Dick. Miffy at the Zoo
Carle, Eric. One, Two, Three to the Zoo
Chalmers, Audrey. Hundreds and
 Hundreds of Pancakes
Colonius, Lillian, and Schroeder, Glen W.
 At the Zoo
Fatio, Louise. The Happy Lion
 The Happy Lion and the Bear
 The Happy Lion in Africa
 The Happy Lion Roars
 The Happy Lion's Rabbits
 The Happy Lion's Treasure
 Hector and Christiana
 The Three Happy Lions
Fay, Hermann. My Zoo
Flora, James. Leopold, the See-Through
 Crumbpicker
Geisel, Theodor Seuss. If I Ran the Zoo
Gordon, Shirley. Grandma Zoo
Graham, Margaret Bloy. Be Nice to
 Spiders
Grosvenor, Donna. Zoo Babies
Hader, Berta Hoerner, and Hader, Elmer
 Stanley. Lost in the Zoo

Hanlon, Emily. What If a Lion Eats Me
 and I Fall into a Hippopotamus' Mud
 Hole?
Hoff, Sydney. Sammy the Seal
Kirn, Ann Minette. Leopard on a String
Kishida, Eriko. The Hippo Boat
Knight, Hilary. Where's Wallace?
Koffler, Camilla, and Bonsall, Crosby
 Newell. Look Who's Talking
Lewis, Stephen. Zoo City
Lippman, Peter. New at the Zoo
Lisker, Sonia O. Lost
Lobel, Arnold Stark. A Holiday for Mister
 Muster
 A Zoo for Mister Muster
McGovern, Ann. Zoo, Where Are You?
Meeks, Esther K. Something New at the
 Zoo
Miklowitz, Gloria D. The Zoo That Moved
Munari, Bruno. Bruno Munari's Zoo
Panek, Dennis. Catastrophe Cat at the Zoo
Rey, Hans Augusto. Curious George Takes
 a Job
 Feed the Animals
Rice, Eve. Sam Who Never Forgets
Rietveld, Jane. Monkey Island
Rojankovsky, Feodor Stepanovich. Animals
 in the Zoo
Snyder, Dick. One Day at the Zoo
 Talk to Me, Tiger
Tensen, Ruth Marjorie. Come to the Zoo!
Unteracker, John. The Dreaming Zoo
Wondriska, William. Which Way to the
 Zoo?
Young, Miriam Burt. Please Don't Feed
 Horace

Bibliographic Guide

This section is arranged alphabetically by author or by title when the author is unknown. Included are subjects to which the books relate, listed according to the numerical classification in the Subject Headings section.

Aardema, Verna, reteller. *Why Mosquitoes Buzz in People's Ears.* Illus. by Leo Dillon, and Diane Dillon. New York: Dial Pr., 1975.
062 Folk and fairy tales; 064.01 Foreign lands—Africa; 090 Insects and spiders.

Abisch, Roslyn Kroop. *The Clever Turtle.* Illus. by Boche Kaplan. Englewood Cliffs, NJ: Prentice-Hall, 1969.
062 Folk and fairy tales; 064.01 Foreign lands—Africa; 142.05 Reptiles—turtles.

Abisch, Roslyn Kroop. *Do You Know What Time It Is?* Illus. by Boche Kaplan. Englewood Cliffs, NJ: Prentice-Hall, 1968.
174 Time.

Abisch, Roslyn Kroop. *Open Your Eyes.* Illus. by Boche Kaplan. New York: Parents, 1964.
032.01 Concepts—color;
089 Imagination.

Abisch, Roslyn Kroop. *The Pumpkin Heads.* Illus. by Boche Kaplan. Englewood Cliffs, NJ: Prentice-Hall, 1968.
062 Folk and fairy tales; 076 Hair;
189 U.S. history.

Abisch, Roslyn Kroop. *'Twas in the Moon of Wintertime.* Illus. by Boche Kaplan. Adapted by Roz Abisch. Englewood Cliffs, NJ: Prentice-Hall, 1969.
064.11 Foreign lands—France;
083.03 Holidays—Christmas; 116 Music;
154.04 Seasons—winter; 164 Songs.

Abisch, Roz (pseud.). See Abisch, Roslyn Kroop.

Adams, Adrienne. *The Christmas Party.* Illus. by author. New York: Scribner's, 1978.
008.46 Animals—rabbits;
083.03 Holidays—Christmas;
130 Parties.

Adams, Adrienne. *The Easter Egg Artists.* Illus. by author. New York: Scribner's, 1976.
002.09 Activities—painting;
002.17 Activities—vacationing;
008.46 Animals—rabbits;
083.04 Holidays—Easter.

Adams, Adrienne, jt. author. *Two Hundred Rabbits.* By Lonzo Anderson, and Adrienne Adams.

Adams, Adrienne. *A Woggle of Witches.* Illus. by author. New York: Scribner's, 1971.
083.07 Holidays—Halloween;
199 Witches.

Adams, Richard George. *The Tyger Voyage.* Illus. by Nicola Bayley. New York: Knopf, 1976.
008.10 Animals—cats, wild; 134 Poetry, rhyme.

Adams, Ruth Joyce. *Fidelia.* Illus. by author. New York: Lothrop, 1970.
053.06 Ethnic groups in the U.S.—Mexican-Americans.

Adelson, Leone. *All Ready for School.* Illus. by Kathleen Elgin. New York: McKay, 1957.
151 School; 154.01 Seasons—fall.

Adelson, Leone. *All Ready for Summer.* Illus. by Kathleen Elgin. New York: McKay, 1955.
154.03 Seasons—summer.

Adelson, Leone. *All Ready for Winter.* Illus. by Kathleen Elgin. New York: McKay, 1952.
154.04 Seasons—winter.

Adelson, Leone. *Please Pass the Grass.* Illus. by Roger Antoine Duvoisin. New York: McKay, 1960.
090 Insects and spiders; 133 Plants;
134 Poetry, rhyme.

Adler, David A. *The House on the Roof.* Illus. by author. New York: Hebrew Pub., 1976.
086 Houses; 093 Jewish culture.

Adler, David A. *A Little at a Time.* Illus. by author. New York: Random House, 1976.
026.28 Character traits—questioning; 057.02 Family life—grandparents; great-grandparents.

Adoff, Arnold. *Big Sister Tells Me That I'm Black.* Illus. by Lorenzo Lynch. New York: Holt, 1976.
053.01 Ethnic groups in the U.S.—Afro-Americans; 057 Family life; 134 Poetry, rhyme.

Adoff, Arnold. *Black Is Brown Is Tan.* Illus. by Emily Arnold McCully. New York: Harper, 1973.
057 Family life; 105 Marriage, interracial; 121 Non-sexist.

Adoff, Arnold. *Ma nDa La.* Illus. by Emily Arnold McCully. New York: Harper, 1971.
057 Family life; 064.01 Foreign lands—Africa.

Adoff, Arnold. *Where Wild Willie?* Illus. by Emily Arnold McCully. New York: Harper, 1978.
016.27 Behavior—running away; 029 City; 053.01 Ethnic groups in the U.S.—Afro-Americans; 134 Poetry, rhyme.

Adshead, Gladys L. *Brownies—Hush!* Illus. by Elizabeth Orton Jones. New York: Oxford Univ. Pr., 1938.
026.14 Character traits—helpfulness; 051 Elves and little people; 062 Folk and fairy tales.

Adshead, Gladys L. *Brownies—It's Christmas.* Illus. by Velma Ilsley. New York: Oxford Univ. Pr., 1955.
051 Elves and little people; 083.03 Holidays—Christmas.

Aesopus. *The Miller, His Son, and Their Donkey.* Illus. by Roger Antoine Duvoisin. New York: McGraw-Hill, 1962.
008.16 Animals—donkeys; 026.25 Character traits—perseverance; 087 Humor; 062 Folk and fairy tales.

Aesopus. *Three Fox Fables.* Illus. by Paul Galdone. New York: Seabury Pr., 1971.
008.18 Animals—foxes; 016.36 Behavior—trickery; 026.11 Character traits—flattery; 062 Folk and fairy tales.

Agostinelli, Maria Enrica. *I Know Something You Don't Know.* Illus. by author. New York: Watts, 1970.
069 Games; 129 Participation.

Ahlberg, Allan, jt. author. *Burglar Bill.* By Janet Ahlberg, and Allan Ahlberg.

Ahlberg, Allan, jt. author. *Each Peach Pear Plum; An "I Spy" Story.* By Janet Ahlberg, and Allan Ahlberg.

Ahlberg, Janet, and Ahlberg, Allan. *Burglar Bill.* Illus. by authors. New York: Greenwillow, 1977.
013 Babies; 036 Crime.

Ahlberg, Janet, and Ahlberg, Allan. *Each Peach Pear Plum; An "I Spy" Story.* Illus. by authors. New York: Viking, 1978.
069 Games; 134 Poetry, rhyme.

Aitken, Amy. *Ruby!* Illus. by author. New York: Bradbury Pr., 1979.
016.14 Behavior—growing up; 026.01 Character traits—ambition.

Alan, Sandy. *The Plaid Peacock.* Illus. by Kelly Oechsli. New York: Pantheon, 1965.
017.16 Birds—peacocks, peahens; 064.16 Foreign lands—India.

Albert, Burton, Jr. *Mine, Yours, Ours.* Illus. by Lois Axeman. Chicago: Albert Whitman, 1977.
016.31 Behavior—sharing; 032 Concepts.

Alderson, Brian. *Cakes and Custard.* Illus. by Helen Oxenbury. New York: Morrow, 1975.
122 Nursery rhymes.

Aldridge, Josephine Haskell. *The Best of Friends.* Illus. by Betty F. Peterson. Berkeley: Parnassus, 1963.
008 Animals; 068 Friendship.

Aldridge, Josephine Haskell. *Fisherman's Luck.* Illus. by Ruth Robbins. Berkeley: Parnassus, 1966.
023.11 Careers—fishermen; 026.21 Character traits—luck; 166.05 Sports—fishing; 195.05 Weather—rain.

Aldridge, Josephine Haskell. *A Peony and a Periwinkle.* Illus. by Ruth Robbins. Berkeley: Parnassus, 1961.
166.05 Sports—fishing.

Alexander, Anne. *ABC of Cars and Trucks.* Illus. by Ninon MacKnight. Garden City, NY: Doubleday, 1956.
001 ABC Books; 012 Automobiles; 184 Trucks.

Alexander, Anne. *I Want to Whistle*. Illus. by Abner Graboff. New York: Abelard-Schuman, 1958.
002.19 Activities—whistling; 134 Poetry, rhyme.

Alexander, Anne. *Noise in the Night*. Illus. by Abner Graboff. Skokie, IL: Rand McNally, 1960.
052.04 Emotions—fear; 119 Night; 120 Noise.

Alexander, Cecil Frances. *All Things Bright and Beautiful*. Illus. by Leo Politi. New York: Scribner's, 1962.
116 Music; 141 Religion; 164 Songs.

Alexander, Lloyd. *The King's Fountain*. Illus. by Ezra Jack Keats. New York: Dutton, 1971.
135 Poverty; 147 Royalty.

Alexander, Martha G. *And My Mean Old Mother Will Be Sorry, Blackboard Bear*. Illus. by author. New York: Dial Pr., 1972.
008.06 Animals—bears; 016.27 Behavior—running away; 052.01 Emotions—anger; 089.01 Imagination—imaginary friends.

Alexander, Martha G. *Blackboard Bear*. Illus. by author. New York: Dial Pr., 1969.
008.06 Animals—bears; 089.01 Imagination—imaginary friends.

Alexander, Martha G. *Bobo's Dream*. Illus. by author. New York: Dial Pr., 1970.
008.14 Animals—dogs; 047 Dreams; 053.01 Ethnic groups in the U.S.—Afro-Americans; 089 Imagination; 201 Wordless.

Alexander, Martha G. *I Sure Am Glad to See You, Blackboard Bear*. Illus. by author. New York: Dial Pr., 1976.
008.06 Animals—bears; 016.05 Behavior—bullying; 089.01 Imagination—imaginary friends.

Alexander, Martha G. *I'll Be the Horse If You'll Play with Me*. Illus. by author. New York: Dial Pr., 1975.
002.12 Activities—playing; 016.10 Behavior—fighting, arguing; 016.32 Behavior—sibling rivalry; 057 Family life.

Alexander, Martha G. *I'll Protect You from the Jungle Beasts*. Illus. by author. New York: Dial Pr., 1973.
052.04 Emotions—fear; 089.01 Imagination—imaginary friends; 137 Problem solving; 162 Sleep; 177.08 Toys—teddy bears.

Alexander, Martha G. *No Ducks in Our Bathtub*. Illus. by author. New York: Dial Pr., 1973.
005 Amphibians; 131 Pets.

Alexander, Martha G. *Nobody Asked Me If I Wanted a Baby Sister*. Illus. by author. New York: Dial Pr., 1971.
013 Babies; 016.32 Behavior—sibling rivalry; 052.03 Emotions—envy, jealousy.

Alexander, Martha G. *Out! Out! Out!* Illus. by author. New York: Dial Pr., 1968.
017 Birds; 137 Problem solving; 201 Wordless.

Alexander, Martha G. *Sabrina*. Illus. by author. New York: Dial Pr., 1971.
052.02 Emotions—embarrassment; 118 Names; 151 School.

Alexander, Martha G. *The Story Grandmother Told*. Illus. by author. New York: Dial Pr., 1969.
053.01 Ethnic groups in the U.S.—Afro-Americans; 057.02 Family life—grandparents; great-grandparents; 177 Toys.

Alexander, Martha G. *We Never Get to Do Anything*. Illus. by author. New York: Dial Pr., 1970.
016.04 Behavior—boredom; 069 Games; 137 Problem solving; 166.15 Sports—swimming.

Alexander, Sue. *Marc the Magnificent*. Illus. by Thomas Anthony de Paola. New York: Pantheon, 1978.
026.23 Character traits—optimism; 103 Magic.

Alexander, Sue. *More Witch, Goblin and Ghost Stories*. Illus. by Jeanette Winter. New York: Pantheon, 1978.
071 Ghosts; 074 Goblins; 199 Witches.

Alexander, Sue. *Seymour the Prince*. Illus. by Lillian Hoban. New York: Pantheon, 1979.
070 Gangs, clubs; 173 Theater.

Alger, Leclaire. *All in the Morning Early*. Illus. by Evaline Ness. New York: Holt, 1963.
062 Folk and fairy tales; 064.31 Foreign lands—Scotland; 134 Poetry, rhyme; 164 Songs.

Alger, Leclaire. *Always Room for One More*. Illus. by Nonny Hogrogian. New York: Holt, 1965.
038 Cumulative tales; 062 Folk and fairy tales; 064.310 Foreign lands—Scotland; 086 Houses; 116 Music; 164 Songs.

Alger, Leclaire. *Kellyburn Braes.* Illus. by Evaline Ness. New York: Harcourt, 1968.
042 Devil; 064.31 Foreign lands—Scotland; 065 Foreign languages; 116 Music; 134 Poetry, rhyme; 164 Songs.

Aliki (pseud.). See Brandenberg, Aliki Liacouras.

Allard, Harry. *I Will Not Go to Market Today.* Illus. by James Marshall. New York: Dial Pr., 1979.
017.04 Birds—chickens; 160 Shopping.

Allard, Harry. *It's So Nice to Have a Wolf Around the House.* Illus. by James Marshall. Garden City, NY: Doubleday, 1977.
036 Crime; 125 Old age; 131 Pets.

Allard, Harry. *May I Stay?* Illus. by F. A. Fitzgerald. Englewood Cliffs, NJ: Prentice-Hall, 1977.
026.28 Character traits—questioning; 062 Folk and fairy tales; 064.12 Foreign lands—Germany; 064.25 Foreign lands—Norway.

Allard, Harry. *The Stupids Step Out.* Illus. by James Marshall. Boston: Houghton, 1974.
087 Humor.

Allard, Harry, and Marshall, James. *Miss Nelson Is Missing!* Illus. by James Marshall. Boston: Houghton, 1977.
016.22 Behavior—misbehavior; 023.27 Careers—teachers; 151 School.

Allard, Harry, and Marshall, James. *The Stupids Have a Ball.* Illus. by James Marshall. Boston: Houghton, 1978.
087 Humor; 130 Parties; 151 School.

Allen, Frances. *Little Hippo.* Illus. by Laura J. Allen. New York: Putnam's, 1971.
008.27 Animals—hippopotami; 052.09 Emotions—sadness.

Allen, Jeffrey. *Bonzini! The Tattooed Man.* Illus. by James Marshall. Boston: Little, 1976.
028 Circus, clowns.

Allen, Jeffrey. *Mary Alice, Operator Number 9.* Illus. by James Marshall. Boston: Little, 1975.
002.20 Activities—working; 008 Animals; 017.08 Birds—ducks; 023.28 Careers—telephone operators; 172 Telephone; 174 Time.

Allen, Marjorie N., jt. author. *The Remarkable Ride of Israel Bissell As Related by Molly the Crow.* By Alice Schick, and Marjorie N. Allen.

Allen, Robert. *Numbers; A First Counting Book.* Illus. by Mottke Weissman. New York: Platt, 1968.
033 Counting.

Ambler, Christopher Gifford. *Ten Little Foxhounds.* Illustrated. Chicago: Children's Pr., 1968.
008.14 Animals—dogs; 033 Counting; 064.10 Foreign lands—England.

Ambrus, Victor G. *Brave Soldier Janosch.* Illus. by author. New York: Harcourt, 1967.
023.17 Careers—military; 064.15 Foreign lands—Hungary; 193 War.

Ambrus, Victor G. *A Country Wedding.* Illus. by author. Reading: Addison-Wesley, 1975.
008.18 Animals—foxes; 008.61 Animals—wolves; 063 Food; 196 Weddings.

Ambrus, Victor G. *The Sultan's Bath.* Illus. by author. New York: Harcourt, 1971.
002.02 Activities—bathing; 062 Folk and fairy tales; 064.16 Foreign lands—India; 147 Royalty.

Ambrus, Victor G. *The Three Poor Tailors.* Illus. by author. New York: Harcourt, 1966.
002.19 Activities—whistling; 008.21 Animals—goats; 023.25 Careers—tailors; 062 Folk and fairy tales; 064.15 Foreign lands—Hungary; 135 Poverty.

Amoss, Berthe. *It's Not Your Birthday.* Illus. by author. New York: Harper, 1966.
018 Birthdays; 016.32 Behavior—sibling rivalry.

Amoss, Berthe. *Tom in the Middle.* Illus. by author. New York: Harper, 1968.
016.32 Behavior—sibling rivalry; 057 Family life.

Ancona, George. *I Feel; A Picture Book of Emotions.* Illus. by author. New York: Dutton, 1977.
052 Emotions.

Andersen, Hans Christian. *The Emperor's New Clothes.* Illus. by Erik Blegvad. Translated by Erik Blegvad. New York: Harcourt, 1959.
026.27 Character traits—pride; 031 Clothing; 062 Folk and fairy tales; 087 Humor; 089 Imagination; 147 Royalty.

Andersen, Hans Christian. *The Emperor's New Clothes.* Illus. by Virginia Lee Burton. Boston: Houghton, 1949.
026.27 Character traits—pride;
031 Clothing; 062 Folk and fairy tales;
087 Humor; 089 Imagination;
147 Royalty.

Andersen, Hans Christian. *The Emperor's New Clothes.* Illus. by Jack Delano, and Irene Delano. Adapted from Hans Christian Andersen and other sources by Jean van Leeuwen. New York: Random House, 1971.
026.27 Character traits—pride;
031 Clothing; 062 Folk and fairy tales;
087 Humor; 089 Imagination;
147 Royalty.

Andersen, Hans Christian. *The Emperor's New Clothes.* Illus. by Monika Laimgruber. Reading: Addison-Wesley, 1973.
026.27 Character traits—pride;
031 Clothing; 062 Folk and fairy tales;
087 Humor; 089 Imagination;
147 Royalty.

Andersen, Hans Christian. *The Little Match Girl.* Illus. by Blair Lent. Boston: Houghton, 1968.
062 Folk and fairy tales;
083.03 Holidays—Christmas;
135 Poverty.

Andersen, Hans Christian. *The Princess and the Pea.* Illus. by Paul Galdone. New York: Seabury Pr., 1978.
062 Folk and fairy tales; 147 Royalty.

Andersen, Hans Christian. *Thumbelina.* Illus. by Adrienne Adams. Translated by R. P. Keigwin. New York: Scribner's, 1961.
026.31 Character traits—smallness;
062 Folk and fairy tales.

Andersen, Hans Christian. *The Ugly Duckling.* Illus. by Adrienne Adams. Translated by R. P. Keigwin. New York: Scribner's, 1965.
017.04 Birds—chickens; 017.25 Birds—swans; 026.02 Character traits—appearance; 026.03 Character traits—being different; 062 Folk and fairy tales.

Andersen, Hans Christian. *The Ugly Duckling.* Illus. by Johannes Larsen. Translated by R. P. Keigwin. New York: Macmillan, 1956.
017.04 Birds—chickens; 017.25 Birds—swans; 026.02 Character traits—appearance; 026.03 Character traits—being different; 062 Folk and fairy tales.

Andersen, Hans Christian. *The Ugly Duckling.* Illus. by Will Nickless. Boston: Houghton, 1948.
017.04 Birds—chickens; 017.25 Birds—swans; 026.02 Character traits—appearance; 026.03 Character traits—being different; 062 Folk and fairy tales.

Andersen, Hans Christian. *The Ugly Duckling.* Illus. by Josef Palecek. Translated by Phyllis Palecek. New York: Abelard-Schuman, 1971.
017.04 Birds—chickens; 017.25 Birds—swans; 026.02 Character traits—appearance; 026.03 Character traits—being different; 062 Folk and fairy tales.

Andersen, Hans Christian. *The Woman with the Eggs.* Illus. by Ray Cruz. Adapted by Jan Wahl. New York: Crown, 1974.
016.13 Behavior—greed; 062 Folk and fairy tales.

Anderson, Clarence William. *Billy and Blaze.* Illus. by author. New York: Macmillan, 1936.
008.28 Animals—horses; 018 Birthdays; 057 Family life.

Anderson, Clarence William. *Blaze and the Forest Fire.* Illus. by author. New York: Macmillan, 1938/1948.
008.28 Animals—horses; 059 Fire.

Anderson, Clarence William. *Blaze and the Gray Spotted Pony.* Illus. by author. New York: Macmillan, 1968.
008.28 Animals—horses.

Anderson, Clarence William. *Blaze and the Gypsies.* Illus. by author. New York: Macmillan, 1937.
008.28 Animals—horses; 036 Crime;
075 Gypsies.

Anderson, Clarence William. *Blaze and the Indian Cave.* Illus. by author. New York: Macmillan, 1964.
008.28 Animals—horses; 035 Cowboys.

Anderson, Clarence William. *Blaze and the Lost Quarry.* Illus. by author. New York: Macmillan, 1966.
008.28 Animals—horses; 035 Cowboys.

Anderson, Clarence William. *Blaze and the Mountain Lion.* Illus. by author. New York: Macmillan, 1959.
008.10 Animals—cats, wild;
008.28 Animals—horses; 035 Cowboys.

Anderson, Clarence William. *Blaze and Thunderbolt.* Illus. by author. New York: Macmillan, 1955.
008.28 Animals—horses; 035 Cowboys.

Anderson, Clarence William. *Blaze Finds Forgotten Roads.* Illus. by author. New York: Macmillan, 1970.
008.28 Animals—horses;
016.20 Behavior—lost; 035 Cowboys.

Anderson, Clarence William. *Blaze Finds the Trail.* Illus. by author. New York: Macmillan, 1950.
008.28 Animals—horses;
016.20 Behavior—lost; 035 Cowboys.

Anderson, Clarence William. *Blaze Shows the Way.* Illus. by author. New York: Macmillan, 1969.
008.28 Animals—horses.

Anderson, Clarence William. *The Crooked Colt.* Illus. by author. New York: Macmillan, 1954.
008.28 Animals—horses.

Anderson, Clarence William. *Lonesome Little Colt.* Illus. by author. New York: Macmillan, 1961.
008.28 Animals—horses;
026.18 Character traits—kindness to animals.

Anderson, Clarence William. *A Pony for Linda.* Illus. by author. New York: Macmillan, 1951.
008.28 Animals—horses.

Anderson, Clarence William. *A Pony for Three.* Illus. by author. New York: Macmillan, 1958.
008.28 Animals—horses.

Anderson, Clarence William. *Rumble Seat Pony.* Illus. by author. New York: Macmillan, 1971.
008.28 Animals—horses;
026.18 Character traits—kindness to animals; 128 Parades.

Anderson, Lonzo. *Halloween Party.* Illus. by Adrienne Adams. New York: Scribner's, 1974.
083.07 Holidays—Halloween;
130 Parties.

Anderson, Lonzo. *Izzard.* Illus. by Adrienne Adams. New York: Scribner's, 1973.
064.05 Foreign lands—Caribbean Islands; 142.03 Reptiles—lizards.

Anderson, Lonzo. *Mr. Biddle and the Birds.* Illus. by Adrienne Adams. New York: Scribner's, 1971.
002.05 Activities—flying; 017 Birds.

Anderson, Lonzo, and Adams, Adrienne. *Two Hundred Rabbits.* Illus. by Adrienne Adams. New York: Viking, 1968.
008.46 Animals—rabbits; 055 Fairies;
103 Magic; 147 Royalty.

Anderson, Paul S. *Red Fox and the Hungry Tiger.* Illus. by Robert Kraus. Reading: Addison-Wesley, 1962.
008.10 Animals—cats, wild;
008.18 Animals—foxes;
026.06 Character traits—cleverness;
068 Friendship.

Andrews, Frank Emerson. *Nobody Comes to Dinner.* Illus. by Lydia Dabcovich. Boston: Little, 1976.
016.02 Behavior—bad day;
052.01 Emotions—anger;
089.01 Imagination—imaginary friends.

Andry, Andrew C., and Kratka, Suzanne C. *Hi, New Baby.* Illus. by Thomas di Grazia. New York: Simon & Schuster, 1970.
013 Babies.

Angelis, Nancy de (pseud.). See Angelo, Nancy Carolyn Harris.

Angelo, Nancy Carolyn Harris. *Camembert.* Illus. by author. Boston: Houghton, 1958.
008.34 Animals—mice; 011 Art;
023.02 Careers—artists; 064.11 Foreign lands—France.

Anglund, Joan Walsh. *The Brave Cowboy.* Illus. by author. New York: Harcourt, 1959.
026.04 Character traits—bravery;
035 Cowboys; 069 Games.

Anglund, Joan Walsh. *A Child's Book of Old Nursery Rhymes.* Illus. by author. New York: Atheneum, 1973.
122 Nursery rhymes.

Anglund, Joan Walsh. *Christmas Is a Time of Giving.* Illus. by author. New York: Harcourt, 1961.
026.13 Character traits—generosity;
083.03 Holidays—Christmas.

Anglund, Joan Walsh. *Cowboy and His Friend.* Illus. by author. New York: Harcourt, 1961.
035 Cowboys; 068 Friendship.

Anglund, Joan Walsh. *The Cowboy's Christmas.* Illus. by author. New York: Atheneum, 1972.
035 Cowboys; 083.03 Holidays—Christmas.

Anglund, Joan Walsh. *Cowboy's Secret Life.* Illus. by author. New York: Harcourt, 1963.
035 Cowboys; 069 Games.

Anglund, Joan Walsh. *A Friend Is Someone Who Likes You.* Illus. by author. New York: Harcourt, 1958.
068 Friendship.

Anglund, Joan Walsh. *The Joan Walsh Anglund Storybook.* Illus. by author. New York: Random House, 1978.
134 Poetry, rhyme.

Anglund, Joan Walsh. *Look out the Window.* Illus. by author. New York: Harcourt, 1959.
026.16 Character traits—individuality.

Anglund, Joan Walsh. *Love Is a Special Way of Feeling.* Illus. by author. New York: Harcourt, 1960.
052.08 Emotions—love.

Annett, Cora. *The Dog Who Thought He Was a Boy.* Illus. by Walter Lorraine. Boston: Houghton, 1965.
008.14 Animals—dogs; 018 Birthdays; 151 School.

Annett, Cora. *When the Porcupine Moved In.* Illus. by Peter Parnall. New York: Watts, 1971.
008.43 Animals—porcupines;
008.46 Animals—rabbits;
016.36 Behavior—trickery.

Anno, Mitsumasa. *Anno's Alphabet.* Illus. by author. New York: Crowell, 1974.
001 ABC Books; 089 Imagination; 126 Optical illusions.

Anno, Mitsumasa. *Anno's Counting Book.* Illus. by author. New York: Crowell, 1975.
033 Counting; 089 Imagination; 126 Optical illusions.

Anno, Mitsumasa. *Anno's Journey.* Illus. by author. Cleveland: Collins, 1978.
089 Imagination; 126 Optical illusions; 201 Wordless.

Anno, Mitsumasa. *Dr. Anno's Magical Midnight Circus.* Illus. by author. Rutland, VT: Weatherhill, 1972.
028 Circus, clowns; 087 Humor;
089 Imagination; 126 Optical illusions; 201 Wordless.

Anno, Mitsumasa. *The King's Flower.* Illus. by author. Cleveland: Collins, 1976/1979.
032.08 Concepts—size; 061 Flowers; 147 Royalty.

Anno, Mitsumasa. *Topsy-Turvies.* Illus. by author. Rutland, VT: Weatherhill, 1970.
087 Humor; 089 Imagination;
126 Optical illusions; 201 Wordless.

Anno, Mitsumasa. *Upside-Downers.* Illus. by author. Rutland, VT: Weatherhill, 1971.
087 Humor; 089 Imagination;
126 Optical illusions; 201 Wordless.

Applebaum, Neil. *Is There a Hole in Your Head?* Illus. by author. New York: Astor-Honor, 1963.
008.60 Animals—whales; 069 Games.

Ardizzone, Aingelda, jt. author. *The Little Girl and the Tiny Doll.* By Edward Jeffrey Irving Ardizzone, and Aingelda Ardizzone.

Ardizzone, Aingelda. *The Night Ride.* Illus. by Edward Jeffrey Irving Ardizzone. New York: Dutton, 1973.
083.03 Holidays—Christmas; 119 Night; 177 Toys; 177.04 Toys—dolls; 177.08 Toys—teddy bears.

Ardizzone, Edward Jeffrey Irving. *Johnny the Clock Maker.* Illus. by author. New York: Walck, 1960.
023.06 Careers—clockmakers; 030 Clocks.

Ardizzone, Edward Jeffrey Irving. *Little Tim and the Brave Sea Captain.* Illus. by author. New York: Walck, 1955.
019 Boats, ships; 026.04 Character traits—bravery; 153 Sea and seashore.

Ardizzone, Edward Jeffrey Irving. *Peter the Wanderer.* Illus. by author. New York: Walck, 1963.
026.04 Character traits—bravery;
026.06 Character traits—cleverness;
153 Sea and seashore.

Ardizzone, Edward Jeffrey Irving. *Ship's Cook Ginger.* Illus. by author. New York: Macmillan, 1977.
019 Boats, ships; 153 Sea and seashore.

Ardizzone, Edward Jeffrey Irving. *Tim All Alone.* Illus. by author. New York: Oxford Univ. Pr., 1957.
019 Boats, ships; 153 Sea and seashore.

Ardizzone, Edward Jeffrey Irving. *Tim and Charlotte.* Illus. by author. New York: Oxford Univ. Pr., 1951.
019 Boats, ships; 026.04 Character traits—bravery; 153 Sea and seashore.

Ardizzone, Edward Jeffrey Irving. *Tim and Ginger.* Illus. by author. New York: Walck, 1965.
019 Boats, ships; 153 Sea and seashore.

Ardizzone, Edward Jeffrey Irving. *Tim and Lucy Go to Sea.* Illus. by author. New York: Walck, 1958.
019 Boats, ships; 068 Friendship; 153 Sea and seashore.

Ardizzone, Edward Jeffrey Irving. *Tim in Danger.* Illus. by author. New York: Oxford Univ. Pr., 1953.
019 Boats, ships; 153 Sea and seashore.

Ardizzone, Edward Jeffrey Irving. *Tim to the Rescue*. Illus. by author. New York: Oxford Univ. Pr., 1949.
019 Boats, ships; 026.04 Character traits—bravery; 026.20 Character traits—loyalty; 153 Sea and seashore; 195 Weather.

Ardizzone, Edward Jeffrey Irving. *Tim's Friend Towser*. Illus. by author. New York: Walck, 1962.
008.14 Animals—dogs; 019 Boats, ships; 153 Sea and seashore.

Ardizzone, Edward Jeffrey Irving. *Tim's Last Voyage*. Illus. by author. New York: Walck, 1972.
019 Boats, ships; 153 Sea and seashore; 195.08 Weather—wind.

Ardizzone, Edward Jeffrey Irving, and Ardizzone, Aingelda. *The Little Girl and the Tiny Doll*. Illus. by Edward Jeffrey Irving Ardizzone. New York: Delacorte Pr., 1966.
016.19 Behavior—losing things; 160 Shopping; 177.04 Toys—dolls.

Arkin, Alan. *Tony's Hard Work Day*. Illus. by James Stevenson. New York: Harper, 1972.
002.20 Activities—working; 057 Family life; 086 Houses.

Armour, Richard Willard. *The Adventures of Egbert the Easter Egg*. Illus. by Paul Galdone. New York: McGraw-Hill, 1965.
083.04 Holidays—Easter; 134 Poetry, rhyme.

Armour, Richard Willard. *Animals on the Ceiling*. Illus. by Paul Galdone. New York: McGraw-Hill, 1966.
008 Animals; 087 Humor; 089 Imagination; 134 Poetry, rhyme.

Armour, Richard Willard. *The Year Santa Went Modern*. Illus. by Paul Galdone. New York: McGraw-Hill, 1964.
083.03 Holidays—Christmas; 134 Poetry, rhyme.

Arneson, D. J. *Secret Places*. Illus. by Peter Arnold. New York: Holt, 1971.
049 Ecology; 066 Forest, woods.

Arnstein, Helen S. *Billy and Our New Baby*. Illus. by M. Jane Smyth. New York: Human Sci. Pr., 1973.
013 Babies; 016.32 Behavior—sibling rivalry.

Aruego, José. *Juan and the Asuangs*. Illus. by author. New York: Scribner's, 1970.
062 Folk and fairy tales; 064.33 Foreign lands—South Sea Islands; 071 Ghosts; 110 Monsters.

Aruego, José. *The King and His Friends*. Illus. by author. New York: Scribner's, 1969.
046 Dragons; 068 Friendship; 117 Mythical creatures; 147 Royalty.

Aruego, José. *Look What I Can Do*. Illus. by author. New York: Scribner's, 1971.
008 Animals; 016.07 Behavior—copying; 064.33 Foreign lands—South Sea Islands; 069 Games.

Aruego, José. *Pilyo the Piranha*. Illus. by author. New York: Macmillan, 1971.
060 Fish; 064.32 Foreign lands—South America.

Arundel, Jocelyn. *Shoes for Punch*. Illus. by Wesley Dennis. New York: McGraw-Hill, 1964.
008.28 Animals—horses.

Asbjørnsen, Peter Christen. *The Squire's Bride*. Illus. by Marcia Sewall. A Norwegian folktale originally collected and told by P. C. Asbjørnsen. New York: Atheneum, 1975.
062 Folk and fairy tales; 064.25 Foreign lands—Norway; 196 Weddings.

Asbjørnsen, Peter Christen. *The Three Billy Goats Gruff*. Illus. by Paul Galdone. New York: Seabury Pr., 1973.
008.21 Animals—goats; 026.06 Character traits—cleverness; 038 Cumulative tales; 062 Folk and fairy tales; 117 Mythical creatures; 183 Trolls.

Asbjørnsen, Peter Christen. *The Three Billy Goats Gruff*. Illus. by William Stobbs. New York: McGraw-Hill, 1967.
008.21 Animals—goats; 026.06 Character traits—cleverness; 038 Cumulative tales; 062 Folk and fairy tales; 117 Mythical creatures; 183 Trolls.

Asbjørnsen, Peter Christen, and Moe, Jørgen Engebretsen. *The Three Billy Goats Gruff*. Illus. by Marcia Brown. Translated by G. W. Dasent. New York: Harcourt, 1957.
008.21 Animals—goats; 026.06 Character traits—cleverness; 038 Cumulative tales; 062 Folk and fairy tales; 117 Mythical creatures; 183 Trolls.

Asch, Frank. *Good Lemonade*. Illus. by Marie Zimmerman. New York: Watts, 1976.
063 Food.

Asch, Frank. *Yellow Yellow*. Illus. by Mark Alan Stamaty. New York: McGraw-Hill, 1971.
031 Clothing; 032.01 Concepts—color.

Asimov, Isaac. *The Best New Thing.* Illus. by Symeon Shimin. Cleveland: Collins, 1971.
048 Earth; 152 Science; 165 Space and space ships.

Attenberger, Walburga. *The Little Man in Winter.* Illus. by author. New York: Random House, 1972.
064.12 Foreign lands—Germany; 134 Poetry, rhyme; 154.04 Seasons—winter.

Attenberger, Walburga. *Who Knows the Little Man?* Illus. by author. New York: Random House, 1972.
064.12 Foreign lands—Germany; 134 Poetry, rhyme.

Atwood, Ann. *The Little Circle.* Illus. by author. New York: Scribner's, 1967.
032.07 Concepts—shape; 134 Poetry, rhyme.

Auerbach, Marjorie. *King Lavra and the Barber.* Illus. by author. New York: Knopf, 1964.
016.29 Behavior—secrets; 023.04 Careers—barbers; 147 Royalty.

Augarde, Stephen Andre. *Pig.* Illus. by author. New York: Bradbury Pr., 1975.
008.42 Animals—pigs; 058 Farms; 059 Fire.

Augarde, Steve. See Augarde, Stephen Andre.

Aulaire, Edgar Parin d', jt. author. *Animals Everywhere.* By Ingri Mortenson d'Aulaire, and Edgar Parin d'Aulaire.

Aulaire, Edgar Parin d', jt. author. *Don't Count Your Chicks.* By Ingri Mortenson d'Aulaire, and Edgar Parin d'Aulaire.

Aulaire, Edgar Parin d', jt. author. *Foxie, the Singing Dog.* By Ingri Mortenson d'Aulaire, and Edgar Parin d'Aulaire.

Aulaire, Edgar Parin d', jt. author. *Nils.* By Ingri Mortenson d'Aulaire, and Edgar Parin d'Aulaire.

Aulaire, Edgar Parin d', jt. author. *Ola.* By Ingri Mortenson d'Aulaire, and Edgar Parin d'Aulaire.

Aulaire, Edgar Parin d', jt. author. *The Terrible Troll-Bird.* By Ingri Mortenson d'Aulaire, and Edgar Parin d'Aulaire.

Aulaire, Edgar Parin d', jt. author. *Too Big.* By Ingri Mortenson d'Aulaire, and Edgar Parin d'Aulaire.

Aulaire, Ingri Mortenson d', and Aulaire, Edgar Parin d'. *Animals Everywhere.* Illus. by authors. Garden City, NY: Doubleday, 1940.
008 Animals.

Aulaire, Ingri Mortenson d', and Aulaire, Edgar Parin d'. *Don't Count Your Chicks.* Illus. by authors. Garden City, NY: Doubleday, 1943.
016.13 Behavior—greed; 017.04 Birds—chickens; 062 Folk and fairy tales; 087 Humor.

Aulaire, Ingri Mortenson d', and Aulaire, Edgar Parin d'. *Foxie, the Singing Dog.* Illus. by authors. Garden City, NY: Doubleday, 1949.
008.09 Animals—cats; 008.14 Animals—dogs; 017.04 Birds—chickens.

Aulaire, Ingri Mortenson d', and Aulaire, Edgar Parin d'. *Nils.* Illus. by authors. Garden City, NY: Doubleday, 1948.
026.03 Character traits—being different; 035 Cowboys; 057 Family life; 151 School.

Aulaire, Ingri Mortenson d', and Aulaire, Edgar Parin d'. *Ola.* Illus. by authors. Garden City, NY: Doubleday, 1932.
064.25 Foreign lands—Norway.

Aulaire, Ingri Mortenson d', and Aulaire, Edgar Parin d'. *The Terrible Troll-Bird.* Illus. by authors. Garden City, NY: Doubleday, 1976.
064.25 Foreign lands—Norway; 117 Mythical creatures; 183 Trolls.

Aulaire, Ingri Mortenson d', and Aulaire, Edgar Parin d'. *Too Big.* Illus. by authors. Garden City, NY: Doubleday, 1945.
032.08 Concepts—size.

Austin, Margot. *Barney's Adventure.* Illus. by author. New York: Dutton, 1941.
028 Circus, clowns.

Austin, Margot. *Growl Bear.* Illus. by author. New York: Dutton, 1951.
008.06 Animals—bears; 052.07 Emotions—loneliness.

Averill, Esther Holden. *The Fire Cat.* Illus. by author. New York: Harper, 1960.
008.09 Animals—cats; 023.10 Careers—firefighters.

Averill, Esther Holden. *Jenny's Birthday Book.* Illus. by author. New York: Harper, 1954.
008.09 Animals—cats; 018 Birthdays; 130 Parties.

Avery, Kay. *Wee Willow Whistle*. Illus. by Winifred Bromhall. New York: Knopf, 1947.
002.19 Activities—whistling; 057 Family life; 177 Toys.

Ayars, James, jt. author. *Contrary Jenkins*. By Rebecca Caudill, and James Ayars.

Ayer, Jacqueline Brandford. *Little Silk*. Illus. by author. New York: Harcourt, 1970.
016.20 Behavior—lost; 177.04 Toys—dolls.

Ayer, Jacqueline Brandford. *Nu Dang and His Kite*. Illus. by author. New York: Harcourt, 1959.
016.19 Behavior—losing things; 064.37 Foreign lands—Thailand; 094 Kites; 177 Toys.

Ayer, Jacqueline Brandford. *The Paper Flower Tree*. Illus. by author. New York: Harcourt, 1962.
026.23 Character traits—optimism; 064.37 Foreign lands—Thailand; 133 Plants.

Ayer, Jacqueline Brandford. *A Wish for Little Sister*. Illus. by author. New York: Harcourt, 1960.
016.38 Behavior—wishing; 017 Birds; 018 Birthdays; 057 Family life; 064.37 Foreign lands—Thailand.

Azaad, Meyer. *Half for You*. Illus. by Naheed Hakeeget. Minneapolis: Carolrhoda Books, 1971.
016.31 Behavior—sharing; 017 Birds; 023 Careers; 0310 Clothing.

Babbitt, Lorraine. *Pink Like the Geranium*. Illus. by author. Chicago: Children's Pr., 1973.
016 Behavior; 031 Clothing; 057 Family life; 151 School.

Babbitt, Natalie. *The Something*. Illus. by author. New York: Farrar, 1970.
052.04 Emotions—fear; 110 Monsters; 119 Night.

Babbitt, Samuel F. *The Forty-Ninth Magician*. Illus. by Natalie Babbitt. New York: Pantheon, 1966.
103 Magic; 147 Royalty.

Bach, Alice. *The Day After Christmas*. Illus. by Mary Eileen Chalmers. New York: Harper, 1975.
052 Emotions; 083.03 Holidays—Christmas.

Bacon, Joan Chase (pseud.). See Bowden, Joan Chase.

Baker, Betty. *Little Runner of the Longhouse*. Illus. by Arnold Stark Lobel. New York: Harcourt, 1962.
038 Cumulative tales; 053.04 Ethnic groups in the U.S.—Indians; 057 Family life.

Baker, Betty. *Partners*. Illus. by Emily Arnold McCully. New York: Morrow, 1978.
008 Animals; 026.06 Character traits—cleverness; 026.19 Character traits—laziness; 068 Friendship.

Baker, Betty. *The Pig War*. Illus. by Robert Martin Lopshire. New York: Harper, 1969.
189 U.S. history.

Baker, Betty. *Three Fools and a Horse*. Illus. by Glen H. Rounds. New York: Macmillan, 1975.
008.28 Animals—horses; 053.04 Ethnic groups in the U.S.—Indians; 087 Humor.

Balet, Jan B. *Amos and the Moon*. Illus. by author. New York: Oxford Univ. Pr., 1948.
111 Moon.

Balet, Jan B. *The Fence*. Illus. by author. New York: Delacorte Pr., 1969.
057 Family life; 064.24 Foreign lands—Mexico; 135 Poverty; 137 Problem solving.

Balet, Jan B. *The Gift; A Portuguese Christmas Tale*. Illus. by author. New York: Delacorte Pr., 1967.
064.28 Foreign lands—Portugal; 083.03 Holidays—Christmas; 141 Religion.

Balet, Jan B. *Joanjo; A Portuguese Tale*. Illus. by author. New York: Delacorte Pr., 1967.
026.01 Character traits—ambition; 047 Dreams; 060 Fish; 064.28 Foreign lands—Portugal.

Balet, Jan B. *The King and the Broom Maker*. Illus. by author. New York: Delacorte Pr., 1968.
147 Royalty.

Balian, Lorna. *Bah! Humbug?* Illus. by author. Nashville: Abingdon Pr., 1977.
083.03 Holidays—Christmas.

Balian, Lorna. *Humbug Rabbit.* Illus. by author. Nashville: Abingdon Pr., 1974.
008.46 Animals—rabbits; 057.02 Family life—grandparents; great-grandparents; 083.04 Holidays—Easter.

Balian, Lorna. *Humbug Witch.* Illus. by author. Nashville: Abingdon Pr., 1965.
083.07 Holidays—Halloween; 199 Witches.

Balian, Lorna. *Sometimes It's Turkey—Sometimes It's Feathers.* Illus. by author. Nashville: Abingdon Pr., 1973.
017.26 Birds—turkeys; 083.10 Holidays—Thanksgiving.

Banchek, Linda. *Snake In, Snake Out.* Illus. by Elaine Arnold. New York: Crowell, 1978.
032.03 Concepts—in and out; 032.06 Concepts—opposites; 142.04 Reptiles—snakes; 201 Wordless.

Bang, Betsy. *The Old Woman and the Red Pumpkin.* Illus. by Molly G. Bang. New York: Macmillan, 1975.
008 Animals; 026.06 Character traits—cleverness; 064.01 Foreign lands—Africa.

Bang, Molly G. *Wiley and the Hairy Man.* Illus. by author. Adapted from an American folk tale. New York: Macmillan, 1976.
015 Bedtime; 026.06 Character traits—cleverness; 053.01 Ethnic groups in the U.S.—Afro-Americans; 062 Folk and fairy tales; 110 Monsters.

Bangs, Edward. *Yankee Doodle.* Illus. by Steven Kellogg. New York: Parents, 1976.
164 Songs; 189 U.S. history.

Banigan, Sharon Stearns. *Circus Magic.* Illus. by Katharina Maillard. New York: Dutton, 1958.
028 Circus, clowns; 103 Magic.

Bank Street College of Education. *Around the City.* Illus. by Aurelius Battaglia, and others. New York: Macmillan, 1972.
029 City.

Bank Street College of Education. *Green Light, Go.* Illus. by Jack Endewelt, and others. Rev. ed. New York: Macmillan, 1972.
029 City; 178 Traffic signs.

Bank Street College of Education. *In the City.* Illus. by Dan Dickas. Rev. ed. New York: Macmillan, 1972.
029 City.

Bank Street College of Education. *My City.* Illus. by Ron Becker, and others. New York: Macmillan, 1965.
029 City.

Bank Street College of Education. *People Read.* Illus. by Dan Dickas. New York: Macmillan, 1972.
002.13 Activities—reading; 023 Careers.

Bank Street College of Education. *Uptown, Downtown.* Illus. by Ron Becker, and others. New York: Macmillan, 1965.
029 City.

Bannerman, Helen Brodie Cowan. *The Story of Little Black Sambo.* Illus. by author. Philadelphia: Lippincott, 1943.
008.10 Animals—cats, wild; 026.06 Character traits—cleverness; 064.16 Foreign lands—India.

Bannon, Laura May. *Little People of the Night.* Illus. by author. Boston: Houghton, 1963.
052.04 Emotions—fear; 119 Night.

Bannon, Laura May. *Manuela's Birthday in Old Mexico.* Illus. by author. Chicago: Albert Whitman, 1939/1972.
018 Birthdays; 064.24 Foreign lands—Mexico; 177.04 Toys—dolls.

Bannon, Laura May. *The Scary Thing.* Illus. by author. Boston: Houghton, 1956.
008 Animals; 052.04 Emotions—fear.

Barchilon, Jacques, and Pettit, Henry. *The Authentic Mother Goose Fairy Tales and Nursery Rhymes.* Illustrated. Denver: Alan Swallow, 1960.
122 Nursery rhymes.

Barrett, Judith. *An Apple a Day.* Illus. by Tim Lewis. New York: Atheneum, 1973.
063 Food; 088 Illness.

Barrett, Judith. *Benjamin's 365 Birthdays.* Illus. by Ron Barrett. New York: Atheneum, 1974.
018 Birthdays.

Barrett, Judith. *I Hate to Take a Bath.* Illus. by Charles B. Slackman. New York: Four Winds Pr., 1975.
002.02 Activities—bathing.

Barrett, Judith. *Old MacDonald Had an Apartment House.* Illus. by Ron Barrett. New York: Atheneum, 1969.
002.06 Activities—gardening; 029 City; 058 Farms.

Barrett, Judith. *Peter's Pocket.* Illus. by Julia Noonan. New York: Atheneum, 1974.
031 Clothing.

Barry, Katharina. *A Is for Anything; An ABC Book of Pictures and Rhymes.* Illus. by author. New York: Harcourt, 1961.
001 ABC Books; 008 Animals.

Barry, Robert E. *Mr. Willowby's Christmas Tree.* Illus. by Paul Galdone. New York: McGraw-Hill, 1963.
083.03 Holidays—Christmas;
134 Poetry, rhyme.

Barry, Robert E. *Next Please.* Illus. by author. Boston: Houghton, 1961.
023.04 Careers—barbers; 204 Zoos.

Bartoli, Jennifer. *In a Meadow, Two Hares Hide.* Illus. by Takeo Ashida. Edited by Kathy Pacini. Chicago: Albert Whitman, 1978.
008.46 Animals—rabbits;
154.04 Seasons—winter.

Bartoli, Jennifer. *Nonna.* Illus. by Joan Drescher. New York: Harvey House, 1975.
040 Death; 052.09 Emotions—sadness;
057 Family life; 057.02 Family life—grandparents; great-grandparents.

Bartoli, Jennifer. *Snow on Bear's Nose.* Illus. by Takeo Ishida. Edited by Caroline Rubin. Chicago: Albert Whitman, 1972.
008.06 Animals—bears; 064.19 Foreign lands—Japan; 081 Hibernation;
154.01 Seasons—fall; 154.04 Seasons—winter.

Barton, Byron. *Buzz, Buzz, Buzz.* Illus. by author. New York: Macmillan, 1973.
038 Cumulative tales; 090 Insects and spiders.

Barton, Byron. *Jack and Fred.* Illus. by author. New York: Macmillan, 1974.
008.14 Animals—dogs; 131 Pets.

Barton, Byron. *Wheels.* Illus. by author. New York: Crowell, 1979.
138 Progress; 197 Wheels.

Barton, Byron. *Where's Al?* Illus. by author. New York: Seabury Pr., 1972.
008.14 Animals—dogs;
016.20 Behavior—lost; 201 Wordless.

Baskin, Leonard. *Hosie's Alphabet.* Illus. by author. Words by Hosea, Tobias and Lisa Baskin. New York: Viking, 1972.
001 ABC Books.

Baskin, Tobias. *Hosie's Aviary.* Illus. by Leonard Baskin. Words mostly by Tobias Baskin and others. New York: Viking, 1979.
017 Birds.

Bason, Lillian. *Pick a Raincoat, Pick a Whistle.* Illus. by Allan Eitzen. New York: Lothrop, 1966.
002.19 Activities—whistling; 181 Trees.

Bate, Lucy. *Little Rabbit's Loose Tooth.* Illus. by Diane de Groat. New York: Crown, 1975.
008.46 Animals—rabbits; 171 Teeth.

Bate, Norman. *Who Built the Bridge?* Illus. by author. New York: Scribner's, 1954.
102 Machines.

Bate, Norman. *Who Built the Highway?* Illus. by author. New York: Scribner's, 1953.
102 Machines.

Batherman, Muriel. *Some Things You Should Know about My Dog.* Illus. by author. Englewood Cliffs, NJ: Prentice-Hall, 1976.
008.14 Animals—dogs.

Battles, Edith. *One to Teeter-Totter.* Illus. by Rosalind Fry. Chicago: Albert Whitman, 1973.
052.07 Emotions—loneliness;
057 Family life; 068 Friendship;
069 Games.

Battles, Edith. *The Terrible Terrier.* Illus. by Tom Funk. Reading: Addison-Wesley, 1972.
008.14 Animals—dogs;
016.13 Behavior—greed.

Battles, Edith. *The Terrible Trick or Treat.* Illus. by Tom Funk. Reading: Addison-Wesley, 1970.
016.13 Behavior—greed;
083.07 Holidays—Halloween.

Battles, Edith. *What Does the Rooster Say, Yoshio?* Illus. by Toni Hormann. Edited by Kathy Pacini. Chicago: Albert Whitman, 1978.
008 Animals; 064.19 Foreign lands—Japan; 096 Language.

Baugh, Dolores M., and Pulsifer, Marjorie P. *Bikes.* Illus. by Eve Hoffmann. New York: Noble, 1965.
166.03 Sports—bicycling; 178 Traffic signs.

Baugh, Dolores M., and Pulsifer, Marjorie P. *Let's Go.* Illus. by Eve Hoffmann. New York: Noble, 1970.
168 Stores.

Baugh, Dolores M., and Pulsifer, Marjorie P. *Let's See the Animals.* Illus. by Eve Hoffmann. New York: Noble, 1965.
008 Animals.

Baugh, Dolores M., and Pulsifer, Marjorie P. *Let's Take a Trip*. Illus. by Richard Szumski, and others. New York: Noble, 1966.
100 Libraries; 102 Machines.

Baugh, Dolores M., and Pulsifer, Marjorie P. *Slides*. Illus. by Eve Hoffmann. New York: Noble, 1970.
002.12 Activities—playing.

Baugh, Dolores M., and Pulsifer, Marjorie P. *Supermarket*. Illus. by Eve Hoffmann. New York: Noble, 1970.
160 Shopping; 168 Stores.

Baugh, Dolores M., and Pulsifer, Marjorie P. *Swings*. Illus. by Eve Hoffmann. New York: Noble, 1970.
002.12 Activities—playing.

Baugh, Dolores M., and Pulsifer, Marjorie P. *Trucks and Cars to Ride*. Illus. by Eve Hoffmann. New York: Noble, 1970.
012 Automobiles; 184 Trucks.

Baum, Arline, and Baum, Joseph. *One Bright Monday Morning*. Illus. by Joseph Baum. New York: Random House, 1962.
033 Counting; 154.02 Seasons—spring; 195 Weather.

Baum, Joseph, jt. author. *One Bright Monday Morning*. By Arline Baum, and Joseph Baum.

Baum, Lyman Frank. *Mother Goose in Prose*. Illus. by Maxfield Parrish. New York: Bounty Books, 1901.
122 Nursery rhymes.

Baum, Willi. *Birds of a Feather*. Illus. by author. Reading: Addison-Wesley, 1969.
017 Birds; 201 Wordless.

Bayley, Nicola. *Nicola Bayley's Book of Nursery Rhymes*. Illus. by author. New York: Knopf, 1975.
122 Nursery rhymes.

Bayley, Nicola. *One Old Oxford Ox*. Illus. by author. New York: Atheneum, 1977.
033 Counting.

Baylor, Byrd. *Everybody Needs a Rock*. Illus. by Peter Parnall. New York: Scribner's, 1974.
146 Rocks.

Baylor, Byrd. *Guess Who My Favorite Person Is*. Illus. by Robert Andrew Parker. New York: Scribner's, 1977.
068 Friendship; 069 Games.

Baylor, Byrd. *Hawk, I'm Your Brother*. Illus. by Peter Parnall. New York: Scribner's, 1976.
017.12 Birds—hawks; 026.12 Character traits—freedom; 053.04 Ethnic groups in the U.S.—Indians.

Baylor, Byrd. *We Walk in Sandy Places*. Illus. by Marilyn Schweitzer. New York: Scribner's, 1976.
008 Animals.

Beach, Stewart. *Good Morning, Sun's Up*. Illus. by Yutaka Sugita. New York: Scroll Pr., 1970.
008 Animals; 069 Games; 112 Morning.

Beatty, Hetty Burlingame. *Bucking Horse*. Illus. by author. Boston: Houghton, 1957.
008.28 Animals—horses; 035 Cowboys.

Beatty, Hetty Burlingame. *Little Owl Indian*. Illus. by author. Boston: Houghton, 1951.
053.04 Ethnic groups in the U.S.—Indians.

Becker, Edna. *Nine Hundred Buckets of Paint*. Illus. by Margaret Bradfield. Nashville: Abingdon Pr., 1945.
002.09 Activities—painting; 086 Houses; 114 Moving.

Becker, John L. *Seven Little Rabbits*. Illus. by Barbara Cooney. New York: Walker, 1973.
008.46 Animals—rabbits; 033 Counting.

Beckman, Kaj. *Lisa Cannot Sleep*. Illus. by Per Beckman. New York: Watts, 1969.
015 Bedtime; 057 Family life; 162 Sleep; 177 Toys.

Beer, Kathleen Costello. *What Happens in the Spring*. Illustrated. Washington, DC: National Geographic Soc., 1977.
154.02 Seasons—spring.

Bees. Illus. by Tancy Baran. New York: Grosset, 1971.
090 Insects and spiders; 152 Science.

Behn, Harry. *All Kinds of Time*. Illus. by author. New York: Harcourt, 1950.
102 Machines; 174 Time.

Behn, Harry. *What a Beautiful Noise*. Illus. by Harold Berson. Cleveland: Collins, 1970.
087 Humor; 116 Music; 120 Noise.

Behrens, June. *Who Am I?* Illus. by Ray Ambraziunas. Chicago: Children's Pr., 1968.
053.07 Ethnic groups in the U.S.—Multi-ethnic.

Behrens, June York. *Can You Walk the Plank?* Illus. by Tom Grimm, and Michele Grimm. Chicago: Children's Pr., 1976.
069 Games; 089 Imagination.

Behrens, June York. *Soo Ling Finds a Way.* Illus. by Jun Iwamatsu. Chicago: Children's Pr., 1965.
053.02 Ethnic groups in the U.S.—Chinese-Americans; 057.02 Family life—grandparents; great-grandparents; 064.06 Foreign lands—China; 097 Laundry.

Beim, Jerrold, jt. author. *Little Igloo.* By Lorraine Levy Beim, and Jerrold Beim.

Beim, Jerrold. *Sir Halloween.* Illus. by Tracy Sugarman. New York: Morrow, 1959.
083.07 Holidays—Halloween.

Beim, Jerrold. *The Smallest Boy in Class.* Illus. by Meg Wohlberg. New York: Morrow, 1949.
016.31 Behavior—sharing; 026.31 Character traits—smallness; 118 Names.

Beim, Jerrold. *The Swimming Hole.* Illus. by Louis Darling. New York: Morrow, 1950.
016 Behavior; 053.01 Ethnic groups in the U.S.—Afro-Americans; 068 Friendship; 154.03 Seasons—summer; 166.15 Sports—swimming.

Beim, Jerrold, jt. author. *Two Is a Team.* By Lorraine Levy Beim, and Jerrold Beim.

Beim, Jerrold. *With Dad Alone.* Illus. by Don Sibley. New York: Harcourt, 1954.
040 Death; 057.01 Family life—fathers.

Beim, Lorraine Levy, and Beim, Jerrold. *Little Igloo.* Illus. by Howard Simon. New York: Harcourt, 1941.
053.03 Ethnic groups in the U.S.—Eskimos.

Beim, Lorraine Levy, and Beim, Jerrold. *Two Is a Team.* Illus. by Ernest Crichlow. New York: Harcourt, 1945.
016.10 Behavior—fighting, arguing; 053.01 Ethnic groups in the U.S.—Afro-Americans; 068 Friendship; 137 Problem solving.

Bell, Norman. *Linda's Air Mail Letter.* Illus. by Patricia Villemain. Chicago: Follett, 1964.
018 Birthdays; 023.16 Careers—mail carriers; 068 Friendship; 099 Letters; 195 Weather.

Bell-Zano, Gina. *The Wee Moose.* Illus. by Enrico Arno. New York: Parents, 1964.
008.34 Animals—mice; 058 Farms.

Belpré, Pura. *Perez and Martina.* Illus. by Sanchez M. Carlos. New York: Warne, 1932.
008.34 Animals—mice; 062 Folk and fairy tales; 064.05 Foreign lands—Caribbean Islands; 090 Insects and spiders.

Belpré, Pura. *Santiago.* Illus. by Symeon Shimin. New York: Warne, 1969.
053.07 Ethnic groups in the U.S.—Multi-ethnic; 053.08 Ethnic groups in the U.S.—Puerto Rican-Americans.

Belting, Natalie Maree. *Summer's Coming In.* Illus. by Adrienne Adams. New York: Holt, 1970.
154.02 Seasons—spring.

Bemelmans, Ludwig. *Hansi.* Illus. by author. New York: Viking, 1934.
002.17 Activities—vacationing; 064.39 Foreign lands—Tyrol; 083.03 Holidays—Christmas.

Bemelmans, Ludwig. *Madeline.* Illus. by author. New York: Simon & Schuster, 1939.
064.11 Foreign lands—France; 084 Hospitals; 127 Orphans; 134 Poetry, rhyme; 151 School.

Bemelmans, Ludwig. *Madeline and the Bad Hat.* Illus. by author. New York: Viking, 1956.
016.01 Behavior—animals, dislike of; 064.11 Foreign lands—France; 127 Orphans; 134 Poetry, rhyme.

Bemelmans, Ludwig. *Madeline and the Gypsies.* Illus. by author. New York: Viking, 1958.
016.20 Behavior—lost; 064.11 Foreign lands—France; 075 Gypsies; 127 Orphans; 134 Poetry, rhyme.

Bemelmans, Ludwig. *Madeline in London.* Illus. by author. New York: Viking, 1961.
008.28 Animals—horses; 018 Birthdays; 064.10 Foreign lands—England; 127 Orphans; 134 Poetry, rhyme.

Bemelmans, Ludwig. *Madeline's Rescue.* Illus. by author. New York: Viking, 1953.
008.14 Animals—dogs; 064.11 Foreign lands—France; 127 Orphans; 134 Poetry, rhyme.

Bemelmans, Ludwig. *Marina.* Illus. by author. New York: Harper, 1962.
008.10 Animals—cats, wild; 008.47 Animals—raccoons.

Bemelmans, Ludwig. *Parsley.* Illus. by author. New York: Harper, 1955.
008.13 Animals—deer; 166.08 Sports—hunting; 181 Trees.

Bemelmans, Ludwig. *Welcome Home.* Illus. by author. New York: Harper, 1959.
008.18 Animals—foxes;
026.06 Character traits—cleverness;
134 Poetry, rhyme.

Benarde, Anita. *The Pumpkin Smasher.* Illus. by author. New York: Walker, 1972.
083.07 Holidays—Halloween;
137 Problem solving; 199 Witches.

Benchley, Nathaniel. *The Deep Dives of Stanley Whale.* Illus. by Mischa Richter. New York: Harper, 1973.
008.60 Animals—whales;
026.04 Character traits—bravery.

Benchley, Nathaniel. *The Flying Lessons of Gerald Pelican.* Illus. by Mamoru R. Funai. New York: Harper, 1970.
002.05 Activities—flying; 017.17 Birds— pelicans.

Benchley, Nathaniel. *George the Drummer Boy.* Illus. by Donald Alan Bolognese. New York: Harper, 1977.
189 U.S. history; 193 War.

Benchley, Nathaniel. *A Ghost Named Fred.* Illus. by Ben Shecter. New York: Harper, 1968.
071 Ghosts; 137 Problem solving.

Benchley, Nathaniel. *Oscar Otter.* Illus. by Arnold Stark Lobel. New York: Harper, 1966.
008.40 Animals—otters; 016 Behavior.

Benchley, Nathaniel. *Red Fox and His Canoe.* Illus. by Arnold Stark Lobel. New York: Harper, 1964.
008.06 Animals—bears; 019 Boats, ships; 053.04 Ethnic groups in the U.S.—Indians.

Benchley, Nathaniel. *Sam the Minuteman.* Illus. by Arnold Stark Lobel. New York: Harper, 1969.
189 U.S. history; 193 War.

Benchley, Nathaniel. *The Several Tricks of Edgar Dolphin.* Illus. by Mamoru R. Funai. New York: Harper, 1970.
008.15 Animals—dolphins;
026.06 Character traits—cleverness.

Benchley, Nathaniel. *Small Wolf.* Illus. by Joan Sandin. New York: Harper, 1972.
053.04 Ethnic groups in the U.S.— Indians; 189 U.S. history.

Benchley, Nathaniel. *Snorri and the Strangers.* Illus. by Donald Alan Bolognese. New York: Harper, 1976.
064.25 Foreign lands—Norway;
189 U.S. history.

Benchley, Nathaniel. *The Strange Disappearance of Arthur Cluck.* Illus. by Arnold Stark Lobel. New York: Harper, 1967.
017.04 Birds—chickens; 017.14 Birds— owls; 058 Farms; 083.04 Holidays— Easter.

Benét, William Rose. *Timothy's Angels.* Illus. by Constantin Alajalov. New York: Crowell, 1947.
002.12 Activities—playing; 007 Angels;
134 Poetry, rhyme.

Bennett, Rainey. *After the Sun Goes Down.* Illus. by author. Cleveland: Collins, 1961.
017.14 Birds—owls; 119 Night.

Bennett, Rainey. *The Secret Hiding Place.* Illus. by author. Cleveland: Collins, 1960.
008.27 Animals—hippopotami;
016.33 Behavior—solitude.

Benton, Robert. *Little Brother, No More.* Illus. by author. New York: Knopf, 1960.
057 Family life; 118 Names.

Berenstain, Janice, jt. author. *Bears in the Night.* By Stanley Berenstain, and Janice Berenstain.

Berenstain, Janice, jt. author. *Bears on Wheels.* By Stanley Berenstain, and Janice Berenstain.

Berenstain, Janice, jt. author. *The Berenstain Bears and the Spooky Old Tree.* By Stanley Berenstain, and Janice Berenstain.

Berenstain, Janice, jt. author. *The Berenstain Bears' Counting Book.* By Stanley Berenstain, and Janice Berenstain.

Berenstain, Janice, jt. author. *The Berenstains' B Book.* By Stanley Berenstain, and Janice Berenstain.

Berenstain, Janice, jt. author. *He Bear, She Bear.* By Stanley Berenstain, and Janice Berenstain.

Berenstain, Janice, jt. author. *Inside Outside Upside Down.* By Stanley Berenstain, and Janice Berenstain.

Berenstain, Stanley. *The Bear Detectives: The Case of the Missing Pumpkin.* Illus. by author. New York: Random House, 1975.
008.06 Animals—bears;
023.08 Careers—detectives; 134 Poetry, rhyme; 137 Problem solving.

Berenstain, Stanley, and Berenstain, Janice. *Bears in the Night.* Illus. by authors. New York: Random House, 1971.
008.06 Animals—bears; 015 Bedtime;
119 Night; 120 Noise.

Berenstain, Stanley, and Berenstain, Janice. *Bears on Wheels.* Illus. by authors. New York: Random House, 1969.
008.06 Animals—bears; 033 Counting; 197 Wheels.

Berenstain, Stanley, and Berenstain, Janice. *The Berenstain Bears and the Spooky Old Tree.* Illus. by authors. New York: Random House, 1978.
008.06 Animals—bears; 134 Poetry, rhyme.

Berenstain, Stanley, and Berenstain, Janice. *The Berenstain Bears' Counting Book.* Illus. by authors. New York: Random House, 1976.
033 Counting.

Berenstain, Stanley, and Berenstain, Janice. *The Berenstains' B Book.* Illus. by authors. New York: Random House, 1971.
001 ABC Books; 008.06 Animals—bears.

Berenstain, Stanley, and Berenstain, Janice. *He Bear, She Bear.* Illus. by authors. New York: Random House, 1974.
008.06 Animals—bears; 121 Non-sexist.

Berenstain, Stanley, and Berenstain, Janice. *Inside Outside Upside Down.* Illus. by authors. New York: Random House, 1968.
008.06 Animals—bears; 032 Concepts.

Beresford, Elisabeth. *Snuffle to the Rescue.* Illus. by Gunvor Edwards. New York: Penguin, 1975.
008.14 Animals—dogs.

Berg, Jean Horton. *The O'Learys and Friends.* Illus. by Mary Stevens. Chicago: Follett, 1961.
008.09 Animals—cats; 016.24 Behavior—misunderstanding; 114 Moving; 137 Problem solving.

Berg, Jean Horton. *The Wee Little Man.* Illus. by Charles Geer. Chicago: Follett, 1963.
008.09 Animals—cats; 051 Elves and little people; 119 Night; 120 Noise; 134 Poetry, rhyme.

Berger, Terry. *I Have Feelings.* Illus. by I. Howard Spivak. New York: Human Sci. Pr., 1971.
052 Emotions.

Bergere, Thea. *Paris in the Rain with Jean and Jacqueline.* Illus. by Richard Bergere. New York: McGraw-Hill, 1963.
029 City; 064.11 Foreign lands—France; 195.05 Weather—rain.

Bernadette (pseud.). See Watts, Bernadette.

Bernstein, Joanne, and Gullo, Steven V. *When People Die.* Illus. by Rosmarie Hauscherr. New York: Dutton, 1977.
040 Death.

Bernstein, Margery, and Kobrin, Janet. *Coyote Goes Hunting for Fire.* Illus. by Ed Heffernan. A California Indian myth retold by Margery Bernstein and Janet Kobrin. New York: Scribner's, 1974.
008 Animals; 053.04 Ethnic groups in the U.S.—Indians; 059 Fire; 062 Folk and fairy tales.

Bernstein, Margery, and Kobrin, Janet. *Earth Namer.* Illustrated. A California Indian myth retold by Margery Bernstein and Janet Kobrin. New York: Scribner's, 1974.
048 Earth; 062 Folk and fairy tales; 053.04 Ethnic groups in the U.S.—Indians.

Berson, Harold. *Balarin's Goat.* Illus. by author. New York: Crown, 1972.
008.21 Animals—goats; 062 Folk and fairy tales; 121 Non-sexist.

Berson, Harold. *The Boy, the Baker, the Miller and More.* Illus. by author. New York: Crown, 1974.
038 Cumulative tales; 062 Folk and fairy tales.

Berson, Harold. *Henry Possum.* Illus. by author. New York: Crown, 1973.
008.18 Animals—foxes; 008.44 Animals—possums; 016.20 Behavior—lost.

Berson, Harold. *A Moose Is Not a Moose.* Illus. by author. New York: Crown, 1975.
008.34 Animals—mice; 096 Language.

Berson, Harold. *Pop Goes the Turnip.* Illus. by author. New York: Grosset, 1966.
002.06 Activities—gardening; 008.46 Animals—rabbits; 063 Food; 133 Plants.

Berson, Harold. *The Rats Who Lived in the Delicatessen.* Illus. by author. New York: Crown, 1976.
008.48 Animals—rats; 016.13 Behavior—greed; 063 Food.

Berson, Harold. *The Thief Who Hugged a Moonbeam.* Illus. by author. New York: Seabury Pr., 1972.
016.12 Behavior—gossip; 036 Crime; 103 Magic; 147 Royalty.

Beskow, Elsa Maartman. *Children of the Forest*. Illus. by author. Adapted from the Swedish by William Jay Smith. New York: Delacorte Pr., 1969.
064.35 Foreign lands—Sweden;
066 Forest, woods; 134 Poetry, rhyme;
154 Seasons.

Beskow, Elsa Maartman. *Pelle's New Suit*. Illus. by author. Translated from the Swedish by Marion Letcher Woodburn. New York: Harper, 1929.
008.52 Animals—sheep; 031 Clothing;
064.35 Foreign lands—Sweden.

Beskow, Elsa Maartman. *Peter's Adventures in Blueberry Land*. Illus. by author. Translated from the Swedish by Sheila La Farge. New York: Delacorte Pr., 1975.
018 Birthdays; 051 Elves and little people; 063 Food; 064.35 Foreign lands—Sweden; 103 Magic; 134 Poetry, rhyme.

Bethell, Jean. *Bathtime*. Illustrated. New York: Holt, 1979.
002.02 Activities—bathing; 008 Animals.

Bettina (pseud.). See Ehrlich, Bettina.

Bettinger, Craig. *Follow Me, Everybody*. Illus. by Edward S. Hollander. Garden City, NY: Doubleday, 1968.
053.07 Ethnic groups in the U.S.—Multi-ethnic.

Bible. The First Seven Days. Illus. by Paul Galdone. Bible. O. T. Genesis I-II, 3. English. 1962. Authorized. New York: Crowell, 1962.
141 Religion.

Bible. Shadrach, Meshack, and Abednego. Illus. by Paul Galdone. Bible. O. T. Daniel III. English. 1965. Authorized. New York: McGraw-Hill, 1965.
141 Religion.

Bible, Charles. *Jennifer's New Chair*. Illus. by author. New York: Holt, 1978.
018 Birthdays; 057 Family life;
057.02 Family life—grandparents; great-grandparents; 059 Fire;
130 Parties.

Bileck, Marvin, jt. author. *Penny*. By Beatrice Schenk De Regniers, and Marvin Bileck.

Billy Boy. Illus. by Glen H. Rounds. Verses selected by Richard Chase. Chicago: Children's Pr., 1966.
062 Folk and fairy tales; 134 Poetry, rhyme; 164 Songs.

Binzen, Bill. *Alfred Goes House Hunting*. Illus. by author. Garden City, NY: Doubleday, 1974.
008 Animals; 086 Houses; 177 Toys.

Biro, Val. *Gumdrop, the Adventures of a Vintage Car*. Illus. by author. Chicago: Follett, 1966.
012 Automobiles.

Bishop, Bonnie. *No One Noticed Ralph*. Illus. by Jack Kent. Garden City, NY: Doubleday, 1979.
016.37 Behavior—unnoticed, unseen;
017.15 Birds—parrots, parakeets.

Bishop, Claire Huchet. *The Man Who Lost His Head*. Illus. by Robert John McCloskey. New York: Viking, 1962.
006 Anatomy; 087 Humor.

Bishop, Claire Huchet. *The Truffle Pig*. Illus. by Kurt Wiese. New York: Coward, 1971.
008.42 Animals—pigs; 064.11 Foreign lands—France; 131 Pets.

Bishop, Claire Huchet. *Twenty Two Bears*. Illus. by Kurt Wiese. New York: Viking, 1964.
008.06 Animals—bears; 033 Counting;
038 Cumulative tales.

Bishop, Claire Huchet, and Wiese, Kurt. *The Five Chinese Brothers*. Illus. by Kurt Wiese. Chicago: Follett, 1966.
026.06 Character traits—cleverness;
057 Family life; 062 Folk and fairy tales;
064.06 Foreign lands—China.

Black, Irma Simonton. *Big Puppy and Little Puppy*. Illus. by Theresa Sherman. New York: Holiday, 1960.
008.14 Animals—dogs;
032.08 Concepts—size.

Black, Irma Simonton. *Is This My Dinner?* Illus. by Rosalind Fry. Chicago: Albert Whitman, 1972.
063 Food; 129 Participation; 134 Poetry, rhyme.

Black, Irma Simonton. *The Little Old Man Who Could Not Read*. Illus. by Seymour Fleishman. Chicago: Albert Whitman, 1968.
002.13 Activities—reading;
160 Shopping.

Blaine, Marge. *The Terrible Thing That Happened at Our House*. Illus. by John C. Wallner. New York: Parents, 1975.
057 Family life; 057.03 Family life—mothers; 137 Problem solving.

Blake, Quentin. *Snuff*. Illus. by author. Philadelphia: Lippincott, 1973.
036 Crime; 095 Knights.

Blech, Dietlind. *Hello Irina*. Illus. by author. Adapted from the German text by Yaak Karsunke. New York: Holt, 1970.
002.16 Activities—traveling;
008.28 Animals—horses.

Blegvad, Erik. *Burnie's Hill*. Illus. by author. New York: Atheneum, 1977.
038 Cumulative tales; 064.31 Foreign lands—Scotland; 134 Poetry, rhyme;
154 Seasons.

Blegvad, Erik, jt. author. *One Is for the Sun*. By Lenore Hochman Blegvad, and Erik Blegvad.

Blegvad, Lenore Hochman, ed. *Hark! Hark! The Dogs Do Bark, and Other Rhymes about Dogs*. Illus. by Erik Blegvad. New York: Atheneum, 1975.
008.14 Animals—dogs; 122 Nursery rhymes.

Blegvad, Lenore Hochman, ed. *Mittens for Kittens, and Other Rhymes about Cats*. Illus. by Erik Blegvad. New York: Atheneum, 1974.
008.09 Animals—cats; 122 Nursery rhymes.

Blegvad, Lenore Hochman, and Blegvad, Erik. *One Is for the Sun*. Illus. by Erik Blegvad. New York: Harcourt, 1968.
033 Counting.

Blood, Charles L., and Link, Martin. *The Goat in the Rug*. Illus. by Nancy Winslow Parker. New York: Parents, 1976.
008.21 Animals—goats; 062 Folk and fairy tales.

Blue, Rose. *Black, Black, Beautiful Black*. Illus. by Emmett Wigglesworth. New York: Watts, 1969.
053.01 Ethnic groups in the U.S.—Afro-Americans; 204 Zoos.

Blue, Rose. *How Many Blocks Is the World?* Illus. by Harold James. New York: Watts, 1970.
029 City; 032.08 Concepts—size;
053.01 Ethnic groups in the U.S.—Afro-Americans; 057 Family life; 151 School.

Blue, Rose. *I Am Here: Yo Estoy Aqui*. Illus. by Moneta Barnett. New York: Watts, 1971.
026.03 Character traits—being different; 053.07 Ethnic groups in the U.S.—Multi-ethnic; 053.08 Ethnic groups in the U.S.—Puerto Rican-Americans; 065 Foreign languages;
151 School.

Bodecker, N. M. See Bodecker, Nils Mogens.

Bodecker, Nils Mogens, jt. author. *Good Night Little One*. By Robert Kraus, and Nils Mogens Bodecker.

Bodecker, Nils Mogens, jt. author. *Good Night Richard Rabbit*. By Robert Kraus, and Nils Mogens Bodecker.

Bodecker, Nils Mogens, translator. *"It's Raining," Said John Twaining*. Illus. by Nils Mogens Bodecker. New York: Atheneum, 1973.
064.08 Foreign lands—Denmark;
087 Humor; 122 Nursery rhymes.

Bodwell, Gaile. *The Long Day of the Giants*. Illus. by Leon Shtainmets. New York: McGraw-Hill, 1975.
072 Giants; 174 Time.

Boegehold, Betty. *Pawpaw's Run*. Illus. by Christine Price. New York: Dutton, 1968.
008.09 Animals—cats;
016.20 Behavior—lost; 026.06 Character traits—cleverness; 052.08 Emotions—love; 131 Pets.

Boegehold, Betty. *Pippa Mouse*. Illus. by Cyndy Szekeres. New York: Knopf, 1973.
008.34 Animals—mice.

Boegehold, Betty. *Pippa Pops Out!* Illus. by Cyndy Szekeres. New York: Knopf, 1979.
008.34 Animals—mice.

Boegehold, Betty. *Three to Get Ready*. Illus. by Mary Eileen Chalmers. New York: Harper, 1965.
008.09 Animals—cats; 016 Behavior.

Boegehold, Betty, and Szekeres, Cyndy. *Here's Pippa Again!* Illus. by Cyndy Szekeres. New York: Knopf, 1975.
008.34 Animals—mice.

Bolliger, Max. *The Fireflies*. Illus. by Jeri Trinka. Translated by Roseanna Hoover. New York: Atheneum, 1970.
057 Family life; 062 Folk and fairy tales; 064.07 Foreign lands—Czechoslovakia; 090 Insects and spiders.

Bolliger, Max. *The Giants' Feast*. Illus. by Monika Laimgruber. English version by Barbara Willard. Reading: Addison-Wesley, 1975.
063 Food; 072 Giants.

Bolliger, Max. *The Golden Apple*. Illus. by Celestino Piatti. Translated by Roseanna Hoover. New York: Atheneum, 1970.
016.13 Behavior—greed; 057 Family life; 063 Food.

Bolliger, Max. *Sandy at the Children's Zoo*. Illus. by Klaus Brunner. Translated from German by Elisabeth Gemming. New York: Crowell, 1966.
016.20 Behavior—lost; 204 Zoos.

Bolliger, Max. *The Wooden Man*. Illus. by Fred Baver. New York: Seabury Pr., 1974.
150 Scarecrows; 194 Weapons; 195 Weather.

Bolognese, Donald Alan. *A New Day*. Illus. by author. New York: Delacorte Pr., 1970.
002.16 Activities—traveling; 013 Babies; 053.06 Ethnic groups in the U.S.—Mexican-Americans; 057 Family life; 083.03 Holidays—Christmas.

Bolognese, Donald Alan, jt. author. *The Sleepy Watchdog*. By Elaine Bolognese, and Donald Alan Bolognese.

Bolognese, Elaine, and Bolognese, Donald Alan. *The Sleepy Watchdog*. Illus. by Donald Alan Bolognese. New York: Lothrop, 1964.
008.14 Animals—dogs; 026.19 Character traits—laziness.

Bond, Jean Carey. *A Is for Africa*. Illus. by author. New York: Watts, 1969.
001 ABC Books; 064.01 Foreign lands—Africa.

Bond, Michael. *Paddington at the Circus*. Illus. by Fred Banbery. New York: Random House, 1973.
008.06 Animals—bears; 028 Circus, clowns; 064.10 Foreign lands—England.

Bond, Michael. *Paddington at the Seaside*. Illus. by Fred Banbery. New York: Random House, 1975.
002.17 Activities—vacationing; 008.06 Animals—bears; 064.10 Foreign lands—England; 153 Sea and seashore.

Bond, Michael. *Paddington at the Tower*. Illus. by Fred Banbery. New York: Random House, 1975.
008.06 Animals—bears; 064.10 Foreign lands—England.

Bond, Michael. *Paddington's Lucky Day*. Illus. by Fred Banbery. New York: Random House, 1973.
008.06 Animals—bears; 026.21 Character traits—luck; 064.10 Foreign lands—England; 160 Shopping.

Bonne, Rose. *I Know an Old Lady*. Illus. by Abner Graboff. Music by Alan Mills. Skokie, IL: Rand McNally, 1961.
038 Cumulative tales; 062 Folk and fairy tales; 087 Humor; 116 Music; 164 Songs.

Bonners, Susan. *Panda*. Illus. by author. New York: Delacorte Pr., 1978.
008.06 Animals—bears; 152 Science.

Bonsall, Crosby Newell. *And I Mean It, Stanley*. Illus. by author. New York: Harper, 1974.
002.12 Activities—playing; 008.14 Animals—dogs.

Bonsall, Crosby Newell. *The Case of the Cat's Meow*. Illus. by author. New York: Harper, 1965.
008.09 Animals—cats; 053.01 Ethnic groups in the U.S.—Afro-Americans; 137 Problem solving.

Bonsall, Crosby Newell. *The Case of the Dumb Bells*. Illus. by author. New York: Harper, 1966.
016.23 Behavior—mistakes; 137 Problem solving; 172 Telephone.

Bonsall, Crosby Newell. *The Case of the Hungry Stranger*. Illus. by author. New York: Harper, 1963.
023.08 Careers—detectives; 053.01 Ethnic groups in the U.S.—Afro-Americans; 137 Problem solving.

Bonsall, Crosby Newell. *The Case of the Scaredy Cats*. Illus. by author. New York: Harper, 1971.
121 Non-sexist; 137 Problem solving.

Bonsall, Crosby Newell. *The Day I Had to Play with My Sister*. Illus. by author. New York: Harper, 1972.
069 Games.

Bonsall, Crosby Newell. *It's Mine! A Greedy Book*. Illus. by author. New York: Harper, 1964.
016.13 Behavior—greed; 068 Friendship.

Bonsall, Crosby Newell. *Listen, Listen!* Illus. by Camilla Koffler. New York: Harper, 1961.
008.09 Animals—cats; 008.14 Animals—dogs; 026.02 Character traits—appearance.

Bonsall, Crosby Newell, jt. author. *Look Who's Talking*. By Camilla Koffler, and Crosby Newell Bonsall.

Bonsall, Crosby Newell. *Mine's the Best*. Illus. by author. New York: Harper, 1973.
016.03 Behavior—boasting;
016.32 Behavior—sibling rivalry;
153 Sea and seashore; 177.01 Toys—balloons.

Bonsall, Crosby Newell. *Piggle*. Illus. by author. New York: Harper, 1973.
002.12 Activities—playing;
068 Friendship; 069 Games.

Bonsall, Crosby Newell, jt. author. *Polar Bear Brothers*. By Camilla Koffler, and Crosby Newell Bonsall.

Bonsall, Crosby Newell. *Tell Me Some More*. Illus. by Fritz Siebel. New York: Harper, 1961.
100 Libraries.

Bonsall, Crosby Newell. *Twelve Bells for Santa*. Illus. by author. New York: Harper, 1977.
083.03 Holidays—Christmas;
130 Parties.

Bonsall, Crosby Newell. *What Spot?* Illus. by author. New York: Harper, 1963.
008.58 Animals—walruses; 010 Arctic.

Bonsall, Crosby Newell. *Who's a Pest*. Illus. by author. New York: Harper, 1962.
016.10 Behavior—fighting, arguing;
026.14 Character traits—helpfulness.

Bontemps, Arna Wendell, and Conroy, Jack. *The Fast Sooner Hound*. Illus. by George Van Sautvoord, and Archibald C. Coolidge. Boston: Houghton, 1942.
008.14 Animals—dogs; 179 Trains.

Bornstein, Ruth. *Annabelle*. Illus. by author. New York: Crowell, 1978.
016.20 Behavior—lost; 177 Toys.

Bornstein, Ruth. *Indian Bunny*. Illus. by author. Chicago: Children's Pr., 1973.
008.46 Animals—rabbits; 053.04 Ethnic groups in the U.S.—Indians.

Borten, Helen. *Do You Go Where I Go?* Illus. by author. New York: Abelard-Schuman, 1972.
087 Humor; 134 Poetry, rhyme.

Borten, Helen. *Do You Know What I Know?* Illus. by author. New York: Abelard-Schuman, 1970.
134 Poetry, rhyme; 157 Senses.

Bossom, Naomi. *A Scale Full of Fish and Other Turnabouts*. Illus. by author. New York: Greenwillow, 1970.
087 Humor; 096 Language.

Bourke, Linda. *Ethel's Exceptional Egg*. Illus. by author. New York: Harvey House, 1977.
017.04 Birds—chickens; 050 Eggs;
056 Fairs.

Bourne, Miriam Anne. *Emilio's Summer Day*. Illus. by Ben Shecter. New York: Harper, 1966.
029 City; 053.08 Ethnic groups in the U.S.—Puerto Rican-Americans;
154.03 Seasons—summer.

Bowden, Joan Chase. *The Bean Boy*. Illus. by Salvatore Murdocca. New York: Macmillan, 1979.
038 Cumulative tales; 062 Folk and fairy tales; 087 Humor.

Bowden, Joan Chase. *Bear's Surprise Party*. Illus. by Jerry Scott. Racine, WI: Western Pub., 1975.
008.06 Animals—bears; 130 Parties.

Bowden, Joan Chase. *Boo and the Flying Flews*. Illus. by Don Leake. Racine, WI: Western Pub., 1974.
008.14 Animals—dogs; 028 Circus, clowns.

Bowden, Joan Chase. *A Hat for the Queen*. Illus. by Olindo Giacomini. Racine, WI: Western Pub., 1974.
031 Clothing; 147 Royalty.

Bowden, Joan Chase. *A New Home for Snow Ball*. Illus. by Jan Pyk. Racine, WI: Western Pub., 1974.
008.28 Animals—horses; 147 Royalty.

Bowden, Joan Chase. *Who Took the Top Hat Trick*. Illus. by Jim Cummins. Racine, WI: Western Pub., 1974.
016.19 Behavior—losing things;
103 Magic.

Bowen, Vernon. *The Lazy Beaver*. Illus. by Jim Davis. New York: McKay, 1948.
008.07 Animals—beavers;
026.19 Character traits—laziness.

Boynton, Sandra. *Hester in the Wild*. Illus. by author. New York: Harper, 1979.
008.27 Animals—hippopotami;
008.42 Animals—pigs; 166.04 Sports—camping.

Bradbury, Ray. *Switch on the Night*. Illus. by Madeleine Gekiere. New York: Pantheon, 1955.
119 Night.

Bradfield, Roger. *The Flying Hockey Stick*. Illus. by author. Skokie, IL: Rand McNally, 1966.
002.05 Activities—flying; 087 Humor;
102 Machines.

Bradfield, Roger. *Giants Come in Different Sizes*. Illus. by author. Skokie, IL: Rand McNally, 1966.
072 Giants; 200 Wizards.

Bradfield, Roger. *A Good Knight for Dragons*. Illus. by author. Reading: Addison-Wesley, 1967.
046 Dragons; 095 Knights.

Bram, Elizabeth. *I Don't Want to Go to School*. Illus. by author. New York: Greenwillow, 1977.
151 School.

Bram, Elizabeth. *Saturday Morning Lasts Forever*. Illus. by author. New York: Dial Pr., 1978.
002.12 Activities—playing.

Brand, Millen. *This Little Pig Named Curly*. Illus. by John F. Hamberger. New York: Crown, 1968.
008.42 Animals—pigs; 058 Farms.

Brand, Oscar. *When I First Came to This Land*. Illus. by Doris Burn. New edition. New York: Putnam's, 1974.
038 Cumulative tales; 062 Folk and fairy tales; 135 Poverty; 164 Songs.

Brande, Marlie. *Sleepy Nicholas*. Illustrated. Adapted by Noel Streatfield. Chicago: Follett, 1969.
064.08 Foreign lands—Denmark; 162 Sleep.

Brandenberg, Aliki Liacouras. *June 7!* Illus. by author. New York: Macmillan, 1972.
018 Birthdays; 038 Cumulative tales; 057 Family life.

Brandenberg, Aliki Liacouras. *Keep Your Mouth Closed, Dear*. Illus. by author. New York: Dial Pr., 1966.
016.06 Behavior—carelessness; 057 Family life; 142.01 Reptiles—alligators, crocodiles.

Brandenberg, Aliki Liacouras. *My Five Senses*. Illus. by author. New York: Crowell, 1962.
157 Senses.

Brandenberg, Franz. *Fresh Cider and Apple Pie*. Illus. by Aliki Liacouras Brandenberg. New York: Macmillan, 1973.
063 Food; 090 Insects and spiders.

Brandenberg, Franz. *I Wish I Was Sick, Too!* Illus. by Aliki Liacouras Brandenberg. New York: Greenwillow, 1976.
016.38 Behavior—wishing; 088 Illness.

Brandenberg, Franz. *Nice New Neighbors*. Illus. by Aliki Liacouras Brandenberg. New York: Greenwillow, 1977.
008.34 Animals—mice; 068 Friendship; 114 Moving.

Brandenberg, Franz. *No School Today!* Illus. by Aliki Liacouras Brandenberg. New York: Macmillan, 1975.
008.09 Animals—cats; 016.23 Behavior—mistakes; 151 School.

Brandenberg, Franz. *A Picnic, Hurrah!* Illus. by Aliki Liacouras Brandenberg. New York: Greenwillow, 1978.
002.11 Activities—picnicking; 008.09 Animals—cats; 137 Problem solving; 195.05 Weather—rain.

Brandenberg, Franz. *A Secret for Grandmother's Birthday*. Illus. by Aliki Liacouras Brandenberg. New York: Greenwillow, 1975.
016.29 Behavior—secrets; 018 Birthdays; 057.02 Family life—grandparents; great-grandparents.

Brandenberg, Franz. *What Can You Make of It?* Illus. by Aliki Liacouras Brandenberg. New York: Greenwillow, 1977.
008.34 Animals—mice; 011 Art; 016.28 Behavior—saving things; 114 Moving.

Braun, Kathy. *Kangaroo and Kangaroo*. Illus. by Jim McMullan. Garden City, NY: Doubleday, 1965.
008.30 Animals—kangaroos; 016.28 Behavior—saving things; 134 Poetry, rhyme.

Brecht, Bertolt. *Uncle Eddie's Moustache*. Illus. by Ursula Kirchberg. English by Muriel Rukeyser. New York: Pantheon, 1974.
087 Humor; 134 Poetry, rhyme.

Breinburg, Petronella. *Doctor Shawn*. Illus. by Errol Lloyd. New York: Crowell, 1974.
002.12 Activities—playing; 023.09 Careers—doctors; 053.01 Ethnic groups in the U.S.—Afro-Americans.

Breinburg, Petronella. *Shawn Goes to School*. Illus. by Errol Lloyd. New York: Crowell, 1973.
053.01 Ethnic groups in the U.S.—Afro-Americans; 068 Friendship; 151 School.

Breinburg, Petronella. *Shawn's Red Bike*. Illus. by Errol Lloyd. New York: Crowell, 1975.
053.01 Ethnic groups in the U.S.—Afro-Americans; 166.03 Sports—bicycling.

Brenner, Barbara. *Faces, Faces.* Illus. by George Ancona. New York: Dutton, 1970.
006 Anatomy; 052 Emotions; 053.07 Ethnic groups in the U.S.—Multiethnic; 157 Senses.

Brenner, Barbara. *The Flying Patchwork Quilt.* Illus. by Fred Brenner. Reading: Addison-Wesley, 1965.
002.05 Activities—flying; 103 Magic.

Brenner, Barbara. *Wagon Wheels.* Illus. by Donald Alan Bolognese. New York: Harper, 1978.
026.25 Character traits—perseverance; 053.01 Ethnic groups in the U.S.—Afro-Americans; 058 Farms; 189 U.S. history.

Bridgman, Elizabeth P. *New Dog Next Door.* Illus. by author. New York: Harper, 1978.
008.14 Animals—dogs.

Bridwell, Norman. *Clifford's Good Deeds.* Illus. by author. New York: Four Winds Pr., 1975.
008.14 Animals—dogs; 012 Automobiles; 016.23 Behavior—mistakes; 023.10 Careers—firefighters; 026.14 Character traits—helpfulness.

Bridwell, Norman. *Clifford's Halloween.* Illus. by author. New York: Four Winds Pr., 1966.
008.14 Animals—dogs; 083.07 Holidays—Halloween.

Bridwell, Norman. *The Witch Next Door.* Illus. by author. New York: Four Winds Pr., 1965.
199 Witches.

Briggs, Raymond. *Father Christmas.* Illus. by author. New York: Coward, 1973.
083.03 Holidays—Christmas; 201 Wordless.

Briggs, Raymond. *Father Christmas Goes on Holiday.* Illus. by author. New York: Coward, 1975.
002.17 Activities—vacationing; 083.03 Holidays—Christmas; 201 Wordless.

Briggs, Raymond. *Fee Fi Fo Fum.* Illus. by author. New York: Coward, 1964.
122 Nursery rhymes.

Briggs, Raymond. *Ring-A-Ring O' Roses.* Illus. by author. New York: Coward, 1962.
122 Nursery rhymes.

Briggs, Raymond. *The Snowman.* Illus. by author. New York: Random House, 1978.
068 Friendship; 163 Snowmen; 201 Wordless.

Briggs, Raymond. *The White Land.* Illus. by author. New York: Coward, 1963.
122 Nursery rhymes; 164 Songs.

Bright, Robert. *Georgie.* Illus. by author. Garden City, NY: Doubleday, 1944.
057 Family life; 058 Farms; 071 Ghosts.

Bright, Robert. *Georgie and the Noisy Ghost.* Illus. by author. Garden City, NY: Doubleday, 1971.
002.17 Activities—vacationing; 071 Ghosts; 120 Noise; 153 Sea and seashore.

Bright, Robert. *Georgie and the Robbers.* Illus. by author. Garden City, NY: Doubleday, 1963.
036 Crime; 071 Ghosts.

Bright, Robert. *Georgie Goes West.* Illus. by author. Garden City, NY: Doubleday, 1973.
035 Cowboys; 071 Ghosts.

Bright, Robert. *Georgie to the Rescue.* Illus. by author. Garden City, NY: Doubleday, 1956.
029 City; 071 Ghosts.

Bright, Robert. *Georgie's Christmas Carol.* Illus. by author. Garden City, NY: Doubleday, 1975.
071 Ghosts; 083.03 Holidays—Christmas.

Bright, Robert. *Georgie's Halloween.* Illus. by author. Garden City, NY: Doubleday, 1958.
071 Ghosts; 083.07 Holidays—Halloween.

Bright, Robert. *Gregory, the Noisiest and Strongest Boy in Grangers Grove.* Illus. by author. Garden City, NY: Doubleday, 1969.
026.19 Character traits—laziness; 063 Food; 120 Noise.

Bright, Robert. *Hurrah for Freddie!* Illus. by author. Garden City, NY: Doubleday, 1953.
128 Parades; 147 Royalty; 177 Toys.

Bright, Robert. *I Like Red.* Illus. by author. Garden City, NY: Doubleday, 1955.
032.01 Concepts—color; 076 Hair.

Bright, Robert. *Me and the Bears.* Illus. by author. Garden City, NY: Doubleday, 1951.
008.06 Animals—bears; 016.38 Behavior—wishing; 162 Sleep; 204 Zoos.

Bright, Robert. *Miss Pattie.* Illus. by author. Garden City, NY: Doubleday, 1954.
008.09 Animals—cats.

Bright, Robert. *My Hopping Bunny*. Illus. by author. Garden City, NY: Doubleday, 1960.
002.07 Activities—jumping;
008.46 Animals—rabbits; 134 Poetry, rhyme.

Bright, Robert. *My Red Umbrella*. Illus. by author. New York: Morrow, 1959.
033 Counting; 187 Umbrellas;
195.05 Weather—rain.

Brightman, Alan. *Like Me*. Illus. by author. Boston: Little, 1976.
026.03 Character traits—being different; 077 Handicaps.

Brincklae, Julie. *Gordon's House*. Illus. by author. Garden City, NY: Doubleday, 1976.
008.06 Animals—bears.

Bring a Torch, Jeannette, Isabella. Illus. by Adrienne Adams. A Provencial Carol attributed to Nicholas Saboly, seventeenth century. New York: Scribner's, 1963.
064.11 Foreign lands—France;
083.03 Holidays—Christmas; 116 Music;
164 Songs.

Brock, Emma Lillian. *The Birds' Christmas Tree*. Illus. by author. New York: Knopf, 1946.
017 Birds; 026.18 Character traits—kindness to animals; 083.03 Holidays—Christmas.

Brock, Emma Lillian. *One Little Indian Boy*. Illus. by author. New York: Knopf, 1932.
053.04 Ethnic groups in the U.S.—Indians.

Brock, Emma Lillian. *To Market! To Market!* Illus. by author. New York: Knopf, 1930.
122 Nursery rhymes; 160 Shopping.

Brodsky, Beverly. See McDermott, Beverly Brodsky.

Brook, Judy. *Tim Mouse Goes Downstream*. Illus. by author. New York: Lothrop, 1969.
008.26 Animals—hedgehogs;
008.34 Animals—mice; 019 Boats, ships;
058 Farms; 144 Rivers.

Brook, Judy. *Tim Mouse Visits the Farm*. Illus. by author. New York: Lothrop, 1977.
008.26 Animals—hedgehogs;
008.34 Animals—mice; 058 Farms.

Brooke, L. Leslie. See Brooke, Leonard Leslie.

Brooke, Leonard Leslie. *The Golden Goose Book*. Illus. by author. New York: Warne, 1906.
062 Folk and fairy tales.

Brooke, Leonard Leslie. *Johnny Crow's Garden*. Illus. by author. New York: Warne, 1903.
008 Animals; 087 Humor; 134 Poetry, rhyme.

Brooke, Leonard Leslie. *Johnny Crow's New Garden*. Illus. by author. New York: Warne, 1935.
008 Animals; 087 Humor; 134 Poetry, rhyme.

Brooke, Leonard Leslie. *Johnny Crow's Party*. Illus. by author. New York: Warne, 1907.
008 Animals; 087 Humor; 130 Parties.

Brooke, Leonard Leslie. *Oranges and Lemons*. Illus. by author. New York: Warne, 1913.
122 Nursery rhymes.

Brooks, Ron. *This Little Pig Went to Market*. Illus. by author. New York: Warne, 1922.
008.42 Animals—pigs; 122 Nursery rhymes.

Brooks, Ron. *Timothy and Gramps*. Illus. by author. New York: Bradbury Pr., 1978.
057.02 Family life—grandparents;
great-grandparents; 151 School.

Brothers, Aileen. *Jiffy, Miss Boo and Mr. Roo*. Illus. by Audean Johnson. Chicago: Follett, 1966.
017.04 Birds—chickens; 131 Pets.

Brothers and Sisters Are Like That! Illus. by Michael Hampshire. Selected by The Child Study Association of America. New York: Crowell, 1971.
016.32 Behavior—sibling rivalry;
057 Family life.

Brown, Jeff. *Flat Stanley*. Illus. by Tomi Ungerer. New York: Harper, 1964.
057 Family life; 087 Humor;
137 Problem solving.

Brown, Judith Gwyn. *Alphabet Dreams*. Illus. by author. Englewood Cliffs, NJ: Prentice-Hall, 1976.
001 ABC Books.

Brown, Judith Gwyn. *The Happy Voyage*. Illus. by author. New York: Macmillan, 1965.
019 Boats, ships.

Brown, Judith Gwyn. *Max and the Truffle Pig*. Illus. by author. Nashville: Abingdon Pr., 1963.
008.42 Animals—pigs;
016.20 Behavior—lost; 064.11 Foreign lands—France.

Brown, Marc Tolon. *Arthur's Eyes*. Illus. by author. Boston: Little, 1979.
073 Glasses.

Brown, Marcia. *All Butterflies.* Illus. by author. New York: Scribner's, 1974.
001 ABC Books.

Brown, Marcia. *The Blue Jackal.* Illus. by author. New York: Scribner's, 1977.
008 Animals; 016.36 Behavior—trickery; 062 Folk and fairy tales; 064.16 Foreign lands—India.

Brown, Marcia. *The Bun.* Illus. by author. New York: Harcourt, 1972.
008 Animals; 008.18 Animals—foxes; 016.13 Behavior—greed; 026.06 Character traits—cleverness; 038 Cumulative tales; 062 Folk and fairy tales; 064.30 Foreign lands—Russia.

Brown, Marcia. *Felice.* Illus. by author. New York: Scribner's, 1958.
008.09 Animals—cats; 064.18 Foreign lands—Italy.

Brown, Marcia. *How, Hippo!* Illus. by author. New York: Scribner's, 1969.
008.27 Animals—hippopotami.

Brown, Marcia. *The Little Carousel.* Illus. by author. New York: Scribner's, 1946.
029 City; 052.07 Emotions—loneliness; 094 Kites; 106 Merry-go-rounds; 109 Money.

Brown, Marcia. *The Neighbors.* Illus. by author. New York: Scribner's, 1967.
008.18 Animals—foxes; 008.46 Animals—rabbits; 038 Cumulative tales; 064.30 Foreign lands—Russia; 086 Houses.

Brown, Marcia. *Once a Mouse.* Illus. by author. New York: Scribner's, 1961.
008.10 Animals—cats, wild; 008.34 Animals—mice; 032.08 Concepts—size; 062 Folk and fairy tales; 064.16 Foreign lands—India; 103 Magic.

Brown, Marcia. *Peter Piper's Alphabet.* Illus. by author. New York: Scribner's, 1959.
001 ABC Books; 122 Nursery rhymes; 175 Tongue twisters.

Brown, Marcia. *Tamarindo.* Illus. by author. New York: Scribner's, 1960.
008.16 Animals—donkeys; 016.20 Behavior—lost; 064.13 Foreign lands—Greece.

Brown, Margaret Wise. *A Child's Good-Night Book.* Illus. by Jean Charlot. New York: Abelard-Schuman, 1950.
015 Bedtime; 162 Sleep.

Brown, Margaret Wise. *Country Noisy Book.* Illus. by Leonard Weisgard. New York: Harper, 1940.
008.14 Animals—dogs; 034 Country; 120 Noise; 129 Participation.

Brown, Margaret Wise. *The Dead Bird.* Illus. by Remy Charlip. New York: Abelard-Schuman, 1958.
040 Death.

Brown, Margaret Wise. *Four Fur Feet.* Illus. by Remy Charlip. New York: Abelard-Schuman, 1961.
002.18 Activities—walking; 134 Poetry, rhyme; 202 World.

Brown, Margaret Wise. *Fox Eyes.* Illus. by Garth Montgomery Williams. New York: Pantheon, 1977.
008 Animals; 008.18 Animals—foxes.

Brown, Margaret Wise. *The Golden Egg Book.* Illus. by Leonard Weisgard. New York: Simon & Schuster, 1947.
008.46 Animals—rabbits; 017.08 Birds—ducks; 050 Eggs; 083.04 Holidays—Easter.

Brown, Margaret Wise. *Goodnight, Moon.* Illus. by Clement Hurd. New York: Harper, 1947.
008.46 Animals—rabbits; 015 Bedtime; 111 Moon.

Brown, Margaret Wise. *Indoor Noisy Book.* Illus. by Leonard Weisgard. New York: Harper, 1942.
008.14 Animals—dogs; 069 Games; 120 Noise; 129 Participation.

Brown, Margaret Wise. *Little Chicken.* Illus. by Leonard Weisgard. New York: Harper, 1943.
008.46 Animals—rabbits; 017.04 Birds—chickens.

Brown, Margaret Wise. *The Little Farmer.* Illus. by Esphyr Slobodkina. Reading: Addison-Wesley, 1947.
032.08 Concepts—size; 058 Farms.

Brown, Margaret Wise. *The Little Fir Tree.* Illus. by Barbara Cooney. New York: Crowell, 1954.
083.03 Holidays—Christmas; 088 Illness; 181 Trees.

Brown, Margaret Wise. *The Little Fireman.* Illus. by Esphyr Slobodkina. Reading: Addison-Wesley, 1938.
023.10 Careers—firefighters; 059 Fire.

Brown, Margaret Wise. *The Little Island.* Illus. by Leonard Weisgard. Garden City, NY: Doubleday, 1946.
091 Islands; 154 Seasons.

Brown, Margaret Wise. *Little Lost Lamb.* Illus. by Leonard Weisgard. Garden City, NY: Doubleday, 1945.
008.52 Animals—sheep;
016.20 Behavior—lost.

Brown, Margaret Wise. *Noisy Book.* Illus. by Leonard Weisgard. New York: Harper, 1939.
120 Noise; 129 Participation.

Brown, Margaret Wise. *On Christmas Eve.* Illus. by Beni Montresor. Reading: Addison-Wesley, 1961.
083.03 Holidays—Christmas;
141 Religion.

Brown, Margaret Wise. *A Pussycat's Christmas.* Illus. by Helen Stone. New York: Crowell, 1949.
008.09 Animals—cats;
083.03 Holidays—Christmas.

Brown, Margaret Wise. *The Quiet Noisy Book.* Illus. by Leonard Weisgard. New York: Harper, 1950.
008.14 Animals—dogs; 112 Morning;
120 Noise; 129 Participation.

Brown, Margaret Wise. *Red Light, Green Light.* Illus. by Leonard Weisgard. Garden City, NY: Doubleday, 1944.
032.01 Concepts—color; 148 Safety;
178 Traffic signs.

Brown, Margaret Wise. *The Runaway Bunny.* Illus. by Clement Hurd. New York: Harper, 1942.
008.46 Animals—rabbits;
016.27 Behavior—running away;
083.04 Holidays—Easter.

Brown, Margaret Wise. *The Seashore Noisy Book.* Illus. by Leonard Weisgard. Reading: Addison-Wesley, 1941.
129 Participation; 153 Sea and seashore.

Brown, Margaret Wise. *SHHhhh......Bang: A Whispering Book.* Illus. by Robert De Veyrac. New York: Harper, 1943.
120 Noise.

Brown, Margaret Wise. *Sleepy ABC.* Illus. by Esphyr Slobodkina. New York: Lothrop, 1953.
001 ABC Books; 134 Poetry, rhyme;
162 Sleep.

Brown, Margaret Wise. *The Sleepy Little Lion.* Illus. by Camilla Koffler. New York: Harper, 1947.
008.10 Animals—cats, wild; 162 Sleep.

Brown, Margaret Wise. *The Steamroller.* Illus. by Evaline Ness. New York: Walker, 1974.
083.03 Holidays—Christmas;
102 Machines; 121 Non-sexist.

Brown, Margaret Wise. *Summer Noisy Book.* Illus. by Leonard Weisgard. New York: Harper, 1951.
058 Farms; 120 Noise; 129 Participation;
154.03 Seasons—summer.

Brown, Margaret Wise. *Wait Till the Moon Is Full.* Illus. by Garth Montgomery Williams. New York: Harper, 1948.
008 Animals; 008.47 Animals—raccoons; 026.28 Character traits—questioning; 111 Moon; 119 Night.

Brown, Margaret Wise. *When the Wind Blew.* Illus. by Geoffrey Hayes. New York: Harper, 1977.
008.09 Animals—cats; 088 Illness;
195.08 Weather—wind.

Brown, Margaret Wise. *Whistle for the Train.* Illus. by Leonard Weisgard. Garden City, NY: Doubleday, 1956.
134 Poetry, rhyme; 179 Trains.

Brown, Margaret Wise. *Winter Noisy Book.* Illus. by Charles Green Shaw. New York: Harper, 1947.
008.14 Animals—dogs; 120 Noise;
129 Participation; 154.04 Seasons—winter; 195.07 Weather—snow.

Brown, Margaret Wise, and Gergely, Tibor. *Wheel on the Chimney.* Illus. by Tibor Gergely. Philadelphia: Lippincott, 1954.
017.24 Birds—storks; 026.21 Character traits—luck; 064.15 Foreign lands—Hungary.

Brown, Myra Berry. *Benjy's Blanket.* Illus. by Dorothy Bronson Marino. New York: Watts, 1962.
008.09 Animals—cats;
016.14 Behavior—growing up.

Brown, Myra Berry. *Best Friends.* Illus. by Don Freeman. Chicago: Children's Pr., 1967.
068 Friendship; 134 Poetry, rhyme.

Brown, Myra Berry. *Best of Luck.* Illus. by Don Freeman. Chicago: Children's Pr., 1969.
026.21 Character traits—luck;
134 Poetry, rhyme.

Brown, Myra Berry. *First Night Away from Home.* Illus. by Dorothy Bronson Marino. New York: Watts, 1960.
002.12 Activities—playing;
068 Friendship; 162 Sleep;
177.08 Toys—teddy bears.

Brown, Myra Berry. *Pip Camps Out*. Illus. by Phyllis Graham. Chicago: Children's Pr., 1966.
057 Family life; 119 Night;
166.04 Sports—camping.

Brown, Myra Berry. *Pip Moves Away*. Illus. by Polly Jackson. Chicago: Children's Pr., 1967.
057 Family life; 114 Moving.

Brown, Palmer. *Cheerful*. Illus. by author. New York: Harper, 1957.
008.34 Animals—mice.

Brown, Palmer. *Something for Christmas*. Illus. by author. New York: Harper, 1958.
008.34 Animals—mice;
026.13 Character traits—generosity;
052.08 Emotions—love;
083.03 Holidays—Christmas.

Browner, Richard. *Look Again!* Illus. by Emma Landau. New York: Atheneum, 1962.
032 Concepts.

Bruna, Dick. *Another Story to Tell*. Illus. by author. New York: Methuen, 1974.
201 Wordless.

Bruna, Dick. *B Is for Bear; An ABC*. Illus. by author. New York: Methuen, 1972.
001 ABC Books.

Bruna, Dick. *Christmas*. Illus. by author. English verse by Eve Merriam. Garden City, NY: Doubleday, 1969.
083.03 Holidays—Christmas.

Bruna, Dick. *The Christmas Book*. Illus. by author. New York: Methuen, 1964.
083.03 Holidays—Christmas.

Bruna, Dick. *The Fish*. Illus. by author. Chicago: Follett, 1963.
060 Fish; 063 Food; 134 Poetry, rhyme.

Bruna, Dick. *I Can Dress Myself*. Illus. by author. New York: Methuen, 1977.
016.14 Behavior—growing up.

Bruna, Dick. *Little Bird Tweet*. Illus. by author. Chicago: Follett, 1963.
017 Birds; 058 Farms; 134 Poetry, rhyme.

Bruna, Dick. *Miffy*. Illus. by author. Chicago: Follett, 1970.
008.46 Animals—rabbits; 057 Family life.

Bruna, Dick. *Miffy at the Seaside*. Illus. by author. Chicago: Follett, 1970.
008.46 Animals—rabbits; 153 Sea and seashore.

Bruna, Dick. *Miffy at the Zoo*. Illus. by author. Chicago: Follett, 1970.
008.46 Animals—rabbits; 204 Zoos.

Bruna, Dick. *Miffy in the Hospital*. Illus. by author. New York: Methuen, 1976.
008.46 Animals—rabbits; 084 Hospitals.

Bruna, Dick. *Miffy in the Snow*. Illus. by author. Chicago: Follett, 1970.
008.46 Animals—rabbits;
154.04 Seasons—winter;
195.07 Weather—snow.

Brunhoff, Jean de. *Babar and Father Christmas*. Illus. by author. New York: Random House, 1940.
008.17 Animals—elephants;
083.03 Holidays—Christmas.

Brunhoff, Jean de. *Babar and His Children*. Illus. by author. Translated by Merle S. Haas. New York: Random House, 1938.
008.17 Animals—elephants;
182 Triplets.

Brunhoff, Jean de. *Babar and Zephir*. Illus. by author. Translated by Merle S. Haas. New York: Random House, 1937.
008.17 Animals—elephants;
008.37 Animals—monkeys.

Brunhoff, Jean de. *Babar the King*. Illus. by author. New York: Random House, 1935.
008.17 Animals—elephants.

Brunhoff, Jean de. *The Story of Babar, the Little Elephant*. Illus. by author. Translated by Merle S. Haas. New York: Random House, 1960.
008.17 Animals—elephants;
016.27 Behavior—running away;
064.11 Foreign lands—France.

Brunhoff, Jean de. *The Travels of Babar*. Illus. by author. New York: Random House, 1934/1961.
002.16 Activities—traveling;
008.17 Animals—elephants.

Brunhoff, Laurent de. *Babar and the Willy-Wully*. Illus. by author. New York: Random House, 1975.
008.17 Animals—elephants; 131 Pets.

Brunhoff, Laurent de. *Babar Comes to America*. Illus. by author. Translated by M. Jean Craig. New York: Random House, 1965.
008.17 Animals—elephants.

Brunhoff, Laurent de. *Babar Loses His Crown*. Illus. by author. New York: Random House, 1967.
008.17 Animals—elephants;
016.19 Behavior—losing things.

Brunhoff, Laurent de. *Babar Visits Another Planet*. Illus. by author. New York: Random House, 1972.
008.17 Animals—elephants; 165 Space and space ships.

Brunhoff, Laurent de. *Babar's Birthday Surprise*. Illus. by author. New York: Random House, 1970.
008.17 Animals—elephants;
018 Birthdays.

Brunhoff, Laurent de. *Babar's Castle*. Illus. by author. Translated by Merle S. Haas. New York: Random House, 1962.
008.17 Animals—elephants.

Brunhoff, Laurent de. *Babar's Cousin, That Rascal Arthur*. Illus. by author. Translated by Merle S. Haas. New York: Random House, 1948.
002.17 Activities—vacationing;
008.17 Animals—elephants;
016.22 Behavior—misbehavior.

Brunhoff, Laurent de. *Babar's Fair Will Be Opened Next Sunday*. Illus. by author. Translated by Merle S. Haas. New York: Random House, 1954.
008.17 Animals—elephants; 056 Fairs.

Brunhoff, Laurent de. *Babar's Mystery*. Illus. by author. New York: Random House, 1978.
002.17 Activities—vacationing;
008.17 Animals—elephants; 036 Crime.

Brustlein, Janice. *Little Bear Marches in the St. Patrick's Day Parade*. Illus. by Marian Curtis Foster. New York: Lothrop, 1967.
008.06 Animals—bears;
083.09 Holidays—St. Patrick's Day;
128 Parades.

Brustlein, Janice. *Little Bear's Christmas*. Illus. by Marian Curtis Foster. New York: Lothrop, 1964.
008.06 Animals—bears;
026.13 Character traits—generosity;
081 Hibernation; 083.03 Holidays—Christmas.

Brustlein, Janice. *Little Bear's New Year's Party*. Illus. by Marian Curtis Foster. New York: Lothrop, 1973.
008.06 Animals—bears;
083.08 Holidays—New Year's Day;
130 Parties.

Brustlein, Janice. *Little Bear's Pancake Party*. Illus. by Marian Curtis Foster. New York: Lothrop, 1960.
008.06 Animals—bears; 063 Food;
130 Parties; 154.02 Seasons—spring.

Brustlein, Janice. *Little Bear's Thanksgiving*. Illus. by Marian Curtis Foster. New York: Lothrop, 1967.
008.06 Animals—bears;
083.10 Holidays—Thanksgiving.

Brustlein, Janice. *Mr. and Mrs. Button's Wonderful Watchdogs*. Illus. by Roger Antoine Duvoisin. New York: Lothrop, 1978.
008.14 Animals—dogs; 036 Crime.

Bryant, Sara Cone. *Epaminondas and His Auntie*. Illus. by Inez Hogan. Boston: Houghton, 1938.
016.24 Behavior—misunderstanding;
062 Folk and fairy tales; 087 Humor.

Buck, Pearl Sydenstricker. *Welcome Child*. Illus. by Alan D. Haas. New York: Harper, 1963.
003 Adoption.

Buckley, Helen Elizabeth. *Grandfather and I*. Illus. by Paul Galdone. New York: Lothrop, 1959.
002.18 Activities—walking;
057.02 Family life—grandparents; great-grandparents.

Buckley, Helen Elizabeth. *Josie and the Snow*. Illus. by Evaline Ness. New York: Lothrop, 1964.
134 Poetry, rhyme; 154.04 Seasons—winter; 195.07 Weather—snow.

Buckley, Helen Elizabeth. *Josie's Buttercup*. Illus. by Evaline Ness. New York: Lothrop, 1967.
008.14 Animals—dogs; 134 Poetry, rhyme.

Budney, Blossom. *After Dark*. Illus. by Tony Chen. New York: Lothrop, 1975.
119 Night.

Budney, Blossom. *A Kiss Is Round*. Illus. by Vladimir Bobri. New York: Lothrop, 1954.
032.07 Concepts—shape; 134 Poetry, rhyme.

Budney, Blossom. *N Is for Nursery School*. Illus. by Vladimir Bobri. New York: Lothrop, 1956.
001 ABC Books; 151 School.

Bulette, Sara. *The Elf in the Singing Tree*. Illus. by Tom Dunnington. Reading consultant: Morton Botel. Chicago: Follett, 1964.
051 Elves and little people;
089 Imagination.

Bulette, Sara. *The Splendid Belt of Mr. Big.* Illus. by Lou Myers. Chicago: Follett, 1964.
008.37 Animals—monkeys;
031 Clothing; 032.08 Concepts—size;
137 Problem solving.

Bulla, Clyde Robert. *Keep Running, Allen!* Illus. by Satomi Ichikawa. New York: Crowell, 1978.
016.32 Behavior—sibling rivalry;
016.33 Behavior—solitude.

Bulla, Clyde Robert. *Washington's Birthday.* Illus. by Donald Alan Bolognese. New York: Crowell, 1967.
083.12 Holidays—Washington's
Birthday; 189 U.S. history.

Bunin, Catherine, and Bunin, Sherry. *Is That Your Sister?* Illustrated. A true story about adoption. New York: Pantheon, 1976.
003 Adoption; 057 Family life.

Bunin, Sherry, jt. author. *Is That Your Sister?* By Catherine Bunin, and Sherry Bunin.

Bunting, Eve. *Winter's Coming.* Illus. by Howard Clayton Knotts. New York: Harcourt, 1977.
058 Farms; 154.01 Seasons—fall;
154.04 Seasons—winter.

Burch, Robert. *The Hunting Trip.* Illus. by Susanne Suba. New York: Scribner's, 1971.
026.18 Character traits—kindness to animals; 057 Family life; 063 Food;
166.08 Sports—hunting.

Burch, Robert. *Joey's Cat.* Illus. by Don Freeman. New York: Viking, 1969.
008.09 Animals—cats; 008.44 Animals—possums; 053.01 Ethnic groups in the U.S.—Afro-Americans; 057 Family life.

Burgert, Hans-Joachim. *Samulo and the Giant.* Illus. by author. New York: Holt, 1970.
026.04 Character traits—bravery;
195 Weather.

Burgess, Anthony. *The Land Where the Ice Cream Grows.* Illus. by Fulvio Testa. Story by Fulvio Testa as told by Anthony Burgess. Garden City, NY: Doubleday, 1979.
063 Food; 089 Imagination.

Burlingham, Mary, jt. author. *The Climbing Book.* By Charlotte Steiner, and Mary Burlingham.

Burn, Doris. *The Summerfolk.* Illus. by author. New York: Coward, 1968.
019 Boats, ships; 091 Islands;
154.03 Seasons—summer.

Burnett, Carol. *What I Want to Be When I Grow Up.* Illus. by Sheldon Secunda. Created by George Mendoza and Sheldon Secunda. New York: Simon & Schuster, 1975.
023 Careers.

Burningham, John Mackintosh. *The Blanket.* Illus. by author. New York: Crowell, 1976.
016.19 Behavior—losing things.

Burningham, John Mackintosh. *Borka, the Adventures of a Goose with No Feathers.* Illus. by author. New York: Random House, 1963.
017.11 Birds—geese; 026.03 Character traits—being different;
026.22 Character traits—meanness;
064.10 Foreign lands—England.

Burningham, John Mackintosh. *Cannonball Simp.* Illus. by author. Indianapolis: Bobbs-Merrill, 1966.
008.14 Animals—dogs; 028 Circus, clowns.

Burningham, John Mackintosh. *Come Away from the Water, Shirley.* Illus. by author. New York: Crowell, 1977.
153 Sea and seashore.

Burningham, John Mackintosh. *The Cupboard.* Illus. by author. New York: Crowell, 1975.
063 Food.

Burningham, John Mackintosh. *The Dog.* Illus. by author. New York: Crowell, 1975.
008.14 Animals—dogs.

Burningham, John Mackintosh. *The Friend.* Illus. by author. New York: Crowell, 1975.
068 Friendship.

Burningham, John Mackintosh. *Harquin, the Fox Who Went Down to the Valley.* Illus. by author. Indianapolis: Bobbs-Merrill, 1968.
008.18 Animals—foxes;
026.06 Character traits—cleverness;
166.08 Sports—hunting.

Burningham, John Mackintosh. *John Burningham's ABC.* Illus. by author. Indianapolis: Bobbs-Merrill, 1967.
001 ABC Books.

Burningham, John Mackintosh. *Mr. Gumpy's Motor Car.* Illus. by author. New York: Macmillan, 1975.
012 Automobiles;
195.05 Weather—rain.

Burningham, John Mackintosh. *Mr. Gumpy's Outing.* Illus. by author. New York: Macmillan, 1971.
008 Animals; 016.10 Behavior—fighting, arguing; 019 Boats, ships; 038 Cumulative tales.

Burningham, John Mackintosh. *Seasons.* Illus. by author. New York: Crowell, 1975.
154 Seasons.

Burningham, John Mackintosh. *Time to Get Out of the Bath, Shirley.* Illus. by author. New York: Crowell, 1978.
002.02 Activities—bathing; 089 Imagination; 147 Royalty.

Burningham, John Mackintosh. *Would You Rather...* Illus. by author. New York: Crowell, 1978.
089 Imagination.

Burroway, Janet. *The Truck on the Track.* Illus. by John Vernon Lord. Indianapolis: Bobbs-Merrill, 1970.
087 Humor; 134 Poetry, rhyme; 184 Trucks.

Burton, Virginia Lee. *Calico the Wonder Horse, or The Saga of Stewy Slinker.* Illus. by author. Boston: Houghton, 1941.
008.28 Animals—horses; 026.06 Character traits—cleverness; 035 Cowboys; 036 Crime.

Burton, Virginia Lee. *Choo Choo, the Story of a Little Engine Who Ran Away.* Illus. by author. Boston: Houghton, 1937.
016.27 Behavior—running away; 179 Trains.

Burton, Virginia Lee. *Katy and the Big Snow.* Illus. by author. Boston: Houghton, 1943.
029 City; 038 Cumulative tales; 102 Machines; 154.04 Seasons—winter; 195.07 Weather—snow.

Burton, Virginia Lee. *The Little House.* Illus. by author. Boston: Houghton, 1942.
029 City; 034 Country; 049 Ecology; 086 Houses; 138 Progress.

Burton, Virginia Lee. *Maybelle, the Cable Car.* Illus. by author. Boston: Houghton, 1952.
022 Cable cars; 029 City; 180 Transportation.

Burton, Virginia Lee. *Mike Mulligan and His Steam Shovel.* Illus. by author. Boston: Houghton, 1939.
002.20 Activities—working; 102 Machines.

Byars, Betsy Cromer. *Go and Hush the Baby.* Illus. by Emily Arnold McCully. New York: Viking, 1971.
002.01 Activities—babysitting; 013 Babies; 057 Family life; 069 Games; 121 Non-sexist.

Byars, Betsy Cromer. *The Groober.* Illus. by author. New York: Harper, 1967.
008 Animals; 016.09 Behavior—dissatisfaction.

Byfield, Barbara Ninde. *The Haunted Churchbell.* Illus. by author. Garden City, NY: Doubleday, 1971.
026.06 Character traits—cleverness; 052.04 Emotions—fear; 087 Humor.

Caines, Jeannette Franklin. *Abby.* Illus. by Steven Kellogg. New York: Harper, 1973.
003 Adoption; 016.32 Behavior—sibling rivalry; 053.01 Ethnic groups in the U.S.—Afro-Americans; 057 Family life.

Caines, Jeannette Franklin. *Daddy.* Illus. by Ronald Norbert Himler. New York: Harper, 1977.
045 Divorce; 053.01 Ethnic groups in the U.S.—Afro-Americans; 057.01 Family life—fathers.

Caldecott, Randolph. *The Diverting History of John Gilpin.* Illus. by author. New York: Warne, 1878.
122 Nursery rhymes.

Caldecott, Randolph. *Hey Diddle Diddle, and Baby Bunting.* Illus. by author. New York: Warne, 1882.
122 Nursery rhymes.

Caldecott, Randolph. *Hey Diddle Diddle Picture Book.* Illus. by author. New York: Warne, 1883.
122 Nursery rhymes.

Caldecott, Randolph. *Panjandrum Picture Book.* Illus. by author. New York: Warne, 1885.
122 Nursery rhymes.

Caldecott, Randolph. *The Queen of Hearts.* Illus. by author. New York: Warne, 1881.
122 Nursery rhymes.

Caldecott, Randolph. *Randolph Caldecott's John Gilpin and Other Stories*. Illus. by author. Contains The Diverting History of John Gilpin, The House That Jack Built, The Frog He Would A-Wooing Go and The Milkmaid. New York: Warne, 1977.
122 Nursery rhymes.

Caldecott, Randolph. *Randolph Caldecott's Picture Book, No. 1*. Illus. by author. New York: Warne, 1879.
122 Nursery rhymes.

Caldecott, Randolph. *Randolph Caldecott's Picture Book, No. 2*. Illus. by author. New York: Warne, 1879.
122 Nursery rhymes.

Caldecott, Randolph. *Sing a Song for Sixpence*. Illus. by author. New York: Warne, 1880.
122 Nursery rhymes.

Caldecott, Randolph. *The Three Jovial Huntsmen*. Illus. by author. New York: Warne, 1880.
122 Nursery rhymes.

Calhoun, Mary. *Cross-Country Cat*. Illus. by Erick Ingraham. New York: Morrow, 1979.
008.09 Animals—cats; 166.12 Sports—skiing.

Calhoun, Mary. *Euphonia and the Flood*. Illus. by Simms Taback. New York: Parents, 1976.
008 Animals; 019 Boats, ships;
026.14 Character traits—helpfulness;
195.05 Weather—rain.

Calhoun, Mary. *Houn' Dog*. Illus. by Roger Antoine Duvoisin. New York: Morrow, 1959.
008.14 Animals—dogs;
008.18 Animals—foxes; 166.08 Sports—hunting.

Calhoun, Mary. *The Hungry Leprechaun*. Illus. by Roger Antoine Duvoisin. New York: Harper, 1962.
051 Elves and little people; 063 Food;
064.17 Foreign lands—Ireland;
083.09 Holidays—St. Patrick's Day.

Calhoun, Mary. *Mrs. Dog's Own House*. Illus. by Janet McCaffery. New York: Morrow, 1972.
008.14 Animals—dogs; 086 Houses.

Calhoun, Mary. *Old Man Whickutt's Donkey*. Illus. by Thomas Anthony de Paola. New York: Parents, 1975.
008.16 Animals—donkeys;
026.25 Character traits—perseverance;
062 Folk and fairy tales; 087 Humor.

Calhoun, Mary. *The Traveling Ball of String*. Illus. by Janet McCaffery. New York: Morrow, 1969.
016.28 Behavior—saving things;
087 Humor; 177.07 Toys—string.

Calhoun, Mary. *The Witch of Hissing Hill*. Illus. by Janet McCaffery. New York: Morrow, 1964.
008.09 Animals—cats;
083.07 Holidays—Halloween;
199 Witches.

Calhoun, Mary. *Wobble the Witch Cat*. Illus. by Roger Antoine Duvoisin. New York: Morrow, 1958.
008.09 Animals—cats;
083.07 Holidays—Halloween.

Calloway, Northern J. *Northern J. Calloway Presents Super-Vroomer!* Illus. by Sammis McLean. Written by Carol Hall. Conceived by Northern J. Calloway. Garden City, NY: Doubleday, 1978.
053.01 Ethnic groups in the U.S.—Afro-Americans; 166.11 Sports—racing.

Cameron, Polly. *The Cat Who Thought He Was a Tiger*. Illus. by author. New York: Coward, 1956.
008.09 Animals—cats; 028 Circus, clowns.

Cameron, Polly. *A Child's Book of Nonsense*. Illus. by author. New York: Coward, 1960.
087 Humor; 134 Poetry, rhyme.

Cameron, Polly. *"I Can't," Said the Ant*. Illus. by author. New York: Coward, 1961.
057 Family life; 090 Insects and spiders;
129 Participation; 134 Poetry, rhyme.

Campbell, M. Rudolph, adapter. *The Talking Crocodile*. Illus. by Judy Piussi-Campbell. New York: Atheneum, 1968.
064.30 Foreign lands—Russia;
142.01 Reptiles—alligators, crocodiles.

Canfield, Jane White. *The Frog Prince*. Illus. by Winn Smith. New York: Harper, 1970.
005 Amphibians.

Canfield, Jane White. *Swan Cove*. Illus. by Jo Polseno. New York: Harper, 1978.
017.25 Birds—swans.

Carigiet, Alois. *The Pear Tree, the Birch Tree and the Barberry Bush*. Illus. by author. New York: Walck, 1967.
064.36 Foreign lands—Switzerland;
181 Trees.

Carle, Eric. *All About Arthur*. Illus. by author. New York: Watts, 1974.
001 ABC Books; 008.37 Animals—monkeys; 175 Tongue twisters.

Carle, Eric. *Do You Want to Be My Friend?* Illus. by author. New York: Crowell, 1971.
008.34 Animals—mice; 068 Friendship; 121 Non-sexist; 201 Wordless.

Carle, Eric. *The Grouchy Ladybug.* Illus. by author. New York: Crowell, 1977.
016 Behavior; 090 Insects and spiders; 174 Time.

Carle, Eric. *Have You Seen My Cat?* Illus. by author. New York: Watts, 1973.
008.09 Animals—cats;
016.20 Behavior—lost.

Carle, Eric. *I See a Song.* Illus. by author. New York: Crowell, 1973.
116 Music; 201 Wordless.

Carle, Eric. *The Mixed-Up Chameleon.* Illus. by author. New York: Crowell, 1975.
026.03 Character traits—being different; 032.01 Concepts—color; 142.03 Reptiles—lizards; 156 Self-concept.

Carle, Eric. *One, Two, Three to the Zoo.* Illus. by author. Cleveland: Collins, 1968.
033 Counting; 204 Zoos.

Carle, Eric. *Pancakes, Pancakes.* Illus. by author. New York: Knopf, 1970.
038 Cumulative tales; 063 Food.

Carle, Eric. *The Rooster Who Set Out to See the World.* Illus. by author. New York: Watts, 1972.
002.16 Activities—traveling;
017.04 Birds—chickens; 033 Counting.

Carle, Eric. *Secret Birthday Message.* Illus. by author. New York: Crowell, 1972.
018 Birthdays; 067 Format, unusual.

Carle, Eric. *The Tiny Seed.* Illus. by author. New York: Crowell, 1970.
133 Plants.

Carle, Eric. *The Very Hungry Caterpillar.* Illus. by author. Cleveland: Collins, 1969.
039 Days of the week, months of the year; 063 Food; 067 Format, unusual; 090 Insects and spiders.

Carle, Eric. *Walter the Baker.* Illus. by author. New York: Knopf, 1972.
002.20 Activities—working;
023.03 Careers—bakers; 063 Food.

Carle, Eric. *Watch Out! A Giant!* Illus. by author. Cleveland: Collins, 1978.
067 Format, unusual; 072 Giants.

Carleton, Barbee Oliver. *Benny and the Bear.* Illus. by Dagmar Wilson. Chicago: Follett, 1960.
008.06 Animals—bears;
026.04 Character traits—bravery.

Carlson, Natalie Savage. *Marie Louise's Heyday.* Illus. by José Aruego. New York: Scribner's, 1975.
002.01 Activities—babysitting;
008.36 Animals—mongooses;
008.44 Animals—possums.

Carlson, Natalie Savage. *Runaway Marie Louise.* Illus. by José Aruego, and Ariane Dewey. New York: Scribner's, 1977.
008.36 Animals—mongooses;
016.27 Behavior—running away.

Carrick, Carol. *The Accident.* Illus. by Donald Carrick. New York: Seabury Pr., 1976.
008.14 Animals—dogs; 040 Death;
131 Pets.

Carrick, Carol. *The Foundling.* Illus. by Donald Carrick. New York: Seabury Pr., 1977.
008.14 Animals—dogs; 131 Pets.

Carrick, Carol. *The Old Barn.* Illus. by Donald Carrick. Indianapolis: Bobbs-Merrill, 1966.
014 Barns; 154 Seasons.

Carrick, Carol. *Old Mother Witch.* Illus. by Donald Carrick. New York: Seabury Pr., 1975.
016.24 Behavior—misunderstanding;
026.22 Character traits—meanness;
083.07 Holidays—Halloween;
088 Illness.

Carrick, Carol. *A Rabbit for Easter.* Illus. by Donald Carrick. New York: Greenwillow, 1979.
008.46 Animals—rabbits;
016.06 Behavior—carelessness;
016.19 Behavior—losing things;
151 School.

Carrick, Carol. *Sleep Out.* Illus. by Donald Carrick. New York: Seabury Pr., 1973.
016.33 Behavior—solitude;
166.04 Sports—camping;
195.05 Weather—rain.

Carrick, Carol. *The Washout.* Illus. by Donald Carrick. New York: Seabury Pr., 1978.
002.17 Activities—vacationing;
019 Boats, ships; 195.05 Weather—rain.

Carrick, Carol, and Carrick, Donald. *A Clearing in the Forest.* Illus. by Donald Carrick. New York: Dial Pr., 1970.

049 Ecology; 066 Forest, woods;
131 Pets.

Carrick, Carol, and Carrick, Donald. *The Highest Balloon on the Common.* Illus. by Donald Carrick. New York: Greenwillow, 1977.
016.20 Behavior—lost; 056 Fairs;
177.01 Toys—balloons.

Carrick, Donald, jt. author. *A Clearing in the Forest.* By Carol Carrick, and Donald Carrick.

Carrick, Donald. *The Deer in the Pasture.* Illus. by author. New York: Greenwillow, 1976.
008.12 Animals—cows, bulls;
008.13 Animals—deer; 058 Farms;
166.08 Sports—hunting.

Carrick, Donald, jt. author. *The Highest Balloon on the Common.* By Carol Carrick, and Donald Carrick.

Carrick, Malcolm. *Happy Jack.* Illus. by author. New York: Harper, 1979.
062 Folk and fairy tales.

Carrick, Malcolm. *Today Is Shrew's Day.* Illus. by author. New York: Harper, 1978.
005 Amphibians; 008 Animals;
068 Friendship.

Carroll, Latrobe, jt. author. *Pet Tale.* By Ruth Robinson Carroll, and Latrobe Carroll.

Carroll, Lewis (pseud.). See Dodgson, Charles Lutwidge.

Carroll, Ruth Robinson. *What Whiskers Did.* Illus. by author. New York: Walck, 1965.
008.14 Animals—dogs;
008.18 Animals—foxes;
008.46 Animals—rabbits;
016.27 Behavior—running away;
201 Wordless.

Carroll, Ruth Robinson. *Where's the Bunny?* Illus. by author. New York: Oxford Univ. Pr., 1950.
002.12 Activities—playing;
008.46 Animals—rabbits; 069 Games;
129 Participation; 201 Wordless.

Carroll, Ruth Robinson, and Carroll, Latrobe. *Pet Tale.* Illus. by Ruth Robinson Carroll. New York: Oxford Univ. Pr., 1949.
131 Pets.

Cartlidge, Michelle. *Pippin and Pod.* Illus. by author. New York: Pantheon, 1978.
002.12 Activities—playing;
008.34 Animals—mice;
016.20 Behavior—lost;
016.22 Behavior—misbehavior.

Cass, Joan. *The Cats Go to Market.* Illus. by William Stobbs. New York: Abelard-Schuman, 1969.
008.09 Animals—cats; 160 Shopping.

Cassedy, Sylvia, and Thampi, Parvathi. *Moon-Uncle, Moon-Uncle.* Illus. by Susanne Suba. Rhymes from India selected and translated by Sylvia Cassedy and Parvathi Thampi. Garden City, NY: Doubleday, 1973.
064.16 Foreign lands—India;
122 Nursery rhymes.

Castle, Sue. *Face Talk, Hand Talk, Body Talk.* Illus. by Frances McLaughlin-Gill. Garden City, NY: Doubleday, 1977.
006 Anatomy; 052 Emotions.

Cathon, Laura E. *Tot Botot and His Little Flute.* Illus. by Arnold Stark Lobel. New York: Macmillan, 1970.
008 Animals; 064.16 Foreign lands—India; 116 Music.

Caudill, Rebecca. *A Pocketful of Cricket.* Illus. by Evaline Ness. New York: Holt, 1964.
016.31 Behavior—sharing; 058 Farms;
090 Insects and spiders; 151 School.

Caudill, Rebecca. *Wind, Sand and Sky.* Illus. by Donald Carrick. New York: Dutton, 1976.
041 Desert; 134 Poetry, rhyme.

Caudill, Rebecca, and Ayars, James. *Contrary Jenkins.* Illus. by Glen H. Rounds. New York: Holt, 1969.
016 Behavior; 034 Country;
087 Humor.

Cauley, Lorinda Bryan. *Pease Porridge Hot: A Mother Goose Cookbook.* Illus. by author. New York: Putnam's, 1977.
122 Nursery rhymes; 063 Food.

Cerf, Bennett Alfred. *Bennett Cerf's Book of Animal Riddles.* Illus. by Roy McKie. New York: Random House, 1964.
087 Humor; 143 Riddles.

Cerf, Bennett Alfred. *Bennett Cerf's Book of Laughs.* Illus. by Carl Rose. New York: Random House, 1959.
087 Humor; 143 Riddles.

Cerf, Bennett Alfred. *Bennett Cerf's Book of Riddles.* Illus. by Roy McKie. New York: Random House, 1960.
087 Humor; 143 Riddles.

Cerf, Bennett Alfred. *More Riddles.* Illus. by Roy McKie. New York: Random House, 1961.
087 Humor; 143 Riddles.

Chaffin, Lillie D. *Tommy's Big Problem.* Illus. by Haris Petie. Mt. Vernon: Lantern Pr., 1965.
013 Babies; 016.14 Behavior—growing up; 057 Family life; 137 Problem solving.

Chalmers, Audrey. *A Birthday for Obash.* Illus. by author. New York: Viking, 1937/1952.
018 Birthdays.

Chalmers, Audrey. *Hector and Mr. Murfit.* Illus. by author. New York: Viking, 1953.
008.14 Animals—dogs; 032.08 Concepts—size.

Chalmers, Audrey. *Hundreds and Hundreds of Pancakes.* Illus. by author. New York: Viking, 1942.
008 Animals; 063 Food; 087 Humor; 204 Zoos.

Chalmers, Audrey. *A Kitten's Tale.* Illus. by author. New York: Viking, 1946.
008.09 Animals—cats; 026.23 Character traits—optimism.

Chalmers, Mary Eileen. *Be Good, Harry.* Illus. by author. New York: Harper, 1967.
002.01 Activities—babysitting; 008.09 Animals—cats.

Chalmers, Mary Eileen. *A Christmas Story.* Illus. by author. New York: Harper, 1956.
083.03 Holidays—Christmas.

Chalmers, Mary Eileen. *George Appleton.* Illus. by author. New York: Harper, 1957.
008.09 Animals—cats; 046 Dragons.

Chalmers, Mary Eileen. *A Hat for Amy Jean.* Illus. by author. New York: Harper, 1956.
018 Birthdays; 026.13 Character traits—generosity; 031 Clothing.

Chalmers, Mary Eileen. *Kevin.* Illus. by author. New York: Harper, 1957.
008.46 Animals—rabbits; 029 City.

Chalmers, Mary Eileen. *Merry Christmas, Harry.* Illus. by author. New York: Harper, 1977.
008.09 Animals—cats; 083.03 Holidays—Christmas.

Chalmers, Mary Eileen. *Take a Nap, Harry.* Illus. by author. New York: Harper, 1964.
008.09 Animals—cats; 057 Family life; 162 Sleep.

Chalmers, Mary Eileen. *Throw a Kiss, Harry.* Illus. by author. New York: Harper, 1958.

008.09 Animals—cats; 023.10 Careers—firefighters.

Chandler, Edna Walker. *Cattle Drive.* Illus. by Jack Merryweather. Chicago: Benefic Pr., 1966.
035 Cowboys.

Chandler, Edna Walker. *Cowboy Andy.* Illus. by Raymond Kinstler. New York: Random House, 1959.
035 Cowboys.

Chandler, Edna Walker. *Pony Rider.* Illus. by Jack Merryweather. Chicago: Benefic Pr., 1966.
008.28 Animals—horses; 035 Cowboys.

Chandler, Edna Walker. *Secret Tunnel.* Illus. by Jack Merryweather. Chicago: Benefic Pr., 1967.
035 Cowboys.

Chandoha, Walter. *A Baby Bunny for You.* Illus. by author. Cleveland: Collins, 1968.
008.46 Animals—rabbits.

Chandoha, Walter. *A Baby Goat for You.* Illus. by author. Cleveland: Collins, 1968.
008.21 Animals—goats.

Chandoha, Walter. *A Baby Goose for You.* Illus. by author. Cleveland: Collins, 1968.
017.11 Birds—geese.

Chapin, Cynthia. *Squad Car 55.* Illus. by Dale Fleming. Chicago: Albert Whitman, 1966.
023.21 Careers—police officers.

Chapman, Carol. *Barney Bipple's Magic Dandelions.* Illus. by Steven Kellogg. New York: Dutton, 1977.
016.38 Behavior—wishing; 061 Flowers; 103 Magic; 133 Plants.

Chapman, Gaynor. *The Luck Child.* Illus. by author. Based on a story of the Brothers Grimm. New York: Atheneum, 1968.
062 Folk and fairy tales; 147 Royalty.

Chapman, Noralee. *The Story of Barbara.* Illus. by Helen Schuyler Hull. Atlanta: John Knox Pr., 1963.
003 Adoption.

Chardiet, Bernice. *C Is for Circus.* Illus. by Brinton Cassady Turkle. New York: Walker, 1971.
001 ABC Books; 028 Circus, clowns; 134 Poetry, rhyme.

Charles, Robert H. *The Roundabout Turn.* Illus. by Leonard Leslie Brooke. New York: Warne, 1930.

005 Amphibians; 106 Merry-go-rounds; 134 Poetry, rhyme.

Charlip, Remy. *Arm in Arm*. Illus. by author. New York: Parents, 1969.
087 Humor.

Charlip, Remy. *Fortunately*. Illus. by author. New York: Parents, 1964.
087 Humor; 129 Participation.

Charlip, Remy, jt. author. *The Tree Angel*. By Judith Martin, and Remy Charlip.

Charlip, Remy. *Where Is Everybody?* Illus. by author. Reading: Addison-Wesley, 1957.
069 Games; 195.05 Weather—rain.

Charlip, Remy, and Joyner, Jerry. *Thirteen*. Illus. by Remy Charlip. New York: Parents, 1975.
033 Counting; 087 Humor.

Charlip, Remy, and Supree, Burton. *Harlequin and the Gift of Many Colors*. Illus. by Remy Charlip. New York: Parents, 1973.
032.01 Concepts—color; 062 Folk and fairy tales; 064.11 Foreign lands—France.

Charlip, Remy, and Supree, Burton. *"Mother, Mother I Feel Sick."* Illus. by Remy Charlip. New York: Parents, 1966.
023.09 Careers—doctors; 087 Humor; 088 Illness.

Charlot, Martin. *Sunnyside Up*. Illus. by author. Rutland, VT: Weatherhill, 1972.
201 Wordless.

Charters, Janet, and Foreman, Michael. *The General*. Illus. by Michael Foreman. New York: Dutton, 1961.
191 Violence, anti-violence.

Chasek, Judith. *Have You Seen Wilhelmina Krumpf?* Illus. by Salvatore Murdocca. New York: Lothrop, 1973.
064.14 Foreign lands—Holland.

Chaucer, Geoffrey. *Chanticleer and the Fox*. Illus. by Barbara Cooney. Adapted by Barbara Cooney. New York: Crowell, 1958.
008.18 Animals—foxes; 017.04 Birds—chickens; 026.11 Character traits—flattery; 058 Farms; 062 Folk and fairy tales.

Chenery, Janet. *Pickles and Jack*. Illus. by Lilian Obligado. New York: Viking, 1975.
008.09 Animals—cats; 008.14 Animals—dogs; 131 Pets.

Chenery, Janet. *The Toad Hunt*. Illus. by Ben Hunt. New York: Harper, 1967.
005 Amphibians.

Chenery, Janet. *Wolfie*. Illus. by Marc Simont. New York: Harper, 1969.
016.32 Behavior—sibling rivalry; 090 Insects and spiders.

Cheng, Hou-Tien. *Chinese New Year*. Illus. by author. New York: Holt, 1976.
083.02 Holidays—Chinese New Year.

Chicken Little. *Chicken Licken*. Illus. by Jutta Ash. Text by Kenneth McLeish. New York: Bradbury Pr., 1972.
008 Animals; 016.12 Behavior—gossip; 016.36 Behavior—trickery; 017.04 Birds—chickens; 038 Cumulative tales; 062 Folk and fairy tales.

Chicken Little. *Henny Penny*. Illus. by Paul Galdone. New York: Seabury Pr., 1968.
008 Animals; 016.12 Behavior—gossip; 016.36 Behavior—trickery; 017.04 Birds—chickens; 038 Cumulative tales; 062 Folk and fairy tales.

Chicken Little. *Henny Penny*. Illus. by William Stobbs. Chicago: Follett, 1968.
008 Animals; 016.12 Behavior—gossip; 016.36 Behavior—trickery; 017.04 Birds—chickens; 038 Cumulative tales; 062 Folk and fairy tales.

Child, Lydia Maria. *Over the River and Through the Wood*. Illus. by Brinton Cassady Turkle. New York: Coward, 1974.
057.02 Family life—grandparents; great-grandparents; 058 Farms; 083.10 Holidays—Thanksgiving; 164 Songs.

Chönz, Selina. *A Bell for Ursli*. Illus. by Alois Carigiet. New York: Walck, 1950.
064.36 Foreign lands—Switzerland; 134 Poetry, rhyme; 154.02 Seasons—spring.

Chönz, Selina. *Florina and the Wild Bird*. Illus. by Alois Carigiet. Translated from the German by Anne and Ian Serraillier. New York: Walck, 1966.
017 Birds; 064.36 Foreign lands—Switzerland; 134 Poetry, rhyme; 154.03 Seasons—summer.

Chönz, Selina. *The Snowstorm*. Illus. by Alois Carigiet. New York: Walck, 1958.
064.36 Foreign lands—Switzerland; 134 Poetry, rhyme; 154.04 Seasons—winter; 195.07 Weather—snow.

Chorao, Kay. *The Baby's Lap Book*. Illus. by author. New York: Dutton, 1977.
122 Nursery rhymes.

Chorao, Kay. *Lester's Overnight*. Illus. by author. New York: Dutton, 1977.
052.04 Emotions—fear; 057 Family life; 089 Imagination; 162 Sleep.

Chorao, Kay. *Molly's Lies*. Illus. by author. New York: Seabury Pr., 1979.
016.19 Behavior—losing things; 016.21 Behavior—lying; 068 Friendship; 151 School.

Chorao, Kay. *Molly's Moe*. Illus. by author. New York: Seabury Pr., 1976.
016.19 Behavior—losing things; 160 Shopping; 177 Toys.

Christian, Mary Blount. *Devin and Goliath*. Illus by Normand Chartier. Reading: Addison-Wesley, 1974.
131 Pets; 142.05 Reptiles—turtles.

Christian, Mary Blount. •*No Dogs Allowed, Jonathan!* Illus. by Don Madden. Reading: Addison-Wesley, 1975.
008.14 Animals—dogs.

Christian, Mary Blount. *Nothing Much Happened Today*. Illus. by Don Madden. Reading: Addison-Wesley, 1973.
038 Cumulative tales; 087 Humor.

Christian, Mary Blount. *The Sand Lot*. Illus. by Dennis Kendrick. New York: Harvey House, 1978.
002.12 Activities—playing; 016.10 Behavior—fighting, arguing; 166.01 Sports—baseball.

Christopher, Matthew F. *Jackrabbit Goalie*. Illus. by Ed Parker. Boston: Little, 1978.
016.21 Behavior—lying; 166 Sports.

Christopher, Matthew F. *Johnny No Hit*. Illus. by Ray Burns. Boston: Little, 1977.
016.05 Behavior—bullying; 166.01 Sports—baseball.

Chukovsky, Kornei. *The Telephone*. Illus. by Blair Lent. Adapted from the Russian by William Jay Smith in collaboration with Max Hayward. New York: Delacorte Pr., 1977.
134 Poetry, rhyme; 172 Telephone.

Chwast, Seymour. *The House That Jack Built*. Illus. by author. New York: Random House, 1973.
038 Cumulative tales; 067 Format, unusual; 122 Nursery rhymes; 129 Participation.

Chwast, Seymour, and Moskof, Martin Stephen. *Still Another Alphabet Book*. Illus. by authors. New York: McGraw-Hill, 1970.
001 ABC Books.

Chwast, Seymour, and Moskof, Martin Stephen. *Still Another Children's Book*. Illus. by authors. New York: McGraw-Hill, 1972.
047 Dreams; 154.03 Seasons—summer.

Chwast, Seymour, and Moskof, Martin Stephen. *Still Another Number Book*. Illus. by authors. New York: McGraw-Hill, 1971.
033 Counting.

Ciardi, John. *I Met a Man*. Illus. by Robert Osborn. Boston: Houghton, 1961.
087 Humor; 134 Poetry, rhyme.

Ciardi, John. *Scrappy the Pup*. Illus. by Jane Miller. Philadelphia: Lippincott, 1960.
008.14 Animals—dogs; 016.14 Behavior—growing up; 162 Sleep.

Clark, Ann Nolan. *The Little Indian Basket Maker*. Illus. by Harrison Begay. Chicago: Melmont, 1957.
053.04 Ethnic groups in the U.S.—Indians.

Clark, Ann Nolan. *The Little Indian Pottery Maker*. Illus. by Don Perceval. Chicago: Melmont, 1955.
002.20 Activities—working; 053.04 Ethnic groups in the U.S.—Indians.

Claude-Lafontaine, Pascale. *Monsieur Bussy, the Celebrated Hamster*. Illus. by Annick Delhumeau. New York: McGraw-Hill, 1968.
008.25 Animals—hamsters; 026.01 Character traits—ambition.

Cleary, Beverly. *The Hullabaloo ABC*. Illus. by Earl Thollander. Berkeley: Parnassus, 1960.
001 ABC Books; 058 Farms; 120 Noise.

Cleary, Beverly. *The Real Hole*. Illus. by Mary Stevens. New York: Morrow, 1960.
181 Trees; 186 Twins.

Cleary, Beverly. *Two Dog Biscuits*. Illus. by Mary Stevens. New York: Morrow, 1961.
186 Twins.

Clifford, David (pseud.). See Rosenberg, David.

Clifford, Eth (pseud.). See Rosenberg, Ethel Clifford.

Clifton, Lucille B. *All Us Come Across the Water*. Illus. by John Steptoe. New York: Holt, 1973.
026.27 Character traits—pride; 053.01 Ethnic groups in the U.S.—Afro-Americans; 151 School.

Clifton, Lucille B. *Amifika.* Illus. by Thomas di Grazia. New York: Dutton, 1977.
052.04 Emotions—fear; 053.01 Ethnic groups in the U.S.—Afro-Americans; 057 Family life; 057.01 Family life—fathers.

Clifton, Lucille B. *The Boy Who Didn't Believe in Spring.* Illus. by Brinton Cassady Turkle. New York: Dutton, 1973.
029 City; 053.01 Ethnic groups in the U.S.—Afro-Americans; 121 Non-sexist; 154.02 Seasons—spring.

Clifton, Lucille B. *Don't You Remember?* Illus. by Evaline Ness. New York: Dutton, 1973.
018 Birthdays; 053.01 Ethnic groups in the U.S.—Afro-Americans; 057 Family life.

Clifton, Lucille B. *Everett Anderson's Christmas Coming.* Illus. by Evaline Ness. New York: Holt, 1971.
029 City; 053.01 Ethnic groups in the U.S.—Afro-Americans; 083.03 Holidays—Christmas.

Clifton, Lucille B. *Everett Anderson's Friend.* Illus. by Ann Grifalconi. New York: Holt, 1976.
053.01 Ethnic groups in the U.S.—Afro-Americans; 068 Friendship; 121 Non-sexist; 134 Poetry, rhyme.

Clifton, Lucille B. *Everett Anderson's Nine Months Long.* Illus. by Ann Grifalconi. New York: Holt, 1978.
013 Babies; 053.01 Ethnic groups in the U.S.—Afro-Americans; 057 Family life; 134 Poetry, rhyme.

Clifton, Lucille B. *Everett Anderson's 1, 2, 3.* Illus. by Ann Grifalconi. New York: Holt, 1977.
053.01 Ethnic groups in the U.S.—Afro Americans; 057.01 Family life—fathers; 134 Poetry, rhyme.

Clifton, Lucille B. *Everett Anderson's Year.* Illus. by Ann Grifalconi. New York: Holt, 1974.
053.01 Ethnic groups in the U.S.—Afro-Americans; 134 Poetry, rhyme; 154 Seasons.

Clifton, Lucille B. *My Brother Fine with Me.* Illus. by Moneta Barnett. New York: Holt, 1975.
016.27 Behavior—running away; 016.32 Behavior—sibling rivalry; 053.01 Ethnic groups in the U.S.—Afro-Americans; 057 Family life.

Clifton, Lucille B. *Some of the Days of Everett Anderson.* Illus. by Evaline Ness. New York: Holt, 1970.
039 Days of the week, months of the year; 053.01 Ethnic groups in the U.S.—Afro-Americans; 057 Family life; 134 Poetry, rhyme.

Clifton, Lucille B. *Three Wishes.* Illus. by Stephanie Douglas. New York: Viking, 1974.
016.38 Behavior—wishing; 053.01 Ethnic groups in the U.S.—Afro-Americans; 068 Friendship.

Clithero, Sally. *Beginning-to-Read Poetry.* Illustrated. Chicago: Follett, 1967.
134 Poetry, rhyme.

Clymer, Eleanor Lowenton. *Horatio.* Illus. by Robert Mead Quackenbush. New York: Atheneum, 1968.
008.09 Animals—cats; 053.01 Ethnic groups in the U.S.—Afro-Americans.

Clymer, Eleanor Lowenton. *Horatio Goes to the Country.* Illus. by Robert Mead Quackenbush. New York: Atheneum, 1978.
008.09 Animals—cats; 186 Twins.

Clymer, Eleanor Lowenton. *The Tiny Little House.* Illus. by Ingrid Fetz. New York: Atheneum, 1964.
086 Houses.

Coatsworth, Elizabeth Jane. *Good Night.* Illus. by José Aruego. New York: Macmillan, 1972.
015 Bedtime; 167 Stars.

Cock Robin. *The Courtship, Merry Marriage, and Feast of Cock Robin and Jenny Wren, to Which Is Added The Doleful Death of Cock Robin.* Illus. by Barbara Cooney. New York: Holiday, 1935.
017.20 Birds—robins; 017.29 Birds—wrens; 040 Death; 122 Nursery rhymes; 196 Weddings.

Cohen, Carol L. *Wake Up Groundhog!* Illus. by author. New York: Crown, 1975.
008.23 Animals—groundhogs; 030 Clocks; 081 Hibernation; 083.06 Holidays—Groundhog Day; 154.02 Seasons—spring.

Cohen, Miriam. *Bee My Valentine!* Illus. by Lillian Hoban. New York: Greenwillow, 1978.
083.11 Holidays—Valentine's Day; 151 School.

Cohen, Miriam. *Best Friends.* Illus. by Lillian Hoban. New York: Macmillan, 1971.
068 Friendship; 151 School.

Cohen; Miriam. *Lost in the Museum.* Illus. by Lillian Hoban. New York: Greenwillow, 1979.
016.20 Behavior—lost; 115 Museums; 151 School.

Cohen, Miriam. *The New Teacher.* Illus. by Lillian Hoban. New York: Macmillan, 1972.
151 School.

Cohen, Miriam. *Tough Jim.* Illus. by Lillian Hoban. New York: Macmillan, 1974.
016.05 Behavior—bullying; 130 Parties; 151 School.

Cohen, Miriam. *When Will I Read?* Illus. by Lillian Hoban. New York: Greenwillow, 1977.
002.13 Activities—reading; 151 School.

Cohen, Miriam. *Will I Have a Friend?* Illus. by Lillian Hoban. New York: Macmillan, 1967.
053.07 Ethnic groups in the U.S.— Multi-ethnic; 068 Friendship; 151 School.

Cohen, Peter Zachary. *Authorized Autumn Charts of the Upper Red Canoe River Country.* Illus. by Thomas Anthony de Paola. New York: Atheneum, 1972.
001 ABC Books; 019 Boats, ships; 069 Games; 154.01 Seasons—fall.

Coker, Gylbert. *Naptime.* Illus. by author. New York: Delacorte Pr., 1978.
151 School; 162 Sleep; 201 Wordless.

Cole, Joanna. *Fun on Wheels.* Illus. by Whitney Darrow, Jr. New York: Morrow, 1976.
033 Counting.

Cole, Joanna. *The Secret Box.* Illus. by Joan Sandin. New York: Morrow, 1971.
016.34 Behavior—stealing.

Cole, William. *Aunt Bella's Umbrella.* Illus. by Jacqueline Chwast. Garden City, NY: Doubleday, 1970.
026.14 Character traits—helpfulness; 187 Umbrellas; 195.05 Weather—rain.

Cole, William. *Frances Face-Maker.* Illus. by Tomi Ungerer. Cleveland: Collins, 1963.
015 Bedtime; 052 Emotions; 057 Family life; 129 Participation; 134 Poetry, rhyme.

Cole, William. *That Pest Jonathan.* Illus. by Tomi Ungerer. New York: Harper, 1970.
016.22 Behavior—misbehavior; 057 Family life; 134 Poetry, rhyme.

Cole, William. *What's Good for a Four-Year-Old?* Illus. by Tomi Ungerer. New York: Holt, 1967.
002.12 Activities—playing; 134 Poetry, rhyme.

Cole, William. *What's Good for a Six-Year-Old?* Illus. by Ingrid Fetz. New York: Holt, 1965.
002.12 Activities—playing; 134 Poetry, rhyme.

Cole, William. *What's Good for a Three-Year-Old?* Illus. by Lillian Hoban. New York: Holt, 1974.
002.01 Activities—babysitting; 134 Poetry, rhyme.

Coletta, Hallie, jt. author. *From A to Z.* By Irene Coletta, and Hallie Coletta.

Coletta, Irene, and Coletta, Hallie. *From A to Z.* Illus. by Hallie Coletta. Englewood Cliffs, NJ: Prentice-Hall, 1979.
001 ABC Books; 134 Poetry, rhyme; 140 Rebuses.

Coley, Pete, jt. author. *Peter Pumpkin.* By John Ott, and Pete Coley.

Collier, Ethel. *I Know a Farm.* Illus. by Honore Guilbeau. Reading: Addison-Wesley, 1960.
058 Farms.

Collier, James Lincoln. *Danny Goes to the Hospital.* Illus. by Yale Joel. New York: Norton, 1970.
084 Hospitals.

Colman, Hila. *Peter's Brownstone House.* Illus. by Leonard Weisgard. New York: Morrow, 1963.
029 City; 086 Houses.

Colonius, Lillian, and Schroeder, Glen W. *At the Zoo.* Illus. by Glen W. Schroeder. Chicago: Melmont, 1954.
204 Zoos.

Conaway, Judith. *I'll Get Even.* Illus. by Mark Gubin. Chicago: Children's Pr., 1977.
016.32 Behavior—sibling rivalry; 052.07 Emotions—loneliness.

Conford, Ellen. *Eugene the Brave.* Illus. by John M. Larrecq. Boston: Little, 1978.
008.43 Animals—porcupines; 026.04 Character traits—bravery; 052.04 Emotions—fear; 119 Night.

Conford, Ellen. *Impossible Possum.* Illus. by Rosemary Wells. Boston: Little, 1971.
008.44 Animals—possums; 026.16 Character traits—individuality; 121 Non-sexist.

Conford, Ellen. *Just the Thing for Geraldine.* Illus. by John M. Larrecq. Boston: Little, 1974.
008.44 Animals—possums;
026.25 Character traits—perseverance.

Conford, Ellen. *Why Can't I Be William?* Illus. by Philip Wende. Boston: Little, 1972.
052.03 Emotions—envy, jealousy;
057 Family life; 057.04 Family life—the only child; 068 Friendship.

Conklin, Gladys Plemon. *Lucky Ladybugs.* Illus. by Glen H. Rounds. New York: Holiday, 1968.
090 Insects and spiders; 152 Science.

Conover, Chris. *Six Little Ducks.* Illus. by author. New York: Crowell, 1976.
017.08 Birds—ducks; 033 Counting;
116 Music; 134 Poetry, rhyme;
164 Songs.

Conroy, Jack, jt. author. *The Fast Sooner Hound.* By Arna Wendell Bontemps, and Jack Conroy.

Conta, Marcia Maher, and Reardon, Maureen. *Feelings Between Brothers and Sisters.* Illus. by Jules M. Rosenthal. Milwaukee: Raintree Pub., 1974.
052 Emotions.

Conta, Marcia Maher, and Reardon, Maureen. *Feelings Between Friends.* Illus. by Jules M. Rosenthal. Milwaukee: Raintree Pub., 1974.
052 Emotions; 068 Friendship.

Conta, Marcia Maher, and Reardon, Maureen. *Feelings Between Kids and Grownups.* Illus. by Jules M. Rosenthal. Milwaukee: Raintree Pub., 1974.
052 Emotions.

Conta, Marcia Maher, and Reardon, Maureen. *Feelings Between Kids and Parents.* Illus. by Jules M. Rosenthal. Milwaukee: Raintree Pub., 1974.
052 Emotions.

Cook, Bernadine. *The Little Fish That Got Away.* Illus. by David Johnson Leisk. Reading: Addison-Wesley, 1956.
060 Fish; 166.05 Sports—fishing.

Cook, Bernadine. *Looking for Susie.* Illus. by Judith Shahn. Reading: Addison-Wesley, 1959.
008.09 Animals—cats; 057 Family life;
058 Farms.

Coombs, Patricia. *Dorrie and the Amazing Magic Elixir.* Illus. by author. New York: Lothrop, 1974.
103 Magic; 199 Witches; 200 Wizards.

Coombs, Patricia. *Dorrie and the Birthday Eggs.* Illus. by author. New York: Lothrop, 1971.
018 Birthdays; 050 Eggs; 199 Witches.

Coombs, Patricia. *Dorrie and the Blue Witch.* Illus. by author. New York: Lothrop, 1964.
103 Magic; 199 Witches.

Coombs, Patricia. *Dorrie and the Dreamyard Monsters.* Illus. by author. New York: Lothrop, 1977.
026.10 Character traits—curiosity;
047 Dreams; 103 Magic; 110 Monsters;
199 Witches.

Coombs, Patricia. *Dorrie and the Fortune Teller.* Illus. by author. New York: Lothrop, 1973.
023.12 Careers—fortune tellers;
138 Progress; 199 Witches.

Coombs, Patricia. *Dorrie and the Goblin.* Illus. by author. New York: Lothrop, 1972.
002.01 Activities—babysitting;
074 Goblins; 199 Witches.

Coombs, Patricia. *Dorrie and the Halloween Plot.* Illus. by author. New York: Lothrop, 1976.
002.05 Activities—flying;
083.07 Holidays—Halloween;
199 Witches.

Coombs, Patricia. *Dorrie and the Haunted House.* Illus. by author. New York: Lothrop, 1970.
036 Crime; 199 Witches.

Coombs, Patricia. *Dorrie and the Screebit Ghost.* Illus. by author. New York: Lothrop, 1979.
071 Ghosts; 199 Witches.

Coombs, Patricia. *Dorrie and the Weather-Box.* Illus. by author. New York: Lothrop, 1966.
002.11 Activities—picnicking;
103 Magic; 195 Weather; 199 Witches.

Coombs, Patricia. *Dorrie and the Witch Doctor.* Illus. by author. New York: Lothrop, 1967.
088 Illness; 199 Witches.

Coombs, Patricia. *Dorrie and the Witch's Imp.* Illus. by author. New York: Lothrop, 1975.
103 Magic; 199 Witches.

Coombs, Patricia. *Dorrie and the Wizard's Spell.* Illus. by author. New York: Lothrop, 1968.
103 Magic; 199 Witches; 200 Wizards.

Coombs, Patricia. *Dorrie's Magic.* Illus. by author. New York: Lothrop, 1962.
103 Magic; 199 Witches.

Coombs, Patricia. *Dorrie's Play.* Illus. by author. New York: Lothrop, 1965.
016.23 Behavior—mistakes;
173 Theater; 199 Witches.

Coombs, Patricia. *Lisa and the Grompet.* Illus. by author. New York: Lothrop, 1970.
016.27 Behavior—running away;
055 Fairies; 057 Family life.

Coombs, Patricia. *The Lost Playground.* Illus. by author. New York: Lothrop, 1963.
016.19 Behavior—losing things;
026.03 Character traits—being different; 177 Toys.

Coombs, Patricia. *The Magic Pot.* Illus. by author. New York: Lothrop, 1970.
026.06 Character traits—cleverness;
042 Devil; 103 Magic; 135 Poverty.

Coombs, Patricia. *Molly Mullett.* Illus. by author. New York: Lothrop, 1975.
026.04 Character traits—bravery;
110 Monsters; 121 Non-sexist.

Coombs, Patricia. *Mouse Cafe.* Illus. by author. New York: Lothrop, 1972.
008.34 Animals—mice; 196 Weddings.

Coombs, Patricia. *Tilabel.* Illus. by author. New York: Lothrop, 1978.
008.23 Animals—groundhogs;
083.06 Holidays—Groundhog Day;
147 Royalty.

Cooney, Barbara. *A Garland of Games and Other Diversions.* Illus. by author. Initial letters by Suzanne R. Morse. New York: Holt, 1969.
001 ABC Books; 069 Games; 189 U.S. history.

Cooney, Barbara. *A Little Prayer.* Illus. by author. New York: Hastings, 1967.
141 Religion.

Coontz, Otto. *The Quiet House.* Illus. by author. Boston: Little, 1978.
008.14 Animals—dogs; 050 Eggs;
052.07 Emotions—loneliness;
068 Friendship.

Coontz, Otto. *A Real Class Clown.* Illus. by author. Boston: Little, 1979.
028 Circus, clowns; 151 School.

Cooper, Elizabeth K. *The Fish from Japan.* Illus. by Beth Krush, and Joe Krush. New York: Harcourt, 1969.
060 Fish; 089 Imagination; 094 Kites;
131 Pets.

Cooper, Lettice Ulpha. *The Bear Who Was Too Big.* Illus. by Ruth Ives. Chicago: Follett, 1963.
168 Stores; 177.08 Toys—teddy bears.

Copeland, Helen. *Meet Miki Takino.* Illus. by Kurt Werth. New York: Lothrop, 1963.
053.05 Ethnic groups in the U.S.—Japanese-Americans; 057.02 Family life—grandparents; great-grandparents.

Copp, Jim. *Martha Matilda O'Toole.* Illus. by Steven Kellogg. New York: Bradbury Pr., 1969.
016.11 Behavior—forgetfulness;
087 Humor; 134 Poetry, rhyme;
151 School.

Corbett, Scott. *Dr. Merlin's Magic Shop.* Illus. by Joe Mathieu. Boston: Little, 1973.
103 Magic.

Corbett, Scott. *The Foolish Dinosaur Fiasco.* Illus. by Jon McIntosh. Boston: Little, 1978.
044 Dinosaurs; 103 Magic.

Corbett, Scott. *The Great Custard Pie Panic.* Illus. by Joe Mathieu. Boston: Atlantic Monthly Pr., 1974.
103 Magic.

Corey, Dorothy. *Tomorrow You Can.* Illus. by Lois Axeman. Chicago: Albert Whitman, 1977.
016.14 Behavior—growing up.

Cortesi, Wendy W. *Explore a Spooky Swamp.* Illus. by Joseph H. Bailey. Washington, DC: National Geographic Soc., 1979.
005 Amphibians; 008 Animals;
017 Birds; 142 Reptiles.

Counting Rhymes. Illus. by Corinne Malvern. New York: Simon & Schuster, 1946.
033 Counting; 134 Poetry, rhyme.

Coville, Bruce, and Coville, Katherine. *The Foolish Giant.* Illus. by Katherine Coville. Philadelphia: Lippincott, 1978.
026.04 Character traits—bravery;
026.17 Character traits—kindness;
068 Friendship; 072 Giants; 103 Magic;
200 Wizards.

Coville, Katherine, jt. author. *The Foolish Giant.* By Bruce Coville, and Katherine Coville.

Craft, Ruth. *The Winter Bear.* Illus. by Erik Blegvad. New York: Atheneum, 1974.
134 Poetry, rhyme; 154.04 Seasons—winter; 177.08 Toys—teddy bears.

Craig, M. Jean. *Boxes*. Illus. by Joseph Leon Lasker. New York: Norton, 1964.
032.07 Concepts—shape; 032.08 Concepts—size; 069 Games; 129 Participation; 177 Toys.

Craig, M. Jean. *The Dragon in the Clock Box*. Illus. by Kelly Oechsli. New York: Norton, 1962.
046 Dragons; 057 Family life; 089 Imagination.

Craig, M. Jean. *Spring Is Like the Morning*. Illus. by Don Almquist. New York: Putnam's, 1965.
112 Morning; 154.02 Seasons—spring.

Craig, M. Jean. *What Did You Dream?* Illus. by Margery Gill. New York: Abelard-Schuman, 1964.
112 Morning.

Credle, Ellis. *Down, Down the Mountain*. Illus. by author. New York: Nelson, 1934.
031 Clothing; 057 Family life; 133 Plants.

Cressey, James. *Fourteen Rats and a Rat-Catcher*. Illus. by Tamasin Cole. Englewood Cliffs, NJ: Prentice-Hall, 1976.
008.48 Animals—rats; 057 Family life; 137 Problem solving.

Cressey, James. *Max the Mouse*. Illus. by Tamasin Cole. Englewood Cliffs, NJ: Prentice-Hall, 1977.
008.34 Animals—mice.

Cretan, Gladys Yessayan. *Lobo and Brewster*. Illus. by Patricia Coombs. New York: Lothrop, 1971.
008.09 Animals—cats; 052.03 Emotions—envy, jealousy.

Cretan, Gladys Yessayan. *Ten Brothers with Camels*. Illus. by Piero Ventura. Racine, WI: Western Pub., 1975.
033 Counting.

Cretien, Paul D., Jr. *Sir Henry and the Dragon*. Illus. by author. Chicago: Follett, 1958.
008.28 Animals—horses; 046 Dragons; 095 Knights; 147 Royalty; 199 Witches.

Crews, Donald. *Freight Train*. Illus. by author. New York: Greenwillow, 1978.
032.01 Concepts—color; 179 Trains.

Crews, Donald. *Ten Black Dots*. Illus. by author. New York: Scribner's, 1968.
032.07 Concepts—shape; 033 Counting.

Crews, Donald. *We Read: A to Z*. Illus. by author. New York: Harper, 1967.
001 ABC Books; 032 Concepts.

Cromie, William J. *Steven and the Green Turtle*. Illus. by Tom Eaton. New York: Harper, 1970.
009 Animals—endangered; 142.05 Reptiles—turtles; 152 Science.

Croswell, Volney. *How to Hide a Hippopotamus*. Illus. by author. New York: Dodd, 1958.
008.27 Animals—hippopotami; 016.16 Behavior—hiding things; 032.08 Concepts—size.

Crowe, Robert L. *Clyde Monster*. Illus. by Kay Chorao. New York: Dutton, 1976.
052.04 Emotions—fear; 110 Monsters; 119 Night.

Crume, Marion W. *Let Me See You Try*. Illus. by Jacques Rupp. Los Angeles: Bowmar, 1968.
002 Activities; 129 Participation.

Crume, Marion W. *Listen!* Illus. by Cliff Roe, and Judy Houston. Los Angeles: Bowmar, 1968.
002 Activities; 053.07 Ethnic groups in the U.S.—Multi-ethnic; 129 Participation.

Crume, Marion W. *What Do You Say?* Illus. by Harvey Mandlin. Los Angeles: Bowmar, 1967.
002 Activities; 129 Participation.

Cummings, W. T. *Miss Esta Maude's Secret*. Illus. by author. New York: McGraw-Hill, 1961.
012 Automobiles; 016.29 Behavior—secrets; 023.27 Careers—teachers.

Curry, Nancy. *The Littlest House*. Illus. by Jacques Rupp. Los Angeles: Bowmar, 1968.
057 Family life; 086 Houses.

Dalgliesh, Alice. *The Little Wooden Farmer*. Illus. by Anita Lobel. New York: Macmillan, 1930/1968.
058 Farms.

Dalgliesh, Alice. *The Thanksgiving Story*. Illus. by Helen Moore Sewell. New York: Scribner's, 1954.
083.10 Holidays—Thanksgiving; 189 U.S. history.

Daly, Maureen. *Patrick Visits the Library*. Illus. by Paul Lantz. New York: Dodd, 1961.
018 Birthdays; 100 Libraries.

Daly, Niki. *Vim the Rag Mouse.* Illus. by author. New York: Atheneum, 1979.
036 Crime; 177 Toys.

Damjan, Mischa (pseud.). *The Little Prince and the Tiger Cat.* Illus. by Ralph Steadman. New York: McGraw-Hill, 1967.
008.09 Animals—cats; 064.19 Foreign lands—Japan; 147 Royalty.

Damjan, Mischa (pseud.). *The Wolf and the Kid.* Illus. by Max Velthuijs. New York: McGraw-Hill, 1967.
008.21 Animals—goats;
008.61 Animals—wolves;
026.06 Character traits—cleverness.

Daniels, Guy, translator. *The Peasant's Pea Patch.* Illus. by Robert Mead Quackenbush. New York: Delacorte Pr., 1971.
017 Birds; 062 Folk and fairy tales; 064.30 Foreign lands—Russia.

Daudet, Alphonse. *The Brave Little Goat of Monsieur Seguin.* Illus. by Chiyoko Nakatani. Translated and adapted by Alphonse Daudet. Cleveland: Collins, 1968.
008.21 Animals—goats;
008.61 Animals—wolves; 064.11 Foreign lands—France.

Dauer, Rosamond. *Bullfrog Builds a House.* Illus. by Byron Barton. New York: Greenwillow, 1977.
005 Amphibians; 068 Friendship;
086 Houses.

Dauer, Rosamond. *Bullfrog Grows Up.* Illus. by Byron Barton. New York: Greenwillow, 1976.
005 Amphibians; 008.34 Animals—mice; 016.14 Behavior—growing up.

Daugherty, Charles Michael. *Wisher.* Illus. by James Henry Daugherty. New York: Viking, 1960.
008.09 Animals—cats;
016.38 Behavior—wishing; 047 Dreams.

Daugherty, James Henry. *Andy and the Lion.* Illus. by author. New York: Viking, 1938.
008.10 Animals—cats, wild;
026.18 Character traits—kindness to animals; 087 Humor; 100 Libraries.

Daugherty, James Henry. *The Picnic.* Illus. by author. New York: Viking, 1958.
002.11 Activities—picnicking;
008.10 Animals—cats, wild;
008.34 Animals—mice.

d'Aulaire, Edgar Parin. See Aulaire, Edgar Parin d'.

d'Aulaire, Ingri Mortenson. See Aulaire, Ingri Mortenson d'.

Davies, Sumiko. *Kittymouse.* Illus. by author. New York: Harcourt, 1976.
008.09 Animals—cats; 008.34 Animals—mice.

Davis, Alice V. *Timothy Turtle.* Illus. by Guy B. Wiser. New York: Harcourt, 1940/1972.
026.14 Character traits—helpfulness;
142.05 Reptiles—turtles.

Davis, Reda. *Martin's Dinosaur.* Illus. by author. New York: Crowell, 1959.
046 Dragons; 064.10 Foreign lands—England.

Dayrell, Elphinstone. *Why the Sun and the Moon Live in the Sky.* Illus. by Blair Lent. Boston: Houghton, 1968.
062 Folk and fairy tales; 064.01 Foreign lands—Africa; 111 Moon; 161 Sky;
169 Sun.

Dayton, Mona. *Earth and Sky.* Illus. by Roger Antoine Duvoisin. New York: Harper, 1969.
016.10 Behavior—fighting, arguing;
048 Earth; 161 Sky.

Dean, Leigh, jt. author. *Two Special Cards.* By Sonia O. Lisker, and Leigh Dean.

De Angeli, Marguerite Lofft. *The Book of Nursery and Mother Goose Rhymes.* Illus. by author. Compiled by Marguerite De Angeli. Garden City, NY: Doubleday, 1954.
122 Nursery rhymes.

de Angelis, Nancy (pseud.). See Angelo, Nancy Carolyn Harris.

de Brunhoff, Jean. See Brunhoff, Jean de.

de Brunhoff, Laurent. See Brunhoff, Laurent de.

De Caprio, Annie. *One, Two.* Illus. by Seymour Nydorf. New York: Grosset, 1965.
033 Counting.

DeForest, Charlotte B. *The Prancing Pony.* Illus. by Keiko Hida. Adapted into English verse for children by Charlotte B. DeForest. "Kusa-e" illustrations by Keiko Hida. New York: Walker, 1967.
064.19 Foreign lands—Japan;
122 Nursery rhymes.

de Groat, Diane. *Alligator's Toothache.* Illus. by author. New York: Crown, 1977.
088 Illness; 142.01 Reptiles—alligators, crocodiles; 171 Teeth; 201 Wordless.

Delaney, A. *The Butterfly.* Illus. by author. New York: Delacorte Pr., 1977.
038 Cumulative tales; 090 Insects and spiders.

Delaney, Ned. *One Dragon to Another*. Illus. by author. Boston: Houghton, 1976.
026.16 Character traits—individuality; 046 Dragons; 069 Games; 090 Insects and spiders.

Delaunay, Sonia. *Sonia Delaunay's Alphabet*. Illus. by author. New York: Crowell, 1970.
001 ABC Books; 134 Poetry, rhyme.

Delton, Judy, and Knox-Wagner, Elaine. *The Best Mom in the World*. Illus. by John Faulkner. Chicago: Albert Whitman, 1979.
016.14 Behavior—growing up; 057.03 Family life—mothers.

Delton, Judy. *Brimhall Comes to Stay*. Illus. by Cyndy Szekeres. New York: Lothrop, 1978.
008.06 Animals—bears; 057 Family life.

Delton, Judy. *Brimhall Turns to Magic*. Illus. by Bruce Deghen. New York: Lothrop, 1979.
008.06 Animals—bears; 008.46 Animals—rabbits; 103 Magic.

Delton, Judy. *It Happened on Thursday*. Illus. by June Goldsborough. Chicago: Albert Whitman, 1978.
026.21 Character traits—luck; 057 Family life; 088 Illness.

Delton, Judy. *My Mom Hates Me in January*. Illus. by John Faulkner. Chicago: Albert Whitman, 1977.
016.04 Behavior—boredom; 154.04 Seasons—winter.

Delton, Judy. *The New Girl at School*. Illus. by Lillian Hoban. New York: Dutton, 1979.
151 School.

Delton, Judy. *Penny Wise, Fun Foolish*. Illus. by Giulio Maestro. New York: Crown, 1977.
008.17 Animals—elephants; 016.28 Behavior—saving things; 017 Birds; 056 Fairs.

Delton, Judy. *Three Friends Find Spring*. Illus. by Giulio Maestro. New York: Crown, 1977.
008.46 Animals—rabbits; 017.08 Birds—ducks; 068 Friendship; 154.02 Seasons—spring; 154.04 Seasons—winter.

Den Honert, Dorry Van. See Van Den Honert, Dorry.

Denney, Diana. *The Little Red Engine Gets a Name*. Illus. by Lewitt-Him. New York: Transatlantic, 1945.
118 Names; 179 Trains.

Dennis, Morgan. *Burlap*. Illus. by author. New York: Viking, 1945.
008.06 Animals—bears; 008.14 Animals—dogs.

Dennis, Morgan. *The Pup Himself*. Illus. by author. New York: Viking, 1943.
008.14 Animals—dogs.

Dennis, Morgan. *Skit and Skat*. Illus. by author. New York: Viking, 1952.
008.09 Animals—cats; 008.14 Animals—dogs.

Dennis, Suzanne E. *Answer Me That*. Illus. by Owen Wood. Indianapolis: Bobbs-Merrill, 1969.
008 Animals; 087 Humor; 134 Poetry, rhyme.

Dennis, Wesley. *Flip*. Illus. by author. New York: Viking, 1941.
008.28 Animals—horses; 047 Dreams; 058 Farms.

Dennis, Wesley. *Flip and the Cows*. Illus. by author. New York: Viking, 1942.
008.12 Animals—cows, bulls; 008.28 Animals—horses; 058 Farms.

Dennis, Wesley. *Flip and the Morning*. Illus. by author. New York: Viking, 1951.
008.28 Animals—horses; 112 Morning.

Dennis, Wesley. *Tumble, the Story of a Mustang*. Illus. by author. New York: Hastings, 1966.
008.28 Animals—horses; 026.12 Character traits—freedom.

de Paola, Thomas Anthony. *Andy (That's My Name)*. Illus. by author. Englewood Cliffs, NJ: Prentice-Hall, 1973.
016.13 Behavior—greed; 026.31 Character traits—smallness; 068 Friendship; 069 Games; 118 Names.

de Paola, Thomas Anthony. *Big Anthony and the Magic Ring*. Illus. by author. New York: Harcourt, 1979.
026.02 Character traits—appearance; 103 Magic.

de Paola, Thomas Anthony. *Bill and Pete*. Illus. by author. New York: Putnam's, 1978.
064.01 Foreign lands—Africa; 087 Humor; 142.01 Reptiles—alligators, crocodiles; 151 School.

de Paola, Thomas Anthony. *Charlie Needs a Cloak*. Illus. by author. Englewood Cliffs, NJ: Prentice-Hall, 1973.
008.34 Animals—mice; 008.52 Animals—sheep; 031 Clothing; 121 Non-sexist; 137 Problem solving.

de Paola, Thomas Anthony. *The Christmas Pageant.* Illus. by author. Minneapolis: Winston Pr., 1978.
083.03 Holidays—Christmas;
173 Theater.

de Paola, Thomas Anthony. *The Clown of God.* Illus. by author. New York: Harcourt, 1978.
064.18 Foreign lands—Italy;
083.03 Holidays—Christmas;
141 Religion.

de Paola, Thomas Anthony. *Fight the Night.* Illus. by author. Philadelphia: Lippincott, 1968.
015 Bedtime; 162 Sleep.

de Paola, Thomas Anthony. *Four Stories for Four Seasons.* Illus. by author. Englewood Cliffs, NJ: Prentice-Hall, 1977.
002.06 Activities—gardening; 019 Boats, ships; 081 Hibernation; 154 Seasons.

de Paola, Thomas Anthony. *Helga's Dowry.* Illus. by author. New York: Harcourt, 1977.
052.08 Emotions—love; 135 Poverty; 183 Trolls; 196 Weddings.

de Paola, Thomas Anthony. *Michael Bird-Boy.* Illus. by author. Englewood Cliffs, NJ: Prentice-Hall, 1975.
049 Ecology.

de Paola, Thomas Anthony. *Nana Upstairs and Nana Downstairs.* Illus. by author. New York: Putnam's, 1973.
040 Death; 052.09 Emotions—sadness; 057.02 Family life—grandparents; great-grandparents.

de Paola, Thomas Anthony. *Oliver Button Is a Sissy.* Illus. by author. New York: Harcourt, 1979.
002.04 Activities—dancing;
026.16 Character traits—individuality;
121 Non-sexist.

de Paola, Thomas Anthony. *Pancakes for Breakfast.* Illus. by author. New York: Harcourt, 1978.
002.03 Activities—cooking; 063 Food;
201 Wordless.

de Paola, Thomas Anthony. *The Popcorn Book.* Illus. by author. New York: Holiday, 1978.
002.03 Activities—cooking; 063 Food.

de Paola, Thomas Anthony. *The Quicksand Book.* Illus. by author. New York: Holiday, 1977.
016.06 Behavior—carelessness.

de Paola, Thomas Anthony. *Songs of the Fog Maiden.* Illus. by author. New York: Holiday, 1979.
134 Poetry, rhyme.

de Paola, Thomas Anthony. *Strega Nona.* Illus. by author. Englewood Cliffs, NJ: Prentice-Hall, 1975.
016.11 Behavior—forgetfulness;
087 Humor; 103 Magic; 199 Witches.

de Paola, Thomas Anthony. *When Everyone Was Fast Asleep.* Illus. by author. New York: Holiday, 1976.
162 Sleep.

de Paola, Thomas Anthony. *The Wonderful Dragon of Timlin.* Illus. by author. Indianapolis: Bobbs-Merrill, 1966.
046 Dragons; 095 Knights; 147 Royalty.

de Paola, Tomie. See de Paola, Thomas Anthony.

De Regniers, Beatrice Schenk. *Cats Cats Cats Cats Cats.* Illus. by Bill Sokol. New York: Pantheon, 1958.
008.09 Animals—cats; 134 Poetry, rhyme.

De Regniers, Beatrice Schenk. *David and Goliath.* Illus. by Richard M. Powers. New York: Viking, 1965.
141 Religion.

De Regniers, Beatrice Schenk. *The Giant Story.* Illus. by Maurice Sendak. New York: Harper, 1953.
057 Family life; 072 Giants.

De Regniers, Beatrice Schenk. *It Does Not Say Meow!* Illus. by Paul Galdone. New York: Seabury Pr., 1972.
008 Animals; 129 Participation;
134 Poetry, rhyme; 143 Riddles.

De Regniers, Beatrice Schenk. *Laura's Story.* Illus. by Jack Kent. New York: Atheneum, 1979.
089 Imagination.

De Regniers, Beatrice Schenk. *A Little House of Your Own.* Illus. by Irene Haas. New York: Harcourt, 1954.
057 Family life; 086 Houses;
089 Imagination.

De Regniers, Beatrice Schenk. *Little Sister and the Month Brothers.* Illus. by Margot Ladd Tomes. New York: Seabury Pr., 1976.
039 Days of the week, months of the year; 062 Folk and fairy tales;
064 Foreign lands.

De Regniers, Beatrice Schenk. *May I Bring a Friend?* Illus. by Beni Montresor. New York: Atheneum, 1964.
008 Animals; 068 Friendship; 087 Humor; 134 Poetry, rhyme; 147 Royalty.

De Regniers, Beatrice Schenk. *Red Riding Hood.* Illus. by Edward St. John Gorey. Retold in verse for boys and girls to read themselves. New York: Atheneum, 1972.
008.61 Animals—wolves; 016.35 Behavior—talking to strangers; 062 Folk and fairy tales; 134 Poetry, rhyme.

De Regniers, Beatrice Schenk. *Was It a Good Trade?* Illus. by Irene Haas. New York: Harcourt, 1956.
002.15 Activities—trading; 134 Poetry, rhyme; 164 Songs.

De Regniers, Beatrice Schenk. *What Can You Do with a Shoe?* Illus. by Maurice Sendak. New York: Harper, 1955.
069 Games; 089 Imagination.

De Regniers, Beatrice Schenk, and Bileck, Marvin. *Penny.* Illus. by Marvin Bileck. New York: Viking, 1966.
051 Elves and little people.

De Regniers, Beatrice Schenk, and Gordon, Isabel. *The Shadow Book.* Illus. by Isabel Gordon. New York: Harcourt, 1960.
158 Shadows.

De Regniers, Beatrice Schenk, and Pierce, Leona. *Who Likes the Sun?* Illus. by Leona Pierce. New York: Harcourt, 1961.
169 Sun.

Deveaux, Alexis. *Na-Ni.* Illus. by author. New York: Harper, 1973.
026.28 Character traits—questioning; 029 City; 052.09 Emotions—sadness; 135 Poverty.

Devlin, Harry, jt. author. *Aunt Agatha, There's a Lion under the Couch!* By Wende Devlin, and Harry Devlin.

Devlin, Harry, jt. author. *Cranberry Christmas.* By Wende Devlin, and Harry Devlin.

Devlin, Harry, jt. author. *Old Black Witch.* By Wende Devlin, and Harry Devlin.

Devlin, Harry, jt. author. *Old Witch and the Polka-Dot Ribbon.* By Wende Devlin, and Harry Devlin.

Devlin, Harry, jt. author. *Old Witch Rescues Halloween.* By Wende Devlin, and Harry Devlin.

Devlin, Harry. *The Walloping Window Blind.* Illus. by author. New York: Van Nostrand, 1968.
019 Boats, ships; 132 Pirates; 164 Songs.

Devlin, Wende. *Cranberry Thanksgiving.* Illus. by Harry Devlin. New York: Parents, 1971.
083.10 Holidays—Thanksgiving.

Devlin, Wende, and Devlin, Harry. *Aunt Agatha, There's a Lion under the Couch!* Illus. by authors. New York: Van Nostrand, 1968.
008.10 Animals—cats, wild; 052.04 Emotions—fear; 089 Imagination.

Devlin, Wende, and Devlin, Harry. *Cranberry Christmas.* Illus. by authors. New York: Parents, 1976.
016.31 Behavior—sharing; 026.14 Character traits—helpfulness; 083.03 Holidays—Christmas.

Devlin, Wende, and Devlin, Harry. *Old Black Witch.* Illus. by Harry Devlin. Chicago: Encyclopaedia Brit., 1963.
002.03 Activities—cooking; 199 Witches.

Devlin, Wende, and Devlin, Harry. *Old Witch and the Polka-Dot Ribbon.* Illus. by Harry Devlin. New York: Parents, 1970.
002.03 Activities—cooking; 056 Fairs; 063 Food; 199 Witches.

Devlin, Wende, and Devlin, Harry. *Old Witch Rescues Halloween.* Illus. by Harry Devlin. New York: Parents, 1972.
002.03 Activities—cooking; 083.07 Holidays—Halloween; 199 Witches.

Dines, Glen. *Gilly and the Wicharoo.* Illus. by author. New York: Lothrop, 1968.
016.36 Behavior—trickery; 026.06 Character traits—cleverness; 064.10 Foreign lands—England.

Dines, Glen. *Pitidoe the Color Maker.* Illus. by author. New York: Macmillan, 1959.
032.01 Concepts—color; 200 Wizards.

Dines, Glen. *A Tiger in the Cherry Tree.* Illus. by author. New York: Macmillan, 1958.
008.10 Animals—cats, wild; 016.11 Behavior—forgetfulness; 026.30 Character traits—shyness; 064.19 Foreign lands—Japan; 103 Magic.

Dinosaurs. Illus. by Laurent Sauveur Sant. New York: Grosset, 1971.
044 Dinosaurs.

Diska, Pat. *Andy Says Bonjour!* Illus. by Chris Jenkyns. New York: Vanguard, 1954.
008.09 Animals—cats; 064.11 Foreign lands—France; 065 Foreign languages.

Dobrin, Arnold Jack. *Josephine's 'magination.* Illus. by author. New York: Four Winds Pr., 1973.
064.05 Foreign lands—Caribbean Islands; 089 Imagination; 177 Toys.

Dodd, Lynley. *The Nickle Nackle Tree.* Illus. by author. New York: Macmillan, 1976.
033 Counting; 134 Poetry, rhyme.

Dodgson, Charles Lutwidge. *Jabberwocky.* Illus. by Jane Breskin Zalben. New York: Warne, 1977.
087 Humor; 134 Poetry, rhyme.

Domanska, Janina. *The Best of the Bargain.* Illus. by author. New York: Greenwillow, 1977.
002.06 Activities—gardening;
008.18 Animals—foxes;
008.26 Animals—hedgehogs;
016.36 Behavior—trickery;
026.06 Character traits—cleverness;
062 Folk and fairy tales;
064.27 Foreign lands—Poland.

Domanska, Janina. *Din Dan Don, It's Christmas.* Illus. by author. New York: Greenwillow, 1975.
064.27 Foreign lands—Poland;
083.03 Holidays— Christmas;
141 Religion; 164 Songs.

Domanska, Janina. *I Saw a Ship A-Sailing.* Illus. by author. New York: Macmillan, 1972.
019 Boats, ships; 083.03 Holidays— Christmas; 122 Nursery rhymes.

Domanska, Janina. *If All the Seas Were One Sea.* Illus. by author. New York: Macmillan, 1971.
122 Nursery rhymes; 153 Sea and seashore.

Domanska, Janina. *King Krakus and the Dragon.* Illus. by author. New York: Greenwillow, 1979.
026.06 Character traits—cleverness;
046 Dragons; 062 Folk and fairy tales;
064.27 Foreign lands—Poland; 147 Royalty.

Domanska, Janina. *The Tortoise and the Tree.* Illus. by author. New York: Greenwillow, 1978.
062 Folk and fairy tales; 064.01 Foreign lands—Africa; 142.05 Reptiles—turtles.

Domanska, Janina. *What Do You See?* Illus. by author. New York: Macmillan, 1974.
008 Animals; 134 Poetry, rhyme;
202 World.

Domanska, Janina. *Why So Much Noise?* Illus. by author. New York: Harper, 1965.
008.10 Animals—cats, wild;
008.17 Animals—elephants;
026.06 Character traits—cleverness;
062 Folk and fairy tales; 064.16 Foreign lands—India; 120 Noise.

Donaldson, Lois. *Karl's Wooden Horse.* Illus. by Annie Bergmann. Chicago: Albert Whitman, 1970.
047 Dreams; 083.03 Holidays— Christmas; 119 Night; 177.05 Toys— rocking horses.

Dorian, Marguerite. *When the Snow Is Blue.* Illus. by author. New York: Lothrop, 1960.
008.06 Animals—bears;
089 Imagination; 195.07 Weather— snow.

Dorsky, Blanche. *Harry, a True Story.* Illus. by Muriel Batherman. Englewood Cliffs, NJ: Prentice-Hall, 1977.
008.46 Animals—rabbits; 151 School.

Doty, Roy. *Old One Eye Meets His Match.* Illus. by author. New York: Lothrop, 1978.
008.34 Animals—mice;
008.48 Animals—rats.

Dragonwagon, Crescent. *Wind Rose.* Illus. by Ronald Norbert Himler. New York: Harper, 1976.
013 Babies; 052.08 Emotions—love;
118 Names.

Drdek, Richard E. *Horace the Friendly Octopus.* Illus. by Joseph Veno. Reading consultants: William D. Sheldon and Mary C. Austin. Boston: Allyn & Bacon, 1965.
068 Friendship; 123 Octopod.

Dreifus, Miriam W. *Brave Betsy.* Illus. by Sheila Greenwald. New York: Putnam's, 1961.
026.04 Character traits—bravery;
151 School; 177.04 Toys—dolls.

Drummond, Violet H. *The Flying Postman.* Illus. by author. New York: Walck, 1964.
023.16 Careers—mail carriers;
064.10 Foreign lands—England;
080 Helicopters.

Du Bois, William Pène. *Bear Circus.* Illus. by author. New York: Viking, 1971.
008 Animals; 026.14 Character traits— helpfulness; 028 Circus, clowns;
090 Insects and spiders.

Du Bois, William Pène. *Bear Party*. Illus. by author. New York: Viking, 1951.
008 Animals; 052.01 Emotions—anger; 130 Parties.

Du Bois, William Pène. *Giant Otto*. Illus. by author. New York: Viking, n.d.
008.14 Animals—dogs; 072 Giants.

Du Bois, William Pène. *Lazy Tommy Pumpkinhead*. Illus. by author. New York: Harper, 1966.
026.19 Character traits—laziness; 102 Machines.

Du Bois, William Pène. *Otto and the Magic Potatoes*. Illus. by author. New York: Viking, 1970.
002.17 Activities—vacationing; 008.14 Animals—dogs; 059 Fire; 072 Giants.

Du Bois, William Pène. *Otto at Sea*. Illus. by author. New York: Viking, 1936.
008.14 Animals—dogs; 019 Boats, ships; 072 Giants.

Du Bois, William Pène. *Otto in Africa*. Illus. by author. New York: Viking, 1961.
008.14 Animals—dogs; 064.01 Foreign lands—Africa; 072 Giants.

Du Bois, William Pène. *Otto in Texas*. Illus. by author. New York: Viking, 1959.
008.14 Animals—dogs; 072 Giants.

Duff, Maggie. *Rum Pum Pum*. Illus. by José Aruego. New York: Macmillan, 1978.
017 Birds; 062 Folk and fairy tales; 064.16 Foreign lands—India.

Dukas, Paul Abraham. *The Sorcerer's Apprentice*. Illus. by Ryohei Yanagihara. Adapted by Makoto Oishi. Translated by Ann Brannen. Tokyo, Japan: Gakken, 1971.
062 Folk and fairy tales; 103 Magic.

Dunn, Judy. *The Little Duck*. Illus. by Phoebe Dunn. New York: Random House, 1976.
017.08 Birds—ducks.

Dunn, Judy. *The Little Goat*. Illus. by Phoebe Dunn. New York: Random House, 1978.
008.21 Animals—goats; 131 Pets.

Dunn, Judy. *The Little Lamb*. Illus. by Phoebe Dunn. New York: Random House, 1977.
008.52 Animals—sheep; 026.18 Character traits—kindness to animals; 058 Farms.

Duplaix, Georges. *Animal Stories*. Illus. by Feodor Stepanovich Rojankovsky. Racine, WI: Western Pub., 1944.
008 Animals.

Dupre, Ramona Dorrel. *Too Many Dogs*. Illus. by Howard Baer. Chicago: Follett, 1960.
008.14 Animals—dogs.

Duvoisin, Roger Antoine. *A for the Ark*. Illus. by author. New York: Lothrop, 1952.
001 ABC Books; 008 Animals; 141.01 Religion—Noah.

Duvoisin, Roger Antoine. *The Christmas Whale*. Illus. by author. New York: Knopf, 1945.
008.60 Animals—whales; 083.03 Holidays—Christmas; 088 Illness.

Duvoisin, Roger Antoine. *The Crocodile in the Tree*. Illus. by author. New York: Knopf, 1973.
008 Animals; 058 Farms; 068 Friendship; 142.01 Reptiles—alligators, crocodiles.

Duvoisin, Roger Antoine. *Crocus*. Illus. by author. New York: Knopf, 1977.
023.07 Careers—dentists; 026.27 Character traits—pride; 058 Farms; 142.01 Reptiles—alligators, crocodiles; 171 Teeth.

Duvoisin, Roger Antoine. *Day and Night*. Illus. by author. New York: Knopf, 1960.
008.14 Animals—dogs; 017.14 Birds—owls.

Duvoisin, Roger Antoine. *Donkey-Donkey*. Illus. by author. New York: Parents, 1968.
008.16 Animals—donkeys.

Duvoisin, Roger Antoine. *Easter Treat*. Illus. by author. New York: Knopf, 1954.
083.04 Holidays—Easter.

Duvoisin, Roger Antoine. *Happy Hunter*. Illus. by author. New York: Lothrop, 1961.
026.18 Character traits—kindness to animals; 049 Ecology; 166.08 Sports—hunting; 191 Violence, anti-violence; 194 Weapons.

Duvoisin, Roger Antoine. *The House of Four Seasons*. Illus. by author. New York: Lothrop, 1956.
002.09 Activities—painting; 032.01 Concepts—color; 154 Seasons.

Duvoisin, Roger Antoine. *Jasmine*. Illus. by author. New York: Knopf, 1973.
008 Animals; 026.16 Character traits—individuality; 031 Clothing; 058 Farms.

Duvoisin, Roger Antoine. *Lonely Veronica*. Illus. by author. New York: Knopf, 1963.
008.27 Animals—hippopotami; 029 City; 138 Progress.

Duvoisin, Roger Antoine, jt. author. *Marc and Pixie and the Walls in Mrs. Jones's Garden.* By Louise Fatio, and Roger Antoine Duvoisin.

Duvoisin, Roger Antoine. *One Thousand Christmas Beards.* Illus. by author. New York: Knopf, 1955.
083.03 Holidays—Christmas.

Duvoisin, Roger Antoine. *Our Veronica Goes to Petunia's Farm.* Illus. by author. New York: Knopf, 1962.
008 Animals; 008.27 Animals—hippopotami; 026.03 Character traits—being different; 058 Farms.

Duvoisin, Roger Antoine. *Periwinkle.* Illus. by author. New York: Knopf, 1976.
005 Amphibians; 008.20 Animals—giraffes; 052.07 Emotions—loneliness; 054 Etiquette; 068 Friendship.

Duvoisin, Roger Antoine. *Petunia.* Illus. by author. New York: Knopf, 1950.
002.13 Activities—reading;
008 Animals; 017.11 Birds—geese;
026.27 Character traits—pride;
058 Farms; 068 Friendship.

Duvoisin, Roger Antoine. *Petunia and the Song.* Illus. by author. New York: Knopf, 1951.
008 Animals; 017.11 Birds—geese;
036 Crime; 058 Farms; 068 Friendship;
120 Noise; 164 Songs.

Duvoisin, Roger Antoine. *Petunia, Beware!* Illus. by author. New York: Knopf, 1958.
008 Animals; 016.09 Behavior—dissatisfaction; 017.11 Birds—geese;
058 Farms.

Duvoisin, Roger Antoine. *Petunia, I Love You!* Illus. by author. New York: Knopf, 1965.
008.47 Animals—raccoons;
016.36 Behavior—trickery;
017.11 Birds—geese; 017.27 Birds—vultures; 058 Farms; 068 Friendship.

Duvoisin, Roger Antoine. *Petunia Takes a Trip.* Illus. by author. New York: Knopf, 1953.
002.05 Activities—flying;
002.17 Activities— vacationing;
008 Animals; 017.11 Birds—geese.

Duvoisin, Roger Antoine. *Petunia's Christmas.* Illus. by author. New York: Knopf, 1952.
017.11 Birds—geese; 083.03 Holidays—Christmas; 087 Humor.

Duvoisin, Roger Antoine. *Petunia's Treasure.* Illus. by author. New York: Knopf, 1975.
008 Animals; 017.11 Birds—geese;
058 Farms.

Duvoisin, Roger Antoine. *See What I Am.* Illus. by author. New York: Lothrop, 1974.
016.03 Behavior—boasting;
032.01 Concepts—color.

Duvoisin, Roger Antoine. *Two Lonely Ducks.* Illus. by author. New York: Knopf, 1955.
017.08 Birds—ducks; 058 Farms.

Duvoisin, Roger Antoine. *Veronica.* Illus. by author. New York: Knopf, 1961.
008.27 Animals—hippopotami;
026.03 Character traits —being different; 029 City; 058 Farms.

Duvoisin, Roger Antoine. *Veronica and the Birthday Present.* Illus. by author. New York: Knopf, 1971.
008.09 Animals—cats; 008.27 Animals—hippopotami; 018 Birthdays; 058 Farms.

Duvoisin, Roger Antoine. *Veronica's Smile.* Illus. by author. New York: Knopf, 1964.
008.27 Animals—hippopotami;
016.04 Behavior—boredom.

Dyke, John. *Pigwig.* Illus. by author. New York: Methuen, 1978.
008.42 Animals—pigs;
016.34 Behavior—stealing;
026.04 Character traits—bravery;
052.08 Emotions—love.

Eastman, Philip Day. *Are You My Mother?* Illus. by author. New York: Random House, 1960.
016.24 Behavior—misunderstanding;
017 Birds; 057.03 Family life—mothers.

Eastman, Philip Day. *Flap Your Wings.* Illus. by author. New York: Random House, 1969.
017 Birds; 050 Eggs; 142.01 Reptiles—alligators, crocodiles.

Eastman, Philip Day. *Go, Dog, Go!* Illus. by author. New York: Random House, 1961.
008.14 Animals—dogs.

Eastman, Philip Day. *Sam and the Firefly.* Illus. by author. New York: Random House, 1958.
017.14 Birds—owls; 090 Insects and spiders.

Eastman, Philip Day, jt. author. *Snow.* By Roy McKie, and Philip Day Eastman.

Eckert, Horst. *Dear Snowman.* Illus. by author. Cleveland: Collins, 1969.
154.04 Seasons—winter; 163 Snowmen; 195.07 Weather—snow.

Eckert, Horst. *Joshua and the Magic Fiddle.* Illus. by author. Cleveland: Collins, 1967.
103 Magic; 111 Moon; 116 Music.

Eckert, Horst. *Just One Apple.* Illus. by author. New York: Walck, 1965.
046 Dragons.

Eckert, Horst. *The Magic Auto.* Illus. by author. New York: Crown, 1971.
012 Automobiles; 103 Magic.

Eckert, Horst. *Tonight at Nine.* Illus. by author. New York: Walck, 1967.
008 Animals; 116 Music; 134 Poetry, rhyme.

Economakis, Olga. *Oasis of the Stars.* Illus. by Blair Lent. New York: Coward, 1955.
064.01 Foreign lands—Africa; 137 Problem solving.

Edwards, Dorothy, and Williams, Jenny. *A Wet Monday.* Illus. by Jenny Williams. New York: Morrow, 1975.
016.02 Behavior—bad day; 052 Emotions; 057 Family life; 195.05 Weather—rain.

Eggs. Illus. by Esmé Eve. New York: Grosset, 1971.
050 Eggs.

Ehrhardt, Reinhold. *Kikeri or The Proud Red Rooster.* Illus. by Bernadette Watts. Cleveland: Collins, 1969.
017.04 Birds—chickens; 026.27 Character traits—pride.

Ehrlich, Amy. *The Everyday Train.* Illus. by Martha Alexander. New York: Dial Pr., 1977.
016.33 Behavior—solitude; 179 Trains.

Ehrlich, Amy. *Zeek Silver Moon.* Illus. by Robert Andrew Parker. New York: Dial Pr., 1972.
053.04 Ethnic groups in the U.S.—Indians; 057 Family life.

Ehrlich, Bettina. *Cocolo Comes to America.* Illus. by author. New York: Harper, 1949.
008.16 Animals—donkeys.

Ehrlich, Bettina. *Cocolo's Home.* Illus. by author. New York: Harper, 1950.
008.16 Animals—donkeys.

Ehrlich, Bettina. *Of Uncles and Aunts.* Illus. by author. New York: Norton, 1964.
057 Family life.

Ehrlich, Bettina. *Pantaloni.* Illus. by author. New York: Harper, 1957.
008.14 Animals—dogs; 064.18 Foreign lands—Italy; 135 Poverty; 166.05 Sports—fishing.

Ehrlich, Bettina. *Piccolo.* Illus. by author. New York: Harper, 1954.
008.16 Animals—donkeys.

Eichenberg, Fritz. *Ape in Cape.* Illus. by author. New York: Harcourt, 1952.
001 ABC Books; 008 Animals.

Eichenberg, Fritz. *Dancing in the Moon.* Illus. by author. New York: Harcourt, 1955.
008 Animals; 033 Counting.

Elkin, Benjamin. *The Big Jump and Other Stories.* Illus. by Katherine Evans. New York: Random House, 1958.
008.14 Animals—dogs; 062 Folk and fairy tales; 147 Royalty.

Elkin, Benjamin. *Gillespie and the Guards.* Illus. by James Henry Daugherty. New York: Viking, 1956.
006 Anatomy; 016.36 Behavior—trickery; 026.06 Character traits—cleverness; 147 Royalty.

Elkin, Benjamin. *The King Who Could Not Sleep.* Illus. by Victoria Dickerson Chess. New York: Parents, 1975.
038 Cumulative tales; 134 Poetry, rhyme; 147 Royalty; 162 Sleep.

Elkin, Benjamin. *The King's Wish and Other Stories.* Illus. by Leonard W. Shortall. New York: Random House, 1960.
062 Folk and fairy tales; 147 Royalty.

Elkin, Benjamin. *The Loudest Noise in the World.* Illus. by James Henry Daugherty. New York: Viking, 1954.
018 Birthdays; 120 Noise; 147 Royalty.

Elkin, Benjamin. *Lucky and the Giant.* Illus. by Katherine Evans. Chicago: Children's Pr., 1962.
026.06 Character traits—cleverness; 026.29 Character traits—selfishness; 072 Giants.

Elkin, Benjamin. *Six Foolish Fishermen.* Illus. by Katherine Evans. Based on a folktale in Ashton's Chap-Books of the 18th century. Chicago: Children's Pr., 1957.
033 Counting; 062 Folk and fairy tales; 166.05 Sports —fishing.

Elkin, Benjamin. *Such Is the Way of the World.* Illus. by Yoko Mitsuhashi. New York: Parents, 1968.
008.37 Animals—monkeys;
038 Cumulative tales; 062 Folk and fairy tales; 064.01 Foreign lands—Africa;
137 Problem solving.

Elkin, Benjamin. *Why the Sun Was Late.* Illus. by Jerome Snyder. New York: Parents, 1966.
008 Animals; 038 Cumulative tales;
062 Folk and fairy tales; 090 Insects and spiders; 169 Sun.

Ellen, Barbara, jt. author. *Phillip the Flower-Eating Phoenix.* By John Todaro, and Barbara Ellen.

Ellentuck, Shan. *Did You See What I Said?* Illus. by author. Garden City, NY: Doubleday, 1967.
087 Humor; 096 Language.

Ellentuck, Shan. *A Sunflower as Big as the Sun.* Illus. by author. Garden City, NY: Doubleday, 1968.
016.03 Behavior—boasting; 087 Humor;
061 Flowers; 133 Plants.

Emberley, Barbara. *Drummer Hoff.* Illus. by Edward Randolph Emberley. Englewood Cliffs, NJ: Prentice-Hall, 1967.
023.17 Careers—military;
038 Cumulative tales; 134 Poetry, rhyme; 194 Weapons.

Emberley, Barbara. *One Wide River to Cross.* Illus. by Edward Randolph Emberley. Englewood Cliffs, NJ: Prentice-Hall, 1966.
008 Animals; 164 Songs.

Emberley, Barbara. *Simon's Song.* Illus. by Edward Randolph Emberley. Englewood Cliffs, NJ: Prentice-Hall, 1969.
122 Nursery rhymes; 164 Songs.

Emberley, Barbara, and Emberley, Edward Randolph. *Night's Nice.* Illus. by Edward Randolph Emberley. Garden City, NY: Doubleday, 1963.
119 Night; 134 Poetry, rhyme.

Emberley, Ed. See Emberley, Edward Randolph.

Emberley, Edward Randolph. *A Birthday Wish.* Illus. by author. Boston: Little, 1977.
008.34 Animals—mice;
016.38 Behavior—wishing;
018 Birthdays; 063 Food;
201 Wordless.

Emberley, Edward Randolph. *Ed Emberley's ABC.* Illus. by author. Boston: Little, 1978.
001 ABC Books.

Emberley, Edward Randolph. *Ed Emberley's Amazing Look Through Book.* Illus. by author. Boston: Little, 1979.
032 Concepts; 067 Format, unusual;
129 Participation.

Emberley, Edward Randolph. *Green Says Go.* Illus. by author. Boston: Little, 1969.
032.01 Concepts—color.

Emberley, Edward Randolph. *Klippity Klop.* Illus. by author. Boston: Little, 1974.
046 Dragons; 069 Games; 095 Knights;
129 Participation.

Emberley, Edward Randolph, jt. author. *Night's Nice.* By Barbara Emberley, and Edward Randolph Emberley.

Emberley, Edward Randolph. *The Parade Book.* Illus. by author. Boston: Little, 1962.
128 Parades.

Emberley, Edward Randolph. *Rosebud.* Illus. by author. Boston: Little, 1966.
026.03 Character traits—being different; 137 Problem solving;
142.05 Reptiles—turtles.

Emberley, Edward Randolph. *Wing on a Flea.* Illus. by author. Boston: Little, 1961.
032.07 Concepts—shape; 134 Poetry, rhyme.

Emberley, Edward Randolph. *The Wizard of Op.* Illus. by author. Boston: Little, 1975.
126 Optical illusions; 200 Wizards.

Embry, Margaret. *The Blue-Nosed Witch.* Illus. by Carl Rose. New York: Holiday, 1956.
083.07 Holidays—Halloween;
199 Witches.

Emmett, Fredrick Rowland. *New World for Nellie.* Illus. by author. New York: Harcourt, 1952.
087 Humor; 179 Trains.

Emmons, Ramona Ware, jt. author. *Your World: Let's Visit the Hospital.* By Billy N. Pope, and Ramona Ware Emmons.

Erickson, Phoebe. *Just Follow Me.* Illus. by author. Chicago: Follett, 1960.
008.14 Animals—dogs;
016.20 Behavior—lost; 086 Houses.

Erickson, Phoebe. *Uncle Debunkel or Barely Believable Bear.* Illus. by author. New York: Knopf, 1964.
002.12 Activities—playing; 069 Games; 087 Humor.

Erickson, Russell E. *Warton's Christmas Eve Adventure.* Illus. by Lawrence Di Fiori. New York: Lothrop, 1977.
083.03 Holidays—Christmas.

Erskine, Jim. *The Snowman.* Illus. by author. New York: Crown, 1978.
163 Snowmen.

Espenscheid, Gertrude E. *The Oh Ball.* Illus. by author. New York: Harper, 1966.
147 Royalty; 177.02 Toys—balls.

Estes, Eleanor. *A Little Oven.* Illus. by author. New York: Harcourt, 1955.
052.08 Emotions—love.

Ets, Marie Hall. *Another Day.* Illus. by author. New York: Viking, 1953.
008 Animals; 066 Forest, woods; 128 Parades; 173 Theater.

Ets, Marie Hall. *Bad Boy, Good Boy.* Illus. by author. New York: Crowell, 1967.
016 Behavior; 053.06 Ethnic groups in the U.S.—Mexican-Americans; 057 Family life; 151 School.

Ets, Marie Hall. *Beasts and Nonsense.* Illus. by author. New York: Viking, 1952.
008 Animals; 087 Humor; 134 Poetry, rhyme.

Ets, Marie Hall. *The Cow's Party.* Illus. by author. New York: Viking, 1958.
008.12 Animals—cows, bulls; 016.09 Behavior—dissatisfaction; 016.31 Behavior—sharing; 130 Parties.

Ets, Marie Hall. *Elephant in a Well.* Illus. by author. New York: Viking, 1972.
008 Animals; 008.17 Animals—elephants; 026.14 Character traits—helpfulness; 038 Cumulative tales.

Ets, Marie Hall. *Gilberto and the Wind.* Illus. by author. New York: Viking, 1963.
053.06 Ethnic groups in the U.S.—Mexican-Americans; 195.08 Weather—wind.

Ets, Marie Hall. *In the Forest.* Illus. by author. New York: Viking, 1944.
002.11 Activities—picnicking; 008 Animals; 066 Forest, woods; 089 Imagination; 128 Parades.

Ets, Marie Hall. *Just Me.* Illus. by author. New York: Viking, 1965.
008 Animals; 129 Participation.

Ets, Marie Hall. *Little Old Automobile.* Illus. by author. New York: Viking, 1948.
012 Automobiles.

Ets, Marie Hall. *Mister Penny.* Illus. by author. New York: Viking, 1935.
008 Animals; 058 Farms; 087 Humor.

Ets, Marie Hall. *Mr. Penny's Circus.* Illus. by author. New York: Viking, 1961.
008 Animals; 028 Circus, clowns.

Ets, Marie Hall. *Mr. Penny's Race Horse.* Illus. by author. New York: Viking, 1956.
008 Animals; 008.28 Animals—horses; 056 Fairs; 058 Farms.

Ets, Marie Hall. *Mr. T. W. Anthony Woo.* Illus. by author. New York: Viking, 1951.
008.09 Animals—cats; 008.14 Animals—dogs; 008.34 Animals—mice.

Ets, Marie Hall. *Nine Days to Christmas.* Illus. by author. New York: Viking, 1959.
053.06 Ethnic groups in the U.S.—Mexican-Americans; 064.24 Foreign lands—Mexico; 083.03 Holidays—Christmas.

Ets, Marie Hall. *Play with Me.* Illus. by author. New York: Viking, 1955.
002.12 Activities—playing; 008 Animals; 016 Behavior.

Ets, Marie Hall. *Talking Without Words; I Can. Can You?* Illus. by author. New York: Viking, 1968.
129 Participation.

Evans, Eva Knox. *Sleepy Time.* Illus. by Reed Champion. Boston: Houghton, 1962.
008 Animals; 038 Cumulative tales; 081 Hibernation; 162 Sleep.

Evans, Katherine. *The Boy Who Cried Wolf.* Illus. by author. Chicago: Albert Whitman, 1960.
008.61 Animals—wolves; 016.21 Behavior—lying; 016.36 Behavior—trickery; 062 Folk and fairy tales.

Evans, Katherine. *The Maid and Her Pail of Milk.* Illus. by author. Chicago: Albert Whitman, 1959.
016.13 Behavior—greed; 062 Folk and fairy tales; 087 Humor.

Evans, Katherine. *The Man, the Boy, and the Donkey.* Illus. by author. Chicago: Albert Whitman, 1958.
008.16 Animals—donkeys; 026.26 Character traits—practicality; 062 Folk and fairy tales; 087 Humor.

Evers, Alf. *There's No Such Animal.* Illus. by Bogdan Grom. Philadelphia: Lippincott, 1958.
008.06 Animals—bears.

Falls, C. B. See Falls, Charles Buckles.

Falls, Charles Buckles. *ABC Book.* Illus. by author. Garden City, NY: Doubleday, 1923.
001 ABC Books.

Fanshawe, Elizabeth. *Rachel.* Illus. by Michael Charlton. New York: Dutton, 1975.
077 Handicaps; 151 School.

Farber, Norma. *As I Was Crossing Boston Common.* Illus. by Arnold Stark Lobel. New York: Dutton, 1975.
001 ABC Books; 134 Poetry, rhyme.

Farber, Norma. *How Does It Feel to Be Old?* Illus. by Trina Schart Hyman. New York: Dutton, 1979.
125 Old age.

Farber, Norma. *How the Left-Behind Beasts Built Ararat.* Illus. by Antonio Frasconi. New York: Walker, 1978.
008 Animals; 134 Poetry, rhyme; 137 Problem solving; 141.01 Religion—Noah.

Farber, Norma. *Never Say Ugh to a Bug.* Illus. by José Aruego. New York: Greenwillow, 1979.
090 Insects and spiders; 134 Poetry, rhyme.

Farber, Norma. *There Once Was a Woman Who Married a Man.* Illus. by Lydia Dabcovich. Reading: Addison-Wesley, 1978.
087 Humor; 120 Noise; 134 Poetry, rhyme.

Farber, Norma. *Where's Gomer?* Illus. by William Pène Du Bois. New York: Dutton, 1974.
016.20 Behavior—lost; 134 Poetry, rhyme; 141.01 Religion—Noah.

Farjeon, Eleanor. *Mrs. Malone.* Illus. by Edward Jeffery Irving Ardizzone. New York: Walck, 1962.
026.13 Character traits—generosity; 134 Poetry, rhyme.

Farley, Walter. *Little Black, a Pony.* Illus. by James Schucker. New York: Random House, 1961.
008.28 Animals—horses.

Farley, Walter. *Little Black Goes to the Circus.* Illus. by James Schucker. New York: Random House, 1963.
008.28 Animals—horses; 028 Circus, clowns.

The Farmer in the Dell. Illus. by Diane Zuromskia. Boston: Little, 1978.
069 Games; 116 Music; 121 Non-sexist; 164 Songs.

Fassler, Joan. *All Alone with Daddy.* Illus. by Dorothy Lake Gregory. New York: Human Sci. Pr., 1969.
057.01 Family life—fathers.

Fassler, Joan. *Boy with a Problem.* Illus. by Stuart [i.e., Stewart] Kranz. New York: Human Sci. Pr., 1971.
068 Friendship; 137 Problem solving.

Fassler, Joan. *Don't Worry Dear.* Illus. by Stuart [i.e., Stewart] Kranz. New York: Human Sci. Pr., 1971.
016.14 Behavior—growing up; 053.01 Ethnic groups in the U.S.—Afro-Americans.

Fassler, Joan. *Howie Helps Himself.* Illus. by Joseph Leon Lasker. Chicago: Albert Whitman, 1975.
077 Handicaps.

Fassler, Joan. *The Man of the House.* Illus. by Peter Landa. New York: Human Sci. Pr., 1969/1975.
016.14 Behavior—growing up; 046 Dragons; 057.03 Family life—mothers; 110 Monsters.

Fassler, Joan. *My Grandpa Died Today.* Illus. by Stuart [i.e., Stewart] Kranz. New York: Human Sci. Pr., 1971.
040 Death; 057.02 Family life—grandparents; great-grandparents; 093 Jewish culture; 125 Old age.

Fassler, Joan. *One Little Girl.* Illus. by M. Jane Smyth. New York: Human Sci. Pr., 1969.
057 Family life; 077 Handicaps.

Fatio, Louise. *Anna, the Horse.* Illus. by Roger Antoine Duvoisin. New York: Atheneum, 1951.
008.28 Animals—horses; 083.03 Holidays—Christmas.

Fatio, Louise. *A Doll for Marie.* Illus. by Roger Antoine Duvoisin. New York: McGraw-Hill, 1957.
177.04 Toys—dolls.

Fatio, Louise. *The Happy Lion*. Illus. by Roger Antoine Duvoisin. New York: McGraw-Hill, 1954.
008.10 Animals—cats, wild;
064.11 Foreign lands—France;
068 Friendship; 204 Zoos.

Fatio, Louise. *The Happy Lion and the Bear*. Illus. by Roger Antoine Duvoisin. New York: McGraw-Hill, 1964.
008.06 Animals—bears;
008.10 Animals—cats, wild;
026.02 Character traits—appearance;
064.11 Foreign lands—France;
204 Zoos.

Fatio, Louise. *The Happy Lion in Africa*. Illus. by Roger Antoine Duvoisin. New York: McGraw-Hill, 1955.
008.10 Animals—cats, wild;
064.01 Foreign lands—Africa;
064.11 Foreign lands—France;
204 Zoos.

Fatio, Louise. *The Happy Lion Roars*. Illus. by Roger Antoine Duvoisin. New York: McGraw-Hill, 1957.
008.10 Animals—cats, wild;
052.07 Emotions—loneliness;
064.11 Foreign lands—France;
204 Zoos.

Fatio, Louise. *The Happy Lion's Quest*. Illus. by Roger Antoine Duvoisin. New York: McGraw-Hill, 1961.
008.10 Animals—cats, wild;
064.11 Foreign lands—France.

Fatio, Louise. *The Happy Lion's Rabbits*. Illus. by Roger Antoine Duvoisin. New York: McGraw-Hill, 1974.
008.10 Animals—cats, wild;
008.46 Animals—rabbits;
026.17 Character traits—kindness;
064.11 Foreign lands—France;
204 Zoos.

Fatio, Louise. *The Happy Lion's Treasure*. Illus. by Roger Antoine Duvoisin. New York: McGraw-Hill, 1970.
008.10 Animals—cats, wild;
052.08 Emotions—love; 064.11 Foreign lands—France; 204 Zoos.

Fatio, Louise. *The Happy Lion's Vacation*. Illus. by Roger Antoine Duvoisin. New York: McGraw-Hill, 1967.
002.17 Activities—vacationing;
008.10 Animals—cats, wild.

Fatio, Louise. *Hector and Christiana*. Illus. by Roger Antoine Duvoisin. New York: McGraw-Hill, 1977.
017.17 Birds—pelicans; 204 Zoos.

Fatio, Louise. *Hector Penguin*. Illus. by Roger Antoine Duvoisin. New York: McGraw-Hill, 1973.
017.18 Birds—penguins;
026.16 Character traits—individuality.

Fatio, Louise. *The Red Bantam*. Illus. by Roger Antoine Duvoisin. New York: McGraw-Hill, 1963.
008.18 Animals—foxes; 017.04 Birds—chickens; 026.04 Character traits—bravery; 058 Farms.

Fatio, Louise. *The Three Happy Lions*. Illus. by Roger Antoine Duvoisin. New York: McGraw-Hill, 1959.
008.10 Animals—cats, wild;
064.11 Foreign lands—France;
204 Zoos.

Fatio, Louise, and Duvoisin, Roger Antoine. *Marc and Pixie and the Walls in Mrs. Jones's Garden*. Illus. by Roger Antoine Duvoisin. New York: McGraw-Hill, 1975.
008.09 Animals—cats; 008.11 Animals—chipmunks.

Fay, Hermann. *My Zoo*. Illus. by author. Northbrook, IL: Hubbard Sci., 1972.
008 Animals; 204 Zoos.

Feder, Jane. *Beany*. Illus. by Karen Gundersheimer. New York: Pantheon, 1979.
008.09 Animals—cats.

Feder, Paula Kurzband. *Where Does the Teacher Live?* Illus. by Lillian Hoban. New York: Dutton, 1979.
023.27 Careers—teachers; 086 Houses;
137 Problem solving; 151 School.

Feelings, Muriel L. *Jambo Means Hello; A Swahili Alphabet Book*. Illus. by Tom Feelings. New York: Dial Pr., 1974.
001 ABC Books; 064.01 Foreign lands—Africa; 065 Foreign languages.

Feelings, Muriel L. *Monjo Means One; A Swahili Counting Book*. Illus. by Tom Feelings. New York: Dial Pr., 1971.
033 Counting; 064.01 Foreign lands—Africa; 065 Foreign languages.

Feistel, Sally, jt. author. *The Guinea Pigs That Went to School*. By Leonard Meshover, and Sally Feistel.

Feistel, Sally, jt. author. *The Monkey That Went to School*. By Leonard Meshover, and Sally Feistel.

Felt, Sue. *Rosa-Too-Little*. Illus. by author. Garden City, NY: Doubleday, 1950.
002.21 Activities—writing;
016.14 Behavior—growing up;
053.06 Ethnic groups in the U.S.—Mexican-Americans; 057 Family life;
100 Libraries.

Felton, Harold W. *Pecos Bill and the Mustang*. Illus. by Leonard W. Shortall. Englewood Cliffs, NJ: Prentice-Hall, 1965.
008.28 Animals—horses; 035 Cowboys;
062 Folk and fairy tales.

Fender, Kay. *Odette, a Bird in Paris*. Illus. by Philippe Dumas. Englewood Cliffs, NJ: Prentice-Hall, 1978.
017 Birds; 064.11 Foreign lands—France; 125 Old age.

Fenner, Carol Elizabeth. *Christmas Tree on the Mountain*. Illus. by author. New York: Harcourt, 1966.
083.03 Holidays—Christmas.

Fenner, Carol Elizabeth. *Tigers in the Cellar*. Illus. by author. New York: Harcourt, 1963.
008.10 Animals—cats, wild;
089 Imagination; 119 Night.

Fenton, Edward. *The Big Yellow Balloon*. Illus. by Ib Ohlsson. Garden City, NY: Doubleday, 1967.
038 Cumulative tales; 087 Humor.

Fenton, Edward. *Fierce John*. Illus. by William Pène Du Bois. Garden City, NY: Doubleday, 1959.
057 Family life; 089 Imagination.

Fern, Eugene. *Birthday Presents*. Illus. by author. New York: Farrar, 1967.
018 Birthdays; 164 Songs.

Fern, Eugene. *The King Who Was Too Busy*. Illus. by author. New York: Ariel, 1966.
147 Royalty.

Fern, Eugene. *Pepito's Story*. Illus. by author. New York: Ariel, 1960.
002.04 Activities—dancing;
026.03 Character traits—being different; 088 Illness.

Field, Eugene. *Wynken, Blynken and Nod*. Illus. by Barbara Cooney. New York: McGraw-Hill, 1964.
134 Poetry, rhyme; 153 Sea and seashore; 162 Sleep.

Field, Rachel Lyman. *Prayer for a Child*. Illus. by Elizabeth Orton Jones. New York: Macmillan, 1944.
141 Religion.

Fife, Dale. *Adam's ABC*. Illus. by Don Robertson. New York: Coward, 1971.
001 ABC Books; 029 City; 053.01 Ethnic groups in the U.S.—Afro-Americans.

Fife, Dale. *The Little Park*. Illus. by Janet La Salle. Chicago: Albert Whitman, 1973.
008 Animals; 049 Ecology; 138 Progress.

Fifield, Flora. *Pictures for the Palace*. Illus. by Nola Langner. New York: Vanguard, 1957.
011 Art; 064.19 Foreign lands—Japan.

Finfer, Celentha; Wasserberg, Esther; and Weinberg, Florence. *Grandmother Dear*. Illus. by Roy Mathews. Chicago: Follett, 1966.
002.01 Activities—babysitting;
057.02 Family life—grandparents;
great-grandparents; 134 Poetry, rhyme.

Fire. Illus. by Michael Ricketts. New York: Grosset, 1972.
059 Fire.

Firmin, Peter. *Basil Brush and a Dragon*. Illus. by author. Englewood Cliffs, NJ: Prentice-Hall, 1971.
008.18 Animals—foxes;
008.35 Animals—moles; 046 Dragons;
089 Imagination.

Firmin, Peter. *Basil Brush Builds a House*. Illus. by author. Englewood Cliffs, NJ: Prentice-Hall, 1973.
008.18 Animals—foxes;
008.35 Animals—moles; 086 Houses.

Firmin, Peter. *Basil Brush Finds Treasure*. Illus. by author. Englewood Cliffs, NJ: Prentice-Hall, 1979.
008.18 Animals—foxes;
008.35 Animals—moles;
154.03 Seasons—summer.

Firmin, Peter. *Basil Brush Gets a Medal*. Illus. by author. Englewood Cliffs, NJ: Prentice-Hall, 1978.
008.18 Animals—foxes;
008.35 Animals—moles; 038 Cumulative tales.

Firmin, Peter. *Basil Brush Goes Flying*. Illus. by author. Englewood Cliffs, NJ: Prentice-Hall, 1969.
004 Airplanes; 008.18 Animals—foxes;
008.35 Animals —moles;
016.23 Behavior—mistakes;
080 Helicopters.

Firmin, Peter, jt. author. *Noggin and the Whale*. By Oliver Postgate, and Peter Firmin.

Firmin, Peter, jt. author. *Noggin the King*. By Oliver Postgate, and Peter Firmin.

First Graces. Illus. by Tasha Tudor. New York: Oxford Univ. Pr., 1955.
134 Poetry, rhyme; 141 Religion.

First Prayers. Illus. by Tasha Tudor. New York: Oxford Univ. Pr., 1952.
134 Poetry, rhyme; 141 Religion.

Fischer, Hans. *The Birthday.* Illus. by author. New York: Harcourt, 1954.
008 Animals; 018 Birthdays.

Fischer, Hans. *Pitschi, the Kitten Who Always Wanted to Do Something Else.* Illus. by author. New York: Harcourt, 1953.
008.09 Animals—cats;
016.09 Behavior—dissatisfaction.

Fish, Helen Dean. *When the Root Children Wake Up.* Illus. by Sibylle V. Olfers. A picture book by Sibylle V. Olfers, with text by Helen Dean Fish. Philadelphia: Lippincott, 1930.
051 Elves and little people;
154.02 Seasons—spring.

Fisher, Aileen Lucia. *And a Sunflower Grew.* Illus. by Trina Schart Hyman. New York: Noble, 1977.
061 Flowers; 133 Plants; 134 Poetry, rhyme; 152 Science.

Fisher, Aileen Lucia. *As the Leaves Fall Down.* Illus. by Barbara Smith. New York: Noble, 1977.
133 Plants; 152 Science; 154 Seasons; 181 Trees.

Fisher, Aileen Lucia. *Best Little House.* Illus. by Arnold Spilka. New York: Crowell, 1966.
086 Houses; 114 Moving; 134 Poetry, rhyme.

Fisher, Aileen Lucia. *Do Bears Have Mothers Too?* Illus. by Eric Carle. New York: Crowell, 1973.
008 Animals; 057.03 Family life—mothers; 134 Poetry, rhyme.

Fisher, Aileen Lucia. *Going Barefoot.* Illus. by Adrienne Adams. New York: Crowell, 1960.
134 Poetry, rhyme; 154 Seasons.

Fisher, Aileen Lucia. *Like Nothing at All.* Illus. by Leonard Weisgard. New York: Crowell, 1962.
134 Poetry, rhyme; 152 Science; 154 Seasons.

Fisher, Aileen Lucia. *My Mother and I.* Illus. by Kazue Mizumura. New York: Crowell, 1967.
057.03 Family life—mothers;
134 Poetry, rhyme; 154.02 Seasons—spring.

Fisher, Aileen Lucia. *Mysteries in the Garden.* Illus. by Ati Forberg. New York: Noble, 1977.
133 Plants; 134 Poetry, rhyme;
152 Science.

Fisher, Aileen Lucia. *Now That Spring Is Here.* Illus. by Symeon Shimin. New York: Noble, 1977.
133 Plants; 134 Poetry, rhyme;
152 Science; 154.02 Seasons—spring.

Fisher, Aileen Lucia. *Petals Yellow and Petals Red.* Illus. by Albert John Pucci. New York: Noble, 1977.
061 Flowers; 134 Poetry, rhyme;
152 Science.

Fisher, Aileen Lucia. *Plant Magic.* Illus. by Barbara Cooney. New York: Noble, 1977.
133 Plants; 134 Poetry, rhyme;
152 Science.

Fisher, Aileen Lucia. *Prize Performance.* Illus. by Margot Ladd Tomes. New York: Noble, 1977.
133 Plants; 134 Poetry, rhyme;
152 Science.

Fisher, Aileen Lucia. *Seeds on the Go.* Illus. by Hans Zander. New York: Noble, 1977.
133 Plants; 134 Poetry, rhyme;
152 Science.

Fisher, Aileen Lucia. *Sing Little Mouse.* Illus. by Symeon Shimin. New York: Crowell, 1969.
008.34 Animals—mice; 134 Poetry, rhyme.

Fisher, Aileen Lucia. *Swords and Daggers.* Illus. by James Higa. New York: Noble, 1977.
133 Plants; 134 Poetry, rhyme;
152 Science.

Fisher, Aileen Lucia. *A Tree with a Thousand Uses.* Illus. by James R. Endicott. New York: Noble, 1977.
134 Poetry, rhyme; 152 Science;
181 Trees.

Fisher, Aileen Lucia. *We Went Looking.* Illus. by Marie Angel. New York: Crowell, 1968.
008 Animals; 017 Birds; 090 Insects and spiders; 133 Plants; 134 Poetry, rhyme.

Fisher, Aileen Lucia. *Where Does Everyone Go?* Illus. by Adrienne Adams. New York: Crowell, 1961.
008 Animals; 081 Hibernation;
134 Poetry, rhyme; 154.04 Seasons—winter.

Fitch, Florence Mary. *A Book about God.* Illus. by Leonard Weisgard. New York: Lothrop, 1953.
141 Religion.

Fitzhugh, Louise, and Scoppetone, Sandra. *Bang Bang You're Dead.* Illus. by Louise Fitzhugh. New York: Harper, 1969.
002.12 Activities—playing;
035 Cowboys; 191 Violence, anti-violence; 193 War; 194 Weapons.

Flack, Marjorie. *Angus and the Cat.* Illus. by author. Garden City, NY: Doubleday, 1931.
008.09 Animals—cats; 008.14 Animals—dogs; 026.07 Character traits—completing things; 026.10 Character traits—curiosity.

Flack, Marjorie. *Angus and the Ducks.* Illus. by author. Garden City, NY: Doubleday, 1930.
008.14 Animals—dogs; 017.08 Birds—ducks; 026.09 Character traits—conceit; 026.10 Character traits—curiosity.

Flack, Marjorie. *Angus Lost.* Illus. by author. Garden City, NY: Doubleday, 1932.
008.14 Animals—dogs;
016.20 Behavior—lost;
154.04 Seasons—winter.

Flack, Marjorie. *Ask Mr. Bear.* Illus. by author. New York: Macmillan, 1932.
008 Animals; 008.06 Animals—bears;
018 Birthdays; 052.08 Emotions—love;
057.03 Family life—mothers.

Flack, Marjorie. *The Boats on the River.* Illus. by author. New York: Viking, 1946.
019 Boats, ships; 144 Rivers.

Flack, Marjorie. *The New Pet.* Illus. by author. Garden City, NY: Doubleday, 1943.
013 Babies; 057 Family life.

Flack, Marjorie. *The Restless Robin.* Illus. by author. Boston: Houghton, 1937.
017.20 Birds—robins.

Flack, Marjorie, and Wiese, Kurt. *The Story about Ping.* Illus. by Kurt Wiese. New York: Viking, 1933.
016.22 Behavior—misbehavior;
017.08 Birds—ducks; 064.06 Foreign lands—China.

Flack, Marjorie. *Tim Tadpole and the Great Bullfrog.* Illus. by author. Garden City, NY: Doubleday, 1934.
005 Amphibians.

Flack, Marjorie. *Wait for William.* Illus. by Marjorie Flack, and Richard A. Holberg. Boston: Houghton, 1935.
028 Circus, clowns; 057 Family life.

Flack, Marjorie. *William and His Kitten.* Illus. by author. Boston: Houghton, 1938.
008.09 Animals—cats.

Fleischman, Albert Sidney. *Kate's Secret Riddle.* Illus. by Barbara Bottner. New York: Watts, 1977.
088 Illness; 143 Riddles.

Fleischman, Albert Sidney. *Longbeard the Wizard.* Illus. by Charles Bragg. Boston: Little, 1970.
147 Royalty; 200 Wizards.

Fleischman, Sid. See Fleischman, Albert Sidney.

Fleisher, Robbin. *Quilts in the Attic.* Illus. by Ati Forberg. New York: Macmillan, 1978.
057 Family life; 069 Games.

Flora, James. *The Day the Cow Sneezed.* Illus. by author. New York: Harcourt, 1957.
008 Animals; 038 Cumulative tales;
087 Humor.

Flora, James. *Grandpa's Farm.* Illus. by author. New York: Harcourt, 1965.
057.02 Family life—grandparents; great-grandparents; 058 Farms;
087 Humor.

Flora, James. *Leopold, the See-Through Crumbpicker.* Illus. by author. New York: Harcourt, 1961.
110 Monsters; 204 Zoos.

Flora, James. *My Friend Charlie.* Illus. by author. New York: Harcourt, 1964.
087 Humor.

Flora, James. *Sherwood Walks Home.* Illus. by author. New York: Harcourt, 1966.
038 Cumulative tales; 177 Toys;
177.08 Toys—teddy bears.

Flory, Jane. *The Unexpected Grandchild.* Illus. by Carolyn Croll. Boston: Houghton, 1977.
016.31 Behavior—sharing;
057.02 Family life— grandparents; great-grandparents.

Flory, Jane. *We'll Have a Friend for Lunch.* Illus. by Carolyn Croll. Boston: Houghton, 1974.
008.09 Animals—cats; 063 Food;
068 Friendship.

Flower, Phyllis. *Barn Owl.* Illus. by Cherryl Pape. New York: Harper, 1978.
017.14 Birds—owls; 152 Science.

Floyd, Lucy, and Lasky, Kathryn. *Agatha's Alphabet, with Her Very Own Dictionary*. Illustrated. Skokie, IL: Rand McNally, 1975.
001 ABC Books; 043 Dictionaries; 121 Non-sexist.

Ford, George, jt. author. *Walk On!* By Mel Williamson, and George Ford.

Foreman, Michael, jt. author. *The General*. By Janet Charters, and Michael Foreman.

Foreman, Michael. *Moose*. Illus. by author. New York: Pantheon, 1972.
008.06 Animals—bears; 008.38 Animals—moose; 017.09 Birds—eagles; 191 Violence, anti-violence.

Foreman, Michael. *War and Peas*. Illus. by author. New York: Crowell, 1974.
008.10 Animals—cats, wild; 063 Food; 147 Royalty; 193 War.

Foster, Doris Van Liew. *A Pocketful of Seasons*. Illus. by Talivaldis Stubis. New York: Lothrop, 1961.
016.28 Behavior—saving things; 154 Seasons.

Foster, Doris Van Liew. *Tell Me, Mr. Owl*. Illus. by Helen Stone. New York: Lothrop, 1957.
017.14 Birds—owls; 083.07 Holidays—Halloween.

Foster, Marian Curtis. *Doki, the Lonely Papoose*. Illus. by author. New York: Lothrop, 1955.
053.04 Ethnic groups in the U.S.—Indians.

Foster, Marian Curtis. *The Journey of Bangwell Putt*. Illus. by author. New York: Lothrop, 1965.
083.03 Holidays—Christmas; 177.04 Toys—dolls.

Foulds, Elfrida Vipont. *The Elephant and the Bad Baby*. Illus. by Raymond Briggs. New York: Coward, 1969.
008.17 Animals—elephants; 013 Babies; 016.34 Behavior—stealing; 038 Cumulative tales.

Fox, Dorothea Warren. *Follow Me the Leader*. Illus. by author. New York: Parents, 1968.
069 Games.

Fox, Robin. *Le Poulet, the Rooster Who Laid Eggs*. Illus. by Laszlo Matulay. New York: Lion, 1967.
017.04 Birds—chickens; 058 Farms; 064.11 Foreign lands—France; 131 Pets.

The Fox Went Out on a Chilly Night. Illus. by Peter Spier. Garden City, NY: Doubleday, 1961.
008.18 Animals—foxes; 062 Folk and fairy tales; 116 Music; 164 Songs.

Frances, Esteban, jt. author. *The Thread Soldiers*. By Anne Heathers, and Esteban Frances.

Francis, Frank. *The Magic Wallpaper*. Illus. by author. New York: Abelard-Schuman, 1970.
008 Animals; 016.20 Behavior—lost; 047 Dreams; 089 Imagination.

Francis, Frank. *Natasha's New Doll*. Illus. by author. New York: O'Hara, 1971.
062 Folk and fairy tales; 064.30 Foreign lands—Russia; 177.04 Toys—dolls; 199 Witches.

Françoise (pseud.). See Seignobosc, Françoise.

Frasconi, Antonio. *See Again, Say Again*. Illus. by author. New York: Harcourt, 1964.
065 Foreign languages.

Frasconi, Antonio. *See and Say*. Illus. by author. New York: Harcourt, 1955.
065 Foreign languages.

Fraser, James Howard. *Los Posadas, a Christmas Story*. Illus. by Nick De Grazia. Flagstaff: Northland, 1963.
053.06 Ethnic groups in the U.S.—Mexican-Americans; 064.24 Foreign lands—Mexico; 083.03 Holidays—Christmas; 141 Religion.

Fraser, Kathleen, and Levy, Miriam F. *Adam's World, San Francisco*. Illus. by Helen D. Hipshman. Chicago: Albert Whitman, 1971.
029 City; 053.01 Ethnic groups in the U.S.—Afro-Americans; 057 Family life.

Freeman, Don. *Add-A-Line Alphabet*. Illus. by author. Chicago: Children's Pr., 1968.
001 ABC Books; 008 Animals.

Freeman, Don. *Beady Bear*. Illus. by author. New York: Viking, 1954.
016.27 Behavior—running away; 177.08 Toys—teddy bears.

Freeman, Don. *Bearymore*. Illus. by author. New York: Viking, 1976.
008.06 Animals—bears; 028 Circus, clowns; 081 Hibernation.

Freeman, Don. *The Chalk Box Story*. Illus. by author. Philadelphia: Lippincott, 1976.
002.09 Activities—painting; 032.01 Concepts—color.

Freeman, Don. *Come Again, Pelican*. Illus. by author. New York: Viking, 1961.
017.17 Birds—pelicans; 153 Sea and seashore.

Freeman, Don. *Corduroy*. Illus. by author. New York: Viking, 1968.
016.19 Behavior—losing things; 031 Clothing; 052.08 Emotions—love; 053.01 Ethnic groups in the U.S.—Afro-Americans; 168 Stores; 177.08 Toys—teddy bears.

Freeman, Don. *Dandelion*. Illus. by author. New York: Viking, 1964.
008.10 Animals—cats, wild; 026.02 Character traits—appearance; 130 Parties; 195.05 Weather—rain.

Freeman, Don. *Fly High, Fly Low*. Illus. by author. New York: Viking, 1957.
017 Birds; 029 City.

Freeman, Don. *Forever Laughter*. Illus. by author. Chicago: Children's Pr., 1970.
087 Humor; 092 Jesters; 147 Royalty; 201 Wordless.

Freeman, Don. *The Guard Mouse*. Illus. by author. New York: Viking, 1967.
008.34 Animals—mice; 018 Birthdays; 029 City; 064.100 Foreign lands—England.

Freeman, Don. *Hattie the Backstage Bat*. Illus. by author. New York: Viking, 1970.
008.05 Animals—bats; 173 Theater.

Freeman, Don. *Mop Top*. Illus. by author. New York: Viking, 1955.
018 Birthdays; 023.04 Careers—barbers; 076 Hair; 134 Poetry, rhyme.

Freeman, Don. *The Night the Lights Went Out*. Illus. by author. New York: Viking, 1958.
119 Night.

Freeman, Don. *Norman the Doorman*. Illus. by author. New York: Viking, 1959.
008.34 Animals—mice; 011 Art; 115 Museums.

Freeman, Don. *The Paper Party*. Illus. by author. New York: Viking, 1974.
089 Imagination; 130 Parties; 139 Puppets.

Freeman, Don. *A Pocket for Corduroy*. Illus. by author. New York: Viking, 1978.
031 Clothing; 053.01 Ethnic groups in the U.S.—Afro-Americans; 097 Laundry; 177.08 Toys—teddy bears.

Freeman, Don. *Quiet! There's a Canary in the Library*. Illus. by author. Chicago: Children's Pr., 1969.
017.03 Birds—canaries; 052.02 Emotions—embarrassment; 089 Imagination; 100 Libraries.

Freeman, Don. *A Rainbow of My Own*. Illus. by author. New York: Viking, 1966.
032.01 Concepts—color; 195.06 Weather—rainbows.

Freeman, Don. *The Seal and the Slick*. Illus. by author. New York: Viking, 1974.
008.51 Animals—seals; 026.18 Character traits—kindness to animals; 049 Ecology; 124 Oil.

Freeman, Don. *Ski Pup*. Illus. by author. New York: Viking, 1963.
008.14 Animals—dogs; 064.36 Foreign lands—Switzerland; 166.12 Sports—skiing.

Freeman, Don. *Space Witch*. Illus. by author. New York: Viking, 1959.
083.07 Holidays—Halloween; 165 Space and space ships; 199 Witches.

Freeman, Don. *Tilly Witch*. Illus. by author. New York: Viking, 1969.
026.22 Character traits—meanness; 083.07 Holidays—Halloween; 199 Witches.

Freeman, Don. *The Turtle and the Dove*. Illus. by author. New York: Viking, 1964.
017.07 Birds—doves; 142.05 Reptiles—turtles.

Freeman, Don. *Will's Quill*. Illus. by author. New York: Viking, 1975.
017.11 Birds—geese; 064.10 Foreign lands—England; 159 Shakespeare; 173 Theater.

Freeman, Don, and Freeman, Lydia. *Pet of the Met*. Illus. by Don Freeman. New York: Viking, 1953.
008.34 Animals—mice; 116 Music; 173 Theater.

Freeman, Ira, jt. author. *You Will Go to the Moon*. By Mae Freeman, and Ira Freeman.

Freeman, Jean Todd. *Cynthia and the Unicorn*. Illus. by Leonard Weisgard. New York: Norton, 1967.
083.03 Holidays—Christmas; 117 Mythical creatures; 134 Poetry, rhyme.

Freeman, Lydia, jt. author. *Pet of the Met*. By Don Freeman, and Lydia Freeman.

Freeman, Mae, and Freeman, Ira. *You Will Go to the Moon.* Illus. by Lee Ames. New York: Random House, 1971.
111 Moon; 165 Space and space ships.

French, Fiona Mary. *The Blue Bird.* Illus. by author. New York: Walck, 1972.
017 Birds.

French, Fiona Mary. *Hunt the Thimble.* Illus. by author. New York: Oxford Univ. Pr., 1978.
069 Games; 129 Participation.

Freschet, Berniece. *The Ants Go Marching.* Illus. by Stefan Martin. New York: Scribner's, 1973.
002.11 Activities—picnicking; 033 Counting; 090 Insects and spiders; 134 Poetry, rhyme.

Freschet, Berniece. *Bear Mouse.* Illus. by Donald Carrick. New York: Scribner's, 1973.
008.34 Animals—mice; 152 Science.

Freschet, Berniece. *The Old Bullfrog.* Illus. by Roger Antoine Duvoisin. New York: Scribner's, 1968.
005 Amphibians.

Freschet, Berniece. *Turtle Pond.* Illus. by Donald Carrick. New York: Scribner's, 1971.
142.05 Reptiles—turtles.

Freschet, Berniece. *The Web in the Grass.* Illus. by Roger Antoine Duvoisin. New York: Scribner's, 1972.
090 Insects and spiders.

Freudberg, Judy. *Some, More, Most.* Illus. by Richard Hefter. New York: Larousse, 1976.
032 Concepts.

Fribourg, Marjorie G. *Ching-Ting and the Ducks.* Illus. by Artur Marokvia. New York: Sterling, 1957.
016.14 Behavior—growing up; 017.08 Birds—ducks; 064.06 Foreign lands—China.

Friedrich, Otto, jt. author. *The Easter Bunny That Overslept.* By Priscilla Friedrich, and Otto Friedrich.

Friedrich, Otto, jt. author. *The Marshmallow Ghosts.* By Priscilla Friedrich, and Otto Friedrich.

Friedrich, Priscilla, and Friedrich, Otto. *The Easter Bunny That Overslept.* Illus. by Adrienne Adams. New York: Lothrop, 1957.
083.04 Holidays—Easter.

Friedrich, Priscilla, and Friedrich, Otto. *The Marshmallow Ghosts.* Illus. by Louis Slobodkin. New York: Lothrop, 1960.
071 Ghosts; 083.07 Holidays—Halloween.

The Friendly Beasts and A Partridge in a Pear Tree. Illus. by Virginia Parsons. Calligraphy by Sheila Waters. Garden City, NY: Doubleday, 1966/1977.
083.03 Holidays—Christmas; 116 Music; 141 Religion; 164 Songs.

Friskey, Margaret. *Chicken Little Count-To-Ten.* Illus. by Katherine Evans. Chicago: Children's Pr., 1946.
033 Counting.

Friskey, Margaret. *Indian Two Feet and His Eagle Feather.* Illus. by John Hawkinson, and Lucy Ozone Hawkinson. Chicago: Children's Pr., 1967.
053.04 Ethnic groups in the U.S.—Indians.

Friskey, Margaret. *Indian Two Feet and His Horse.* Illus. by Katherine Evans. Chicago: Children's Pr., 1959.
053.04 Ethnic groups in the U.S.—Indians.

Friskey, Margaret. *Indian Two Feet and the Wolf Cubs.* Illus. by John Hawkinson. Chicago: Children's Pr., 1971.
008.61 Animals—wolves; 053.04 Ethnic groups in the U.S.—Indians.

Friskey, Margaret. *Mystery of the Gate Sign.* Illus. by Katherine Evans. Chicago: Children's Pr., 1958.
002.13 Activities—reading; 008.46 Animals—rabbits.

Friskey, Margaret. *Seven Diving Ducks.* Illus. by Jean Morey. Chicago: Children's Pr., 1965.
017.08 Birds—ducks; 033 Counting.

Friskey, Margaret. *Three Sides and the Round One.* Illus. by Mary Gehr. Chicago: Children's Pr., 1973.
032.07 Concepts—shape.

Frith, Michael K. *I'll Teach My Dog 100 Words.* Illus. by Philip Day Eastman. New York: Random House, 1973.
008.14 Animals—dogs; 087 Humor; 134 Poetry, rhyme.

Frith, Michael K. *Some of Us Walk, Some Fly, Some Swim.* Illus. by author. New York: Random House, 1971.
008 Animals; 152 Science.

A Frog He Would A-Wooing Go. Illus. by William Stobbs. Chicago: Follett, 1969.
005 Amphibians; 087 Humor;
164 Songs.

Frog Went A-Courtin'. Illus. by Feodor Stepanovich Rojankovsky. Retold by John Meredith Langstaff. New York: Harcourt, 1955.
005 Amphibians; 087 Humor;
164 Songs.

Fromm, Lilo. *Muffel and Plums.* Illus. by author. New York: Macmillan, 1972.
008 Animals; 201 Wordless.

Fry, Christopher. *The Boat That Mooed.* Illus. by Leonard Weisgard. New York: Macmillan, 1965.
019 Boats, ships; 195.04 Weather—fog.

Fuchs, Eric. *Journey to the Moon.* Illus. by author. New York: Delacorte Pr., 1969.
111 Moon; 165 Space and space ships;
201 Wordless.

Fuchshuber, Annegert. *The Wishing Hat.* Illus. by author. Translated by Elizabeth D. Crawford. New York: Morrow, 1977.
016.38 Behavior—wishing; 087 Humor;
103 Magic.

Fujikawa, Gyo. *Gyo Fujikawa's A to Z Picture Book.* Illus. by author. New York: Grosset, 1974.
001 ABC Books.

Fujita, Tamao. *The Boy and the Bird.* Illus. by Chiyo Ono. Translated by Kiyoko Tucker. New York: Harper, 1972.
017 Birds; 026.12 Character traits—
freedom; 064.19 Foreign lands—Japan;
131 Pets.

Funai, Mamoru R. *Moke and Poki in the Rain Forest.* Illus. by author. New York: Harper, 1972.
051 Elves and little people; 078 Hawaii.

Futamata, Eigoro. *How Not to Catch a Mouse.* Illus. by author. Rutland, VT: Weatherhill, 1972.
008 Animals; 008.34 Animals—mice.

Gackenbach, Dick. *Claude and Pepper.* Illus. by author. New York: Seabury Pr., 1976.
008.14 Animals—dogs;
016.27 Behavior—running away.

Gackenbach, Dick. *Claude the Dog.* Illus. by author. New York: Seabury Pr., 1974.
008.14 Animals—dogs;
016.31 Behavior—sharing;
083.03 Holidays—Christmas.

Gackenbach, Dick. *Crackle, Gluck and the Sleeping Toad.* Illus. by author. New York: Seabury Pr., 1979.
005 Amphibians; 016.21 Behavior—
lying; 058 Farms.

Gackenbach, Dick. *Harry and the Terrible Whatzit.* Illus. by author. New York: Seabury Pr., 1977.
052.04 Emotions—fear;
089 Imagination; 110 Monsters.

Gackenbach, Dick. *Hattie Be Quiet, Hattie Be Good.* Illus. by author. New York: Harper, 1977.
008.46 Animals—rabbits; 016 Behavior;
088 Illness.

Gackenbach, Dick. *Hattie Rabbit.* Illus. by author. New York: Harper, 1971.
008.46 Animals—rabbits;
016.38 Behavior—wishing.

Gackenbach, Dick. *Ida Fanfanny.* Illus. by author. New York: Harper, 1978.
103 Magic; 154 Seasons; 195 Weather.

Gackenbach, Dick. *Mother Rabbit's Son Tom.* Illus. by author. New York: Harper, 1977.
008.46 Animals—rabbits;
016.09 Behavior—dissatisfaction;
063 Food; 131 Pets.

Gackenbach, Dick. *Pepper and All the Legs.* Illus. by author. New York: Seabury Pr., 1968.
008.14 Animals—dogs;
016.22 Behavior—misbehavior.

Gackenbach, Dick. *The Pig Who Saw Everything.* Illus. by author. New York: Seabury Pr., 1978.
008.42 Animals—pigs; 026.10 Character traits—curiosity; 058 Farms;
087 Humor.

Gaeddert, Lou Ann Bigge. *Noisy Nancy Nora.* Illus. by Gioia Fiammenghi. Garden City, NY: Doubleday, 1965.
016 Behavior; 120 Noise.

Gág, Wanda. *ABC Bunny.* Illus. by author. Hand lettered by Howard Gág. New York: Coward, 1933.
001 ABC Books; 008.46 Animals—
rabbits; 134 Poetry, rhyme.

Gág, Wanda. *The Funny Thing.* Illus. by author. New York: Coward, 1929.
046 Dragons; 063 Food; 110 Monsters.

Gág, Wanda. *Gone Is Gone*. Illus. by author. New York: Coward, 1935.
002.20 Activities—working; 016.23 Behavior—mistakes; 121 Nonsexist.

Gág, Wanda. *Millions of Cats*. Illus. by author. New York: Coward, 1928.
008.09 Animals—cats; 026.26 Character traits—practicality; 038 Cumulative tales.

Gág, Wanda. *Nothing at All*. Illus. by author. New York: Coward, 1941.
008.14 Animals—dogs; 052.07 Emotions—loneliness; 103 Magic.

Gág, Wanda. *Snippy and Snappy*. Illus. by author. New York: Coward, 1931.
008.34 Animals—mice.

Gage, Wilson. *Down in the Boondocks*. Illus. by Glen H. Rounds. New York: Greenwillow, 1977.
036 Crime; 077 Handicaps; 120 Noise; 134 Poetry, rhyme.

Galbraith, Kathryn Osebold. *Sports Are Special*. Illus. by Diane Dawson. New York: Atheneum, 1976.
088 Illness; 089 Imagination.

Galdone, Joanna. *Amber Day*. Illus. by Paul Galdone. New York: McGraw-Hill, 1978.
042 Devil; 062 Folk and fairy tales.

Galdone, Joanna. *Gertrude, the Goose Who Forgot*. Illus. by Paul Galdone. New York: Watts, 1975.
016.11 Behavior—forgetfulness; 017.11 Birds—geese; 134 Poetry, rhyme.

Galdone, Joanna. *Honeybee's Party*. Illus. by Paul Galdone. New York: Watts, 1972.
090 Insects and spiders; 130 Parties.

Galdone, Joanna. *The Tailypo, a Ghost Story*. Illus. by Paul Galdone. New York: Seabury Pr., 1977.
071 Ghosts; 134 Poetry, rhyme.

Galdone, Paul. *Androcles and the Lion*. Illus. by author. New York: McGraw-Hill, 1970.
008.10 Animals—cats, wild; 026.18 Character traits—kindness to animals; 062 Folk and fairy tales; 064.18 Foreign lands—Italy.

Galdone, Paul. *The Horse, the Fox, and the Lion*. Illus. by author. New York: Seabury Pr., 1968.
008.10 Animals—cats, wild; 008.14 Animals—dogs; 008.18 Animals—foxes; 008.28 Animals—horses; 016.36 Behavior—trickery; 062 Folk and fairy tales; 125 Old age.

Galdone, Paul. *The Magic Porridge Pot*. Illus. by author. New York: Seabury Pr., 1976.
016.11 Behavior—forgetfulness; 016.31 Behavior—sharing; 062 Folk and fairy tales; 063 Food; 103 Magic.

Galdone, Paul. *The Monkey and the Crocodile*. Illus. by author. A Jataka tale from India. New York: Seabury Pr., 1969.
008.37 Animals—monkeys; 026.06 Character traits—cleverness; 062 Folk and fairy tales; 142.01 Reptiles—alligators, crocodiles.

Galdone, Paul. *Obedient Jack*. Illus. by author. New York: Watts, 1971.
016.23 Behavior—mistakes; 057 Family life; 062 Folk and fairy tales.

Galdone, Paul. *The Table, the Donkey and the Stick*. Illus. by author. New York: McGraw-Hill, 1976.
038 Cumulative tales; 062 Folk and fairy tales.

Galdone, Paul. *The Town Mouse and the Country Mouse*. Illus. by author. New York: McGraw-Hill, 1971.
008.34 Animals—mice; 062 Folk and fairy tales.

Gannett, Ruth Stiles. *Katie and the Sad Noise*. Illus. by Ellie Simmons. New York: Random House, 1961.
008.14 Animals—dogs; 026.17 Character traits—kindness; 083.03 Holidays—Christmas.

Gantos, John B. *Rotten Ralph*. Illus. by Nicole Rubel. Boston: Houghton, 1976.
008.09 Animals—cats; 016.22 Behavior—misbehavior.

Garcia Lorca, Federico. *The Lieutenant Colonel and the Gypsy*. Illus. by Marc Simont. Translated by Marc Simont. Garden City, NY: Doubleday, 1971.
064.34 Foreign lands—Spain; 075 Gypsies; 134 Poetry, rhyme.

Garelick, May. *Down to the Beach*. Illus. by Barbara Cooney. New York: Four Winds Pr., 1973.
153 Sea and seashore; 154.03 Seasons—summer.

Garelick, May. *Look at the Moon.* Illus. by Leonard Weisgard. Reading: Addison-Wesley, 1969.
008 Animals; 111 Moon; 134 Poetry, rhyme.

Garelick, May. *Sounds of a Summer Night.* Illus. by Beni Montresor. Reading: Addison-Wesley, 1963.
119 Night; 120 Noise.

Garelick, May. *Where Does the Butterfly Go When It Rains?* Illus. by Leonard Weisgard. Reading: Addison-Wesley, 1961.
090 Insects and spiders; 134 Poetry, rhyme; 195.05 Weather—rain.

Garrett, Helen. *Angelo the Naughty One.* Illus. by Leo Politi. New York: Viking, 1944.
053.06 Ethnic groups in the U.S.—Mexican-Americans.

Garrison, Christian. *The Dream Eater.* Illus. by Diane Goode. New York: Dutton, 1978.
046 Dragons; 047 Dreams; 064.19 Foreign lands—Japan.

Garrison, Christian. *Little Pieces of the West Wind.* Illus. by Diane Goode. New York: Dutton, 1975.
038 Cumulative tales; 195.08 Weather—wind.

Garten, Jan. *The Alphabet Tale.* Illus. by Muriel Batherman. New York: Random House, 1964.
001 ABC Books; 008 Animals; 129 Participation; 134 Poetry, rhyme.

Gaston, Susan. *New Boots for Salvador.* Illus. by Lydia Schwartz. Pasadena, CA: Ritchie, 1972.
008.28 Animals—horses.

Gay, Zhenya. *Look!* Illus. by author. New York: Viking, 1952.
008 Animals; 100 Libraries; 134 Poetry, rhyme.

Gay, Zhenya. *Small One.* Illus. by author. New York: Viking, 1958.
008.46 Animals—rabbits; 016.20 Behavior—lost.

Gay, Zhenya. *What's Your Name?* Illus. by author. New York: Viking, 1955.
008 Animals; 134 Poetry, rhyme; 143 Riddles.

Gay, Zhenya. *Who's Afraid?* Illus. by author. New York: Viking, 1965.
052.04 Emotions—fear.

Gay, Zhenya. *Wonderful Things.* Illus. by author. New York: Viking, 1954.
008.28 Animals—horses.

Geisel, Theodor Seuss. *And to Think That I Saw It on Mulberry Street.* Illus. by author. New York: Vanguard, 1937.
087 Humor; 089 Imagination; 134 Poetry, rhyme.

Geisel, Theodor Seuss. *Bartholomew and the Oobleck.* Illus. by author. New York: Random House, 1949.
087 Humor; 147 Royalty.

Geisel, Theodor Seuss. *Because a Little Bug Went Ka-choo!* Illus. by author. New York: Random House, 1975.
038 Cumulative tales; 087 Humor; 090 Insects and spiders; 134 Poetry, rhyme.

Geisel, Theodor Seuss. *The Cat in the Hat.* Illus. by author. New York: Random House, 1957.
008.09 Animals—cats; 087 Humor; 134 Poetry, rhyme.

Geisel, Theodor Seuss. *The Cat in the Hat Beginner Book Dictionary.* Illus. by author. New York: Random House, 1964.
043 Dictionaries; 087 Humor.

Geisel, Theodor Seuss. *The Cat in the Hat Comes Back!* Illus. by author. New York: Random House, 1958.
008.09 Animals—cats; 087 Humor; 134 Poetry, rhyme.

Geisel, Theodor Seuss. *The Cat's Quizzer.* Illus. by author. New York: Random House, 1976.
087 Humor; 134 Poetry, rhyme; 143 Riddles.

Geisel, Theodor Seuss. *Come Over to My House.* Illus. by Richard Erdoes. New York: Random House, 1966.
064 Foreign lands; 086 Houses; 087 Humor; 134 Poetry, rhyme.

Geisel, Theodor Seuss. *Did I Ever Tell You How Lucky You Are?* Illus. by author. New York: Random House, 1973.
026.21 Character traits—luck; 087 Humor; 134 Poetry, rhyme; 137 Problem solving.

Geisel, Theodor Seuss. *Dr. Seuss's ABC.* Illus. by author. New York: Random House, 1963.
001 ABC Books; 087 Humor; 134 Poetry, rhyme.

Geisel, Theodor Seuss. *Dr. Seuss's Sleep Book.* Illus. by author. New York: Random House, 1962.
087 Humor; 134 Poetry, rhyme; 162 Sleep.

Geisel, Theodor Seuss. *The Foot Book*. Illus. by author. New York: Random House, 1968.
006 Anatomy; 087 Humor; 134 Poetry, rhyme.

Geisel, Theodor Seuss. *Fox in Socks*. Illus. by author. New York: Random House, 1965.
087 Humor; 134 Poetry, rhyme.

Geisel, Theodor Seuss. *A Great Day for Up*. Illus. by Quentin Blake. New York: Random House, 1974.
032.10 Concepts—up and down; 087 Humor; 134 Poetry, rhyme.

Geisel, Theodor Seuss. *Green Eggs and Ham*. Illus. by author. New York: Random House, 1960.
038 Cumulative tales; 063 Food; 087 Humor; 134 Poetry, rhyme.

Geisel, Theodor Seuss. *Happy Birthday to You*. Illus. by author. New York: Random House, 1959.
018 Birthdays; 087 Humor; 134 Poetry, rhyme.

Geisel, Theodor Seuss. *Hooper Humperdink...? Not Him!* Illus. by Charles E. Martin. New York: Random House, 1976.
001 ABC Books; 018 Birthdays; 087 Humor; 130 Parties; 134 Poetry, rhyme.

Geisel, Theodor Seuss. *Hop on Pop*. Illus. by author. New York: Random House, 1963.
087 Humor; 134 Poetry, rhyme.

Geisel, Theodor Seuss. *Horton Hatches the Egg*. Illus. by author. New York: Random House, 1940.
008.17 Animals—elephants; 017 Birds; 026.17 Character traits—kindness; 050 Eggs; 087 Humor; 134 Poetry, rhyme.

Geisel, Theodor Seuss. *Horton Hears a Who*. Illus. by author. New York: Random House, 1954.
008.17 Animals—elephants; 026.17 Character traits—kindness; 087 Humor; 134 Poetry, rhyme.

Geisel, Theodor Seuss. *How the Grinch Stole Christmas*. Illus. by author. New York: Random House, 1957.
026.22 Character traits—meanness; 083.03 Holidays—Christmas; 087 Humor; 134 Poetry, rhyme.

Geisel, Theodor Seuss. *I Can Lick 30 Tigers Today and Other Stories*. Illus. by author. New York: Random House, 1969.
008.10 Animals—cats, wild; 087 Humor; 134 Poetry, rhyme.

Geisel, Theodor Seuss. *I Can Read with My Eyes Shut!* Illus. by author. New York: Random House, 1978.
002.13 Activities—reading; 087 Humor; 134 Poetry, rhyme.

Geisel, Theodor Seuss. *I Can Write! A Book by Me, Myself, with a Little Help from Theo. LeSieg*. Illus. by author. New York: Random House, 1971.
002.21 Activities—writing; 087 Humor; 134 Poetry, rhyme.

Geisel, Theodor Seuss. *I Had Trouble Getting to Solla Sollew*. Illus. by author. New York: Random House, 1965.
002.16 Activities—traveling; 087 Humor; 134 Poetry, rhyme.

Geisel, Theodor Seuss. *I Wish That I Had Duck Feet*. Illus. by author. New York: Random House, 1965.
016.38 Behavior—wishing; 087 Humor; 134 Poetry, rhyme.

Geisel, Theodor Seuss. *If I Ran the Circus*. Illus. by author. New York: Random House, 1956.
028 Circus, clowns; 087 Humor; 134 Poetry, rhyme.

Geisel, Theodor Seuss. *If I Ran the Zoo*. Illus. by author. New York: Random House, 1950.
087 Humor; 134 Poetry, rhyme; 204 Zoos.

Geisel, Theodor Seuss. *In a People House*. Illus. by author. New York: Random House, 1972.
086 Houses; 087 Humor; 134 Poetry, rhyme.

Geisel, Theodor Seuss. *The King's Stilts*. Illus. by author. New York: Random House, 1939.
087 Humor; 134 Poetry, rhyme; 147 Royalty; 177 Toys.

Geisel, Theodor Seuss. *The Lorax*. Illus. by author. New York: Random House, 1971.
049 Ecology; 087 Humor; 134 Poetry, rhyme.

Geisel, Theodor Seuss. *McElligot's Pool*. Illus. by author. New York: Random House, 1947.
060 Fish; 087 Humor; 089 Imagination; 134 Poetry, rhyme.

Geisel, Theodor Seuss. *Marvin K. Mooney, Will You Please Go Now!* Illus. by author. New York: Random House, 1972.
087 Humor; 134 Poetry, rhyme.

Geisel, Theodor Seuss. *Mr. Brown Can Moo, Can You?* Illus. by author. New York: Random House, 1970.
008 Animals; 087 Humor; 129 Participation; 134 Poetry, rhyme.

Geisel, Theodor Seuss. *Oh Say Can You Say?* Illus. by author. New York: Random House, 1979.
087 Humor; 175 Tongue twisters.

Geisel, Theodor Seuss. *Oh, the Thinks You Can Think!* Illus. by author. New York: Random House, 1975.
087 Humor; 089 Imagination; 134 Poetry, rhyme.

Geisel, Theodor Seuss. *On Beyond Zebra.* Illus. by author. New York: Random House, 1955.
087 Humor; 099 Letters; 134 Poetry, rhyme.

Geisel, Theodor Seuss. *One Fish, Two Fish, Red Fish, Blue Fish.* Illus. by author. New York: Random House, 1960.
060 Fish; 087 Humor; 134 Poetry, rhyme.

Geisel, Theodor Seuss. *Please Try to Remember the First of Octember!* Illus. by author. New York: Random House, 1977.
016.38 Behavior—wishing; 087 Humor; 134 Poetry, rhyme.

Geisel, Theodor Seuss. *Scrambled Eggs Super!* Illus. by author. New York: Random House, 1953.
063 Food; 087 Humor; 134 Poetry, rhyme.

Geisel, Theodor Seuss. *The Shape of Me and Other Stuff.* Illus. by author. New York: Random House, 1973.
032.07 Concepts—shape; 087 Humor; 134 Poetry, rhyme.

Geisel, Theodor Seuss. *The Sneetches and Other Stories.* Illus. by author. New York: Random House, 1961.
052.04 Emotions—fear; 087 Humor; 134 Poetry, rhyme.

Geisel, Theodor Seuss. *Ten Apples Up on Top!* Illus. by author. New York: Random House, 1961.
033 Counting; 063 Food; 087 Humor; 134 Poetry, rhyme.

Geisel, Theodor Seuss. *There's a Wocket in My Pocket!* Illus. by author. New York: Random House, 1974.
087 Humor; 134 Poetry, rhyme.

Geisel, Theodor Seuss. *Thidwick, the Big Hearted Moose.* Illus. by author. New York: Random House, 1948.
008.38 Animals—moose; 017 Birds; 087 Humor; 134 Poetry, rhyme.

Geisel, Theodor Seuss. *Wacky Wednesday.* Illus. by author. New York: Random House, 1974.
087 Humor; 129 Participation; 134 Poetry, rhyme.

Geisel, Theodor Seuss. *Would You Rather Be a Bullfrog?* Illus. by Roy McKie. New York: Random House, 1975.
005 Amphibians; 008 Animals; 026.23 Character traits—optimism.

Gelman, Rita Golden. *Dumb Joey.* Illus. by Cheryl Pelavin. New York: Holt, 1973.
002.12 Activities—playing; 029 City; 068 Friendship.

Gelman, Rita Golden. *Hey, Kid.* Illus. by Karol Nicklaus. New York: Watts, 1977.
087 Humor; 134 Poetry, rhyme.

Gelman, Rita Golden. *Professor Coconut and the Thief.* Illus. by Emily Arnold McCully. New York: Holt, 1977.
008.37 Animals—monkeys; 137 Problem solving.

Gelman, Rita Golden. *Uncle Hugh, a Fishing Story.* Illus. by Eros Keith. New York: Harcourt, 1978.
166.05 Sports—fishing.

Gendel, Evelyn. *Tortoise and Turtle Abroad.* Illus. by Hilary Knight. New York: Simon & Schuster, 1963.
008 Animals; 130 Parties; 142.05 Reptiles—turtles.

George, Jean Craighead. *All Upon a Stone.* Illus. by Donald Alan Bolognese. New York: Crowell, 1971.
090 Insects and spiders; 152 Science.

George, Jean Craighead. *The Wentletrap Trap.* Illus. by Symeon Shimin. New York: Dutton, 1978.
053.01 Ethnic groups in the U.S.—Afro-Americans; 064.05 Foreign lands—Caribbean Islands; 153 Sea and seashore.

Georgiady, Nicholas P. *Gertie the Duck.* Illus. by Dagmar Wilson. Chicago: Follett, 1959.
017.08 Birds—ducks; 026.18 Character traits—kindness to animals.

Gergely, Tibor, jt. author. *Wheel on the Chimney*. By Margaret Wise Brown, and Tibor Gergely.

Gibson, Myra Tomback. *What Is Your Favorite Thing to Touch?* Illus. by author. New York: Grosset, 1965.
134 Poetry, rhyme; 157 Senses.

Gilbert, Helen Earle. *Dr. Trotter and His Big Gold Watch.* Illus. by Margaret Bradfield. Nashville: Abingdon Pr., 1948.
023.09 Careers—doctors; 030 Clocks.

Gilbert, Helen Earle. *Mr. Plum and the Little Green Tree.* Illus. by Margaret Bradfield. Nashville: Abingdon Pr., 1946.
023.24 Careers—shoemakers;
181 Trees.

Gilchrist, Theo E. *Halfway up the Mountain.* Illus. by Glen H. Rounds. Philadelphia: Lippincott, 1978.
016.10 Behavior—fighting, arguing;
134 Poetry, rhyme.

Gill, Bob, and Reid, Alastair. *A Balloon for a Blunderbuss.* Illus. by Bob Gill. New York: Harper, 1961.
002.15 Activities—trading.

Gill, Joan. *Hush, Jon!* Illus. by Tracy Sugarman. Garden City, NY: Doubleday, 1968.
013 Babies; 052.03 Emotions—envy, jealousy; 053.01 Ethnic groups in the U.S.—Afro-Americans; 057 Family life.

The Gingerbread Boy. Illus. by Paul Galdone. New York: Seabury Pr., 1975.
016.27 Behavior—running away;
038 Cumulative tales; 062 Folk and fairy tales; 063 Food; 134 Poetry, rhyme.

The Gingerbread Boy. Illus. by William Curtis Holdsworth. New York: Farrar, 1968.
016.27 Behavior—running away;
038 Cumulative tales; 062 Folk and fairy tales; 063 Food.

The Gingerbread Man. Illus. by Gerald Rose. Retold by Barbara Ireson. New York: Norton, 1963/1965.
016.27 Behavior—running away;
038 Cumulative tales; 062 Folk and fairy tales; 063 Food.

Ginsburg, Mirra. *The Chick and the Duckling.* Illus. by José Aruego, and Ariane Dewey. New York: Macmillan, 1972.
017.04 Birds—chickens; 017.08 Birds—ducks; 166.15 Sports—swimming.

Ginsburg, Mirra. *The Fox and the Hare.* Illus. by Victor Nolden. New York: Crown, 1969.
008 Animals; 008.18 Animals—foxes; 008.46 Animals—rabbits; 062 Folk and fairy tales; 064.30 Foreign lands—Russia; 068 Friendship.

Ginsburg, Mirra. *Mushroom in the Rain.* Illus. by José Aruego. Adapted by Vladimir Suteyer. New York: Macmillan, 1974.
008 Animals; 008.18 Animals—foxes;
133 Plants; 195.05 Weather—rain.

Ginsburg, Mirra. *The Strongest One of All.* Illus. by José Aruego. New York: Greenwillow, 1977.
008.52 Animals—sheep;
026.04 Character traits—bravery;
064.30 Foreign lands—Russia.

Ginsburg, Mirra. *Two Greedy Bears.* Illus. by José Aruego, and Ariane Dewey. New York: Macmillan, 1976.
008.06 Animals—bears;
008.18 Animals—foxes;
016.13 Behavior—greed;
016.32 Behavior—sibling rivalry;
064.15 Foreign lands—Hungary.

Ginsburg, Mirra. *Which Is the Best Place?* Illus. by Roger Antoine Duvoisin. Adapted by Pyotr Dubochkin. New York: Macmillan, 1976.
015 Bedtime; 064.30 Foreign lands—Russia.

Gipson, Morrell. *Hello, Peter.* Illus. by Clement Hurd. Garden City, NY: Doubleday, 1948.
002 Activities.

Glovach, Linda. *The Little Witch's Black Magic Book of Disguises.* Illus. by author. Englewood Cliffs, NJ: Prentice-Hall, 1973.
083 Holidays.

Glovach, Linda. *The Little Witch's Black Magic Book of Games.* Illus. by author. Englewood Cliffs, NJ: Prentice-Hall, 1974.
069 Games; 148 Safety.

Glovach, Linda. *The Little Witch's Christmas Book.* Illus. by author. Englewood Cliffs, NJ: Prentice-Hall, 1974.
083.03 Holidays—Christmas.

Glovach, Linda. *The Little Witch's Halloween Book.* Illus. by author. Englewood Cliffs, NJ: Prentice-Hall, 1975.
083.07 Holidays—Halloween.

Glovach, Linda. *The Little Witch's Thanksgiving Book.* Illus. by author. Englewood Cliffs, NJ: Prentice-Hall, 1976.
083.10 Holidays—Thanksgiving.

Go Tell Aunt Rhody. Illus. by Aliki Liacouras Brandenberg. New York: Macmillan, 1974.
062 Folk and fairy tales; 069 Games; 164 Songs.

Go Tell Aunt Rhody. Illus. by Robert Mead Quackenbush. Philadelphia: Lippincott, 1973.
069 Games; 116 Music; 164 Songs.

Gobhai, Mehlli. *Lakshmi the Water Buffalo Who Wouldn't.* Illus. by author. New York: Hawthorn, 1969.
008 Animals; 064.16 Foreign lands—India.

Goble, Paul. *The Friendly Wolf.* Illus. by author. New York: Dutton, 1974.
008.61 Animals—wolves; 016.20 Behavior—lost; 053.04 Ethnic groups in the U.S.—Indians.

Goble, Paul. *The Girl Who Loved Wild Horses.* Illus. by author. New York: Dutton, 1978.
008.28 Animals—horses; 053.04 Ethnic groups in the U.S.—Indians.

Goddard, Carrie Lou. *Isn't It a Wonder!* Illus. by Leigh Grant. Nashville: Abingdon Pr., 1976.
141 Religion.

Goff, Beth. *Where's Daddy?* Illus. by Susan Perl. Boston: Beacon Pr., 1969.
045 Divorce.

Goffstein, M. B. See Goffstein, Marilyn Brooks.

Goffstein, Marilyn Brooks. *Fish for Supper.* Illus. by author. New York: Dial Pr., 1976.
057.02 Family life—grandparents; great-grandparents; 125 Old age; 166.05 Sports—fishing.

Goffstein, Marilyn Brooks. *Goldie the Doll-maker.* Illus. by author. New York: Farrar, 1969.
052.07 Emotions—loneliness; 093 Jewish culture; 127 Orphans; 177.04 Toys—dolls.

Goffstein, Marilyn Brooks. *A Little Schubert.* Illus. by author. New York: Harper, 1972.
116 Music.

Goffstein, Marilyn Brooks. *Me and My Captain.* Illus. by author. New York: Farrar, 1974.
177.04 Toys—dolls.

Goffstein, Marilyn Brooks. *My Noah's Ark.* Illus. by author. New York: Harper, 1978.
141.01 Religion—Noah.

Goffstein, Marilyn Brooks. *Sleepy People.* Illus. by author. New York: Farrar, 1966.
015 Bedtime.

The Golden Goose. Illus. by William Stobbs. New York: McGraw-Hill, 1967.
017.04 Birds—chickens; 038 Cumulative tales; 062 Folk and fairy tales; 087 Humor; 147 Royalty.

Goldfrank, Helen Colodny. *An Egg Is for Wishing.* Illus. by Yaroslava Surmach Mills. New York: Abelard-Schuman, 1966.
016.01 Behavior—animals, dislike of; 016.38 Behavior—wishing; 050 Eggs; 064.40 Foreign lands—Ukraine; 083.04 Holidays—Easter.

Goldfrank, Helen Colodny. *One Mitten Lewis.* Illus. by Kurt Werth. New York: Lothrop, 1955.
016.19 Behavior—losing things.

Goldman, Susan. *Grandma Is Somebody Special.* Illus. by author. Edited by Caroline Rubin. Chicago: Albert Whitman, 1976.
057.02 Family life—grandparents; great-grandparents.

Goodall, John Strickland. *The Adventures of Paddy Pork.* Illus. by author. New York: Harcourt, 1968.
008.42 Animals—pigs; 016.27 Behavior—running away; 028 Circus, clowns; 067 Format, unusual; 201 Wordless.

Goodall, John Strickland. *The Ballooning Adventures of Paddy Pork.* Illus. by author. New York: Harcourt, 1969.
008.42 Animals—pigs; 067 Format, unusual; 201 Wordless.

Goodall, John Strickland. *Creepy Castle.* Illus. by author. New York: Atheneum, 1975.
008.34 Animals—mice; 067 Format, unusual; 095 Knights; 110 Monsters; 201 Wordless.

Goodall, John Strickland. *An Edwardian Christmas.* Illus. by author. New York: Atheneum, 1978.
064.10 Foreign lands—England; 067 Format, unusual; 083.03 Holidays—Christmas; 201 Wordless.

Goodall, John Strickland. *An Edwardian Summer.* Illus. by author. New York: Atheneum, 1976.
064.10 Foreign lands—England; 067 Format, unusual; 154.03 Seasons—summer; 201 Wordless.

Goodall, John Strickland. *Jacko.* Illus. by author. New York: Harcourt, 1971.
008.37 Animals—monkeys; 067 Format, unusual; 201 Wordless.

Goodall, John Strickland. *The Midnight Adventures of Kelly, Dot and Esmeralda.* Illus. by author. New York: Atheneum, 1972.
067 Format, unusual; 201 Wordless.

Goodall, John Strickland. *Naughty Nancy.* Illus. by author. New York: Atheneum, 1975.
016.22 Behavior—misbehavior; 067 Format, unusual; 196 Weddings; 201 Wordless.

Goodall, John Strickland. *Paddy Pork's Holiday.* Illus. by author. New York: Atheneum, 1976.
002.17 Activities—vacationing; 008.42 Animals—pigs; 067 Format, unusual; 201 Wordless.

Goodall, John Strickland. *Paddy's Evening Out.* Illus. by author. New York: Atheneum, 1973.
008.42 Animals—pigs; 067 Format, unusual; 173 Theater; 201 Wordless.

Goodall, John Strickland. *Shrewbettina's Birthday.* Illus. by author. New York: Harcourt, 1970.
018 Birthdays; 067 Format, unusual; 201 Wordless.

Goodall, John Strickland. *The Story of an English Village.* Illus. by author. New York: Atheneum, 1979.
064.10 Foreign lands—England; 067 Format, unusual; 138 Progress; 201 Wordless.

Goodall, John Strickland. *The Surprise Picnic.* Illus. by author. New York: Atheneum, 1977.
002.11 Activities—picnicking; 008.09 Animals—cats; 063 Food; 067 Format, unusual; 201 Wordless.

Goodenow, Earle. *The Last Camel.* Illus. by author. New York: Walck, 1968.
008.08 Animals—camels; 064.09 Foreign lands—Egypt.

Goodenow, Earle. *The Owl Who Hated the Dark.* Illus. by author. New York: Walck, 1969.
017.14 Birds—owls; 052.04 Emotions—fear; 119 Night.

Goodsell, Jane. *Katie's Magic Glasses.* Illus. by Barbara Cooney. Boston: Houghton, 1965.
023.09 Careers—doctors; 073 Glasses.

Goodspeed, Peter. *Hugh and Fitzhugh.* Illus. by author. New York: Grosset, 1974.
008.14 Animals—dogs; 096 Language.

Goody Two Shoes' Picture Book. Illus. by Walter Crane. London: Routledge, n.d.
001 ABC Books; 062 Folk and fairy tales; 064.10 Foreign lands—England.

Gordon, Isabel, jt. author. *The Shadow Book.* By Beatrice Schenk De Regniers, and Isabel Gordon.

Gordon, Margaret. *A Paper of Pins.* Illus. by author. New York: Seabury Pr., 1975.
164 Songs.

Gordon, Shirley. *Crystal Is My Friend.* Illus. by Edward Frascino. New York: Harper, 1978.
068 Friendship; 151 School.

Gordon, Shirley. *Crystal Is the New Girl.* Illus. by Edward Frascino. New York: Harper, 1976.
068 Friendship; 121 Non-sexist; 151 School.

Gordon, Shirley. *Grandma Zoo.* Illus. by Whitney Darrow, Jr. New York: Harper, 1978.
008 Animals; 057.02 Family life—grandparents; great-grandparents; 204 Zoos.

Goudey, Alice E. *The Day We Saw the Sun Come Up.* Illus. by Adrienne Adams. New York: Scribner's, 1961.
057 Family life; 169 Sun.

Goudey, Alice E. *The Good Rain.* Illus. by Nora Spicer Unwin. New York: Dutton, 1950.
195.05 Weather—rain.

Grabianski, Janusz. *Androcles and the Lion.* Illus. by author. New York: Watts, 1970.
008.10 Animals—cats, wild; 026.14 Character traits—helpfulness; 026.18 Character traits—kindness to animals; 062 Folk and fairy tales; 064.18 Foreign lands—Italy; 141 Religion.

Grabianski, Janusz. *Cats.* Illus. by author. New York: Watts, 1966.
008.09 Animals—cats.

Grabianski, Janusz. *Dogs.* Illus. by author. New York: Watts, 1968.
008.14 Animals—dogs.

Grabianski, Janusz. *Grabianski's Wild Animals.* Illus. by author. New York: Watts, 1969.
008 Animals.

Grabianski, Janusz. *Horses.* Illus. by author. New York: Watts, 1966.
008.28 Animals—horses.

Graham, Al. *Timothy Turtle.* Illus. by Tony Palazzo. New York: Walck, 1946.
026.01 Character traits—ambition; 026.14 Character traits—helpfulness; 068 Friendship; 142.05 Reptiles—turtles.

Graham, John. *A Crowd of Cows.* Illus. by Feodor Stepanovich Rojankovsky. New York: Harcourt, 1968.
008 Animals; 120 Noise.

Graham, John. *I Love You, Mouse.* Illus. by Thomas Anthony de Paola. New York: Harcourt, 1976.
008 Animals.

Graham, Lorenz. *David He No Fear.* Illus. by Ann Grifalconi. New York: Crowell, 1971.
141 Religion.

Graham, Lorenz. *Every Man Heart Lay Down.* Illus. by Colleen Browning. New York: Crowell, 1970.
141 Religion.

Graham, Lorenz. *God Wash the World and Start Again.* Illus. by Clare Romano Ross. New York: Crowell, 1971.
141.01 Religion—Noah.

Graham, Lorenz. *Hongry Catch the Foolish Boy.* Illus. by James Brown, Jr. New York: Crowell, 1973.
141 Religion.

Graham, Lorenz. *A Road Down in the Sea.* Illus. by Gregorio Prestopino. New York: Crowell, 1970.
141 Religion.

Graham, Lorenz. *Song of the Boat.* Illus. by Leo Dillon, and Diane Dillon. New York: Crowell, 1975.
019 Boats, ships; 047 Dreams; 064.01 Foreign lands—Africa; 134 Poetry, rhyme.

Graham, Margaret Bloy. *Be Nice to Spiders.* Illus. by author. New York: Harper, 1967.
090 Insects and spiders; 204 Zoos.

Graham, Margaret Bloy. *Benjy and the Barking Bird.* Illus. by author. New York: Harper, 1971.
008.14 Animals—dogs; 017.15 Birds—parrots, parakeets; 052.03 Emotions—envy, jealousy.

Graham, Margaret Bloy. *Benjy's Boat Trip.* Illus. by author. New York: Harper, 1977.
008.14 Animals—dogs; 019 Boats, ships.

Graham, Margaret Bloy. *Benjy's Dog House.* Illus. by author. New York: Harper, 1973.
008.14 Animals—dogs.

Graham, Mary Stuart Campbell. *The Pirates' Bridge.* Illus. by Winifred Milius Lubell. New York: Lothrop, 1960.
132 Pirates.

Gramatky, Hardie. *Bolivar.* Illus. by author. New York: Putnam's, 1961.
008.16 Animals—donkeys; 064.32 Foreign lands—South America.

Gramatky, Hardie. *Hercules.* Illus. by author. New York: Putnam's, 1940.
023.10 Careers—firefighters; 059 Fire; 115 Museums; 184 Trucks.

Gramatky, Hardie. *Homer and the Circus Train.* Illus. by author. New York: Putnam's, 1957.
028 Circus, clowns; 179 Trains.

Gramatky, Hardie. *Little Toot.* Illus. by author. New York: Putnam's, 1939.
019 Boats, ships; 026.01 Character traits—ambition.

Gramatky, Hardie. *Little Toot on the Thames.* Illus. by author. New York: Putnam's, 1964.
019 Boats, ships; 064.10 Foreign lands—England.

Gramatky, Hardie. *Little Toot through the Golden Gate.* Illus. by author. New York: Putnam's, 1975.
019 Boats, ships; 029 City; 026.16 Character traits—individuality.

Gramatky, Hardie. *Loopy.* Illus. by author. New York: Putnam's, 1941.
002.05 Activities—flying; 004 Airplanes.

Gramatky, Hardie. *Nikos and the Sea God.* Illus. by author. New York: Putnam's, 1963.
023.11 Careers—fishermen; 062 Folk and fairy tales; 117 Mythical creatures; 141 Religion.

Gramatky, Hardie. *Sparky.* Illus. by author. New York: Putnam's, 1952.
022 Cable cars; 180 Transportation.

Grant, Anne. *Danbury's Burning! The Story of Sybil Ludington's Ride.* Illus. by Pat Howell. New York: Walck, 1976.
121 Non-sexist; 189 U.S. history.

Grant, Sandy. *Hey, Look at Me! A City ABC*. Illus. by Larry Mulvehill. New York: Dutton, 1973.
001 ABC Books; 029 City.

Gray, Genevieve. *How Far, Felipe?* Illus. by Ann Grifalconi. New York: Harper, 1978.
002.16 Activities—traveling;
008.16 Animals—donkeys;
026.25 Character traits—perseverance.

Gray, Genevieve. *Keep an Eye on Kevin: Safety Begins at Home*. Illus. by Don Madden. New York: Lothrop, 1973.
013 Babies; 016.32 Behavior—sibling rivalry; 148 Safety.

Gray, Genevieve. *Send Wendell*. Illus. by Symeon Shimin. New York: McGraw-Hill, 1974.
026.14 Character traits—helpfulness;
053.01 Ethnic groups in the U.S.—Afro-Americans; 057 Family life.

Grayson, Marion F., comp. *Let's Count and Count Out*. Illus. by Deborah Derr McClintock. Bethesda, MD: Luce, 1975.
033 Counting; 134 Poetry, rhyme.

Green, Adam. *The Funny Bunny Factory*. Illus. by Leonard Weisgard. New York: Grosset, 1950.
008.46 Animals—rabbits;
083.04 Holidays—Easter.

The Green Grass Grows All Around. Illus. by Hilde Hoffmann. A traditional folk song. New York: Macmillan, 1968.
133 Plants; 134 Poetry, rhyme;
164 Songs.

Green, Mary McBurney. *Everybody Has a House and Everybody Eats*. Illus. by Louis Klein. New York: Abelard-Schuman, 1944.
058 Farms; 086 Houses.

Green, Mary McBurney. *Is It Hard? Is It Easy?* Illus. by Lucienne Bloch. New York: Abelard-Schuman, 1948.
032 Concepts.

Green, Norma B. *The Hole in the Dike*. Illus. by Eric Carle. New York: Crowell, 1974.
026.14 Character traits—helpfulness;
064.14 Foreign lands—Holland.

Greenaway, Kate. *A Apple Pie*. Illus. by author. New York: Warne, 1886.
001 ABC Books.

Greenaway, Kate. *Marigold Garden*. Illus. by author. New York: Warne, 1885.
134 Poetry, rhyme.

Greenaway, Kate. *Under the Window*. Illus. by author. New York: Warne, 1879.
134 Poetry, rhyme.

Greenberg, Barbara. *The Bravest Babysitter*. Illus. by Diane Paterson. New York: Dial Pr., 1977.
002.01 Activities—babysitting;
013 Babies; 052.04 Emotions—fear;
195 Weather.

Greenberg, Polly. *O Lord, I Wish I Was a Buzzard*. Illus. by Aliki Liacouras Brandenberg. New York: Macmillan, 1968.
053.01 Ethnic groups in the U.S.—Afro-Americans; 057 Family life; 058 Farms;
133 Plants.

Greene, Carla. *Animal Doctors: What Do They Do?* Illus. by Leonard P. Kessler. New York: Harper, 1967.
023.30 Careers—veterinarians.

Greene, Carla. *Cowboys: What Do They Do?* Illus. by Leonard P. Kessler. New York: Harper, 1972.
035 Cowboys.

Greene, Carla. *Doctors and Nurses: What Do They Do?* Illus. by Leonard P. Kessler. New York: Harper, 1963.
023.09 Careers—doctors;
023.19 Careers—nurses.

Greene, Carla. *A Hotel Holiday*. Illus. by William L. Hoffman. Chicago: Melmont, 1954.
085 Hotels.

Greene, Carla. *I Want to Be a Carpenter*. Illus. by Frances Eckart. Chicago: Children's Pr., 1959.
023.05 Careers—carpenters.

Greene, Carla. *A Motor Holiday*. Illus. by Harold L. Van Pelt. Chicago: Melmont, 1956.
002.16 Activities—traveling.

Greene, Carla. *Railroad Engineers and Airplane Pilots: What Do They Do?* Illus. by Leonard P. Kessler. New York: Harper, 1964.
023.01 Careers—airplane pilots;
023.22 Careers—railroad engineers.

Greene, Carla. *Soldiers and Sailors: What Do They Do?* Illus. by Leonard P. Kessler. New York: Harper, 1963.
023.17 Careers—military.

Greene, Carla. *Truck Drivers: What Do They Do?* Illus. by Leonard P. Kessler. New York: Harper, 1967.
023.29 Careers—truck drivers;
184 Trucks.

Greene, Ellin, reteller. *Princess Rosetta and the Popcorn Man.* Illus. by Trina Schart Hyman. From The Pot of Gold by Mary E. Wilkins. New York: Lothrop, 1971.
062 Folk and fairy tales; 147 Royalty.

Greene, Ellin. *The Pumpkin Giant.* Illus. by Trina Schart Hyman. New York: Lothrop, 1970.
063 Food; 072 Giants;
083.07 Holidays—Halloween.

Greene, Graham. *The Little Fire Engine.* Illus. by Edward Jeffrey Irving Ardizzone. Garden City, NY: Doubleday, 1973.
059 Fire; 138 Progress.

Greene, Graham. *The Little Train.* Illus. by Edward Jeffrey Irving Ardizzone. Garden City, NY: Doubleday, 1973.
016.27 Behavior—running away;
179 Trains.

Greene, Roberta. *Two and Me Makes Three.* Illus. by Paul Galdone. New York: Coward, 1970.
053.07 Ethnic groups in the U.S.—Multi-ethnic.

Greenfield, Eloise. *Africa Dream.* Illus. by Carole Byard. Scranton, PA: John Day, 1977.
047 Dreams; 064.01 Foreign lands—Africa.

Greenfield, Eloise. *First Pink Light.* Illus. by Moneta Barnett. New York: Crowell, 1976.
053.01 Ethnic groups in the U.S.—Afro-Americans; 057.01 Family life—fathers.

Greenfield, Eloise. *Me and Nessie.* Illus. by Moneta Barnett. New York: Crowell, 1975.
053.01 Ethnic groups in the U.S.—Afro-Americans; 057 Family life;
089.01 Imagination—imaginary friends.

Greenfield, Eloise. *She Come Bringing Me That Little Baby Girl.* Illus. by John Steptoe. Philadelphia: Lippincott, 1974.
013 Babies; 016.32 Behavior—sibling rivalry; 052.03 Emotions—envy, jealousy; 053.01 Ethnic groups in the U.S.—Afro-Americans.

Greenwood, Ann. *A Pack of Dreams.* Illus. by Bernard Colonna. Englewood Cliffs, NJ: Prentice-Hall, 1978.
008 Animals; 047 Dreams; 134 Poetry, rhyme.

Gregor, Arthur, jt. author. *Animal Babies.* By Camilla Koffler, and Arthur Gregor.

Gregor, Arthur. *One, Two, Three, Four, Five.* Illus. by Robert Doisneau. Philadelphia: Lippincott, 1956.
033 Counting.

Greisman, Joan, jt. author. *Things I Hate!* By Harriet Wittels, and Joan Greisman.

Gretz, Susanna. *Teddybears ABC.* Illus. by author. Chicago: Follett, 1975.
001 ABC Books; 033 Counting;
177.08 Toys—teddy bears.

Gretz, Susanna. *Teddybears One to Ten.* Illus. by author. Chicago: Follett, 1969.
033 Counting; 177.08 Toys—teddy bears.

Grieg, Edvard Hagerup. *E. H. Grieg's Peer Gynt.* Illus. by Yoshiharu Suzuki. Adapted by Makoto Oishi. Translated by Ann Brannen. Tokyo, Japan: Japan Pub., 1971.
062 Folk and fairy tales; 064.25 Foreign lands—Norway.

Grifalconi, Ann. *City Rhythms.* Illus. by author. Indianapolis: Bobbs-Merrill, 1965.
029 City; 053.01 Ethnic groups in the U.S.—Afro-Americans.

Grifalconi, Ann. *The Toy Trumpet.* Illus. by author. Indianapolis: Bobbs-Merrill, 1968.
064.24 Foreign lands—Mexico;
116 Music; 177 Toys.

Grimm, Jakob Ludwig Karl, and Grimm, Wilhelm Karl. *The Bearskinner.* Illus. by Felix Hoffmann. New York: Atheneum, 1978.
042 Devil; 062 Folk and fairy tales.

Grimm, Jakob Ludwig Karl, and Grimm, Wilhelm Karl. *The Bremen Town Musicians.* Illus. by Paul Galdone. New York: McGraw-Hill, 1968.
008 Animals; 062 Folk and fairy tales;
125 Old age.

Grimm, Jakob Ludwig Karl, and Grimm, Wilhelm Karl. *Hans in Luck.* Illus. by Felix Hoffmann. New York: Atheneum, 1975.
026.21 Character traits—luck; 062 Folk and fairy tales.

Grimm, Wilhelm Karl, jt. author. *The Bearskinner.* By Jakob Ludwig Karl Grimm, and Wilhelm Karl Grimm.

Grimm, Wilhelm Karl, jt. author. *The Bremen Town Musicians.* By Jakob Ludwig Karl Grimm, and Wilhelm Karl Grimm.

Grimm, Wilhelm Karl, jt. author. *Hans in Luck.* By Jakob Ludwig Karl Grimm, and Wilhelm Karl Grimm.

Grossbart, Francine B. *A Big City*. Illus. by author. New York: Harper, 1966.
001 ABC Books; 029 City.

Grosvenor, Donna. *Zoo Babies*. Illus. by author. Washington, DC: National Geographic Soc., 1979.
008 Animals; 204 Zoos.

Groves-Raines, Antony, jt. author. *On Christmas Day in the Morning!* By John Meredith Langstaff, and Antony Groves-Raines.

Groves-Raines, Antony. *The Tidy Hen*. Illus. by author. New York: Harcourt, 1961.
017.04 Birds—chickens;
026.05 Character traits—cleanliness.

Guilfoile, Elizabeth. *Have You Seen My Brother*. Illus. by Mary Stevens. Chicago: Follett, 1962.
016.20 Behavior—lost; 023.21 Careers—police officers; 029 City.

Guilfoile, Elizabeth. *Nobody Listens to Andrew*. Illus. by Mary Stevens. Chicago: Follett, 1957.
008.06 Animals—bears;
016.26 Behavior—needing someone.

Gullo, Steven V., jt. author. *When People Die*. By Joanne Bernstein, and Steven V. Gullo.

Gunning, Monica. *The Two Georges: Los Dos Jorges*. Illus. by Veronica Mary Miracle. Detroit: Blaine-Ethridge, 1976.
001 ABC Books; 065 Foreign languages; 134 Poetry, rhyme.

Gunthrop, Karen. *Adam and the Wolf*. Illus. by Attilio Cassinelli. Garden City, NY: Doubleday, 1967.
008.61 Animals—wolves;
016.08 Behavior—disbelief; 063 Food.

Gurney, Eric, jt. author. *The King, the Mice and the Cheese*. By Nancy Gurney, and Eric Gurney.

Gurney, Nancy, and Gurney, Eric. *The King, the Mice and the Cheese*. Illus. by Jean Vallier. New York: Random House, 1965.
008.34 Animals—mice; 063 Food;
147 Royalty.

Haas, Irene. *The Maggie B*. Illus. by author. New York: Atheneum, 1975.
016.38 Behavior—wishing; 019 Boats, ships; 134 Poetry, rhyme; 153 Sea and seashore.

Hader, Berta Hoerner, and Hader, Elmer Stanley. *The Big Snow*. Illus. by authors. New York: Macmillan, 1948.
195.07 Weather—snow.

Hader, Berta Hoerner, and Hader, Elmer Stanley. *Cock-A-Doodle-Do; The Story of a Little Red Rooster*. Illus. by authors. New York: Macmillan, 1939.
017.04 Birds—chickens; 017.08 Birds—ducks; 058 Farms.

Hader, Berta Hoerner, and Hader, Elmer Stanley. *Lost in the Zoo*. Illus. by authors. New York: Macmillan, 1951.
016.20 Behavior—lost; 204 Zoos.

Hader, Berta Hoerner, and Hader, Elmer Stanley. *The Mighty Hunter*. Illus. by authors. New York: Macmillan, 1943.
049 Ecology; 053.04 Ethnic groups in the U.S.—Indians; 151 School;
166.08 Sports—hunting.

Hader, Berta Hoerner, and Hader, Elmer Stanley. *Mister Billy's Gun*. Illus. by authors. New York: Macmillan, 1960.
002.06 Activities—gardening; 017 Birds; 026.18 Character traits—kindness to animals; 191 Violence, anti-violence;
194 Weapons.

Hader, Berta Hoerner, and Hader, Elmer Stanley. *The Story of Pancho and the Bull with the Crooked Tail*. Illus. by authors. New York: Oxford Univ. Pr., 1933.
008.12 Animals—cows, bulls;
064.24 Foreign lands—Mexico.

Hader, Elmer Stanley, jt. author. *The Big Snow*. By Berta Hoerner Hader, and Elmer Stanley Hader.

Hader, Elmer Stanley, jt. author. *Cock-A-Doodle-Do; The Story of a Little Red Rooster*. By Berta Hoerner Hader, and Elmer Stanley Hader.

Hader, Elmer Stanley, jt. author. *Lost in the Zoo*. By Berta Hoerner Hader, and Elmer Stanley Hader.

Hader, Elmer Stanley, jt. author. *The Mighty Hunter*. By Berta Hoerner Hader, and Elmer Stanley Hader.

Hader, Elmer Stanley, jt. author. *Mister Billy's Gun*. By Berta Hoerner Hader, and Elmer Stanley Hader.

Hader, Elmer Stanley, jt. author. *The Story of Pancho and the Bull with the Crooked Tail*. By Berta Hoerner Hader, and Elmer Stanley Hader.

Hahn, Hannelore. *Take a Giant Step*. Illus. by Margot Zemach. Boston: Little, 1960.
069 Games.

Hair. Illus. by Christine Sharr. New York: Grosset, 1971.
076 Hair.

Haiz, Danah. *Jonah's Journey.* Illus. by H. Hechtkopf. Minneapolis: Lerner, 1973.
008.60 Animals—whales; 141 Religion.

Haley, Gail Diana Einhart. *Go Away, Stay Away.* Illus. by author. New York: Scribner's, 1977.
074 Goblins; 154 Seasons.

Haley, Gail Diana Einhart. *Jack Jouett's Ride.* Illus. by author. New York: Viking, 1973.
189 U.S. history.

Haley, Gail Diana Einhart. *Noah's Ark.* Illus. by author. New York: Atheneum, 1971.
008 Animals; 019 Boats, ships; 049 Ecology; 141.01 Religion—Noah.

Haley, Gail Diana Einhart. *The Post Office Cat.* Illus. by author. New York: Scribner's, 1976.
008.09 Animals—cats; 023.16 Careers—mail carriers; 064.10 Foreign lands—England.

Haley, Gail Diana Einhart. *A Story, a Story.* Illus. by author. New York: Atheneum, 1970.
062 Folk and fairy tales; 064.01 Foreign lands—Africa.

Hall, Bill. *Fish Tale.* Illus. by John E. Johnson. New York: Norton, 1967.
060 Fish; 166.05 Sports—fishing.

Hall, Bill. *A Year in the Forest.* Illus. by Feodor Stepanovich Rojankovsky. New York: McGraw-Hill, 1973.
008 Animals; 154 Seasons.

Hall, Donald. *Andrew the Lion Farmer.* Illus. by Jane Miller. New York: Watts, 1959.
087 Humor.

Hallinan, P. K. See Hallinan, Patrick K.

Hallinan, Patrick K. *I'm Glad to Be Me.* Illus. by author. Chicago: Children's Pr., 1977.
002 Activities; 057.04 Family life—the only child.

Hallinan, Patrick K. *Just Being Alone.* Illus. by author. Chicago: Children's Pr., 1976.
002 Activities; 016.33 Behavior—solitude; 057.04 Family life—the only child.

Hallinan, Patrick K. *That's What a Friend Is.* Illus. by author. Chicago: Children's Pr., 1977.
068 Friendship; 134 Poetry, rhyme.

Hamberger, John F. *The Day the Sun Disappeared.* Illus. by author. New York: Norton, 1964.
008 Animals; 049 Ecology; 152 Science; 169 Sun.

Hamberger, John F. *Hazel Was an Only Pet.* Illus. by author. New York: Norton, 1968.
008.14 Animals—dogs; 057.04 Family life—the only child; 131 Pets.

Hamberger, John F. *The Lazy Dog.* Illus. by author. New York: Four Winds Pr., 1971.
008.14 Animals—dogs; 177.02 Toys—balls; 201 Wordless.

Hamberger, John F. *The Peacock Who Lost His Tail.* Illus. by author. New York: Norton, 1967.
017.16 Birds—peacocks, peahens; 026.27 Character traits—pride.

Hamberger, John F. *This Is the Day.* Illus. by author. New York: Grosset, 1971.
008.23 Animals—groundhogs; 083.06 Holidays—Groundhog Day.

Hamil, Thomas A. *Brother Alonzo.* Illus. by author. New York: Macmillan, 1957.
141 Religion.

Handforth, Thomas Scofield. *Mei Li.* Illus. by author. Garden City, NY: Doubleday, 1938.
064.06 Foreign lands—China; 083.02 Holidays—Chinese New Year.

Hanlon, Emily. *What If a Lion Eats Me and I Fall into a Hippopotamus' Mud Hole?* Illus. by Leigh Grant. New York: Delacorte Pr., 1975.
052.04 Emotions—fear; 089 Imagination; 204 Zoos.

Hanson, Joan. *I Don't Like Timmy.* Illus. by author. Minneapolis: Carolrhoda Books, 1972.
013 Babies; 068 Friendship.

Hanson, Joan. *I Won't Be Afraid.* Illus. by author. Minneapolis: Carolrhoda Books, 1974.
016.14 Behavior—growing up; 052.04 Emotions—fear.

Hapgood, Miranda. *Martha's Mad Day.* Illus. by Emily Arnold McCully. New York: Crown, 1977.
052.01 Emotions—anger.

Harper, Anita. *How We Work.* Illus. by Christine Roche. New York: Harper, 1977.
002.20 Activities—working; 023 Careers.

Harper, Wilhelmina, reteller. *The Gunniwolf.* Illus. by William Wiesner. New York: Dutton, 1967.
008.61 Animals—wolves; 016.22 Behavior—misbehavior; 061 Flowers; 064.12 Foreign lands—Germany.

Harris, Leon A. *The Great Picture Robbery.* Illus. by Joseph Schindelman. New York: Atheneum, 1963.
008.34 Animals—mice; 011 Art; 036 Crime; 064.11 Foreign lands—France.

Harris, Robie H. *Don't Forget to Come Back.* Illus. by Tony De Luna. New York: Knopf, 1978.
057 Family life.

Harrison, David Lee. *The Case of Og, the Missing Frog.* Illus. by Jerry Warshaw. Skokie, IL: Rand McNally, 1972.
005 Amphibians; 134 Poetry, rhyme.

Harrison, David Lee. *Little Turtle's Big Adventure.* Illus. by J. P. Miller. New York: Random House, 1969.
026.18 Character traits—kindness to animals; 138 Progress; 142.05 Reptiles—turtles.

Hart, Jeanne McGahey. *Scareboy.* Illus. by Gerhardt Hurt. Berkeley: Parnassus, 1957.
087 Humor; 150 Scarecrows.

Hartclius, Margaret A. *The Chicken's Child.* Illus. by author. Garden City, NY: Doubleday, 1975.
017.04 Birds—chickens; 142.01 Reptiles—alligators, crocodiles; 201 Wordless.

Haskins, Ilma. *Color Seems.* Illus. by author. New York: Vanguard, 1973.
032.01 Concepts—color.

Hastings, Evelyn Belmont. *The Department Store.* Illus. by Lewis A. Ogan. Chicago: Melmont, 1956.
160 Shopping; 168 Stores.

Hautzig, Esther. *At Home; A Visit in Four Languages.* Illus. by Aliki Liacouras Brandenberg. New York: Macmillan, 1968.
057 Family life; 064.11 Foreign lands—France; 064.30 Foreign lands—Russia; 064.34 Foreign lands—Spain; 065 Foreign languages.

Hautzig, Esther. *In the Park; An Excursion in Four Languages.* Illus. by Ezra Jack Keats. New York: Macmillan, 1968.
064.11 Foreign lands—France; 064.30 Foreign lands—Russia; 064.34 Foreign lands—Spain; 065 Foreign languages.

Hawes, Judy. *Fireflies in the Night.* Illus. by Kazue Mizumura. New York: Crowell, 1963.
057.02 Family life—grandparents; great-grandparents; 058 Farms; 090 Insects and spiders; 152 Science.

Hawkins, Mark. *A Lion Under Her Bed.* Illus. by Jean Vallario. New York: Holt, 1978.
015 Bedtime; 008.10 Animals—cats, wild.

Hawkinson, John. *The Old Stump.* Illus. by author. Chicago: Albert Whitman, 1965.
008.34 Animals—mice; 181 Trees.

Hawkinson, John. *Where the Wild Apples Grow.* Illus. by author. Chicago: Albert Whitman, 1967.
026.12 Character traits—freedom.

Hawkinson, John, and Hawkinson, Lucy Ozone. *Robins and Rabbits.* Illus. by John Hawkinson. Chicago: Albert Whitman, 1960.
008 Animals; 017.20 Birds—robins.

Hawkinson, Lucy Ozone. *Dance, Dance, Amy-Chan!* Illus. by author. Chicago: Albert Whitman, 1964.
053.05 Ethnic groups in the U.S.—Japanese-Americans.

Hawkinson, Lucy Ozone, jt. author. *Robins and Rabbits.* By John Hawkinson, and Lucy Ozone Hawkinson.

Hay, Dean. *I See a Lot of Things.* Illus. by author. New York: Lion, 1966.
157 Senses.

Hay, Dean. *Now I Can Count.* Illus. by author. New York: Lion, 1968.
033 Counting; 174 Time.

Hayes, Geoffrey. *Bear by Himself.* Illus. by author. New York: Harper, 1976.
016.33 Behavior—solitude; 177.08 Toys—teddy bears.

Hayes, William D., jt. author. *Mexicallie Soup.* By Kathryn Hitte, and William D. Hayes.

Haynes, Robert, jt. author. *The Elephant That Ga-lumphed.* By Nanda Weedon Ward, and Robert Haynes.

Hays, Daniel, jt. author. *Charley Sang a Song.* By Hoffman Reynolds Hays, and Daniel Hays.

Hays, H. R. See Hays, Hoffman Reynolds.

Hays, Hoffman Reynolds, and Hays, Daniel. *Charley Sang a Song.* Illus. by Uri Shulevitz. New York: Harper, 1964.
002.05 Activities—flying.

Hays, Wilma Pitchford. *Little Yellow Fur.* Illus. by Richard Cuffari. New York: Coward, 1973.
053.04 Ethnic groups in the U.S.—Indians.

Haywood, Carolyn. *A Christmas Fantasy.* Illus by Glenys Ambrus, and Victor G. Ambrus. New York: Morrow, 1972.
083.03 Holidays—Christmas.

Hazelton, Elizabeth Baldwin. *Sammy, the Crow Who Remembered.* Illus. by Ann Atwood. New York: Scribner's, 1969.
017.06 Birds—crows; 057 Family life.

Hazen, Barbara Shook. *The Gorilla Did It!* Illus. by Ray Cruz. New York: Atheneum, 1974.
008.22 Animals—gorillas;
089.01 Imagination—imaginary friends.

Hazen, Barbara Shook. *Happy, Sad, Silly, Mad: A Beginning Book about Emotions.* Illus. by Elizabeth Dauber. Editorial consultant: Mary Elting. New York: Grosset, 1971.
052 Emotions.

Hazen, Barbara Shook. *Tight Times.* Illus. by Trina Schart Hyman. New York: Viking, 1979.
008.09 Animals—cats; 057 Family life; 057.04 Family life—the only child; 135 Poverty.

Hazen, Barbara Shook. *Two Homes to Live In.* Illus. by Peggy Luks. New York: Human Sci. Pr., 1978.
045 Divorce; 052 Emotions.

Hazen, Barbara Shook. *Where Do Bears Sleep?* Illus. by Ian E. Staunton. Reading: Addison-Wesley, 1970.
008 Animals; 134 Poetry, rhyme; 162 Sleep.

Hazen, Barbara Shook. *Why Couldn't I Be an Only Kid Like You, Wigger?* Illus. by Leigh Grant. New York: Atheneum, 1975.
013 Babies; 016.32 Behavior—sibling rivalry; 052.03 Emotions—envy, jealousy; 057.04 Family life—the only child.

Hazen, Barbara Shook, and Ungerer, Tomi. *The Sorcerer's Apprentice.* Illus. by Tomi Ungerer. New York: Lancelot Pr., 1969.
016.22 Behavior—misbehavior; 103 Magic.

Heathers, Anne, and Frances, Esteban. *The Thread Soldiers.* Illus. by Esteban Frances. New York: Harcourt, 1960.
008.34 Animals—mice; 177.06 Toys—soldiers; 177.07 Toys—string.

Hefter, Richard. *The Strawberry Book of Shapes.* Illus. by author. New York: Larousse, 1976.
032.07 Concepts—shape.

Heide, Florence Parry. *The Shrinking of Treehorn.* Illus. by Edward St. John Gorey. New York: Holiday, 1971.
057 Family life; 087 Humor; 137 Problem solving.

Heilbroner, Joan. *Robert the Rose Horse.* Illus. by Philip Day Eastman. New York: Random House, 1972.
008.28 Animals—horses; 061 Flowers; 087 Humor.

Heilbroner, Joan. *This Is the House Where Jack Lives.* Illus. by Aliki Liacouras Brandenberg. New York: Harper, 1962.
038 Cumulative tales; 129 Participation.

Helena, Ann. *The Lie.* Illus. by Ellen Pizer. Chicago: Children's Pr., 1977.
016.21 Behavior—lying; 052 Emotions; 068 Friendship.

Heller, George. *Hiroshi's Wonderful Kite.* Illus. by Kyuzo Tsugami. Morristown, NJ: Silver Burdett, 1968.
036 Crime; 064.19 Foreign lands—Japan; 094 Kites.

Hellsing, Lennart. *The Wonderful Pumpkin.* Illus. by Svend Otto. New York: Atheneum, 1976.
008.06 Animals—bears; 063 Food; 083.07 Holidays—Halloween.

Henrioud, Charles. *Mr. Noah and the Animals. Monsieur Noe et les Animaux.* Illus. by author. New York: Walck, 1960.
008 Animals; 065 Foreign languages; 141.01 Religion—Noah.

Herrmann, Frank. *The Giant Alexander.* Illus. by George Him. New York: McGraw-Hill, 1964.
064.10 Foreign lands—England; 072 Giants.

Herrmann, Frank. *The Giant Alexander and the Circus.* Illus. by George Him. New York: McGraw-Hill, 1966.
028 Circus, clowns; 064.10 Foreign lands—England; 072 Giants.

Hewett, Anita. *The Little White Hen.* Illus. by William Stobbs. New York: McGraw-Hill, 1963.
017.04 Birds—chickens; 038 Cumulative tales; 062 Folk and fairy tales.

Hewett, Anita. *The Tale of the Turnip.* Illus. by Margery Gill. New York: McGraw-Hill, 1961.
038 Cumulative tales; 129 Participation; 133 Plants.

Heymans, Margriet. *Pippin and Robber Grumblecroak's Big Baby.* Illus. by author. Reading: Addison-Wesley, 1973.
036 Crime; 139 Puppets.

Heyward, Dubose. *The Country Bunny and the Little Gold Shoes.* Illus. by Marjorie Flack. Boston: Houghton, 1939.
008.46 Animals—rabbits; 026.17 Character traits—kindness; 083.04 Holidays—Easter.

Hickman, Martha Whitmore. *My Friend William Moved Away.* Illus. by Bill Myers. Nashville: Abingdon Pr., 1979.
068 Friendship; 114 Moving.

Hill, Elizabeth Starr. *Evan's Corner.* Illus. by Nancy Grossman. New York: Holt, 1967.
026.14 Character traits—helpfulness; 053.01 Ethnic groups in the U.S.—Afro-Americans; 057 Family life.

Hille-Brandts, Lene. *The Little Black Hen.* Illus. by Sigrid Heuck. Chicago: Children's Pr., 1968.
016.09 Behavior—dissatisfaction; 017.04 Birds—chickens.

Hillert, Margaret. *The Birthday Car.* Illus. by Kelly Oechsli. Chicago: Follett, 1966.
018 Birthdays; 177 Toys.

Hillert, Margaret. *The Funny Baby.* Illus. by Hertha Depper. Chicago: Follett, 1963.
017.08 Birds—ducks; 062 Folk and fairy tales.

Hillert, Margaret. *The Little Runaway.* Illus. by Irv Anderson. Chicago: Follett, 1966.
008.09 Animals—cats; 016.27 Behavior—running away.

Hillert, Margaret. *The Magic Beans.* Illus. by Mel Pekarsky. Chicago: Follett, 1966.
062 Folk and fairy tales; 072 Giants.

Hillert, Margaret. *Play Ball.* Illus. by Dick Martin. Chicago: Follett, 1978.
002.12 Activities—playing; 069 Games; 166.01 Sports—baseball.

Hillert, Margaret. *The Three Goats.* Illus. by Mel Pekarsky. Chicago: Follett, 1963.
008.21 Animals—goats; 062 Folk and fairy tales; 117 Mythical creatures; 183 Trolls.

Hillert, Margaret. *The Yellow Boat.* Illus. by Ed Young. Chicago: Follett, 1966.
019 Boats, ships.

Himler, Ronald Norbert. *The Girl on the Yellow Giraffe.* Illus. by author. New York: Harper, 1976.
029 City; 089 Imagination.

Hippel, Ursula Von. See Von Hippel, Ursula.

Hirawa, Yasuko, comp. *Song of the Sour Plum and Other Japanese Children's Songs.* Illus. by Setsuko Majima. Translated by Yasuko Hirawa. New York: Walker, 1968.
064.19 Foreign lands—Japan; 062 Folk and fairy tales; 164 Songs.

Hirsh, Marilyn Joyce. *Captain Jeri and Rabbi Jacob.* Illus. by author. Adapted from a Jewish folktale. New York: Holiday, 1976.
062 Folk and fairy tales; 093 Jewish culture.

Hirsh, Marilyn Joyce. *Could Anything Be Worse?* Illus. by author. A Yiddish tale. New York: Holiday, 1974.
087 Humor; 093 Jewish culture.

Hirsh, Marilyn Joyce. *Deborah the Dybbuk, a Ghost Story.* Illus. by author. New York: Holiday, 1978.
064.15 Foreign lands—Hungary; 071 Ghosts; 093 Jewish culture.

Hirsh, Marilyn Joyce. *The Pink Suit.* Illus. by author. New York: Crown, 1970.
002.15 Activities—trading; 052.02 Emotions—embarrassment; 057 Family life; 093 Jewish culture.

Hirsh, Marilyn Joyce. *The Rabbi and the Twenty-Nine Witches.* Illus. by author. New York: Holiday, 1976.
026.06 Character traits—cleverness; 093 Jewish culture; 199 Witches.

Hirsh, Marilyn Joyce. *Where Is Yonkela?* Illus. by author. New York: Crown, 1969.
013 Babies; 016.20 Behavior—lost; 093 Jewish culture.

Hirsh, Marilyn Joyce, and Narayan, Maya. *Leela and the Watermelon*. Illus. by Marilyn Joyce Hirsh. New York: Crown, 1971.
013 Babies; 063 Food; 064.16 Foreign lands—India.

The History of Mother Twaddle and the Marvelous Achievements of Her Son Jack. Illus. by Paul Galdone. New York: Seabury Pr., 1974.
062 Folk and fairy tales; 072 Giants; 134 Poetry, rhyme.

Hitte, Kathryn, and Hayes, William D. *Mexicallie Soup*. Illus. by Anne F. Rockwell. New York: Parents, 1970.
002.03 Activities—cooking;
053.06 Ethnic groups in the U.S.—Mexican-Americans; 057 Family life;
063 Food; 064.24 Foreign lands—Mexico.

Hoban, Lillian. *Arthur's Christmas Cookies*. Illus. by author. New York: Harper, 1972.
002.03 Activities—cooking;
008.37 Animals—monkeys;
083.03 Holidays—Christmas.

Hoban, Lillian. *Arthur's Honey Bear*. Illus. by author. New York: Harper, 1973.
008.37 Animals—monkeys;
177.08 Toys—teddy bears.

Hoban, Lillian. *Arthur's Pen Pal*. Illus. by author. New York: Harper, 1976.
002.21 Activities—writing;
008.37 Animals—monkeys;
016.32 Behavior—sibling rivalry.

Hoban, Lillian. *Arthur's Prize Reader*. Illus. by author. New York: Harper, 1978.
002.13 Activities—reading;
008.37 Animals—monkeys; 057 Family life.

Hoban, Lillian. *Here Come Raccoons*. Illus. by author. New York: Holt, 1977.
008.47 Animals—raccoons; 186 Twins.

Hoban, Lillian. *Mr. Pig and Sonny Too*. Illus. by author. New York: Harper, 1977.
008.42 Animals—pigs; 166.09 Sports—ice skating; 196 Weddings.

Hoban, Lillian, jt. author. *Some Snow Said Hello*. By Russell Conwell Hoban, and Lillian Hoban.

Hoban, Lillian. *Stick-in-the-Mud Turtle*. Illus. by author. New York: Greenwillow, 1977.
016.09 Behavior—dissatisfaction;
135 Poverty; 142.05 Reptiles—turtles.

Hoban, Lillian. *The Sugar Snow Spring*. Illus. by author. New York: Harper, 1973.
008.34 Animals—mice;
154.02 Seasons—spring;
195.02 Weather—cold;
195.07 Weather—snow.

Hoban, Lillian. *Turtle Spring*. Illus. by author. New York: Greenwillow, 1978.
142.05 Reptiles—turtles;
154.02 Seasons—spring.

Hoban, Russell Conwell. *Arthur's New Power*. Illus. by Byron Barton. New York: Crowell, 1978.
138 Progress; 142.01 Reptiles—alligators, crocodiles.

Hoban, Russell Conwell. *A Baby Sister for Frances*. Illus. by Lillian Hoban. New York: Harper, 1964.
013 Babies; 016.27 Behavior—running away; 016.32 Behavior—sibling rivalry;
052.03 Emotions—envy, jealousy;
057 Family life.

Hoban, Russell Conwell. *A Bargain for Frances*. Illus. by Lillian Hoban. New York: Harper, 1970.
068 Friendship.

Hoban, Russell Conwell. *Bedtime for Frances*. Illus. by Garth Montgomery Williams. New York: Harper, 1960.
015 Bedtime.

Hoban, Russell Conwell. *Best Friends for Frances*. Illus. by Lillian Hoban. New York: Harper, 1969.
068 Friendship.

Hoban, Russell Conwell. *A Birthday for Frances*. Illus. by Lillian Hoban. New York: Harper, 1968.
018 Birthdays; 052.03 Emotions—envy, jealousy.

Hoban, Russell Conwell. *Bread and Jam for Frances*. Illus. by Lillian Hoban. New York: Harper, 1964.
063 Food; 151 School.

Hoban, Russell Conwell. *Dinner at Alberta's*. Illus. by James Marshall. New York: Crowell, 1975.
016 Behavior; 054 Etiquette; 063 Food;
142.01 Reptiles—alligators, crocodiles.

Hoban, Russell Conwell. *Emmet Otter's Jug-Band Christmas*. Illus. by Lillian Hoban. New York: Parents, 1971.
008.40 Animals—otters;
026.13 Character traits—generosity;
083.03 Holidays—Christmas; 116 Music.

Hoban, Russell Conwell. *Goodnight*. Illus. by Lillian Hoban. New York: Norton, 1966.
015 Bedtime; 052.04 Emotions—fear; 089 Imagination; 134 Poetry, rhyme.

Hoban, Russell Conwell. *Harvey's Hideout*. Illus. by Lillian Hoban. New York: Parents, 1969.
008.39 Animals—muskrats; 016.10 Behavior—fighting, arguing; 057 Family life.

Hoban, Russell Conwell. *How Tom Beat Captain Najork and His Hired Sportsmen*. Illus. by Quentin Blake. New York: Atheneum, 1974.
016.22 Behavior—misbehavior; 069 Games.

Hoban, Russell Conwell. *The Little Brute Family*. Illus. by Lillian Hoban. New York: Macmillan, 1966.
026.22 Character traits—meanness; 054 Etiquette.

Hoban, Russell Conwell. *The Mole Family's Christmas*. Illus. by Lillian Hoban. New York: Parents, 1969.
008.35 Animals—moles; 026.13 Character traits—generosity; 083.03 Holidays—Christmas.

Hoban, Russell Conwell. *A Near Thing for Captain Najork*. Illus. by Quentin Blake. New York: Atheneum, 1976.
087 Humor.

Hoban, Russell Conwell. *Nothing to Do*. Illus. by Lillian Hoban. New York: Harper, 1964.
008.44 Animals—possums; 016.04 Behavior—boredom.

Hoban, Russell Conwell. *The Sorely Trying Day*. Illus. by Lillian Hoban. New York: Harper, 1964.
016.02 Behavior—bad day; 016.10 Behavior—fighting, arguing.

Hoban, Russell Conwell. *The Stone Doll of Sister Brute*. Illus. by Lillian Hoban. New York: Macmillan, 1968.
008.14 Animals—dogs; 052 Emotions; 177.04 Toys—dolls.

Hoban, Russell Conwell, and Hoban, Lillian. *Some Snow Said Hello*. Illus. by Lillian Hoban. New York: Harper, 1963.
016.32 Behavior—sibling rivalry; 154.04 Seasons—winter; 195.07 Weather—snow.

Hoban, Tana. *Big Ones, Little Ones*. Illus. by author. New York: Greenwillow, 1976.
008 Animals; 032.08 Concepts—size; 201 Wordless.

Hoban, Tana. *Circles, Triangles, and Squares*. Illus. by author. New York: Macmillan, 1974.
032.07 Concepts—shape; 201 Wordless.

Hoban, Tana. *Count and See*. Illus. by author. New York: Macmillan, 1972.
033 Counting.

Hoban, Tana. *Dig, Drill, Dump, Fill*. Illus. by author. New York: Greenwillow, 1975.
102 Machines; 201 Wordless.

Hoban, Tana. *Is It Red? Is It Yellow? Is It Blue?* Illus. by author. New York: Greenwillow, 1978.
029 City; 032.01 Concepts—color; 201 Wordless.

Hoban, Tana. *Look Again*. Illus. by author. New York: Macmillan, 1971.
129 Participation; 157 Senses; 201 Wordless.

Hoban, Tana. *Push-Pull, Empty-Full*. Illus. by author. New York: Macmillan, 1972.
032.06 Concepts—opposites.

Hoban, Tana. *Shapes and Things*. Illus. by author. New York: Macmillan, 1970.
032.07 Concepts—shape; 201 Wordless.

Hoban, Tana. *Where Is It?* Illus. by author. New York: Macmillan, 1974.
008.46 Animals—rabbits; 134 Poetry, rhyme.

Hoberman, Mary Ann. *A House Is a House for Me*. Illus. by Betty Fraser. New York: Viking, 1978.
086 Houses; 134 Poetry, rhyme.

Hoberman, Mary Ann. *I Like Old Clothes*. Illus. by Jacqueline Chwast. New York: Knopf, 1976.
031 Clothing; 121 Non-sexist; 134 Poetry, rhyme.

Hoberman, Mary Ann, and Hoberman, Norman. *How Do I Go?* Illus. by authors. Boston: Little, 1958.
180 Transportation.

Hoberman, Norman, jt. author. *How Do I Go?* By Mary Ann Hoberman, and Norman Hoberman.

Hochman, Sandra. *The Magic Convention*. Illus. by Ben Shecter. Garden City, NY: Doubleday, 1971.
026.01 Character traits—ambition; 103 Magic.

Hoff, Carol. *The Four Friends*. Illus. by Jim Ponter. Chicago: Follett, 1958.
008 Animals; 008.34 Animals—mice.

Hoff, Sydney. *Albert the Albatross.* Illus. by author. New York: Harper, 1961.
017.01 Birds—albatrosses; 153 Sea and seashore.

Hoff, Sydney. *Barkley.* Illus. by author. New York: Harper, 1975.
008.14 Animals—dogs; 028 Circus, clowns; 125 Old age.

Hoff, Sydney. *Chester.* Illus. by author. New York: Harper, 1961.
008.28 Animals—horses.

Hoff, Sydney. *Danny and the Dinosaur.* Illus. by author. New York: Harper, 1958.
044 Dinosaurs; 115 Museums.

Hoff, Sydney. *Dinosaur Do's and Don'ts.* Illus. by author. New York: Dutton, 1975.
044 Dinosaurs; 054 Etiquette.

Hoff, Sydney. *Grizzwold.* Illus. by author. New York: Harper, 1963.
008.06 Animals—bears; 049 Ecology.

Hoff, Sydney. *The Horse in Harry's Room.* Illus. by author. New York: Harper, 1970.
008.28 Animals—horses;
089.01 Imagination—imaginary friends.

Hoff, Sydney. *Julius.* Illus. by author. New York: Harper, 1959.
008.22 Animals—gorillas.

Hoff, Sydney. *Katy's Kitty; Three Kitty Stories.* Illus. by author. New York: Dutton, 1975.
008.09 Animals—cats; 131 Pets.

Hoff, Sydney. *Lengthy.* Illus. by author. New York: Putnam's, 1964.
008.14 Animals—dogs.

Hoff, Sydney. *The Littlest Leaguer.* Illus. by author. New York: Dutton, 1976.
026.31 Character traits—smallness;
069 Games; 166.01 Sports—baseball.

Hoff, Sydney. *My Aunt Rosie.* Illus. by author. New York: Harper, 1972.
057 Family life.

Hoff, Sydney. *Oliver.* Illus. by author. New York: Harper, 1960.
008.17 Animals—elephants;
026.23 Character traits—optimism;
028 Circus, clowns.

Hoff, Sydney. *Pete's Pup; Three Puppy Stories.* Illus. by author. New York: Dutton, 1975.
008.14 Animals—dogs; 131 Pets.

Hoff, Sydney. *Sammy the Seal.* Illus. by author. New York: Harper, 1959.
008.51 Animals—seals; 204 Zoos.

Hoff, Sydney. *Santa's Moose.* Illus. by author. New York: Harper, 1979.
008.38 Animals—moose;
083.03 Holidays—Christmas.

Hoff, Sydney. *Slithers.* Illus. by author. New York: Putnam's, 1968.
142.04 Reptiles—snakes.

Hoff, Sydney. *Slugger Sal's Slump.* Illus. by author. New York: Dutton, 1979.
026.25 Character traits—perseverance;
166.06 Sports—football.

Hoff, Sydney. *Stanley.* Illus. by author. New York: Harper, 1962.
024 Cavemen; 086 Houses.

Hoff, Sydney. *Thunderhoff.* Illus. by author. New York: Harper, 1971.
008.28 Animals—horses; 035 Cowboys.

Hoff, Sydney. *A Walk Past Ellen's House.* Illus. by author. New York: McGraw-Hill, 1973.
068 Friendship.

Hoff, Sydney. *Walpole.* Illus. by author. New York: Harper, 1977.
008.58 Animals—walruses.

Hoff, Sydney. *When Will It Snow?* Illus. by Mary Eileen Chalmers. New York: Harper, 1971.
154.04 Seasons—winter;
195.07 Weather—snow.

Hoff, Sydney. *Where's Prancer?* Illus. by author. New York: Harper, 1960.
083.03 Holidays—Christmas.

Hoff, Sydney. *Who Will Be My Friends?* Illus. by author. New York: Harper, 1960.
068 Friendship; 114 Moving.

Hoffman, Phyllis. *Steffie and Me.* Illus. by Emily Arnold McCully. New York: Harper, 1970.
053.01 Ethnic groups in the U.S.—Afro-Americans; 057 Family life;
068 Friendship; 151 School.

Hoffmann, Felix. *A Boy Went Out to Gather Pears.* Illus. by author. New York: Harcourt, 1963.
038 Cumulative tales.

Hogan, Inez. *About Nono, the Baby Elephant.* Illus. by author. New York: Dutton, 1947.
008.17 Animals—elephants;
016.22 Behavior—misbehavior;
118 Names.

Hogrogian, Nonny. *Apples.* Illus. by author. New York: Macmillan, 1973.
133 Plants; 201 Wordless.

Hogrogian, Nonny. *Billy Goat and His Well-Fed Friends.* Illus. by author. New York: Harper, 1972.
008 Animals; 008.21 Animals—goats; 016.27 Behavior—running away.

Hogrogian, Nonny. *Carrot Cake.* Illus. by author. New York: Greenwillow, 1977.
008.46 Animals—rabbits; 016 Behavior; 026.08 Character traits—compromising; 026.30 Character traits—shyness; 196 Weddings.

Hogrogian, Nonny. *The Hermit and Harry and Me.* Illus. by author. Boston: Little, 1972.
016.18 Behavior—indifference; 068 Friendship.

Hogrogian, Nonny. *One Fine Day.* Illus. by author. New York: Macmillan, 1971.
008.18 Animals—foxes; 038 Cumulative tales.

Hoke, Helen L. *The Biggest Family in the Town.* Illus. by Vance Locke. New York: McKay, 1947.
057 Family life.

Holden, Edith B. *The Hedgehog Feast.* Illus. by author. Words by Rowena Stott. New York: Dutton, 1978.
008.26 Animals—hedgehogs; 063 Food.

Holding, James. *The Lazy Little Zulu.* Illus. by Aliki Liacouras Brandenberg. New York: Morrow, 1962.
026.19 Character traits—laziness; 064.01 Foreign lands—Africa.

Holl, Adelaide. *The ABC of Cars, Trucks and Machines.* Illus. by William Dugan. New York: American Heritage, 1970.
001 ABC Books; 012 Automobiles; 102 Machines; 184 Trucks.

Holl, Adelaide. *Mrs. McGarrity's Peppermint Sweater.* Illus. by Abner Graboff. New York: Lothrop, 1966.
002.08 Activities—knitting; 028 Circus, clowns; 134 Poetry, rhyme.

Holl, Adelaide. *My Father and I.* Illus. by Kjell Ringi. New York: Watts, 1972.
026.01 Character traits—ambition; 057.01 Family life—fathers; 089 Imagination.

Holl, Adelaide. *The Rain Puddle.* Illus. by Roger Antoine Duvoisin. New York: Lothrop, 1965.
008 Animals; 195.05 Weather—rain.

Holl, Adelaide. *The Remarkable Egg.* Illus. by Roger Antoine Duvoisin. New York: Lothrop, 1968.
017 Birds; 177.02 Toys—balls.

Holl, Adelaide. *The Runaway Giant.* Illus. by Mamoru R. Funai. New York: Lothrop, 1967.
016.12 Behavior—gossip; 163 Snowmen.

Holl, Adelaide. *Sir Kevin of Devon.* Illus. by Leonard Weisgard. New York: Lothrop, 1963.
026.04 Character traits—bravery; 095 Knights; 134 Poetry, rhyme.

Holland, Marion. *A Big Ball of String.* Illus. by author. New York: Random House, 1958.
134 Poetry, rhyme; 177.07 Toys—string.

Holland, Viki. *We Are Having a Baby.* Illus. by author. New York: Scribner's, 1972.
013 Babies; 057 Family life.

Holm, Mayling Mack. *A Forest Christmas.* Illus. by author. New York: Harper, 1977.
008 Animals; 083.03 Holidays—Christmas.

Holman, Felice. *Victoria's Castle.* Illus. by Lillian Hoban. New York: Norton, 1966.
017.15 Birds—parrots, parakeets; 087 Humor; 089 Imagination.

Holmes, Efner Tudor. *Amy's Goose.* Illus. by Tasha Tudor. New York: Crowell, 1977.
017.11 Birds—geese; 026.14 Character traits—helpfulness; 026.18 Character traits—kindness to animals.

Holmes, Efner Tudor. *The Christmas Cat.* Illus. by Tasha Tudor. New York: Crowell, 1976.
008.09 Animals—cats; 083.03 Holidays—Christmas.

Holt, Margaret. *David McCheever's Twenty-Nine Dogs.* Illus. by Walter Lorraine. Boston: Houghton, 1963.
008.14 Animals—dogs; 033 Counting; 128 Parades; 160 Shopping.

Holzenthaler, Jean. *My Feet Do.* Illus. by George Ancona. New York: Dutton, 1979.
002 Activities; 006 Anatomy.

Holzenthaler, Jean. *My Hands Can.* Illus. by Nancy Tafuri. New York: Dutton, 1978.
002 Activities; 006 Anatomy.

Homes. Illus. by Christine Sharr. New York: Grosset, 1971.
057 Family life; 086 Houses.

Honert, Dorry Van Den. See Van Den Honert, Dorry.

Hood, Flora. *Living in Navajoland.* Illus. by Mamoru R. Funai. New York: Putnam's, 1970.
053.04 Ethnic groups in the U.S.—Indians.

Hopkins, Lee Bennett. *I Loved Rose Ann.* Illus. by Ingrid Fetz. New York: Knopf, 1976.
016.24 Behavior—misunderstanding; 052 Emotions.

Hopkins, Lee Bennett, comp. *I Think I Saw a Snail.* Illus. by Harold James. Young poems for city seasons. New York: Crown, 1969.
029 City; 053.01 Ethnic groups in the U.S.—Afro-Americans; 134 Poetry, rhyme.

Hopkins, Marjorie. *Three Visitors.* Illus. by Anne F. Rockwell. New York: Parents, 1967.
053.03 Ethnic groups in the U.S.—Eskimos.

Horn, Grace Van. See Van Horn, Grace.

Horvath, Betty F. *Be Nice to Josephine.* Illus. by Pat Grant Porter. New York: Watts, 1970.
016 Behavior; 057 Family life; 121 Non-sexist.

Horvath, Betty F. *The Cheerful Quiet.* Illus. by Jo Ann Stover. New York: Watts, 1969.
120 Noise; 137 Problem solving.

Horvath, Betty F. *Hooray for Jasper.* Illus. by Fermin Rocker. New York: Watts, 1966.
026.31 Character traits—smallness; 053.01 Ethnic groups in the U.S.—Afro-Americans.

Horvath, Betty F. *Jasper and the Hero Business.* Illus. by Donald Alan Bolognese. New York: Watts, 1977.
026.04 Character traits—bravery; 053.01 Ethnic groups in the U.S.—Afro-Americans.

Horvath, Betty F. *Jasper Makes Music.* Illus. by Fermin Rocker. New York: Watts, 1967.
002.20 Activities—working; 053.01 Ethnic groups in the U.S.—Afro-Americans; 116 Music.

Horvath, Betty F. *Will the Real Tommy Wilson Please Stand Up?* Illus. by Charles Robinson. New York: Watts, 1969.
026.16 Character traits—individuality; 052 Emotions; 068 Friendship.

Horwitz, Elinor. *When the Sky Is Like Lace.* Illus. by Barbara Cooney. Philadelphia: Lippincott, 1975.
119 Night.

The House That Jack Built. Illus. by Paul Galdone. New York: McGraw-Hill, 1961.
038 Cumulative tales; 122 Nursery rhymes.

The House That Jack Built. Illus. by Rodney Peppé. New York: Delacorte Pr., 1970.
038 Cumulative tales.

The House That Jack Built. La Maison que Jacques a Batie. Illus. by Antonio Frasconi. New York: Harcourt, 1958.
038 Cumulative tales; 065 Foreign languages; 122 Nursery rhymes.

Houston, John A. *The Bright Yellow Rope.* Illus. by Winnie Fitch. Reading: Addison-Wesley, 1973.
016.31 Behavior—sharing; 026.13 Character traits—generosity; 026.14 Character traits—helpfulness; 137 Problem solving; 164 Songs.

Houston, John A. *A Mouse in My House.* Illus. by Winnie Fitch. Reading: Addison-Wesley, 1973.
008.34 Animals—mice; 038 Cumulative tales; 137 Problem solving; 164 Songs.

Houston, John A. *A Room Full of Animals.* Illus. by Winnie Fitch. Reading: Addison-Wesley, 1973.
008 Animals; 164 Songs.

Howells, Mildred. *The Woman Who Lived in Holland.* Illus. by William Curtis Holdsworth. New York: Farrar, 1973.
026.05 Character traits—cleanliness; 064.14 Foreign lands—Holland; 134 Poetry, rhyme.

Hughes, Peter. *The Emperor's Oblong Pancake.* Illus. by Gerald Rose. New York: Abelard-Schuman, 1961.
032.07 Concepts—shape; 063 Food; 147 Royalty.

Hughes, Shirley. *David and Dog.* Illus. by author. Englewood Cliffs, NJ: Prentice-Hall, 1978.
002.15 Activities—trading; 057 Family life; 177 Toys.

Hughes, Shirley. *George the Babysitter.* Illus. by author. Englewood Cliffs, NJ: Prentice-Hall, 1975.
002.01 Activities—babysitting; 121 Non-sexist.

Hunt, Bernice Kohn. *Your Ant Is a Which, Fun with Homophones.* Illus. by Jan Pyk. New York: Harcourt, 1976.
096 Language; 134 Poetry, rhyme.

Hurd, Edith Thacher. *Caboose.* Illus. by Clement Hurd. New York: Lothrop, 1950.
134 Poetry, rhyme; 179 Trains.

Hurd, Edith Thacher. *Christmas Eve.* Illus. by Clement Hurd. New York: Harper, 1962.
008 Animals; 083.03 Holidays—Christmas.

Hurd, Edith Thacher. *Come and Have Fun.* Illus. by Clement Hurd. New York: Harper, 1962.
008.09 Animals—cats; 008.34 Animals—mice; 134 Poetry, rhyme.

Hurd, Edith Thacher. *The Day the Sun Danced.* Illus. by Clement Hurd. New York: Harper, 1965.
154 Seasons; 154.02 Seasons—spring; 169 Sun.

Hurd, Edith Thacher. *Dinosaur, My Darling.* Illus. by Don Freeman. New York: Harper, 1978.
044 Dinosaurs.

Hurd, Edith Thacher. *Engine, Engine Number 9.* Illus. by Clement Hurd. New York: Lothrop, 1940.
179 Trains.

Hurd, Edith Thacher. *Hurry Hurry.* Illus. by Clement Hurd. New York: Harper, 1960.
002.01 Activities—babysitting; 016.17 Behavior—hurrying.

Hurd, Edith Thacher. *Johnny Lion's Bad Day.* Illus. by Clement Hurd. New York: Harper, 1970.
008.10 Animals—cats, wild; 088 Illness.

Hurd, Edith Thacher. *Johnny Lion's Book.* Illus. by Clement Hurd. New York: Harper, 1965.
002.13 Activities—reading; 008.10 Animals—cats, wild.

Hurd, Edith Thacher. *Johnny Lion's Rubber Boots.* Illus. by Clement Hurd. New York: Harper, 1972.
008.10 Animals—cats, wild; 195.05 Weather—rain.

Hurd, Edith Thacher. *Last One Home Is a Green Pig.* Illus. by Clement Hurd. New York: Harper, 1959.
008.37 Animals—monkeys; 017.08 Birds—ducks; 069 Games; 166.11 Sports—racing.

Hurd, Edith Thacher. *Little Dog, Dreaming.* Illus. by Clement Hurd. New York: Harper, 1967.
008.14 Animals—dogs; 047 Dreams.

Hurd, Edith Thacher. *No Funny Business.* Illus. by Clement Hurd. New York: Harper, 1962.
002.11 Activities—picnicking; 008.09 Animals—cats.

Hurd, Edith Thacher. *Sandpipers.* Illus. by Lucienne Bloch. New York: Crowell, 1961.
017.21 Birds—sandpipers; 152 Science.

Hurd, Edith Thacher. *The So-So Cat.* Illus. by Clement Hurd. New York: Harper, 1964.
008.09 Animals—cats; 083.07 Holidays—Halloween; 199 Witches.

Hurd, Edith Thacher. *Stop, Stop.* Illus. by Clement Hurd. New York: Harper, 1961.
002.01 Activities—babysitting; 026.05 Character traits—cleanliness.

Hurd, Edith Thacher. *What Whale? Where?* Illus. by Clement Hurd. New York: Harper, 1966.
008.60 Animals—whales; 019 Boats, ships.

Hurd, Edith Thacher. *The White Horse.* Illus. by Tony Chen. New York: Harper, 1970.
089 Imagination.

Hurd, Edith Thacher. *Wilson's World.* Illus. by Clement Hurd. New York: Harper, 1971.
011 Art; 049 Ecology.

Hurd, Thacher. *The Quiet Evening.* Illus. by author. New York: Greenwillow, 1978.
119 Night.

Hürlimann, Ruth. *The Mouse with the Daisy Hat.* Illus. by author. Port Washington, NY: White, 1971.
008.34 Animals—mice; 031 Clothing; 196 Weddings.

Hürlimann, Ruth. *The Proud White Cat.* Illus. by author. Translated by Anthea Bell. New York: Morrow, 1977.
008.09 Animals—cats; 026.27 Character traits—pride; 062 Folk and fairy tales; 064.12 Foreign lands—Germany.

Hush Little Baby. Illus. by Aliki Liacouras Brandenberg. A folk lullaby. Englewood Cliffs, NJ: Prentice-Hall, 1968.
013 Babies; 026.13 Character traits—generosity; 038 Cumulative tales; 062 Folk and fairy tales; 164 Songs.

Hutchins, Pat. *The Best Train Set Ever.* Illus. by author. New York: Greenwillow, 1978. 018 Birthdays; 083.03 Holidays—Christmas; 083.07 Holidays—Halloween; 088 Illness.

Hutchins, Pat. *Changes, Changes.* Illus. by author. New York: Macmillan, 1971. 177.03 Toys—blocks; 201 Wordless.

Hutchins, Pat. *Clocks and More Clocks.* Illus. by author. New York: Macmillan, 1970. 030 Clocks; 087 Humor; 174 Time.

Hutchins, Pat. *Don't Forget the Bacon!* Illus. by author. New York: Greenwillow, 1976. 016.11 Behavior—forgetfulness; 038 Cumulative tales; 063 Food; 087 Humor; 160 Shopping.

Hutchins, Pat. *Good-Night Owl.* Illus. by author. New York: Macmillan, 1972. 038 Cumulative tales; 120 Noise; 129 Participation; 162 Sleep.

Hutchins, Pat. *Happy Birthday, Sam.* Illus. by author. New York: Greenwillow, 1978. 018 Birthdays; 057.02 Family life—grandparents; great-grandparents.

Hutchins, Pat. *Rosie's Walk.* Illus. by author. New York: Macmillan, 1968. 008.18 Animals—foxes; 017.04 Birds—chickens; 058 Farms; 087 Humor.

Hutchins, Pat. *The Silver Christmas Tree.* Illus. by author. New York: Macmillan, 1974. 008 Animals; 083.03 Holidays—Christmas; 181 Trees.

Hutchins, Pat. *Surprise Party.* Illus. by author. New York: Macmillan, 1969. 008 Animals; 016.12 Behavior—gossip; 130 Parties.

Hutchins, Pat. *Titch.* Illus. by author. New York: Macmillan, 1971. 032.08 Concepts—size; 038 Cumulative tales; 057 Family life; 133 Plants.

Hutchins, Pat. *The Wind Blew.* Illus. by author. New York: Macmillan, 1974. 134 Poetry, rhyme; 195.08 Weather—wind.

Hymes, James L., jt. author. *Oodles of Noodles and Other Rhymes.* By Lucia Hymes, and James L. Hymes.

Hymes, Lucia, and Hymes, James L. *Oodles of Noodles and Other Rhymes.* Illus. by authors. Written and illus. by Lucia and James L. Hymes, Jr. Reading: Addison-Wesley, 1964. 134 Poetry, rhyme.

Ichikawa, Satomi. *Suzanne and Nicholas at the Market.* Illus. by author. Translated by Denise Sheldon. New York: Watts, 1977. 064.11 Foreign lands—France.

Ichikawa, Satomi. *Suzanne and Nicholas in the Garden.* Illus. by author. Translated by Denise Sheldon. New York: Watts, 1976. 002.06 Activities—gardening; 049 Ecology.

Ilsley, Velma. *A Busy Day for Chris.* Illus. by author. Philadelphia: Lippincott, 1957. 001 ABC Books; 134 Poetry, rhyme.

Ilsley, Velma. *M Is for Moving.* Illus. by author. New York: Walck, 1966. 001 ABC Books; 114 Moving.

Ilsley, Velma. *The Pink Hat.* Illus. by author. Philadelphia: Lippincott, 1956. 016.06 Behavior—carelessness; 134 Poetry, rhyme.

Ipcar, Dahlov Zorach. *Animal Hide and Seek.* Illus. by author. Reading: Addison-Wesley, 1947. 008 Animals.

Ipcar, Dahlov Zorach. *The Biggest Fish in the Sea.* Illus. by author. New York: Viking, 1972. 032.08 Concepts—size; 060 Fish; 166.05 Sports—fishing.

Ipcar, Dahlov Zorach. *Black and White.* Illus. by author. New York: Knopf, 1963. 008.14 Animals—dogs; 134 Poetry, rhyme.

Ipcar, Dahlov Zorach. *Bright Barnyard.* Illus. by author. New York: Knopf, 1966. 008 Animals; 017 Birds; 058 Farms.

Ipcar, Dahlov Zorach. *Brown Cow Farm.* Illus. by author. Garden City, NY: Doubleday, 1959. 008 Animals; 033 Counting; 058 Farms.

Ipcar, Dahlov Zorach. *Bug City.* Illus. by author. New York: Holiday, 1975. 090 Insects and spiders.

Ipcar, Dahlov Zorach. *The Cat at Night.* Illus. by author. Garden City, NY: Doubleday, 1969. 008.09 Animals—cats; 119 Night.

Ipcar, Dahlov Zorach. *The Cat Came Back.*
Illus. by author. New York: Knopf, 1971.
008.09 Animals—cats; 116 Music;
134 Poetry, rhyme; 164 Songs.

Ipcar, Dahlov Zorach. *A Flood of Creatures.*
Illus. by author. New York: Holiday,
1973.
008 Animals; 195.03 Weather—floods.

Ipcar, Dahlov Zorach. *Hard Scrabble Harvest.*
Illus. by author. Garden City, NY: Doubleday, 1976.
058 Farms; 083.10 Holidays—
Thanksgiving; 133 Plants; 134 Poetry,
rhyme.

Ipcar, Dahlov Zorach. *I Like Animals.* Illus.
by author. New York: Knopf, 1960.
008 Animals.

Ipcar, Dahlov Zorach. *I Love My Anteater with
an A.* Illus. by author. New York: Knopf,
1964.
001 ABC Books; 008 Animals.

Ipcar, Dahlov Zorach. *The Land of Flowers.*
Illus. by author. New York: Viking, 1974.
002.06 Activities—gardening;
008.52 Animals—sheep;
032.08 Concepts—size; 061 Flowers.

Ipcar, Dahlov Zorach. *One Horse Farm.* Illus.
by author. Garden City, NY: Doubleday,
1950.
008.28 Animals—horses; 058 Farms;
102 Machines; 138 Progress.

Ipcar, Dahlov Zorach. *Sir Addlepate and the
Unicorn.* Illus. by author. Garden City,
NY: Doubleday, 1971.
095 Knights; 117 Mythical creatures.

Ipcar, Dahlov Zorach. *The Song of the Day
Birds and the Night Birds.* Illus. by author.
Garden City, NY: Doubleday, 1967.
017 Birds; 119 Night; 164 Songs.

Ipcar, Dahlov Zorach. *Stripes and Spots.* Illus.
by author. Garden City, NY: Doubleday,
1953.
008.10 Animals—cats, wild.

Ipcar, Dahlov Zorach. *Ten Big Farms.* Illus.
by author. New York: Knopf, 1958.
033 Counting; 058 Farms.

Ipcar, Dahlov Zorach. *Wild and Tame Animals.* Illus. by author. Garden City, NY:
Doubleday, 1962.
008 Animals.

Ipcar, Dahlov Zorach. *World Full of Horses.*
Illus. by author. Garden City, NY: Doubleday, 1955.
008.28 Animals—horses.

Isadora, Rachel. *Max.* Illus. by author. New
York: Macmillan, 1976.
002.04 Activities—dancing; 121 Non-
sexist; 166.01 Sports—baseball.

Isadora, Rachel. *The Potters' Kitchen.* Illus. by
author. New York: Greenwillow, 1977.
114 Moving.

Isadora, Rachel. *Willaby.* Illus. by author.
New York: Macmillan, 1977.
151 School.

Israel, Marion Louise. *The Tractor on the
Farm.* Illus. by Robert Dranko. Chicago:
Melmont, 1958.
058 Farms; 102 Machines.

Ivanko and the Dragon. Illus. by Yaroslava
Surmach Mills. An old Ukrainian folk tale
from the original collection of Ivan Ru-
dehenko. Translated by Marie Halun
Bloch. New York: Atheneum, 1969.
046 Dragons; 062 Folk and fairy tales.

Ivimey, John William. *The Complete Version
of Ye Three Blind Mice.* Illus. by Walton
Corbould. New York: Warne, 1909.
008.34 Animals—mice; 116 Music;
122 Nursery rhymes; 164 Songs.

Iwamatsu, Jun. *Crow Boy.* Illus. by author.
New York: Viking, 1955.
052.07 Emotions—loneliness;
064.19 Foreign lands—Japan;
151 School.

Iwamatsu, Jun. *Seashore Story.* Illus. by author. New York: Viking, 1967.
062 Folk and fairy tales; 064.19 Foreign
lands—Japan; 142.05 Reptiles—turtles;
153 Sea and seashore.

Iwamatsu, Jun. *Umbrella.* Illus. by author.
New York: Viking, 1958.
018 Birthdays; 026.16 Character traits—
individuality; 053.05 Ethnic groups in
the U.S.—Japanese-Americans;
064.19 Foreign lands—Japan;
187 Umbrellas;
195.05 Weather—rain.

Iwamatsu, Jun. *The Village Tree.* Illus. by author. New York: Viking, 1953.
064.19 Foreign lands—Japan;
181 Trees.

Iwamatsu, Jun. *The Youngest One.* Illus. by
author. New York: Viking, 1962.
026.30 Character traits—shyness;
053.05 Ethnic groups in the U.S.—
Japanese-Americans; 068 Friendship.

Iwamatsu, Tomoe Sasako. *Momo's Kitten.* Illus. by Jun Iwamatsu. New York: Viking, 1961.
008.09 Animals—cats; 053.05 Ethnic groups in the U.S.—Japanese-Americans.

Iwamatsu, Tomoe Sasako. *Plenty to Watch.* Illus. by Jun Iwamatsu. New York: Viking, 1954.
064.19 Foreign lands—Japan.

Iwasaki, Chihiro. *The Birthday Wish.* Illus. by author. New York: McGraw-Hill, 1974.
016.38 Behavior—wishing; 018 Birthdays; 195.07 Weather—snow.

Iwasaki, Chihiro. *Staying Home Alone on a Rainy Day.* Illus. by author. New York: McGraw-Hill, 1968.
052.07 Emotions—loneliness; 057 Family life; 057.04 Family life—the only child; 195.05 Weather—rain.

Iwasaki, Chihiro. *What's Fun Without a Friend?* Illus. by author. New York: McGraw-Hill, 1972.
008.14 Animals—dogs; 153 Sea and seashore.

Iwasaki, Chihiro. *Will You Be My Friend?* Illus. by author. New York: McGraw-Hill, 1970.
068 Friendship.

Jack Sprat. *The Life of Jack Sprat, His Wife and His Cat.* Illus. by Paul Galdone. New York: McGraw-Hill, 1969.
008.09 Animals—cats; 057 Family life; 063 Food; 122 Nursery rhymes.

Jackson, Jacqueline. *Chicken Ten Thousand.* Illus. by Barbara Morrow. Boston: Little, 1968.
017.04 Birds—chickens; 152 Science.

Jacobs, Joseph. *The Crock of Gold, Being "The Pedlar of Swaffham."* Illus. by William Stobbs. Chicago: Follett, 1971.
023.20 Careers—peddlers; 047 Dreams; 062 Folk and fairy tales; 064.10 Foreign lands—England.

Jacobs, Joseph. *Hereafterthis.* Illus. by Paul Galdone. Adapted by Paul Galdone. New York: McGraw-Hill, 1973.
008 Animals; 016.23 Behavior—mistakes; 036 Crime; 058 Farms; 062 Folk and fairy tales.

Jacobs, Joseph. *Johnny-Cake.* Illus. by Emma Lillian Brock. New York: Putnam's, 1967.
038 Cumulative tales; 062 Folk and fairy tales; 063 Food.

Jacobs, Joseph. *Johnny-Cake.* Illus. by William Stobbs. New York: Viking, 1972.
038 Cumulative tales; 062 Folk and fairy tales; 063 Food.

Jacobs, Joseph. *Lazy Jack.* Illus. by Barry Wilkinson. Cleveland: Collins, 1969.
026.19 Character traits—laziness; 038 Cumulative tales; 062 Folk and fairy tales.

Jacobs, Joseph. *Master of All Masters.* Illus. by Anne F. Rockwell. New York: Grosset, 1972.
016.24 Behavior—misunderstanding; 062 Folk and fairy tales.

Jaffe, Rona. *Last of the Wizards.* Illus. by Erik Blegvad. New York: Simon & Schuster, 1961.
016.38 Behavior—wishing; 026.06 Character traits—cleverness; 200 Wizards.

Jameson, Cynthia. *The Clay Pot Boy.* Illus. by Arnold Stark Lobel. New York: Coward, 1973.
016.22 Behavior—misbehavior; 038 Cumulative tales; 062 Folk and fairy tales; 064.30 Foreign lands—Russia.

Jameson, Cynthia. *A Day with Whisker Wickles.* Illus. by James Marshall. New York: Coward, 1975.
008.46 Animals—rabbits; 069 Games.

Janice (pseud.). See Brustlein, Janice.

Janosch (pseud.). See Eckert, Horst.

Jarrell, Mary. *Knee Baby.* Illus. by Symeon Shimin. New York: Farrar, 1973.
013 Babies; 057 Family life.

Jasner, W. K. (pseud.). See Watson, Jane Werner.

Jaynes, Ruth. *Benny's Four Hats.* Illus. by Harvey Mandlin. Los Angeles: Bowmar, 1967.
031 Clothing; 053.07 Ethnic groups in the U.S.—Multi-ethnic; 129 Participation; 195 Weather.

Jaynes, Ruth. *The Biggest House.* Illus. by Jacques Rupp. Los Angeles: Bowmar, 1968.
086 Houses.

Jaynes, Ruth. *Friends, Friends, Friends.* Illus. by Harvey Mandlin. Los Angeles: Bowmar, 1967.
053.07 Ethnic groups in the U.S.—Multi-ethnic; 068 Friendship; 151 School.

Jaynes, Ruth. *Melinda's Christmas Stocking.* Illus. by Richard George. Los Angeles: Bowmar, 1968.
053.06 Ethnic groups in the U.S.—Mexican-Americans; 083.03 Holidays—Christmas; 157 Senses.

Jaynes, Ruth. *Tell Me Please! What's That?* Illus. by Harvey Mandlin. Los Angeles: Bowmar, 1968.
008 Animals; 053.06 Ethnic groups in the U.S.—Mexican-Americans; 053.07 Ethnic groups in the U.S.—Multi-ethnic; 065 Foreign languages.

Jaynes, Ruth. *That's What It Is!* Illus. by Harvey Mandlin. Los Angeles: Bowmar, 1968.
053.07 Ethnic groups in the U.S.—Multi-ethnic; 090 Insects and spiders.

Jaynes, Ruth. *Three Baby Chicks.* Illus. by Harvey Mandlin. Los Angeles: Bowmar, 1967.
017.04 Birds—chickens; 151 School.

Jaynes, Ruth. *What Is a Birthday Child?* Illus. by Harvey Mandlin. Los Angeles: Bowmar, 1967.
018 Birthdays; 026.16 Character traits—individuality; 053.06 Ethnic groups in the U.S.—Mexican-Americans; 053.07 Ethnic groups in the U.S.—Multi-ethnic.

Jeffers, Susan. *All the Pretty Horses.* Illus. by author. New York: Macmillan, 1974.
008.28 Animals—horses; 015 Bedtime; 162 Sleep.

Jeffers, Susan. *Wild Robin.* Illus. by author. New York: Dutton, 1976.
016.22 Behavior—misbehavior; 064.31 Foreign lands—Scotland.

Jenny, Anne. *The Fantastic Story of King Brioche the First.* Illus. by Joycelyne Pache. Translated by Catherine Barton. New York: Lothrop, 1970.
002.05 Activities—flying; 151 School.

Jensen, Virginia Allen. *Sara and the Door.* Illus. by Ann Strugnell. Reading: Addison-Wesley, 1977.
026.25 Character traits—perseverance; 031 Clothing; 053.01 Ethnic groups in the U.S.—Afro-Americans.

Jerome, Judson. *I Never Saw.* Illus. by Helga Aichinger. Chicago: Albert Whitman, 1974.
134 Poetry, rhyme.

Jeschke, Susan. *Angela and Bear.* Illus. by author. New York: Holt, 1979.
008.06 Animals—bears; 089.01 Imagination—imaginary friends; 103 Magic.

Jeschke, Susan. *The Devil Did It.* Illus. by author. New York: Holt, 1975.
042 Devil; 057.02 Family life—grandparents; great-grandparents; 089.01 Imagination—imaginary friends.

Jeschke, Susan. *Firerose.* Illus. by author. New York: Holt, 1974.
023.12 Careers—fortune tellers; 046 Dragons; 087 Humor; 103 Magic.

Jeschke, Susan. *Mia, Grandma and the Genie.* Illus. by author. New York: Holt, 1978.
055 Fairies; 057.02 Family life—grandparents; great-grandparents.

Jeschke, Susan. *Rima and Zeppo.* Illus. by author. New York: Dutton, 1976.
103 Magic; 199 Witches.

Jewell, Nancy. *Bus Ride.* Illus. by Ronald Norbert Himler. New York: Harper, 1978.
021 Buses.

Jewell, Nancy. *The Snuggle Bunny.* Illus. by Mary Eileen Chalmers. New York: Harper, 1972.
008.46 Animals—rabbits; 052.08 Emotions—love.

Jewell, Nancy. *Try and Catch Me.* Illus. by Leonard Weisgard. New York: Harper, 1972.
002.12 Activities—playing; 049 Ecology; 068 Friendship; 089 Imagination.

Johnson, Crockett (pseud.). See Leisk, David Johnson.

Johnson, Elizabeth. *All in Free but Janey.* Illus. by Trina Schart Hyman. Boston: Little, 1968.
069 Games; 089 Imagination.

Johnson, Ryerson. *Let's Walk Up the Wall.* Illus. by Eva Cellini. New York: Holiday, 1967.
129 Participation.

Johnston, Johanna. *Edie Changes Her Mind.* Illus. by Paul Galdone. New York: Putnam's, 1964.
015 Bedtime; 137 Problem solving.

Johnston, Johanna. *Speak Up, Edie.* Illus. by Paul Galdone. New York: Putnam's, 1974.
096 Language; 173 Theater.

Johnston, Johanna. *Sugarplum.* Illus. by Marvin Bileck. New York: Knopf, 1955.
026.31 Character traits—smallness; 177.04 Toys—dolls.

Johnston, Johanna. *That's Right Edie.* Illus. by Paul Galdone. New York: Putnam's, 1966.
002.21 Activities—writing.

Johnston, Tony. *The Adventures of Mole and Troll.* Illus. by Wallace Tripp. New York: Putnam's, 1972.
008.35 Animals—moles; 183 Trolls.

Johnston, Tony. *Four Scary Stories.* Illus. by Thomas Anthony de Paola. New York: Putnam's, 1978.
071 Ghosts; 074 Goblins; 110 Monsters.

Jones, Harold. *There and Back Again.* Illus. by author. New York: Atheneum, 1977.
177 Toys.

Jones, Hettie, comp. *The Trees Stand Shining; Poetry of the North American Indians.* Illus. by Robert Andrew Parker. New York: Dial Pr., 1971.
053.04 Ethnic groups in the U.S.—Indians; 134 Poetry, rhyme.

Jones, Jessie Mae Orton, comp. *A Little Child.* Illus. by Elizabeth Orton Jones. The Christmas miracle told in Bible verses chosen by Jessie Orton Jones. New York: Viking, 1946.
141 Religion.

Jones, Jessie Mae Orton, comp. *Small Rain.* Illus. by Elizabeth Orton Jones. Verses from the Bible chosen by Jessie Orton Jones. New York: Viking, 1943.
134 Poetry, rhyme; 141 Religion.

Jones, Jessie Mae Orton, comp. *This Is the Way.* Illus. by Elizabeth Orton Jones. Prayers and precepts from world religions. New York: Viking, 1951.
141 Religion.

Joslin, Sesyle. *Baby Elephant and the Secret Wishes.* Illus. by Leonard Weisgard. New York: Harcourt, 1962.
008.17 Animals—elephants; 083.03 Holidays—Christmas.

Joslin, Sesyle. *Baby Elephant Goes to China.* Illus. by Leonard Weisgard. New York: Harcourt, 1963.
008.17 Animals—elephants; 065 Foreign languages; 153 Sea and seashore.

Joslin, Sesyle. *Baby Elephant's Trunk.* Illus. by Leonard Weisgard. New York: Harcourt, 1961.
008.17 Animals—elephants; 064.11 Foreign lands—France; 065 Foreign languages.

Joslin, Sesyle. *Brave Baby Elephant.* Illus. by Leonard Weisgard. New York: Harcourt, 1960.
008.17 Animals—elephants; 015 Bedtime.

Joslin, Sesyle. *Dear Dragon and Other Useful Letter Forms for Young Ladies and Gentlemen, Engaged in Everyday Correspondence.* Illus. by Irene Haas. New York: Harcourt, 1962.
002.21 Activities—writing; 046 Dragons; 054 Etiquette; 087 Humor; 099 Letters.

Joslin, Sesyle. *Senor Baby Elephant, the Pirate.* Illus. by Leonard Weisgard. New York: Harcourt, 1962.
008.17 Animals—elephants; 065 Foreign languages; 132 Pirates.

Joslin, Sesyle. *What Do You Do, Dear?* Illus. by Maurice Sendak. Reading: Addison-Wesley, 1961.
054 Etiquette; 087 Humor.

Joslin, Sesyle. *What Do You Say, Dear?* Illus. by Maurice Sendak. Reading: Addison-Wesley, 1958.
054 Etiquette; 087 Humor.

Joyce, Irma. *Never Talk to Strangers.* Illus. by George Buckett. Racine, WI: Western Pub., 1967.
016.35 Behavior—talking to strangers; 087 Humor; 148 Safety.

Joyner, Jerry, jt. author. *Thirteen.* By Remy Charlip, and Jerry Joyner.

Jüchen, Aurel von. *The Holy Night, the Story of the First Christmas.* Illus. by Celestino Piatti. Translated from the German by Cornelia Schaeffer. New York: Atheneum, 1968.
083.03 Holidays—Christmas; 141 Religion.

Kahl, Virginia Caroline. *Away Went Wolfgang.* Illus. by author. New York: Scribner's, 1954.
008.14 Animals—dogs; 064.03 Foreign lands—Austria.

Kahl, Virginia Caroline. *The Baron's Booty.* Illus. by author. New York: Scribner's, 1963.
107 Middle ages; 134 Poetry, rhyme; 147 Royalty.

Kahl, Virginia Caroline. *Droopsi.* Illus. by author. New York: Scribner's, 1958.
064.12 Foreign lands—Germany;
116 Music.

Kahl, Virginia Caroline. *The Duchess Bakes a Cake.* Illus. by author. New York: Scribner's, 1955.
002.03 Activities—cooking; 063 Food;
107 Middle ages; 134 Poetry, rhyme;
147 Royalty.

Kahl, Virginia Caroline. *Giants, Indeed!* Illus. by author. New York: Scribner's, 1974.
072 Giants; 110 Monsters.

Kahl, Virginia Caroline. *Gunhilde and the Halloween Spell.* Illus. by author. New York: Scribner's, 1975.
083.07 Holidays—Halloween;
107 Middle ages; 134 Poetry, rhyme;
147 Royalty; 199 Witches.

Kahl, Virginia Caroline. *Gunhilde's Christmas Booke.* Illus. by author. New York: Scribner's, 1972.
083.03 Holidays—Christmas;
107 Middle ages; 116 Music; 134 Poetry, rhyme; 147 Royalty.

Kahl, Virginia Caroline. *The Habits of Rabbits.* Illus. by author. New York: Scribner's, 1957.
008.46 Animals—rabbits; 107 Middle ages; 131 Pets; 134 Poetry, rhyme;
147 Royalty.

Kahl, Virginia Caroline, jt. author. *Here Is Henri!* By Edith Vacheron, and Virginia Caroline Kahl.

Kahl, Virginia Caroline. *How Do You Hide a Monster?* Illus. by author. New York: Scribner's, 1971.
110 Monsters; 134 Poetry, rhyme;
166.08 Sports—hunting.

Kahl, Virginia Caroline. *Maxie.* Illus. by author. New York: Scribner's, 1956.
008.14 Animals—dogs;
026.25 Character traits—perseverance;
064.12 Foreign lands—Germany;
125 Old age.

Kahl, Virginia Caroline, jt. author. *More about Henri!* By Edith Vacheron, and Virginia Caroline Kahl.

Kahl, Virginia Caroline. *The Perfect Pancake.* Illus. by author. New York: Scribner's, 1960.
026.29 Character traits—selfishness;
063 Food; 134 Poetry, rhyme.

Kahl, Virginia Caroline. *Plum Pudding for Christmas.* Illus. by author. New York: Scribner's, 1956.
063 Food; 083.03 Holidays—Christmas;
134 Poetry, rhyme; 147 Royalty.

Kahn, Joan. *Seesaw.* Illus. by Crosby Newell Bonsall. New York: Harper, 1964.
069 Games; 177 Toys.

Kalab, Theresa. See Smith, Theresa Kalab.

Kalan, Robert. *Blue Sea.* Illus. by Donald Crews. New York: Greenwillow, 1979.
032.08 Concepts—size; 060 Fish.

Kalan, Robert. *Rain.* Illus. by Donald Crews. New York: Greenwillow, 1978.
195.05 Weather—rain.

Kantor, MacKinlay. *Angleworms on Toast.* Illus. by Kurt Wiese. New York: Putnam's, 1942.
063 Food.

Kantrowitz, Mildred. *I Wonder If Herbie's Home Yet.* Illus. by Tony De Luna. New York: Parents, 1971.
068 Friendship.

Kantrowitz, Mildred. *When Violet Died.* Illus. by Emily Arnold McCully. New York: Parents, 1973.
017 Birds; 040 Death.

Kantrowitz, Mildred. *Willy Bear.* Illus. by Nancy Winslow Parker. New York: Parents, 1976.
151 School; 162 Sleep; 177.08 Toys—teddy bears.

Kauffman, Lois. *What's That Noise?* Illus. by Allan Eitzen. New York: Lothrop, 1965.
057.01 Family life—fathers; 119 Night;
120 Noise.

Kaune, Merriman B. *My Own Little House.* Illus. by author. Chicago: Follett, 1957.
086 Houses.

Kavanaugh, James. *The Crooked Angel.* Illus. by Elaine Havelock. Los Angeles: Nash, 1970.
007 Angels; 134 Poetry, rhyme.

Kay, Helen (pseud.). See Goldfrank, Helen Colodny.

Kaye, Geraldine. *The Sea Monkey.* Illus. by Gay Galsworthy. A picture story from Malaysia. Cleveland: Collins, 1968.
008.37 Animals—monkeys;
064.23 Foreign lands—Malaysia.

Keats, Ezra Jack. *Apartment 3.* Illus. by author. New York: Macmillan, 1971.
029 City; 053.01 Ethnic groups in the U.S.—Afro-Americans; 057 Family life; 077.01 Handicaps—blindness; 116 Music.

Keats, Ezra Jack. *Dreams.* Illus. by author. New York: Macmillan, 1974.
047 Dreams; 053.01 Ethnic groups in the U.S.—Afro-Americans; 089 Imagination; 119 Night; 162 Sleep.

Keats, Ezra Jack. *God Is in the Mountain.* Illus. by author. New York: Holt, 1966.
141 Religion.

Keats, Ezra Jack. *Goggles.* Illus. by author. New York: Macmillan, 1969.
016.05 Behavior—bullying; 029 City; 053.01 Ethnic groups in the U.S.—Afro-Americans; 137 Problem solving.

Keats, Ezra Jack. *Hi, Cat!* Illus. by author. New York: Macmillan, 1970.
008.09 Animals—cats; 029 City; 053.01 Ethnic groups in the U.S.—Afro-Americans.

Keats, Ezra Jack. *Jennie's Hat.* Illus. by author. New York: Harper, 1966.
031 Clothing; 016.09 Behavior—dissatisfaction; 026.18 Character traits—kindness to animals.

Keats, Ezra Jack. *John Henry.* Illus. by author. New York: Pantheon, 1965.
026.25 Character traits—perseverance; 026.27 Character traits—pride; 053.01 Ethnic groups in the U.S.—Afro-Americans; 062 Folk and fairy tales.

Keats, Ezra Jack. *Kitten for a Day.* Illus. by author. New York: Watts, 1974.
008.09 Animals—cats; 008.14 Animals—dogs; 201 Wordless.

Keats, Ezra Jack. *A Letter to Amy.* Illus. by author. New York: Harper, 1968.
018 Birthdays; 023.16 Careers—mail carriers; 053.01 Ethnic groups in the U.S.—Afro-Americans;

068 Friendship; 099 Letters; 130 Parties; 195.05 Weather—rain; 195.08 Weather—wind.

Keats, Ezra Jack. *The Little Drummer Boy.* Illus. by author. Words and music by Katherine Davis, Henry Onorati and Harry Simeone. New York: Macmillan, 1968.
083.03 Holidays—Christmas; 141 Religion; 164 Songs.

Keats, Ezra Jack. *Louie.* Illus. by author. New York: Greenwillow, 1975.
026.30 Character traits—shyness; 053.01 Ethnic groups in the U.S.—Afro-Americans; 139 Puppets.

Keats, Ezra Jack. *My Dog Is Lost!* Illus. by author. New York: Crowell, 1960.
008.14 Animals—dogs; 016.20 Behavior—lost; 023.21 Careers—police officers; 053.07 Ethnic groups in the U.S.—Multi-ethnic; 053.08 Ethnic groups in the U.S.—Puerto Rican-Americans; 065 Foreign languages.

Keats, Ezra Jack. *Over in the Meadow.* Illus. by author. New York: Scholastic, 1971.
008 Animals; 033 Counting; 062 Folk and fairy tales; 134 Poetry, rhyme; 164 Songs.

Keats, Ezra Jack. *Pet Show!* Illus. by author. New York: Macmillan, 1972.
008 Animals; 053.01 Ethnic groups in the U.S.—Afro-Americans; 131 Pets.

Keats, Ezra Jack. *Peter's Chair.* Illus. by author. New York: Harper, 1967.
013 Babies; 016.31 Behavior—sharing; 016.32 Behavior—sibling rivalry; 053.01 Ethnic groups in the U.S.—Afro-Americans; 057 Family life; 068 Friendship; 156 Self-concept.

Keats, Ezra Jack. *Psst, Doggie.* Illus. by author. New York: Watts, 1973.
008.09 Animals—cats; 008.14 Animals—dogs; 201 Wordless.

Keats, Ezra Jack. *Skates.* Illus. by author. New York: Watts, 1972.
002.12 Activities—playing; 008.14 Animals—dogs; 053.01 Ethnic groups in the U.S.—Afro-Americans; 087 Humor; 201 Wordless.

Keats, Ezra Jack. *The Snowy Day.* Illus. by author. New York: Viking, 1962.
002.12 Activities—playing;

053.01 Ethnic groups in the U.S.—Afro-Americans; 154.04 Seasons—winter; 195.07 Weather—snow.

Keats, Ezra Jack. *The Trip*. Illus. by author. New York: Greenwillow, 1978.
053.01 Ethnic groups in the U.S.—Afro-Americans; 089 Imagination.

Keats, Ezra Jack. *Whistle for Willie*. Illus. by author. New York: Viking, 1964.
002.19 Activities—whistling;
008.14 Animals—dogs; 053.01 Ethnic groups in the U.S.—Afro-Americans; 137 Problem solving; 156 Self-concept.

Keenan, Martha. *The Mannerly Adventures of Little Mouse*. Illus. by Meri Shardin. New York: Crown, 1977.
008.34 Animals—mice; 054 Etiquette.

Keenen, George. *The Preposterous Week*. Illus. by Stanley Mack. New York: Dial Pr., 1971.
016.02 Behavior—bad day; 049 Ecology; 087 Humor.

Keeping, Charles William James. *Alfie Finds the Other Side of the World*. Illus. by author. New York: Watts, 1968.
029 City; 064.10 Foreign lands—England; 144 Rivers; 195.04 Weather—fog.

Keeping, Charles William James. *Joseph's Yard*. Illus. by author. New York: Watts, 1969.
002.06 Activities—gardening;
135 Poverty.

Keeping, Charles William James. *Molly o' the Moors, the Story of a Pony*. Illus. by author. Cleveland: Collins, 1966.
008.28 Animals—horses; 125 Old age.

Keeping, Charles William James. *Through the Window*. Illus. by author. New York: Watts, 1970.
029 City; 064.10 Foreign lands—England.

Keeshan, Robert. *She Loves Me, She Loves Me Not*. Illus. by Maurice Sendak. New York: Harper, 1963.
069 Games; 083.11 Holidays—Valentine's Day; 117 Mythical creatures.

Keith, Eros. *Bedita's Bad Day*. Illus. by author. New York: Bradbury Pr., 1971.
016.02 Behavior—bad day; 199 Witches.

Keith, Eros. *Nancy's Backyard*. Illus. by author. New York: Harper, 1973.
047 Dreams; 195.05 Weather—rain.

Keith, Eros. *Rrra-ah*. Illus. by author. New York: Bradbury Pr., 1969.
005 Amphibians; 131 Pets.

Keller, Beverly. *Fiona's Bee*. Illus. by Diane Paterson. New York: Coward, 1975.
026.30 Character traits—shyness;
090 Insects and spiders.

Keller, John G. *Krispin's Fair*. Illus. by author. Boston: Little, 1976.
054 Etiquette.

Kellogg, Stephen. See Kellogg, Steven.

Kellogg, Steven. *Can I Keep Him?* Illus. by author. New York: Dial Pr., 1971.
057 Family life; 131 Pets.

Kellogg, Steven. *The Island of the Skog*. Illus. by author. New York: Dial Pr., 1973.
008.34 Animals—mice; 019 Boats, ships; 091 Islands; 110 Monsters.

Kellogg, Steven. *The Mysterious Tadpole*. Illus. by author. New York: Dial Pr., 1977.
005 Amphibians; 110 Monsters.

Kellogg, Steven. *The Mystery of the Magic Green Ball*. Illus. by author. New York: Dial Pr., 1978.
016.19 Behavior—losing things;
075 Gypsies; 177.02 Toys—balls.

Kellogg, Steven. *The Mystery of the Missing Red Mitten*. Illus. by author. New York: Dial Pr., 1974.
016.19 Behavior—losing things;
137 Problem solving; 163 Snowmen.

Kennedy, Richard. *The Contests at Cowlick*. Illus. by Marc Simont. Boston: Little, 1975.
026.06 Character traits—cleverness;
035 Cowboys.

Kennedy, Richard. *The Leprechaun's Story*. Illus. by Marcia Sewall. New York: Dutton, 1979.
051 Elves and little people;
064.17 Foreign lands—Ireland.

Kennedy, Richard. *The Porcelain Man*. Illus. by Marcia Sewall. Boston: Little, 1976.
103 Magic.

Kent, Jack. *The Christmas Pinata*. Illus. by author. New York: Parents, 1975.
064.24 Foreign lands—Mexico;
083.03 Holidays—Christmas.

Kent, Jack. *Clotilda*. Illus. by author. New York: Random House, 1978.
026.17 Character traits—kindness;
055 Fairies.

Kent, Jack. *The Egg Book*. Illus. by author. New York: Macmillan, 1975.
050 Eggs; 201 Wordless.

Kent, Jack. *The Fat Cat.* Illus. by author. New York: Parents, 1971.
008.09 Animals—cats; 038 Cumulative tales.

Kent, Jack. *Hoddy Doddy.* Illus. by author. New York: Greenwillow, 1979.
064.08 Foreign lands—Denmark; 087 Humor.

Kent, Jack. *There's No Such Thing as a Dragon.* Illus. by author. Racine, WI: Western Pub., 1975.
016.26 Behavior—needing someone; 046 Dragons.

Kepes, Charles. *Run, Little Monkeys, Run, Run, Run.* Illus. by author. New York: Pantheon, 1974.
008.10 Animals—cats, wild; 008.37 Animals—monkeys; 129 Participation.

Kepes, Juliet. *Five Little Monkeys.* Illus. by author. Boston: Houghton, 1965.
008 Animals; 008.37 Animals—monkeys.

Kepes, Juliet. *Frogs, Merry.* Illus. by author. New York: Pantheon, 1961.
005 Amphibians; 081 Hibernation.

Kepes, Juliet. *Lady Bird, Quickly.* Illus. by author. Boston: Little, 1964.
090 Insects and spiders; 122 Nursery rhymes.

Kepes, Juliet. *The Seed That Peacock Planted.* Illus. by author. Boston: Little, 1967.
017.16 Birds—peacocks, peahens; 103 Magic; 116 Music; 133 Plants.

Kerr, Judith. *Mog's Christmas.* Illus. by author. Cleveland: Collins, 1976.
083.03 Holidays—Christmas.

Kesselman, Wendy Ann. *Angelita.* Illus. by Norma Holt. New York: Hill & Wang, 1970.
053.07 Ethnic groups in the U.S.—Multi-ethnic; 053.08 Ethnic groups in the U.S.—Puerto Rican-Americans.

Kesselman, Wendy Ann. *Time for Jody.* Illus. by Gerald Dumas. New York: Harper, 1975.
008.23 Animals—groundhogs; 081 Hibernation; 083.06 Holidays—Groundhog Day; 154.02 Seasons—spring.

Kessler, Ethel. *What's inside the Box?* Illus. by Leonard P. Kessler. New York: Dodd, 1978.
008 Animals.

Kessler, Ethel, and Kessler, Leonard P. *All Aboard the Train.* Illus. by authors. Garden City, NY: Doubleday, 1964.
179 Trains.

Kessler, Ethel, and Kessler, Leonard P. *Do Baby Bears Sit in Chairs?* Illus. by authors. Garden City, NY: Doubleday, 1961.
008 Animals; 134 Poetry, rhyme.

Kessler, Leonard P., jt. author. *All Aboard the Train.* By Ethel Kessler, and Leonard P. Kessler.

Kessler, Leonard P. *Are We Lost, Daddy?* Illus. by author. New York: Grosset, 1967.
002.17 Activities—vacationing; 016.20 Behavior—lost; 057 Family life; 057.01 Family life—fathers.

Kessler, Leonard P., jt. author. *Do Baby Bears Sit in Chairs?* By Ethel Kessler, and Leonard P. Kessler.

Kessler, Leonard P. *Here Comes the Strikeout.* Illus. by author. New York: Harper, 1965.
166.01 Sports—baseball.

Kessler, Leonard P. *Kick, Pass and Run.* Illus. by author. New York: Harper, 1966.
008 Animals; 166.06 Sports—football.

Kessler, Leonard P. *Last One in Is a Rotten Egg.* Illus. by author. New York: Harper, 1969.
016.05 Behavior—bullying; 166.15 Sports—swimming.

Kessler, Leonard P. *Mr. Pine's Mixed-Up Signs.* Illus. by author. New York: Grosset, 1961.
073 Glasses.

Kessler, Leonard P. *Mr. Pine's Purple House.* Illus. by author. New York: Grosset, 1965.
002.09 Activities—painting; 032.01 Concepts—color.

Kessler, Leonard P. *Mrs. Pine Takes a Trip.* Illus. by author. New York: Grosset, 1966.
002.16 Activities—traveling.

Kessler, Leonard P. *On Your Mark, Get Set, Go!* Illus. by author. New York: Harper, 1972.
008 Animals; 166.10 Sports—Olympics.

Kessler, Leonard P. *Soup for the King.* Illus. by author. New York: Grosset, 1969.
023.03 Careers—bakers; 063 Food; 147 Royalty.

Key, Francis Scott. *The Star-Spangled Banner.* Illus. by Paul Galdone. New York: Crowell, 1966.
164 Songs; 189 U.S. history.

Key, Francis Scott. *The Star-Spangled Banner.* Illus. by Peter Spier. Garden City, NY: Doubleday, 1973.
164 Songs; 189 U.S. history.

Kimmel, Eric. *Why Worry?* Illus. by Elizabeth Cannon. New York: Pantheon, 1979.
090 Insects and spiders; 116 Music; 164 Songs.

Kimmel, Margaret Mary. *Magic in the Mist.* Illus. by Trina Schart Hyman. New York: Atheneum, 1975.
046 Dragons; 103 Magic; 200 Wizards.

King, Patricia. *Mabel the Whale.* Illus. by Katherine Evans. Chicago: Follett, 1958.
008.60 Animals—whales.

Kingman, Lee. *Peter's Long Walk.* Illus. by Barbara Cooney. Garden City, NY: Doubleday, 1953.
002.18 Activities—walking;
008 Animals; 034 Country;
068 Friendship.

Kipling, Rudyard. *The Miracle of the Mountain.* Illus. by Willi Baum. Adapted by Aroline Beecher Leach. Reading: Addison-Wesley, 1969.
008 Animals; 064.16 Foreign lands—India; 141 Religion.

Kirk, Barbara. *Grandpa, Me and Our House in the Tree.* Illus. by author. New York: Macmillan, 1978.
057.02 Family life—grandparents; great-grandparents; 086 Houses; 181 Trees.

Kirn, Ann Minette. *Beeswax Catches a Thief.* Illus. by author. From a Congo folktale. New York: Norton, 1968.
008 Animals; 053.01 Ethnic groups in the U.S.—Afro-Americans.

Kirn, Ann Minette. *I Spy.* Illus. by author. New York: Norton, 1965.
017.14 Birds—owls; 036 Crime.

Kirn, Ann Minette. *Leopard on a String.* Illus. by author. Cleveland: Collins, 1959.
008.10 Animals—cats, wild; 204 Zoos.

Kirn, Ann Minette. *The Tale of a Crocodile.* Illus. by author. From a Congo folktale. New York: Norton, 1968.
008.46 Animals—rabbits; 059 Fire; 062 Folk and fairy tales; 064.01 Foreign lands—Africa; 142.01 Reptiles—alligators, crocodiles.

Kishida, Eriko. *The Hippo Boat.* Illus. by Chiyoko Nakatani. Cleveland: Collins, 1964.
008.27 Animals—hippopotami;
195.05 Weather—rain; 204 Zoos.

Kishida, Eriko. *The Lion and the Bird's Nest.* Illus. by Chiyoko Nakatani. New York: Crowell, 1972.
008.10 Animals—cats, wild; 017 Birds; 026.14 Character traits—helpfulness; 068 Friendship.

Kitt, Tamara. *Sam and the Impossible Thing.* Illus. by Brinton Cassady Turkle. New York: Norton, 1967.
002.03 Activities—cooking; 063 Food; 110 Monsters; 134 Poetry, rhyme.

Kitt, Tamara. *A Special Birthday Party for Someone Very Special.* Illus. by Brinton Cassady Turkle. New York: Norton, 1966.
008.53 Animals—skunks; 018 Birthdays.

Klein, Leonore. *Henri's Walk to Paris.* Illus. by Saul Bass. Reading: Addison-Wesley, 1962.
002.18 Activities—walking;
064.11 Foreign lands—France.

Klein, Leonore. *Just Like You.* Illus. by Audrey Walters. New York: Harvey House, 1968.
053.07 Ethnic groups in the U.S.—Multi-ethnic.

Klein, Norma. *Girls Can Be Anything.* Illus. by Roy Doty. New York: Dutton, 1973.
023 Careers; 121 Non-sexist.

Klein, Suzanne. *An Elephant in My Bed.* Illus. by Sharleen Pederson. Chicago: Follett, 1974.
008.17 Animals—elephants.

Klimowicz, Barbara. *The Strawberry Thumb.* Illus. by Gloria Kamen. Nashville: Abingdon Pr., 1968.
134 Poetry, rhyme; 137 Problem solving; 139 Puppets.

Knight, Hilary. *Angels and Berries and Candy Canes.* Illus. by author. New York: Harper, 1963.
007 Angels; 083.03 Holidays—Christmas.

Knight, Hilary. *A Firefly in a Fir Tree.* Illus. by author. New York: Harper, 1963.
090 Insects and spiders.

Knight, Hilary. *Sylvia the Sloth.* Illus. by author. New York: Harper, 1969.
008.54 Animals—sloths;
032.10 Concepts—up and down.

Knight, Hilary. *Where's Wallace?* Illus. by author. New York: Harper, 1964.
008.37 Animals—monkeys;
016.27 Behavior—running away;
204 Zoos.

Knotts, Howard Clayton. *The Lost Christmas.* Illus. by author. New York: Harcourt, 1978.
047 Dreams; 083.03 Holidays—
Christmas; 088 Illness.

Knotts, Howard Clayton. *The Winter Cat.* Illus. by author. New York: Harper, 1972.
008.09 Animals—cats; 154.04 Seasons—winter.

Knox-Wagner, Elaine, jt. author. *The Best Mom in the World.* By Judy Delton, and Elaine Knox-Wagner.

Kobrin, Janet, jt. author. *Coyote Goes Hunting for Fire.* By Margery Bernstein, and Janet Kobrin.

Kobrin, Janet, jt. author. *Earth Namer.* By Margery Bernstein, and Janet Kobrin.

Koch, Dorothy Clarke. *Gone Is My Goose.* Illus. by Doris Lee. New York: Holiday, 1956.
017.11 Birds—geese.

Koch, Dorothy Clarke. *I Play at the Beach.* Illus. by Feodor Stepanovich Rojankovsky. New York: Random House, 1955.
057 Family life; 069 Games; 153 Sea and seashore.

Koch, Dorothy Clarke. *When the Cows Got Out.* Illus. by Paul Lantz. New York: Holiday, 1958.
008.12 Animals—cows, bulls;
058 Farms.

Koenig, Marion. *The Wonderful World of Night.* Illus. by David Parry. New York: Grosset, 1969.
008.09 Animals—cats;
016.22 Behavior—misbehavior;
119 Night.

Koffler, Camilla. *I'll Show You Cats.* Illus. by author. New York: Harper, 1964.
008.09 Animals—cats.

Koffler, Camilla. *The Little Elephant.* Illus. by author. New York: Harper, 1956.
008.17 Animals—elephants.

Koffler, Camilla. *Two Little Bears.* Illus. by author. New York: Harper, 1954.
008.06 Animals—bears;
016.20 Behavior—lost.

Koffler, Camilla, and Bonsall, Crosby Newell. *Look Who's Talking.* Illus. by Camilla Koffler. New York: Harper, 1962.
017.13 Birds—ostriches; 204 Zoos.

Koffler, Camilla, and Bonsall, Crosby Newell. *Polar Bear Brothers.* Illus. by Camilla Koffler. New York: Harper, 1960.
008.06 Animals—bears.

Koffler, Camilla, and Gregor, Arthur. *Animal Babies.* Illus. by Camilla Koffler. Designed by Luc Bouchage. New York: Harper, 1959.
008 Animals.

Kopczynski, Anna. *Jerry and Ami.* Illus. by author. New York: Scribner's, 1963.
008.14 Animals—dogs; 068 Friendship.

Koren, Edward. *Behind the Wheel.* Illus. by author. New York: Holt, 1972.
180 Transportation.

Kotzwinkle, William. *The Day the Gang Got Rich.* Illus. by Joe Servello. New York: Viking, 1970.
068 Friendship; 070 Gangs, clubs.

Kotzwinkle, William. *Up the Alley with Jack and Joe.* Illus. by Joe Servello. New York: Macmillan, 1974.
068 Friendship.

Kouts, Anne. *Kenny's Rat.* Illus. by Betty Fraser. New York: Viking, 1970.
008.48 Animals—rats; 131 Pets.

Krahn, Fernando. *April Fools.* Illus. by author. New York: Dutton, 1974.
083.01 Holidays—April Fools' Day;
087 Humor; 201 Wordless.

Krahn, Fernando. *The Biggest Christmas Tree on Earth.* Illus. by author. Boston: Little, 1978.
008 Animals; 083.03 Holidays—
Christmas; 177.02 Toys—balls;
181 Trees; 201 Wordless.

Krahn, Fernando. *Catch That Cat!* Illus. by author. New York: Dutton, 1978.
008.09 Animals—cats; 201 Wordless.

Krahn, Fernando. *A Funny Friend from Heaven.* Illus. by author. Philadelphia: Lippincott, 1977.
007 Angels; 028 Circus, clowns;
201 Wordless.

Krahn, Fernando. *The Great Ape.* Illus. by author. New York: Viking, 1978.
008.22 Animals—gorillas;
068 Friendship; 201 Wordless.

Krahn, Fernando. *How Santa Claus Had a Long and Difficult Journey Delivering His Presents.* Illus. by author. New York: Delacorte Pr., 1970.
083.03 Holidays—Christmas; 201 Wordless.

Krahn, Fernando. *Little Love Story.* Illus. by author. Philadelphia: Lippincott, 1976.
083.11 Holidays—Valentine's Day; 201 Wordless.

Krahn, Fernando. *The Mystery of the Giant Footprints.* Illus. by author. New York: Dutton, 1977.
038 Cumulative tales; 110 Monsters; 201 Wordless.

Krahn, Fernando. *Robot-Bot-Bot.* Illus. by author. New York: Dutton, 1979.
002.12 Activities—playing;
002.20 Activities—working; 145 Robots; 201 Wordless.

Krahn, Fernando. *Sebastian and the Mushroom.* Illus. by author. New York: Delacorte Pr., 1976.
047 Dreams; 201 Wordless.

Krahn, Fernando. *Who's Seen the Scissors?* Illus. by author. New York: Dutton, 1975.
201 Wordless.

Krasilovsky, Phyllis. *The Cow Who Fell in the Canal.* Illus. by Peter Spier. Garden City, NY: Doubleday, 1953.
008.12 Animals—cows, bulls;
064.14 Foreign lands—Holland.

Krasilovsky, Phyllis. *The Girl Who Was a Cowboy.* Illus. by Cyndy Szekeres. Garden City, NY: Doubleday, 1965.
031 Clothing.

Krasilovsky, Phyllis. *The Man Who Did Not Wash His Dishes.* Illus. by Barbara Cooney. Garden City, NY: Doubleday, 1950.
026.05 Character traits—cleanliness;
026.19 Character traits—laziness.

Krasilovsky, Phyllis. *Scaredy Cat.* Illus. by Ninon MacKnight. New York: Macmillan, 1959.
008.09 Animals—cats.

Krasilovsky, Phyllis. *The Shy Little Girl.* Illus. by Trina Schart Hyman. Boston: Houghton, 1970.
026.30 Character traits—shyness;
068 Friendship.

Krasilovsky, Phyllis. *The Very Little Boy.* Illus. by Ninon MacKnight. Garden City, NY: Doubleday, 1962.
013 Babies; 016.14 Behavior—growing up; 057 Family life.

Krasilovsky, Phyllis. *The Very Little Girl.* Illus. by Ninon MacKnight. Garden City, NY: Doubleday, 1953.
013 Babies; 016.14 Behavior—growing up; 057 Family life.

Krasilovsky, Phyllis. *The Very Tall Little Girl.* Illus. by Olivia H. Cole. Garden City, NY: Doubleday, 1969.
026.03 Character traits—being different; 057 Family life.

Kratka, Suzanne C., jt. author. *Hi, New Baby.* By Andrew C. Andry, and Suzanne C. Kratka.

Kraus, Robert. *Big Brother.* Illus. by author. New York: Parents, 1973.
008.46 Animals—rabbits; 013 Babies; 057 Family life.

Kraus, Robert. *Boris Bad Enough.* Illus. by José Aruego, and Ariane Dewey. New York: Dutton, 1976.
008.17 Animals—elephants.

Kraus, Robert. *Daddy Long Ears.* Illus. by author. New York: Simon & Schuster, 1970.
008.46 Animals—rabbits;
083.04 Holidays—Easter.

Kraus, Robert. *Herman the Helper.* Illus. by José Aruego, and Ariane Dewey. New York: Dutton, 1974.
026.14 Character traits—helpfulness;
123 Octopod; 153 Sea and seashore.

Kraus, Robert. *I, Mouse.* Illus. by author. New York: Harper, 1958.
008.34 Animals—mice.

Kraus, Robert. *Ladybug! Ladybug!* Illus. by author. New York: Harper, 1957.
016.24 Behavior—misunderstanding;
090 Insects and spiders.

Kraus, Robert. *Leo the Late Bloomer.* Illus. by José Aruego. New York: Dutton, 1971.
008.10 Animals—cats, wild;
016.14 Behavior—growing up.

Kraus, Robert. *The Little Giant.* Illus. by author. New York: Harper, 1967.
032.08 Concepts—size; 072 Giants.

Kraus, Robert. *The Littlest Rabbit.* Illus. by author. New York: Harper, 1961.
008.46 Animals—rabbits;
026.31 Character traits—smallness.

Kraus, Robert. *Milton the Early Riser.* Illus. by José Aruego. New York: Dutton, 1972.
008.06 Animals—bears; 162 Sleep.

Kraus, Robert. *Noel the Coward.* Illus. by José Aruego. New York: Dutton, 1977.
052.04 Emotions—fear.

Kraus, Robert. *Owliver*. Illus. by José Aruego, and Ariane Dewey. New York: Dutton, 1974.
017.14 Birds—owls; 023 Careers.

Kraus, Robert. *Rebecca Hatpin*. Illus. by Robert Byrd. New York: Dutton, 1974.
023.19 Careers—nurses;
026.14 Character traits—helpfulness;
026.29 Character traits—selfishness;
057.02 Family life—grandparents;
great-grandparents.

Kraus, Robert. *Springfellow*. Illus. by Sam Savitt. New York: Dutton, 1978.
008.28 Animals—horses.

Kraus, Robert. *The Three Friends*. Illus. by José Aruego, and Ariane Dewey. New York: Dutton, 1975.
068 Friendship.

Kraus, Robert. *The Trouble with Spider*. Illus. by author. New York: Harper, 1962.
068 Friendship; 090 Insects and spiders.

Kraus, Robert. *Whose Mouse Are You?* Illus. by José Aruego. New York: Macmillan, 1970.
008.34 Animals—mice.

Kraus, Robert, and Bodecker, Nils Mogens. *Good Night Little One*. Illus. by Nils Mogens Bodecker. New York: Dutton, 1972.
015 Bedtime; 119 Night; 162 Sleep.

Kraus, Robert, and Bodecker, Nils Mogens. *Good Night Richard Rabbit*. Illus. by Nils Mogens Bodecker. New York: Dutton, 1972.
008.46 Animals—rabbits; 015 Bedtime; 033 Counting; 119 Night; 162 Sleep.

Krauss, Ruth. *The Backward Day*. Illus. by Marc Simont. New York: Harper, 1950.
057 Family life.

Krauss, Ruth. *Bears*. Illus. by Phyllis Rowand. New York: Harper, 1948.
008.06 Animals—bears; 134 Poetry, rhyme.

Krauss, Ruth. *A Bouquet of Littles*. Illus. by Jane Flora. New York: Harper, 1963.
032.08 Concepts—size; 134 Poetry, rhyme.

Krauss, Ruth. *The Bundle Book*. Illus. by Helen Stone. New York: Harper, 1951.
015 Bedtime; 052 Emotions;
057.03 Family life—mothers;
069 Games.

Krauss, Ruth. *The Carrot Seed*. Illus. by David Johnson Leisk. New York: Harper, 1945.
002.06 Activities—gardening;
026.23 Character traits—optimism;
133 Plants; 156 Self-concept.

Krauss, Ruth. *Charlotte and the White Horse*. Illus. by Maurice Sendak. New York: Harper, 1955.
008.28 Animals—horses.

Krauss, Ruth. *Eyes, Nose, Fingers, Toes*. Illus. by Elizabeth Schneider. New York: Harper, 1964.
006 Anatomy.

Krauss, Ruth. *A Good Man and His Good Wife*. Illus. by Marc Simont. New York: Harper, 1962.
016.04 Behavior—boredom;
068 Friendship.

Krauss, Ruth. *The Growing Story*. Illus. by Phyllis Rowand. New York: Harper, 1947.
016.14 Behavior—growing up.

Krauss, Ruth. *The Happy Day*. Illus. by David Johnson Leisk. New York: Harper, 1949.
081 Hibernation; 154.02 Seasons—spring; 154.04 Seasons—winter;
195.07 Weather—snow.

Krauss, Ruth. *The Happy Egg*. Illus. by David Johnson Leisk. New York: O'Hara, 1967.
017 Birds; 050 Eggs.

Krauss, Ruth. *A Hole Is to Dig*. Illus. by Maurice Sendak. New York: Harper, 1952.
068 Friendship.

Krauss, Ruth. *I Write It*. Illus. by Mary Eileen Chalmers. New York: Harper, 1970.
002.21 Activities—writing.

Krauss, Ruth. *I'll Be You and You Be Me*. Illus. by Maurice Sendak. New York: Harper, 1954.
068 Friendship; 087 Humor.

Krauss, Ruth. *Mama, I Wish I Was Snow. Child, You'd Be Very Cold*. Illus. by Ellen Raskin. New York: Atheneum, 1962.
016.38 Behavior—wishing; 069 Games.

Krauss, Ruth. *A Moon or a Button*. Illus. by Remy Charlip. New York: Harper, 1959.
089 Imagination.

Krauss, Ruth. *Open House for Butterflies*. Illus. by Maurice Sendak. New York: Harper, 1960.
089 Imagination.

Krauss, Ruth. *Somebody Else's Nut Tree, and Other Tales from Children*. Illus. by Maurice Sendak. New York: Harper, 1958.
027 Children as authors;
089 Imagination.

Krauss, Ruth. *This Thumbprint*. Illus. by author. New York: Harper, 1967.
087 Humor; 089 Imagination.

Krauss, Ruth. *A Very Special House.* Illus. by Maurice Sendak. New York: Harper, 1953.
086 Houses; 089 Imagination.

Kroll, Steven. *The Candy Witch.* Illus. by Marylin Hafner. New York: Holiday, 1979.
016.37 Behavior—unnoticed, unseen; 083.07 Holidays—Halloween; 103 Magic; 199 Witches.

Kroll, Steven. *Fat Magic.* Illus. by Thomas Anthony de Paola. New York: Holiday, 1978.
103 Magic; 147 Royalty.

Kroll, Steven. *If I Could Be My Grandmother.* Illus. by Lady McCrady. New York: Pantheon, 1977.
057.02 Family life—grandparents; great-grandparents.

Kroll, Steven. *Santa's Crash-Bang Christmas.* Illus. by Thomas Anthony de Paola. New York: Holiday, 1977.
083.03 Holidays—Christmas.

Kroll, Steven. *The Tyrannosaurus Game.* Illus. by Thomas Anthony de Paola. New York: Holiday, 1976.
038 Cumulative tales; 044 Dinosaurs; 069 Games; 089 Imagination.

Krum, Gertrude. *The Four Riders.* Illus. by Katherine Evans. Chicago: Follett, 1953.
008.28 Animals—horses.

Krüss, James. *3 X 3, Three by Three.* Illus. by Eva Johnson Rubin. English text by Geoffrey Strachan. New York: Macmillan, 1963.
008 Animals; 033 Counting; 134 Poetry, rhyme.

Kumin, Maxine W. *The Beach Before Breakfast.* Illus. by Leonard Weisgard. New York: Putnam's, 1964.
153 Sea and seashore.

Kumin, Maxine W. *Follow the Fall.* Illus. by Artur Marokvia. New York: Putnam's, 1961.
083 Holidays; 089 Imagination; 134 Poetry, rhyme; 154.01 Seasons—fall.

Kumin, Maxine W. *Mittens in May.* Illus. by Eliott Gilbert. New York: Putnam's, 1962.
017 Birds; 026.18 Character traits—kindness to animals; 031 Clothing.

Kumin, Maxine W. *Sebastian and the Dragon.* Illus. by William D. Hayes. New York: Putnam's, 1960.
026.31 Character traits—smallness; 046 Dragons; 134 Poetry, rhyme.

Kumin, Maxine W. *Speedy Digs Downside Up.* Illus. by Ezra Jack Keats. New York: Putnam's, 1964.
026.01 Character traits—ambition; 087 Humor; 134 Poetry, rhyme.

Kumin, Maxine W. *Spring Things.* Illus. by Artur Marokvia. New York: Putnam's, 1961.
134 Poetry, rhyme; 154.02 Seasons—spring.

Kumin, Maxine W. *A Winter Friend.* Illus. by Artur Marokvia. New York: Putnam's, 1961.
134 Poetry, rhyme; 154.04 Seasons—winter.

Kumin, Maxine W. *The Wizard's Tears.* Illus. by Evaline Ness. New York: McGraw-Hill, 1975.
103 Magic; 200 Wizards.

Kumin, Maxine W., and Sexton, Anne. *Eggs of Things.* Illus. by Leonard Shortall. New York: Putnam's, 1963.
005 Amphibians; 050 Eggs; 152 Science.

Kumin, Maxine W., and Sexton, Anne. *Joey and the Birthday Present.* Illus. by Evaline Ness. New York: McGraw-Hill, 1971.
008.34 Animals—mice; 018 Birthdays.

Kunhardt, Dorothy. *Billy the Barber.* Illus. by William Pène Du Bois. New York: Harper, 1961.
023.04 Careers—barbers; 076 Hair; 125 Old age.

Kuratomi, Chizuko. *Mr. Bear and the Robbers.* Illus. by Kozo Kakimoto. New York: Dial Pr., 1970.
008.06 Animals—bears; 008.46 Animals—rabbits.

Kuskin, Karla Seidman. *ABCDEFGHIJKLMNOPQRSTUVWXYZ.* Illus. by author. New York: Harper, 1963.
001 ABC Books.

Kuskin, Karla Seidman. *All Sizes of Noises.* Illus. by author. New York: Harper, 1962.
032 Concepts; 120 Noise; 134 Poetry, rhyme.

Kuskin, Karla Seidman. *The Animals and the Ark.* Illus. by author. New York: Harper, 1958.
008 Animals; 019 Boats, ships; 134 Poetry, rhyme; 141.01 Religion—Noah.

Kuskin, Karla Seidman. *In the Flaky Frosty Morning.* Illus. by author. New York: Harper, 1969.
134 Poetry, rhyme; 154.04 Seasons—winter; 163 Snowmen;
195.07 Weather—snow.

Kuskin, Karla Seidman. *James and the Rain.* Illus. by author. New York: Harper, 1957.
008 Animals; 134 Poetry, rhyme;
195.05 Weather—rain.

Kuskin, Karla Seidman. *Just Like Everyone Else.* Illus. by author. New York: Harper, 1959.
002.05 Activities—flying.

Kuskin, Karla Seidman. *Roar and More.* Illus. by author. New York: Harper, 1956.
008 Animals; 120 Noise;
129 Participation; 134 Poetry, rhyme.

Kuskin, Karla Seidman. *Sand and Snow.* Illus. by author. New York: Harper, 1965.
134 Poetry, rhyme; 153 Sea and seashore; 154.03 Seasons—summer;
154.04 Seasons—winter.

Kuskin, Karla Seidman. *A Space Story.* Illus. by Marc Simont. New York: Harper, 1978.
015 Bedtime; 165 Space and space ships; 167 Stars.

Kuskin, Karla Seidman. *Watson, the Smartest Dog in the U.S.A.* Illus. by author. New York: Harper, 1968.
002.13 Activities—reading;
008.14 Animals—dogs.

Kuskin, Karla Seidman. *What Did You Bring Me?* Illus. by author. New York: Harper, 1973.
008.34 Animals—mice;
016.13 Behavior—greed; 156 Self-concept; 199 Witches.

Kuskin, Karla Seidman. *Which Horse Is William?* Illus. by author. New York: Harper, 1959.
026.16 Character traits—individuality;
089 Imagination.

Kwitz, Mary DeBall. *Little Chick's Story.* Illus. by Cyndy Szekeres. New York: Harper, 1978.
017.04 Birds—chickens; 050 Eggs.

Kwitz, Mary DeBall. *Mouse at Home.* Illus. by author. New York: Harper, 1966.
008.34 Animals—mice; 154 Seasons.

Kwitz, Mary DeBall. *When It Rains.* Illus. by author. Chicago: Follett, 1974.
008 Animals; 134 Poetry, rhyme;
195.05 Weather—rain;
195.06 Weather—rainbows.

LaFarge, Phyllis. *Joanna Runs Away.* Illus. by Trina Schart Hyman. New York: Holt, 1973.
016.27 Behavior—running away.

La Fontaine, Jean de. *The Hare and the Tortoise.* Illus. by Brian Wildsmith. New York: Watts, 1966.
008.46 Animals—rabbits; 062 Folk and fairy tales; 142.05 Reptiles—turtles;
166.11 Sports—racing.

La Fontaine, Jean de. *The Lion and the Rat.* Illus. by Brian Wildsmith. New York: Watts, 1963.
008.10 Animals—cats, wild;
008.48 Animals—rats; 026.14 Character traits—helpfulness; 062 Folk and fairy tales.

La Fontaine, Jean de. *The Miller, the Boy and the Donkey.* Illus. by Brian Wildsmith. New York: Watts, 1969.
008.16 Animals—donkeys;
026.26 Character traits—practicality;
062 Folk and fairy tales; 087 Humor.

La Fontaine, Jean de. *The North Wind and the Sun.* Illus. by Brian Wildsmith. New York: Watts, 1964.
062 Folk and fairy tales; 169 Sun;
195.08 Weather—wind.

La Fontaine, Jean de. *The Rich Man and the Shoemaker.* Illus. by Brian Wildsmith. New York: Watts, 1965.
016.13 Behavior—greed;
023.24 Careers—shoemakers; 062 Folk and fairy tales; 135 Poverty.

Lane, Carolyn. *The Voices of Greenwillow Pond.* Illus. by Wallace Tripp. Boston: Houghton, 1972.
005 Amphibians; 026.25 Character traits—perseverance.

Langstaff, John Meredith. *Oh, A-Hunting We Will Go.* Illus. by Nancy Winslow Parker. New York: Atheneum, 1974.
116 Music; 164 Songs; 166.08 Sports—hunting.

Langstaff, John Meredith. *Ol' Dan Tucker.* Illus. by Joe Krush. New York: Harcourt, 1963.
062 Folk and fairy tales; 116 Music; 164 Songs.

Langstaff, John Meredith. *Over in the Meadow.* Illus. by Feodor Stepanovich Rojankovsky. New York: Harcourt, 1957.
008 Animals; 033 Counting; 062 Folk and fairy tales; 164 Songs.

Langstaff, John Meredith. *Soldier, Soldier, Won't You Marry Me?* Illus. by Anita Lobel. Compiled by John Langstaff. Garden City, NY: Doubleday, 1972.
023.17 Careers—military; 116 Music; 164 Songs.

Langstaff, John Meredith. *The Swapping Boy.* Illus. by Beth Krush, and Joe Krush. New York: Harcourt, 1960.
002.15 Activities—trading; 062 Folk and fairy tales; 116 Music; 164 Songs.

Langstaff, John Meredith. *The Two Magicians.* Illus. by Fritz Eichenberg. Adapted by John Langstaff from an ancient ballad. New York: Atheneum, 1973.
062 Folk and fairy tales; 103 Magic; 116 Music; 164 Songs; 199 Witches.

Langstaff, John Meredith, and Groves-Raines, Antony. *On Christmas Day in the Morning!* Illus. by Antony Groves-Raines. New York: Harcourt, 1959.
062 Folk and fairy tales; 083.03 Holidays—Christmas; 116 Music; 164 Songs.

Langstaff, Nancy. *A Tiny Baby for You.* Illus. by Suzanne Szasz. New York: Harcourt, 1955.
013 Babies.

Lansdown, Brenda. *Galumpf.* Illus. by Ernest Crichlow. Boston: Houghton, 1963.
008.09 Animals—cats; 053.01 Ethnic groups in the U.S.—Afro-Americans; 053.07 Ethnic groups in the U.S.—Multi-ethnic; 131 Pets.

Lapp, Carolyn. *The Dentists' Tools.* Illus. by George Overlie. Minneapolis: Lerner, 1961.
023.07 Careers—dentists.

Lapp, Eleanor J. *In the Morning Mist.* Illus. by David Cunningham. Chicago: Albert Whitman, 1978.
057.02 Family life—grandparents; great-grandparents; 112 Morning.

Lapp, Eleanor J. *The Mice Came in Early This Year.* Illus. by David Cunningham. Chicago: Albert Whitman, 1976.
008 Animals; 058 Farms; 154.01 Seasons—fall; 154.04 Seasons—winter.

Lapsley, Susan. *I Am Adopted.* Illus. by Michael Alan Charlton. New York: Bradbury Pr., 1974.
003 Adoption; 057 Family life.

Lasell, Fen. *Michael Grows a Wish.* Illus. by author. Boston: Houghton, 1962.
008.28 Animals—horses; 016.38 Behavior—wishing; 018 Birthdays.

Lasher, Faith B. *Hubert Hippo's World.* Illus. by Leonard Lee Rue, III. Chicago: Children's Pr., 1971.
008.27 Animals—hippopotami.

Lasker, Joseph Leon. *He's My Brother.* Illus. by author. Chicago: Albert Whitman, 1974.
026.20 Character traits—loyalty; 057 Family life; 077 Handicaps.

Lasker, Joseph Leon. *Lentil Soup.* Illus. by author. Chicago: Albert Whitman, 1977.
002.03 Activities—cooking; 033 Counting; 039 Days of the week, months of the year; 063 Food.

Lasker, Joseph Leon. *Mothers Can Do Anything.* Illus. by author. Chicago: Albert Whitman, 1972.
002.20 Activities—working; 023 Careers; 057.03 Family life—mothers; 121 Non-sexist.

Laskowski, Jerzy. *Master of the Royal Cats.* Illus. by Janina Domanska. New York: Seabury Pr., 1965.
008.09 Animals—cats; 008.14 Animals—dogs; 064.01 Foreign lands—Africa; 064.09 Foreign lands—Egypt; 147 Royalty.

Lasky, Kathryn, jt. author. *Agatha's Alphabet, with Her Very Own Dictionary.* By Lucy Floyd, and Kathryn Lasky.

Lasky, Kathryn. *I Have Four Names for My Grandfather.* Illus. by Christopher G. Knight. Boston: Little, 1976.
057.02 Family life—grandparents; great-grandparents; 052.08 Emotions—love.

Lasson, Robert. *Orange Oliver.* Illus. by Chuck Hayden. New York: McKay, 1957.
008.09 Animals—cats; 058 Farms; 073 Glasses.

Lathrop, Dorothy Pulis. *An Angel in the Woods.* Illus. by author. New York: Macmillan, 1947.
007 Angels; 083.03 Holidays—Christmas.

Lathrop, Dorothy Pulis. *Puppies for Keeps.* Illus. by author. New York: Macmillan, 1943.
008.14 Animals—dogs; 131 Pets.

Lathrop, Dorothy Pulis. *Who Goes There?* Illus. by author. New York: Macmillan, 1935.
002.11 Activities—picnicking;
008 Animals; 026.18 Character traits—kindness to animals; 154.04 Seasons—winter.

Lattin, Anne. *Peter's Policeman.* Illus. by Gertrude E. Espenscheid. Chicago: Follett, 1958.
023.21 Careers—police officers.

Laurin, Anne. *Little Things.* Illus. by Marcia Sewall. New York: Atheneum, 1978.
002.08 Activities—knitting;
026.24 Character traits—patience;
087 Humor.

Lawrence, James D. *Binky Brothers and the Fearless Four.* Illus. by Leonard P. Kessler. New York: Harper, 1970.
023.08 Careers—detectives; 186 Twins.

Lawrence, James D. *Binky Brothers, Detectives.* Illus. by Leonard P. Kessler. New York: Harper, 1968.
023.08 Careers—detectives.

Lawrence, John D. *The Giant of Grabbist.* Illus. by author. Port Washington, NY: White, 1969.
064.10 Foreign lands—England;
072 Giants.

Lawrence, John D. *Pope Leo's Elephant.* Illus. by author. Cleveland: Collins, 1970.
008.17 Animals—elephants; 059 Fire;
064.41 Foreign lands—Vatican City.

Leaf, Munro. *Boo, Who Used to Be Scared of the Dark.* Illus. by author. New York: Random House, 1948.
015 Bedtime; 052.04 Emotions—fear;
119 Night.

Leaf, Munro. *A Flock of Watchbirds.* Illus. by author. Philadelphia: Lippincott, 1946.
016.22 Behavior—misbehavior;
054 Etiquette.

Leaf, Munro. *Gordon, the Goat.* Illus. by author. Philadelphia: Lippincott, 1944.
008.21 Animals—goats.

Leaf, Munro. *Grammar Can Be Fun.* Illus. by author. Philadelphia: Lippincott, 1934.
096 Language.

Leaf, Munro. *Health Can Be Fun.* Illus. by author. New York: Stokes, 1943.
079 Health.

Leaf, Munro. *How to Behave and Why.* Illus. by author. Philadelphia: Lippincott, 1946.
054 Etiquette.

Leaf, Munro. *Manners Can Be Fun.* Illus. by author. Philadelphia: Lippincott, 1958.
054 Etiquette.

Leaf, Munro. *Noodle.* Illus. by author. New York: Four Winds Pr., 1965.
008.14 Animals—dogs; 156 Self-concept.

Leaf, Munro. *Robert Francis Weatherbee.* Illus. by author. Philadelphia: Lippincott, 1935.
151 School.

Leaf, Munro. *Safety Can Be Fun.* Illus. by author. Philadelphia: Lippincott, 1961.
148 Safety.

Leaf, Munro. *The Story of Ferdinand the Bull.* Illus. by Robert Lawson. New York: Viking, 1936.
008.12 Animals—cows, bulls;
026.16 Character traits—individuality;
064.34 Foreign lands—Spain;
191 Violence, anti-violence.

Leaf, Munro. *Wee Gillis.* Illus. by Robert Lawson. New York: Viking, 1938.
064.31 Foreign lands—Scotland.

Lear, Edward. *ABC.* Illus. by author. New York: McGraw-Hill, 1965.
001 ABC Books; 134 Poetry, rhyme.

Lear, Edward. *The Dong with the Luminous Nose.* Illus. by Edward St. John Gorey. Reading: Addison-Wesley, 1969.
087 Humor; 134 Poetry, rhyme.

Lear, Edward. *Edward Lear's Nonsense Book.* Illus. by Tony Palazzo. Garden City, NY: Doubleday, 1956.
087 Humor; 116 Music; 134 Poetry, rhyme.

Lear, Edward. *Lear's Nonsense Verses.* Illus. by Tomi Ungerer. New York: Grosset, 1967.
087 Humor; 134 Poetry, rhyme.

Lear, Edward. *Nonsense Alphabets.* Illus. by Richard McClure Scarry. Garden City, NY: Doubleday, 1962.
001 ABC Books; 134 Poetry, rhyme.

Lear, Edward. *The Nutcrackers and the Sugar-Tongs.* Illus. by Marcia Sewall. Boston: Little, 1978.
087 Humor; 134 Poetry, rhyme.

Lear, Edward. *The Owl and the Pussy-Cat.* Illus. by Barbara Cooney. Boston: Little, 1961/1969.
008.09 Animals—cats; 017.14 Birds—owls; 134 Poetry, rhyme.

Lear, Edward. *The Owl and the Pussy-Cat.* Illus. by William Pène Du Bois. Garden City, NY: Doubleday, 1961.
008.09 Animals—cats; 017.14 Birds—owls; 134 Poetry, rhyme.

Lear, Edward. *The Owl and the Pussy-Cat.* Illus. by Gwen Fulton. New York: Atheneum, 1977.
008.09 Animals—cats; 017.14 Birds—owls; 134 Poetry, rhyme.

Lear, Edward. *The Pelican Chorus.* Illus. by Harold Berson. New York: Parents, 1967.
017.17 Birds—pelicans; 087 Humor; 116 Music; 134 Poetry, rhyme; 164 Songs.

Lear, Edward. *The Pobble Who Has No Toes.* Illus. by Kevin W. Maddison. New York: Viking, 1977.
087 Humor; 134 Poetry, rhyme.

Lear, Edward. *The Quangle Wangle's Hat.* Illus. by Helen Oxenbury. New York: Watts, 1969.
031 Clothing; 087 Humor; 134 Poetry, rhyme.

Lear, Edward. *Whizz!* Illus. by Janina Domanska. Completed by Ogden Nash. New York: Macmillan, 1973.
038 Cumulative tales; 087 Humor; 134 Poetry, rhyme.

Leavens, George. *Kippy the Koala.* Illus. by Crosby Newell Bonsall. New York: Harper, 1960.
008.32 Animals—koala bears; 134 Poetry, rhyme; 154.02 Seasons—spring.

Leichman, Seymour. *Shaggy Dogs and Spotty Dogs and Shaggy and Spotty Dogs.* Illus. by author. New York: Harcourt, 1973.
008.14 Animals—dogs; 134 Poetry, rhyme.

Leichman, Seymour. *The Wicked Wizard and the Wicked Witch.* Illus. by author. New York: Harcourt, 1972.
103 Magic; 134 Poetry, rhyme; 199 Witches; 200 Wizards.

Leisk, David Johnson. *The Blue Ribbon Puppies.* Illus. by author. New York: Harper, 1958.
008.14 Animals—dogs.

Leisk, David Johnson. *Ellen's Lion.* Illus. by author. New York: Harper, 1959.
089 Imagination; 177 Toys.

Leisk, David Johnson. *The Emperor's Gift.* Illus. by author. New York: Holt, 1965.
026 Character traits; 026.13 Character traits—generosity; 147 Royalty.

Leisk, David Johnson. *The Frowning Prince.* Illus. by author. New York: Harper, 1959.
147 Royalty.

Leisk, David Johnson. *Harold and the Purple Crayon.* Illus. by author. New York: Harper, 1955.
011 Art; 087 Humor; 089 Imagination.

Leisk, David Johnson. *Harold at the North Pole.* Illus. by author. New York: Harper, 1957.
083.03 Holidays—Christmas; 089 Imagination.

Leisk, David Johnson. *Harold's ABC's.* Illus. by author. New York: Harper, 1963.
001 ABC Books.

Leisk, David Johnson. *Harold's Circus.* Illus. by author. New York: Harper, 1959.
028 Circus, clowns; 087 Humor; 089 Imagination.

Leisk, David Johnson. *Harold's Fairy Tale.* Illus. by author. New York: Harper, 1956.
062 Folk and fairy tales; 089 Imagination.

Leisk, David Johnson. *Harold's Trip to the Sky.* Illus. by author. New York: Harper, 1957.
089 Imagination; 165 Space and space ships.

Leisk, David Johnson. *A Picture for Harold's Room.* Illus. by author. New York: Harper, 1960.
011 Art; 089 Imagination.

Leisk, David Johnson. *Terrible Terrifying Toby.* Illus. by author. New York: Harper, 1957.
008.14 Animals—dogs.

Leisk, David Johnson. *Time for Spring.* Illus. by author. New York: Harper, 1957.
154.02 Seasons—spring; 163 Snowmen.

Leisk, David Johnson. *Upside Down*. Illus. by author. Chicago: Albert Whitman, 1969.
008.30 Animals—kangaroos;
032.10 Concepts—up and down;
087 Humor; 202 World.

Leisk, David Johnson. *We Wonder What Will Walter Be, When He Grows Up?* Illus. by author. New York: Holt, 1964.
008 Animals; 016.14 Behavior—growing up.

Leisk, David Johnson. *Will Spring Be Early?* Illus. by author. New York: Crowell, 1959.
008.23 Animals—groundhogs;
083.06 Holidays—Groundhog Day;
154.02 Seasons—spring.

Leister, Mary. *The Silent Concert*. Illus. by Yoko Mitsuhashi. Indianapolis: Bobbs-Merrill, 1970.
066 Forest, woods; 120 Noise.

Lemke, Horst. *Places and Faces*. Illus. by author. New York: Scroll Pr., 1971.
201 Wordless.

Lenski, Lois L. *Animals for Me*. Illus. by author. New York: Oxford Univ. Pr., 1941.
008 Animals.

Lenski, Lois L. *At Our House*. Illus. by author. Music by Clyde Robert Bulla. New York: Walck, 1959.
057 Family life; 116 Music; 164 Songs.

Lenski, Lois L. *Big Little Davy*. Illus. by author. New York: Walck, 1956.
008 Animals.

Lenski, Lois L. *Cowboy Small*. Illus. by author. New York: Oxford Univ. Pr., 1949.
035 Cowboys.

Lenski, Lois L. *Davy and His Dog*. Illus. by author. New York: Walck, 1957.
008.14 Animals—dogs; 116 Music;
164 Songs.

Lenski, Lois L. *Davy Goes Places*. Illus. by author. New York: Walck, 1961.
002.16 Activities—traveling; 116 Music;
164 Songs; 180 Transportation.

Lenski, Lois L. *Debbie and Her Dolls*. Illus. by author. New York: Walck, 1970.
008.14 Animals—dogs; 177.04 Toys—dolls.

Lenski, Lois L. *Debbie and Her Family*. Illus. by author. New York: Walck, 1969.
057 Family life.

Lenski, Lois L. *Debbie and Her Grandma*. Illus. by author. New York: Walck, 1967.
057.02 Family life—grandparents;
great-grandparents; 116 Music;
164 Songs.

Lenski, Lois L. *Debbie Goes to Nursery School*. Illus. by author. New York: Walck, 1970.
151 School.

Lenski, Lois L. *A Dog Came to School*. Illus. by author. New York: Oxford Univ. Pr., 1955.
008.14 Animals—dogs; 116 Music;
151 School; 164 Songs.

Lenski, Lois L. *I Like Winter*. Illus. by author. New York: Oxford Univ. Pr., 1950.
116 Music; 134 Poetry, rhyme;
154.04 Seasons—winter; 164 Songs.

Lenski, Lois L. *I Went for a Walk*. Illus. by author. New York: Walck, 1958.
002.18 Activities—walking; 116 Music;
164 Songs.

Lenski, Lois L. *Let's Play House*. Illus. by author. New York: Walck, 1944.
002.12 Activities—playing;
177.04 Toys—dolls.

Lenski, Lois L. *The Little Airplane*. Illus. by author. New York: Oxford Univ. Pr., 1938.
004 Airplanes.

Lenski, Lois L. *The Little Auto*. Illus. by author. New York: Oxford Univ. Pr., 1934.
012 Automobiles.

Lenski, Lois L. *The Little Family*. Illus. by author. Garden City, NY: Doubleday, 1932.
057 Family life.

Lenski, Lois L. *The Little Farm*. Illus. by author. New York: Oxford Univ. Pr., 1942.
058 Farms.

Lenski, Lois L. *The Little Fire Engine*. Illus. by author. New York: Oxford Univ. Pr., 1946.
023.10 Careers—firefighters.

Lenski, Lois L. *The Little Sail Boat*. Illus. by author. New York: Oxford Univ. Pr., 1937.
019 Boats, ships.

Lenski, Lois L. *The Little Train*. Illus. by author. New York: Oxford Univ. Pr., 1940.
023.22 Careers—railroad engineers;
179 Trains.

Lenski, Lois L. *Mr. and Mrs. Noah*. Illus. by author. New York: Crowell, 1948.
019 Boats, ships; 141.01 Religion—Noah.

Lenski, Lois L. *Now It's Fall.* Illus. by author. New York: Walck, 1948.
134 Poetry, rhyme; 154.01 Seasons—fall.

Lenski, Lois L. *On a Summer Day.* Illus. by author. New York: Oxford Univ. Pr., 1953.
134 Poetry, rhyme; 154.03 Seasons—summer.

Lenski, Lois L. *Papa Small.* Illus. by author. New York: Oxford Univ. Pr., 1951.
057 Family life; 057.01 Family life—fathers.

Lenski, Lois L. *Policeman Small.* Illus. by author. New York: Walck, 1962.
023.21 Careers—police officers; 029 City.

Lenski, Lois L. *Spring Is Here.* Illus. by author. New York: Oxford Univ. Pr., 1945.
134 Poetry, rhyme; 154.02 Seasons—spring.

Lenski, Lois L. *A Surprise for Davy.* Illus. by author. New York: Walck, 1947.
018 Birthdays; 130 Parties.

Lenski, Lois L. *Susie Mariar.* Illus. by author. New York: Walck, 1939/1967.
038 Cumulative tales; 062 Folk and fairy tales; 134 Poetry, rhyme.

Lent, Blair. *From King Boggen's Hall to Nothing at All.* Illus. by author. A collection of improbable houses and unusual places found in traditional rhymes and limericks. Boston: Little, 1967.
086 Houses; 087 Humor; 122 Nursery rhymes.

Lent, Blair. *John Tabor's Ride.* Illus. by author. Boston: Little, 1966.
008.60 Animals—whales; 062 Folk and fairy tales; 087 Humor.

Lent, Blair. *Pistachio.* Illus. by author. Boston: Little, 1964.
008.12 Animals—cows, bulls; 028 Circus, clowns.

Leodhas, Sorche Nic (pseud.). See Alger, Leclaire.

Lerner, Marguerite Rush. *Dear Little Mumps Child.* Illus. by George Overlie. Minneapolis: Lerner, 1959.
088 Illness; 134 Poetry, rhyme.

Lerner, Marguerite Rush. *Doctors' Tools.* Illus. by George Overlie. Rev. 2nd ed. Minneapolis: Lerner, 1960.
023.09 Careers—doctors; 176 Tools.

Lerner, Marguerite Rush. *Lefty: The Story of Left-Handedness.* Illus. by Rov Andre. Minneapolis: Lerner, 1960.
026.03 Character traits—being different; 098 Left-handedness.

Lerner, Marguerite Rush. *Michael Gets the Measles.* Illus. by George Overlie. Minneapolis: Lerner, 1959.
088 Illness.

Lerner, Marguerite Rush. *Peter Gets the Chickenpox.* Illus. by George Overlie. Minneapolis: Lerner, 1959.
088 Illness.

LeSieg, Theo (pseud.). See Geisel, Theodor Seuss.

Levine, Joan. *A Bedtime Story.* Illus. by Gail Owens. New York: Dutton, 1975.
015 Bedtime.

Levine, Rhoda. *Harrison Loved His Umbrella.* Illus. by Karla Seidman Kuskin. New York: Atheneum, 1964.
026.03 Character traits—being different; 026.16 Character traits—individuality; 187 Umbrellas.

Levy, Elizabeth. *Nice Little Girls.* Illus. by Mordicai Gerstein. New York: Delacorte Pr., 1974.
121 Non-sexist; 151 School.

Levy, Elizabeth. *Something Queer Is Going On.* Illus. by Mordicai Gerstein. New York: Delacorte Pr., 1973.
008.14 Animals—dogs; 137 Problem solving.

Levy, Miriam F., jt. author. *Adam's World, San Francisco.* By Kathleen Fraser, and Miriam F. Levy.

Levy, Sara G. *Mother Goose Rhymes for Jewish Children.* Illus. by Jessie B. Robinson. New York: Bloch, 1945.
093 Jewish culture; 122 Nursery rhymes.

Lewis, Claudia I. *When I Go to the Moon.* Illus. by Leonard Weisgard. New York: Macmillan, 1961.
048 Earth; 111 Moon.

Lewis, Richard, ed. *In a Spring Garden.* Illus. by Ezra Jack Keats. New York: Dial Pr., 1965.
134 Poetry, rhyme.

Lewis, Stephen. *Zoo City.* Illus. by author. New York: Greenwillow, 1976.
008 Animals; 029 City; 067 Format, unusual; 089 Imagination; 201 Wordless; 204 Zoos.

Lewis, Thomas. *Hill of Fire*. Illus. by Joan Sandin. New York: Harper, 1971.
064.24 Foreign lands—Mexico;
192 Volcanoes.

Lewiton, Mina. See Simon, Mina Lewiton.

Lexau, Joan M. *Benjie*. Illus. by Donald Alan Bolognese. New York: Dial Pr., 1964.
026.30 Character traits—shyness;
053.01 Ethnic groups in the U.S.—Afro-Americans; 057 Family life;
057.02 Family life—grandparents;
great-grandparents; 137 Problem solving.

Lexau, Joan M. *Benjie on His Own*. Illus. by Donald Alan Bolognese. New York: Dial Pr., 1970.
026.16 Character traits—individuality;
029 City; 053.01 Ethnic groups in the U.S.—Afro-Americans; 057.02 Family life—grandparents; great-grandparents;
088 Illness; 137 Problem solving.

Lexau, Joan M. *Cathy Is Company*. Illus. by Aliki Liacouras Brandenberg. New York: Dial Pr., 1961.
054 Etiquette; 068 Friendship.

Lexau, Joan M. *Come Here, Cat*. Illus. by Steven Kellogg. New York: Harper, 1973.
008.09 Animals—cats; 029 City.

Lexau, Joan M. *Crocodile and Hen*. Illus. by Joan Sandin. New York: Harper, 1969.
017.04 Birds—chickens; 038 Cumulative tales; 062 Folk and fairy tales;
064.01 Foreign lands—Africa;
142.01 Reptiles—alligators, crocodiles.

Lexau, Joan M. *Every Day a Dragon*. Illus. by Ben Schecter. New York: Harper, 1967.
057 Family life; 057.01 Family life—fathers; 069 Games.

Lexau, Joan M. *Finders Keepers, Losers Weepers*. Illus. by Thomas Anthony de Paola. Philadelphia: Lippincott, 1967.
013 Babies; 016.19 Behavior—losing things; 016.21 Behavior—lying;
057 Family life.

Lexau, Joan M. *Go Away, Dog*. Illus. by Crosby Newell Bonsall. New York: Harper, 1963.
008.14 Animals—dogs; 018 Birthdays.

Lexau, Joan M. *The Homework Caper*. Illus. by Sydney Hoff. New York: Harper, 1966.
016.32 Behavior—sibling rivalry.

Lexau, Joan M. *A House So Big*. Illus. by Sydney Hoff. New York: Harper, 1968.
026.13 Character traits—generosity;
052.08 Emotions—love; 057.03 Family life—mothers; 089 Imagination.

Lexau, Joan M. *I Should Have Stayed in Bed*. Illus. by Sydney Hoff. New York: Harper, 1965.
016.02 Behavior—bad day;
052.02 Emotions—embarrassment;
053.01 Ethnic groups in the U.S.—Afro-Americans.

Lexau, Joan M. *It All Began with a Drip, Drip, Drip*. Illus. by Joan Sandin. New York: McCall, 1970.
016.23 Behavior—mistakes;
026.04 Character traits—bravery;
062 Folk and fairy tales; 064.16 Foreign lands—India.

Lexau, Joan M. *Me Day*. Illus. by Robert Weaver. New York: Dial Pr., 1971.
018 Birthdays; 029 City; 045 Divorce;
053.01 Ethnic groups in the U.S.—Afro-Americans; 057 Family life; 057.01 Family life—fathers.

Lexau, Joan M. *Millicent's Ghost*. Illus. by Ben Shecter. New York: Dial Pr., 1962.
071 Ghosts; 119 Night.

Lexau, Joan M. *Olaf Is Late*. Illus. by Harvey Weiss. New York: Dial Pr., 1963.
016.17 Behavior—hurrying; 151 School.

Lexau, Joan M. *Olaf Reads*. Illus. by Harvey Weiss. New York: Dial Pr., 1961.
002.13 Activities—reading.

Lexau, Joan M. *The Rooftop Mystery*. Illus. by Sydney Hoff. New York: Harper, 1968.
053.01 Ethnic groups in the U.S.—Afro-Americans; 114 Moving; 177.04 Toys—dolls.

Lexau, Joan M. *Who Took the Farmer's Hat?* Illus. by Fritz Siebel. New York: Harper, 1963.
031 Clothing; 058 Farms;
195.08 Weather—wind.

Lifton, Betty Jean. *Goodnight Orange Monster*. Illus. by Cyndy Szekeres. New York: Atheneum, 1972.
015 Bedtime; 052.04 Emotions—fear;
110 Monsters; 119 Night.

Lifton, Betty Jean. *Joji and the Amanojaku*. Illus. by Eiichi Mitsui. New York: Norton, 1965.
017 Birds; 064.19 Foreign lands—Japan; 074 Goblins; 150 Scarecrows.

Lifton, Betty Jean. *Joji and the Dragon.* Illus. by Eiichi Mitsui. New York: Morrow, 1957.
017 Birds; 046 Dragons; 064.19 Foreign lands—Japan; 150 Scarecrows.

Lifton, Betty Jean. *Joji and the Fog.* Illus. by Eiichi Mitsui. New York: Morrow, 1959.
017 Birds; 150 Scarecrows; 195.04 Weather—fog.

Lifton, Betty Jean. *The Many Lives of Chio and Goro.* Illus. by Yasuo Segawa. New York: Norton, 1968.
008.18 Animals—foxes; 017.04 Birds—chickens; 064.19 Foreign lands—Japan.

Lifton, Betty Jean. *The Rice-Cake Rabbit.* Illus. by Eiichi Mitsui. New York: Norton, 1966.
008.46 Animals—rabbits; 064.19 Foreign lands—Japan; 111 Moon.

Lifton, Betty Jean. *The Secret Seller.* Illus. by Etienne Delessert, and Norma Holt. New York: Norton, 1967.
016.29 Behavior—secrets; 089 Imagination.

Linch, Elizabeth Johanna. *Samson.* Illus. by author. New York: Harper, 1964.
008.34 Animals—mice; 083.03 Holidays—Christmas; 154.04 Seasons—winter.

Lindgren, Astrid Ericsson. *Christmas in the Stable.* Illus. by Harald Wiberg. New York: Coward, 1962.
083.03 Holidays—Christmas; 064.35 Foreign lands—Sweden; 141 Religion.

Lindgren, Astrid Ericsson. *The Tomten.* Illus. by Harald Wiberg. Adapted from a poem by Victor Rydberg. New York: Coward, 1961.
058 Farms; 064.35 Foreign lands—Sweden; 154.04 Seasons—winter; 183 Trolls.

Lindgren, Astrid Ericsson. *The Tomten and the Fox.* Illus. by Harald Wiberg. Adapted from a poem by Victor Rydberg. New York: Coward, 1966.
008.18 Animals—foxes; 064.35 Foreign lands—Sweden; 154.04 Seasons—winter; 183 Trolls.

Lindgren, Astrid Ericsson, and Wikland, Ilon. *Christmas in Noisy Village.* Illus. by Ilon Wikland. Translated by Florence Lamborn. New York: Viking, 1964.
064.35 Foreign lands—Sweden; 083.03 Holidays—Christmas.

Lindman, Maj Jan. *Flicka, Ricka, Dicka and a Little Dog.* Illus. by author. Chicago: Albert Whitman, 1946.
008.14 Animals—dogs; 057 Family life; 064.35 Foreign lands—Sweden.

Lindman, Maj Jan. *Flicka, Ricka, Dicka and the Big Red Hen.* Illus. by author. Chicago: Albert Whitman, 1960.
017.04 Birds—chickens; 057 Family life; 182 Triplets.

Lindman, Maj Jan. *Flicka, Ricka, Dicka and the New Dotted Dress.* Illus. by author. Chicago: Albert Whitman, 1939.
026.14 Character traits—helpfulness; 057 Family life; 064.35 Foreign lands—Sweden; 182 Triplets.

Lindman, Maj Jan. *Flicka, Ricka, Dicka and the Three Kittens.* Illus. by author. Chicago: Albert Whitman, 1941.
008.09 Animals—cats; 057 Family life; 182 Triplets.

Lindman, Maj Jan. *Flicka, Ricka, Dicka and Their New Skates.* Illus. by author. Chicago: Albert Whitman, 1950.
008.14 Animals—dogs; 057 Family life; 064.35 Foreign lands—Sweden; 166.09 Sports—ice skating; 182 Triplets.

Lindman, Maj Jan. *Flicka, Ricka, Dicka Bake a Cake.* Illus. by author. Chicago: Albert Whitman, 1955.
002.03 Activities—cooking; 018 Birthdays; 057 Family life; 064.35 Foreign lands—Sweden; 182 Triplets.

Lindman, Maj Jan. *Sailboat Time.* Illus. by author. Chicago: Albert Whitman, 1951.
019 Boats, ships; 064.35 Foreign lands—Sweden.

Lindman, Maj Jan. *Snipp, Snapp, Snurr and the Buttered Bread.* Illus. by author. Chicago: Albert Whitman, 1934/1937.
038 Cumulative tales; 057 Family life; 058 Farms; 064.35 Foreign lands—Sweden; 182 Triplets.

Lindman, Maj Jan. *Snipp, Snapp, Snurr and the Gingerbread.* Illus. by author. Chicago: Albert Whitman, 1932.
057 Family life; 182 Triplets.

Lindman, Maj Jan. *Snipp, Snapp, Snurr and the Magic Horse.* Illus. by author. Chicago: Albert Whitman, 1935.
057 Family life; 064.35 Foreign lands—Sweden; 103 Magic; 177.05 Toys—rocking horses; 182 Triplets.

Lindman, Maj Jan. *Snipp, Snapp, Snurr and the Red Shoes.* Illus. by author. Chicago: Albert Whitman, 1932.
002.17 Activities—vacationing;
018 Birthdays; 026.13 Character traits—generosity; 026.14 Character traits—helpfulness; 057 Family life;
064.21 Foreign lands—Lapland;
166.12 Sports—skiing; 182 Triplets.

Lindman, Maj Jan. *Snipp, Snapp, Snurr and the Reindeer.* Illus. by author. Chicago: Albert Whitman, 1957.
008.13 Animals—deer; 057 Family life;
064.35 Foreign lands—Sweden;
182 Triplets.

Lindman, Maj Jan. *Snipp, Snapp, Snurr and the Seven Dogs.* Illus. by author. Chicago: Albert Whitman, 1959.
008.14 Animals—dogs; 057 Family life;
064.35 Foreign lands—Sweden;
182 Triplets.

Lindman, Maj Jan. *Snipp, Snapp, Snurr and the Yellow Sled.* Illus. by author. Chicago: Albert Whitman, 1936.
002.20 Activities—working;
026.13 Character traits—generosity;
057 Family life; 064.35 Foreign lands—Sweden; 182 Triplets.

Link, Martin, jt. author. *The Goat in the Rug.* By Charles L. Blood, and Martin Link.

Lionni, Leo. *Alexander and the Wind-Up Mouse.* Illus. by author. New York: Pantheon, 1969.
008.34 Animals—mice;
052.03 Emotions—envy, jealousy;
068 Friendship; 177 Toys.

Lionni, Leo. *The Biggest House in the World.* Illus. by author. New York: Pantheon, 1968.
008 Animals; 016.13 Behavior—greed.

Lionni, Leo. *A Color of His Own.* Illus. by author. New York: Pantheon, 1975.
026.16 Character traits—individuality;
032.01 Concepts—color;
142.03 Reptiles—lizards.

Lionni, Leo. *Fish Is Fish.* Illus. by author. New York: Pantheon, 1970.
005 Amphibians; 016.24 Behavior—misunderstanding; 060 Fish;
068 Friendship.

Lionni, Leo. *Frederick.* Illus. by author. New York: Pantheon, 1967.
008.34 Animals—mice;
154.04 Seasons—winter.

Lionni, Leo. *Geraldine, the Music Mouse.* Illus. by author. New York: Pantheon, 1979.
008.34 Animals—mice; 116 Music.

Lionni, Leo. *The Greentail Mouse.* Illus. by author. New York: Pantheon, 1973.
008.34 Animals—mice; 104 Mardi Gras.

Lionni, Leo. *In the Rabbitgarden.* Illus. by author. New York: Pantheon, 1975.
008.18 Animals—foxes;
008.34 Animals—mice;
142.04 Reptiles—snakes.

Lionni, Leo. *Inch by Inch.* Illus. by author. New York: Astor-Honor, 1960.
017 Birds; 032.05 Concepts—measurement; 090 Insects and spiders.

Lionni, Leo. *Little Blue and Little Yellow.* Illus. by author. New York: Astor-Honor, 1959.
032.01 Concepts—color;
068 Friendship.

Lionni, Leo. *On My Beach There Are Many Pebbles.* Illus. by author. New York: Astor-Honor, 1961.
146 Rocks; 153 Sea and seashore.

Lionni, Leo. *Pezzettino.* Illus. by author. New York: Pantheon, 1975.
026.16 Character traits—individuality;
032.07 Concepts—shape; 156 Self-concept.

Lionni, Leo. *Swimmy.* Illus. by author. New York: Pantheon, 1963.
060 Fish; 153 Sea and seashore.

Lionni, Leo. *Tico and the Golden Wings.* Illus. by author. New York: Pantheon, 1964.
017 Birds; 026.13 Character traits—generosity; 026.16 Character traits—individuality; 026.28 Character traits—questioning.

Lipkind, William. *Nubber Bear.* Illus. by Roger Antoine Duvoisin. New York: Harcourt, 1966.
008.06 Animals—bears;
016.22 Behavior—misbehavior.

Lipkind, William, and Mordvinoff, Nicolas. *Billy the Kid.* Illus. by Nicolas Mordvinoff. New York: Harcourt, 1961.
008.21 Animals—goats.

Lipkind, William, and Mordvinoff, Nicolas. *The Boy and the Forest.* Illus. by Nicolas Mordvinoff. New York: Harcourt, 1964.
008 Animals; 026.18 Character traits—kindness to animals; 066 Forest, woods; 103 Magic.

Lipkind, William, and Mordvinoff, Nicolas. *Chaga.* Illus. by Nicolas Mordvinoff. New York: Harcourt, 1955.
008.17 Animals—elephants;
032.08 Concepts—size.

Lipkind, William, and Mordvinoff, Nicolas. *The Christmas Bunny*. Illus. by Nicolas Mordvinoff. New York: Harcourt, 1953.
008.18 Animals—foxes;
008.46 Animals—rabbits;
083.03 Holidays—Christmas;
130 Parties.

Lipkind, William, and Mordvinoff, Nicolas. *Circus Rucus*. Illus. by Nicolas Mordvinoff. New York: Harcourt, 1954.
028 Circus, clowns.

Lipkind, William, and Mordvinoff, Nicolas. *Even Steven*. Illus. by Nicolas Mordvinoff. New York: Harcourt, 1952.
008.28 Animals—horses; 035 Cowboys.

Lipkind, William, and Mordvinoff, Nicolas. *Finders Keepers*. Illus. by Nicolas Mordvinoff. New York: Harcourt, 1951.
008.14 Animals—dogs;
026.29 Character traits—selfishness.

Lipkind, William, and Mordvinoff, Nicolas. *Four-Leaf Clover*. Illus. by Nicolas Mordvinoff. New York: Harcourt, 1959.
053.01 Ethnic groups in the U.S.—Afro-Americans.

Lipkind, William, and Mordvinoff, Nicolas. *The Little Tiny Rooster*. Illus. by Nicolas Mordvinoff. New York: Harcourt, 1960.
008.18 Animals—foxes; 017.04 Birds—chickens; 026.31 Character traits—smallness; 156 Self-concept.

Lipkind, William, and Mordvinoff, Nicolas. *The Magic Feather Duster*. Illus. by Nicolas Mordvinoff. New York: Harcourt, 1958.
026.17 Character traits—kindness;
062 Folk and fairy tales; 103 Magic.

Lipkind, William, and Mordvinoff, Nicolas. *Russet and the Two Reds*. Illus. by Nicolas Mordvinoff. New York: Harcourt, 1962.
008.09 Animals—cats.

Lipkind, William, and Mordvinoff, Nicolas. *Sleepyhead*. Illus. by Nicolas Mordvinoff. New York: Harcourt, 1957.
002.12 Activities—playing; 069 Games;
134 Poetry, rhyme.

Lipkind, William, and Mordvinoff, Nicolas. *The Two Reds*. Illus. by Nicolas Mordvinoff. New York: Harcourt, 1950.
008.09 Animals—cats; 068 Friendship.

Lipkind, William, and Schreiber, Georges. *Professor Bull's Umbrella*. Illus. by Georges Schreiber. New York: Viking, 1954.
187 Umbrellas.

Lippman, Peter. *New at the Zoo*. Illus. by author. New York: Harper, 1969.
008 Animals; 015 Bedtime; 204 Zoos.

Lisker, Sonia O. *Lost*. Illus. by author. New York: Harcourt, 1975.
016.20 Behavior—lost; 201 Wordless;
204 Zoos.

Lisker, Sonia O., and Dean, Leigh. *Two Special Cards*. Illus. by Sonia O. Lisker. New York: Harcourt, 1976.
045 Divorce; 057 Family life.

Lisowski, Gabriel. *How Tevye Became a Milkman*. Illus. by author. New York: Holt, 1976.
064.40 Foreign lands—Ukraine;
093 Jewish culture.

Litchfield, Ada Bassett. *A Button in Her Ear*. Illus. by Eleanor Mill. Chicago: Albert Whitman, 1976.
077.02 Handicaps—deafness.

Litchfield, Ada Bassett. *A Cane in Her Hand*. Illus. by Eleanor Mill. Chicago: Albert Whitman, 1977.
077.01 Handicaps—blindness.

Little, Mary E. *ABC for the Library*. Illus. by author. New York: Atheneum, 1975.
001 ABC Books; 100 Libraries.

Little, Mary E. *Ricardo and the Puppets*. Illus. by author. New York: Scribner's, 1958.
008.34 Animals—mice; 100 Libraries;
139 Puppets.

The Little Red Hen. Illus. by Janina Domanska. New York: Macmillan, 1973.
008 Animals; 017.04 Birds—chickens;
026.19 Character traits—laziness;
038 Cumulative tales; 058 Farms;
062 Folk and fairy tales; 133 Plants.

The Little Red Hen. Illus. by Paul Galdone. New York: Seabury Pr., 1973.
008 Animals; 017.04 Birds—chickens;
026.19 Character traits—laziness;
038 Cumulative tales; 058 Farms;
062 Folk and fairy tales; 133 Plants.

The Little Red Hen. Illus. by Mel Pekarsky. Retold by Jean Horton Berg. Reading consultant: Morton Betel. Chicago: Follett, 1963.
008 Animals; 017.04 Birds—chickens;
026.19 Character traits—laziness;
038 Cumulative tales; 058 Farms;
062 Folk and fairy tales; 133 Plants.

Little Red Riding Hood. Illus. by Paul Galdone. Adapted from the retelling of the Brothers Grimm by Paul Galdone. New York: McGraw-Hill, 1974.
008.61 Animals—wolves;
016.35 Behavior—talking to strangers;
062 Folk and fairy tales.

Little Red Riding Hood. Illus. by Bernadette Watts. Cleveland: Collins, 1969.
008.61 Animals—wolves;
016.35 Behavior—talking to strangers;
062 Folk and fairy tales.

Little Tom Tucker. Illus. by Paul Galdone. New York: McGraw-Hill, 1970.
122 Nursery rhymes.

Little Tuppen: An Old Tale. Illus. by Paul Galdone. New York: Seabury Pr., 1967.
017.04 Birds—chickens; 038 Cumulative tales; 062 Folk and fairy tales.

Littlefield, William. *The Whiskers of Ho Ho.* Illus. by Vladimir Bobri. New York: Lothrop, 1958.
008.46 Animals—rabbits;
017.04 Birds—chickens;
083.04 Holidays—Easter.

Livermore, Elaine. *Find the Cat.* Illus. by author. Boston: Houghton, 1973.
008.09 Animals—cats; 069 Games.

Livermore, Elaine. *Lost and Found.* Illus. by author. Boston: Houghton, 1975.
016.19 Behavior—losing things;
069 Games.

Livermore, Elaine. *One to Ten Count Again.* Illus. by author. Boston: Houghton, 1973.
033 Counting; 069 Games.

Lobel, Anita. *A Birthday for the Princess.* Illus. by author. New York: Harper, 1973.
016.26 Behavior—needing someone;
018 Birthdays; 147 Royalty.

Lobel, Anita. *King Rooster, Queen Hen.* Illus. by author. New York: Greenwillow, 1975.
017.04 Birds—chickens.

Lobel, Anita. *The Pancake.* Illus. by author. New York: Greenwillow, 1978.
038 Cumulative tales; 063 Food.

Lobel, Anita. *Potatoes, Potatoes.* Illus. by author. New York: Harper, 1967.
191 Violence, anti-violence.

Lobel, Anita. *The Seamstress of Salzburg.* Illus. by author. New York: Harper, 1970.
016.32 Behavior—sibling rivalry;
023.23 Careers—seamstresses;
031 Clothing; 147 Royalty.

Lobel, Anita. *Sven's Bridge.* Illus. by author. New York: Harper, 1965.
020 Bridges; 147 Royalty.

Lobel, Anita. *The Troll Music.* Illus. by author. New York: Harper, 1966.
103 Magic; 116 Music; 183 Trolls.

Lobel, Arnold Stark. *Days with Frog and Toad.* Illus. by author. New York: Harper, 1979.
005 Amphibians; 068 Friendship.

Lobel, Arnold Stark. *Frog and Toad All Year.* Illus. by author. New York: Harper, 1976.
005 Amphibians; 068 Friendship;
154 Seasons.

Lobel, Arnold Stark. *Frog and Toad Are Friends.* Illus. by author. New York: Harper, 1970.
005 Amphibians; 068 Friendship.

Lobel, Arnold Stark. *Frog and Toad Together.* Illus. by author. New York: Harper, 1971.
005 Amphibians; 068 Friendship.

Lobel, Arnold Stark. *Giant John.* Illus. by author. New York: Harper, 1964.
072 Giants.

Lobel, Arnold Stark. *Grasshopper on the Road.* Illus. by author. New York: Harper, 1978.
090 Insects and spiders.

Lobel, Arnold Stark. *The Great Blueness and Other Predicaments.* Illus. by author. New York: Harper, 1968.
032.01 Concepts—color; 200 Wizards.

Lobel, Arnold Stark. *Gregory Griggs and Other Nursery Rhyme People.* Illus. by author. New York: Greenwillow, 1978.
122 Nursery rhymes.

Lobel, Arnold Stark. *A Holiday for Mister Muster.* Illus. by author. New York: Harper, 1963.
008 Animals; 088 Illness; 204 Zoos.

Lobel, Arnold Stark. *How the Rooster Saved the Day.* Illus. by Anita Lobel. New York: Greenwillow, 1977.
017.04 Birds—chickens;
026.06 Character traits—cleverness;
036 Crime.

Lobel, Arnold Stark. *Lucille.* Illus. by author. New York: Harper, 1964.
008.28 Animals—horses; 087 Humor.

Lobel, Arnold Stark. *Martha the Movie Mouse.* Illus. by author. New York: Harper, 1966.
008.34 Animals—mice; 134 Poetry, rhyme; 173 Theater.

Lobel, Arnold Stark. *Mouse Soup.* Illus. by author. New York: Harper, 1977.
008.34 Animals—mice;
008.59 Animals—weasels;
026.06 Character traits—cleverness.

Lobel, Arnold Stark. *Mouse Tales.* Illus. by author. New York: Harper, 1972.
008.34 Animals—mice; 087 Humor.

Lobel, Arnold Stark. *On the Day Peter Stuyvesant Sailed into Town.* Illus. by author. New York: Harper, 1971.
134 Poetry, rhyme; 137 Problem solving; 189 U.S. history.

Lobel, Arnold Stark. *Owl at Home.* Illus. by author. New York: Harper, 1975.
017.14 Birds—owls.

Lobel, Arnold Stark. *Prince Bertram the Bad.* Illus. by author. New York: Harper, 1963.
016.22 Behavior—misbehavior; 046 Dragons; 147 Royalty; 199 Witches.

Lobel, Arnold Stark. *Small Pig.* Illus. by author. New York: Harper, 1969.
008.42 Animals—pigs; 016.27 Behavior—running away; 058 Farms.

Lobel, Arnold Stark. *A Treeful of Pigs.* Illus. by Anita Lobel. New York: Greenwillow, 1979.
008.42 Animals—pigs; 026.19 Character traits—laziness; 058 Farms; 087 Humor.

Lobel, Arnold Stark. *A Zoo for Mister Muster.* Illus. by author. New York: Harper, 1962.
008 Animals; 204 Zoos.

Löfgren, Ulf. *The Color Trumpet.* Illus. by author. English text by Alison Winn; adapted by Ray Broekel. Reading: Addison-Wesley, 1973.
032.01 Concepts—color.

Löfgren, Ulf. *The Flying Orchestra.* Illus. by author. English text by Alison Winn; adapted by Ray Broekel. Reading: Addison-Wesley, 1973.
116 Music.

Löfgren, Ulf. *One-Two-Three.* Illus. by author. English text by Alison Winn; adapted by Ray Broekel. Reading: Addison-Wesley, 1973.
008 Animals; 033 Counting; 129 Participation.

Löfgren, Ulf. *The Traffic Stopper That Became a Grandmother Visitor.* Illus. by author. English text by Alison Winn: adapted by Ray Broekel. Reading: Addison-Wesley, 1973.
008.17 Animals—elephants; 012 Automobiles; 102 Machines.

Löfgren, Ulf. *The Wonderful Tree.* Illus. by author. New York: Delacorte Pr., 1969.
089 Imagination; 181 Trees.

Lopshire, Robert Martin. *I Am Better Than You!* Illus. by author. New York: Harper, 1968.
016.03 Behavior—boasting; 142.03 Reptiles—lizards.

Lopshire, Robert Martin. *It's Magic?* Illus. by author. New York: Macmillan, 1969.
103 Magic.

Lopshire, Robert Martin. *Put Me in the Zoo.* Illus. by author. New York: Macmillan, 1960.
008.14 Animals—dogs; 028 Circus, clowns; 032.01 Concepts—color.

Lord, Beman. *The Days of the Week.* Illus. by Walter Erhard. New York: Walck, 1968.
039 Days of the week, months of the year; 134 Poetry, rhyme; 164 Songs.

The Lord's Prayer. Illus. by George Kraus. New York: Dutton, 1970.
141 Religion.

Lorimer, Lawrence T. *Noah's Ark.* Illus. by Charles E. Martin. New York: Random House, 1978.
141.01 Religion—Noah.

Low, Alice. *David's Windows.* Illus. by Thomas Anthony de Paola. New York: Putnam's, 1974.
029 City; 057.02 Family life—grandparents; great-grandparents; 086 Houses.

Low, Alice. *The Witch Who Was Afraid of Witches.* Illus. by Karen Gundersheimer. New York: Pantheon, 1978.
016.32 Behavior—sibling rivalry; 083.07 Holidays—Halloween; 199 Witches.

Low, Alice. *Witch's Holiday.* Illus. by Tony Walton. New York: Pantheon, 1971.
083.07 Holidays—Halloween; 134 Poetry, rhyme; 199 Witches.

Low, Joseph. *Adam's Book of Odd Creatures.* Illus. by author. New York: Atheneum, 1962.
001 ABC Books; 008 Animals; 118 Names; 134 Poetry, rhyme.

Low, Joseph. *Benny Rabbit and the Owl.* Illus. by author. New York: Greenwillow, 1978.
008.46 Animals—rabbits; 015 Bedtime; 052.04 Emotions—fear; 089 Imagination.

Low, Joseph. *Boo to a Goose.* Illus. by author. New York: Atheneum, 1975.
017.11 Birds—geese; 026.04 Character traits—bravery; 052.04 Emotions—fear; 058 Farms.

Low, Joseph. *The Christmas Grump*. Illus. by author. New York: Atheneum, 1977.
008.34 Animals—mice;
052.05 Emotions—happiness;
052.09 Emotions—sadness;
083.03 Holidays—Christmas.

Lowitz, Anson, jt. author. *The Pilgrims' Party*. By Sadyebeth Lowitz, and Anson Lowitz.

Lowitz, Sadyebeth, and Lowitz, Anson. *The Pilgrims' Party*. Illus. by Anson Lowitz. Minneapolis: Lerner, 1931.
083.10 Holidays—Thanksgiving;
189 U.S. history.

Lowrey, Janette Sebring. *Six Silver Spoons*. Illus. by Robert Mead Quackenbush. New York: Harper, 1971.
018 Birthdays; 189 U.S. history.

Lubell, Cicil, jt. author. *Rosalie, the Bird Market Turtle*. By Winifred Milius Lubell, and Cicil Lubell.

Lubell, Winifred Milius. *Here Comes Daddy; A Book for Twos and Threes*. Illus. by author. Reading: Addison-Wesley, 1944.
057.01 Family life—fathers.

Lubell, Winifred Milius, jt. author. *I Wish I Had Another Name*. By Jay Williams, and Winifred Milius Lubell.

Lubell, Winifred Milius, and Lubell, Cicil. *Rosalie, the Bird Market Turtle*. Illus. by Winifred Milius Lubell. Skokie, IL: Rand McNally, 1962.
016.20 Behavior—lost; 017 Birds;
064.11 Foreign lands—France;
142.05 Reptiles—turtles.

Lund, Doris Herold. *The Paint-Box Sea*. Illus. by Symeon Shimin. New York: McGraw-Hill, 1973.
134 Poetry, rhyme; 153 Sea and seashore; 154.03 Seasons—summer.

Lund, Doris Herold. *You Ought to See Herbert's House*. Illus. by Steven Kellogg. New York: Watts, 1973.
016.03 Behavior—boasting;
068 Friendship.

Lynch, Marietta, jt. author. *Mommy and Daddy Are Divorced*. By Patricia Perry, and Marietta Lynch.

Lystad, Mary. *That New Boy*. Illus. by Emily Arnold McCully. New York: Crown, 1973.
026.16 Character traits—individuality;
068 Friendship; 114 Moving.

MacArthur-Onslow, Annette. *Minnie*. Illus. by author. Skokie, IL: Rand McNally, 1971.
008.09 Animals—cats.

MacBean, Dilla Wittemore. *Picture Book Dictionary*. Illus. by Pauline Batchelder Adams. Chicago: Children's Pr., 1962.
043 Dictionaries.

MacBeth, George. *Jonah and the Lord*. Illus. by Margaret Gordon. New York: Holt, 1970.
062 Folk and fairy tales; 141 Religion.

MacCabe, Lorin, jt. author. *Cable Car Joey*. By Naomi MacCabe, and Lorin MacCabe.

MacCabe, Naomi, and MacCabe, Lorin. *Cable Car Joey*. Illus. by authors. Stanford: Stanford Univ. Pr., 1949.
022 Cable cars.

McClintock, Marshall. *A Fly Went By*. Illus. by Fritz Siebel. New York: Random House, 1958.
016.24 Behavior—misunderstanding;
038 Cumulative tales; 090 Insects and spiders.

McClintock, Marshall. *Stop That Ball*. Illus. by Fritz Siebel. New York: Random House, 1959.
177.02 Toys—balls.

McClintock, Marshall. *What Have I Got?* Illus. by Leonard P. Kessler. New York: Harper, 1961.
031 Clothing; 089 Imagination;
134 Poetry, rhyme.

McClintock, Mike (pseud.). See McClintock, Marshall.

McCloskey, Robert John. *Blueberries for Sal*. Illus. by author. New York: Viking, 1948.
008.06 Animals—bears;
016.20 Behavior—lost; 057 Family life;
063 Food.

McCloskey, Robert John. *Burt Dow, Deep Water Man*. Illus. by author. New York: Viking, 1963.
008.60 Animals—whales; 019 Boats, ships; 153 Sea and seashore.

McCloskey, Robert John. *Lentil*. Illus. by author. New York: Viking, 1940.
116 Music; 120 Noise; 137 Problem solving.

McCloskey, Robert John. *Make Way for Duck-lings*. Illus. by author. New York: Viking, 1941.
017.08 Birds—ducks; 023.21 Careers—police officers; 029 City.

McCloskey, Robert John. *One Morning in Maine*. Illus. by author. New York: Viking, 1952.
057 Family life; 121 Non-sexist; 153 Sea and seashore; 171 Teeth.

McCloskey, Robert John. *Time of Wonder*. Illus. by author. New York: Viking, 1957.
091 Islands; 153 Sea and seashore; 154.03 Seasons—summer; 195 Weather.

McCrea, James, and McCrea, Ruth. *The King's Procession*. Illus. by authors. New York: Atheneum, 1963.
008.16 Animals—donkeys; 026.20 Character traits—loyalty; 135 Poverty; 147 Royalty.

McCrea, James, and McCrea, Ruth. *The Magic Tree*. Illus. by authors. New York: Atheneum, 1965.
026.22 Character traits—meanness; 052 Emotions; 052.05 Emotions—happiness; 147 Royalty.

McCrea, James, and McCrea, Ruth. *The Story of Olaf*. Illus. by authors. New York: Atheneum, 1964.
046 Dragons; 095 Knights; 200 Wizards.

McCrea, Ruth, jt. author. *The King's Procession*. By James McCrea, and Ruth McCrea.

McCrea, Ruth, jt. author. *The Magic Tree*. By James McCrea, and Ruth McCrea.

McCrea, Ruth, jt. author. *The Story of Olaf*. By James McCrea, and Ruth McCrea.

McCready, Tasha Tudor. See Tudor, Tasha.

McDermott, Beverly Brodsky. *The Golem, a Jewish Legend*. Illus. by author. Philadelphia: Lippincott, 1976.
062 Folk and fairy tales; 093 Jewish culture.

McDermott, Beverly Brodsky. *Jonah, an Old Testament Story*. Illus. by author. Philadelphia: Lippincott, 1977.
141 Religion.

McDermott, Gerald. *Anansi the Spider*. Illus. by author. New York: Holt, 1972.
062 Folk and fairy tales; 064.01 Foreign lands—Africa; 090 Insects and spiders; 111 Moon.

McDermott, Gerald. *Arrow to the Sun; A Pueblo Indian Tale*. Illus. by author. New York: Viking, 1974.
053.04 Ethnic groups in the U.S.—Indians; 062 Folk and fairy tales.

McDermott, Gerald. *The Magic Tree; A Tale from the Congo*. Illus. by author. New York: Holt, 1973.
026.02 Character traits—appearance; 103 Magic; 186 Twins.

McDermott, Gerald. *The Stonecutter; A Japanese Folk Tale*. Illus. by author. New York: Viking, 1975.
016.09 Behavior—dissatisfaction; 062 Folk and fairy tales; 064.19 Foreign lands—Japan.

MacDonald, Golden (pseud.). See Brown, Margaret Wise.

McGinley, Phyllis. *All Around the Town*. Illus. by Helen Stone. Philadelphia: Lippincott, 1948.
001 ABC Books; 029 City; 134 Poetry, rhyme.

McGinley, Phyllis. *The Horse Who Lived Upstairs*. Illus. by Helen Stone. Philadelphia: Lippincott, 1944.
008.28 Animals—horses; 016.09 Behavior—dissatisfaction.

McGinley, Phyllis. *How Mrs. Santa Claus Saved Christmas*. Illus. by Kurt Werth. Philadelphia: Lippincott, 1963.
083.03 Holidays—Christmas; 134 Poetry, rhyme.

McGinley, Phyllis. *Lucy McLockett*. Illus. by Helen Stone. Philadelphia: Lippincott, 1958.
016.19 Behavior—losing things; 057 Family life; 134 Poetry, rhyme; 171 Teeth.

McGovern, Ann. *Black Is Beautiful*. Illus. by Hope Wurmfeld. New York: Four Winds Pr., 1969.
053.01 Ethnic groups in the U.S.—Afro-Americans.

McGovern, Ann. *Feeling Mad, Feeling Sad, Feeling Bad, Feeling Glad*. Illus. by Hope Wurmfeld. New York: Walker, 1977.
052 Emotions; 134 Poetry, rhyme.

McGovern, Ann. *Too Much Noise*. Illus. by Simms Taback. Boston: Houghton, 1967.
087 Humor; 120 Noise.

McGovern, Ann. *Zoo, Where Are You?* Illus. by Ezra Jack Keats. New York: Harper, 1964.
204 Zoos.

McGowen, Tom. *The Only Glupmaker in the U.S. Navy.* Illus. by author. Chicago: Albert Whitman, 1966.
002.20 Activities—working;
023.17 Careers—military.

MacGregor, Ellen. *Mr. Pingle and Mr. Buttonhouse.* Illus. by Paul Galdone. New York: McGraw-Hill, 1957.
068 Friendship.

MacGregor, Ellen. *Theodor Turtle.* Illus. by Paul Galdone. New York: McGraw-Hill, 1955.
016.11 Behavior—forgetfulness;
129 Participation; 142.05 Reptiles—turtles.

Machetanz, Fred, jt. author. *A Puppy Named Gia.* By Sara Machetanz, and Fred Machetanz.

Machetanz, Sara, and Machetanz, Fred. *A Puppy Named Gia.* Illus. by Fred Machetanz. New York: Scribner's, 1957.
008.14 Animals—dogs; 053.03 Ethnic groups in the U.S.—Eskimos.

McIntire, Alta. *Follett Beginning to Read Picture Dictionary.* Illus. by Janet La Salle. Chicago: Follett, 1959.
043 Dictionaries.

Mack, Stan. See Mack, Stanley.

Mack, Stanley. *Ten Bears in My Bed, a Goodnight Countdown.* Illus. by author. New York: Pantheon, 1974.
008.06 Animals—bears; 015 Bedtime;
033 Counting; 164 Songs.

McKee, David. *The Day the Tide Went Out and Out and Out.* Illus. by author. New York: Abelard-Schuman, 1975.
008.08 Animals—camels; 041 Desert;
153 Sea and seashore.

McKee, David. *Elmer, the Story of a Patchwork Elephant.* Illus. by author. New York: McGraw-Hill, 1968.
008.17 Animals—elephants;
026.16 Character traits—individuality.

McKee, David. *The Man Who Was Going to Mind the House.* Illus. by author. New York: Abelard-Schuman, 1972.
062 Folk and fairy tales.

McKee, David. *123456789 Benn.* Illus. by author. New York: McGraw-Hill, 1970.
036 Crime; 137 Problem solving.

McKee, David. *Two Can Toucan.* Illus. by author. New York: Abelard-Schuman, 1964.
017 Birds; 118 Names.

McKie, Roy, and Eastman, Philip Day. *Snow.* Illus. by Philip Day Eastman. New York: Random House, 1962.
134 Poetry, rhyme; 195.07 Weather—snow.

McLeod, Emilie Warren. *The Bear's Bicycle.* Illus. by David McPhail. Boston: Little, 1975.
148 Safety; 166.03 Sports—bicycling;
177.08 Toys—teddy bears.

McLeod, Emilie Warren. *One Snail and Me.* Illus. by Walter Lorraine. Boston: Little, 1961.
002.02 Activities—bathing; 008 Animals;
033 Counting.

McMillan, Bruce. *The Alphabet Symphony.* Illus. by author. New York: Greenwillow, 1977.
001 ABC Books; 116 Music.

McNeely, Jeannette. *Where's Izzy?* Illus. by Bill Morrison. Chicago: Follett, 1972.
016.19 Behavior—losing things;
142.03 Reptiles—lizards.

McNeer, May Yonge. *Little Baptiste.* Illus. by Lynd Kendall Ward. Boston: Houghton, 1954.
008 Animals; 058 Farms.

McNeer, May Yonge. *My Friend Mac.* Illus. by Lynd Kendall Ward. The story of Little Baptiste and the Moose. Boston: Houghton, 1960.
008.38 Animals—moose;
052.07 Emotions—loneliness.

McNeill, Janet. *The Giant's Birthday.* Illus. by Walter Erhard. New York: Walck, 1964.
018 Birthdays; 072 Giants.

McNulty, Faith. *Mouse and Tim.* Illus. by Marc Simont. New York: Harper, 1978.
008.34 Animals—mice;
026.18 Character traits—kindness to animals; 131 Pets.

McNulty, Faith. *When a Boy Wakes Up in the Morning.* Illus. by Leonard Weisgard. New York: Knopf, 1962.
002.12 Activities—playing;
112 Morning; 120 Noise.

McNulty, Faith. *Woodchuck.* Illus. by Joan Sandin. New York: Harper, 1974.
008.23 Animals—groundhogs;
152 Science.

McPhail, David. *The Bear's Toothache.* Illus. by author. Boston: Little, 1972.
008.06 Animals—bears;
026.18 Character traits—kindness to animals; 088 Illness.

McPhail, David. *Captain Toad and the Motorbike.* Illus. by author. New York: Atheneum, 1978.
005 Amphibians; 113 Motorcycles.

McPhail, David. *The Cereal Box.* Illus. by author. Boston: Little, 1974.
087 Humor; 089 Imagination;
160 Shopping.

McPhail, David. *Henry Bear's Park.* Illus. by author. Boston: Little, 1976.
008.06 Animals—bears.

McPhail, David. *Mistletoe.* Illus. by author. New York: Dutton, 1978.
047 Dreams; 083.03 Holidays—Christmas; 089 Imagination; 177 Toys.

McPhail, David. *The Train.* Illus. by author. Boston: Little, 1977.
047 Dreams; 089 Imagination;
177.09 Toys—trains; 179 Trains.

Madden, Don. *Lemonade Serenade or the Thing in the Garden.* Illus. by author. Chicago: Albert Whitman, 1966.
051 Elves and little people; 120 Noise.

Maestro, Betsy. *Busy Day.* Illus. by Giulio Maestro. New York: Crown, 1978.
002 Activities; 028 Circus, clowns.

Maestro, Betsy. *Fat Polka-Dot Cat and Other Haiku.* Illus. by Giulio Maestro. New York: Dutton, 1976.
134 Poetry, rhyme.

Maestro, Betsy, and Maestro, Giulio. *Harriet Goes to the Circus.* Illus. by Giulio Maestro. New York: Crown, 1977.
028 Circus, clowns; 033 Counting.

Maestro, Betsy, and Maestro, Giulio. *Leopard Is Sick.* Illus. by Giulio Maestro. New York: Morrow, 1978.
008 Animals; 008.10 Animals—cats, wild; 088 Illness.

Maestro, Giulio, jt. author. *Harriet Goes to the Circus.* By Betsy Maestro, and Giulio Maestro.

Maestro, Giulio, jt. author. *Leopard Is Sick.* By Betsy Maestro, and Giulio Maestro.

Maestro, Giulio. *One More and One Less.* Illus. by author. New York: Crown, 1974.
008 Animals; 033 Counting.

Maestro, Giulio. *The Remarkable Plant in Apartment 4.* Illus. by author. New York: Bradbury Pr., 1973.
087 Humor; 133 Plants.

Maestro, Giulio. *The Tortoise's Tug of War.* Illus. by author. New York: Bradbury Pr., 1971.
008.57 Animals—tapirs;
008.60 Animals—whales; 062 Folk and fairy tales; 064.32 Foreign lands—South America; 069 Games; 142.05 Reptiles—turtles.

Mahood, Kenneth. *The Laughing Dragon.* Illus. by author. New York: Scribner's, 1970.
046 Dragons; 059 Fire; 087 Humor;
147 Royalty.

Mahy, Margaret. *The Boy Who Was Followed Home.* Illus. by Steven Kellogg. New York: Watts, 1975.
008.27 Animals—hippopotami;
087 Humor; 199 Witches.

Mahy, Margaret. *The Boy with Two Shadows.* Illus. by Jenny Williams. New York: Watts, 1971.
026.22 Character traits—meanness;
158 Shadows; 199 Witches.

Mahy, Margaret. *The Dragon of an Ordinary Family.* Illus. by Helen Oxenbury. New York: Watts, 1969.
046 Dragons.

Mahy, Margaret. *A Lion in the Meadow.* Illus. by Jenny Williams. New York: Watts, 1969.
008.10 Animals—cats, wild;
046 Dragons.

Mahy, Margaret. *Mrs. Discombobulous.* Illus. by Jan Brychta. New York: Watts, 1969.
016.25 Behavior—nagging; 057 Family life; 075 Gypsies.

Mahy, Margaret. *Pillycock's Shop.* Illus. by Carol Barker. New York: Watts, 1969.
055 Fairies; 190 Values.

Mahy, Margaret. *Rooms for Rent.* Illus. by Jenny Williams. New York: Watts, 1974.
016.13 Behavior—greed; 085 Hotels.

Mahy, Margaret. *Sailor Jack and the Twenty Orphans.* Illus. by Robert Bartlet. New York: Watts, 1970.
019 Boats, ships; 023.17 Careers—military; 127 Orphans; 132 Pirates;
153 Sea and seashore.

Maiorano, Robert. *Backstage.* Illus. by Rachel Isadora. New York: Greenwillow, 1978.
173 Theater.

Maiorano, Robert. *Francisco.* Illus. by Rachel Isadora. New York: Macmillan, 1978.
008.16 Animals—donkeys;
064.32 Foreign lands—South America;
135 Poverty; 137 Problem solving.

Makower, Sylvia. *Samson's Breakfast*. Illus. by author. New York: Watts, 1961.
008.10 Animals—cats, wild.

Maley, Anne. *Have You Seen My Mother?* Illus. by Yutaka Sugita. Minneapolis: Carolrhoda Books, 1969.
028 Circus, clowns; 177.02 Toys—balls.

Mallett, Anne. *Here Comes Tagalong*. Illus. by Steven Kellogg. New York: Parents, 1971.
016.32 Behavior—sibling rivalry; 057 Family life; 068 Friendship.

Mandry, Kathy. *The Cat and the Mouse and the Mouse and the Cat*. Illus. by Joe Toto. New York: Pantheon, 1972.
008.09 Animals—cats; 008.34 Animals—mice; 068 Friendship.

Mann, Peggy. *King Laurence the Alarm Clock*. Illus. by Ray Cruz. Garden City, NY: Doubleday, 1976.
008 Animals; 008.10 Animals—cats, wild; 088 Illness; 112 Morning.

Manushkin, Fran. *Baby*. Illus. by Ronald Norbert Himler. New York: Harper, 1972.
013 Babies.

Manushkin, Fran. *Bubblebath*. Illus. by Ronald Norbert Himler. New York: Harper, 1974.
002.02 Activities—bathing.

Marceau, Marcel. *The Story of Bip*. Illus. by author. New York: Harper, 1976.
028 Circus, clowns; 089 Imagination.

Marcin, Marietta. *A Zoo in Her Bed*. Illus. by Sofia Zeiger. New York: Coward, 1963.
015 Bedtime; 134 Poetry, rhyme; 177 Toys.

Margalit, Avi. *The Hebrew Alphabet Book*. Illus. by author. New York: Funk & Wagnells, 1968.
001 ABC Books; 093 Jewish culture.

Mari, Iela. *The Magic Balloon*. Illus. by author. New York: S. G. Phillips, 1970.
177.01 Toys—balloons; 201 Wordless.

Mariana (pseud.). See Foster, Marian Curtis.

Maril, Lee. *Mr. Bunny Paints the Eggs*. Illus. by Irena Lorentowica. New York: Roy Pub., 1945.
008.46 Animals—rabbits; 032.01 Concepts—color; 050 Eggs; 083.04 Holidays—Easter; 116 Music; 164 Songs.

Marino, Barbara Pavis. *Eric Needs Stitches*. Illus. by Richard Rudinski. Reading: Addison-Wesley, 1979.
084 Hospitals.

Marino, Dorothy Bronson. *Buzzy Bear and the Rainbow*. Illus. by author. New York: Watts, 1962.
008.06 Animals—bears; 195.06 Weather—rainbows.

Marino, Dorothy Bronson. *Buzzy Bear Goes Camping*. Illus. by author. New York: Watts, 1964.
008.06 Animals—bears; 166.04 Sports—camping.

Marino, Dorothy Bronson. *Buzzy Bear Goes South*. Illus. by author. New York: Watts, 1961.
008.06 Animals—bears; 081 Hibernation.

Marino, Dorothy Bronson. *Buzzy Bear in the Garden*. Illus. by author. New York: Watts, 1963.
002.06 Activities—gardening; 008.06 Animals—bears.

Marino, Dorothy Bronson. *Buzzy Bear's Busy Day*. Illus. by author. New York: Watts, 1965.
008.06 Animals—bears.

Marino, Dorothy Bronson. *Edward and the Boxes*. Illus. by author. Philadelphia: Lippincott, 1957.
002.12 Activities—playing; 162 Sleep.

Marino, Dorothy Bronson. *Good-Bye Thunderstorm*. Illus. by author. Philadelphia: Lippincott, 1958.
195.05 Weather—rain.

Marks, Marcia Bliss. *Swing Me, Swing Tree*. Illus. by David Berger. Boston: Little, 1959.
002.14 Activities—swinging; 134 Poetry, rhyme.

Marokvia, Merelle. *A French School for Paul*. Illus. by Artur Marokvia. Philadelphia: Lippincott, 1963.
028 Circus, clowns; 064.11 Foreign lands—France; 151 School.

Marsh, Jeri. *Hurrah for Alexander*. Illus. by Joan Hanson. Minneapolis: Carolrhoda Books, 1977.
087 Humor.

Marshall, James. *Four Little Troubles*. Illus. by author. Boston: Houghton, 1975.
008 Animals; 137 Problem solving.

Marshall, James. *George and Martha.* Illus. by author. Boston: Houghton, 1972.
008.27 Animals—hippopotami;
068 Friendship.

Marshall, James. *George and Martha Encore.* Illus. by author. Boston: Houghton, 1973.
002.04 Activities—dancing;
008.27 Animals—hippopotami;
068 Friendship.

Marshall, James. *George and Martha One Fine Day.* Illus. by author. Boston: Houghton, 1978.
008.27 Animals—hippopotami;
068 Friendship.

Marshall, James. *George and Martha Rise and Shine.* Illus. by author. Boston: Houghton, 1976.
008.27 Animals—hippopotami;
068 Friendship.

Marshall, James. *The Guest.* Illus. by author. Boston: Houghton, 1975.
008.38 Animals—moose;
008.55 Animals—snails; 068 Friendship.

Marshall, James. *Miss Dog's Christmas Treat.* Illus. by author. Boston: Houghton, 1973.
008.14 Animals—dogs; 063 Food;
083.03 Holidays—Christmas.

Marshall, James, jt. author. *Miss Nelson Is Missing!* By Harry Allard, and James Marshall.

Marshall, James. *Portly McSwine.* Illus. by author. Boston: Houghton, 1979.
008.42 Animals—pigs;
016.39 Behavior—worrying.

Marshall, James. *Speedboat.* Illus. by author. Boston: Houghton, 1976.
008.14 Animals—dogs; 019 Boats, ships;
068 Friendship.

Marshall, James, jt. author. *The Stupids Have a Ball.* By Harry Allard, and James Marshall.

Marshall, James. *What's the Matter with Carruthers?* Illus. by author. Boston: Houghton, 1972.
008.06 Animals—bears; 015 Bedtime;
026.14 Character traits—helpfulness;
081 Hibernation.

Marshall, James. *Willis.* Illus. by author. Boston: Houghton, 1974.
008 Animals.

Marshall, James. *Yummers!* Illus. by author. Boston: Houghton, 1973.
008.42 Animals—pigs; 063 Food;
088 Illness.

Martel, Cruz. *Yagua Days.* Illus. by Jerry Pinkney. New York: Dial Pr., 1976.
057 Family life; 064.29 Foreign lands—Puerto Rico.

Martin, Bernard Herman, jt. author. *Brave Little Indian.* By William Ivan Martin, and Bernard Herman Martin.

Martin, Bernard Herman, jt. author. *Smoky Poky.* By William Ivan Martin, and Bernard Herman Martin.

Martin, Bill. See Martin, William Ivan, Jr.

Martin, Janet. *Round and Square.* Illus. by Philippe Thomas. New York: Platt, 1965.
032.07 Concepts—shape.

Martin, Judith, and Charlip, Remy. *The Tree Angel.* Illus. by Remy Charlip. New York: Knopf, 1962.
007 Angels; 083.03 Holidays—Christmas; 173 Theater.

Martin, Patricia Miles. *Friend of Miguel.* Illus. by Genia. Skokie, IL: Rand McNally, 1967.
008.28 Animals—horses; 064.24 Foreign lands—Mexico.

Martin, Patricia Miles. *Jump Frog Jump.* Illus. by Earl Thollander. New York: Putnam's, 1965.
005 Amphibians; 056 Fairs.

Martin, Patricia Miles. *No, No, Rosina.* Illus. by Earl Thollander. New York: Putnam's, 1964.
019 Boats, ships; 023.11 Careers—fishermen; 026.31 Character traits—smallness; 029 City; 166.05 Sports—fishing.

Martin, Patricia Miles. *The Pointed Brush.* Illus. by Roger Antoine Duvoisin. New York: Lothrop, 1959.
002.21 Activities—writing;
064.06 Foreign lands—China.

Martin, Patricia Miles. *The Raccoon and Mrs. McGinnis.* Illus. by Leonard Weisgard. New York: Putnam's, 1961.
008.47 Animals—raccoons; 014 Barns;
036 Crime.

Martin, Patricia Miles. *The Rice Bowl Pet.* Illus. by Ezra Jack Keats. New York: Crowell, 1962.
131 Pets.

Martin, Patricia Miles. *Rolling the Cheese.* Illus. by Alton Raible. New York: Atheneum, 1966.
029 City; 069 Games; 121 Non-sexist.

Martin, Patricia Miles. *Show and Tell*. Illus. by Thomas A. Hamil. New York: Putnam's, 1962.
008.14 Animals—dogs; 151 School.

Martin, Patricia Miles. *Sylvester Jones and the Voice in the Forest*. Illus. by Leonard Weisgard. New York: Lothrop, 1958.
008 Animals; 066 Forest, woods.

Martin, Sarah Catherine. *The Comic Adventures of Old Mother Hubbard and Her Dog*. Illus. by Arnold Stark Lobel. New York: Bradbury Pr., 1968.
008.14 Animals—dogs; 122 Nursery rhymes.

Martin, Sarah Catherine. *Old Mother Hubbard and Her Dog*. Illus. by Paul Galdone. New York: McGraw-Hill, 1960.
008.14 Animals—dogs; 122 Nursery rhymes.

Martin, Sarah Catherine. *Old Mother Hubbard and Her Dog*. Illus. by Evaline Ness. New York: Holt, 1972.
008.14 Animals—dogs; 122 Nursery rhymes.

Martin, William Ivan, Jr. *My Days Are Made of Butterflies*. Illus. by Vic Herman. Written by Sano M. Galea'i Fa'apouli. Adapted by William Ivan Martin, Jr. New York: Holt, 1970.
064.24 Foreign lands—Mexico.

Martin, William Ivan, Jr. and Martin, Bernard Herman. *Brave Little Indian*. Illus. by Bernard Herman Martin. Kansas City, MO: Tell-Well Pr., 1951.
053.04 Ethnic groups in the U.S.—Indians; 129 Participation.

Martin, William Ivan., Jr. and Martin, Bernard Herman. *Smoky Poky*. Illus. by Bernard Herman Martin. Kansas City, MO: Tell-Well Pr., 1947.
008.17 Animals—elephants; 179 Trains.

Marzollo, Jean. *Close Your Eyes*. Illus. by Susan Jeffers. New York: Dial Pr., 1978.
015 Bedtime; 057.01 Family life—fathers; 134 Poetry, rhyme.

Massey, Jeanne. *The Littlest Witch*. Illus. by Adrienne Adams. New York: Knopf, 1959.
083.07 Holidays—Halloween; 199 Witches.

Massie, Diane Redfield. *The Baby Beebee Bird*. Illus. by author. New York: Harper, 1963.
008 Animals; 017 Birds; 120 Noise; 162 Sleep.

Massie, Diane Redfield. *The Komodo Dragon's Jewels*. Illus. by author. New York: Macmillan, 1975.
019 Boats, ships; 046 Dragons; 142.03 Reptiles—lizards.

Massie, Diane Redfield. *Tiny Pin*. Illus. by author. New York: Harper, 1964.
008.43 Animals—porcupines; 016.14 Behavior—growing up; 134 Poetry, rhyme.

Massie, Diane Redfield. *Walter Was a Frog*. Illus. by author. New York: Simon & Schuster, 1970.
005 Amphibians; 016.09 Behavior—dissatisfaction.

Mathews, Louise. *Bunches and Bunches of Bunnies*. Illus. by Jeni Bassett. New York: Dodd, 1978.
008.46 Animals—rabbits; 033 Counting; 134 Poetry, rhyme.

Mathieson, Egon. *Oswald, the Monkey*. Illus. by author. Adapted from the Danish by Nancy and Edward Maze. New York: Astor-Honor, 1959.
008.37 Animals—monkeys.

Matias (pseud.). See Henrioud, Charles.

Matsuno, Masako. *A Pair of Red Clogs*. Illus. by Kazue Mizumura. Cleveland: Collins, 1960.
026.15 Character traits—honesty; 031 Clothing; 064.19 Foreign lands—Japan.

Matsuno, Masako. *Taro and the Bamboo Shoot*. Illus. by Yasuo Segawa. New York: Pantheon, 1964.
064.19 Foreign lands—Japan.

Matsuno, Masako. *Taro and the Tofu*. Illus. by Kazue Mizumura. Cleveland: Collins, 1962.
026.15 Character traits—honesty; 064.19 Foreign lands—Japan.

Matsutani, Miyoko. *The Fisherman under the Sea*. Illus. by Chihiro Iwasaki. English version by Alvin Tresselt. New York: Parents, 1969.
023.11 Careers—fishermen; 064.19 Foreign lands—Japan; 142.05 Reptiles—turtles; 147 Royalty; 153 Sea and seashore.

Matsutani, Miyoko. *How the Withered Trees Blossomed.* Illus. by Yasuo Segawa. Philadelphia: Lippincott, 1969.
016.13 Behavior—greed;
064.19 Foreign lands—Japan;
065 Foreign languages.

Matsutani, Miyoko. *The Witch's Magic Cloth.* Illus. by Yasuo Segawa. English version by Alvin Tresselt. New York: Parents, 1969.
026.04 Character traits—bravery;
064.19 Foreign lands—Japan;
199 Witches.

Matus, Greta. *Where Are You, Jason?* Illus. by author. New York: Lothrop, 1974.
016.15 Behavior—hiding;
089 Imagination; 119 Night.

Maury, Inez. *My Mother the Mail Carrier: Mi Mama la Cartera.* Illus. by Lady McCrady. Translated by Norah E. Alemany. Old Westbury, NY: Feminist Pr., 1976.
023.16 Careers—mail carriers;
065 Foreign languages; 121 Non-sexist.

May, Charles Paul. *High-Noon Rocket.* Illus. by Brinton Cassady Turkle. New York: Holiday, 1966.
002.16 Activities—traveling;
152 Science; 165 Space and space ships;
174 Time.

May, Julian. *Why People Are Different Colors.* Illus. by Symeon Shimin. New York: Holiday, 1971.
053.07 Ethnic groups in the U.S.—Multi-ethnic.

Mayer, Mercer. *Ah-choo.* Illus. by author. New York: Dial Pr., 1976.
008.17 Animals—elephants; 088 Illness;
201 Wordless.

Mayer, Mercer. *A Boy, a Dog, a Frog, and a Friend.* Illus. by author. New York: Dial Pr., 1971.
005 Amphibians; 008.14 Animals—dogs; 068 Friendship; 166.05 Sports—fishing; 201 Wordless.

Mayer, Mercer. *A Boy, a Dog and a Frog.* Illus. by author. New York: Dial Pr., 1967.
005 Amphibians; 008.14 Animals—dogs; 068 Friendship; 201 Wordless.

Mayer, Mercer. *Bubble, Bubble.* Illus. by author. New York: Parents, 1973.
201 Wordless.

Mayer, Mercer. *Frog Goes to Dinner.* Illus. by author. New York: Dial Pr., 1974.
005 Amphibians; 063 Food;
201 Wordless.

Mayer, Mercer. *Frog on His Own.* Illus. by author. New York: Dial Pr., 1973.
005 Amphibians; 201 Wordless.

Mayer, Mercer. *Frog, Where Are You?* Illus. by author. New York: Dial Pr., 1969.
005 Amphibians; 068 Friendship;
201 Wordless.

Mayer, Mercer. *The Great Cat Chase.* Illus. by author. New York: Four Winds Pr., 1974.
008.09 Animals—cats; 201 Wordless.

Mayer, Mercer. *Hiccup.* Illus. by author. New York: Dial Pr., 1976.
008.27 Animals—hippopotami;
088 Illness; 201 Wordless.

Mayer, Mercer. *I Am a Hunter.* Illus. by author. New York: Dial Pr., 1969.
089 Imagination.

Mayer, Mercer. *Just for You.* Illus. by author. Racine, WI: Western Pub., 1975.
026.14 Character traits—helpfulness;
052.08 Emotions—love; 057.03 Family life—mothers.

Mayer, Mercer. *Liza Lou and the Yeller Belly Swamp.* Illus. by author. New York: Parents, 1976.
026.04 Character traits—bravery;
053.01 Ethnic groups in the U.S.—Afro-Americans; 110 Monsters; 121 Non-sexist.

Mayer, Mercer. *Mine!* Illus. by author. New York: Simon & Schuster, 1970.
032 Concepts; 052 Emotions.

Mayer, Mercer. *Mrs. Beggs and the Wizard.* Illus. by author. New York: Parents, 1973.
103 Magic; 110 Monsters; 200 Wizards.

Mayer, Mercer. *One Frog Too Many.* Illus. by author. New York: Dial Pr., 1975.
005 Amphibians; 052.03 Emotions—envy, jealousy; 201 Wordless.

Mayer, Mercer. *Oops.* Illus. by author. New York: Dial Pr., 1977.
008.27 Animals—hippopotami;
016.06 Behavior—carelessness;
201 Wordless.

Mayer, Mercer. *The Queen Always Wanted to Dance.* Illus. by author. New York: Simon & Schuster, 1971.
002.04 Activities—dancing; 087 Humor;
147 Royalty.

Mayer, Mercer. *A Special Trick.* Illus. by author. New York: Dial Pr., 1970.
103 Magic; 110 Monsters.

Mayer, Mercer. *Terrible Troll.* Illus. by author. New York: Dial Pr., 1968.
089 Imagination; 095 Knights;
110 Monsters; 117 Mythical creatures;
183 Trolls.

Mayer, Mercer. *There's a Nightmare in My Closet.* Illus. by author. New York: Dial Pr., 1968.
015 Bedtime; 052.04 Emotions—fear;
110 Monsters.

Mayer, Mercer. *Two Moral Tales.* Illus. by author. New York: Four Winds Pr., 1974.
008.06 Animals—bears; 017 Birds;
031 Clothing; 201 Wordless.

Mayer, Mercer. *What Do You Do with a Kangaroo?* Illus. by author. New York: Four Winds Pr., 1973.
008 Animals; 087 Humor; 121 Non-sexist; 137 Problem solving.

Mayer, Mercer. *You're the Scaredy Cat.* Illus. by author. New York: Parents, 1974.
052.04 Emotions—fear; 119 Night;
166.04 Sports—camping.

Mayers, Patrick. *Just One More Block.* Illus. by Lucy Ozone Hawkinson. Chicago: Albert Whitman, 1970.
002.12 Activities—playing;
016.32 Behavior—sibling rivalry;
052 Emotions; 177.03 Toys—blocks.

Meddaugh, Susan. *Too Short Fred.* Illus. by author. Boston: Houghton, 1978.
008.09 Animals—cats; 026.31 Character traits—smallness.

Meeks, Esther K. *Curious Cow.* Illus. by Mel Pekarsky. Chicago: Follett, 1960.
008.12 Animals—cows, bulls;
026.10 Character traits—curiosity.

Meeks, Esther K. *Friendly Farm Animals.* Illustrated. Chicago: Follett, 1956.
008 Animals; 058 Farms.

Meeks, Esther K. *The Hill That Grew.* Illus. by Lazlo Roth. Chicago: Follett, 1959.
002.12 Activities—playing.

Meeks, Esther K. *One Is the Engine.* Illus. by Ernie King. Chicago: Follett, 1947/1956.
033 Counting; 179 Trains.

Meeks, Esther K. *One Is the Engine.* Illus. by Joe Rogers. Chicago: Follett, 1972.
033 Counting; 179 Trains.

Meeks, Esther K. *Playland Pony.* Illus. by Mary Miller Salem. Chicago: Follett, 1951.
008.28 Animals—horses.

Meeks, Esther K. *Something New at the Zoo.* Illus. by Hazel Hoecker. Chicago: Follett, 1957.
008 Animals; 204 Zoos.

Memling, Carl. *What's in the Dark?* Illus. by John E. Johnson. New York: Parents, 1971.
110 Monsters; 119 Night.

Mendoza, George. *The Alphabet Boat; A Sea-going Alphabet Book.* Illus. by author. New York: American Heritage, 1972.
001 ABC Books; 019 Boats, ships.

Mendoza, George. *The Marcel Marceau Counting Book.* Illus. by Milton H. Greene. Garden City, NY: Doubleday, 1971.
028 Circus, clowns; 033 Counting.

Mendoza, George. *Norman Rockwell's American ABC.* Illus. by Norman Rockwell. New York: Abrams, 1975.
001 ABC Books.

Mendoza, George. *The Scribbler.* Illus. by Robert Mead Quackenbush. New York: Holt, 1971.
017 Birds; 134 Poetry, rhyme; 153 Sea and seashore.

Mendoza, George. *Sesame Street Book of Opposites with Zero Mostel.* Illus. by Sheldon Secunda. Book design by Nicole Sekora-Mendoza. New York: Grosset, 1974.
032.06 Concepts—opposites.

Merriam, Eve. *Boys and Girls, Girls and Boys.* Illus. by Harriet Sherman. New York: Holt, 1972.
121 Non-sexist.

Merriam, Eve. *Epaminondas.* Illus. by Trina Schart Hyman. Chicago: Follett, 1968.
053.01 Ethnic groups in the U.S.—Afro-Americans; 062 Folk and fairy tales.

Merriam, Eve. *A Gaggle of Geese.* Illus. by Paul Galdone. New York: Knopf, 1960.
096 Language.

Merriam, Eve. *Mommies at Work.* Illus. by Beni Montresor. New York: Knopf, 1961.
002.20 Activities—working;
023 Careers; 057.03 Family life—mothers; 121 Non-sexist.

Merrill, Jean. *Tell about the Cowbarn, Daddy.* Illus. by Lili Cassel Wronker. Reading: Addison-Wesley, 1963.
008.12 Animals—cows, bulls;
058 Farms; 014 Barns.

Merrill, Jean, and Scott, Frances Gruse. *How Many Kids Are Hiding on My Block?* Illus. by Frances Gruse Scott. Chicago: Albert Whitman, 1970.
033 Counting; 053.07 Ethnic groups in the U.S.—Multi-ethnic; 069 Games.

Merrill, Jean, and Solbert, Romaine G. *Emily Emerson's Moon.* Illus. by Romaine G. Solbert. Boston: Little, 1960.
057 Family life; 111 Moon.

Meshover, Leonard, and Feistel, Sally. *The Guinea Pigs That Went to School.* Illus. by Eve Hoffmann. Chicago: Follett, 1968.
008.24 Animals—guinea pigs; 151 School; 152 Science.

Meshover, Leonard, and Feistel, Sally. *The Monkey That Went to School.* Illus. by Eve Hoffmann. Chicago: Follett, 1978.
008.37 Animals—monkeys; 151 School; 152 Science.

Meyer, Elizabeth. *The Blue China Pitcher.* Illus. by author. Nashville: Abingdon Pr., 1974.
083 Holidays; 130 Parties.

Meyer, Louis A., Jr. *The Clean Air and Peaceful Contentment Dirigible Airline.* Illus. by author. Boston: Little, 1972.
049 Ecology.

Michaels, Ruth, jt. author. *The Family That Grew.* By Florence Rondell, and Ruth Michaels.

Miklowitz, Gloria D. *Barefoot Boy.* Illus. by Jim Collins. Chicago: Follett, 1964.
018 Birthdays; 031 Clothing.

Miklowitz, Gloria D. *Save That Raccoon!* Illus. by St. Tamara. New York: Harcourt, 1978.
008.47 Animals—raccoons; 026.18 Character traits—kindness to animals; 059 Fire; 066 Forest, woods.

Miklowitz, Gloria D. *The Zoo That Moved.* Illus. by Don Madden. Chicago: Follett, 1968.
204 Zoos.

Miles, Betty. *Around and Around...Love.* Illustrated with photographs. New York: Knopf, 1975.
052.08 Emotions—love; 134 Poetry, rhyme.

Miles, Betty. *Having a Friend.* Illus. by Erik Blegvad. New York: Knopf, 1959.
068 Friendship.

Miles, Betty. *A House for Everyone.* Illus. by Jo Lowery. New York: Knopf, 1958.
086 Houses.

Miles, Miska. *Apricot ABC.* Illus. by Peter Parnall. Boston: Little, 1969.
001 ABC Books; 134 Poetry, rhyme; 181 Trees.

Miles, Miska. *Chicken Forgets.* Illus. by Jim Arnosky. Boston: Little, 1976.
016.11 Behavior—forgetfulness; 017.04 Birds—chickens; 087 Humor.

Miles, Miska. *The Fox and the Fire.* Illus. by John Carl Schoenherr. Boston: Little, 1966.
008.18 Animals—foxes; 059 Fire; 066 Forest, woods.

Miles, Miska. *Mouse Six and the Happy Birthday.* Illus. by Leslie Morrill. New York: Dutton, 1978.
008.34 Animals—mice; 018 Birthdays.

Miles, Miska. *Noisy Gander.* Illus. by Leslie Morrill. New York: Dutton, 1978.
008 Animals; 017.08 Birds—ducks; 058 Farms.

Miles, Miska. *Rabbit Garden.* Illus. by John Carl Schoenherr. Boston: Little, 1967.
008.46 Animals—rabbits; 049 Ecology.

Miles, Miska. *Small Rabbit.* Illus. by Jim Arnosky. Boston: Little, 1977.
008.46 Animals—rabbits.

Miles, Miska. *Somebody's Dog.* Illus. by John Carl Schoenherr. Boston: Little, 1973.
008.14 Animals—dogs.

Miles, Miska. *Wharf Rat.* Illus. by John Carl Schoenherr. Boston: Little, 1972.
008.48 Animals—rats.

Milgram, Mary. *Brothers Are All the Same.* Illus. by Rosmarie Hausherr. New York: Dutton, 1978.
003 Adoption; 016.32 Behavior—sibling rivalry; 057 Family life.

Milius, Winifred. See Lubell, Winifred Milius.

Miller, Albert. *The Hungry Goat.* Illus. by Abner Graboff. Skokie, IL: Rand McNally, 1964.
008.21 Animals—goats; 087 Humor; 116 Music; 164 Songs.

Miller, Alice P. *The Little Store on the Corner.* Illus. by John D. Lawrence. New York: Abelard-Schuman, 1961.
168 Stores.

Miller, Edna Anita. *Mousekin Finds a Friend.* Illus. by author. Englewood Cliffs, NJ: Prentice-Hall, 1967.
008.34 Animals—mice; 068 Friendship.

Miller, Edna Anita. *Mousekin's ABC.* Illus. by author. Englewood Cliffs, NJ: Prentice-Hall, 1972.
001 ABC Books; 008.34 Animals—mice; 134 Poetry, rhyme.

Miller, Edna Anita. *Mousekin's Christmas Eve.* Illus. by author. Englewood Cliffs, NJ: Prentice-Hall, 1965.
008.34 Animals—mice; 083.03 Holidays—Christmas.

Miller, Edna Anita. *Mousekin's Close Call.* Illus. by author. Englewood Cliffs, NJ: Prentice-Hall, 1978.
008.34 Animals—mice.

Miller, Edna Anita. *Mousekin's Family.* Illus. by author. Englewood Cliffs, NJ: Prentice-Hall, 1969.
008.34 Animals—mice.

Miller, Edna Anita. *Mousekin's Golden House.* Illus. by author. Englewood Cliffs, NJ: Prentice-Hall, 1964.
008.34 Animals—mice; 081 Hibernation; 083.07 Holidays—Halloween; 154.04 Seasons—winter.

Miller, Edna Anita. *Pebbles, a Pack Rat.* Illus. by author. Englewood Cliffs, NJ: Prentice-Hall, 1976.
008.41 Animals—pack rats; 150 Scarecrows.

Miller, Jane. *Birth of a Foal.* Illus. by author. Philadelphia: Lippincott, 1977.
008.28 Animals—horses.

Miller, Judith R. *Nabob and the Geranium.* Illus. by Marilyn Neuhart. Chicago: Children's Pr., 1967.
008 Animals; 133 Plants.

Miller, Warren. *The Goings On at Little Wishful.* Illus. by Edward Sorel. Boston: Little, 1959.
016.03 Behavior—boasting; 052.03 Emotions—envy, jealousy.

Miller, Warren. *Pablo Paints a Picture.* Illus. by Edward Sorel. Boston: Little, 1959.
002.09 Activities—painting; 023.02 Careers—artists.

Mills, Alan (pseud.). See Miller, Albert.

Milne, A. A. See Milne, Alan Alexander.

Milne, Alan Alexander. *Pooh's Quiz Book.* Illus. by Ernest Howard Shepard. New York: Dutton, 1977.
087 Humor; 177.08 Toys—teddy bears.

Minarik, Else Holmelund. *Cat and Dog.* Illus. by Fritz Siebel. New York: Harper, 1960.
008.09 Animals—cats; 008.14 Animals—dogs.

Minarik, Else Holmelund. *Father Bear Comes Home.* Illus. by Maurice Sendak. New York: Harper, 1959.
008.06 Animals—bears; 057.01 Family life—fathers.

Minarik, Else Holmelund. *A Kiss for Little Bear.* Illus. by Maurice Sendak. New York: Harper, 1968.
008.06 Animals—bears.

Minarik, Else Holmelund. *Little Bear.* Illus. by Maurice Sendak. New York: Harper, 1957.
008.06 Animals—bears; 018 Birthdays.

Minarik, Else Holmelund. *Little Bear's Friend.* Illus. by Maurice Sendak. New York: Harper, 1960.
008.06 Animals—bears; 068 Friendship.

Minarik, Else Holmelund. *Little Bear's Visit.* Illus. by Maurice Sendak. New York: Harper, 1961.
008.06 Animals—bears; 057.02 Family life—grandparents; great-grandparents.

Minarik, Else Holmelund. *The Little Giant Girl and the Elf Boy.* Illus. by Garth Montgomery Williams. New York: Harper, 1963.
051 Elves and little people; 072 Giants.

Minarik, Else Holmelund. *No Fighting, No Biting!* Illus. by Maurice Sendak. New York: Harper, 1958.
016.10 Behavior—fighting, arguing; 142.01 Reptiles—alligators, crocodiles.

Mitchell, Cynthia. *Playtime.* Illus. by Satomi Ichikawa. Cleveland: Collins, 1978.
002.12 Activities—playing; 134 Poetry, rhyme.

Miyoshi, Sekiya. *Singing David.* Illus. by author. New York: Watts, 1969.
141 Religion.

Mizumura, Kazue. *If I Built a Village.* Illus. by author. New York: Crowell, 1971.
026.17 Character traits—kindness; 029 City; 049 Ecology; 086 Houses.

Mizumura, Kazue. *If I Were a Cricket...* Illus. by author. New York: Crowell, 1973.
052.08 Emotions—love; 090 Insects and spiders.

Mizumura, Kazue. *If I Were a Mother.* Illus. by author. New York: Crowell, 1967.
057.03 Family life—mothers.

Modell, Frank. *Tooley! Tooley!* Illus. by author. New York: Greenwillow, 1979.
008.14 Animals—dogs; 087 Humor.

Moe, Jørgen Engebretsen, jt. author. *The Three Billy Goats Gruff.* By Peter Christen Asbjørnsen, and Jørgen Engebretsen Moe.

Moeschlin, Elsa. *Red Horse.* Illus. by author. New York: Coward, 1944.
047 Dreams; 083.03 Holidays— Christmas; 119 Night; 177.05 Toys— rocking horses.

Moffett, Martha. *A Flower Pot Is Not a Hat.* Illus. by Susan Perl. New York: Dutton, 1972.
087 Humor.

Monjo, Ferdinand N. *The Drinking Gourd.* Illus. by Fred Brenner. New York: Harper, 1970.
053.01 Ethnic groups in the U.S.—Afro-Americans; 053.04 Ethnic groups in the U.S.—Indians; 189 U.S. history.

Monjo, Ferdinand N. *Indian Summer.* Illus. by Anita Lobel. New York: Harper, 1968.
053.04 Ethnic groups in the U.S.— Indians; 189 U.S. history.

Monjo, Ferdinand N. *The One Bad Thing About Father.* Illus. by Rocco Negri. New York: Harper, 1970.
057.01 Family life—fathers; 189 U.S. history.

Monjo, Ferdinand N. *Poor Richard in France.* Illus. by Brinton Cassady Turkle. New York: Holt, 1973.
189 U.S. history.

Monjo, Ferdinand N. *Rudi and the Distelfink.* Illus. by George Kraus. New York: Dutton, 1972.
057 Family life.

Monsell, Helen Albee. *Paddy's Christmas.* Illus. by Kurt Wiese. New York: Knopf, 1942.
008.06 Animals—bears; 083.03 Holidays—Christmas.

Montgomerie, Norah Mary, comp. *This Little Pig Went to Market; Play Rhymes.* Illus. by Margery Gill. New York: Watts, 1967.
069 Games; 122 Nursery rhymes; 129 Participation.

Montresor, Beni. *A for Angel.* Illus. by author. New York: Knopf, 1969.
001 ABC Books.

Moon, Grace. *One Little Indian.* Illus. by Carl Moon. Chicago: Albert Whitman, 1950/1967.
018 Birthdays; 053.04 Ethnic groups in the U.S.—Indians.

The Moon's the North Wind's Cookie. Illus. by Susan Russo. Edited by Susan Russo. New York: Lothrop, 1979.
134 Poetry, rhyme.

Moore, Clement Clarke. *The Night Before Christmas.* Illus. by Gyo Fujikawa. New York: Grosset, 1961.
083.03 Holidays—Christmas; 134 Poetry, rhyme.

Moore, Clement Clarke. *The Night Before Christmas.* Illus. by Gustaf Tenggren. New York: Simon & Schuster, 1951.
083.03 Holidays—Christmas; 134 Poetry, rhyme.

Moore, Clement Clarke. *The Night Before Christmas.* Illus. by Tasha Tudor. New York: Random House, 1975.
083.03 Holidays—Christmas; 134 Poetry, rhyme.

Moore, Clement Clarke. *A Visit from St. Nicholas; 'Twas the Night Before Christmas.* Illus. by Paul Galdone. New York: McGraw-Hill, 1968.
083.03 Holidays—Christmas; 134 Poetry, rhyme.

Moore, Lilian. *Little Raccoon and No Trouble at All.* Illus. by Gioia Fiammenghi. New York: McGraw-Hill, 1972.
002.01 Activities—babysitting; 008.11 Animals—chipmunks; 008.47 Animals—raccoons; 186 Twins.

Moore, Lilian. *Little Raccoon and the Outside World.* Illus. by Gioia Fiammenghi. New York: McGraw-Hill, 1965.
008.47 Animals—raccoons.

Moore, Lilian. *Little Raccoon and the Thing in the Pool.* Illus. by Gioia Fiammenghi. New York: McGraw-Hill, 1963.
008.47 Animals—raccoons; 052.04 Emotions—fear.

Moore, Lilian. *Papa Albert.* Illus. by Gioia Fiammenghi. New York: Atheneum, 1964.
023.26 Careers—taxi drivers; 057 Family life; 064.11 Foreign lands— France; 065 Foreign languages; 170 Taxis.

Mooser, Stephen. *The Ghost with the Halloween Hiccups.* Illus. by Thomas Anthony de Paola. New York: Watts, 1977.
083.07 Holidays—Halloween.

Mordvinoff, Nicolas, jt. author. *Billy the Kid.* By William Lipkind, and Nicolas Mordvinoff.

Mordvinoff, Nicolas, jt. author. *The Boy and the Forest.* By William Lipkind, and Nicolas Mordvinoff.

Mordvinoff, Nicolas, jt. author. *Chaga.* By William Lipkind, and Nicolas Mordvinoff.

Mordvinoff, Nicolas, jt. author. *The Christmas Bunny.* By William Lipkind, and Nicolas Mordvinoff.

Mordvinoff, Nicolas, jt. author. *Circus Rucus.* By William Lipkind, and Nicolas Mordvinoff.

Mordvinoff, Nicolas. *Coral Island.* Illus. by author. Garden City, NY: Doubleday, 1957.
016.14 Behavior—growing up;
064.33 Foreign lands—South Sea Islands; 091 Islands.

Mordvinoff, Nicolas, jt. author. *Even Steven.* By William Lipkind, and Nicolas Mordvinoff.

Mordvinoff, Nicolas, jt. author. *Finders Keepers.* By William Lipkind, and Nicolas Mordvinoff.

Mordvinoff, Nicolas, jt. author. *Four-Leaf Clover.* By William Lipkind, and Nicolas Mordvinoff.

Mordvinoff, Nicolas, jt. author. *The Little Tiny Rooster.* By William Lipkind, and Nicolas Mordvinoff.

Mordvinoff, Nicolas, jt. author. *The Magic Feather Duster.* By William Lipkind, and Nicolas Mordvinoff.

Mordvinoff, Nicolas, jt. author. *Russet and the Two Reds.* By William Lipkind, and Nicolas Mordvinoff.

Mordvinoff, Nicolas, jt. author. *Sleepyhead.* By William Lipkind, and Nicolas Mordvinoff.

Mordvinoff, Nicolas, jt. author. *The Two Reds.* By William Lipkind, and Nicolas Mordvinoff.

Morel, Eve, comp. *Fairy Tales and Fables.* Illus. by Gyo Fujikawa. New York: Grosset, 1970.
062 Folk and fairy tales.

Moreman, Grace E. *No, No, Natalie.* Illus. by Geoffrey P. Fulton. Chicago: Children's Pr., 1973.
008.46 Animals—rabbits;
016.22 Behavior—misbehavior;
151 School.

Morgenstern, Elizabeth. *The Little Gardeners.* Illus. by Marigard Bantzer. From the German of Elizabeth Morgenstern; retold by Louise F. Encking. Chicago: Albert Whitman, 1933.
002.06 Activities—gardening;
064.12 Foreign lands—Germany.

Morris, Robert A. *Dolphin.* Illus. by Mamoru R. Funai. New York: Harper, 1975.
008.15 Animals—dolphins; 152 Science.

Morris, Robert A. *Seahorse.* Illus. by Arnold Stark Lobel. New York: Harper, 1972.
037 Crustacea; 152 Science.

Morrison, Bill. *Louis James Hates School.* Illus. by author. Boston: Houghton, 1978.
023 Careers; 151 School.

Morrison, Sean. *Is That a Happy Hippopotamus?* Illus. by Aliki Liacouras Brandenberg. New York: Crowell, 1966.
008 Animals; 087 Humor; 120 Noise.

Morrow, Elizabeth Reeve Cutter. *The Painted Pig.* Illus. by Rene D'harnoncourt. New York: Knopf, 1930.
064.24 Foreign lands—Mexico.

Morrow, Suzanne Stark. *Inatuck's Friend.* Illus. by Ellen Raskin. Boston: Little, 1968.
053.03 Ethnic groups in the U.S.—Eskimos; 068 Friendship.

Morse, Samuel French. *All in a Suitcase.* Illus. by Barbara Cooney. Boston: Little, 1966.
001 ABC Books; 008 Animals.

Morse, Samuel French. *Sea Sums.* Illus. by Fuku Akino. Boston: Little, 1970.
033 Counting; 134 Poetry, rhyme;
153 Sea and seashore;
195.04 Weather—fog.

Mosel, Arlene. *The Funny Little Woman.* Illus. by Blair Lent. New York: Dutton, 1972.
064.19 Foreign lands—Japan;
110 Monsters.

Mosel, Arlene. *Tikki Tikki Tembo.* Illus. by Blair Lent. New York: Holt, 1968.
064.06 Foreign lands—China;
118 Names.

Moskin, Marietta D. *Lysbet and the Fire Kittens.* Illus. by Margot Ladd Tomes. New York: Coward, 1973.
008.09 Animals—cats; 189 U.S. history.

Moskof, Martin Stephen, jt. author. *Still Another Alphabet Book.* By Seymour Chwast, and Martin Stephen Moskof.

Moskof, Martin Stephen, jt. author. *Still Another Children's Book.* By Seymour Chwast, and Martin Stephen Moskof.

Moskof, Martin Stephen, jt. author. *Still Another Number Book*. By Seymour Chwast, and Martin Stephen Moskof.

Moss, Jeffrey; Stiles, Norman; and Wilcox, Daniel. *The Sesame Street ABC Storybook*. Illus. by Peter Cross, and others. Featuring Jim Henson's Muppets. New York: Random House, 1974.
001 ABC Books.

Most, Bernard. *If the Dinosaurs Came Back*. Illus. by author. Boston: Houghton, 1978.
044 Dinosaurs; 089 Imagination.

Mother Goose. *The Annotated Mother Goose*. Illus. by Walter Crane, and others. Nursery rhymes old and new, arranged and explained by William S. Baring-Gould and Ceil Baring-Gould. Chapter decorations by E. M. Simon. New York: Potter, 1962.
122 Nursery rhymes.

Mother Goose. *Blessed Mother Goose; Favorite Nursery Rhymes for Today's Children*. Illus. by Kaye Luke. By Frank Scully. Hollywood, CA: House-Warven, 1951.
122 Nursery rhymes.

Mother Goose. *Brian Wildsmith's Mother Goose*. Illus. by Brian Wildsmith. New York: Watts, 1964.
122 Nursery rhymes.

Mother Goose. *Carolyn Wells Edition of Mother Goose*. Illus. by Margeria Cooper, and others. Garden City, NY: Doubleday, 1946.
122 Nursery rhymes.

Mother Goose. *The Charles Addams Mother Goose*. Illus. by Charles Addams. New York: Harper, 1967.
122 Nursery rhymes.

Mother Goose. *The City and Country Mother Goose*. Illus. by Hilde Hoffmann. New York: American Heritage, 1969.
122 Nursery rhymes.

Mother Goose. *Frank Baber's Mother Goose Nursery Rhymes*. Illus. by Frank Baber. Selected by Ruth Spriggs. New York: Crown, 1976.
122 Nursery rhymes.

Mother Goose. *The Gay Mother Goose*. Illus. by Françoise Seignobosc. New York: Scribner's, 1938.
122 Nursery rhymes.

Mother Goose. *Grafa' Grig Had a Pig, and Other Rhymes without Reason from Mother Goose*. Illus. by Wallace Tripp. Boston: Little, 1976.
122 Nursery rhymes.

Mother Goose. *Hurrah, We're Outward Bound!* Illus. by Peter Spier. Garden City, NY: Doubleday, 1968.
019 Boats, ships; 122 Nursery rhymes.

Mother Goose. *In a Pumpkin Shell; A Mother Goose ABC*. Illus. by Joan Walsh Anglund. New York: Harcourt, 1960.
001 ABC Books; 122 Nursery rhymes.

Mother Goose. *Jack Horner and Song of Sixpence*. Illus. by Emily Newton Barto. New York: Longman, 1943.
122 Nursery rhymes.

Mother Goose. *James Marshall's Mother Goose*. Illus. by James Marshall. New York: Farrar, 1979.
122 Nursery rhymes.

Mother Goose. *The Little Mother Goose*. Illus. by Jessie Wilcox Smith. New York: Dodd, 1918.
122 Nursery rhymes.

Mother Goose. *London Bridge Is Falling Down*. Illus. by Edward Randolph Emberley. Boston: Little, 1976.
062 Folk and fairy tales; 064.10 Foreign lands—England; 069 Games; 122 Nursery rhymes; 164 Songs.

Mother Goose. *London Bridge Is Falling Down!* Illus. by Peter Spier. Garden City, NY: Doubleday, 1967.
062 Folk and fairy tales; 064.10 Foreign lands—England; 069 Games; 122 Nursery rhymes; 164 Songs.

Mother Goose. Illus. by Roger Antoine Duvoisin. A comprehensive collection of rhymes, made by William Rose Benét. New York: Heritage Pr., 1943.
122 Nursery rhymes.

Mother Goose. Illus. by Miss Elliott (pseud.). Selected by Phyllis Maurine Fraser. New York: Simon & Schuster, 1942.
122 Nursery rhymes.

Mother Goose. Illus. by Charles Buckles Falls. Garden City, NY: Doubleday, 1924.
122 Nursery rhymes.

Mother Goose. Illus. by Gyo Fujikawa. Chicago: Donohue, 1968.
122 Nursery rhymes.

Mother Goose. Illus. by Frederick Richardson. The Volland ed., arranged and edited by Eulalie Osgood Grover. Chicago: Volland, 1915.
122 Nursery rhymes.

Mother Goose, Illus. By Frederick Richardson. The classic Volland edition, re-arranged and edited in this form by Eulalie Osgood Grover. Northbrook, IL: Hubbard Sci., 1971.
122 Nursery rhymes.

Mother Goose. Illus. by Frederick Richardson. Re-arranged and edited in this form by Eulalie Osgood Grover. The classic Volland edition. Skokie, IL: Rand McNally, 1971, 1976.
122 Nursery rhymes.

Mother Goose. Illus. by Gustaf Tenggren. Boston: Little, 1940.
122 Nursery rhymes.

Mother Goose. Illustrated. The Volland edition; a reproduction of the 1825 edition. Chicago: Donohue, 1968.
122 Nursery rhymes.

Mother Goose. *Mother Goose and Nursery Rhymes.* Illus. by Philip Reed. New York: Atheneum, 1963.
122 Nursery rhymes.

Mother Goose. *Mother Goose as Told by Kellogg's Singing Lady.* Illus. by Vernon Grant. Battle Creek: Kellogg Co., 1933.
122 Nursery rhymes.

Mother Goose. *The Mother Goose Book.* Illus. by Alice Provensen, and Martin Provensen. New York: Random House, 1976.
122 Nursery rhymes.

Mother Goose. *The Mother Goose Book.* Illus. by Sonia Roetter. Gathered from many sources. Mount Vernon, NY: Peter Pauper Pr., 1946.
122 Nursery rhymes.

Mother Goose. *Mother Goose in French; Poesies de la vraie Mere Oie.* Illus. by Barbara Cooney. Translations by Hugh Latham. New York: Crowell, 1964.
065 Foreign languages; 122 Nursery rhymes.

Mother Goose. *Mother Goose in Hieroglyphics.* Illus. by George S. Appleton. Reproduction of the 1st ed. published in 1849. Boston: Houghton, 1962.
069 Games; 082 Hieroglyphics; 122 Nursery rhymes; 140 Rebuses.

Mother Goose. *Mother Goose in Spanish. Poesias de la Madre Oca.* Illus. by Barbara Cooney. Translations by Alastair Reid and Anthony Kerrigan. New York: Crowell, 1968.
065 Foreign languages; 122 Nursery rhymes.

Mother Goose. *Mother Goose Melodies.* Illustrated. Introduction and bibliographic note by E. F. Bleiler. Facsimile edition of the Munroe and Francis "copyright 1833" version. Illus. with engravings. New York: Dover, 1970.
122 Nursery rhymes.

Mother Goose. *Mother Goose Nursery Rhymes.* Illus. by Arthur Rackham. New York: Watts, 1969.
122 Nursery rhymes.

Mother Goose. *Mother Goose Nursery Rhymes.* Illus. by Arthur Rackham. New York: Viking, 1975.
122 Nursery rhymes.

Mother Goose. *Mother Goose; Or, The Old Nursery Rhymes.* Illus. by Kate Greenaway. Illustrated as originally engraved and printed by Edmund Evans. London: Routledge, 1881.
122 Nursery rhymes.

Mother Goose. *Mother Goose Rhymes.* Illus. by Eulalie M. Banks, and Lois L. Lenski. Edited by Watty Piper (pseud.). New York: Platt, 1947/1956.
122 Nursery rhymes.

Mother Goose. *Mother Goose; Seventy-Seven Verses.* Illus. by Tasha Tudor. New York: Oxford Univ. Pr., 1944.
122 Nursery rhymes.

Mother Goose. *Mother Goose, Sixty-Seven Favorite Rhymes.* Illus. by Violet La Mont. New York: Simon & Schuster, 1957.
122 Nursery rhymes.

Mother Goose. *Mother Goose; The Old Nursery Rhymes.* Illus. by Arthur Rackham. Watkins Glen, NY: Century, 1913.
122 Nursery rhymes.

Mother Goose. *The Mother Goose Treasury.* Illus. by Raymond Briggs. New York: Coward, 1966.
122 Nursery rhymes.

Mother Goose. *Mother Goose's Melodies; Or, Songs for the Nursery.* Illustrated. Edited by William Adolphus Wheeler. Boston: Houghton, 189?.
122 Nursery rhymes; 164 Songs.

Mother Goose. *Mother Goose's Melody; Or, Sonnets for the Cradle.* Illustrated. In two parts; facsimile of John Newbery's collection of Mother Goose rhymes, reproduced from the earliest known perfect copy of the 1794 printing. New York: Frederic G. Melcher, 1945.
122 Nursery rhymes.

Mother Goose. *Mother Goose's Rhymes and Melodies.* Illus. by J. L. Webb. Music and melodies by E. I. Lane. New York: Cassell, 1888.
116 Music; 122 Nursery rhymes.

Mother Goose. *Nursery Rhyme Book.* Illus. by Leonard Leslie Brooke. Edited by Andrew Lang. New York: Warne, 1897.
122 Nursery rhymes.

Mother Goose. *Nursery Rhymes from Mother Goose in Signed English.* Illustrated. Prepared under the supervision of the staff of the Pre-School Signed English Project: Barbara M. Kanapell and others. Washington, DC: Gallaudet College Pr., 1972.
077.02 Handicaps—deafness;
122 Nursery rhymes.

Mother Goose. *One I Love, Two I Love, and Other Loving Mother Goose Rhymes.* Illus. by Nonny Hogrogian. New York: Dutton, 1972.
122 Nursery rhymes.

Mother Goose. *One Misty Moisty Morning; Rhymes from Mother Goose.* Illus. by Mitchell Miller. New York: Farrar, 1971.
122 Nursery rhymes.

Mother Goose. *One, Two, Buckle My Shoe.* Illus. by Gail Diana Einhart Haley. Garden City, NY: Doubleday, 1964.
033 Counting; 122 Nursery rhymes.

Mother Goose. *The Only True Mother Goose Melodies.* Illustrated. An exact and full-size reproduction of the original edition published and copyrighted in Boston in the year 1833 by Munroe and Francis. New York: Lothrop, 1905.
122 Nursery rhymes.

Mother Goose. *The Piper's Son.* Illus. by Emily Newton Barto. New York: Longman, 1942.
122 Nursery rhymes.

Mother Goose. *A Pocket Full of Posies.* Illus. by Marguerite Lofft De Angeli. Garden City, NY: Doubleday, 1954/1961.
122 Nursery rhymes.

Mother Goose. *The Rainbow Mother Goose.* Illus. by Lili Cassel. Edited, with an introduction, by May Lamberton Becker. Cleveland: Collins, 1947.
122 Nursery rhymes.

Mother Goose. *The Real Mother Goose.* Illus. by Blanche Fisher Wright. Skokie, IL: Rand McNally, 1916.
122 Nursery rhymes.

Mother Goose. *Richard Scarry's Best Mother Goose Ever.* Illus. by Richard McClure Scarry. Racine, WI: Western Pub., 1964.
122 Nursery rhymes.

Mother Goose. *Richard Scarry's Favorite Mother Goose Rhymes.* Illus. by Richard McClure Scarry. Racine, WI: Western Pub., 1976.
122 Nursery rhymes.

Mother Goose. *Rimes de la Mere Oie.* Illus. by Seymour Chwast; Milton Glaser; and Barry Zaid. Mother Goose rhymes rendered into French by Ormonde De Kay, Jr. Boston: Little, 1971.
065 Foreign languages; 122 Nursery rhymes.

Mother Goose. *Ring O' Roses.* Illus. by Leonard Leslie Brooke. New York: Warne, 1923.
122 Nursery rhymes.

Mother Goose. *Songs from Mother Goose.* Illus. by Maginel Wright Enright Barney. For voice and piano; set to music by Sidney Homer. New York: Macmillan, 1920.
116 Music; 122 Nursery rhymes;
164 Songs.

Mother Goose. *The Tall Book of Mother Goose.* Illus. by Feodor Stepanovich Rojankovsky. New York: Harper, 1942.
122 Nursery rhymes.

Mother Goose. *The Three Jovial Huntsmen.* Illus. by Susan Jeffers. New York: Bradbury Pr., 1973.
122 Nursery rhymes.

Mother Goose. *To Market! To Market!* Illus. by Peter Spier. Garden City, NY: Doubleday, 1967.
058 Farms; 122 Nursery rhymes.

Mother Goose. *Tom Tom the Piper's Son.* Illus. by Paul Galdone. New York: McGraw-Hill, 1964.
122 Nursery rhymes.

Mother Goose. *Twenty Nursery Rhymes.* Illus. by Philip Van Aver. San Francisco: Grabhorn-Hoyem, 1970.
122 Nursery rhymes.

Mother Goose. *Willy Pogany's Mother Goose.* Illus. by William Andrew Pogany. New York: Nelson, 1928.
122 Nursery rhymes.

The Moving Adventures of Old Dame Trot and Her Comical Cat. Illus. by Paul Galdone. New York: McGraw-Hill, 1973.
008.09 Animals—cats; 122 Nursery rhymes.

Müller, Jörg, jt. author. *The Bear Who Wanted to Be a Bear.* By Jörg Steiner, and Jörg Müller.

Munari, Bruno. *ABC.* Illus. by author. Cleveland: Collins, 1960.
001 ABC Books.

Munari, Bruno. *Animals for Sale.* Illus. by author. Cleveland: Collins, 1957.
008 Animals.

Munari, Bruno. *The Birthday Present.* Illus. by author. Cleveland: Collins, 1959.
018 Birthdays; 069 Games.

Munari, Bruno. *Bruno Munari's Zoo.* Illus. by author. Cleveland: Collins, 1963.
008 Animals; 017 Birds; 204 Zoos.

Munari, Bruno. *The Circus in the Mist.* Illus. by author. Cleveland: Collins, 1968.
028 Circus, clowns; 067 Format, unusual; 195.04 Weather—fog.

Munari, Bruno. *The Elephant's Wish.* Illus. by author. Cleveland: Collins, 1945/1959.
008 Animals; 016.38 Behavior—wishing; 067 Format, unusual.

Munari, Bruno. *Jimmy Has Lost His Cap.* Illus. by author. Cleveland: Collins, 1959.
016.19 Behavior—losing things; 067 Format, unusual.

Munari, Bruno. *Tic, Tac and Toc.* Illus. by author. Cleveland: Collins, 1957.
017 Birds; 067 Format, unusual.

Munari, Bruno. *Who's There? Open the Door.* Illus. by author. Cleveland: Collins, 1957.
008 Animals; 067 Format, unusual.

Murdocca, Salvatore. *Tuttle's Shell.* Illus. by author. New York: Lothrop, 1976.
142.05 Reptiles—turtles.

Murphey, Sara. *The Animal Hat Shop.* Illus. by Mel Pekarsky. Chicago: Follett, 1964.
008.09 Animals—cats; 017.04 Birds—chickens; 031 Clothing.

Murphey, Sara. *The Roly Poly Cookie.* Illus. by Leonard W. Shortall. Chicago: Follett, 1963.
038 Cumulative tales; 063 Food.

Murschetz, Luis. *Mister Mole.* Illus. by author. Translated from the German by Diane Martin. Englewood Cliffs, NJ: Prentice-Hall, 1976.
008.35 Animals—moles; 049 Ecology; 138 Progress.

Myller, Lois. *No! No!* Illus. by Cyndy Szekeres. New York: Simon & Schuster, 1971.
008.26 Animals—hedgehogs; 016 Behavior; 016.22 Behavior—misbehavior; 054 Etiquette; 057 Family life; 148 Safety.

Myller, Rolf. *How Big Is a Foot?* Illus. by author. New York: Atheneum, 1962.
018 Birthdays; 032.05 Concepts—measurement; 087 Humor; 147 Royalty.

Myller, Rolf. *Rolling Round.* Illus. by author. New York: Atheneum, 1963.
147 Royalty; 197 Wheels.

Myrick, Jean Lockwood. *Ninety-Nine Pockets.* Illus. by Haris Petie. Mt. Vernon: Lantern Pr., 1966.
018 Birthdays; 031 Clothing; 137 Problem solving.

Myrick, Mildred. *Ants Are Fun.* Illus. by Arnold Stark Lobel. New York: Harper, 1968.
090 Insects and spiders; 152 Science.

Myrick, Mildred. *The Secret Three.* Illus. by Arnold Stark Lobel. New York: Harper, 1963.
070 Gangs, clubs; 101 Lighthouses; 155 Secret codes.

Nakàno, Hirotaka. *Elephant Blue.* Illus. by author. Translated by Fukuinkan Shoten. Indianapolis: Bobbs-Merrill, 1970.
008 Animals; 008.17 Animals—elephants; 026.14 Character traits—helpfulness.

Nakatani, Chiyoko. *The Day Chiro Was Lost.* Illus. by author. Cleveland: Collins, 1969.
008.14 Animals—dogs; 016.20 Behavior—lost.

Nakatani, Chiyoko. *Fumio and the Dolphins.* Illus. by author. Reading: Addison-Wesley, 1970.
008.15 Animals—dolphins; 026.18 Character traits—kindness to animals; 064.19 Foreign lands—Japan; 153 Sea and seashore.

Nakatani, Chiyoko. *My Day on the Farm*. Illus. by author. New York: Crowell, 1976.
058 Farms.

Nakatani, Chiyoko. *My Teddy Bear*. Illus. by author. New York: Crowell, 1975.
177.08 Toys—teddy bears.

Nakatani, Chiyoko. *The Zoo in My Garden*. Illus. by author. New York: Crowell, 1973.
008 Animals.

Napoli, Guillier. *Adventure at Mont St. Michael*. Illus. by author. New York: McGraw-Hill, 1966.
023.11 Careers—fishermen;
026.10 Character traits—curiosity;
064.11 Foreign lands—France; 153 Sea and seashore.

Narayan, Maya, jt. author. *Leela and the Watermelon*. By Marilyn Joyce Hirsh, and Maya Narayan.

Nash, Ogden. *The Adventures of Isabel*. Illus. by Walter Lorraine. Boston: Little, 1963.
052.04 Emotions—fear; 087 Humor;
134 Poetry, rhyme.

Nash, Ogden. *The Animal Garden*. Illus. by Hilary Knight. Philadelphia: Lippincott, 1965.
087 Humor; 133 Plants; 134 Poetry, rhyme.

Nash, Ogden. *A Boy Is a Boy*. Illus. by Arthur Shilstone. New York: Watts, 1960.
087 Humor; 134 Poetry, rhyme.

Nash, Ogden. *Custard the Dragon and the Wicked Knight*. Illus. by Linell Nash. Boston: Little, 1959.
046 Dragons; 134 Poetry, rhyme.

Ness, Evaline. *Do You Have the Time, Lydia?* Illus. by author. New York: Dutton, 1971.
017.22 Birds—sea gulls;
026.07 Character traits—completing things; 121 Non-sexist; 137 Problem solving; 174 Time.

Ness, Evaline. *Exactly Alike*. Illus. by author. New York: Scribner's, 1964.
057 Family life.

Ness, Evaline. *The Girl and the Goatherd*. Illus. by author. New York: Dutton, 1970.
026.02 Character traits—appearance.

Ness, Evaline. *Josefina February*. Illus. by author. New York: Scribner's, 1963.
018 Birthdays; 026.13 Character traits—generosity; 064.05 Foreign lands—Caribbean Islands.

Ness, Evaline. *Marcella's Guardian Angel*. Illus. by author. New York: Holiday, 1979.
007 Angels.

Ness, Evaline. *Pavo and the Princess*. Illus. by author. New York: Scribner's, 1964.
017 Birds; 026.14 Character traits—helpfulness; 052 Emotions; 147 Royalty.

Ness, Evaline. *Sam, Bangs and Moonshine*. Illus. by author. New York: Holt, 1966.
089 Imagination; 166.05 Sports—fishing.

Ness, Evaline. *Tom Tit Tot*. Illus. by author. New York: Scribner's, 1965.
062 Folk and fairy tales; 103 Magic;
118 Names.

Newberry, Clare Turlay. *April's Kittens*. Illus. by author. New York: Harper, 1940.
008.09 Animals—cats; 131 Pets.

Newberry, Clare Turlay. *Barkis*. Illus. by author. New York: Harper, 1938.
008.14 Animals—dogs; 131 Pets.

Newberry, Clare Turlay. *Cousin Toby*. Illus. by author. New York: Harper, 1939.
013 Babies.

Newberry, Clare Turlay. *Herbert the Lion*. Illus. by author. New York: Harper, 1931/1956.
008.10 Animals—cats, wild; 131 Pets.

Newberry, Clare Turlay. *The Kittens' ABC*. Illus. by author. New York: Harper, 1965.
001 ABC Books; 008.09 Animals—cats;
134 Poetry, rhyme.

Newberry, Clare Turlay. *Lambert's Bargain*. Illus. by author. New York: Harper, 1941.
008.29 Animals—hyenas.

Newberry, Clare Turlay. *Marshmallow*. Illus. by author. New York: Harper, 1942.
008.09 Animals—cats; 008.46 Animals—rabbits.

Newberry, Clare Turlay. *Mittens*. Illus. by author. New York: Harper, 1937.
008.09 Animals—cats.

Newberry, Clare Turlay. *Pandora*. Illus. by author. New York: Harper, 1944.
008.09 Animals—cats.

Newberry, Clare Turlay. *Percy, Polly and Pete*. Illus. by author. New York: Harper, 1952.
008.09 Animals—cats;
016.14 Behavior—growing up;
026.18 Character traits—kindness to animals; 131 Pets.

Newberry, Clare Turlay. *Smudge*. Illus. by author. New York: Harper, 1948.
008.09 Animals—cats.

Newberry, Clare Turlay. *T-Bone, the Baby-Sitter*. Illus. by author. New York: Harper, 1950.
002.01 Activities—babysitting;
008.09 Animals—cats; 013 Babies.

Newberry, Clare Turlay. *Widget*. Illus. by author. New York: Harper, 1958.
008.09 Animals—cats.

Newbolt, Sir Henry John. *Rilloby-Rill*. Illus. by Susanna Gretz. New York: O'Hara, 1973.
090 Insects and spiders; 116 Music;
164 Songs.

Newell, Crosby. See Bonsall, Crosby Newell.

Newell, Peter. *Topsys and Turvys*. Illus. by author. New York: Dover, 1965.
067 Format, unusual; 087 Humor.

Newfield, Marcia. *Iggy*. Illus. by Jacqueline Chwast. Boston: Houghton, 1972.
131 Pets; 142.02 Reptiles—iguanas.

Nicholson, William. *Clever Bill*. Illus. by author. New York: Farrar, 1977.
177.06 Toys—soldiers.

Nic Leodhas, Sorche (pseud.). See Alger, Leclaire.

Nicolas (pseud.). See Mordvinoff, Nicolas.

Nicoll, Helen. *Meg and Mog*. Illus. by Jan Pienkowski. New York: Atheneum, 1972.
008.09 Animals—cats;
083.07 Holidays—Halloween;
103 Magic; 199 Witches.

Nicoll, Helen. *Meg at Sea*. Illus. by Jan Pienkowski. New York: Harvey House, 1974.
008.09 Animals—cats; 017.14 Birds—owls; 103 Magic; 153 Sea and seashore;
199 Witches.

Nicoll, Helen. *Meg on the Moon*. Illus. by Jan Pienkowski. New York: Harvey House, 1974.
008.09 Animals—cats; 103 Magic;
111 Moon; 199 Witches.

Nicoll, Helen. *Meg's Eggs*. Illus. by Jan Pienkowski. New York: Atheneum, 1972.
008.09 Animals—cats; 017.14 Birds—owls; 044 Dinosaurs; 050 Eggs;
103 Magic; 199 Witches.

Niland, Deborah. *ABC of Monsters*. Illus. by author. New York: McGraw-Hill, 1978.
001 ABC Books; 110 Monsters.

Nodset, Joan L. See Lexau, Joan M.

Nolan, Dennis. *Wizard McBean and His Flying Machine*. Illus. by author. Englewood Cliffs, NJ: Prentice-Hall, 1977.
004 Airplanes; 038 Cumulative tales;
103 Magic; 134 Poetry, rhyme;
200 Wizards.

Nolan, Madeena Spray. *My Daddy Don't Go to Work*. Illus. by Jim LaMarche. Minneapolis: Carolrhoda Books, 1978.
053.01 Ethnic groups in the U.S.—Afro-Americans; 057 Family life;
057.01 Family life—fathers;
135 Poverty.

Northrop, Mili. *The Watch Cat*. Illus. by Adrina Zanazanian. Designed by Kent Salisbury. Indianapolis: Bobbs-Merrill, 1968.
008.09 Animals—cats; 064.37 Foreign lands—Thailand.

Norton, Natalie. *A Little Old Man*. Illus. by Will Huntington. Skokie, IL: Rand McNally, 1959.
052.07 Emotions—loneliness.

Nourse, Alan Edward. *Lumps, Bumps and Rashes; A Look at Kids' Diseases*. Illustrated. New York: Watts, 1976.
088 Illness.

Numeroff, Laura Joffe. *Amy for Short*. Illus. by author. New York: Macmillan, 1976.
026.02 Character traits—appearance;
068 Friendship.

Numeroff, Laura Joffe. *Phoebe Dexter Has Harriet Peterson's Sniffles*. Illus. by author. New York: Greenwillow, 1977.
088 Illness.

Numeroff, Laura Joffe, jt. author. *You Can't Put Braces on Spaces*. By Alice Richter, and Laura Joffe Numeroff.

Nursery Rhymes. Illus. by Gertrude Elliott. New York: Simon & Schuster, 1948.
122 Nursery rhymes.

Nussbaumer, Mares, and Nussbaumer, Paul. *Away in a Manger*. Illus. by Paul Nussbaumer. A Story of the Nativity. New York: Harcourt, 1965.
083.03 Holidays—Christmas; 116 Music;
141 Religion.

Nussbaumer, Paul, jt. author. *Away in a Manger*. By Mares Nussbaumer, and Paul Nussbaumer.

Oakley, Graham. *The Church Cat Abroad*. Illus. by author. New York: Atheneum, 1973.

008.09 Animals—cats; 008.34 Animals—mice; 064.10 Foreign lands—England.

Oakley, Graham. *The Church Mice Adrift.* Illus. by author. New York: Atheneum, 1976.
008.09 Animals—cats; 008.34 Animals—mice; 008.48 Animals—rats; 064.10 Foreign lands—England.

Oakley, Graham. *The Church Mice and the Moon.* Illus. by author. New York: Atheneum, 1974.
008.09 Animals—cats; 008.34 Animals—mice; 064.10 Foreign lands—England.

Oakley, Graham. *The Church Mice at Bay.* Illus. by author. New York: Atheneum, 1978.
008.09 Animals—cats; 008.34 Animals—mice; 064.10 Foreign lands—England.

Oakley, Graham. *The Church Mice Spread Their Wings.* Illus. by author. New York: Atheneum, 1975.
008.09 Animals—cats; 008.34 Animals—mice; 064.10 Foreign lands—England.

Oakley, Graham. *The Church Mouse.* Illus. by author. New York: Atheneum, 1972.
008.09 Animals—cats; 008.34 Animals—mice; 064.10 Foreign lands—England.

Oberhansli, Gertrud. *Sleep, Baby, Sleep.* Illus. by author. New York: Atheneum, 1967.
015 Bedtime; 116 Music; 164 Songs.

Ogle, Lucille. *I Spy with My Little Eye.* Illus. by Joe Kaufman. New York: McGraw-Hill, 1970.
157 Senses; 201 Wordless.

Ogle, Lucille, and Thoburn, Tine. *A B See.* Illus. by Ralph Stobart. New York: McGraw-Hill, 1973.
001 ABC Books.

Ogle, Lucille, and Thoburn, Tine. *I Hear.* Illus. by Eloise Wilkin. New York: McGraw-Hill, 1971.
120 Noise; 129 Participation; 157 Senses.

O'Hare, Colette. *What Do You Feed Your Donkey On?* Illus. by Jenny Rodwell. Rhymes from a Belfast childhood. Cleveland: Collins, 1978.
064.10 Foreign lands—England; 134 Poetry, rhyme.

Oksner, Robert M. *The Incompetent Wizard.* Illus. by Janet McCaffery. New York: Morrow, 1965.
046 Dragons; 103 Magic; 200 Wizards.

Old MacDonald Had a Farm. Illus. by Mel Crawford. Racine, WI: Western Pub., 1967.
008 Animals; 038 Cumulative tales; 058 Farms; 116 Music; 164 Songs.

Old MacDonald Had a Farm. Illus. by Abner Graboff. New York: Four Winds Pr., 1970.
008 Animals; 038 Cumulative tales; 058 Farms; 116 Music; 164 Songs.

Old MacDonald Had a Farm. Illus. by Robert Mead Quackenbush. Philadelphia: Lippincott, 1972.
008 Animals; 038 Cumulative tales; 058 Farms; 116 Music; 164 Songs.

The Old Woman and Her Pig. Illus. by Paul Galdone. New York: McGraw-Hill, 1960.
038 Cumulative tales; 062 Folk and fairy tales.

Olds, Elizabeth. *Feather Mountain.* Illus. by author. Boston: Houghton, 1951.
017 Birds.

Olds, Elizabeth. *Little Una.* Illus. by author. New York: Scribner's, 1963.
029 City.

Olds, Elizabeth. *Plop, Plop, Ploppie.* Illus. by author. New York: Scribner's, 1962.
008.50 Animals—sea lions; 028 Circus, clowns.

Olds, Helen Diehl. *Miss Hattie and the Monkey.* Illus. by Dorothy Bronson Marino. Chicago: Follett, 1958.
008.37 Animals—monkeys; 023.23 Careers—seamstresses.

Oleson, Claire. *For Pepita, an Orange Tree.* Illus. by Margot Ladd Tomes. Garden City, NY: Doubleday, 1967.
018 Birthdays; 064.34 Foreign lands—Spain; 133 Plants.

Olschewski, Alfred. *We Fly.* Illus. by author. Boston: Little, 1967.
004 Airplanes.

Olschewski, Alfred. *The Wheel Rolls Over.* Illus. by author. Boston: Little, 1962.
197 Wheels.

Olsen, Ib Spang. *The Boy in the Moon.* Illus. by author. Translated by Virginia Allen Jensen. New York: Parents, 1962/1971.
111 Moon.

Olsen, Ib Spang. *Cat Alley.* Illus. by author. Translated by Virginia Allen Jensen. New York: Coward, 1971.
016.20 Behavior—lost; 029 City.

O'Neill, Mary. *Big Red Hen.* Illus. by Judy P. Campbell. Garden City, NY: Doubleday, 1971.
017.04 Birds—chickens; 050 Eggs; 134 Poetry, rhyme.

Opie, Iona Archibald, comp., and Opie, Peter, comp. *A Family Book of Nursery Rhymes.* Illus. by Pauline Baynes. New York: Oxford Univ. Pr., 1964.
122 Nursery rhymes.

Opie, Iona Archibald, comp., and Opie, Peter, comp. *The Oxford Nursery Rhyme Book.* Illus. by Joan Hassall. New York: Oxford Univ. Pr., 1955.
122 Nursery rhymes.

Opie, Iona Archibald, comp., and Opie, Peter, comp. *The Puffin Book of Nursery Rhymes.* Illus. by Pauline Baynes. New York: Penguin, 1963.
122 Nursery rhymes.

Opie, Peter, comp., jt. author. *A Family Book of Nursery Rhymes.* By Iona Archibald Opie, comp., and Peter Opie, comp.

Opie, Peter, comp., jt. author. *The Oxford Nursery Rhyme Book.* By Iona Archibald Opie, comp., and Peter Opie, comp.

Opie, Peter, comp., jt. author. *The Puffin Book of Nursery Rhymes.* By Iona Archibald Opie, comp., and Peter Opie, comp.

Oppenheim, Joanne. *Have You Seen Roads?* Illus. by Gerard Nook. Reading: Addison-Wesley, 1969.
134 Poetry, rhyme; 180 Transportation.

Oppenheim, Joanne. *Have You Seen Trees?* Illus. by Irwin Rosenhouse. Reading: Addison-Wesley, 1967.
134 Poetry, rhyme; 154 Seasons; 181 Trees.

Oppenheim, Joanne. *On the Other Side of the River.* Illus. by Aliki Liacouras Brandenberg. New York: Watts, 1972.
016.26 Behavior—needing someone; 020 Bridges; 023 Careers.

Orgel, Doris. *On the Sand Dune.* Illus. by Leonard Weisgard. New York: Harper, 1968.
026.31 Character traits—smallness; 153 Sea and seashore.

Ormondroyd, Edward. *Broderick.* Illus. by John M. Larrecq. Berkeley: Parnassus, 1969.
002.13 Activities—reading; 008.34 Animals—mice; 166.14 Sports—surfing.

Ormondroyd, Edward. *Theodore.* Illus. by John M. Larrecq. Berkeley: Parnassus, 1966.
026.02 Character traits—appearance; 026.17 Character traits—kindness; 097 Laundry; 177.08 Toys—teddy bears.

Ormondroyd, Edward. *Theodore's Rival.* Illus. by John M. Larrecq. Berkeley: Parnassus, 1971.
016.32 Behavior—sibling rivalry; 052.03 Emotions—envy, jealousy; 177.08 Toys—teddy bears.

Ormsby, Virginia H. *Twenty-One Children Plus Ten.* Illus. by author. Philadelphia: Lippincott, 1971.
053.06 Ethnic groups in the U.S.—Mexican-Americans; 151 School.

Ott, John, and Coley, Pete. *Peter Pumpkin.* Illus. by Ivan Chermayeff. Garden City, NY: Doubleday, 1963.
083.07 Holidays—Halloween; 083.10 Holidays—Thanksgiving; 154.01 Seasons—fall.

Otto, Margaret Glover. *The Little Brown Horse.* Illus. by Barbara Cooney. New York: Knopf, 1959.
008.09 Animals—cats; 008.28 Animals—horses; 017.04 Birds—chickens.

Overbeck, Cynthia. *Rusty the Irish Setter.* Illus. by Antoinette Barrere. Translated by Dyan Hammarberg. Minneapolis: Carolrhoda Books, 1977.
008.14 Animals—dogs.

Overbeck, Cynthia, jt. author. *The Winds That Blow.* By Brenda Thompson, and Cynthia Overbeck.

Oxenbury, Helen. *The Animal House.* Illus. by author. New York: Morrow, 1977.
008 Animals.

Oxenbury, Helen. *Helen Oxenbury's ABC of Things.* Illus. by author. New York: Watts, 1971.
001 ABC Books.

Oxenbury, Helen. *Numbers of Things.* Illus. by author. New York: Watts, 1968.
033 Counting.

Oxenbury, Helen. *The Queen and Rosie Randall.* Illus. by author. From an idea by Jill Butterfield-Campbell. New York: Morrow, 1979.
064.10 Foreign lands—England; 069 Games; 130 Parties; 147 Royalty.

Pack, Robert. *How to Catch a Crocodile.* Illus. by Nola Langner. New York: Knopf, 1964.
026.19 Character traits—laziness;
089 Imagination; 134 Poetry, rhyme;
142.01 Reptiles—alligators, crocodiles.

Pack, Robert. *Then What Did You Do?* Illus. by Nola Langner. New York: Macmillan, 1961.
008 Animals; 038 Cumulative tales;
087 Humor.

Palazzo, Anthony D. See Palazzo, Tony.

Palazzo, Tony. *Animal Babies.* Illus. by author. Garden City, NY: Doubleday, 1960.
008 Animals.

Palazzo, Tony. *Animals 'Round the Mulberry Bush.* Illus. by author. Garden City, NY: Doubleday, 1958.
008 Animals; 122 Nursery rhymes.

Palazzo, Tony. *Bianco and the New World.* Illus. by author. New York: Viking, 1957.
008.16 Animals—donkeys; 028 Circus, clowns.

Palazzo, Tony. *Federico, the Flying Squirrel.* Illus. by author. New York: Viking, 1951.
008.56 Animals—squirrels.

Palazzo, Tony. *Noah's Ark.* Illus. by author. Garden City, NY: Doubleday, 1955.
141.01 Religion—Noah.

Palazzo, Tony. *Waldo the Woodchuck.* Illus. by author. New York: Duell, 1964.
008.23 Animals—groundhogs;
083.06 Holidays—Groundhog Day.

Palmer, Helen Marion. *A Fish Out of Water.* Illus. by Philip Day Eastman. New York: Random House, 1961.
060 Fish; 087 Humor.

Palmer, Helen Marion. *I Was Kissed by a Seal at the Zoo.* Illus. by Lynn Fayman. New York: Random House, 1962.
008 Animals; 087 Humor.

Palmer, Helen Marion. *Why I Built the Boogle House.* Illus. by Lynn Fayman. New York: Random House, 1964.
008 Animals; 086 Houses; 131 Pets.

Palmer, Mary. *The No-Sort-of-Animal.* Illus. by Abner Graboff. Boston: Houghton, 1964.
008 Animals; 016.09 Behavior—dissatisfaction; 156 Self-concept.

Panek, Dennis. *Catastrophe Cat.* Illus. by author. New York: Bradbury Pr., 1978.
008.09 Animals—cats;
016.06 Behavior—carelessness.

Panek, Dennis. *Catastrophe Cat at the Zoo.* Illus. by author. New York: Bradbury Pr., 1979.
008.09 Animals—cats; 201 Wordless;
204 Zoos.

Papas, William. *Taresh the Tea Planter.* Illus. by author. Cleveland: Collins, 1968.
026.19 Character traits—laziness;
064.16 Foreign lands—India.

Parish, Peggy. *Amelia Bedelia.* Illus. by Fritz Siebel. New York: Harper, 1963.
016.24 Behavior—misunderstanding;
023.15 Careers—maids; 087 Humor;
096 Language.

Parish, Peggy. *Amelia Bedelia and the Surprise Shower.* Illus. by Fritz Siebel. New York: Harper, 1966.
016.24 Behavior—misunderstanding;
023.15 Careers—maids; 087 Humor;
096 Language; 130 Parties.

Parish, Peggy. *Amelia Bedelia Helps Out.* Illus. by Lynn Sweat. New York: Greenwillow, 1979.
016.24 Behavior—misunderstanding;
023.15 Careers—maids; 087 Humor;
096 Language.

Parish, Peggy. *Come Back, Amelia Bedelia.* Illus. by Wallace Tripp. New York: Harper, 1971.
016.24 Behavior—misunderstanding;
023.15 Careers—maids; 087 Humor;
096 Language.

Parish, Peggy. *Dinosaur Time.* Illus. by Arnold Stark Lobel. New York: Harper, 1974.
044 Dinosaurs.

Parish, Peggy. *Good Hunting, Little Indian.* Illus. by Leonard Weisgard. Reading: Addison-Wesley, 1962.
053.04 Ethnic groups in the U.S.—Indians.

Parish, Peggy. *Good Work, Amelia Bedelia.* Illus. by Lynn Sweat. New York: Greenwillow, 1976.
016.24 Behavior—misunderstanding;
023.15 Careers—maids; 087 Humor;
096 Language.

Parish, Peggy. *Granny and the Desperadoes.* Illus. by Steven Kellogg. New York: Macmillan, 1970.

036 Crime; 057.02 Family life—
grandparents; great-grandparents;
087 Humor.

Parish, Peggy. *Granny and the Indians*. Illus.
by Brinton Cassady Turkle. New York:
Macmillan, 1969.
053.04 Ethnic groups in the U.S.—
Indians; 057.02 Family life—
grandparents; great-grandparents;
087 Humor.

Parish, Peggy. *Granny, the Baby and the Big
Gray Thing*. Illus. by Lynn Sweat. New
York: Macmillan, 1972.
008.61 Animals—wolves; 013 Babies;
053.04 Ethnic groups in the U.S.—
Indians; 057.02 Family life—
grandparents; great-grandparents;
087 Humor.

Parish, Peggy. *Jumper Goes to School*. Illus. by
Cyndy Szekeres. New York: Simon &
Schuster, 1969.
008.37 Animals—monkeys; 151 School.

Parish, Peggy. *Little Indian*. Illus. by John E.
Johnson. New York: Simon & Schuster,
1968.
053.04 Ethnic groups in the U.S.—
Indians; 118 Names.

Parish, Peggy. *Mind Your Manners*. Illus. by
Marylin Hafner. New York: Greenwillow,
1978.
054 Etiquette.

Parish, Peggy. *Ootah's Lucky Day*. Illus. by
Mamoru R. Funai. New York: Harper,
1970.
053.03 Ethnic groups in the U.S.—
Eskimos.

Parish, Peggy. *Play Ball, Amelia Bedelia*. Illus.
by Wallace Tripp. New York: Harper,
1972.
016.24 Behavior—misunderstanding;
023.15 Careers—maids; 087 Humor;
096 Language; 166.01 Sports—baseball.

Parish, Peggy. *Snapping Turtle's All Wrong
Day*. Illus. by John E. Johnson. New York:
Simon & Schuster, 1970.
018 Birthdays; 053.04 Ethnic groups in
the U.S.—Indians.

Parish, Peggy. *Teach Us, Amelia Bedelia*. Illus.
by Lynn Sweat. New York: Greenwillow,
1977.
016.24 Behavior—misunderstanding;
023.15 Careers—maids; 087 Humor;
096 Language; 151 School.

Parish, Peggy. *Thank You, Amelia Bedelia*. Illus. by Fritz Siebel. New York: Harper,
1964.

016.24 Behavior—misunderstanding;
023.15 Careers—maids; 087 Humor.

Parish, Peggy. *Too Many Rabbits*. Illus. by
Leonard P. Kessler. New York: Macmillan, 1974.
008.46 Animals—rabbits.

Parish, Peggy. *Zed and the Monsters*. Illus. by
Paul Galdone. Garden City, NY: Doubleday, 1979.
026.06 Character traits—cleverness;
110 Monsters.

Parker, Dorothy D. *Liam's Catch*. Illus. by
Andrew Parker. New York: Viking, 1972.
023.11 Careers—fishermen;
064.17 Foreign lands—Ireland;
166.05 Sports—fishing.

Parker, Nancy Winslow. *Love from Uncle
Clyde*. Illus. by author. New York: Dodd,
1977.
008.27 Animals—hippopotami;
018 Birthdays.

Parker, Nancy Winslow. *The Ordeal of Byron
B. Blackbear*. Illus. by author. New York:
Dodd, 1979.
008.06 Animals—bears;
081 Hibernation; 152 Science.

Parkin, Rex. *The Red Carpet*. Illus. by author.
New York: Macmillan, 1948.
085 Hotels; 087 Humor.

Parnall, Peter. *The Great Fish*. Illus. by author. Garden City, NY: Doubleday, 1973.
049 Ecology; 053.04 Ethnic groups in
the U.S.—Indians; 060 Fish; 062 Folk
and fairy tales.

Parry, Marian. *King of the Fish*. Illus. by author. New York: Macmillan, 1977.
008.46 Animals—rabbits;
026.06 Character traits—cleverness;
060 Fish; 062 Folk and fairy tales;
064.20 Foreign lands—Korea;
142.05 Reptiles—turtles.

Parsons, Ellen. *Rainy Day Together*. Illus. by
Lillian Hoban. New York: Harper, 1971.
052 Emotions; 057 Family life;
057.04 Family life—the only child;
195.05 Weather—rain.

Partch, Virgil Franklin. *The Christmas Cookie
Sprinkle Snitcher*. Illus. by author. New
York: Simon & Schuster, 1969.
036 Crime; 083.03 Holidays—
Christmas; 140 Rebuses.

Partch, Virgil Franklin. *The VIP's Mistake
Book*. Illus. by author. New York: Dutton,
1970.
087 Humor.

Paterson, Andrew Barton. *Mulga Bill's Bicycle*. Illus. by Kilmeny Niland, and Deborah Niland. New York: Parents, 1975.
008.28 Animals—horses; 064.02 Foreign lands—Australia; 134 Poetry, rhyme; 166.03 Sports—bicycling.

Paterson, Andrew Barton. *Waltzing Matilda*. Illus. by Desmond Ward Digby. New York: Holt, 1970.
064.02 Foreign lands—Australia; 164 Songs.

Paterson, Diane. *Eat*. Illus. by author. New York: Dial Pr., 1975.
063 Food; 087 Humor.

Paterson, Diane. *If I Were a Toad*. Illus. by author. New York: Dial Pr., 1977.
008 Animals; 016.38 Behavior—wishing; 129 Participation.

Paterson, Diane. *Smile for Auntie*. Illus. by author. New York: Dial Pr., 1976.
087 Humor.

Paterson, Diane. *Wretched Rachel*. Illus. by author. New York: Dial Pr., 1978.
016 Behavior; 052.08 Emotions—love; 057 Family life.

Patrick, Gloria. *This Is...* Illus. by Joan Hanson. Minneapolis: Carolrhoda Books, 1970.
038 Cumulative tales; 129 Participation; 134 Poetry, rhyme.

Patz, Nancy. *Pumpernickel Tickle and Mean Green Cheese*. Illus. by author. New York: Watts, 1978.
008.17 Animals—elephants; 016.11 Behavior—forgetfulness; 087 Humor; 160 Shopping; 175 Tongue twisters.

Payne, Emmy. *Katy No-Pocket*. Illus. by Hans Augusto Rey. Boston: Houghton, 1944.
008.30 Animals—kangaroos; 031 Clothing.

Payne, Josephine Balfour. *The Stable That Stayed*. Illus. by author. New York: Ariel, 1952.
008 Animals; 023.02 Careers—artists; 034 Country.

A Peaceable Kingdom; The Shaker Abecedarius. Illus. by Alice Provensen, and Martin Provensen. New York: Viking, 1978.
001 ABC Books; 008 Animals; 134 Poetry, rhyme.

Pearson, Susan. *Everybody Knows That!* Illus. by Diane Paterson. New York: Dial Pr., 1978.
068 Friendship; 121 Non-sexist; 151 School.

Pearson, Susan. *That's Enough for One Day!* Illus. by Kay Chorao. New York: Dial Pr., 1977.
002.12 Activities—playing; 002.13 Activities—reading.

Peck, Richard. *Monster Night at Grandma's House*. Illus. by Don Freeman. New York: Viking, 1977.
057.02 Family life—grandparents; great-grandparents; 110 Monsters; 119 Night.

Peck, Robert Newton. *Hamilton*. Illus. by Laura Lydecker. Boston: Little, 1976.
008.42 Animals—pigs; 008.61 Animals—wolves; 058 Farms; 134 Poetry, rhyme.

Peet, Bill. *The Ant and the Elephant*. Illus. by author. Boston: Houghton, 1972.
008 Animals; 008.17 Animals—elephants; 026.14 Character traits—helpfulness; 026.29 Character traits—selfishness; 038 Cumulative tales; 090 Insects and spiders.

Peet, Bill. *Big Bad Bruce*. Illus. by author. Boston: Houghton, 1977.
008.06 Animals—bears; 016.05 Behavior—bullying; 066 Forest, woods; 087 Humor; 199 Witches.

Peet, Bill. *Buford, the Little Bighorn*. Illus. by author. Boston: Houghton, 1967.
008.52 Animals—sheep; 026.16 Character traits—individuality; 087 Humor; 166.08 Sports—hunting; 166.12 Sports—skiing.

Peet, Bill. *The Caboose Who Got Loose*. Illus. by author. Boston: Houghton, 1971.
016.09 Behavior—dissatisfaction; 049 Ecology; 179 Trains.

Peet, Bill. *Chester the Worldly Pig*. Illus. by author. Boston: Houghton, 1965.
008.42 Animals—pigs; 028 Circus, clowns; 087 Humor; 202 World.

Peet, Bill. *Countdown to Christmas*. Illus. by author. Boston: Houghton, 1972.
083.03 Holidays—Christmas; 087 Humor; 103 Magic; 138 Progress.

Peet, Bill. *Cowardly Clyde*. Illus. by author. Boston: Houghton, 1979.
008.28 Animals—horses; 026.04 Character traits—bravery; 087 Humor; 095 Knights.

Peet, Bill. *Cyrus the Unsinkable Sea Serpent*. Illus. by author. Boston: Houghton, 1975.

026.14 Character traits—helpfulness;
110 Monsters; 117 Mythical creatures;
153 Sea and seashore.

Peet, Bill. *Eli.* Illus. by author. Boston:
Houghton, 1978.
008.10 Animals—cats, wild; 017 Birds;
068 Friendship; 087 Humor.

Peet, Bill. *Ella.* Illus. by author. Boston:
Houghton, 1964.
008.17 Animals—elephants;
016.20 Behavior—lost; 026.09 Character
traits—conceit; 028 Circus, clowns;
134 Poetry, rhyme.

Peet, Bill. *Farewell to Shady Glade.* Illus. by
author. Boston: Houghton, 1966.
008 Animals; 049 Ecology; 138 Progress.

Peet, Bill. *Fly, Homer, Fly.* Illus. by author.
Boston: Houghton, 1969.
017.19 Birds—pigeons; 029 City;
049 Ecology.

Peet, Bill. *The Gnats of Knotty Pine.* Illus. by
author. Boston: Houghton, 1975.
008 Animals; 049 Ecology; 090 Insects
and spiders; 166.08 Sports—hunting.

Peet, Bill. *How Droofus the Dragon Lost His
Head.* Illus. by author. Boston: Houghton, 1971.
046 Dragons; 095 Knights; 147 Royalty.

Peet, Bill. *Hubert's Hair Raising Adventures.*
Illus. by author. Boston: Houghton,
1959.
008.10 Animals—cats, wild;
023.04 Careers—barbers; 087 Humor;
134 Poetry, rhyme.

Peet, Bill. *Huge Harold.* Illus. by author. Boston: Houghton, 1961.
008.46 Animals—rabbits;
026.18 Character traits—kindness to
animals; 032.08 Concepts—size;
087 Humor; 134 Poetry, rhyme.

Peet, Bill. *Jennifer and Josephine.* Illus. by author. Boston: Houghton, 1967.
008.09 Animals—cats; 012 Automobiles;
087 Humor.

Peet, Bill. *Kermit the Hermit.* Illus. by author.
Boston: Houghton, 1965.
016.13 Behavior—greed; 037 Crustacea;
087 Humor; 134 Poetry, rhyme; 153 Sea
and seashore.

Peet, Bill. *Merle the High Flying Squirrel.* Illus.
by author. Boston: Houghton, 1974.
002.05 Activities—flying;
008.56 Animals—squirrels; 087 Humor;
094 Kites; 181 Trees.

Peet, Bill. *The Pinkish, Purplish, Bluish Egg.*
Illus. by author. Boston: Houghton,
1963.
017 Birds; 017.07 Birds—doves;
050 Eggs; 117 Mythical creatures;
134 Poetry, rhyme; 191 Violence, anti-
violence.

Peet, Bill. *Randy's Dandy Lions.* Illus. by author. Boston: Houghton, 1964.
008.10 Animals—cats, wild; 028 Circus,
clowns; 087 Humor; 134 Poetry, rhyme.

Peet, Bill. *Smokey.* Illus. by author. Boston:
Houghton, 1962.
125 Old age; 134 Poetry, rhyme;
179 Trains.

Peet, Bill. *The Spooky Tail of Prewitt Peacock.*
Illus. by author. Boston: Houghton,
1973.
017.16 Birds—peacocks, peahens;
026.03 Character traits—being
different; 026.16 Character traits—
individuality.

Peet, Bill. *The Whingdingdilly.* Illus. by author. Boston: Houghton, 1970.
008.14 Animals—dogs;
016.09 Behavior—dissatisfaction;
026.23 Character traits—optimism;
199 Witches.

Peet, Bill. *The Wump World.* Illus. by author.
Boston: Houghton, 1970.
049 Ecology; 138 Progress; 165 Space
and space ships.

Pender, Lydia. *Barnaby and the Horses.* Illus.
by Alie Evers. New York: Abelard-Schuman, 1961.
008.28 Animals—horses;
016.06 Behavior—carelessness;
034 Country.

Pendery, Rosemary. *A Home for Hopper.* Illus.
by Robert Mead Quackenbush. New
York: Morrow, 1971.
005 Amphibians.

Pène Du Bois, William. See Du Bois, William
Pène.

Peppé, Rodney. *The Alphabet Book.* Illus. by
author. New York: Four Winds Pr., 1968.
001 ABC Books.

Peppé, Rodney. *Cat and Mouse.* Illus. by author. New York: Holt, 1973.
008.09 Animals—cats; 008.34 Animals—
mice; 122 Nursery rhymes; 134 Poetry,
rhyme.

Peppé, Rodney. *Circus Numbers.* Illus. by author. New York: Delacorte Pr., 1969.
028 Circus, clowns; 033 Counting.

Peppé, Rodney. *Hey Riddle Diddle.* Illus. by author. New York: Holt, 1971.
122 Nursery rhymes; 134 Poetry, rhyme; 143 Riddles.

Peppé, Rodney. *Odd One Out.* Illus. by author. New York: Viking, 1974.
032 Concepts; 069 Games.

Peppé, Rodney. *Rodney Peppé's Puzzle Book.* Illus. by author. New York: Viking, 1977.
032 Concepts; 069 Games.

Perera, Lydia. *Frisky.* Illus. by Oscar Liebman. New York: Holiday, 1955.
029 City; 106 Merry-go-rounds.

Perkins, Al. *The Digging-est Dog.* Illus. by Eric Gurney. New York: Random House, 1967.
008.14 Animals—dogs; 134 Poetry, rhyme.

Perkins, Al. *Don and Donna Go to Bat.* Illus. by Barney Tobey. New York: Random House, 1966.
121 Non-sexist; 166.01 Sports—baseball; 186 Twins.

Perkins, Al. *The Ear Book.* Illus. by William O'Brian. New York: Random House, 1968.
006 Anatomy; 134 Poetry, rhyme; 157 Senses.

Perkins, Al. *Hand, Hand, Fingers, Thumb.* Illus. by Eric Gurney. New York: Random House, 1969.
006 Anatomy; 134 Poetry, rhyme.

Perkins, Al. *King Midas and the Golden Touch.* Illus. by Harold Berson. New York: Random House, 1969.
016.13 Behavior—greed; 016.38 Behavior—wishing; 147 Royalty.

Perkins, Al. *The Nose Book.* Illus. by Roy McKie. New York: Random House, 1970.
006 Anatomy; 134 Poetry, rhyme.

Perkins, Al. *Tubby and the Lantern.* Illus. by Rowland B. Wilson. New York: Random House, 1971.
008.17 Animals—elephants; 018 Birthdays; 064.06 Foreign lands—China; 132 Pirates.

Perkins, Al. *Tubby and the Poo-Bah.* Illus. by Rowland B. Wilson. New York: Random House, 1972.
008.17 Animals—elephants; 019 Boats, ships.

Perrault, Charles. *Puss in Boots.* Illus. by Marcia Brown. A free translation from the French. New York: Scribner's, 1952.
008.09 Animals—cats; 026.06 Character traits—cleverness; 062 Folk and fairy tales; 147 Royalty.

Perrault, Charles. *Puss in Boots.* Illus. by Hans Fischer. New York: Harcourt, 1959.
008.09 Animals—cats; 026.06 Character traits—cleverness; 062 Folk and fairy tales; 147 Royalty.

Perrault, Charles. *Puss in Boots.* Illus. by Paul Galdone. New York: Seabury Pr., 1976.
008.09 Animals—cats; 026.06 Character traits—cleverness; 062 Folk and fairy tales; 147 Royalty.

Perrault, Charles. *Puss in Boots.* Illus. by Julia Noonan. Adapted from *Les Contes de Fees de Charles Perrault* by Arthur Luce Klein. Garden City, NY: Doubleday, 1970.
008.09 Animals—cats; 026.06 Character traits—cleverness; 062 Folk and fairy tales; 147 Royalty.

Perrault, Charles. *Puss in Boots.* Illus. by William Stobbs. Perrault's "Maitre Chat" retold and illustrated by William Stobbs. New York: McGraw-Hill, 1975.
008.09 Animals—cats; 026.06 Character traits—cleverness; 062 Folk and fairy tales; 147 Royalty.

Perrault, Charles. *Puss in Boots.* Illus. by Barry Wilkinson. Cleveland: Collins, 1969.
008.09 Animals—cats; 026.06 Character traits—cleverness; 062 Folk and fairy tales; 147 Royalty.

Perrine, Mary. *Salt Boy.* Illus. by Leonard Weisgard. Boston: Houghton, 1968.
053.04 Ethnic groups in the U.S.—Indians.

Perry, Patricia, and Lynch, Marietta. *Mommy and Daddy Are Divorced.* Illus. by authors. New York: Dial Pr., 1978.
045 Divorce.

Petersham, Maud Fuller, and Petersham, Miska. *The Box with Red Wheels.* Illus. by authors. New York: Macmillan, 1949.
008 Animals; 013 Babies; 058 Farms.

Petersham, Maud Fuller, and Petersham, Miska. *The Circus Baby.* Illus. by authors. New York: Macmillan, 1950.
008.17 Animals—elephants; 028 Circus, clowns; 054 Etiquette.

Petersham, Maud Fuller, and Petersham, Miska. *Off to Bed.* Illus. by authors. Seven stories for wide-awakers. New York: Macmillan, 1954.
015 Bedtime.

Petersham, Maud Fuller, and Petersham, Miska. *The Rooster Crows.* Illus. by authors. New York: Macmillan, 1945.
122 Nursery rhymes.

Petersham, Miska, jt. author. *The Box with Red Wheels.* By Maud Fuller Petersham, and Miska Petersham.

Petersham, Miska, jt. author. *The Circus Baby.* By Maud Fuller Petersham, and Miska Petersham.

Petersham, Miska, jt. author. *Off to Bed.* By Maud Fuller Petersham, and Miska Petersham.

Petersham, Miska, jt. author. *The Rooster Crows.* By Maud Fuller Petersham, and Miska Petersham.

Peterson, Hans. *Erik and the Christmas Horse.* Illus. by Ilon Wikland. New York: Lothrop, 1970.
026.17 Character traits—kindness;
064.35 Foreign lands—Sweden;
083.03 Holidays—Christmas.

Petie, Haris. *Billions of Bugs.* Illus. by author. Englewood Cliffs, NJ: Prentice-Hall, 1975.
033 Counting; 090 Insects and spiders.

Petie, Haris. *The Seed the Squirrel Dropped.* Illus. by author. Englewood Cliffs, NJ: Prentice-Hall, 1976.
002.03 Activities—cooking;
038 Cumulative tales; 063 Food;
133 Plants; 134 Poetry, rhyme;
181 Trees.

Petrides, Heidrun. *Hans and Peter.* Illus. by author. New York: Harcourt, 1962.
002.20 Activities—working;
026.07 Character traits—completing things.

Pettit, Henry, jt. author. *The Authentic Mother Goose Fairy Tales and Nursery Rhymes.* By Jacques Barchilon, and Henry Pettit.

Phleger, Frederick B. *Ann Can Fly.* Illus. by Robert Martin Lopshire. New York: Random House, 1959.
002.05 Activities—flying; 004 Airplanes.

Phleger, Frederick B. *Red Tag Comes Back.* Illus. by Arnold Stark Lobel. New York: Harper, 1961.
060 Fish; 152 Science.

Phleger, Frederick B. *The Whales Go By.* Illus. by Paul Galdone. New York: Random House, 1959.
008.60 Animals—whales; 152 Science.

Phleger, Frederick B., and Phleger, Marjorie. *Off to the Races.* Illus. by Leo Summers. New York: Random House, 1968.
166.03 Sports—bicycling;
166.11 Sports—racing.

Phleger, Frederick B., and Phleger, Marjorie. *You Will Live under the Sea.* Illus. by Ward Brackett. New York: Random House, 1966.
152 Science; 153 Sea and seashore.

Phleger, Marjorie, jt. author. *Off to the Races.* By Frederick B. Phleger, and Marjorie Phleger.

Phleger, Marjorie, jt. author. *You Will Live under the Sea.* By Frederick B. Phleger, and Marjorie Phleger.

Piatti, Celestino. *Celestino Piatti's Animal ABC.* Illus. by author. New York: Atheneum, 1966.
001 ABC Books; 008 Animals;
134 Poetry, rhyme.

Piatti, Celestino. *The Happy Owls.* Illus. by author. New York: Atheneum, 1964.
017.14 Birds—owls; 026.23 Character traits—optimism; 052.05 Emotions—happiness.

Pickett, Carla. *Calvin Crocodile and the Terrible Noise.* Illus. by Carroll Dolezal. Austin: Steck-Vaughn, 1972.
120 Noise; 142.01 Reptiles—alligators, crocodiles.

Pienkowski, Jan. *Colors.* Illus. by author. New York: Harvey House, 1974.
032.01 Concepts—color.

Pienkowski, Jan. *Numbers.* Illus. by author. New York: Harvey House, 1975.
033 Counting.

Pienkowski, Jan. *Shapes.* Illus. by author. New York: Harvey House, 1975.
032.07 Concepts—shape.

Pienkowski, Jan. *Sizes.* Illus. by author. New York: Harvey House, 1974.
032.08 Concepts—size.

Pierce, Leona, jt. author. *Who Likes the Sun?* By Beatrice Schenk De Regniers, and Leona Pierce.

Piers, Helen. *Grasshopper and Butterfly.* Illus. by Pauline Baynes. New York: McGraw-Hill, 1975.
081 Hibernation; 090 Insects and spiders.

Piers, Helen. *A Helen Piers Animal Book.* Illus. by author. New York: Watts, 1968.
008 Animals; 137 Problem solving.

Piers, Helen. *The Mouse Book.* Illus. by author. New York: Watts, 1968.
008.34 Animals—mice.

Pincus, Harriet. *Minna and Pippin.* Illus. by author. New York: Farrar, 1972.
177.04 Toys—dolls.

Pinkwater, Manus. *The Bear's Picture.* Illus. by author. New York: Holt, 1972.
008.06 Animals—bears; 011 Art;
023.02 Careers—artists;
032.01 Concepts—color.

Pinkwater, Manus. *Big Orange Splot.* Illus. by author. New York: Hastings, 1977.
002.09 Activities—painting;
026.16 Character traits—individuality;
032.01 Concepts—color; 086 Houses.

Piper, Watty. *The Little Engine That Could.* Illus. by George Hauman, and Doris Hauman. Retold from The Pony Engine, by Mabel C. Bragg. New York: Platt, 1955/1961.
026.25 Character traits—perseverance;
179 Trains.

Pitt, Valerie. *Let's Find Out about the City.* Illus. by Sheila Granda. New York: Watts, 1968.
029 City.

Pitt, Valerie. *Let's Find Out about the Family.* Illus. by Gloria Kamen. New York: Watts, 1970.
057 Family life.

Plath, Sylvia. *The Bed Book.* Illus. by Emily Arnold McCully. New York: Harper, 1976.
015 Bedtime; 134 Poetry, rhyme;
162 Sleep.

Platt, Kin. *Big Max.* Illus. by Robert Martin Lopshire. New York: Harper, 1965.
008.17 Animals—elephants;
023.08 Careers—detectives;
137 Problem solving.

Platt, Kin. *Big Max in the Mystery of the Missing Moose.* Illus. by Robert Martin Lopshire. New York: Harper, 1977.
008.38 Animals—moose;
023.08 Careers—detectives;
137 Problem solving.

Podendorf, Illa. *Color.* Illus. by Wayne Stuart. Chicago: Children's Pr., 1971.
032.01 Concepts—color.

Podendorf, Illa. *Shapes, Sides, Curves, and Corners.* Illus. by Frank Rakoncay. Chicago: Children's Pr., 1970.
032.07 Concepts—shape.

Politi, Leo. *A Boat for Peppe.* Illus. by author. New York: Scribner's, 1950.
053.06 Ethnic groups in the U.S.—Mexican-Americans.

Politi, Leo. *Emmet.* Illus. by author. New York: Scribner's, 1971.
008.14 Animals—dogs; 036 Crime.

Politi, Leo. *Juanita.* Illus. by author. New York: Scribner's, 1948.
053.06 Ethnic groups in the U.S.—Mexican-Americans.

Politi, Leo. *Lito and the Clown.* Illus. by author. New York: Scribner's, 1964.
008.09 Animals—cats; 028 Circus, clowns; 064.24 Foreign lands—Mexico;
131 Pets.

Politi, Leo. *Little Leo.* Illus. by author. New York: Scribner's, 1951.
031 Clothing; 057 Family life;
064.18 Foreign lands—Italy.

Politi, Leo. *Mieko.* Illus. by author. Chicago: Children's Pr., 1969.
026.27 Character traits—pride;
053.05 Ethnic groups in the U.S.—Japanese-Americans.

Politi, Leo. *The Mission Bell.* Illus. by author. New York: Scribner's, 1953.
053.06 Ethnic groups in the U.S.—Mexican-Americans.

Politi, Leo. *Moy Moy.* Illus. by author. New York: Scribner's, 1960.
053.02 Ethnic groups in the U.S.—Chinese-Americans; 083.02 Holidays—Chinese New Year.

Politi, Leo. *Mr. Fong's Toy Shop.* Illus. by author. New York: Scribner's, 1978.
016.31 Behavior—sharing;
053.02 Ethnic groups in the U.S.—Chinese-Americans; 068 Friendship;
139 Puppets; 177 Toys.

Politi, Leo. *The Nicest Gift.* Illus. by author. New York: Scribner's, 1973.
008.14 Animals—dogs;
016.20 Behavior—lost;
083.03 Holidays—Christmas.

Politi, Leo. *Pedro, the Angel of Olvera Street.* Illus. by author. New York: Scribner's, 1946.
053.06 Ethnic groups in the U.S.—Mexican-Americans.

Politi, Leo. *Rosa.* Illus. by author. New York: Scribner's, 1963.
013 Babies; 016.32 Behavior—sibling rivalry; 064.24 Foreign lands—Mexico; 177.04 Toys—dolls.

Politi, Leo. *Song of the Swallows.* Illus. by author. New York: Scribner's, 1949.
053.06 Ethnic groups in the U.S.—Mexican-Americans; 108 Missions.

Polushkin, Maria. *The Little Hen and the Giant.* Illus. by Yuri Salzman. New York: Harper, 1977.
017.04 Birds—chickens; 026.04 Character traits—bravery; 062 Folk and fairy tales; 064.30 Foreign lands—Russia; 072 Giants.

Polushkin, Maria. *Mother, Mother, I Want Another.* Illus. by Diane Dawson. New York: Crown, 1978.
008.34 Animals—mice; 015 Bedtime; 016.24 Behavior—misunderstanding; 057.03 Family life—mothers.

Polushkin, Maria. *Who Said Meow?* Illus. by Giulio Maestro. New York: Crown, 1975.
008 Animals; 120 Noise.

Pomerantz, Charlotte. *The Mango Tooth.* Illus. by Marylin Hafner. New York: Greenwillow, 1977.
057 Family life; 171 Teeth.

Pomerantz, Charlotte. *The Piggy in the Puddle.* Illus. by James Marshall. New York: Macmillan, 1974.
008.42 Animals—pigs; 134 Poetry, rhyme; 175 Tongue twisters.

Pope, Billy N., and Emmons, Ramona Ware. *Your World: Let's Visit the Hospital.* Illustrated. Dallas: Taylor, 1968.
084 Hospitals.

Postgate, Oliver, and Firmin, Peter. *Noggin and the Whale.* Illus. by Peter Firmin. Port Washington, NY: White, 1967.
008.60 Animals—whales; 087 Humor.

Postgate, Oliver, and Firmin, Peter. *Noggin the King.* Illus. by Peter Firmin. Port Washington, NY: White, 1965.
017 Birds; 026.17 Character traits—kindness; 087 Humor; 147 Royalty.

Postma, Lidia. *The Stolen Mirror.* Illus. by author. New York: McGraw-Hill, 1976.
016.32 Behavior—sibling rivalry; 089 Imagination.

Poston, Elizabeth. *Baby's Song Book.* Illus. by William Stobbs. New York: Crowell, 1971.
116 Music; 164 Songs.

Potter, Beatrix. *Appley Dapply's Nursery Rhymes.* Illus. by author. New York: Warne, 1917.
008 Animals; 122 Nursery rhymes.

Potter, Beatrix. *Cecily Parsley's Nursery Rhymes.* Illus. by author. New York: Warne, 1922.
008 Animals; 122 Nursery rhymes.

Potter, Beatrix. *Ginger and Pickles.* Illus. by author. New York: Warne, 1909/1937.
008 Animals; 168 Stores.

Potter, Beatrix. *The Pie and the Patty-Pan.* Illus. by author. New York: Warne, 1905/1933.
008.09 Animals—cats; 008.14 Animals—dogs; 016.36 Behavior—trickery.

Potter, Beatrix. *Rolly-Polly Pudding.* Illus. by author. New York: Warne, 1908/1936.
008.09 Animals—cats.

Potter, Beatrix. *The Sly Old Cat.* Illus. by author. New York: Warne, 1971.
008.09 Animals—cats; 008.48 Animals—rats; 026.06 Character traits—cleverness; 054 Etiquette; 130 Parties.

Potter, Beatrix. *The Story of a Fierce Bad Rabbit.* Illus. by author. New York: Warne, 1906.
008.46 Animals—rabbits.

Potter, Beatrix. *The Story of Miss Moppet.* Illus. by author. New York: Warne, 1906.
008.09 Animals—cats; 016.36 Behavior—trickery.

Potter, Beatrix. *The Tailor of Gloucester.* Illus. by author. New York: Warne, 1931.
008.34 Animals—mice; 023.25 Careers—tailors; 026.14 Character traits—helpfulness.

Potter, Beatrix. *The Tale of Benjamin Bunny.* Illus. by author. New York: Warne, 1904.
008.46 Animals—rabbits; 016.22 Behavior—misbehavior.

Potter, Beatrix. *The Tale of Jemima Puddle-Duck.* Illus. by author. New York: Warne, 1910/1936.
017.08 Birds—ducks; 050 Eggs.

Potter, Beatrix. *The Tale of Johnny Town-Mouse.* Illus. by author. New York: Warne, 1918.
008.34 Animals—mice.

Potter, Beatrix. *The Tale of Little Pig Robinson.* Illus. by author. New York: Warne, 1930.
008.42 Animals—pigs; 016.35 Behavior—talking to strangers; 019 Boats, ships; 160 Shopping.

Potter, Beatrix. *The Tale of Mr. Jeremy Fisher*. Illus. by author. New York: Warne, 1934.
005 Amphibians; 166.05 Sports—fishing.

Potter, Beatrix. *The Tale of Mr. Tod*. Illus. by author. New York: Warne, 1911/1939.
008.04 Animals—badgers;
008.18 Animals—foxes;
008.46 Animals—rabbits.

Potter, Beatrix. *The Tale of Mrs. Tiggy-Winkle*. Illus. by author. New York: Warne, 1905.
008.26 Animals—hedgehogs;
031 Clothing.

Potter, Beatrix. *The Tale of Mrs. Tittlemouse*. Illus. by author. New York: Warne, 1910.
008.34 Animals—mice;
026.05 Character traits—cleanliness.

Potter, Beatrix. *The Tale of Peter Rabbit*. Illus. by author. New York: Warne, 1902.
008.46 Animals—rabbits;
016.22 Behavior—misbehavior.

Potter, Beatrix. *The Tale of Pigling Bland*. Illus. by author. New York: Warne, 1913/1941.
008.42 Animals—pigs.

Potter, Beatrix. *The Tale of Squirrel Nutkin*. Illus. by author. New York: Warne, 1903.
008.56 Animals—squirrels;
017.14 Birds—owls; 143 Riddles;
154.01 Seasons—fall.

Potter, Beatrix. *The Tale of the Faithful Dove*. Illus. by Marie Angel. New York: Warne, 1970.
017.07 Birds—doves; 026.20 Character traits—loyalty.

Potter, Beatrix. *The Tale of the Flopsy Bunnies*. Illus. by author. New York: Warne, 1909/1937.
008.46 Animals—rabbits;
026.06 Character traits—cleverness.

Potter, Beatrix. *The Tale of Timmy Tiptoes*. Illus. by author. New York: Warne, 1911/1939.
008.56 Animals—squirrels.

Potter, Beatrix. *The Tale of Tuppenny*. Illus. by Marie Angel. New York: Warne, 1971.
008.24 Animals—guinea pigs.

Potter, Beatrix. *The Tale of Two Bad Mice*. Illus. by author. New York: Warne, 1904/1934.
008.34 Animals—mice;
016.22 Behavior—misbehavior;
177 Toys.

Potter, Beatrix. *A Treasury of Peter Rabbit and Other Stories*. Illus. by author. New York: Watts, 1978.
008 Animals.

Potter, Russell. *The Little Red Ferry Boat*. Illus. by Marjorie Hill. New York: Holt, 1947.
008.34 Animals—mice; 019 Boats, ships;
180 Transportation.

Potter, Stephen. *Squawky, the Adventures of a Clasperchoice*. Illus. by George Him. Philadelphia: Lippincott, 1964.
017.15 Birds—parrots, parakeets.

Prager, Annabelle. *The Surprise Party*. Illus. by Thomas Anthony de Paola. New York: Pantheon, 1977.
018 Birthdays; 130 Parties.

Prather, Ray. *Double Dog Dare*. Illus. by author. New York: Macmillan, 1975.
008.14 Animals—dogs; 087 Humor.

Pratten, Albra. *Winkie, the Grey Squirrel*. Illus. by Ralph S. Thompson. New York: Oxford Univ. Pr., 1950.
008.56 Animals—squirrels; 131 Pets.

Prelutsky, Jack. *Circus*. Illus. by Arnold Stark Lobel. New York: Macmillan, 1974.
028 Circus, clowns; 134 Poetry, rhyme.

Prelutsky, Jack. *It's Halloween*. Illus. by Marylin Hafner. New York: Greenwillow, 1977.
083.07 Holidays—Halloween;
134 Poetry, rhyme.

Prelutsky, Jack. *The Mean Old Mean Hyena*. Illus. by Arnold Stark Lobel. New York: Greenwillow, 1978.
008.29 Animals—hyenas;
026.22 Character traits—meanness;
134 Poetry, rhyme.

Prelutsky, Jack. *The Terrible Tiger*. Illus. by Arnold Stark Lobel. New York: Macmillan, 1970.
008.10 Animals—cats, wild;
038 Cumulative tales; 134 Poetry, rhyme.

Preston, Edna Mitchell. *Horrible Hepzibah*. Illus. by Ray Cruz. New York: Viking, 1971.
016.22 Behavior—misbehavior;
087 Humor; 121 Non-sexist.

Preston, Edna Mitchell. *Monkey in the Jungle*. Illus. by Clement Hurd. New York: Viking, 1968.
008.37 Animals—monkeys;
015 Bedtime; 119 Night; 162 Sleep.

Preston, Edna Mitchell. *One Dark Night*. Illus. by Kurt Werth. New York: Viking, 1969.
038 Cumulative tales; 083.07 Holidays—Halloween.

Preston, Edna Mitchell. *Pop Corn and Ma Goodness*. Illus. by Robert Andrew Parker. New York: Viking, 1969.
087 Humor; 121 Non-sexist; 134 Poetry, rhyme; 164 Songs; 195.05 Weather—rain.

Preston, Edna Mitchell. *Squawk to the Moon, Little Goose*. Illus. by Barbara Cooney. New York: Viking, 1974.
008.18 Animals—foxes;
016.22 Behavior—misbehavior;
017.11 Birds—geese; 111 Moon.

Price, Christine. *One Is God; Two Old Counting Songs*. Illus. by author. New York: Warne, 1970.
033 Counting; 141 Religion; 164 Songs.

Price, Michelle. *Mean Melissa*. Illus. by author. New York: Bradbury Pr., 1977.
026.22 Character traits—meanness;
151 School.

Price, Roger. *The Last Little Dragon*. Illus. by Mamoru R. Funai. New York: Harper, 1969.
016.09 Behavior—dissatisfaction;
046 Dragons.

Prince, Dorothy E. *Speedy Gets Around*. Illus. by Betsy Warren. Austin: Steck-Vaughn, 1965.
008.11 Animals—chipmunks;
166.04 Sports—camping.

Priolo, Pauline. *Piccolina and the Easter Bells*. Illus. by Rita Fava. Boston: Little, 1962.
026.31 Character traits—smallness;
064.18 Foreign lands—Italy;
083.04 Holidays—Easter.

Prokofiev, Sergei Sergeievitch. *Peter and the Wolf*. Illus. by Warren Chappell. Foreword by Serge Koussevitsky. Calligraphy by Hollis Holland. New York: Knopf, 1940.
008.61 Animals—wolves;
026.06 Character traits—cleverness;
062 Folk and fairy tales; 064.30 Foreign lands—Russia; 116 Music.

Prokofiev, Sergei Sergeievitch. *Peter and the Wolf*. Illus. by Frans Haacken. New York: Watts, 1961.
008.61 Animals—wolves;
026.06 Character traits—cleverness;
062 Folk and fairy tales; 064.30 Foreign lands—Russia; 116 Music.

Prokofiev, Sergei Sergeievitch. *Peter and the Wolf*. Illus. by Alan Howard. New York: Transatlantic, 1954.
008.61 Animals—wolves;
026.06 Character traits—cleverness;
062 Folk and fairy tales; 064.30 Foreign lands—Russia; 116 Music.

Prokofiev, Sergei Sergeievitch. *Peter and the Wolf*. Illus. by Kozo Shimizu. Retold by Ann King Herring. Photographed by Yasugi Yajima. Tokyo, Japan: Gakken, 1971.
008.61 Animals—wolves;
026.06 Character traits—cleverness;
062 Folk and fairy tales; 064.30 Foreign lands—Russia; 116 Music.

Provensen, Alice, and Provensen, Martin. *A Book of Seasons*. Illus. by authors. New York: Random House, 1976.
154 Seasons.

Provensen, Alice, and Provensen, Martin. *Karen's Opposites*. Illus. by authors. Racine, WI: Western Pub., 1963.
032.06 Concepts—opposites; 134 Poetry, rhyme.

Provensen, Alice, and Provensen, Martin. *My Little Hen*. Illus. by authors. New York: Random House, 1973.
017.04 Birds—chickens.

Provensen, Alice, and Provensen, Martin. *Our Animal Friends*. Illus. by authors. New York: Random House, 1974.
008 Animals; 058 Farms.

Provensen, Alice, and Provensen, Martin. *The Year at Maple Hill Farm*. Illus. by authors. New York: Atheneum, 1978.
008 Animals; 039 Days of the week, months of the year; 058 Farms;
154 Seasons.

Provensen, Martin, jt. author. *A Book of Seasons*. By Alice Provensen, and Martin Provensen.

Provensen, Martin, jt. author. *Karen's Opposites*. By Alice Provensen, and Martin Provensen.

Provensen, Martin, jt. author. *My Little Hen*. By Alice Provensen, and Martin Provensen.

Provensen, Martin, jt. author. *Our Animal Friends*. By Alice Provensen, and Martin Provensen.

Provensen, Martin, jt. author. *The Year at Maple Hill Farm*. By Alice Provensen, and Martin Provensen.

Pulsifer, Marjorie P., jt. author. *Bikes*. By Dolores M. Baugh, and Marjorie P. Pulsifer.

Pulsifer, Marjorie P., jt. author. *Let's Go*. By Dolores M. Baugh, and Marjorie P. Pulsifer.

Pulsifer, Marjorie P., jt. author. *Let's See the Animals*. By Dolores M. Baugh, and Marjorie P. Pulsifer.

Pulsifer, Marjorie P., jt. author. *Let's Take a Trip*. By Dolores M. Baugh, and Marjorie P. Pulsifer.

Pulsifer, Marjorie P., jt. author. *Slides*. By Dolores M. Baugh, and Marjorie P. Pulsifer.

Pulsifer, Marjorie P., jt. author. *Supermarket*. By Dolores M. Baugh, and Marjorie P. Pulsifer.

Pulsifer, Marjorie P., jt. author. *Swings*. By Dolores M. Baugh, and Marjorie P. Pulsifer.

Pulsifer, Marjorie P., jt. author. *Trucks and Cars to Ride*. By Dolores M. Baugh, and Marjorie P. Pulsifer.

Puner, Helen Walker. *Daddys, What They Do All Day*. Illus. by Roger Antoine Duvoisin. New York: Lothrop, 1946.
002.20 Activities—working; 023 Careers; 057.01 Family life—fathers; 134 Poetry, rhyme.

Puner, Helen Walker. *The Sitter Who Didn't Sit*. Illus. by Roger Antoine Duvoisin. New York: Lothrop, 1949.
002.01 Activities—babysitting; 087 Humor; 134 Poetry, rhyme.

Pursell, Margaret Sanford. *Jessie the Chicken*. Illus. by Claudie Fayn. Minneapolis: Carolrhoda Books, 1977.
017.04 Birds—chickens; 050 Eggs; 152 Science.

Pursell, Margaret Sanford. *A Look at Birth*. Illus. by Maria S. Forrai. Minneapolis: Lerner, 1978.
013 Babies; 152 Science.

Pursell, Margaret Sanford. *A Look at Divorce*. Illus. by Maria S. Forrai. Minneapolis: Lerner, 1976.
045 Divorce; 052 Emotions.

Pursell, Margaret Sanford. *Polly the Guinea Pig*. Illus. by Antoinette Barrere. Translated by Dyan Hammarberg. Minneapolis: Carolrhoda Books, 1977.
008.24 Animals—guinea pigs; 131 Pets; 152 Science.

Pursell, Margaret Sanford. *Shelley the Sea Gull*. Illus. by L'Ene Matte. Translated by Dyan Hammarberg. Photographs by Jean-Christian David, Guy Dhuit, and Claudie Fayn-Rodriguez. Minneapolis: Carolrhoda Books, 1977.
017.22 Birds—sea gulls; 131 Pets; 152 Science.

Pursell, Margaret Sanford. *Sprig the Tree Frog*. Illus. by Yves Vial. Translated by Dyan Hammarberg. Minneapolis: Carolrhoda Books, 1977.
005 Amphibians; 050 Eggs; 152 Science.

Quackenbush, Robert Mead. *Calling Doctor Quack*. Illus. by author. New York: Lothrop, 1978.
008 Animals; 049 Ecology; 088 Illness.

Quackenbush, Robert Mead. *Clementine*. Illus. by author. Philadelphia: Lippincott, 1974.
062 Folk and fairy tales; 116 Music; 164 Songs; 189 U.S. history.

Quackenbush, Robert Mead. *Detective Mole*. Illus. by author. New York: Lothrop, 1976.
008 Animals; 008.35 Animals—moles; 023.08 Careers—detectives; 087 Humor; 137 Problem solving.

Quackenbush, Robert Mead. *Detective Mole and the Secret Clues*. Illus. by author. New York: Lothrop, 1977.
008 Animals; 008.35 Animals—moles; 023.08 Careers—detectives; 087 Humor; 137 Problem solving.

Quackenbush, Robert Mead. *Detective Mole and the Tip-Top Mystery*. Illus. by author. New York: Lothrop, 1978.
008 Animals; 008.35 Animals—moles; 023.08 Careers—detectives; 087 Humor; 137 Problem solving.

Quackenbush, Robert Mead. *The Man on the Flying Trapeze*. Illus. by author. The circus life of Emmett Kelly, Sr., told with pictures and song! Philadelphia: Lippincott, 1975.
028 Circus, clowns; 116 Music; 164 Songs.

Quackenbush, Robert Mead. *Pete Pack Rat*. Illus. by author. New York: Lothrop, 1976.
008 Animals; 008.41 Animals—pack rats; 035 Cowboys; 087 Humor.

Quackenbush, Robert Mead. *Pop! Goes the Weasel and Yankee Doodle.* Illus. by author. Philadelphia: Lippincott, 1976.
116 Music; 134 Poetry, rhyme; 164 Songs; 189 U.S. history.

Quackenbush, Robert Mead. *She'll Be Comin' 'Round the Mountain.* Illus. by author. Philadelphia: Lippincott, 1973.
116 Music; 164 Songs.

Quackenbush, Robert Mead. *Skip to My Lou.* Illus. by author. Philadelphia: Lippincott, 1975.
116 Music; 164 Songs.

Quackenbush, Robert Mead. *There'll Be a Hot Time in the Old Town Tonight.* Illus. by author. Philadelphia: Lippincott, 1974.
059 Fire; 116 Music; 164 Songs; 189 U.S. history.

Quigley, Lillian. *The Blind Men and the Elephant.* Illus. by Janice Holland. New York: Scribner's, 1959.
008.17 Animals—elephants; 062 Folk and fairy tales; 064.16 Foreign lands—India; 077.01 Handicaps—blindness; 157 Senses.

Quin-Harkin, Janet. *Peter Penny's Dance.* Illus. by Anita Lobel. New York: Dial Pr., 1976.
002.04 Activities—dancing; 196 Weddings; 202 World.

Rabinowitz, Sandy. *What's Happening to Daisy?* Illus. by author. New York: Harper, 1977.
008.28 Animals—horses; 152 Science.

Radlauer, Ruth Shaw. *Of Course, You're a Horse!* Illus. by Abner Graboff, and Sheila Greenwald. New York: Abelard-Schuman, 1959.
079 Health; 089 Imagination.

Raebeck, Lois. *Who Am I?* Illus. by June Goldsborough. Chicago: Follett, 1970.
002.12 Activities—playing; 069 Games; 164 Songs.

Rael, Rick, jt. author. *Baseball Brothers.* By Jeff Rubin, and Rick Rael.

Rand, Ann, and Rand, Paul. *Little 1.* Illus. by Paul Rand. New York: Harcourt, 1962.
033 Counting.

Rand, Ann, and Rand, Paul. *Sparkle and Spin.* Illus. by Paul Rand. New York: Harcourt, 1957.
096 Language.

Rand McNally Picturebook Dictionary. Illus. by Dan Siculan. Compiled by Robert L. Hillerich and others. Skokie, IL: Rand McNally, 1971.
043 Dictionaries.

Rand, Paul, jt. author. *Little 1.* By Ann Rand, and Paul Rand.

Rand, Paul, jt. author. *Sparkle and Spin.* By Ann Rand, and Paul Rand.

Raskin, Ellen. *A & The, or William T. C. Baumgarten Comes to Town.* Illus. by author. New York: Atheneum, 1970.
068 Friendship; 118 Names.

Raskin, Ellen. *And It Rained.* Illus. by author. New York: Atheneum, 1969.
008 Animals; 195.05 Weather—rain.

Raskin, Ellen. *Franklin Stein.* Illus. by author. New York: Atheneum, 1972.
029 City; 087 Humor; 089 Imagination.

Raskin, Ellen. *Ghost in a Four-Room Apartment.* Illus. by author. New York: Atheneum, 1969.
038 Cumulative tales; 057 Family life; 071 Ghosts; 134 Poetry, rhyme.

Raskin, Ellen. *Nothing Ever Happens on My Block.* Illus. by author. New York: Atheneum, 1966.
016.04 Behavior—boredom; 029 City; 087 Humor.

Raskin, Ellen. *Spectacles.* Illus. by author. New York: Atheneum, 1968.
073 Glasses; 089 Imagination.

Raskin, Ellen. *Who, Said Sue, Said Whoo?* Illus. by author. New York: Atheneum, 1973.
008 Animals; 120 Noise; 134 Poetry, rhyme.

Rayner, Mary. *Garth Pig and the Ice Cream Lady.* Illus. by author. New York: Atheneum, 1977.
008.42 Animals—pigs; 008.61 Animals—wolves.

Rayner, Mary. *Mr. and Mrs. Pig's Evening Out.* Illus. by author. New York: Atheneum, 1976.
002.01 Activities—babysitting; 008.42 Animals—pigs; 008.61 Animals—wolves.

Raynor, Dorka. *Grandparents around the World.* Illus. by author. Edited by Caroline Rubin. Chicago: Albert Whitman, 1977.
057.02 Family life—grandparents; great-grandparents.

Reardon, Maureen, jt. author. *Feelings Between Brothers and Sisters.* By Marcia Maher Conta, and Maureen Reardon.

Reardon, Maureen, jt. author. *Feelings Between Friends.* By Marcia Maher Conta, and Maureen Reardon.

Reardon, Maureen, jt. author. *Feelings Between Kids and Grownups.* By Marcia Maher Conta, and Maureen Reardon.

Reardon, Maureen, jt. author. *Feelings Between Kids and Parents.* By Marcia Maher Conta, and Maureen Reardon.

Reavin, Sam. *Hurray for Captain Jane!* Illus. by Emily Arnold McCully. New York: Parents, 1971.
002.02 Activities—bathing; 019 Boats, ships; 089 Imagination; 121 Non-sexist.

Reed, Kit. *When We Dream.* Illus. by Yutaka Sugita. New York: Hawthorn, 1966.
016.38 Behavior—wishing; 047 Dreams.

Reed, Mary M., jt. author. *Biddy and the Ducks.* By Arensa Sondergaard, and Mary M. Reed.

Reesink, Maryke. *The Golden Treasure.* Illus. by Jaap Tol. New York: Harcourt, 1968.
019 Boats, ships; 026.29 Character traits—selfishness; 062 Folk and fairy tales; 064.14 Foreign lands—Holland.

Reeves, James. *Rhyming Will.* Illus. by Edward Jeffrey Irving Ardizzone. New York: McGraw-Hill, 1967.
026.16 Character traits—individuality; 087 Humor; 134 Poetry, rhyme; 147 Royalty.

Regniers, Beatrice Schenk de. See De Regniers, Beatrice Schenk.

Reid, Alastair, jt. author. *A Balloon for a Blunderbuss.* By Bob Gill, and Alastair Reid.

Reid, Alastair. *Supposing.* Illus. by A. Birnbaum. Boston: Little, 1960.
087 Humor; 089 Imagination.

Reidel, Marlene. *Jacob and the Robbers.* Illus. by author. New York: Atheneum, 1967.
036 Crime; 119 Night; 162 Sleep.

Reiss, John J. *Colors.* Illus. by author. New York: Bradbury Pr., 1969.
032.01 Concepts—color.

Reiss, John J. *Numbers.* Illus. by author. New York: Bradbury Pr., 1971.
033 Counting.

Reiss, John J. *Shapes.* Illus. by author. New York: Bradbury Pr., 1974.
032.07 Concepts—shape.

Reit, Seymour. *The King Who Learned to Smile.* Illus. by Gordon Laite. Racine, WI: Western Pub., 1960.
016.04 Behavior—boredom; 147 Royalty.

Reit, Seymour. *Round Things Everywhere.* Illus. by Carol Basen. New York: McGraw-Hill, 1969.
032.07 Concepts—shape; 053.07 Ethnic groups in the U.S.—Multi-ethnic.

Ressner, Phil. *August Explains.* Illus. by Crosby Newell Bonsall. New York: Harper, 1963.
008.06 Animals—bears.

Ressner, Phil. *Dudley Pippin.* Illus. by Arnold Stark Lobel. New York: Harper, 1965.
029 City; 089 Imagination.

Retan, Walter. *The Snowplow That Tried to Go South.* Illus. by John Resko. New York: Atheneum, 1950.
102 Machines; 154.04 Seasons—winter; 195.07 Weather—snow.

Retan, Walter. *The Steam Shovel That Wouldn't Eat Dirt.* Illus. by Roger Antoine Duvoisin. New York: Atheneum, 1948.
063 Food; 102 Machines.

Rey, H. A. See Rey, Hans Augusto.

Rey, Hans Augusto. *Anybody at Home?* Illus. by author. Boston: Houghton, 1942.
067 Format, unusual; 086 Houses.

Rey, Hans Augusto, jt. author. *Billy's Picture.* By Margret Elisabeth Waldstein Rey, and Hans Augusto Rey.

Rey, Hans Augusto. *Cecily G and the Nine Monkeys.* Illus. by author. Boston: Houghton, 1942.
008.20 Animals—giraffes; 008.37 Animals—monkeys; 087 Humor.

Rey, Hans Augusto. *Curious George.* Illus. by author. Boston: Houghton, 1941.
008.37 Animals—monkeys; 023.10 Careers—firefighters; 026.10 Character traits—curiosity; 087 Humor.

Rey, Hans Augusto. *Curious George Gets a Medal*. Illus. by author. Boston: Houghton, 1957.
008.37 Animals—monkeys;
026.10 Character traits—curiosity;
087 Humor; 165 Space and space ships.

Rey, Hans Augusto. *Curious George Learns the Alphabet*. Illus. by author. Boston: Houghton, 1963.
001 ABC Books; 008.37 Animals—monkeys; 026.10 Character traits—curiosity.

Rey, Hans Augusto. *Curious George Rides a Bike*. Illus. by author. Boston: Houghton, 1952.
008.37 Animals—monkeys;
026.10 Character traits—curiosity;
028 Circus, clowns; 087 Humor;
166.03 Sports—bicycling.

Rey, Hans Augusto. *Curious George Takes a Job*. Illus. by author. Boston: Houghton, 1947.
008.37 Animals—monkeys;
023.31 Careers—window cleaners;
026.10 Character traits—curiosity;
087 Humor; 204 Zoos.

Rey, Hans Augusto. *Elizabite, Adventures of a Carnivorous Plant*. Illus. by author. New York: Harper, 1942.
087 Humor; 133 Plants; 134 Poetry, rhyme.

Rey, Hans Augusto. *Feed the Animals*. Illus. by author. Boston: Houghton, 1944.
134 Poetry, rhyme; 204 Zoos.

Rey, Hans Augusto. *How Do You Get There?* Illus. by author. Boston: Houghton, 1941.
067 Format, unusual;
180 Transportation.

Rey, Hans Augusto. *Humpty Dumpty and Other Mother Goose Songs*. Illus. by author. New York: Harper, 1943.
116 Music; 122 Nursery rhymes;
164 Songs.

Rey, Hans Augusto. *Look for the Letters*. Illus. by author. New York: Harper, 1942.
001 ABC Books.

Rey, Hans Augusto. *See the Circus*. Illus. by author. Boston: Houghton, 1956.
028 Circus, clowns; 067 Format, unusual; 134 Poetry, rhyme.

Rey, Hans Augusto. *Tit for Tat*. Illus. by author. New York: Harper, 1942.
008 Animals; 087 Humor.

Rey, Hans Augusto. *Where's My Baby?* Illus. by author. Boston: Houghton, 1943.
008 Animals; 067 Format, unusual;
134 Poetry, rhyme.

Rey, Margret Elisabeth Waldstein. *Curious George Flies a Kite*. Illus. by Hans Augusto Rey. Boston: Houghton, 1958.
008.37 Animals—monkeys;
026.10 Character traits—curiosity;
087 Humor; 094 Kites; 166.05 Sports—fishing.

Rey, Margret Elisabeth Waldstein. *Curious George Goes to the Hospital*. Illus. by Hans Augusto Rey. Boston: Houghton, 1966.
008.37 Animals—monkeys;
016.20 Behavior—lost; 026.10 Character traits—curiosity; 084 Hospitals;
087 Humor.

Rey, Margret Elisabeth Waldstein. *Pretzel*. Illus. by Hans Augusto Rey. New York: Harper, 1944.
008.14 Animals—dogs.

Rey, Margret Elisabeth Waldstein. *Pretzel and the Puppies*. Illus. by Hans Augusto Rey. New York: Harper, 1946.
008.14 Animals—dogs.

Rey, Margret Elisabeth Waldstein. *Spotty*. Illus. by Hans Augusto Rey. New York: Harper, 1945.
008.46 Animals—rabbits;
026.03 Character traits—being different.

Rey, Margret Elisabeth Waldstein, and Rey, Hans Augusto. *Billy's Picture*. Illus. by Hans Augusto Rey. New York: Harper, 1948.
008 Animals; 011 Art; 087 Humor.

Ricciuti, Edward R. *An Animal for Alan*. Illus. by Tom Eaton. New York: Harper, 1970.
008 Animals; 131 Pets; 152 Science.

Ricciuti, Edward R. *Donald and the Fish That Walked*. Illus. by Sydney Hoff. New York: Harper, 1974.
049 Ecology; 060 Fish; 152 Science.

Rice, Eve. *Ebbie*. Illus. by author. New York: Greenwillow, 1975.
057 Family life; 118 Names.

Rice, Eve. *New Blue Shoes*. Illus. by author. New York: Macmillan, 1975.
031 Clothing; 057.03 Family life—mothers; 160 Shopping.

Rice, Eve. *Papa's Lemonade and Other Stories*. Illus. by author. New York: Greenwillow, 1976.
008.14 Animals—dogs; 057 Family life.

Rice, Eve. *Sam Who Never Forgets.* Illus. by author. New York: Greenwillow, 1977.
008 Animals; 063 Food; 204 Zoos.

Rice, Eve. *What Sadie Sang.* Illus. by author. New York: Greenwillow, 1976.
013 Babies; 052.05 Emotions—happiness.

Rice, Inez. *A Long Long Time.* Illus. by Robert Mead Quackenbush. New York: Lothrop, 1964.
026.23 Character traits—optimism; 089 Imagination.

Rice, Inez. *The March Wind.* Illus. by Vladimir Bobri. New York: Lothrop, 1957.
031 Clothing; 089 Imagination; 195.08 Weather—wind.

Richards, Jane. *A Horse Grows Up.* Illus. by Bert Hardy. New York: Walker, 1972.
008.28 Animals—horses; 152 Science.

Richardson, Jack E., Jr., and others. *Six in a Mix.* Illustrated. New York: Macmillan, 1971.
096 Language.

Richter, Alice, and Numeroff, Laura Joffe. *You Can't Put Braces on Spaces.* Illus. by Laura Joffe Numeroff. New York: Greenwillow, 1979.
023.07 Careers—dentists; 171 Teeth.

Richter, Mischa. *Eric and Matilda.* Illus. by author. New York: Harper, 1967.
017.08 Birds—ducks; 128 Parades.

Richter, Mischa. *Quack?* Illus. by author. New York: Harper, 1978.
008 Animals; 017.08 Birds—ducks; 120 Noise.

Rider, Alex. *A la Ferme. At the Farm.* Illus. by Paul Davis. Garden City, NY: Doubleday, 1962.
058 Farms; 064.11 Foreign lands—France; 065 Foreign languages.

Rider, Alex. *Chez nous. At Our House.* Illus. by Isadore Seltzer. Garden City, NY: Doubleday, 1962.
057 Family life; 064.11 Foreign lands—France; 065 Foreign languages.

Ridlon, Marci. *Kittens and More Kittens.* Illus. by Liz Dauber. Chicago: Follett, 1967.
008.09 Animals—cats; 131 Pets.

Rietveld, Jane. *Monkey Island.* Illus. by author. New York: Viking, 1963.
008.37 Animals—monkeys; 204 Zoos.

Ringi, Kjell. *The Sun and the Cloud.* Illus. by author. New York: Harper, 1971.
133 Plants; 169 Sun; 195.01 Weather—clouds.

Ringi, Kjell. *The Winner.* Illus. by author. New York: Harper, 1969.
201 Wordless.

Roach, Marilynne K. *Two Roman Mice.* Illus. by author. New York: Crowell, 1975.
008.34 Animals—mice; 029 City; 034 Country.

Robbins, Ruth. *Baboushka and the Three Kings.* Illus. by Nicolas Sidjakov. Berkeley: Parnassus, 1960.
062 Folk and fairy tales; 064.30 Foreign lands—Russia; 083.03 Holidays—Christmas; 116 Music; 134 Poetry, rhyme; 164 Songs.

Robbins, Ruth. *The Harlequin and Mother Goose; Or, The Magic Stick.* Illus. by Nicolas Sidjakov. Berkeley: Parnassus, 1965.
122 Nursery rhymes.

Roberts, Cliff. *The Dot.* Illus. by author. New York: Watts, 1960.
032.07 Concepts—shape.

Roberts, Cliff. *Start with a Dot.* Illus. by author. New York: Watts, 1960.
032.07 Concepts—shape; 134 Poetry, rhyme.

Roberts, Thom. *Pirates in the Park.* Illus. by Harold Berson. New York: Crown, 1973.
002.12 Activities—playing; 089 Imagination; 132 Pirates.

Robertson, Lilian. *Picnic Woods.* Illus. by author. New York: Harcourt, 1949.
002.11 Activities—picnicking.

Robertson, Lilian. *Runaway Rocking Horse.* Illus. by author. New York: Harcourt, 1948.
177.05 Toys—rocking horses.

Robinson, Adjai. *Femi and Old Grandaddie.* Illus. by Jerry Pinkney. New York: Coward, 1972.
062 Folk and fairy tales; 064.01 Foreign lands—Africa.

Robinson, Irene Bowen, and Robinson, William Wilcox. *Picture Book of Animal Babies.* Illus. by Irene Bowen Robinson. New York: Macmillan, 1947.
008 Animals.

Robinson, Thomas Pendleton. *Buttons.* Illus. by Peggy Bacon. New York: Viking, 1938.
008.09 Animals—cats.

Robinson, William Wilcox. *On the Farm*. Illus. by Irene Clara Robinson. New York: Macmillan, 1939.
008 Animals; 058 Farms.

Robinson, William Wilcox, jt. author. *Picture Book of Animal Babies*. By Irene Bowen Robinson, and William Wilcox Robinson.

Robison, Nancy. *UFO Kidnap*. Illus. by Edward Frascino. New York: Lothrop, 1978.
165 Space and space ships.

Roche, A. K. (pseud.). See Abisch, Roslyn Kroop.

Rockwell, Anne F. *A Bear, a Bobcat and Three Ghosts*. Illus. by author. New York: Macmillan, 1977.
008.06 Animals—bears;
008.10 Animals—cats, wild;
023.20 Careers—peddlers; 071 Ghosts;
083.07 Holidays—Halloween.

Rockwell, Anne F. *Big Boss*. Illus. by author. New York: Macmillan, 1975.
005 Amphibians; 008.10 Animals—cats, wild; 008.18 Animals—foxes;
026.06 Character traits—cleverness.

Rockwell, Anne F. *The Bump in the Night*. Illus. by author. New York: Greenwillow, 1979.
026.14 Character traits—helpfulness;
071 Ghosts.

Rockwell, Anne F. *Gogo's Pay Day*. Illus. by author. Garden City, NY: Doubleday, 1978.
026.13 Character traits—generosity;
028 Circus, clowns; 109 Money.

Rockwell, Anne F. *The Gollywhopper Egg*. Illus. by author. New York: Macmillan, 1974.
016.36 Behavior—trickery; 050 Eggs;
058 Farms.

Rockwell, Anne F. *The Good Llama*. Illus. by author. Cleveland: Collins, 1963.
008 Animals; 008.33 Animals—llamas;
064.32 Foreign lands—South America.

Rockwell, Anne F. *I Like the Library*. Illus. by author. New York: Dutton, 1977.
100 Libraries.

Rockwell, Anne F. *Poor Goose*. Illus. by author. New York: Crowell, 1976.
008 Animals; 017.11 Birds—geese;
038 Cumulative tales; 062 Folk and fairy tales; 064.11 Foreign lands—France.

Rockwell, Anne F. *The Stolen Necklace*. Illus. by author. Cleveland: Collins, 1968.
008.37 Animals—monkeys;
026.06 Character traits—cleverness;
064.16 Foreign lands—India.

Rockwell, Anne F. *The Story Snail*. Illus. by author. New York: Macmillan, 1974.
008.55 Animals—snails; 103 Magic.

Rockwell, Anne F. *The Three Bears and Fifteen Other Stories*. Illus. by author. New York: Crown, 1975.
062 Folk and fairy tales.

Rockwell, Anne F. *Willy Runs Away*. Illus. by author. New York: Dutton, 1978.
008.14 Animals—dogs;
016.27 Behavior—running away.

Rockwell, Anne F. *The Wolf Who Had a Wonderful Dream*. Illus. by author. New York: Crowell, 1973.
008.61 Animals—wolves; 047 Dreams;
062 Folk and fairy tales; 063 Food;
064.11 Foreign lands—France.

Rockwell, Anne F. *The Wonderful Eggs of Furicchia*. Illus. by author. Cleveland: Collins, 1969.
017.04 Birds—chickens; 050 Eggs;
062 Folk and fairy tales; 064.18 Foreign lands—Italy; 103 Magic.

Rockwell, Anne F., and Rockwell, Harlow. *Blackout*. Illus. by authors. New York: Macmillan, 1979.
136 Power failure; 195 Weather.

Rockwell, Anne F., and Rockwell, Harlow. *Machines*. Illus. by Harlow Rockwell. New York: Macmillan, 1972.
102 Machines.

Rockwell, Anne F., and Rockwell, Harlow. *The Supermarket*. Illus. by authors. New York: Macmillan, 1979.
160 Shopping; 168 Stores.

Rockwell, Anne F., and Rockwell, Harlow. *Toad*. Illus. by authors. Garden City, NY: Doubleday, 1972.
005 Amphibians.

Rockwell, Anne F., and Rockwell, Harlow. *The Toolbox*. Illus. by Harlow Rockwell. New York: Macmillan, 1971.
176 Tools.

Rockwell, Harlow, jt. author. *Blackout*. By Anne F. Rockwell, and Harlow Rockwell.

Rockwell, Harlow. *The Compost Heap*. Illus. by author. Garden City, NY: Doubleday, 1974.
002.06 Activities—gardening;
133 Plants.

Rockwell, Harlow. *I Did It*. Illus. by author. New York: Macmillan, 1974.
002 Activities.

Rockwell, Harlow. *Look at This*. Illus. by author. New York: Macmillan, 1978.
002 Activities.

Rockwell, Harlow, jt. author. *Machines*. By Anne F. Rockwell, and Harlow Rockwell.

Rockwell, Harlow. *My Dentist*. Illus. by author. New York: Greenwillow, 1975.
023.07 Careers—dentists.

Rockwell, Harlow. *My Doctor*. Illus. by author. New York: Macmillan, 1973.
023.09 Careers—doctors.

Rockwell, Harlow. *My Nursery School*. Illus. by author. New York: Greenwillow, 1976.
151 School.

Rockwell, Harlow, jt. author. *The Supermarket*. By Anne F. Rockwell, and Harlow Rockwell.

Rockwell, Harlow, jt. author. *Toad*. By Anne F. Rockwell, and Harlow Rockwell.

Rockwell, Harlow, jt. author. *The Toolbox*. By Anne F. Rockwell, and Harlow Rockwell.

Rockwell, Norman. *Counting Book*. Illus. by author. New York: Crown, 1977.
033 Counting; 069 Games.

Rogers, Helen S. *Morris and His Brave Lion*. Illus. by Glo Coalson. New York: McGraw-Hill, 1975.
045 Divorce.

Rojankovsky, Feodor Stepanovich. *ABC, an Alphabet of Many Things*. Illus. by author. Racine, WI: Western Pub., 1970.
001 ABC Books.

Rojankovsky, Feodor Stepanovich. *Animals in the Zoo*. Illus. by author. New York: Knopf, 1962.
001 ABC Books; 008 Animals; 204 Zoos.

Rojankovsky, Feodor Stepanovich. *Animals on the Farm*. Illus. by author. New York: Knopf, 1962.
008 Animals; 058 Farms; 201 Wordless.

Rojankovsky, Feodor Stepanovich. *The Great Big Animal Book*. Illus. by author. New York: Simon & Schuster, 1950.
008 Animals; 058 Farms.

Rojankovsky, Feodor Stepanovich. *The Great Big Wild Animal Book*. Illus. by author. New York: Simon & Schuster, 1951.
008 Animals.

Romanek, Enid Warner. *Teddy*. Illus. by author. New York: Scribner's, 1978.
177.08 Toys—teddy bears.

Rondell, Florence, and Michaels, Ruth. *The Family That Grew*. Illustrated. New York: Crown, 1965.
003 Adoption.

Roscoe, William. *The Butterfly's Ball*. Illus. by Donald Alan Bolognese. New York: McGraw-Hill, 1967.
008 Animals; 090 Insects and spiders; 134 Poetry, rhyme.

Rose, Anne K. *As Right as Right Can Be*. Illus. by Arnold Stark Lobel. New York: Dial Pr., 1976.
016.30 Behavior—seeking better things; 109 Money.

Rose, Anne K. *How Does the Czar Eat Potatoes?* Illus. by Horst Eckert. New York: Lothrop, 1973.
134 Poetry, rhyme; 135 Poverty; 147 Royalty.

Rose, Anne K. *Spider in the Sky*. Illus. by Gail Owens. New York: Harper, 1978.
053.04 Ethnic groups in the U.S.— Indians; 062 Folk and fairy tales.

Rose, Gerald. *The Tiger-Skin Rug*. Illus. by author. Englewood Cliffs, NJ: Prentice-Hall, 1979.
008.10 Animals—cats, wild; 036 Crime.

Rose, Mitchel. *Norman*. Illus. by author. New York: Simon & Schuster, 1970.
008.14 Animals—dogs; 173 Theater.

Rosenberg, David, jt. author. *Your Face Is a Picture*. By Ethel Clifford Rosenberg, and David Rosenberg.

Rosenberg, Ethel Clifford. *Why Is an Elephant Called an Elephant?* Illus. by Jackie Lacy. Indianapolis: Bobbs-Merrill, 1966.
008.17 Animals—elephants; 038 Cumulative tales; 147 Royalty.

Rosenberg, Ethel Clifford, and Rosenberg, David. *Your Face Is a Picture*. Illus. by David Rosenberg. Educational Consultant: Leo Fay. Indianapolis: E. C. Seale, 1963.
053.07 Ethnic groups in the U.S.— Multi-ethnic.

Ross, Diana. *The Story of the Little Red Engine*. Illus. by Leslie Wood. New York: Transatlantic, 1947.
064.10 Foreign lands—England; 179 Trains.

Ross, George Maxim. *When Lucy Went Away*. Illus. by Ingrid Fetz. New York: Dutton, 1976.
008.09 Animals—cats; 131 Pets.

Ross, Jessica. *Ms. Klondike.* Illus. by author. New York: Viking, 1977.
002.20 Activities—working; 023.26 Careers—taxi drivers; 121 Nonsexist; 170 Taxis.

Ross, Tony, reteller. *The Pied Piper of Hamelin.* Illus. by author. New York: Lothrop, 1977.
008.48 Animals—rats; 062 Folk and fairy tales; 064.10 Foreign lands—England.

Rossetti, Christina Georgina. *What Is Pink?* Illus. by José Aruego. New York: Macmillan, 1971.
017.10 Birds—flamingos; 032.01 Concepts—color; 134 Poetry, rhyme.

Rossner, Judith. *What Kind of Feet Does a Bear Have?* Illus. by Irwin Rosenhouse. Indianapolis: Bobbs-Merrill, 1963.
087 Humor.

Roughsey, Dick. *The Giant Devil-Dingo.* Illus. by author. New York: Macmillan, 1973.
008 Animals; 062 Folk and fairy tales; 064.02 Foreign lands—Australia.

Rounds, Glen H. *The Boll Weevil.* Illus. by author. Chicago: Children's Pr., 1967.
062 Folk and fairy tales; 090 Insects and spiders; 116 Music; 164 Songs.

Rounds, Glen H. *Casey Jones.* Illus. by author. Chicago: Children's Pr., 1968.
062 Folk and fairy tales; 116 Music; 164 Songs.

Rounds, Glen H. *The Day the Circus Came to Lone Tree.* Illus. by author. New York: Holiday, 1973.
028 Circus, clowns; 087 Humor; 121 Non-sexist.

Rounds, Glen H. *Once We Had a Horse.* Illus. by author. New York: Holiday, 1971.
008.28 Animals—horses.

Rounds, Glen H. *The Strawberry Roan.* Illus. by author. Chicago: Children's Pr., 1970.
008.28 Animals—horses; 116 Music; 164 Songs.

Rounds, Glen H. *Sweet Betsy from Pike.* Illus. by author. Chicago: Children's Pr., 1973.
062 Folk and fairy tales; 116 Music; 164 Songs.

Routh, Jonathan. *The Nuns Go to Africa.* Illus. by author. Indianapolis: Bobbs-Merrill, 1971.
023.18 Careers—nuns; 064.01 Foreign lands—Africa.

Rowand, Phyllis. *Every Day in the Year.* Illus. by author. Boston: Little, 1959.
052.08 Emotions—love; 083.03 Holidays—Christmas.

Rowand, Phyllis. *George.* Illus. by author. Boston: Little, 1956.
008.14 Animals—dogs.

Rowand, Phyllis. *George Goes to Town.* Illus. by author. Boston: Little, 1958.
008.14 Animals—dogs.

Rowand, Phyllis. *It Is Night.* Illus. by author. New York: Harper, 1953.
119 Night; 162 Sleep.

Rowe, Jeanne A. *City Workers.* Illustrated. New York: Watts, 1969.
023 Careers; 029 City.

Rowe, Jeanne A. *A Trip Through a School.* Illustrated. New York: Watts, 1969.
151 School.

Roy, Ronald. *A Thousand Pails of Water.* Illus. by Yo-Dinh Mai. New York: Knopf, 1978.
008.60 Animals—whales; 026.18 Character traits—kindness to animals; 064.19 Foreign lands—Japan.

Roy, Ronald. *Three Ducks Went Wandering.* Illus. by Paul Galdone. New York: Seabury Pr., 1979.
016.18 Behavior—indifference; 017.08 Birds—ducks; 087 Humor.

Ruben, Patricia. *Apples to Zippers.* Illus. by author. Garden City, NY: Doubleday, 1976.
001 ABC Books.

Ruben, Patricia. *True or False?* Illus. by author. Philadelphia: Lippincott, 1978.
032 Concepts.

Rubin, Jeff, and Rael, Rick. *Baseball Brothers.* Illus. by Sandy Kossin. New York: Lothrop, 1976.
068 Friendship; 166.01 Sports—baseball.

Ruck-Pauguet, Gina. *Little Hedgehog.* Illus. by Marianne Richter. New York: Hastings, 1959.
008.26 Animals—hedgehogs.

Rudolph, Marguerita. *I Am Your Misfortune.* Illus. by Imero Gobbato. New York: Seabury Pr., 1968.

026.29 Character traits—selfishness; 062 Folk and fairy tales; 064.22 Foreign lands—Lithuania; 110 Monsters; 166.01 Sports—baseball.

Rudolph, Marguerita. *Sharp and Shiny.* Illus. by Susan Perl. New York: McGraw-Hill, 1971.
002.02 Activities—bathing;
002.12 Activities—playing;
026.05 Character traits—cleanliness.

Ruskin, John. *Dame Wiggins of Lee and Her Seven Wonderful Cats.* Illus. by Robert Broomfield. Endpapers: reproduction of Kate Greenaway drawings. New York: McGraw-Hill, 1963.
122 Nursery rhymes.

Russ, Lavinia. *Alec's Sand Castle.* Illus. by James Stevenson. New York: Harper, 1972.
002.12 Activities—playing;
089 Imagination; 153 Sea and seashore.

Russell, Betty. *Big Store, Funny Door.* Illus. by Mary Gehr. Chicago: Albert Whitman, 1955.
026.21 Character traits—luck;
160 Shopping.

Russell, Betty. *Run Sheep Run.* Illus. by Mary Gehr. Chicago: Albert Whitman, 1952.
008.52 Animals—sheep.

Russell, Solveig Paulson. *What Good Is a Tail?* Illus. by Ezra Jack Keats. Indianapolis: Bobbs-Merrill, 1962.
008 Animals; 152 Science.

Ryan, Cheli Duran. *Hildilid's Night.* Illus. by Arnold Stark Lobel. New York: Macmillan, 1971.
119 Night.

Ryder, Joanne. *Fireflies.* Illus. by Donald Alan Bolognese. New York: Harper, 1977.
090 Insects and spiders; 152 Science.

Ryder, Joanne. *A Wet and Sandy Day.* Illus. by Donald Carrick. New York: Harper, 1977.
153 Sea and seashore;
195.05 Weather—rain.

Sachs, Marilyn. *Matt's Mitt.* Illus. by Hilary Knight. Garden City, NY: Doubleday, 1975.
166.01 Sports—baseball.

Sage, Michael. *If You Talked to a Boar.* Illus. by Arnold Spilka. Philadelphia: Lippincott, 1960.
087 Humor; 096 Language.

Sage, Michael, and Spilka, Arnold. *Dippy Dos and Don'ts.* Illus. by Arnold Spilka. New York: Viking, 1967.
087 Humor; 134 Poetry, rhyme.

Salazar, Violet. *Squares Are Not Bad.* Illus. by Harlow Rockwell. Racine, WI: Western Pub., 1967.
032.07 Concepts—shape.

Saleh, Harold. *Even Tiny Ants Must Sleep.* Illus. by Jerry Pinkney. New York: McGraw-Hill, 1967.
134 Poetry, rhyme; 162 Sleep.

Sandberg, Inger. *Nicholas' Favorite Pet.* Illus. by Lasse Sandberg. New York: Delacorte Pr., 1969.
008 Animals; 008.14 Animals—dogs;
018 Birthdays; 131 Pets.

Sandberg, Inger, and Sandberg, Lasse. *Come On Out, Daddy.* Illus. by Lasse Sandberg. New York: Delacorte Pr., 1971.
002.20 Activities—working;
023 Careers; 057.01 Family life—fathers.

Sandberg, Inger, and Sandberg, Lasse. *Little Ghost Godfry.* Illus. by Lasse Sandberg. Translated by Nancy Swensen Leupold. New York: Delacorte Pr., 1968.
071 Ghosts.

Sandberg, Inger, and Sandberg, Lasse. *What Little Anna Saved.* Illus. by Lasse Sandberg. New York: Lothrop, 1966.
069 Games.

Sandberg, Lasse, jt. author. *Come On Out, Daddy.* By Inger Sandberg, and Lasse Sandberg.

Sandberg, Lasse, jt. author. *Little Ghost Godfry.* By Inger Sandberg, and Lasse Sandberg.

Sandberg, Lasse, jt. author. *What Little Anna Saved.* By Inger Sandberg, and Lasse Sandberg.

Sandburg, Carl. *The Wedding Procession of the Rag Doll and the Broom Handle and Who Was in It.* Illus. by Harriet Pincus. New York: Harcourt, 1922.
177 Toys; 177.04 Toys—dolls;
196 Weddings.

Sandburg, Helga. *Anna and the Baby Buzzard.* Illus. by Brinton Cassady Turkle. New York: Dutton, 1970.

017.02 Birds—buzzards;
026.18 Character traits—kindness to animals.

Sargent, Robert. *A Trick on a Lion*. Illus. by author. New York: McGraw-Hill, 1966.
008.10 Animals—cats, wild;
008.46 Animals—rabbits; 090 Insects and spiders; 103 Magic.

Sasaki, Jeannie, and Uyeda, Frances. *Chocho Is for Butterfly*. Illus. by authors. Seattle, WA: Uyeda Sasaki Arts, 1975.
064.19 Foreign lands—Japan;
065 Foreign languages.

Sattler, Helen Roney. *Train Whistles; A Language in Code*. Illus. by Tom Funk. New York: Lothrop, 1977.
096 Language; 179 Trains.

Sauer, Julia Lina. *Mike's House*. Illus. by Don Freeman. New York: Viking, 1954.
016.20 Behavior—lost; 029 City;
100 Libraries; 195.07 Weather—snow.

Savage, Kathleen, jt. author. *Bear Hunt*. By Margaret Siewert, and Kathleen Savage.

Sawyer, Ruth. *Journey Cake, Ho!* Illus. by Robert John McCloskey. New York: Viking, 1953.
038 Cumulative tales; 062 Folk and fairy tales; 135 Poverty.

Saxe, John Godfrey. *The Blind Men and the Elephant*. Illus. by Paul Galdone. New York: McGraw-Hill, 1963.
008.17 Animals—elephants;
077.01 Handicaps—blindness.

Saxon, Charles D. *Don't Worry about Poopsie*. Illus. by author. New York: Dodd, 1958.
008.14 Animals—dogs;
016.20 Behavior—lost.

Say, Allen, reteller. *Once under the Cherry Blossom Tree*. Illus. by Allen Say. New York: Harper, 1974.
062 Folk and fairy tales; 064.19 Foreign lands—Japan.

Sazer, Nina. *What Do You Think I Saw?* Illus. by Lois Ehlert. New York: Pantheon, 1976.
033 Counting; 087 Humor; 134 Poetry, rhyme.

Scarry, Patricia M. *Little Richard and Prickles*. Illus. by Cyndy Szekeres. New York: American Heritage, 1971.
008.43 Animals—porcupines;
008.46 Animals—rabbits;
017.14 Birds—owls.

Scarry, Richard McClure. *The Adventures of Tinker and Tanker*. Illus. by author. Garden City, NY: Doubleday, 1968.
008.27 Animals—hippopotami;
008.46 Animals—rabbits.

Scarry, Richard McClure. *Egg in the Hole Book*. Illus. by author. Racine, WI: Western Pub., 1967.
017.04 Birds—chickens; 050 Eggs;
067 Format, unusual.

Scarry, Richard McClure. *The Great Big Car and Truck Book*. Illus. by author. Racine, WI: Western Pub., 1951.
012 Automobiles; 184 Trucks.

Scarry, Richard McClure. *Is This the House of Mistress Mouse?* Illus. by author. Racine, WI: Western Pub., 1964.
008 Animals; 086 Houses.

Scarry, Richard McClure. *Richard Scarry's ABC Word Book*. Illus. by author. New York: Random House, 1971.
001 ABC Books.

Scarry, Richard McClure. *Richard Scarry's Best Counting Book Ever*. Illus. by author. New York: Random House, 1975.
033 Counting.

Scarry, Richard McClure. *Richard Scarry's Best First Book Ever*. Illus. by author. New York: Random House, 1979.
032 Concepts; 039 Days of the week, months of the year.

Scarry, Richard McClure. *Richard Scarry's Best Story Book Ever*. Illus. by author. Racine, WI: Western Pub., 1968.
096 Language.

Scarry, Richard McClure. *Richard Scarry's Best Word Book Ever*. Illus. by author. Racine, WI: Western Pub., 1963.
043 Dictionaries.

Scarry, Richard McClure. *Richard Scarry's Busiest People Ever*. Illus. by author. New York: Random House, 1976.
023 Careers.

Scarry, Richard McClure. *Richard Scarry's Busy Busy World*. Illus. by author. Racine, WI: Western Pub., 1965.
002 Activities.

Scarry, Richard McClure. *Richard Scarry's Cars and Trucks and Things That Go*. Illus. by author. Racine, WI: Western Pub., 1974.
012 Automobiles; 184 Trucks.

Scarry, Richard McClure. *Richard Scarry's Funniest Storybook Ever*. Illus. by author. New York: Random House, 1972.
087 Humor.

Scarry, Richard McClure. *Richard Scarry's Great Big Air Book*. Illus. by author. New York: Random House, 1971.
004 Airplanes; 152 Science.

Scarry, Richard McClure. *Richard Scarry's Great Big Mystery Book*. Illus. by author. New York: Random House, 1969.
008 Animals; 036 Crime; 168 Stores.

Scarry, Richard McClure. *Richard Scarry's Great Big Schoolhouse*. Illus. by author. New York: Random House, 1969.
001 ABC Books; 032 Concepts; 033 Counting; 039 Days of the week, months of the year; 151 School; 174 Time.

Scarry, Richard McClure. *Richard Scarry's Please and Thank You Book*. Illus. by author. New York: Random House, 1973.
054 Etiquette.

Scarry, Richard McClure. *Richard Scarry's Postman Pig and His Busy Neighbors*. Illus. by author. New York: Random House, 1978.
023.16 Careers—mail carriers.

Scarry, Richard McClure. *What Do People Do All Day?* Illus. by author. New York: Random House, 1968.
023 Careers.

Schackburg, Richard. *Yankee Doodle*. Illus. by Edward Randolph Emberley. Englewood Cliffs, NJ: Prentice-Hall, 1965.
116 Music; 164 Songs; 189 U.S. history.

Scharen, Beatrix. *Gigin and Till*. Illus. by author. New York: Atheneum, 1968.
047 Dreams; 089 Imagination; 119 Night; 177 Toys.

Scharen, Beatrix. *Tillo*. Illus. by author. Reading: Addison-Wesley, 1974.
017.14 Birds—owls.

Schatz, Letta. *The Extraordinary Tug-of-War*. Illus. by John Mackintosh Burningham. Chicago: Follett, 1968.
008 Animals; 026.06 Character traits—cleverness; 062 Folk and fairy tales; 064.01 Foreign lands—Africa.

Schatz, Letta. *Whiskers My Cat*. Illus. by Paul Galdone. New York: McGraw-Hill, 1967.
008.09 Animals—cats.

Scheer, Julian. *Rain Makes Applesauce*. Illus. by Marvin Bileck. New York: Holiday, 1964.
087 Humor; 195.05 Weather—rain.

Schenk, Esther M. *Christmas Time*. Illus. by Vera Stone Norman. Chicago: Follett, 1931.
083.03 Holidays—Christmas.

Schermer, Judith. *Mouse in House*. Illus. by author. Boston: Houghton, 1979.
008.34 Animals—mice; 057 Family life; 137 Problem solving.

Schertle, Alice. *The Gorilla in the Hall*. Illus. by Paul Galdone. New York: Lothrop, 1977.
008.22 Animals—gorillas; 026.04 Character traits—bravery; 052.04 Emotions—fear.

Schick, Alice, and Allen, Marjorie N. *The Remarkable Ride of Israel Bissell As Related by Molly the Crow*. Illus. by Joel Schick. Philadelphia: Lippincott, 1976.
189 U.S. history; 193 War.

Schick, Alice, and Schick, Joel. *Just This Once*. Illus. by Joel Schick. Philadelphia: Lippincott, 1978.
008.61 Animals—wolves; 131 Pets.

Schick, Alice, and Schick, Joel. *Santaberry and the Snard*. Illus. by Joel Schick. Philadelphia: Lippincott, 1976/1979.
083.03 Holidays—Christmas.

Schick, Eleanor. *City in the Winter*. Illus. by author. New York: Macmillan, 1970.
029 City; 057.04 Family life—the only child; 121 Non-sexist; 154.04 Seasons—winter; 195.07 Weather—snow; 195.08 Weather—wind.

Schick, Eleanor. *The Little School at Cottonwood Corners*. Illus. by author. New York: Harper, 1965.
151 School.

Schick, Eleanor. *One Summer Night*. Illus. by author. New York: Morrow, 1977.
029 City; 116 Music; 154.03 Seasons—summer.

Schick, Eleanor. *Peggy's New Brother*. Illus. by author. New York: Macmillan, 1970.
013 Babies; 016.32 Behavior—sibling rivalry; 052.03 Emotions—envy, jealousy; 057 Family life.

Schick, Eleanor. *Peter and Mr. Brandon*. Illus. by Donald Carrick. New York: Macmillan, 1973.
002.01 Activities—babysitting.

Schick, Eleanor. *Summer at the Sea*. Illus. by author. New York: Greenwillow, 1979.
002.17 Activities—vacationing; 057.04 Family life—the only child; 153 Sea and seashore; 154.03 Seasons—summer.

Schick, Eleanor. *A Surprise in the Forest*. Illus. by author. New York: Harper, 1964.
008 Animals; 050 Eggs; 066 Forest, woods.

Schick, Joel, jt. author. *Just This Once.* By Alice Schick, and Joel Schick.

Schick, Joel, jt. author. *Santaberry and the Snard.* By Alice Schick, and Joel Schick.

Schiller, Barbara. *The White Rat's Tale.* Illus. by Adrienne Adams. New York: Holt, 1967.
008.48 Animals—rats; 062 Folk and fairy tales; 064.11 Foreign lands—France; 147 Royalty.

Schlein, Miriam. *The Amazing Mr. Pelgrew.* Illus. by Harvey Weiss. New York: Abelard-Schuman, 1957.
023.21 Careers—police officers.

Schlein, Miriam. *Billy, the Littlest One.* Illus. by Lucy Ozone Hawkinson. Chicago: Albert Whitman, 1966.
016.14 Behavior—growing up;
026.31 Character traits—smallness;
057 Family life.

Schlein, Miriam. *Deer in the Snow.* Illus. by Leonard P. Kessler. New York: Abelard-Schuman, 1956.
008.13 Animals—deer;
154.04 Seasons—winter;
195.07 Weather—snow.

Schlein, Miriam. *Elephant Herd.* Illus. by Symeon Shimin. Reading: Addison-Wesley, 1954.
008.17 Animals—elephants.

Schlein, Miriam. *Fast Is Not a Ladybug.* Illus. by Leonard P. Kessler. Reading: Addison-Wesley, 1953.
032.09 Concepts—speed; 090 Insects and spiders.

Schlein, Miriam. *The Four Little Foxes.* Illus. by Louis Quintanilla. Reading: Addison-Wesley, 1953.
008.18 Animals—foxes.

Schlein, Miriam. *Go with the Sun.* Illus. by Symeon Shimin. Reading: Addison-Wesley, 1952.
057.02 Family life—grandparents;
great-grandparents; 154.04 Seasons—winter.

Schlein, Miriam. *Heavy Is a Hippopotamus.* Illus. by Leonard P. Kessler. Reading: Addison-Wesley, 1954.
032.11 Concepts—weight.

Schlein, Miriam. *Here Comes Night.* Illus. by Harvey Weiss. Chicago: Albert Whitman, 1957.
119 Night.

Schlein, Miriam. *Herman McGregor's World.* Illus. by Harvey Weiss. Chicago: Albert Whitman, 1959.
016.14 Behavior—growing up;
202 World.

Schlein, Miriam. *Home, the Tale of a Mouse.* Illus. by E. Harper Johnson. New York: Abelard-Schuman, 1958.
008.34 Animals—mice.

Schlein, Miriam. *It's About Time.* Illus. by Leonard P. Kessler. Reading: Addison-Wesley, 1955.
174 Time.

Schlein, Miriam. *Laurie's New Brother.* Illus. by Elizabeth Donald. New York: Abelard-Schuman, 1961.
013 Babies; 016.32 Behavior—sibling rivalry; 057 Family life.

Schlein, Miriam. *Little Rabbit, the High Jumper.* Illus. by Theresa Sherman. Reading: Addison-Wesley, 1957.
008.46 Animals—rabbits.

Schlein, Miriam. *Little Red Nose.* Illus. by Roger Antoine Duvoisin. New York: Abelard-Schuman, 1955.
154.02 Seasons—spring.

Schlein, Miriam. *My Family.* Illus. by Harvey Weiss. New York: Abelard-Schuman, 1960.
057 Family life.

Schlein, Miriam. *My House.* Illus. by Joseph Leon Lasker. Chicago: Albert Whitman, 1971.
057 Family life; 086 Houses;
114 Moving.

Schlein, Miriam. *The Pile of Junk.* Illus. by Harvey Weiss. New York: Abelard-Schuman, 1962.
026.26 Character traits—practicality;
190 Values.

Schlein, Miriam. *Shapes.* Illus. by Sam Berman. Reading: Addison-Wesley, 1952.
032.07 Concepts—shape.

Schlein, Miriam. *Something for Now, Something for Later.* Illus. by Leonard Weisgard. New York: Harper, 1956.
058 Farms.

Schlein, Miriam. *The Sun Looks Down.* Illus. by Abner Graboff. New York: Abelard-Schuman, 1954.
169 Sun.

Schlein, Miriam. *The Sun, the Wind, the Sea and the Rain*. Illus. by Joseph Leon Lasker. New York: Abelard-Schuman, 1960.
153 Sea and seashore; 169 Sun;
195 Weather; 195.05 Weather—rain;
195.08 Weather—wind.

Schlein, Miriam. *When Will the World Be Mine?* Illus. by Jean Charlot. Reading: Addison-Wesley, 1953.
016.14 Behavior—growing up.

Schmidt, Eric von. *The Young Man Who Wouldn't Hoe Corn*. Illus. by author. Boston: Houghton, 1964.
026.19 Character traits—laziness;
058 Farms; 087 Humor.

Schneider, Herman, and Schneider, Nina. *Follow the Sunset*. Illus. by Lucille Corcos. Garden City, NY: Doubleday, 1952.
152 Science; 169 Sun; 202 World.

Schneider, Nina, jt. author. *Follow the Sunset*. By Herman Schneider, and Nina Schneider.

Schneider, Nina. *While Susie Sleeps*. Illus. by Dagmar Wilson. Reading: Addison-Wesley, 1948.
015 Bedtime; 119 Night; 162 Sleep.

Schoenherr, John Carl. *The Barn*. Illus. by author. Boston: Little, 1968.
008.34 Animals—mice;
008.53 Animals—skunks; 014 Barns;
017.14 Birds—owls; 058 Farms.

Schreiber, Georges. *Bambino Goes Home*. Illus. by author. New York: Viking, 1959.
028 Circus, clowns; 068 Friendship.

Schreiber, Georges. *Bambino the Clown*. Illus. by author. New York: Viking, 1947.
028 Circus, clowns.

Schreiber, Georges, jt. author. *Professor Bull's Umbrella*. By William Lipkind, and Georges Schreiber.

Schroder, William. *Pea Soup and Serpents*. Illus. by author. New York: Lothrop, 1977.
110 Monsters; 117 Mythical creatures;
195.04 Weather—fog.

Schroeder, Glen W., jt. author. *At the Zoo*. By Lillian Colonius, and Glen W. Schroeder.

Schulman, Janet. *The Big Hello*. Illus. by Lillian Hoban. New York: Greenwillow, 1976.
068 Friendship; 114 Moving;
177.04 Toys—dolls.

Schulman, Janet. *Camp Kee Wee's Secret Weapon*. Illus. by Marylin Hafner. New York: Greenwillow, 1979.

121 Non-sexist; 166.01 Sports—baseball;
166.04 Sports—camping.

Schulman, Janet. *Jack the Bum and the Halloween Handout*. Illus. by James Stevenson. New York: Greenwillow, 1977.
016.31 Behavior—sharing;
083.07 Holidays—Halloween;
188 UNICEF.

Schulman, Janet. *Jack the Bum and the Haunted House*. Illus. by James Stevenson. New York: Greenwillow, 1977.
036 Crime; 071 Ghosts; 086 Houses.

Schulman, Janet. *Jack the Bum and the UFO*. Illus. by James Stevenson. New York: Greenwillow, 1978.
026.06 Character traits—cleverness;
138 Progress; 165 Space and space ships.

Schulman, Janet. *Jenny and the Tennis Nut*. Illus. by Marylin Hafner. New York: Greenwillow, 1978.
121 Non-sexist; 166.07 Sports—gymnastics; 166.16 Sports—tennis.

Schurr, Cathleen. *The Long and the Short of It*. Illus. by Dorothy Maas. New York: Vanguard, 1950.
137 Problem solving.

Schwalje, Marjory. *Mr. Angelo*. Illus. by Abner Graboff. New York: Abelard-Schuman, 1960.
002.03 Activities—cooking; 063 Food;
087 Humor.

Schweitzer, Byrd Baylor. *Amigo*. Illus. by Garth Montgomery Williams. New York: Macmillan, 1963.
008.45 Animals—prairie dogs;
053.06 Ethnic groups in the U.S.—Mexican-Americans; 131 Pets;
134 Poetry, rhyme.

Schweninger, Ann. *The Hunt for Rabbit's Galosh*. Illus. by Kay Chorao. Garden City, NY: Doubleday, 1976.
008.46 Animals—rabbits;
016.11 Behavior—forgetfulness;
083.11 Holidays—Valentine's Day.

Scoppetone, Sandra, jt. author. *Bang Bang You're Dead*. By Louise Fitzhugh, and Sandra Scoppetone.

Scott, Ann Herbert. *Big Cowboy Western*. Illus. by Richard L. Lieis. New York: Lothrop, 1965.
031 Clothing; 035 Cowboys;
053.01 Ethnic groups in the U.S.—Afro-Americans; 089 Imagination.

Scott, Ann Herbert. *Let's Catch a Monster.* Illus. by H. Tom Hall. New York: Lothrop, 1967.
029 City; 053.01 Ethnic groups in the U.S.—Afro-Americans; 083.07 Holidays—Halloween.

Scott, Ann Herbert. *On Mother's Lap.* Illus. by Glo Coalson. New York: McGraw-Hill, 1972.
016.26 Behavior—needing someone; 016.32 Behavior—sibling rivalry; 052.08 Emotions—love; 053.03 Ethnic groups in the U.S.—Eskimos; 057 Family life; 057.03 Family life—mothers.

Scott, Ann Herbert. *Sam.* Illus. by Symeon Shimin. New York: McGraw-Hill, 1967.
016.26 Behavior—needing someone; 053.01 Ethnic groups in the U.S.—Afro-Americans; 057 Family life.

Scott, Frances Gruse, jt. author. *How Many Kids Are Hiding on My Block?* By Jean Merrill, and Frances Gruse Scott.

Scott, Natalie. *Firebrand, Push Your Hair Out of Your Eyes.* Illus. by Sandra Smith. Minneapolis: Carolrhoda Books, 1969.
026.02 Character traits—appearance; 076 Hair.

Scott, Rochelle. *Colors, Colors All Around.* Illus. by Leonard P. Kessler. New York: Grosset, 1965.
032.01 Concepts—color.

Scott, Sally. *Little Wiener.* Illus. by Beth Krush. New York: Harcourt, 1951.
008.14 Animals—dogs.

Scott, Sally. *There Was Timmy!* Illus. by Beth Krush. New York: Harcourt, 1957.
008.14 Animals—dogs.

Scott, William Rufus, adapter. *This Is the Milk That Jack Drank.* Illus. by Charles Green Shaw. Adapted from Mother Goose by William R. Scott. Reading: Addison-Wesley, 1944.
038 Cumulative tales.

Sea World Alphabet Book. Illustrated. Concept by Sally and Alan Sloan. San Diego, CA: Sea World Pr., 1979.
001 ABC Books; 153 Sea and seashore.

Seeger, Peter. *Foolish Frog.* Illus. by Miloslav Jagr. New York: Macmillan, 1973.
005 Amphibians; 062 Folk and fairy tales; 116 Music; 164 Songs.

Segal, Lore Groszmann. *All the Way Home.* Illus. by James Marshall. New York: Farrar, 1973.
038 Cumulative tales.

Segal, Lore Groszmann. *Tell Me a Mitzi.* Illus. by Harriet Pincus. New York: Farrar, 1970.
057 Family life; 093 Jewish culture.

Segal, Lore Groszmann. *Tell Me a Trudy.* Illus. by Rosemary Wells. New York: Farrar, 1977.
057 Family life; 093 Jewish culture.

Seidler, Rosalie. *Grumpus and the Venetian Cat.* Illus. by author. New York: Atheneum, 1964.
008.09 Animals—cats; 008.34 Animals—mice; 017 Birds; 064.18 Foreign lands—Italy.

Seignobosc, Françoise. *The Big Rain.* Illus. by author. New York: Scribner's, 1961.
008 Animals; 058 Farms; 064.11 Foreign lands—France; 195.05 Weather—rain.

Seignobosc, Françoise. *Biquette, the White Goat.* Illus. by author. New York: Scribner's, 1953.
008.21 Animals—goats; 064.11 Foreign lands—France; 088 Illness.

Seignobosc, Françoise. *Chouchou.* Illus. by author. New York: Scribner's, 1958.
008.16 Animals—donkeys; 064.11 Foreign lands—France.

Seignobosc, Françoise. *The Gay ABC.* Illus. by author. New York: Scribner's, 1939.
001 ABC Books.

Seignobosc, Françoise. *Jeanne-Marie at the Fair.* Illus. by author. New York: Scribner's, 1959.
056 Fairs; 064.11 Foreign lands—France.

Seignobosc, Françoise. *Jeanne-Marie Counts Her Sheep.* Illus. by author. New York: Scribner's, 1951.
016.38 Behavior—wishing; 033 Counting; 064.11 Foreign lands—France.

Seignobosc, Françoise. *Jeanne-Marie in Gay Paris.* Illus. by author. New York: Scribner's, 1956.
026 Character traits; 064.11 Foreign lands—France.

Seignobosc, Françoise. *Minou.* Illus. by author. New York: Scribner's, 1962.
008.09 Animals—cats; 016.20 Behavior—lost; 064.11 Foreign lands—France.

Seignobosc, Françoise. *Noel for Jeanne-Marie.* Illus. by author. New York: Scribner's, 1953.
064.11 Foreign lands—France; 083.03 Holidays—Christmas.

Seignobosc, Françoise. *Small-Trot*. Illus. by author. New York: Scribner's, 1952.
008.34 Animals—mice; 028 Circus, clowns.

Seignobosc, Françoise. *Springtime for Jeanne-Marie*. Illus. by author. New York: Scribner's, 1955.
008.21 Animals—goats; 016.20 Behavior—lost; 017.08 Birds—ducks; 064.11 Foreign lands—France; 154.02 Seasons—spring.

Seignobosc, Françoise. *The Story of Colette*. Illus. by author. Chippewa Falls, WI: Hale, 1940.
008 Animals; 052.07 Emotions—loneliness; 131 Pets.

Seignobosc, Françoise. *The Thank-You Book*. Illus. by author. New York: Scribner's, 1947.
054 Etiquette; 141 Religion.

Seignobosc, Françoise. *The Things I Like*. Illus. by author. New York: Scribner's, 1960.
129 Participation.

Seignobosc, Françoise. *What Do You Want to Be?* Illus. by author. New York: Scribner's, 1957.
023 Careers; 026.01 Character traits—ambition.

Seignobosc, Françoise. *What Time Is It, Jeanne-Marie?* Illus. by author. New York: Scribner's, 1963.
174 Time.

Selden, George. See Thompson, George Selden.

Seligman, Dorothy Halle. *Run Away Home*. Illus. by Christine Hoffmann. Chicago: Children's Pr., 1969.
016.27 Behavior—running away; 057 Family life.

Selsam, Millicent Ellis. *All Kinds of Babies*. Illus. by Symeon Shimin. New York: Four Winds Pr., 1967.
008 Animals; 013 Babies.

Selsam, Millicent Ellis. *Benny's Animals and How He Put Them in Order*. Illus. by Arnold Stark Lobel. New York: Harper, 1966.
008 Animals; 152 Science.

Selsam, Millicent Ellis. *The Bug That Laid the Golden Eggs*. Illus. by Harold Krieger. New York: Harper, 1967.
050 Eggs; 090 Insects and spiders; 152 Science.

Selsam, Millicent Ellis. *Egg to Chick*. Illus. by Barbara Wolff. New York: Harper, 1970.
017.04 Birds—chickens; 050 Eggs; 152 Science.

Selsam, Millicent Ellis. *Greg's Microscope*. Illus. by Arnold Stark Lobel. New York: Harper, 1963.
152 Science.

Selsam, Millicent Ellis. *Hidden Animals*. Illus. by David Shapiro. New York: Harper, 1947/1969.
008 Animals.

Selsam, Millicent Ellis. *How Kittens Grow*. Illus. by Esther Bubley. New York: Four Winds Pr., 1975.
008.09 Animals—cats; 152 Science.

Selsam, Millicent Ellis. *How Puppies Grow*. Illus. by Esther Bubley. New York: Four Winds Pr., 1971.
008.14 Animals—dogs; 152 Science.

Selsam, Millicent Ellis. *Is This a Baby Dinosaur? And Other Science Picture Puzzles*. Illustrated. New York: Harper, 1972.
069 Games; 152 Science.

Selsam, Millicent Ellis. *Let's Get Turtles*. Illus. by Arnold Stark Lobel. New York: Harper, 1965.
131 Pets; 142.05 Reptiles—turtles; 152 Science.

Selsam, Millicent Ellis. *More Potatoes!* Illus. by Ben Shecter. New York: Harper, 1972.
058 Farms; 133 Plants; 151 School; 152 Science.

Selsam, Millicent Ellis. *Plenty of Fish*. Illus. by Erik Blegvad. New York: Harper, 1960.
060 Fish; 131 Pets; 152 Science.

Selsam, Millicent Ellis. *Seeds and More Seeds*. Illus. by Tomi Ungerer. New York: Harper, 1959.
133 Plants; 152 Science.

Selsam, Millicent Ellis. *Terry and the Caterpillars*. Illus. by Arnold Stark Lobel. New York: Harper, 1962.
090 Insects and spiders; 152 Science.

Selsam, Millicent Ellis. *Tony's Birds*. Illus. by Kurt Werth. New York: Harper, 1961.
017 Birds; 053.01 Ethnic groups in the U.S.—Afro-Americans; 152 Science.

Selsam, Millicent Ellis. *When an Animal Grows*. Illus. by John Kaufman. New York: Harper, 1966.
008 Animals; 152 Science.

Selsam, Millicent Ellis. *You and the World Around You.* Illus. by Greta Elgaard. Garden City, NY: Doubleday, 1963.
152 Science.

Sendak, Maurice. *Alligators All Around.* Illus. by author. New York: Harper, 1962.
001 ABC Books; 142.01 Reptiles—alligators, crocodiles.

Sendak, Maurice. *Chicken Soup with Rice.* Illus. by author. New York: Harper, 1962.
039 Days of the week, months of the year.

Sendak, Maurice. *Hector Protector and As I Went over the Water; Two Nursery Rhymes.* Illus. by author. New York: Harper, 1965.
122 Nursery rhymes.

Sendak, Maurice. *In the Night Kitchen.* Illus. by author. New York: Harper, 1970.
047 Dreams; 089 Imagination.

Sendak, Maurice. *One Was Johnny.* Illus. by author. New York: Harper, 1962.
033 Counting.

Sendak, Maurice. *Pierre, a Cautionary Tale in Five Chapters and a Prologue.* Illus. by author. New York: Harper, 1962.
016.18 Behavior—indifference;
026.16 Character traits—individuality;
087 Humor; 134 Poetry, rhyme.

Sendak, Maurice. *Seven Little Monsters.* Illus. by author. New York: Harper, 1977.
033 Counting; 110 Monsters;
134 Poetry, rhyme.

Sendak, Maurice. *The Sign on Rosie's Door.* Illus. by author. New York: Harper, 1960.
002.12 Activities—playing;
089 Imagination.

Sendak, Maurice. *Very Far Away.* Illus. by author. New York: Harper, 1957.
008 Animals; 016.26 Behavior—needing someone; 016.27 Behavior—running away.

Sendak, Maurice. *Where the Wild Things Are.* Illus. by author. New York: Harper, 1963.
016.22 Behavior—misbehavior;
089 Imagination; 110 Monsters.

Serfozo, Mary. *Welcome Roberto! Bienvenido, Roberto!* Illus. by John Serfozo. Chicago: Follett, 1969.
053.06 Ethnic groups in the U.S.—Mexican-Americans; 065 Foreign languages.

Serraillier, Ian. *Suppose You Met a Witch.* Illus. by Edward Randolph Emberley. Boston: Little, 1973.
134 Poetry, rhyme; 199 Witches.

The Sesame Street Book of Letters. Illustrated. Created in cooperation with the Children's Television Workshop, producers of Sesame Street. Designed by Charles I. Miller and James J. Harvin. New York: Preschool Pr., 1970.
001 ABC Books.

The Sesame Street Book of Numbers. Illustrated. Created in cooperation with the Children's Television Workshop, producers of Sesame Street. Designed by Charles I. Miller and James J. Harvin. New York: Preschool Pr., 1970.
033 Counting.

The Sesame Street Book of People and Things. Illustrated. Created in cooperation with the Children's Television Workshop, producers of Sesame Street. Designed by Charles I. Miller and James J. Harvin. New York: Preschool Pr., 1970.
032 Concepts.

The Sesame Street Book of Shapes. Illustrated. Created in cooperation with the Children's Television Workshop, producers of Sesame Street. New York: Preschool Pr., 1970.
032.07 Concepts—shape.

The Sesame Street Song Book. Illus. by Loretta Trezzo. Created in cooperation with the Children's Television Workshop, producers of Sesame Street. Words and music by Joe Raposo and Jeffrey Moss. New York: Simon & Schuster, 1971.
116 Music; 164 Songs.

Seuling, Barbara. *The Teeny Tiny Woman.* Illus. by author. New York: Viking, 1976.
062 Folk and fairy tales; 064.10 Foreign lands—England; 071 Ghosts.

Seuss, Dr. Theodor (pseud.). See Geisel, Theodor Seuss.

Sewall, Marcia. *The Wee, Wee Mannie and the Big, Big Coo.* Illus. by author. Boston: Little, 1977.
008.12 Animals—cows, bulls; 062 Folk and fairy tales; 064.31 Foreign lands—Scotland.

Sewell, Helen Moore. *Birthdays for Robin.* Illus. by author. New York: Macmillan, 1943.
008.14 Animals—dogs; 018 Birthdays.

Sewell, Helen Moore. *Blue Barns*. Illus. by author. New York: Macmillan, 1933.
014 Barns; 017.08 Birds—ducks; 017.11 Birds—geese; 058 Farms.

Sewell, Helen Moore. *Jimmy and Jemima*. Illus. by author. New York: Macmillan, 1940.
016.32 Behavior—sibling rivalry; 026.04 Character traits—bravery.

Sewell, Helen Moore. *Ming and Mehitable*. Illus. by author. New York: Macmillan, 1936.
008.14 Animals—dogs.

Sewell, Helen Moore. *Peggy and the Pony*. Illus. by author. New York: Oxford Univ. Pr., 1936.
008.28 Animals—horses; 016.38 Behavior—wishing.

Sexton, Anne, jt. author. *Eggs of Things*. By Maxine W. Kumin, and Anne Sexton.

Sexton, Anne, jt. author. *Joey and the Birthday Present*. By Maxine W. Kumin, and Anne Sexton.

Sexton, Gwain. *There Once Was a King*. Illus. by author. New York: Scribner's, 1959.
134 Poetry, rhyme; 147 Royalty.

Seymour, Dorothy Z. *The Tent*. Illus. by Nance Holman. New York: Grosset, 1965.
038 Cumulative tales.

Seyton, Marion. *The Hole in the Hill*. Illus. by Leonard W. Shortall. Chicago: Follett, 1960.
024 Cavemen; 057 Family life.

Shapp, Charles, jt. author. *Let's Find Out about Babies*. By Martha Shapp; Charles Shapp; and Sylvia Shepard.

Shapp, Charles, jt. author. *Let's Find Out about Houses*. By Martha Shapp, and Charles Shapp.

Shapp, Charles, and Shapp, Martha. *Let's Find Out What's Big and What's Small*. Illus. by Vana Earle. New York: Watts, 1959.
032.08 Concepts—size.

Shapp, Martha, jt. author. *Let's Find Out What's Big and What's Small*. By Charles Shapp, and Martha Shapp.

Shapp, Martha, and Shapp, Charles. *Let's Find Out about Houses*. Illus. by Thomas Anthony de Paola. New York: Watts, 1975.
086 Houses.

Shapp, Martha; Shapp, Charles; and Shepard, Sylvia. *Let's Find Out about Babies*. Illus. by Jenny Williams. New York: Watts, 1975.
013 Babies; 152 Science.

Sharmat, Marjorie Weinman. *A Big Fat Enormous Lie*. Illus. by David McPhail. New York: Dutton, 1978.
016.21 Behavior—lying.

Sharmat, Marjorie Weinman. *Burton and Dudley*. Illus. by Barbara Cooney. New York: Holiday, 1975.
008.44 Animals—possums; 026.19 Character traits—laziness; 068 Friendship.

Sharmat, Marjorie Weinman. *Gladys Told Me to Meet Her Here*. Illus. by Edward Frascino. New York: Harper, 1970.
068 Friendship.

Sharmat, Marjorie Weinman. *Goodnight, Andrew. Goodnight, Craig*. Illus. by Mary Eileen Chalmers. New York: Harper, 1969.
015 Bedtime; 057 Family life.

Sharmat, Marjorie Weinman. *I Don't Care*. Illus. by Lillian Hoban. New York: Macmillan, 1977.
016.18 Behavior—indifference; 052.09 Emotions—sadness; 053.01 Ethnic groups in the U.S.—Afro-Americans; 177.01 Toys—balloons.

Sharmat, Marjorie Weinman. *I Want Mama*. Illus. by Emily Arnold McCully. New York: Harper, 1974.
057.04 Family life—the only child; 088 Illness.

Sharmat, Marjorie Weinman. *I'm Not Oscar's Friend Any More*. Illus. by Tony De Luna. New York: Dutton, 1975.
016.10 Behavior—fighting, arguing; 052.01 Emotions—anger; 068 Friendship.

Sharmat, Marjorie Weinman. *I'm Terrific*. Illus. by Kay Chorao. New York: Holiday, 1977.
008.06 Animals—bears; 026.09 Character traits—conceit; 156 Self-concept.

Sharmat, Marjorie Weinman. *Mitchell Is Moving*. Illus. by José Aruego, and Ariane Dewey. New York: Macmillan, 1978.
044 Dinosaurs; 068 Friendship; 114 Moving.

Sharmat, Marjorie Weinman. *Mooch the Messy*. Illus. by Ben Shecter. New York: Harper, 1976.
008.48 Animals—rats; 026.05 Character traits—cleanliness.

Sharmat, Marjorie Weinman. *Nate the Great.* Illus. by Marc Simont. New York: Coward, 1972.
023.08 Careers—detectives; 063 Food; 137 Problem solving.

Sharmat, Marjorie Weinman. *Nate the Great and the Lost List.* Illus. by Marc Simont. New York: Coward, 1975.
023.08 Careers—detectives; 063 Food; 137 Problem solving.

Sharmat, Marjorie Weinman. *Nate the Great and the Phony Clue.* Illus. by Marc Simont. New York: Coward, 1977.
023.08 Careers—detectives; 063 Food; 137 Problem solving.

Sharmat, Marjorie Weinman. *Nate the Great Goes Undercover.* Illus. by Marc Simont. New York: Coward, 1974.
023.08 Careers—detectives; 063 Food; 137 Problem solving.

Sharmat, Marjorie Weinman. *Rex.* Illus. by Emily Arnold McCully. New York: Harper, 1967.
016.27 Behavior—running away.

Sharmat, Marjorie Weinman. *Scarlet Monster Lives Here.* Illus. by Dennis Kendrick. New York: Harper, 1979.
016 Behavior; 068 Friendship; 110 Monsters.

Sharmat, Marjorie Weinman. *Sophie and Gussie.* Illus. by Lillian Hoban. New York: Macmillan, 1973.
008.56 Animals—squirrels.

Sharmat, Marjorie Weinman. *Thornton the Worrier.* Illus. by Kay Chorao. New York: Holiday, 1978.
016.39 Behavior—worrying.

Sharmat, Marjorie Weinman. *The Trip.* Illus. by Lillian Hoban. New York: Macmillan, 1976.
008.56 Animals—squirrels; 016.19 Behavior—losing things; 016.31 Behavior—sharing; 031 Clothing.

Sharmat, Marjorie Weinman. *Walter the Wolf.* Illus. by Kelly Oechsli. New York: Holiday, 1975.
008 Animals; 008.61 Animals—wolves; 191 Violence, anti-violence.

Sharon, Mary Bruce. *Scenes from Childhood.* Illus. by author. New York: Dutton, 1978.
011 Art.

Shaw, Charles Green. *The Blue Guess Book.* Illus. by author. Reading: Addison-Wesley, 1942.
069 Games.

Shaw, Charles Green. *The Guess Book.* Illus. by author. Reading: Addison-Wesley, 1941.
069 Games.

Shaw, Charles Green. *It Looked Like Spilt Milk.* Illus. by author. New York: Harper, 1947.
032.07 Concepts—shape; 069 Games; 129 Participation; 161 Sky; 195.01 Weather—clouds.

Shaw, Evelyn S. *Alligator.* Illus. by Frances Zweifel. New York: Harper, 1972.
142.01 Reptiles—alligators, crocodiles; 152 Science.

Shaw, Evelyn S. *Fish Out of School.* Illus. by Ralph Carpentier. New York: Harper, 1970.
060 Fish; 152 Science; 153 Sea and seashore.

Shaw, Evelyn S. *A Nest of Wood Ducks.* Illus. by Cherryl Pape. New York: Harper, 1976.
017.08 Birds—ducks; 152 Science.

Shaw, Evelyn S. *Octopus.* Illus. by Ralph Carpentier. New York: Harper, 1971.
123 Octopod; 152 Science; 153 Sea and seashore.

Shaw, Richard. *The Kitten in the Pumpkin Patch.* Illus. by Jacqueline Kahane. New York: Warner, 1973.
008.09 Animals—cats; 083.07 Holidays—Halloween; 199 Witches.

Shay, Arthur. *What Happens When You Go to the Hospital.* Illus. by author. Chicago: Contemporary Books, 1969.
084 Hospitals; 088 Illness.

Shearer, John. *The Case of the Sneaker Snatcher.* Illus. by Ted Shearer. New York: Delacorte Pr., 1977.
031 Clothing; 137 Problem solving; 166.02 Sports—basketball.

Shecter, Ben. *Conrad's Castle.* Illus. by author. New York: Harper, 1967.
089 Imagination.

Shecter, Ben. *Emily, Girl Witch of New York.* Illus. by author. New York: Dial Pr., 1963.
029 City; 086 Houses; 103 Magic; 138 Progress; 199 Witches.

Shecter, Ben. *Hester the Jester.* Illus. by author. New York: Harper, 1977.
026.01 Character traits—ambition; 092 Jesters; 121 Non-sexist.

Shecter, Ben. *If I Had a Ship*. Illus. by author. Garden City, NY: Doubleday, 1970.
019 Boats, ships; 026.13 Character traits—generosity; 052.08 Emotions—love; 089 Imagination.

Shecter, Ben. *Partouche Plants a Seed*. Illus. by author. New York: Harper, 1966.
002.06 Activities—gardening; 008.42 Animals—pigs; 064.11 Foreign lands—France; 133 Plants.

Shecter, Ben. *The Stocking Child*. Illus. by author. New York: Harper, 1976.
157 Senses; 177.04 Toys—dolls.

Shecter, Ben. *Stone House Stories*. Illus. by author. New York: Harper, 1973.
008 Animals.

Sheehan, Angela. *The Duck*. Illus. by Maurice Pledger, and Bernard Robinson. New York: Watts, 1979.
017.08 Birds—ducks; 152 Science.

Sheehan, Angela. *The Otter*. Illus. by Bernard Robinson. New York: Watts, 1979.
008.40 Animals—otters; 152 Science.

Sheffield, Margaret. *Where Do Babies Come From?* Illus. by Sheila Bewley. New York: Knopf, 1973.
013 Babies; 152 Science.

Shepard, Sylvia, jt. author. *Let's Find Out about Babies*. By Martha Shapp; Charles Shapp; and Sylvia Shepard.

Sherman, Ivan. *I Am a Giant*. Illus. by author. New York: Harcourt, 1975.
072 Giants; 089 Imagination.

Sherman, Ivan. *I Do Not Like It When My Friend Comes to Visit*. Illus. by author. New York: Harcourt, 1973.
016.31 Behavior—sharing; 054 Etiquette; 068 Friendship.

Sherman, Nancy. *Gwendolyn and the Weathercock*. Illus. by Edward Sorel. Racine, WI: Western Pub., 1963.
017.04 Birds—chickens; 058 Farms; 134 Poetry, rhyme; 195.05 Weather—rain.

Sherman, Nancy. *Gwendolyn the Miracle Hen*. Illus. by Edward Sorel. Racine, WI: Western Pub., 1961.
017.04 Birds—chickens; 046 Dragons; 134 Poetry, rhyme.

Shimin, Symeon. *I Wish There Were Two of Me*. Illus. by author. New York: Warne, 1976.
016.38 Behavior—wishing.

Shimin, Symeon. *A Special Birthday*. Illus. by author. New York: McGraw-Hill, 1976.
018 Birthdays; 201 Wordless.

Short, Mayo. *Andy and the Wild Ducks*. Illus. by Paul M. Souza. Chicago: Melmont, 1959.
008 Animals; 049 Ecology; 058 Farms.

Shortall, Leonard W. *Andy, the Dog Walker*. Illus. by author. New York: Morrow, 1968.
008.14 Animals—dogs; 016.20 Behavior—lost.

Shortall, Leonard W. *Just-in-Time-Joey*. Illus. by author. New York: Morrow, 1973.
049 Ecology.

Shortall, Leonard W. *One Way; A Trip with Traffic Signs*. Illus. by author. Englewood Cliffs, NJ: Prentice-Hall, 1975.
083.05 Holidays—Fourth of July; 134 Poetry, rhyme; 148 Safety; 178 Traffic signs.

Shortall, Leonard W. *Tod on the Tugboat*. Illus. by author. New York: Morrow, 1971.
019 Boats, ships.

Shortall, Leonard W. *Tony's First Dive*. Illus. by author. New York: Morrow, 1972.
052.04 Emotions—fear; 166.15 Sports—swimming.

Showalter, Jean B. *The Donkey Ride*. Illus. by Tomi Ungerer. Garden City, NY: Doubleday, 1967.
008.16 Animals—donkeys; 062 Folk and fairy tales; 087 Humor.

Showers, Paul. *A Baby Starts to Grow*. Illus. by Rosalind Fray. New York: Crowell, 1969.
013 Babies; 152 Science.

Showers, Paul. *Before You Were a Baby*. Illus. by Ingrid Fetz. New York: Crowell, 1968.
013 Babies; 152 Science.

Showers, Paul. *The Listening Walk*. Illus. by Aliki Liacouras Brandenberg. New York: Crowell, 1961.
002.18 Activities—walking; 157 Senses.

Showers, Paul. *Look at Your Eyes*. Illus. by Paul Galdone. New York: Crowell, 1962.
053.01 Ethnic groups in the U.S.—Afro-Americans.

Showers, Paul. *Your Skin and Mine*. Illus. by Paul Galdone. New York: Crowell, 1965.
053.01 Ethnic groups in the U.S.—Afro-Americans.

Shub, Elizabeth. *Clever Kate*. Illus. by Anita Lobel. New York: Macmillan, 1973.
062 Folk and fairy tales; 087 Humor.

Shub, Elizabeth. *Dragon Franz*. Illus. by Ursula Konopka. New York: Greenwillow, 1976.
032.01 Concepts—color; 046 Dragons.

Shulevitz, Uri. *Dawn*. Illus. by author. New York: Farrar, 1974.
057.02 Family life—grandparents; great-grandparents; 112 Morning; 166.04 Sports—camping; 169 Sun.

Shulevitz, Uri. *The Magician*. Illus. by author. Adapted by Isaac Loeb Peretz. New York: Macmillan, 1973.
093 Jewish culture; 103 Magic; 141 Religion.

Shulevitz, Uri. *One Monday Morning*. Illus. by author. New York: Scribner's, 1967.
039 Days of the week, months of the year; 089 Imagination; 147 Royalty.

Shulevitz, Uri. *Rain Rain Rivers*. Illus. by author. New York: Farrar, 1969.
134 Poetry, rhyme; 195.05 Weather—rain.

Shulevitz, Uri. *The Treasure*. Illus. by author. New York: Farrar, 1978.
062 Folk and fairy tales.

Shulman, Milton. *Preep, the Little Pigeon of Trafalgar Square*. Illus. by Dale Maxey. New York: Random House, 1964.
017.19 Birds—pigeons; 064.10 Foreign lands—England.

Shuttlesworth, Dorothy E. *ABC of Buses*. Illus. by Leonard W. Shortall. Garden City, NY: Doubleday, 1965.
001 ABC Books; 021 Buses.

Sicotte, Virginia. *A Riot of Quiet*. Illus. by Edward Jeffrey Irving Ardizzone. New York: Holt, 1969.
089 Imagination; 120 Noise.

Siddiqui, Ashraf. *Bhombal Dass, the Uncle of Lion*. Illus. by Thomas A. Hamil. New York: Macmillan, 1959.
008.10 Animals—cats, wild;
008.21 Animals—goats;
026.06 Character traits—cleverness;
062 Folk and fairy tales; 064.26 Foreign lands—Pakistan.

Sieg, Theo Le (pseud.). See Geisel, Theodor Seuss

Siepmann, Jane. *The Lion on Scott Street*. Illus. by Clement Hurd. New York: Oxford Univ. Pr., 1952.
008.10 Animals—cats, wild; 089 Imagination.

Siewert, Margaret, and Savage, Kathleen. *Bear Hunt*. Illus. by Leonard W. Shortall. Englewood Cliffs, NJ: Prentice-Hall, 1976.
008.06 Animals—bears; 069 Games; 129 Participation; 177.08 Toys—teddy bears.

Silverstein, Shel. *A Giraffe and a Half*. Illus. by author. New York: Harper, 1964.
038 Cumulative tales; 087 Humor; 134 Poetry, rhyme.

Silverstein, Shel. *The Giving Tree*. Illus. by author. New York: Harper, 1964.
026.13 Character traits—generosity; 181 Trees.

Silverstein, Shel. *The Missing Piece*. Illus. by author. New York: Harper, 1976.
026.16 Character traits—individuality; 032.07 Concepts—shape.

Simon, Howard, jt. author. *If You Were an Eel, How Would You Feel?* By Mina Lewiton Simon, and Howard Simon.

Simon, Mina Lewiton. *Is Anyone Here?* Illus. by Howard Simon. New York: Atheneum, 1967.
134 Poetry, rhyme; 153 Sea and seashore.

Simon, Mina Lewiton, and Simon, Howard. *If You Were an Eel, How Would You Feel?* Illus. by Howard Simon. Chicago: Follett, 1963.
008 Animals.

Simon, Norma. *All Kinds of Families*. Illus. by Joseph Leon Lasker. Chicago: Albert Whitman, 1976.
057 Family life.

Simon, Norma. *The Daddy Days*. Illus. by Abner Graboff. New York: Abelard-Schuman, 1958.
045 Divorce; 057.01 Family life—fathers.

Simon, Norma. *How Do I Feel?* Illus. by Joseph Leon Lasker. Chicago: Albert Whitman, 1970.
052 Emotions; 186 Twins.

Simon, Norma. *I Know What I Like*. Illus. by Joseph Leon Lasker. Chicago: Albert Whitman, 1971.
026.16 Character traits—individuality.

Simon, Norma. *I Was So Mad!* Illus. by Joseph Leon Lasker. Chicago: Albert Whitman, 1974.
052.01 Emotions—anger.

Simon, Norma. *The Wet World*. Illus. by Jane Miller. Philadelphia: Lippincott, 1954.
195.05 Weather—rain.

Simon, Norma. *What Do I Do?* Illus. by Joseph Leon Lasker. Chicago: Albert Whitman, 1969.
002 Activities; 026.14 Character traits—helpfulness; 029 City; 053.08 Ethnic groups in the U.S.—Puerto Rican-Americans; 151 School.

Simon, Norma. *What Do I Say?* Illus. by Joseph Leon Lasker. Chicago: Albert Whitman, 1967.
053.07 Ethnic groups in the U.S.—Multi-ethnic; 053.08 Ethnic groups in the U.S.—Puerto Rican-Americans; 057 Family life; 065 Foreign languages; 129 Participation; 151 School.

Simon, Norma. *Why Am I Different?* Illus. by Dora Leder. Chicago: Albert Whitman, 1976.
026.03 Character traits—being different; 026.16 Character traits—individuality; 156 Self-concept.

Simon, Sidney B. *The Armadillo Who Had No Shell.* Illus. by Walter Lorraine. New York: Norton, 1966.
008.03 Animals—armadillos; 026.03 Character traits—being different.

Simon, Sidney B. *Henry the Uncatchable Mouse.* Illus. by Nola Langner. New York: Norton, 1964.
008.34 Animals—mice; 026.06 Character traits—cleverness.

Simont, Marc. *How Come Elephants?* Illus. by author. New York: Harper, 1965.
008.17 Animals—elephants; 026.28 Character traits—questioning.

Simple Simon. *The History of Simple Simon.* Illus. by Paul Galdone. New York: McGraw-Hill, 1966.
122 Nursery rhymes.

Simple Simon. Illus. by Rodney Peppé. New York: Holt, 1973.
122 Nursery rhymes.

Singer, Isaac Bashevis. *Why Noah Chose the Dove.* Illus. by Eric Carle. New York: Farrar, 1973.
008 Animals; 017.07 Birds—doves; 141.01 Religion—Noah.

Singer, Marilyn. *The Dog Who Insisted He Wasn't.* Illus. by Kelly Oechsli. New York: Dutton, 1976.
008.14 Animals—dogs; 026.16 Character traits—individuality; 087 Humor.

Singer, Marilyn. *The Pickle Plan.* Illus. by Steven Kellogg. New York: Dutton, 1978.
016.26 Behavior—needing someone; 026.16 Character traits—individuality.

Sivulich, Sandra Stroner. *I'm Going on a Bear Hunt.* Illus. by Glen H. Rounds. New York: Dutton, 1973.
008.06 Animals—bears; 069 Games; 129 Participation.

Skaar, Grace Marion. *Nothing But (Cats) and All About (Dogs).* Illus. by author. Reading: Addison-Wesley, 1947.
008.09 Animals—cats; 008.14 Animals—dogs.

Skaar, Grace Marion. *What Do the Animals Say?* Illus. by author. Reading: Addison-Wesley, 1968.
008 Animals; 129 Participation.

Skaar, Grace Marion, and Woodcock, Louise Phinney. *The Very Little Dog; and The Smart Little Kitty.* Illus. by Grace Marion Skaar, and Lucienne Bloch. Reading: Addison-Wesley, 1967.
008.09 Animals—cats; 008.14 Animals—dogs.

Skipper, Mervyn. *The Fooling of King Alexander.* Illus. by Gaynor Chapman. New York: Atheneum, 1967.
064.06 Foreign lands—China; 147 Royalty.

Skorpen, Liesel Moak. *All the Lassies.* Illus. by Bruce Martin Scoot. New York: Dial Pr., 1970.
008 Animals; 008.14 Animals—dogs; 026.25 Character traits—perseverance; 038 Cumulative tales; 057.04 Family life—the only child; 129 Participation; 131 Pets.

Skorpen, Liesel Moak. *Charles.* Illus. by Martha G. Alexander. New York: Harper, 1971.
177.08 Toys—teddy bears.

Skorpen, Liesel Moak. *Elizabeth.* Illus. by Martha G. Alexander. New York: Harper, 1970.
177.04 Toys—dolls.

Skorpen, Liesel Moak. *If I Had a Lion.* Illus. by Ursula Landshoff. New York: Harper, 1967.
008.10 Animals—cats, wild; 089 Imagination.

Skorpen, Liesel Moak. *Old Arthur.* Illus. by Wallace Tripp. New York: Harper, 1972.
008.14 Animals—dogs; 125 Old age.

Skorpen, Liesel Moak. *Outside My Window.* Illus. by Mercer Mayer. New York: Harper, 1968.
008.06 Animals—bears; 015 Bedtime.

Skurzynski, Gloria. *The Magic Pumpkin.* Illus. by Rocco Negri. New York: Four Winds Pr., 1971.
008.10 Animals—cats, wild;
008.61 Animals—wolves;
026.06 Character traits—cleverness;
062 Folk and fairy tales; 064.16 Foreign lands—India.

Sloan, Carolyn. *Carter Is a Painter's Cat.* Illus. by Fritz Wegner. New York: Simon & Schuster, 1971.
008.09 Animals—cats; 011 Art;
023.02 Careers—artists.

Slobodkin, Louis. *Clear the Track.* Illus. by author. New York: Macmillan, 1945.
057 Family life; 089 Imagination;
134 Poetry, rhyme; 179 Trains.

Slobodkin, Louis. *Colette and the Princess.* Illus. by author. New York: Dutton, 1965.
008.09 Animals—cats; 064.11 Foreign lands—France; 120 Noise; 147 Royalty.

Slobodkin, Louis. *Dinny and Danny.* Illus. by author. New York: Macmillan, 1951.
024 Cavemen; 026.14 Character traits—helpfulness; 044 Dinosaurs;
068 Friendship.

Slobodkin, Louis. *Friendly Animals.* Illus. by author. New York: Vanguard, 1944.
008 Animals; 134 Poetry, rhyme.

Slobodkin, Louis. *Hustle and Bustle.* Illus. by author. New York: Macmillan, 1962.
008.27 Animals—hippopotami;
016.10 Behavior—fighting, arguing.

Slobodkin, Louis. *The Late Cuckoo.* Illus. by author. New York: Vanguard, 1962.
030 Clocks; 174 Time.

Slobodkin, Louis. *Magic Michael.* Illus. by author. New York: Macmillan, 1944.
057 Family life; 089 Imagination;
103 Magic; 156 Self-concept.

Slobodkin, Louis. *Melvin, the Moose Child.* Illus. by author. New York: Macmillan, 1957.
008 Animals; 008.38 Animals—moose;
066 Forest, woods.

Slobodkin, Louis. *Millions and Millions and Millions!* Illus. by author. New York: Vanguard, 1955.
026.16 Character traits—individuality;
134 Poetry, rhyme.

Slobodkin, Louis. *Moon Blossom and the Golden Penny.* Illus. by author. New York: Vanguard, 1963.
064.06 Foreign lands—China;
109 Money.

Slobodkin, Louis. *One Is Good, but Two Are Better.* Illus. by author. New York: Vanguard, 1956.
068 Friendship; 134 Poetry, rhyme.

Slobodkin, Louis. *Our Friendly Friends.* Illus. by author. New York: Vanguard, 1951.
008 Animals.

Slobodkin, Louis. *The Polka-Dot Goat.* Illus. by author. New York: Macmillan, 1964.
008.21 Animals—goats; 064.16 Foreign lands—India.

Slobodkin, Louis. *The Seaweed Hat.* Illus. by author. New York: Macmillan, 1947.
134 Poetry, rhyme; 153 Sea and seashore.

Slobodkin, Louis. *Thank You—You're Welcome.* Illus. by author. New York: Vanguard, 1957.
054 Etiquette.

Slobodkin, Louis. *Trick or Treat.* Illus. by author. New York: Macmillan, 1959.
083.07 Holidays—Halloween.

Slobodkin, Louis. *Up High and Down Low.* Illus. by author. New York: Macmillan, 1960.
008.21 Animals—goats;
008.52 Animals—sheep;
032.10 Concepts—up and down;
134 Poetry, rhyme.

Slobodkin, Louis. *The Wide-Awake Owl.* Illus. by author. New York: Macmillan, 1958.
017.14 Birds—owls; 116 Music;
162 Sleep; 164 Songs.

Slobodkin, Louis. *Yasu and the Strangers.* Illus. by author. New York: Macmillan, 1965.
016.20 Behavior—lost; 064.19 Foreign lands—Japan.

Slobodkina, Esphyr. *Boris and His Balalaika.* Illus. by Vladimir Bobri. New York: Abelard-Schuman, 1964.
064.30 Foreign lands—Russia.

Slobodkina, Esphyr. *Caps for Sale.* Illus. by author. Reading: Addison-Wesley, 1940.
008.37 Animals—monkeys;
023.20 Careers—peddlers;
031 Clothing; 087 Humor;
129 Participation.

Slobodkina, Esphyr. *Pezzo the Peddler and the Circus Elephant*. Illus. by author. Reading: Addison-Wesley, 1967.
008.17 Animals—elephants;
023.20 Careers—peddlers; 028 Circus, clowns; 031 Clothing; 087 Humor;
128 Parades; 129 Participation.

Slobodkina, Esphyr. *Pezzo the Peddler and the Thirteen Silly Thieves*. Illus. by author. Reading: Addison-Wesley, 1970.
023.20 Careers—peddlers;
031 Clothing; 036 Crime; 087 Humor;
129 Participation.

Slobodkina, Esphyr. *Pinky and the Petunias*. Illus. by author. Based on a story by Tamara Schildkraut. New York: Abelard-Schuman, 1959.
008.09 Animals—cats; 061 Flowers.

Slobodkina, Esphyr. *The Wonderful Feast*. Illus. by author. New York: Lothrop, 1955.
008 Animals; 008.28 Animals—horses;
058 Farms; 063 Food.

Slocum, Rosalie. *Breakfast with the Clowns*. Illus. by author. New York: Viking, 1937.
028 Circus, clowns; 063 Food.

Smaridge, Norah Antoinette. *Peter's Tent*. Illus. by Brinton Cassady Turkle. New York: Viking, 1965.
068 Friendship.

Smaridge, Norah Antoinette. *Watch Out!* Illus. by Susan Perl. Nashville: Abingdon Pr., 1965.
148 Safety.

Smaridge, Norah Antoinette. *You Know Better Than That*. Illus. by Susan Perl. Nashville: Abingdon Pr., 1973.
054 Etiquette; 134 Poetry, rhyme.

Smith, Catriona, jt. author. *The Long Dive*. By Ray Smith, and Catriona Smith.

Smith, Catriona, jt. author. *The Long Slide*. By Ray Smith, and Catriona Smith.

Smith, Donald. *Farm Numbers 1, 2, 3*. Illus. by author. Nashville: Abingdon Pr., 1970.
033 Counting; 058 Farms.

Smith, Elmer Boyd. *The Story of Noah's Ark*. Illus. by author. Boston: Houghton, 1904.
141.01 Religion—Noah.

Smith, Henry Lee, jt. author. *Frog Fun*. By Clara Georgeanna Stratemeyer, and Henry Lee Smith.

Smith, Henry Lee, jt. author. *Pepper*. By Clara Georgeanna Stratemeyer, and Henry Lee Smith.

Smith, Henry Lee, jt. author. *Tuggy*. By Clara Georgeanna Stratemeyer, and Henry Lee Smith.

Smith, Jim. *The Frog Band and Durrington Dormouse*. Illus. by author. Boston: Little, 1977.
005 Amphibians; 008.34 Animals—mice.

Smith, Jim. *The Frog Band and the Onion Seller*. Illus. by author. Boston: Little, 1976.
005 Amphibians; 087 Humor.

Smith, Mary, and Smith, Robert Alan. *Long Ago Elf*. Illus. by authors. Chicago: Follett, 1968.
051 Elves and little people.

Smith, Ray, and Smith, Catriona. *The Long Dive*. Illus. by authors. New York: Atheneum, 1979.
153 Sea and seashore; 177 Toys.

Smith, Ray, and Smith, Catriona. *The Long Slide*. Illus. by authors. New York: Atheneum, 1977.
177 Toys.

Smith, Robert Alan, jt. author. *Long Ago Elf*. By Mary Smith, and Robert Alan Smith.

Smith, Robert Paul. *Jack Mack*. Illus. by Erik Blegvad. New York: Coward, 1960.
087 Humor; 175 Tongue twisters.

Smith, Robert Paul. *Nothingatall, Nothingatall, Nothingatall*. Illus. by Alan E. Cober. New York: Harper, 1965.
015 Bedtime.

Smith, Robert Paul. *When I Am Big*. Illus. by Lillian Hoban. New York: Harper, 1965.
016.14 Behavior—growing up.

Smith, Theresa Kalab. *The Fog Is Secret*. Illus. by author. Englewood Cliffs, NJ: Prentice-Hall, 1966.
153 Sea and seashore;
195.04 Weather—fog.

Smith, William Jay. *Puptents and Pebbles*. Illus. by Juliet Kepes. Boston: Little, 1959.
001 ABC Books; 087 Humor;
134 Poetry, rhyme.

Smith, William Jay. *Typewriter Town*. Illus. by author. New York: Dutton, 1960.
134 Poetry, rhyme.

Snyder, Dick. *One Day at the Zoo*. Illus. by author. New York: Scribner's, 1960.
008 Animals; 008.32 Animals—koala bears; 204 Zoos.

Snyder, Dick. *Talk to Me, Tiger*. Illus. by author. Chicago: Children's Pr., 1965.
008 Animals; 204 Zoos.

Sobol, Harriet L. *Jeff's Hospital Book.* Illus. by Patricia Agre. New York: Walck, 1975. 084 Hospitals.

Sobol, Harriet L. *My Brother Steven Is Retarded.* Illus. by Patricia Agre. New York: Walck, 1977. 077 Handicaps.

Solbert, Romaine G., jt. author. *Emily Emerson's Moon.* By Jean Merrill, and Romaine G. Solbert.

Solbert, Romaine G., ed. *I Wrote My Name on the Wall: Sidewalk Songs.* Illus. by author. Boston: Little, 1971. 053.07 Ethnic groups in the U.S.— Multi-ethnic.

Solbert, Ronni (pseud.). See Solbert, Romaine G.

Sondergaard, Arensa, and Reed, Mary M. *Biddy and the Ducks.* Illus. by Doris Henderson, and Marion Henderson. Lexington, MA: Heath, 1941. 017.04 Birds—chickens; 017.08 Birds— ducks.

Sonneborn, Ruth A. *Friday Night Is Papa Night.* Illus. by Emily Arnold McCully. New York: Viking, 1970. 029 City; 053.08 Ethnic groups in the U.S.—Puerto Rican-Americans; 064.01 Foreign lands—Africa; 135 Poverty.

Sonneborn, Ruth A. *I Love Gram.* Illus. by Leo Carty. New York: Viking, 1971. 029 City; 053.01 Ethnic groups in the U.S.—Afro-Americans; 057.02 Family life—grandparents; great-grandparents; 084 Hospitals; 088 Illness; 125 Old age.

Sonneborn, Ruth A. *Lollipop's Party.* Illus. by Brinton Cassady Turkle. New York: Viking, 1967. 029 City; 052.07 Emotions—loneliness; 053.08 Ethnic groups in the U.S.— Puerto Rican-Americans.

Sonneborn, Ruth A. *Seven in a Bed.* Illus. by Don Freeman. New York: Viking, 1968. 053.08 Ethnic groups in the U.S.— Puerto Rican-Americans; 057 Family life; 162 Sleep.

Sotomayor, Antonio. *Khasa Goes to the Fiesta.* Illus. by author. Garden City, NY: Doubleday, 1967. 016.20 Behavior—lost; 064.32 Foreign lands—South America; 083 Holidays.

Spang, Gunter. *Clelia and the Little Mermaid.* Illus. by Pepperl Off. New York: Abelard-Schuman, 1967. 052.07 Emotions—loneliness; 064.12 Foreign lands—Germany; 068 Friendship; 117 Mythical creatures.

Spiegel, Doris. *Danny and Company 92.* Illus. by author. New York: Coward, 1945. 023.10 Careers—firefighters; 059 Fire.

Spier, Peter. *Bored—Nothing to Do!* Illus. by author. Garden City, NY: Doubleday, 1978. 004 Airplanes; 016.04 Behavior— boredom; 087 Humor.

Spier, Peter. *Crash! Bang! Boom!* Illus. by author. Garden City, NY: Doubleday, 1972. 120 Noise; 128 Parades; 129 Participation.

Spier, Peter. *The Erie Canal.* Illus. by author. Garden City, NY: Doubleday, 1970. 062 Folk and fairy tales; 116 Music; 164 Songs; 189 U.S. history.

Spier, Peter. *Fast—Slow, High—Low.* Illus. by author. Garden City, NY: Doubleday, 1972. 032.06 Concepts—opposites; 032.09 Concepts—speed.

Spier, Peter. *Gobble, Growl, Grunt.* Illus. by author. Garden City, NY: Doubleday, 1971. 008 Animals; 120 Noise; 129 Participation.

Spier, Peter. *The Legend of New Amsterdam.* Illus. by author. Garden City, NY: Doubleday, 1979. 062 Folk and fairy tales; 189 U.S. history.

Spier, Peter. *Noah's Ark.* Illus. by author. Garden City, NY: Doubleday, 1977. 019 Boats, ships; 134 Poetry, rhyme; 141.01 Religion—Noah; 201 Wordless.

Spier, Peter. *Oh, Were They Ever Happy!* Illus. by author. Garden City, NY: Doubleday, 1978. 002.09 Activities—painting; 032.01 Concepts—color; 087 Humor.

Spilka, Arnold. *And the Frog Went "Blah!"* Illus. by author. New York: Scribner's, 1972. 087 Humor; 134 Poetry, rhyme.

Spilka, Arnold, jt. author. *Dippy Dos and Don'ts.* By Michael Sage, and Arnold Spilka.

Spilka, Arnold. *A Lion I Can Do Without.* Illus. by author. New York: Walck, 1964. 087 Humor; 134 Poetry, rhyme.

Spilka, Arnold. *Little Birds Don't Cry*. Illus. by author. New York: Viking, 1965.
008 Animals; 134 Poetry, rhyme.

Spilka, Arnold. *A Rumbudgin of Nonsense*. Illus. by author. New York: Scribner's, 1970.
087 Humor; 134 Poetry, rhyme.

Stafford, Kay. *Ling Tang and the Lucky Cricket*. Illus. by Louise Zibold. New York: McGraw-Hill, 1944.
026.21 Character traits—luck;
064.06 Foreign lands—China.

Stalder, Valerie. *Even the Devil Is Afraid of a Shrew*. Illus. by Richard Brown. Adapted by Ray Broekel. Reading: Addison-Wesley, 1972.
016.25 Behavior—nagging; 042 Devil;
062 Folk and fairy tales; 064.21 Foreign lands—Lapland.

Stamaty, Mark Alan. *Minnie Maloney and Macaroni*. Illus. by author. New York: Dial Pr., 1976.
063 Food; 087 Humor.

Standon, Anna. *The Singing Rhinoceros*. Illus. by Edward Cyril Standon. New York: Coward, 1963.
008.49 Animals—rhinoceros.

Standon, Anna, and Standon, Edward Cyril. *Little Duck Lost*. Illus. by Edward Cyril Standon. New York: Delacorte Pr., 1965.
016.20 Behavior—lost; 017.08 Birds—ducks; 050 Eggs; 057.03 Family life—mothers.

Standon, Edward Cyril, jt. author. *Little Duck Lost*. By Anna Standon, and Edward Cyril Standon.

Stanek, Muriel. *Left, Right, Left, Right*. Illus. by Lucy Ozone Hawkinson. Chicago: Albert Whitman, 1969.
032.04 Concepts—left and right;
052.02 Emotions—embarrassment.

Stanek, Muriel. *One, Two, Three for Fun*. Illus. by Seymour Fleishman. Chicago: Albert Whitman, 1967.
033 Counting; 053.07 Ethnic groups in the U.S.—Multi-ethnic.

Stanley, John. *It's Nice to Be Little*. Illus. by Jean Tamburine. Skokie, IL: Rand McNally, 1965.
026.31 Character traits—smallness.

Steadman, Ralph. *The Bridge*. Illus. by author. Cleveland: Collins, 1972.
016.10 Behavior—fighting, arguing;
020 Bridges; 068 Friendship.

Steadman, Ralph. *The Little Red Computer*. Illus. by author. New York: McGraw-Hill, 1969.
102 Machines; 165 Space and space ships.

Stearns, Monroe, adapter. *Ring-A-Ling*. Illus. by Adolf Zabransky. Adapted and translated by Monroe Stearns. Philadelphia: Lippincott, 1959.
122 Nursery rhymes.

Steger, Hans-Ulrich. *Traveling to Tripiti*. Illus. by author. Translated by Elizabeth D. Crawford. New York: Harcourt, 1967.
002.16 Activities—traveling;
038 Cumulative tales; 177 Toys;
177.08 Toys—teddy bears.

Steig, William. *The Amazing Bone*. Illus. by author. New York: Farrar, 1976.
008.42 Animals—pigs; 103 Magic.

Steig, William. *Amos and Boris*. Illus. by author. New York: Farrar, 1971.
008.34 Animals—mice;
008.60 Animals—whales;
026.14 Character traits—helpfulness;
068 Friendship.

Steig, William. *The Bad Speller*. Illus. by author. New York: Simon & Schuster, 1970.
069 Games; 096 Language.

Steig, William. *Caleb and Kate*. Illus. by author. New York: Farrar, 1977.
008.14 Animals—dogs; 103 Magic;
199 Witches.

Steig, William. *An Eye for Elephants*. Illus. by author. New York: Dutton, 1970.
008.17 Animals—elephants; 134 Poetry, rhyme.

Steig, William. *Farmer Palmer's Wagon Ride*. Illus. by author. New York: Farrar, 1974.
008.16 Animals—donkeys;
008.42 Animals—pigs.

Steig, William. *Roland the Minstrel Pig*. Illus. by author. New York: Dutton, 1968.
008.18 Animals—foxes;
008.42 Animals—pigs; 116 Music;
147 Royalty.

Steig, William. *Sylvester and the Magic Pebble*. Illus. by author. New York: Simon & Schuster, 1969.
008 Animals; 008.16 Animals—donkeys;
057 Family life; 103 Magic.

Stein, Sara Bonnett. *About Dying*. Illus. by Dick Frank. New York: Walker, 1974.
040 Death.

Stein, Sara Bonnett. *About Handicaps*. Illus. by Dick Frank. New York: Walker, 1974.
077 Handicaps.

Stein, Sara Bonnett. *The Adopted One.* Illus. by Erika Stone. New York: Walker, 1979. 003 Adoption; 057 Family life.

Stein, Sara Bonnett. *A Child Goes to School.* Illus. by Don Conners. Garden City, NY: Doubleday, 1978. 151 School.

Stein, Sara Bonnett. *A Hospital Story.* Illus. by Doris Pinney. New York: Walker, 1974. 084 Hospitals; 088 Illness.

Stein, Sara Bonnett. *Making Babies.* Illus. by Doris Pinney. New York: Walker, 1974. 013 Babies; 057 Family life.

Stein, Sara Bonnett. *On Divorce.* Illus. by Erika Stone. New York: Walker, 1979. 045 Divorce; 057 Family life.

Stein, Sara Bonnett. *That New Baby.* Illus. by Dick Frank. New York: Walker, 1974. 013 Babies; 057 Family life.

Steiner, Charlotte. *Birthdays Are for Everyone.* Illus. by author. Garden City, NY: Doubleday, 1964. 018 Birthdays.

Steiner, Charlotte. *Charlotte Steiner's ABC.* Illus. by author. New York: Watts, 1946. 001 ABC Books.

Steiner, Charlotte. *Daddy Comes Home.* Illus. by author. Garden City, NY: Doubleday, 1944. 057 Family life; 057.01 Family life—fathers.

Steiner, Charlotte. *Five Little Finger Playmates.* Illus. by author. New York: Grosset, 1951. 033 Counting; 069 Games.

Steiner, Charlotte. *A Friend Is "Amie."* Illus. by author. New York: Knopf, 1956. 065 Foreign languages; 068 Friendship.

Steiner, Charlotte. *Kiki and Muffy.* Illus. by author. Garden City, NY: Doubleday, 1943. 008.09 Animals—cats; 057.02 Family life—grandparents; great-grandparents.

Steiner, Charlotte. *Kiki Is an Actress.* Illus. by author. Garden City, NY: Doubleday, 1958. 173 Theater.

Steiner, Charlotte. *Kiki's Play House.* Illus. by author. Garden City, NY: Doubleday, 1962. 002.12 Activities—playing.

Steiner, Charlotte. *Listen to My Seashell.* Illus. by author. New York: Knopf, 1959. 120 Noise; 153 Sea and seashore.

Steiner, Charlotte. *Look What Tracy Found.* Illus. by author. New York: Knopf, 1972. 002.12 Activities—playing; 089 Imagination.

Steiner, Charlotte. *Lulu.* Illus. by author. Garden City, NY: Doubleday, 1939. 008.14 Animals—dogs; 089.01 Imagination—imaginary friends.

Steiner, Charlotte. *My Bunny Feels Soft.* Illus. by author. New York: Knopf, 1958. 008.46 Animals—rabbits.

Steiner, Charlotte. *My Slippers Are Red.* Illus. by author. New York: Knopf, 1957. 032.01 Concepts—color.

Steiner, Charlotte. *Pete and Peter.* Illus. by author. Garden City, NY: Doubleday, 1941. 008.14 Animals—dogs; 166.08 Sports—hunting.

Steiner, Charlotte. *Pete's Puppets.* Illus. by author. Garden City, NY: Doubleday, 1952. 139 Puppets.

Steiner, Charlotte. *Polka Dot.* Illus. by author. Garden City, NY: Doubleday, 1947. 131 Pets.

Steiner, Charlotte. *Red Ridinghood's Little Lamb.* Illus. by author. New York: Knopf, 1964. 008.52 Animals—sheep; 051 Elves and little people; 069 Games.

Steiner, Charlotte. *The Sleepy Quilt.* Illus. by author. Garden City, NY: Doubleday, 1947. 015 Bedtime.

Steiner, Charlotte. *What's the Hurry, Harry?* Illus. by author. New York: Lothrop, 1968. 016.17 Behavior—hurrying; 026.24 Character traits—patience.

Steiner, Charlotte, and Burlingham, Mary. *The Climbing Book.* Illus. by Charlotte Steiner. New York: Vanguard, 1943. 067 Format, unusual; 083.03 Holidays—Christmas.

Steiner, Jörg. *Rabbit Island.* Illus. by Jörg Müller. Translated by Ann Conrad Lammers. New York: Harcourt, 1977. 008.46 Animals—rabbits; 026.12 Character traits—freedom.

Steiner, Jörg, and Müller, Jörg. *The Bear Who Wanted to Be a Bear.* Illus. by Jörg Müller. New York: Atheneum, 1977. 008.06 Animals—bears; 168 Stores.

Stephens, Karen. *Jumping*. Illus. by George Wiggins. New York: Grosset, 1965.
002.07 Activities—jumping.

Stephenson, Dorothy. *How to Scare a Lion*. Illus. by John E. Johnson. Chicago: Follett, 1965.
008.10 Animals—cats, wild; 088 Illness.

Stephenson, Dorothy. *The Night It Rained Toys*. Illus. by John E. Johnson. Chicago: Follett, 1963.
083.03 Holidays—Christmas;
134 Poetry, rhyme; 147 Royalty;
177 Toys.

Steptoe, John. *Birthday*. Illus. by author. New York: Holt, 1972.
018 Birthdays; 053.01 Ethnic groups in the U.S.—Afro-Americans.

Steptoe, John. *My Special Best Words*. Illus. by author. New York: Viking, 1974.
053.01 Ethnic groups in the U.S.—Afro-Americans; 057 Family life;
096 Language.

Steptoe, John. *Stevie*. Illus. by author. New York: Harper, 1969.
053.01 Ethnic groups in the U.S.—Afro-Americans; 068 Friendship.

Steptoe, John. *Uptown*. Illus. by author. New York: Harper, 1970.
029 City; 053.01 Ethnic groups in the U.S.—Afro-Americans; 135 Poverty.

Sterling, Helen (pseud.). See Hoke, Helen L.

Stern, Elsie-Jean. *Wee Robin's Christmas Song*. Illus. by Elsie McKean. New York: Nelson, 1945.
017.20 Birds—robins;
083.03 Holidays—Christmas; 116 Music;
164 Songs.

Stevens, Carla. *Hooray for Pig!* Illus. by Rainey Bennett. New York: Seabury Pr., 1974.
008 Animals; 008.42 Animals—pigs;
166.15 Sports—swimming.

Stevens, Carla. *The Pig and the Blue Flag*. Illus. by Rainey Bennett. New York: Seabury Pr., 1977.
008 Animals; 008.42 Animals—pigs;
166.07 Sports—gymnastics.

Stevens, Carla. *Stories from a Snowy Meadow*. Illus. by Eve Rice. New York: Seabury Pr., 1976.
008 Animals; 026.17 Character traits—kindness; 040 Death; 068 Friendship.

Stevenson, James. *The Bear Who Had No Place to Go*. Illus. by author. New York: Harper, 1972.
008.06 Animals—bears;
052.07 Emotions—loneliness.

Stevenson, James. *"Could Be Worse."* Illus. by author. New York: Greenwillow, 1977.
026.23 Character traits—optimism;
057 Family life; 057.02 Family life—grandparents; great-grandparents;
058 Farms; 110 Monsters.

Stevenson, James. *Monty*. Illus. by author. New York: Greenwillow, 1979.
005 Amphibians; 008.46 Animals—rabbits; 017.08 Birds —ducks;
142.01 Reptiles—alligators, crocodiles.

Stevenson, James. *The Sea View Hotel*. Illus. by author. New York: Greenwillow, 1978.
002.17 Activities—vacationing;
008.34 Animals—mice; 085 Hotels.

Stevenson, James. *Wilfred the Rat*. Illus. by author. New York: Greenwillow, 1977.
008.48 Animals—rats; 068 Friendship.

Stevenson, James. *Winston, Newton, Elton, and Ed*. Illus. by author. New York: Greenwillow, 1978.
008.58 Animals—walruses;
016.32 Behavior—sibling rivalry;
017.18 Birds—penguins.

Stevenson, James. *The Worst Person in the World*. Illus. by author. New York: Greenwillow, 1978.
068 Friendship.

Stevenson, Robert Louis. *A Child's Garden of Verses*. Illus. by Erik Blegvad. New York: Random House, 1978.
134 Poetry, rhyme.

Stevenson, Robert Louis. *A Child's Garden of Verses*. Illus. by Pelagie Doane. Garden City, NY: Doubleday, 1942.
134 Poetry, rhyme.

Stevenson, Robert Louis. *A Child's Garden of Verses*. Illus. by Toni Frissell. New York: U.S. Camera, 1944.
134 Poetry, rhyme.

Stevenson, Robert Louis. *A Child's Garden of Verses*. Illus. by Gyo Fujikawa. New York: Grosset, 1957.
134 Poetry, rhyme.

Stevenson, Robert Louis. *A Child's Garden of Verses*. Illus. by Alice Provensen, and Martin Provensen. Racine, WI: Western Pub., 1951.
134 Poetry, rhyme.

Stevenson, Robert Louis. *A Child's Garden of Verses*. Illus. by Tasha Tudor. New York: Oxford Univ. Pr., 1947.
134 Poetry, rhyme.

Stevenson, Robert Louis. *A Child's Garden of Verses*. Illus. by Brian Wildsmith. New York: Watts, 1966.
134 Poetry, rhyme.

Stewart, Elizabeth Laing. *The Lion Twins*. Illus. by Marlin Perkins, and Carol Perkins. New York: Atheneum, 1964.
008.10 Animals—cats, wild; 186 Twins.

Stewart, Robert. *The Daddy Book*. Illus. by Don Madden. New York: American Heritage, 1972.
023 Careers; 052.08 Emotions—love; 057.01 Family life—fathers; 121 Non-sexist.

Stiles, Norman, jt. author. *The Sesame Street ABC Storybook*. By Jeffrey Moss; Norman Stiles; and Daniel Wilcox.

Stockum, Van, Hilda. See Van Stockum, Hilda.

Stolz, Mary Slattery. *Emmett's Pig*. Illus. by Garth Montgomery Williams. New York: Harper, 1959.
008.42 Animals—pigs; 018 Birthdays; 058 Farms.

Stone, A. Harris. *The Last Free Bird*. Illus. by Sheila Heins. Englewood Cliffs, NJ: Prentice-Hall, 1967.
017 Birds; 049 Ecology.

Stone, Bernard. *Emergency Mouse*. Illus. by Ralph Steadman. Englewood Cliffs, NJ: Prentice-Hall, 1978.
008.34 Animals—mice; 084 Hospitals.

Stone, Rosetta (pseud.). See Geisel, Theodor Seuss.

Storm, Theodor. *Little John*. Illus. by Anita Lobel. Retold by Doris Orgel. New York: Farrar, 1972.
015 Bedtime; 047 Dreams.

Stover, Jo Ann. *If Everybody Did*. Illus. by author. New York: McKay, 1960.
016 Behavior; 054 Etiquette; 134 Poetry, rhyme.

Stover, Jo Ann. *Why? Because*. Illus. by author. New York: McKay, 1961.
026.28 Character traits—questioning.

Strahl, Rudi. *Sandman in the Lighthouse*. Illus. by Eberhard Binder. Translated and adapted by Anthea Bell. Chicago: Children's Pr., 1967/1969.
015 Bedtime; 101 Lighthouses; 149 Sandman; 153 Sea and seashore.

Straker, Joan Ann. *Animals That Live in the Sea*. Illustrated. Washington, DC: National Geographic Soc., 1979.
153 Sea and seashore.

Stratemeyer, Clara Georgeanna, and Smith, Henry Lee, Jr. *Frog Fun*. Illustrated. New York: Harper, 1963/1967.
005 Amphibians.

Stratemeyer, Clara Georgeanna, and Smith, Henry Lee, Jr. *Pepper*. Illustrated. New York: Harper, 1971.
008 Animals; 008.09 Animals—cats.

Stratemeyer, Clara Georgeanna, and Smith, Henry Lee, Jr. *Tuggy*. Illustrated. New York: Harper, 1971.
005 Amphibians; 008.14 Animals—dogs.

Stroyer, Poul. *It's a Deal*. Illus. by author. New York: Astor-Honor, 1960.
002.15 Activities—trading; 087 Humor.

Stuart, Mary (pseud.). See Graham, Mary Stuart Campbell.

Suba, Susanne. *The Monkeys and the Pedlar*. Illus. by author. New York: Viking, 1970.
008.37 Animals—monkeys; 023.20 Careers—peddlers; 087 Humor.

Sugita, Yutaka. *The Flower Family*. Illus. by author. New York: McGraw-Hill, 1975.
061 Flowers; 133 Plants; 152 Science.

Sugita, Yutaka. *Good Night 1, 2, 3*. Illus. by author. New York: Scroll Pr., 1971.
015 Bedtime; 033 Counting; 162 Sleep.

Sugita, Yutaka. *Helena the Unhappy Hippopotamus*. Illus. by author. New York: McGraw-Hill, 1972.
008.27 Animals—hippopotami; 016.26 Behavior—needing someone; 052.07 Emotions—loneliness; 052.09 Emotions—sadness; 068 Friendship.

Sugita, Yutaka. *My Friend Little John and Me*. Illus. by author. New York: McGraw-Hill, 1972.
008.14 Animals—dogs; 201 Wordless.

Suhl, Yuri. *Simon Boom Gives a Wedding*. Illus. by Margot Zemach. New York: Four Winds Pr., 1972.
038 Cumulative tales; 087 Humor; 093 Jewish culture; 196 Weddings.

Sumiko (pseud.). See Davies, Sumiko.

Sundgaard, Arnold. *Jethro's Difficult Dinosaur*. Illus. by Stanley Mack. New York: Pantheon, 1977.

044 Dinosaurs; 050 Eggs; 087 Humor;
134 Poetry, rhyme.

Supraner, Robyn. *Would You Rather Be a Tiger?* Illus. by Barbara Cooney. Boston: Houghton, 1973.
016 Behavior; 134 Poetry, rhyme;
156 Self-concept.

Supree, Burton, jt. author. *Harlequin and the Gift of Many Colors.* By Remy Charlip, and Burton Supree.

Supree, Burton, jt. author. *"Mother, Mother I Feel Sick."* By Remy Charlip, and Burton Supree.

Surany, Anico. *Kati and Kormos.* Illus. by Leonard Everett Fisher. New York: Holiday, 1966.
008.14 Animals—dogs;
052.07 Emotions—loneliness;
064.15 Foreign lands—Hungary.

Surany, Anico. *Ride the Cold Wind.* Illus. by Leonard Everett Fisher. New York: Putnam's, 1964.
019 Boats, ships; 064.32 Foreign lands—South America; 166.05 Sports—fishing.

Sutton, Eve. *My Cat Likes to Hide in Boxes.* Illus. by Lynley Dodd. New York: Parents, 1973.
008.09 Animals—cats; 038 Cumulative tales; 129 Participation; 134 Poetry, rhyme.

Svendsen, Carol. *Hulda.* Illus. by Julius Svendsen. Boston: Houghton, 1974.
134 Poetry, rhyme; 183 Trolls.

Swayne, Samuel F., and Swayne, Zoa. *Great-Grandfather in the Honey Tree.* Illus. by Zoa Swayne. New York: Viking, 1949.
057.02 Family life—grandparents; great-grandparents.

Swayne, Zoa, jt. author. *Great-Grandfather in the Honey Tree.* By Samuel F. Swayne, and Zoa Swayne.

Swift, Hildegarde Hoyt, and Ward, Lynd Kendall. *The Little Red Lighthouse and the Great Gray Bridge.* Illus. by Lynd Kendall Ward. New York: Harcourt, 1942.
019 Boats, ships; 020 Bridges;
101 Lighthouses.

Szekeres, Cyndy, jt. author. *Here's Pippa Again!* By Betty Boegehold, and Cyndy Szekeres.

Szekeres, Cyndy. *Long Ago.* Illus. by author. New York: McGraw-Hill, 1977.
008 Animals; 189 U.S. history.

Taback, Simms. *Joseph Had a Little Overcoat.* Illus. by author. New York: Random House, 1977.
031 Clothing; 067 Format, unusual.

Tabor, Troy E. *Mother Goose in Hawaii.* Illus. by Lloyd Sexton. Rutland, VT: Tuttle, 1960.
116 Music; 122 Nursery rhymes;
164 Songs.

Taborin, Gloria. *Norman Rockwell's Counting Book.* Illus. by Norman Rockwell. New York: Crown, 1977.
033 Counting.

Talbot, Toby. *A Bucketful of Moon.* Illus. by Imero Gobbato. New York: Lothrop, 1976.
038 Cumulative tales; 087 Humor;
111 Moon.

The Tall Book of Nursery Rhymes. Illus. by Feodor Stepanovich Rojankovsky. New York: Harper, 1944.
062 Folk and fairy tales.

Tallon, Robert. *Handella.* Illus. by author. Indianapolis: Bobbs-Merrill, 1972.
002.04 Activities—dancing; 137 Problem solving; 173 Theater.

Tallon, Robert. *The Thing in Dolores' Piano.* Illus. by author. Indianapolis: Bobbs-Merrill, 1970.
110 Monsters; 116 Music.

Tallon, Robert. *Zag, a Search through the Alphabet.* Illus. by author. New York: Holt, 1976.
001 ABC Books.

Tamburine, Jean. *I Think I Will Go to the Hospital.* Illus. by author. Nashville: Abingdon Pr., 1965.
084 Hospitals.

Taniuchi, Kota. *Trolley.* Illus. by author. New York: Watts, 1969.
022 Cable cars; 089 Imagination.

Taniuchi, Kota. *Up on a Hilltop.* Illus. by author. New York: Watts, 1969.
089 Imagination; 166.03 Sports—bicycling; 179 Trains.

Tapio, Pat Decker. *The Lady Who Saw the Good Side of Everything.* Illus. by Paul Galdone. New York: Seabury Pr., 1975.
002.16 Activities—traveling;

008.09 Animals—cats; 026.23 Character traits—optimism; 052.05 Emotions—happiness; 087 Humor; 195.03 Weather—floods; 195.05 Weather—rain.

Taylor, Mark. *The Bold Fisherman.* Illus. by Graham Charles Booth. Chicago: Children's Pr., 1967.
062 Folk and fairy tales; 116 Music; 153 Sea and seashore; 164 Songs; 166.05 Sports—fishing.

Taylor, Mark. *The Case of the Missing Kittens.* Illus. by Graham Charles Booth. New York: Atheneum, 1978.
008.09 Animals—cats; 008.14 Animals—dogs; 016.20 Behavior—lost.

Taylor, Mark. *Henry Explores the Jungle.* Illus. by Graham Charles Booth. New York: Atheneum, 1968.
008.10 Animals—cats, wild; 026.04 Character traits—bravery; 028 Circus, clowns; 154.03 Seasons—summer.

Taylor, Mark. *Henry Explores the Mountains.* Illus. by Graham Charles Booth. New York: Atheneum, 1975.
026.04 Character traits—bravery; 059 Fire; 080 Helicopters; 154.01 Seasons—fall.

Taylor, Mark. *Henry the Castaway.* Illus. by Graham Charles Booth. New York: Atheneum, 1972.
016.20 Behavior—lost; 019 Boats, ships; 026.04 Character traits—bravery; 154.02 Seasons—spring; 195.05 Weather—rain.

Taylor, Mark. *Henry the Explorer.* Illus. by Graham Charles Booth. New York: Atheneum, 1966.
008.06 Animals—bears; 016.20 Behavior—lost; 026.04 Character traits—bravery; 154.04 Seasons—winter.

Taylor, Mark. *"Lamb," Said the Lion, "I Am Here."* Illus. by Anne Siberell. Chicago: Children's Pr., 1971.
008 Animals; 141 Religion.

Taylor, Mark. *Old Blue, You Good Dog You.* Illus. by Gene Holtan. Chicago: Children's Pr., 1970.
008.14 Animals—dogs; 008.44 Animals—possums; 062 Folk and fairy tales; 068 Friendship; 069 Games; 116 Music; 164 Songs; 125 Old age.

Taylor, Mark. *A Time for Flowers.* Illus. by Graham Charles Booth. Pasadena, CA: Ritchie, 1967.

002.06 Activities—gardening; 026.17 Character traits—kindness; 053.05 Ethnic groups in the U.S.—Japanese-Americans; 057.02 Family life—grandparents; great-grandparents; 133 Plants.

Taylor, Sydney. *The Dog Who Came to Dinner.* Illus. by John E. Johnson. Chicago: Follett, 1966.
008.14 Animals—dogs; 053.01 Ethnic groups in the U.S.—Afro-Americans.

Taylor, Sydney. *Mr. Barney's Beard.* Illus. by Charles Geer. Chicago: Follett, 1962.
017 Birds; 076 Hair.

Taylor, Talus, jt. author. *The Adventures of the Three Colors.* By Annette Tison, and Talus Taylor.

Taylor, Talus, jt. author. *Animal Hide and Seek.* By Annette Tison, and Talus Taylor.

Taylor, Talus, jt. author. *Inside and Outside.* By Annette Tison, and Talus Taylor.

Teal, Valentine. *Angel Child.* Illus. by Pelagie Doane. Skokie, IL: Rand McNally, 1946.
007 Angels.

Teal, Valentine. *The Little Woman Wanted Noise.* Illus. by Robert Lawson. Skokie, IL: Rand McNally, 1943/1967.
034 Country; 058 Farms; 120 Noise; 157 Senses.

Teeth. Illus. by Michael Ricketts. New York: Grosset, 1971.
171 Teeth.

Telephones. Illus. by Christine Sharr. New York: Grosset, 1971.
172 Telephone.

Tensen, Ruth Marjorie. *Come to the Zoo!* Illustrated. Chicago: Contemporary Books, 1948.
008 Animals; 204 Zoos.

Thaler, Mike. *Madge's Magic Show.* Illus. by Carol Nicklaus. New York: Watts, 1978.
103 Magic.

Thaler, Mike. *There's a Hippopotamus under My Bed.* Illus. by Ray Cruz. New York: Watts, 1977.
008.27 Animals—hippopotami.

Thampi, Parvathi, jt. author. *Moon-Uncle, Moon-Uncle.* By Sylvia Cassedy, and Parvathi Thampi.

Thayer, Jane (pseud.). See Wooley, Catherine.

Thelen, Gerda. *The Toy Maker.* Illus. by Fritz Kükenthal. How a tree becomes a toy village, from the original of Gerda Thelen. Retold by Louise F. Encking. Chicago: Albert Whitman, 1935.
177 Toys; 181 Trees.

Thoburn, Tine, jt. author. *A B See.* By Lucille Ogle, and Tine Thoburn.

Thoburn, Tine, jt. author. *I Hear.* By Lucille Ogle, and Tine Thoburn.

Thomas, Anthony. *Things We Cut.* Illus. by G. W. Hales. New York: Watts, 1976.
176 Tools.

Thomas, Anthony. *Things We Hear.* Illus. by G. W. Hales. New York: Watts, 1976.
157 Senses.

Thomas, Anthony. *Things We See.* Illus. by G. W. Hales. New York: Watts, 1976.
157 Senses.

Thomas, Anthony. *Things We Touch.* Illus. by G. W. Hales. New York: Watts, 1976.
157 Senses.

Thomas, Ianthe. *Eliza's Daddy.* Illus. by Moneta Barnett. New York: Harcourt, 1976.
045 Divorce; 053.01 Ethnic groups in the U.S.—Afro-Americans; 057 Family life; 057.01 Family life—fathers.

Thomas, Ianthe. *Lordy, Aunt Hattie.* Illus. by Thomas di Grazia. New York: Harper, 1973.
053.01 Ethnic groups in the U.S.—Afro-Americans; 154.03 Seasons—summer.

Thomas, Ianthe. *Walk Home Tired, Billy Jenkins.* Illus. by Thomas di Grazia. New York: Harper, 1974.
002.18 Activities—walking; 029 City; 053.01 Ethnic groups in the U.S.—Afro-Americans; 089 Imagination.

Thomas, Katherine Elwes. *The Real Personages of Mother Goose.* Illustrated. New York: Lothrop, 1930.
122 Nursery rhymes.

Thomas, Patricia. *"Stand Back," Said the Elephant, "I'm Going to Sneeze."* Illus. by Wallace Tripp. New York: Lothrop, 1971.
008 Animals; 087 Humor; 134 Poetry, rhyme.

Thompson, Brenda, and Overbeck, Cynthia. *The Winds That Blow.* Illus. by Simon Stern, and Rosemary Giesen. Minneapolis: Lerner, 1977.
195.08 Weather—wind.

Thompson, Elizabeth, jt. author. *The True Book of Time.* By Feenie Ziner, and Elizabeth Thompson.

Thompson, Frances B. *Doctor John.* Illus. by James David Johnson. Chicago: Melmont, 1959.
023.09 Careers—doctors.

Thompson, George Selden. *The Mice, the Monks and the Christmas Tree.* Illus. by Jan B. Balet. New York: Macmillan, 1963.
008.34 Animals—mice;
083.03 Holidays—Christmas.

Thompson, George Selden. *Sparrow Socks.* Illus. by Peter Lippman. New York: Harper, 1965.
017.23 Birds—sparrows; 031 Clothing.

Thompson, Harwood. *The Witch's Cat.* Illus. by Quentin Blake. Reading: Addison-Wesley, 1971.
008.09 Animals—cats; 062 Folk and fairy tales; 064.10 Foreign lands—England; 199 Witches.

Thompson, Vivian Laubach. *Camp-in-the-Yard.* Illus. by Brinton Cassady Turkle. New York: Holiday, 1961.
137 Problem solving; 166.04 Sports—camping; 186 Twins.

Thompson, Vivian Laubach. *The Horse That Liked Sandwiches.* Illus. by Aliki Liacouras Brandenberg. New York: Putnam's, 1962.
008.28 Animals—horses; 063 Food.

Thomson, Ruth. *Peabody All at Sea.* Illus. by Ken Kirkwood. New York: Lothrop, 1978.
002.17 Activities—vacationing;
019 Boats, ships; 023.08 Careers—detectives; 036 Crime; 137 Problem solving.

Thomson, Ruth. *Peabody's First Case.* Illus. by Ken Kirkwood. New York: Lothrop, 1978.
023.08 Careers—detectives; 036 Crime; 137 Problem solving.

Thoreau, Henry David. *What Befell at Mrs. Brook's.* Illus. by George Overlie. Minneapolis: Lerner, 1975.
038 Cumulative tales.

The Three Bears. *The Story of the Three Bears.* Illus. by Leonard Leslie Brooke. New York: Warne, 1934.
008.06 Animals—bears; 062 Folk and fairy tales.

The Three Bears. *The Story of the Three Bears.* Illus. by William Stobbs. New York: McGraw-Hill, 1964/1965.

008.06 Animals—bears; 062 Folk and fairy tales.

The Three Bears. Illus. by Paul Galdone. New York: Seabury Pr., 1972.
008.06 Animals—bears; 062 Folk and fairy tales.

The Three Bears. Illus. by Feodor Stepanovich Rojankovsky. Adapted by Kathleen N. Daly. Racine, WI: Western Pub., 1967.
008.06 Animals—bears; 062 Folk and fairy tales.

The Three Bears. Illus. by Irma Wilde. Text by Margaret Hillert. Chicago: Follett, 1963.
008.06 Animals—bears; 062 Folk and fairy tales.

Three Little Pigs. *The Story of the Three Little Pigs.* Illus. by Leonard Leslie Brooke. New York: Warne, 1934.
008.42 Animals—pigs;
008.61 Animals—wolves;
026.06 Character traits—cleverness;
062 Folk and fairy tales.

Three Little Pigs. *The Story of the Three Little Pigs.* Illus. by William Stobbs. New York: McGraw-Hill, 1965.
008.42 Animals—pigs;
008.61 Animals—wolves;
026.06 Character traits—cleverness;
062 Folk and fairy tales.

The Three Little Pigs. Illus. by William Pène Du Bois. Written in verse; author unknown. New York: Viking, 1962.
008.42 Animals—pigs;
008.61 Animals—wolves;
026.06 Character traits—cleverness;
062 Folk and fairy tales.

The Three Little Pigs. Illus. by Paul Galdone. New York: Seabury Pr., 1970.
008.42 Animals—pigs;
008.61 Animals—wolves;
026.06 Character traits—cleverness;
062 Folk and fairy tales.

The Three Little Pigs. Illus. by Irma Wilde. Text by Margaret Hillert. Chicago: Follett, 1963.
008.42 Animals—pigs;
008.61 Animals—wolves;
026.06 Character traits—cleverness;
062 Folk and fairy tales.

Thurber, James. *Many Moons.* Illus. by Louis Slobodkin. New York: Harcourt, 1943.
088 Illness; 092 Jesters; 111 Moon; 147 Royalty.

Thwaite, Ann. *The Day with the Duke.* Illus. by George Him. Cleveland: Collins, 1969.
069 Games.

Tippett, James Sterling. *Counting the Days.* Illus. by Elizabeth Tyler Wolcott. New York: Harper, 1940.
083.03 Holidays—Christmas;
134 Poetry, rhyme.

Tippett, James Sterling. *I Know Some Little Animals.* Illus. by Flora N. De Muth. New York: Harper, 1941.
008 Animals; 090 Insects and spiders;
134 Poetry, rhyme.

Tippett, James Sterling. *Shadow and the Stocking.* Illus. by Morgan Dennis. New York: Harper, 1937.
008.14 Animals—dogs;
083.03 Holidays—Christmas.

Tison, Annette, and Taylor, Talus. *The Adventures of the Three Colors.* Illustrated. Cleveland: Collins, 1971.
032.01 Concepts—color; 067 Format, unusual.

Tison, Annette, and Taylor, Talus. *Animal Hide and Seek.* Illustrated. Cleveland: Collins, 1972.
008 Animals; 067 Format, unusual;
069 Games; 090 Insects and spiders.

Tison, Annette, and Taylor, Talus. *Inside and Outside.* Illustrated. Cleveland: Collins, 1972.
067 Format, unusual; 086 Houses.

Titus, Eve. *Anatole.* Illus. by Paul Galdone. New York: McGraw-Hill, 1956.
008.34 Animals—mice; 064.11 Foreign lands—France.

Titus, Eve. *Anatole and the Cat.* Illus. by Paul Galdone. New York: McGraw-Hill, 1957.
008.09 Animals—cats; 008.34 Animals—mice; 026.04 Character traits—bravery;
064.11 Foreign lands—France;
137 Problem solving.

Titus, Eve. *Anatole and the Piano.* Illus. by Paul Galdone. New York: McGraw-Hill, 1966.
008.34 Animals—mice; 064.11 Foreign lands—France; 116 Music.

Titus, Eve. *Anatole and the Pied Piper.* Illus. by Paul Galdone. New York: McGraw-Hill, 1979.
008.34 Animals—mice; 064.11 Foreign lands—France; 116 Music; 137 Problem solving.

Titus, Eve. *Anatole and the Poodle.* Illus. by Paul Galdone. New York: McGraw-Hill, 1965.
008.14 Animals—dogs;
008.34 Animals—mice; 064.11 Foreign lands—France; 137 Problem solving.

Titus, Eve. *Anatole and the Robot.* Illus. by Paul Galdone. New York: McGraw-Hill, 1960.
008.34 Animals—mice; 064.11 Foreign lands—France; 137 Problem solving; 145 Robots.

Titus, Eve. *Anatole and the Thirty Thieves.* Illus. by Paul Galdone. New York: McGraw-Hill, 1969.
008.34 Animals—mice; 036 Crime; 064.11 Foreign lands—France; 137 Problem solving.

Titus, Eve. *Anatole and the Toyshop.* Illus. by Paul Galdone. New York: McGraw-Hill, 1970.
008.34 Animals—mice; 064.11 Foreign lands—France; 137 Problem solving; 177 Toys.

Titus, Eve. *Anatole in Italy.* Illus. by Paul Galdone. New York: McGraw-Hill, 1973.
008.34 Animals—mice; 064.18 Foreign lands—Italy; 137 Problem solving.

Titus, Eve. *Anatole Over Paris.* Illus. by Paul Galdone. New York: McGraw-Hill, 1961.
002.05 Activities—flying;
008.34 Animals—mice; 064.11 Foreign lands—France; 094 Kites.

Tobias, Tobi. *At the Beach.* Illus. by Gloria Singer. New York: McKay, 1978.
002.17 Activities—vacationing;
057 Family life; 153 Sea and seashore.

Tobias, Tobi. *Chasing the Goblins Away.* Illus. by Victor G. Ambrus. New York: Warne, 1977.
015 Bedtime; 074 Goblins; 119 Night; 162 Sleep.

Tobias, Tobi. *A Day Off.* Illus. by Ray Cruz. New York: Putnam's, 1973.
088 Illness.

Tobias, Tobi. *Jane, Wishing.* Illus. by Trina Schart Hyman. New York: Viking, 1977.
016.38 Behavior—wishing;
052.05 Emotions—happiness;
057 Family life; 087 Humor; 156 Self-concept.

Tobias, Tobi. *Moving Day.* Illus. by William Pène Du Bois. New York: Knopf, 1976.
052 Emotions; 114 Moving;
177.08 Toys—teddy bears.

Tobias, Tobi. *Petey.* Illus. by Symeon Shimin. New York: Putnam's, 1978.
008.19 Animals—gerbils; 040 Death;
052 Emotions; 131 Pets.

Todaro, John, and Ellen, Barbara. *Phillip the Flower-Eating Phoenix.* Illus. by John Todaro. New York: Abelard-Schuman, 1961.
117 Mythical creatures.

Tolstoy, Alekesi Nikolaevich. *The Great Big Enormous Turnip.* Illus. by Helen Oxenbury. New York: Watts, 1968.
038 Cumulative tales; 058 Farms;
062 Folk and fairy tales; 064.30 Foreign lands—Russia; 133 Plants; 137 Problem solving.

Tom Thumb. *Grimm Tom Thumb.* Illus. by Svend Otto. Translated by Anthea Bell. New York: Larousse, 1976.
051 Elves and little people; 062 Folk and fairy tales.

Tom Thumb. Illus. by Leonard Leslie Brooke. New York: Warne, 1904.
051 Elves and little people; 062 Folk and fairy tales.

Tom Thumb. Illus. by Felix Hoffmann. New York: Atheneum, 1973.
051 Elves and little people; 062 Folk and fairy tales.

Tom Thumb. Illus. by William Wiesner. New York: Walck, 1974.
051 Elves and little people; 062 Folk and fairy tales.

Tompert, Ann. *Badger on His Own.* Illus. by Diane de Groat. New York: Crown, 1978.
008.04 Animals—badgers.

Tompert, Ann. *Little Fox Goes to the End of the World.* Illus. by John C. Wallner. New York: Crown, 1976.
008.18 Animals—foxes;
089 Imagination.

Tompert, Ann. *Little Otter Remembers and Other Stories.* Illus. by John C. Wallner. New York: Crown, 1977.
008.40 Animals—otters; 057.03 Family life—mothers.

Towend, Jack. *Railroad ABC.* Illus. by Denison Budd. New York: Watts, 1944.
001 ABC Books; 134 Poetry, rhyme;
179 Trains.

Townsend, Kenneth. *Felix the Bald-Headed Lion.* Illus. by author. New York: Delacorte Pr., 1967.
008.10 Animals—cats, wild;
031 Clothing; 052.02 Emotions—embarrassment; 076 Hair.

Tredez, Alain. See Trez, Alain.

Tredez, Denise. See Trez, Denise.

Trent, Robbie. *The First Christmas.* Illus. by Marc Simont. New York: Harper, 1948.
083.03 Holidays—Christmas;
134 Poetry, rhyme; 141 Religion.

Tresselt, Alvin R. *Autumn Harvest.* Illus. by Roger Antoine Duvoisin. New York: Lothrop, 1951.
083.10 Holidays—Thanksgiving;
154.01 Seasons—fall.

Tresselt, Alvin R. *The Beaver Pond.* Illus. by Roger Antoine Duvoisin. New York: Lothrop, 1970.
008.07 Animals—beavers.

Tresselt, Alvin R. *A Day with Daddy.* Illus. by Helen Heller. New York: Lothrop, 1953.
045 Divorce; 057 Family life;
057.01 Family life—fathers.

Tresselt, Alvin R. *The Dead Tree.* Illus. by Charles Robinson. New York: Parents, 1972.
049 Ecology; 181 Trees.

Tresselt, Alvin R. *Follow the Road.* Illus. by Roger Antoine Duvoisin. New York: Lothrop, 1953.
134 Poetry, rhyme.

Tresselt, Alvin R. *Follow the Wind.* Illus. by Roger Antoine Duvoisin. New York: Lothrop, 1950.
134 Poetry, rhyme; 195.08 Weather—wind.

Tresselt, Alvin R. *The Frog in the Well.* Illus. by Roger Antoine Duvoisin. New York: Lothrop, 1958.
005 Amphibians.

Tresselt, Alvin R. *Hi, Mr. Robin.* Illus. by Roger Antoine Duvoisin. New York: Lothrop, 1950.
154.02 Seasons—spring.

Tresselt, Alvin R. *Hide and Seek Fog.* Illus. by Roger Antoine Duvoisin. New York: Lothrop, 1965.
153 Sea and seashore;
195.04 Weather—fog.

Tresselt, Alvin R. *How Far Is Far?* Illus. by Ward Brackett. New York: Parents, 1964.
032.02 Concepts—distance.

Tresselt, Alvin R. *I Saw the Sea Come In.* Illus. by Roger Antoine Duvoisin. New York: Lothrop, 1954.
016.33 Behavior—solitude; 153 Sea and seashore.

Tresselt, Alvin R. *It's Time Now!* Illus. by Roger Antoine Duvoisin. New York: Lothrop, 1969.
029 City; 154 Seasons.

Tresselt, Alvin R. *Johnny Maple-Leaf.* Illus. by Roger Antoine Duvoisin. New York: Lothrop, 1948.
154 Seasons; 154.01 Seasons—fall;
181 Trees.

Tresselt, Alvin R. *The Little Lost Squirrel.* Illus. by Leonard Weisgard. New York: Grosset, 1951.
008 Animals; 008.56 Animals—squirrels; 016.20 Behavior—lost;
066 Forest, woods.

Tresselt, Alvin R. *The Mitten.* Illus. by Yaroslava Surmach Mills. Adapted by Alvin Tresselt from the version by E. Rachev. New York: Lothrop, 1964.
008 Animals; 062 Folk and fairy tales;
064.40 Foreign lands—Ukraine.

Tresselt, Alvin R. *The Rabbit Story.* Illus. by Leonard Weisgard. New York: Lothrop, 1957.
008.46 Animals—rabbits.

Tresselt, Alvin R. *Rain Drop Splash.* Illus. by Leonard Weisgard. New York: Lothrop, 1946.
038 Cumulative tales; 152 Science;
195.05 Weather—rain.

Tresselt, Alvin R. *The Smallest Elephant in the World.* Illus. by Milton Glaser. New York: Knopf, 1959.
008.17 Animals—elephants;
026.31 Character traits—smallness;
028 Circus, clowns.

Tresselt, Alvin R. *Sun Up.* Illus. by Roger Antoine Duvoisin. New York: Lothrop, 1949.
058 Farms; 169 Sun; 195 Weather.

Tresselt, Alvin R. *A Thousand Lights and Fireflies.* Illus. by John Moodie. New York: Parents, 1965.
029 City; 034 Country.

Tresselt, Alvin R. *Wake Up, City!* Illus. by Roger Antoine Duvoisin. New York: Lothrop, 1957.
029 City; 112 Morning.

Tresselt, Alvin R. *Wake Up, Farm!* Illus. by Roger Antoine Duvoisin. New York: Lothrop, 1957.
008 Animals; 058 Farms; 112 Morning.

Tresselt, Alvin R. *What Did You Leave Behind?* Illus. by Roger Antoine Duvoisin. New York: Lothrop, 1978.
052 Emotions.

Tresselt, Alvin R. *White Snow, Bright Snow.* Illus. by Roger Antoine Duvoisin. New York: Lothrop, 1947.
154.04 Seasons—winter;
195.07 Weather—snow.

Tresselt, Alvin R. *The Wind and Peter.* Illus. by Garry McKenzie. New York: Oxford Univ. Pr., 1948.
195.08 Weather—wind.

Tresselt, Alvin R. *The World in the Candy Egg.* Illus. by Roger Antoine Duvoisin. New York: Lothrop, 1967.
050 Eggs; 083.04 Holidays—Easter;
103 Magic.

Trez, Alain, jt. author. *Good Night, Veronica.* By Denise Trez, and Alain Trez.

Trez, Alain, jt. author. *The Little Knight's Dragon.* By Denise Trez, and Alain Trez.

Trez, Alain, jt. author. *Maila and the Flying Carpet.* By Denise Trez, and Alain Trez.

Trez, Alain, jt. author. *Rabbit Country.* By Denise Trez, and Alain Trez.

Trez, Alain, jt. author. *The Royal Hiccups.* By Denise Trez, and Alain Trez.

Trez, Denise, and Trez, Alain. *Good Night, Veronica.* Illus. by authors. Translated by Douglas McKee. New York: Viking, 1968.
015 Bedtime; 047 Dreams; 162 Sleep.

Trez, Denise, and Trez, Alain. *The Little Knight's Dragon.* Illus. by authors. Cleveland: Collins, 1963.
046 Dragons; 095 Knights.

Trez, Denise, and Trez, Alain. *Maila and the Flying Carpet.* Illus. by authors. New York: Viking, 1969.
002.05 Activities—flying; 064.16 Foreign lands—India; 103 Magic; 147 Royalty.

Trez, Denise, and Trez, Alain. *Rabbit Country.* Illus. by authors. New York: Viking, 1966.
008.46 Animals—rabbits.

Trez, Denise, and Trez, Alain. *The Royal Hiccups.* Illus. by authors. New York: Viking, 1965.
052.04 Emotions—fear; 088 Illness;
147 Royalty.

Trimby, Elisa. *Mr. Plum's Paradise.* Illus. by author. New York: Lothrop, 1977.
002.06 Activities—gardening; 029 City.

Tripp, Edward. *The Tin Fiddle.* Illus. by Maurice Sendak. New York: Oxford Univ. Pr., 1954.
120 Noise.

Tripp, Paul. *The Strawman Who Smiled by Mistake.* Illus. by Wendy Watson. Garden City, NY: Doubleday, 1967.
052.05 Emotions—happiness;
058 Farms; 068 Friendship;
150 Scarecrows.

Tripp, Wallace. *A Great Big Ugly Man Came Up and Tied His Horse to Me.* Illus. by author. Boston: Little, 1973.
087 Humor; 134 Poetry, rhyme.

Tripp, Wallace. *My Uncle Podger.* Illus. by author. Boston: Little, 1975.
008.46 Animals—rabbits; 087 Humor.

Tripp, Wallace. *The Tale of a Pig.* Illus. by author. New York: McGraw-Hill, 1968.
008.42 Animals—pigs; 062 Folk and fairy tales.

True, Louise. *Number Men.* Illus. by Lillian Owens. Chicago: Children's Pr., 1948.
033 Counting; 134 Poetry, rhyme.

Tucker, Nicholas, comp. *Mother Goose Abroad.* Illus. by Trevor Stubley. New York: Crowell, 1974.
122 Nursery rhymes.

Tucker, Nicholas, comp. *Mother Goose Lost; Nursery Rhymes.* Illus. by Trevor Stubley. New York: Crowell, 1971.
122 Nursery rhymes.

Tudor, Bethany. *Samuel's Tree House.* Illus. by author. Cleveland: Collins, 1979.
017.08 Birds—ducks; 086 Houses;
177 Toys; 181 Trees.

Tudor, Bethany. *Skiddycock Pond.* Illus. by author. Philadelphia: Lippincott, 1965.
017.08 Birds—ducks; 019 Boats, ships.

Tudor, Tasha. *A Is for Annabelle.* Illus. by author. New York: Walck, 1954.
001 ABC Books; 177.04 Toys—dolls.

Tudor, Tasha. *Around the Year.* Illus. by author. New York: Walck, 1957.
039 Days of the week, months of the year; 134 Poetry, rhyme; 154 Seasons.

Tudor, Tasha. *Corgiville Fair.* Illus. by author. New York: Crowell, 1971.
008.21 Animals—goats; 056 Fairs;
183 Trolls.

Tudor, Tasha. *The Doll's Christmas.* Illus. by author. New York: Oxford Univ. Pr., 1950.
083.03 Holidays—Christmas;
177.04 Toys—dolls.

Tudor, Tasha. *1 Is One.* Illus. by author. New York: Walck, 1956.
033 Counting.

Tudor, Tasha. *Snow Before Christmas*. Illus. by author. New York: Oxford Univ. Pr., 1941.
083.03 Holidays—Christmas;
154.04 Seasons—winter;
195.07 Weather—snow.

Tudor, Tasha. *A Tale for Easter*. Illus. by author. New York: Oxford Univ. Pr., 1941.
083.04 Holidays—Easter.

Tudor, Tasha. *Thistly B*. Illus. by author. New York: Oxford Univ. Pr., 1949.
017.03 Birds—canaries; 177 Toys.

Tudor, Tasha. *The White Goose*. Illus. by author. New York: Oxford Univ. Pr., 1943.
017.08 Birds—ducks.

Turkle, Brinton Cassady. *The Adventures of Obadiah*. Illus. by author. New York: Viking, 1972.
016.21 Behavior—lying;
026.15 Character traits—honesty;
189 U.S. history.

Turkle, Brinton Cassady. *Deep in the Forest*. Illus. by author. New York: Dutton, 1976.
008.06 Animals—bears; 062 Folk and fairy tales; 201 Wordless.

Turkle, Brinton Cassady. *It's Only Arnold*. Illus. by author. New York: Viking, 1973.
052.04 Emotions—fear; 057.02 Family life—grandparents; great-grandparents.

Turkle, Brinton Cassady. *The Magic of Millicent Musgrave*. Illus. by author. New York: Viking, 1967.
103 Magic.

Turkle, Brinton Cassady. *Obadiah the Bold*. Illus. by author. New York: Viking, 1965.
016.14 Behavior—growing up; 153 Sea and seashore; 189 U.S. history.

Turkle, Brinton Cassady. *Rachel and Obadiah*. Illus. by author. New York: Dutton, 1978.
016.31 Behavior—sharing;
016.32 Behavior—sibling rivalry;
109 Money.

Turkle, Brinton Cassady. *The Sky Dog*. Illus. by author. New York: Viking, 1969.
008.14 Animals—dogs; 153 Sea and seashore; 195.01 Weather—clouds.

Turkle, Brinton Cassady. *Thy Friend, Obadiah*. Illus. by author. New York: Viking, 1969.
017.22 Birds—sea gulls;
026.18 Character traits—kindness to animals; 154.04 Seasons—winter;
189 U.S. history.

Turner, Nancy Byrd. *When It Rains Cats and Dogs*. Illus. by Tibor Gergely. Philadelphia: Lippincott, 1946.
008.09 Animals—cats; 008.14 Animals—dogs; 087 Humor; 134 Poetry, rhyme;
195.05 Weather—rain.

Turska, Krystyna. *The Magician of Cracow*. Illus. by author. New York: Greenwillow, 1975.
026.01 Character traits—ambition;
042 Devil; 062 Folk and fairy tales;
064.27 Foreign lands—Poland;
103 Magic; 111 Moon.

Turska, Krystyna. *The Woodcutter's Duck*. Illus. by author. New York: Macmillan, 1972.
017.08 Birds—ducks; 062 Folk and fairy tales; 064.27 Foreign lands—Poland.

Tutt, Kay Cunningham. *And Now We Call Him Santa Claus*. Illus. by author. New York: Lothrop, 1963.
083.03 Holidays—Christmas.

Twelve Days of Christmas (English folk song). *Brian Wildsmith's The Twelve Days of Christmas*. Illus. by Brian Wildsmith. New York: Watts, 1972.
038 Cumulative tales; 083.03 Holidays—Christmas; 116 Music; 164 Songs.

Twelve Days of Christmas (English folk song). *Jack Kent's Twelve Days of Christmas*. Illus. by Jack Kent. New York: Parents, 1978.
038 Cumulative tales; 083.03 Holidays—Christmas; 087 Humor; 116 Music;
164 Songs.

The Twelve Days of Christmas. Illus. by Ilonka Karasz. New York: Harper, 1949.
038 Cumulative tales; 083.03 Holidays—Christmas; 116 Music; 164 Songs.

Tworkov, Jack. *The Camel Who Took a Walk*. Illus. by Roger Antoine Duvoisin. New York: Atheneum, 1951.
002.18 Activities—walking;
008 Animals; 008.08 Animals—camels;
008.10 Animals—cats, wild;
038 Cumulative tales; 112 Morning.

Uchida, Yoshiko. *The Rooster Who Understood Japanese*. Illus. by Charles Robinson. New York: Scribner's, 1976.
008 Animals; 017.04 Birds—chickens;
065 Foreign languages.

Uchida, Yoshiko. *Sumi's Prize*. Illus. by Kazue Mizumura. New York: Scribner's,
1964.
026.01 Character traits—ambition;
064.19 Foreign lands—Japan; 094 Kites.

Uchida, Yoshiko. *Sumi's Special Happening*.
Illus. by Kazue Mizumura. New York:
Scribner's, 1966.
018 Birthdays; 064.19 Foreign lands—
Japan; 125 Old age.

Udry, Janice May. *Alfred*. Illus. by Judith S.
Roth. Chicago: Albert Whitman, 1960.
008.14 Animals—dogs;
016.01 Behavior—animals, dislike of;
052.04 Emotions—fear.

Udry, Janice May. *Emily's Autumn*. Illus. by
Erik Blegvad. Chicago: Albert Whitman,
1969.
154.01 Seasons—fall; 177.04 Toys—
dolls.

Udry, Janice May. *How I Faded Away*. Illus.
by Monica De Bruyn. Chicago: Albert
Whitman, 1976.
016.37 Behavior—unnoticed, unseen;
052.02 Emotions—embarrassment;
156 Self-concept.

Udry, Janice May. *Is Susan Here?* Illus. by
Peter Edwards. New York: Abelard-
Schuman, 1962.
008 Animals; 026.14 Character traits—
helpfulness; 057.03 Family life—
mothers; 089 Imagination.

Udry, Janice May. *Let's Be Enemies*. Illus. by
Maurice Sendak. New York: Harper,
1961.
016.10 Behavior—fighting, arguing;
052.06 Emotions—hate; 068 Friendship.

Udry, Janice May. *Mary Ann's Mud Day*. Illus.
by Martha G. Alexander. New York:
Harper, 1967.
002.12 Activities—playing;
053.01 Ethnic groups in the U.S.—Afro-
Americans.

Udry, Janice May. *Mary Jo's Grandmother*. Illus. by Eleanor Mill. Chicago: Albert
Whitman, 1970.
053.01 Ethnic groups in the U.S.—Afro-
Americans; 057.02 Family life—
grandparents; great-grandparents;
088 Illness; 121 Non-sexist;
154.04 Seasons—winter;
195.07 Weather—snow.

Udry, Janice May. *The Mean Mouse and Other
Mean Stories*. Illus. by Ed Young. New
York: Harper, 1962.
026.22 Character traits—meanness.

Udry, Janice May. *The Moon Jumpers*. Illus.
by Maurice Sendak. New York: Harper,
1959.
111 Moon; 185 Twilight.

Udry, Janice May. *"Oh No, Cat!"* Illus. by
Mary Eileen Chalmers. New York: Coward, 1976.
008.09 Animals—cats.

Udry, Janice May. *Theodore's Parents*. Illus.
by Adrienne Adams. New York: Lothrop,
1958.
003 Adoption; 057 Family life.

Udry, Janice May. *A Tree Is Nice*. Illus. by
Marc Simont. New York: Harper, 1956.
134 Poetry, rhyme; 154 Seasons;
181 Trees.

Udry, Janice May. *What Mary Jo Shared*. Illus.
by Eleanor Mill. Chicago: Albert Whitman, 1966.
026.30 Character traits—shyness;
053.01 Ethnic groups in the U.S.—Afro-
Americans; 053.07 Ethnic groups in the
U.S.—Multi-ethnic; 057.01 Family life—
fathers; 151 School.

Udry, Janice May. *What Mary Jo Wanted*. Illus. by Eleanor Mill. Chicago: Albert
Whitman, 1968.
008.14 Animals—dogs; 053.01 Ethnic
groups in the U.S.—Afro-Americans;
057 Family life.

Ueno, Noriko. *Elephant Buttons*. Illus. by author. New York: Harper, 1973.
008 Animals; 032.03 Concepts—in and
out; 032.08 Concepts—size;
038 Cumulative tales; 069 Games;
087 Humor; 129 Participation;
201 Wordless.

Ungerer, Tomi. *Adelaide*. Illus. by author.
New York: Harper, 1959.
002.16 Activities—traveling;
008.30 Animals—kangaroos; 059 Fire;
064.11 Foreign lands—France.

Ungerer, Tomi. *The Beast of Monsieur Racine*.
Illus. by author. New York: Farrar, 1971.
016.36 Behavior—trickery;
064.11 Foreign lands—France;
087 Humor; 110 Monsters.

Ungerer, Tomi. *Christmas Eve at the Mellops'*.
Illus. by author. New York: Harper,
1960. ·
008.42 Animals—pigs;
083.03 Holidays—Christmas.

Ungerer, Tomi. *Crictor*. Illus. by author. New York: Harper, 1958.
087 Humor; 142.04 Reptiles—snakes.

Ungerer, Tomi. *Emile*. Illus. by author. New York: Harper, 1960.
087 Humor; 123 Octopod.

Ungerer, Tomi. *The Hat*. Illus. by author. New York: Parents, 1970.
031 Clothing; 064.18 Foreign lands— Italy; 103 Magic; 195.08 Weather— wind.

Ungerer, Tomi. *The Mellops Go Diving for Treasure*. Illus. by author. New York: Harper, 1957.
008.42 Animals—pigs; 153 Sea and seashore; 166.13 Sports—skin diving.

Ungerer, Tomi. *The Mellops Go Flying*. Illus. by author. New York: Harper, 1957.
002.05 Activities—flying; 004 Airplanes; 008.42 Animals—pigs.

Ungerer, Tomi. *The Mellops Go Spelunking*. Illus. by author. New York: Harper, 1963.
008.42 Animals—pigs; 025 Caves; 026.25 Character traits—perseverance.

Ungerer, Tomi. *The Mellops Strike Oil*. Illus. by author. New York: Harper, 1958.
008.42 Animals—pigs; 059 Fire; 124 Oil.

Ungerer, Tomi. *Moon Man*. Illus. by author. New York: Harper, 1967.
111 Moon; 165 Space and space ships.

Ungerer, Tomi. *No Kiss for Mother*. Illus. by author. New York: Harper, 1973.
008.09 Animals—cats.

Ungerer, Tomi. *One, Two, Where's My Shoe?* Illus. by author. New York: Harper, 1964.
069 Games; 201 Wordless.

Ungerer, Tomi. *Orlando the Brave Vulture*. Illus. by author. New York: Harper, 1966.
017.27 Birds—vultures; 041 Desert.

Ungerer, Tomi. *Rufus*. Illus. by author. New York: Harper, 1961.
008.05 Animals—bats.

Ungerer, Tomi. *Snail Where Are You?* Illus. by author. New York: Harper, 1962.
008.55 Animals—snails; 069 Games; 201 Wordless.

Ungerer, Tomi, jt. author. *The Sorcerer's Apprentice*. By Barbara Shook Hazen, and Tomi Ungerer.

Ungerer, Tomi. *The Three Robbers*. Illus. by author. New York: Atheneum, 1962.
036 Crime; 127 Orphans.

Ungerer, Tomi. *Zeralda's Ogre*. Illus. by author. New York: Harper, 1967.
002.03 Activities—cooking; 026.17 Character traits—kindness; 072 Giants; 110 Monsters.

Unteracker, John. *The Dreaming Zoo*. Illus. by George Weinheimer. New York: Walck, 1965.
008 Animals; 016.38 Behavior—wishing; 047 Dreams; 204 Zoos.

Untermeyer, Louis. *The Kitten Who Barked*. Illus. by Lilian Obligado. Racine, WI: Western Pub., 1962.
008.09 Animals—cats; 008.14 Animals— dogs.

Unwin, Nora Spicer. *Poquito, the Little Mexican Duck*. Illus. by author. New York: McKay, 1959.
017.08 Birds—ducks; 064.24 Foreign lands—Mexico.

Ushinsky, Konstantin. *How a Shirt Grew in the Field*. Illus. by Yaroslava Surmach Mills. Adapted by Marguerita Rudolph. New York: McGraw-Hill, 1967.
031 Clothing; 064.40 Foreign lands— Ukraine; 133 Plants.

Uyeda, Frances, jt. author. *Chocho Is for Butterfly*. By Jeannie Sasaki, and Frances Uyeda.

Vacheron, Edith, and Kahl, Virginia Caroline. *Here Is Henri!* Illus. by Virginia Caroline Kahl. New York: Scribner's, 1959.
008.09 Animals—cats; 064.11 Foreign lands—France; 065 Foreign languages.

Vacheron, Edith, and Kahl, Virginia Caroline. *More about Henri!* Illus. by Virginia Caroline Kahl. New York: Scribner's, 1961.
008.09 Animals—cats; 064.11 Foreign lands—France; 065 Foreign languages.

Valens, Evans G. *Wingfin and Topple*. Illus. by Clement Hurd. Cleveland: Collins, 1962.
002.05 Activities—flying; 060 Fish.

Valentine, Ursula, translator. *Herr Minkipatt and His Friends*. Illus. by Josef Wilkon. New York: Braziller, 1965.
017 Birds.

Vance, Eleanor Graham, comp. *From Little to Big; A Parade of Animal Poems*. Illus. by June Goldsborough. Chicago: Follett, 1972.
008 Animals; 134 Poetry, rhyme.

Vance, Eleanor Graham. *Jonathan*. Illus. by Albert John Pucci. Chicago: Follett, 1966.
026.28 Character traits—questioning; 134 Poetry, rhyme; 195 Weather.

Van Den Honert, Dorry. *Demi the Baby Sitter*. Illus. by Meg Wohlberg. New York: Morrow, 1961.
002.01 Activities—babysitting; 008.14 Animals—dogs.

Vandivert, Rita. *Barnaby*. Illus. by William Vandivert. New York: Dodd, 1963.
008.31 Animals—kinkajous; 131 Pets.

Van Horn, Grace. *Little Red Rooster*. Illus. by Sheila Perry. New York: Abelard-Schuman, 1961.
017.04 Birds—chickens; 058 Farms.

Van Stockum, Hilda. *Day on Skates*. Illus. by author. New York: Viking, 1934.
002.11 Activities—picnicking; 064.14 Foreign lands—Holland; 166.09 Sports—ice skating.

Van Woerkom, Dorothy O. *Abu Ali*. Illus. by Harold Berson. New York: Macmillan, 1976.
064.09 Foreign lands—Egypt; 064.16 Foreign lands—India; 087 Humor.

Van Woerkom, Dorothy O. *Becky and the Bear*. Illus. by Margot Ladd Tomes. New York: Putnam's, 1975.
008.06 Animals—bears; 026.04 Character traits—bravery; 121 Non-sexist; 189 U.S. history.

Van Woerkom, Dorothy O. *Donkey Ysabel*. Illus. by Normand Chartier. New York: Macmillan, 1978.
008.16 Animals—donkeys; 087 Humor.

Van Woerkom, Dorothy O. *The Friends of Abu Ali*. Illus. by Harold Berson. New York: Macmillan, 1978.
064.16 Foreign lands—India; 087 Humor.

Van Woerkom, Dorothy O. *Harry and Shellburt*. Illus. by Erick Ingraham. New York: Macmillan, 1977.
008.46 Animals—rabbits; 142.05 Reptiles—turtles; 166.11 Sports—racing.

Van Woerkom, Dorothy O. *The Queen Who Couldn't Bake Gingerbread*. Illus. by Paul Galdone. New York: Knopf, 1975.
062 Folk and fairy tales; 064.12 Foreign lands—Germany; 087 Humor; 121 Non-sexist; 147 Royalty.

Van Woerkom, Dorothy O. *The Rat, the Ox and the Zodiac*. Illus. by Errol Le Cain. New York: Crown, 1976.
008 Animals; 008.48 Animals—rats; 026.06 Character traits—cleverness; 062 Folk and fairy tales; 064.06 Foreign lands—China; 203 Zodiac.

Van Woerkom, Dorothy O. *Sea Frog, City Frog*. Illus. by José Aruego. New York: Macmillan, 1975.
005 Amphibians; 062 Folk and fairy tales; 064.19 Foreign lands—Japan.

Van Woerkom, Dorothy O. *Tit for Tat*. Illus. by Douglas Florian. New York: Greenwillow, 1977.
062 Folk and fairy tales.

Varga, Judy. *Circus Cannonball*. Illus. by author. New York: Morrow, 1975.
028 Circus, clowns.

Varga, Judy. *The Dragon Who Liked to Spit Fire*. Illus. by author. New York: Morrow, 1961.
046 Dragons; 147 Royalty.

Varga, Judy. *Janko's Wish*. Illus. by author. New York: Morrow, 1969.
016.38 Behavior—wishing; 064.15 Foreign lands—Hungary; 103 Magic; 196 Weddings.

Varga, Judy. *The Mare's Egg*. Illus. by author. New York: Morrow, 1972.
008.18 Animals—foxes; 016.36 Behavior—trickery; 062 Folk and fairy tales; 064.30 Foreign lands—Russia.

Varga, Judy. *Miss Lollipop's Lion*. Illus. by author. New York: Morrow, 1963.
008.10 Animals—cats, wild; 028 Circus, clowns; 131 Pets.

Varga, Judy. *The Monster Behind Black Rock*. Illus. by author. New York: Morrow, 1971.
008 Animals; 016.12 Behavior—gossip; 038 Cumulative tales.

Varga, Judy. *Pig in the Parlor*. Illus. by author. New York: Morrow, 1963.
008.42 Animals—pigs; 131 Pets.

Varley, Dimitry. *The Whirly Bird*. Illus. by
Feodor Stepanovich Rojankovsky. New
York: Knopf, 1961.
017 Birds; 026.18 Character traits—
kindness to animals.

Vasiliu, Marcea. *A Day at the Beach*. Illus. by
author. New York: Random House,
1977.
153 Sea and seashore.

Vasiliu, Marcea. *Everything Is Somewhere*. Illus. by author. Scranton, PA: John Day,
1959.
141 Religion.

Vasiliu, Marcea. *What's Happening?* Illus. by
author. Scranton, PA: John Day, 1970.
002 Activities; 029 City.

Vassel, Matthew F., jt. author. *My Goldfish*.
By Herbert H. Wong, and Matthew F.
Vassel.

Vassel, Matthew F., jt. author. *My Ladybug*.
By Herbert H. Wong, and Matthew F.
Vassel.

Vassel, Matthew F., jt. author. *My Plant*. By
Herbert H. Wong, and Matthew F. Vassel.

Vassel, Matthew F., jt. author. *Our Caterpillars*. By Herbert H. Wong, and Matthew
F. Vassel.

Vassel, Matthew F., jt. author. *Our Earthworms*. By Herbert H. Wong, and Matthew F. Vassel.

Vassel, Matthew F., jt. author. *Our Terrariums*. By Herbert H. Wong, and Matthew
F. Vassel.

Vassel, Matthew F., jt. author. *Our Tree*. By
Herbert H. Wong, and Matthew F. Vassel.

Velthuijs, Max. *The Painter and the Bird*. Illus.
by author. Translated by Ray Broekel.
Reading: Addison-Wesley, 1975.
017 Birds; 023.02 Careers—artists;
089 Imagination.

Venable, Alan. *The Checker Players*. Illus. by
Byron Barton. Philadelphia: Lippincott,
1973.
008.06 Animals—bears;
016.10 Behavior—fighting, arguing;
019 Boats, ships; 068 Friendship;
069 Games; 142.01 Reptiles—alligators,
crocodiles.

Ventura, Marisa, jt. author. *The Painter's
Trick*. By Piero Ventura, and Marisa Ventura.

Ventura, Piero, and Ventura, Marisa. *The
Painter's Trick*. Illus. by Marisa Ventura.
New York: Random House, 1977.
023.02 Careers—artists.

Vigna, Judith. *Couldn't We Have a Turtle Instead?* Illus. by author. Chicago: Albert
Whitman, 1975.
008 Animals; 013 Babies;
052.03 Emotions—envy, jealousy;
057 Family life; 057.03 Family life—
mothers.

Vigna, Judith. *Everyone Goes as a Pumpkin*.
Illus. by author. Chicago: Albert Whitman, 1977.
057.02 Family life—grandparents;
great-grandparents; 083.07 Holidays—
Halloween.

Villarejo, Mary. *The Art Fair*. Illus. by author.
New York: Knopf, 1960.
011 Art.

Villarejo, Mary. *The Tiger Hunt*. Illus. by author. New York: Knopf, 1959.
002.10 Activities—photographing;
008 Animals; 008.10 Animals—cats,
wild.

Vinson, Pauline. *Willie Goes to School*. Illus.
by author. New York: Macmillan, 1953.
008.34 Animals—mice; 151 School.

Vinson, Pauline. *Willie Goes to the Seashore*.
Illus. by author. New York: Macmillan,
1954.
008.34 Animals—mice; 153 Sea and
seashore.

Vinton, Iris. *Look Out for Pirates!* Illus. by
Herman B. Vestal. New York: Random
House, 1961.
019 Boats, ships; 132 Pirates.

Viorst, Judith. *Alexander and the Terrible, Horrible, No Good, Very Bad Day*. Illus. by Ray
Cruz. New York: Atheneum, 1972.
016.02 Behavior—bad day; 057 Family
life.

Viorst, Judith. *Alexander, Who Used to Be Rich
Last Sunday*. Illus. by Ray Cruz. New
York: Atheneum, 1978.
109 Money.

Viorst, Judith. *I'll Fix Anthony!* Illus. by Arnold Stark Lobel. New York: Harper,
1969.
016.32 Behavior—sibling rivalry;
057 Family life.

Viorst, Judith. *My Mama Says There Aren't Any: Zombies, Ghosts, Vampires, Creatures, Demons, Monsters, Fiends, Goblins, or Things.* Illus. by Kay Chorao. New York: Atheneum, 1973.
015 Bedtime; 052.04 Emotions—fear; 057.03 Family life—mothers; 089 Imagination; 110 Monsters.

Viorst, Judith. *Rosie and Michael.* Illus. by Lorna Tomei. New York: Atheneum, 1974.
068 Friendship.

Viorst, Judith. *Sunday Morning.* Illus. by Hilary Knight. New York: Harper, 1968.
002.12 Activities—playing; 057 Family life; 087 Humor.

Viorst, Judith. *The Tenth Good Thing about Barney.* Illus. by Erik Blegvad. New York: Atheneum, 1971.
008.09 Animals—cats; 040 Death; 023.09 Careers—doctors; 131 Pets.

Viorst, Judith. *Try It Again, Sam.* Illus. by Paul Galdone. New York: Lothrop, 1970.
002.18 Activities—walking; 026.16 Character traits—individuality; 148 Safety.

Vogel, Ilse-Margret. *The Don't Be Scared Book.* Illus. by author. New York: Atheneum, 1964.
052.04 Emotions—fear; 089 Imagination; 134 Poetry, rhyme.

Vogel, Ilse-Margret. *One Is No Fun but 20 Is Plenty.* Illus. by author. New York: Atheneum, 1965.
008 Animals; 033 Counting; 134 Poetry, rhyme.

Von Hippel, Ursula. *The Craziest Halloween.* Illus. by author. New York: Coward, 1957.
083.07 Holidays—Halloween.

Von Jüchen, Aurel. See Jüchen, Aurel von.

Von Schmidt, Eric. See Schmidt, Eric von.

Vorse, Mary Ellen. *Skinny Gets Fat.* Illus. by Inez Hogan. Reading: Addison-Wesley, 1940.
008 Animals; 063 Food.

Vorse, Mary Ellen. *Wakey Goes to Bed.* Illus. by Inez Hogan. Reading: Addison-Wesley, 1941.
008 Animals; 015 Bedtime; 162 Sleep.

Vreeken, Elizabeth. *The Boy Who Would Not Say His Name.* Illus. by Leonard W. Shortall. Chicago: Follett, 1959.
016.20 Behavior—lost; 023.21 Careers—police officers; 089 Imagination; 118 Names.

Vreeken, Elizabeth. *Henry.* Illus. by Polly Jackson. Chicago: Follett, 1961.
008.34 Animals—mice; 131 Pets.

Vreeken, Elizabeth. *One Day Everything Went Wrong.* Illus. by Leonard W. Shortall. Chicago: Follett, 1966.
016.02 Behavior—bad day.

Waber, Bernard. *An Anteater Named Arthur.* Illus. by author. Boston: Houghton, 1967.
001 ABC Books; 008.01 Animals—anteaters.

Waber, Bernard. *But Names Will Never Hurt Me.* Illus. by author. Boston: Houghton, 1976.
118 Names.

Waber, Bernard. *A Firefly Named Torchy.* Illus. by author. Boston: Houghton, 1970.
090 Insects and spiders.

Waber, Bernard. *Good-Bye, Funny Dumpy-Lumpy.* Illus. by author. Boston: Houghton, 1977.
008.09 Animals—cats; 057 Family life.

Waber, Bernard. *The House on 88th Street.* Illus. by author. Boston: Houghton, 1962.
068 Friendship; 142.01 Reptiles—alligators, crocodiles.

Waber, Bernard. *How to Go about Laying an Egg.* Illus. by author. Boston: Houghton, 1963.
017.04 Birds—chickens; 050 Eggs; 087 Humor.

Waber, Bernard. *I Was All Thumbs.* Illus. by author. Boston: Houghton, 1975.
123 Octopod; 153 Sea and seashore.

Waber, Bernard. *Ira Sleeps Over.* Illus. by author. Boston: Houghton, 1972.
002.12 Activities—playing; 015 Bedtime; 068 Friendship; 162 Sleep; 177.08 Toys—teddy bears.

Waber, Bernard. *Just Like Abraham Lincoln.* Illus. by author. Boston: Houghton, 1964.
189 U.S. history.

Waber, Bernard. *Lorenzo.* Illus. by author. Boston: Houghton, 1961.
026.10 Character traits—curiosity; 060 Fish.

Waber, Bernard. *Lovable Lyle*. Illus. by author. Boston: Houghton, 1969.
068 Friendship; 142.01 Reptiles—alligators, crocodiles.

Waber, Bernard. *Lyle and the Birthday Party*. Illus. by author. Boston: Houghton, 1966.
018 Birthdays; 052.03 Emotions—envy, jealousy; 084 Hospitals;
142.01 Reptiles—alligators, crocodiles.

Waber, Bernard. *Lyle Finds His Mother*. Illus. by author. Boston: Houghton, 1974.
057.03 Family life—mothers;
142.01 Reptiles—alligators, crocodiles.

Waber, Bernard. *Lyle, Lyle Crocodile*. Illus. by author. Boston: Houghton, 1965.
026.14 Character traits—helpfulness;
142.01 Reptiles—alligators, crocodiles.

Waber, Bernard. *Mice on My Mind*. Illus. by author. Boston: Houghton, 1977.
008.09 Animals—cats; 008.34 Animals—mice.

Waber, Bernard. *Nobody Is Perfick*. Illus. by author. Boston: Houghton, 1971.
016.23 Behavior—mistakes; 087 Humor.

Waber, Bernard. *Rich Cat, Poor Cat*. Illus. by author. Boston: Houghton, 1963.
008.09 Animals—cats.

Waber, Bernard. *A Rose for Mr. Bloom*. Illus. by author. Boston: Houghton, 1968.
061 Flowers; 087 Humor.

Waber, Bernard. *The Snake, a Very Long Story*. Illus. by author. Boston: Houghton, 1978.
067 Format, unusual; 142.04 Reptiles—snakes.

Waber, Bernard. *"You Look Ridiculous," Said the Rhinoceros to the Hippopotamus*. Illus. by author. Boston: Houghton, 1966.
008 Animals; 008.27 Animals—hippopotami; 026.16 Character traits—individuality; 087 Humor; 156 Self-concept.

Waddell, Helen Jane. *The Story of Saul the King*. Illus. by Doreen Roberts. Abridged by Elaine Moss from Helen Waddell's *Stories from Holy Writ*. Port Washington, NY: White, 1966.
141 Religion.

Wagner, Jenny. *Aranea*. Illus. by Ronald George Brooks. New York: Bradbury Pr., 1975/1978.
090 Insects and spiders;
195.05 Weather—rain.

Wagner, Jenny. *The Bunyip of Berkeley's Creek*. Illus. by Ronald George Brooks. New York: Bradbury Pr., 1973.
064.02 Foreign lands—Australia;
110 Monsters; 117 Mythical creatures.

Wagner, Jenny. *John Brown, Rose and the Midnight Cat*. Illus. by Ronald George Brooks. New York: Bradbury Pr., 1978.
008.09 Animals—cats; 008.14 Animals—dogs.

Wahl, Jan. *Cabbage Moon*. Illus. by Adrienne Adams. New York: Holt, 1965.
087 Humor; 111 Moon; 147 Royalty.

Wahl, Jan. *Carrot Nose*. Illus. by James Marshall. New York: Farrar, 1978.
008.46 Animals—rabbits.

Wahl, Jan. *Doctor Rabbit's Foundling*. Illus. by Cyndy Szekeres. New York: Pantheon, 1977.
005 Amphibians; 008.46 Animals—rabbits; 023.09 Careers—doctors.

Wahl, Jan. *The Fishermen*. Illus. by Emily Arnold McCully. New York: Norton, 1969.
057.02 Family life—grandparents; great-grandparents; 166.05 Sports—fishing.

Wahl, Jan. *The Five in the Forest*. Illus. by Erik Blegvad. Chicago: Follett, 1974.
008.46 Animals—rabbits; 050 Eggs;
066 Forest, woods; 083.04 Holidays—Easter.

Wahl, Jan. *Follow Me Cried Bee*. Illus. by John C. Wallner. New York: Crown, 1976.
038 Cumulative tales; 090 Insects and spiders; 134 Poetry, rhyme;
195.05 Weather—rain.

Wahl, Jan. *Frankenstein's Dog*. Illus. by Kay Chorao. Englewood Cliffs, NJ: Prentice-Hall, 1977.
008.14 Animals—dogs; 110 Monsters.

Wahl, Jan. *Hello, Elephant*. Illus. by Edward Jeffrey Irving Ardizzone. New York: Holt, 1964.
008.17 Animals—elephants.

Wahl, Jan. *Jamie's Tiger*. Illus. by Thomas Anthony de Paola. New York: Harcourt, 1978.
077.02 Handicaps—deafness;
088 Illness; 177 Toys.

Wahl, Jan. *The Muffletump Storybook*. Illus. by Cyndy Szekeres. Chicago: Follett, 1975.
177.04 Toys—dolls.

Wahl, Jan. *The Muffletumps*. Illus. by Edward Jeffrey Irving Ardizzone. New York: Holt, 1966.
177.04 Toys—dolls.

Wahl, Jan. *The Muffletumps' Christmas Party.* Illus. by Cyndy Szekeres. Chicago: Follett, 1975.
083.03 Holidays—Christmas;
177.04 Toys—dolls.

Wahl, Jan. *The Muffletumps' Halloween Scare.* Illus. by Cyndy Szekeres. Chicago: Follett, 1977.
083.07 Holidays—Halloween;
177.04 Toys—dolls.

Wahl, Jan. *Pleasant Fieldmouse.* Illus. by Maurice Sendak. New York: Harper, 1964.
008 Animals; 008.34 Animals—mice.

Wahl, Jan. *The Pleasant Fieldmouse Storybook.* Illus. by Erik Blegvad. Englewood Cliffs, NJ: Prentice-Hall, 1977.
008 Animals; 008.34 Animals—mice.

Wahl, Jan. *Pleasant Fieldmouse's Halloween Party.* Illus. by Wallace Tripp. New York: Putnam's, 1974.
008 Animals; 008.34 Animals—mice;
083.07 Holidays—Halloween.

Wahl, Jan. *Push Kitty.* Illus. by Garth Montgomery Williams. New York: Harper, 1968.
002.12 Activities—playing;
008.09 Animals—cats.

Waldman, Dorothy. *Goomer.* Illus. by Marie C. Nichols. New York: Ariel, 1952.
008.09 Animals—cats.

Walker, Barbara K. *Pigs and Pirates.* Illus. by Harold Berson. Port Washington, NY: White, 1969.
008.42 Animals—pigs; 064.13 Foreign lands—Greece; 132 Pirates.

Walker, Barbara K. *Teeny-Tiny and the Witch-Woman.* Illus. by Michael Foreman. New York: Pantheon, 1975.
026.06 Character traits—cleverness;
064.38 Foreign lands—Turkey;
199 Witches.

Walker, Challis. *Three and Three.* Illus. by author. New York: Coward, 1940.
008 Animals; 016.09 Behavior—dissatisfaction; 016.38 Behavior—wishing.

Walker, David E. *Pimpernel and the Poodle.* Illus. by Alan Howard. New York: Barnes, 1960.
008.09 Animals—cats; 008.14 Animals—dogs.

Wallace, Daisy. *Monster Poems.* Illus. by Kay Chorao. New York: Holiday, 1976.
110 Monsters; 134 Poetry, rhyme;
175 Tongue twisters.

Wallner, Alexandra. *Munch.* Illus. by author. New York: Crown, 1976.
063 Food; 134 Poetry, rhyme.

Walters, Marguerite. *The City-Country ABC.* Illus. by Ib Ohlsson. Garden City, NY: Doubleday, 1966.
001 ABC Books; 029 City; 034 Country; 067 Format, unusual.

Walters, Marguerite. *Up and Down and All Around.* Illus. by Susanne Suba. New York: Watts, 1960.
032.10 Concepts—up and down;
134 Poetry, rhyme.

Warburg, Sandol Stoddard. *Curl Up Small.* Illus. by Trina Schart Hyman. Boston: Houghton, 1964.
013 Babies; 015 Bedtime; 134 Poetry, rhyme.

Warburg, Sandol Stoddard. *My Very Own Special Particular Private and Personal Cat.* Illus. by Remy Charlip. Boston: Houghton, 1963.
008.09 Animals—cats; 131 Pets;
134 Poetry, rhyme.

Warburg, Sandol Stoddard. *The Thinking Book.* Illus. by Ivan Chermayeff. Boston: Little, 1960.
057 Family life; 089 Imagination.

Ward, Leila. *I Am Eyes; Ni Macho.* Illus. by Nonny Hogrogian. New York: Greenwillow, 1978.
064.01 Foreign lands—Africa;
065 Foreign languages.

Ward, Lynd Kendall. *The Biggest Bear.* Illus. by author. Boston: Houghton, 1952.
008.06 Animals—bears;
026.18 Character traits—kindness to animals; 064.04 Foreign lands—Canada;
131 Pets.

Ward, Lynd Kendall, jt. author. *The Little Red Lighthouse and the Great Gray Bridge.* By Hildegarde Hoyt Swift, and Lynd Kendall Ward.

Ward, Lynd Kendall. *Nic of the Woods.* Illus. by author. Boston: Houghton, 1965.
008.14 Animals—dogs; 064.04 Foreign lands—Canada.

Ward, Lynd Kendall. *The Silver Pony.* Illus. by author. Boston: Houghton, 1973.
008.28 Animals—horses; 047 Dreams;
201 Wordless.

Ward, Nanda Weedon. *The Black Sombrero.* Illus. by Lynd Kendall Ward. New York: Ariel, 1952.
008 Animals; 031 Clothing;
035 Cowboys.

Ward, Nanda Weedon, and Haynes, Robert. *The Elephant That Ga-lumphed.* Illus. by Robert Haynes. New York: Ariel, 1959.
008 Animals; 008.17 Animals—elephants; 064.16 Foreign lands—India.

Wasserberg, Esther, jt. author. *Grandmother Dear.* By Celentha Finfer; Esther Wasserberg; and Florence Weinberg.

Wasson, Valentine P. *The Chosen Baby.* Illus. by Glo Coalson. Philadelphia: Lippincott, 1977.
003 Adoption.

Watson, Clyde. *Catch Me and Kiss Me and Say It Again.* Illus. by Wendy Watson. Cleveland: Collins, 1978.
057 Family life; 134 Poetry, rhyme.

Watson, Clyde. *Father Fox's Pennyrhymes.* Illus. by Wendy Watson. New York: Crowell, 1971.
122 Nursery rhymes.

Watson, Clyde. *Midnight Moon.* Illus. by Susanna Natti. Cleveland: Collins, 1979.
002.05 Activities—flying; 015 Bedtime; 089 Imagination; 111 Moon.

Watson, Clyde. *Tom Fox and the Apple Pie.* Illus. by Wendy Watson. Cleveland: Collins, 1972.
008.18 Animals—foxes; 016.31 Behavior—sharing; 056 Fairs; 063 Food.

Watson, Jane Werner. *The Marvelous Merry-Go-Round.* Illus. by J. P. Miller. New York: Simon & Schuster, 1950.
008 Animals; 106 Merry-go-rounds; 137 Problem solving.

Watson, Jane Werner. *My Friend the Babysitter.* Illus. by Hilde Hoffmann. Racine, WI: Western Pub., 1971.
002.01 Activities—babysitting.

Watson, Jane Werner. *Noah's Ark.* Illus. by Tibor Gergely. New York: Grosset, 1943.
141.01 Religion—Noah.

Watson, Jane Werner. *Sometimes I Get Angry.* Illus. by Hilde Hoffmann. Racine, WI: Western Pub., 1971.
052.01 Emotions—anger.

Watson, Jane Werner. *Sometimes I'm Afraid.* Illus. by Hilde Hoffmann. Racine, WI: Western Pub., 1971.
052.04 Emotions—fear.

Watson, Jane Werner. *The Tall Book of Make-Believe.* Illus. by Garth Montgomery Williams. New York: Harper, 1950.
089 Imagination; 134 Poetry, rhyme.

Watson, Jane Werner. *Which Is the Witch?* Illus. by Victoria Dickerson Chess. New York: Pantheon, 1979.
083.07 Holidays—Halloween; 199 Witches.

Watson, Nancy Dingman. *Annie's Spending Spree.* Illus. by Aldren A. Watson. New York: Viking, 1957.
018 Birthdays; 109 Money.

Watson, Nancy Dingman. *The Birthday Goat.* Illus. by Wendy Watson. New York: Crowell, 1974.
008.21 Animals—goats; 018 Birthdays; 036 Crime; 056 Fairs.

Watson, Nancy Dingman. *Sugar on Snow.* Illus. by Aldren A. Watson. New York: Viking, 1964.
063 Food; 195.07 Weather—snow.

Watson, Nancy Dingman. *Tommy's Mommy's Fish.* Illus. by Aldren A. Watson. New York: Viking, 1971.
018 Birthdays; 057.03 Family life—mothers; 166.05 Sports—fishing.

Watson, Nancy Dingman. *What Does A Begin With?* Illus. by Aldren A. Watson. New York: Knopf, 1956.
001 ABC Books; 058 Farms.

Watson, Nancy Dingman. *What Is One?* Illus. by Aldren A. Watson. New York: Knopf, 1954.
033 Counting; 058 Farms.

Watson, Nancy Dingman. *When Is Tomorrow?* Illus. by Aldren A. Watson. New York: Knopf, 1955.
153 Sea and seashore; 174 Time.

Watson, Pauline. *Curley Cat Baby-Sits.* Illus. by Lorinda Bryan Cauley. New York: Harcourt, 1977.
002.01 Activities—babysitting; 008.09 Animals—cats.

Watson, Pauline. *Days with Daddy.* Illus. by Joanne Scribner. Englewood Cliffs, NJ: Prentice-Hall, 1977.
057 Family life; 057.01 Family life—fathers.

Watson, Pauline. *Wriggles, the Little Wishing Pig.* Illus. by Paul Galdone. New York: Seabury Pr., 1978.
008.42 Animals—pigs; 016.38 Behavior—wishing; 110 Monsters.

Watson, Wendy. *Fisherman Lullabies.* Illus. by Clyde Watson. Selected and edited by Wendy Watson. Cleveland: Collins, 1968.
015 Bedtime; 116 Music; 164 Songs.

Watson, Wendy. *Has Winter Come?* Illus. by author. Cleveland: Collins, 1978.
008.23 Animals—groundhogs;
081 Hibernation; 154.04 Seasons—winter.

Watson, Wendy. *Lollipop.* Illus. by author. New York: Crowell, 1976.
008.46 Animals—rabbits;
016.22 Behavior—misbehavior.

Watson, Wendy. *Moving.* Illus. by author. New York: Crowell, 1978.
114 Moving.

Watts, Bernadette. *Brigitte and Ferdinand, a Love Story.* Illus. by author. Englewood Cliffs, NJ: Prentice-Hall, 1976.
052.08 Emotions—love; 116 Music.

Watts, Bernadette. *David's Waiting Day.* Illus. by author. Englewood Cliffs, NJ: Prentice-Hall, 1975.
013 Babies; 057 Family life.

Watts, Bernadette, reteller. *Mother Holly.* Illus. by Bernadette Watts. From the Brothers Grimm. New York: Crowell, 1972.
016.13 Behavior—greed;
026.14 Character traits—helpfulness;
026.19 Character traits—laziness;
062 Folk and fairy tales.

Watts, Mabel. *The Boy Who Listened to Everyone.* Illus. by Ervine Metzl. New York: Parents, 1963.
064.17 Foreign lands—Ireland;
109 Money.

Watts, Mabel. *The Day It Rained Watermelons.* Illus. by Lee Albertson. Mt. Vernon: Lantern Pr., 1964.
016.18 Behavior—indifference.

Watts, Mabel. *A Little from Here, a Little from There.* Illus. by Sheila Perry. New York: Abelard-Schuman, 1962.
031 Clothing.

Watts, Mabel. *Something for You, Something for Me.* Illus. by Abner Graboff. New York: Abelard-Schuman, 1960.
002.15 Activities—trading;
016.31 Behavior—sharing.

Watts, Mabel. *Weeks and Weeks.* Illus. by Abner Graboff. New York: Abelard-Schuman, 1962.
002.10 Activities—photographing.

Webb, Clifford Cyril. *The Story of Noah.* Illus. by author. New York: Warne, 1949.
141.01 Religion—Noah.

Weber, Alfons. *Elizabeth Gets Well.* Illus. by Jacqueline Blass. New York: Crowell, 1970.
084 Hospitals; 088 Illness.

Weelen, Guy. *The Little Red Train.* Illus. by Mamoru R. Funai. New York: Lothrop, 1966.
064.11 Foreign lands—France;
179 Trains.

Wegen, Ronald. *Sand Castle.* Illus. by author. New York: Morrow, 1977.
153 Sea and seashore.

Weih, Erica. *Count the Cats.* Illus. by author. Garden City, NY: Doubleday, 1976.
008.09 Animals—cats; 033 Counting.

Weil, Ann. *Animal Families.* Illus. by Roger Vernam. New York: Greenberg, 1956.
008 Animals.

Weil, Ann. *The Very First Day.* Illus. by Jessie B. Robinson. New York: Appleton, 1946.
118 Names; 151 School.

Weil, Lisl. *Bitzli and the Big Bad Wolf.* Illus. by author. Boston: Houghton, 1960.
008.14 Animals—dogs;
016.35 Behavior—talking to strangers;
064.36 Foreign lands—Switzerland.

Weil, Lisl. *The Candy Egg Bunny.* Illus. by author. New York: Holiday, 1975.
008.46 Animals—rabbits;
083.04 Holidays—Easter; 199 Witches.

Weil, Lisl. *Mimi.* Illus. by author. Boston: Houghton, 1961.
023 Careers; 023.21 Careers—police officers.

Weil, Lisl. *Pudding's Wonderful Bone.* Illus. by author. New York: Crowell, 1956.
008.14 Animals—dogs;
016.31 Behavior—sharing.

Weil, Lisl. *The Very First Story Ever Told.* Illus. by author. New York: Atheneum, 1976.
141 Religion.

Weinberg, Florence, jt. author. *Grandmother Dear.* By Celentha Finfer, Esther Wasserberg, and Florence Weinberg.

Weisgard, Leonard. *The Clean Pig.* Illus. by author. New York: Scribner's, 1952.
008.42 Animals—pigs; 026.05 Character traits—cleanliness.

Weisgard, Leonard. *Mr. Peaceable Paints.* Illus. by author. New York: Scribner's, 1956.
002.09 Activities—painting;
023.02 Careers—artists.

Weisgard, Leonard. *Silly Willy Nilly*. Illus. by author. New York: Scribner's, 1953.
008.17 Animals—elephants;
016.11 Behavior—forgetfulness.

Weisgard, Leonard. *Who Dreams of Cheese?* Illus. by author. New York: Scribner's, 1950.
016.38 Behavior—wishing; 047 Dreams;
162 Sleep.

Weiss, Harvey. *My Closet Full of Hats*. Illus. by author. New York: Abelard-Schuman, 1962.
031 Clothing.

Weiss, Harvey. *The Sooner Hound*. Illus. by author. New York: Putnam's, 1959.
008.14 Animals—dogs;
023.10 Careers—firefighters; 062 Folk and fairy tales.

Weiss, Leatie. *Funny Feet*. Illus. by author. New York: Watts, 1978.
006 Anatomy; 017.18 Birds—penguins;
031 Clothing.

Welber, Robert. *Goodbye—Hello*. Illus. by Cyndy Szekeres. New York: Pantheon, 1974.
008 Animals; 016.14 Behavior—growing up; 151 School.

Welber, Robert. *Song of the Seasons*. Illus. by Deborah Ray. New York: Pantheon, 1973.
154 Seasons.

Welles, Winifred. *The Park That Spring Forgot*. Illus. by Marion Downer. New York: Dutton, 1940.
154 Seasons.

Wellington, Anne. *Apple Pie*. Illus. by Nina Sowter. Englewood Cliffs, NJ: Prentice-Hall, 1978.
154 Seasons.

Wells, H. G. See Wells, Herbert George.

Wells, Herbert George. *The Adventures of Tommy*. Illus. by author. New York: Knopf, 1967.
008.17 Animals—elephants;
026.04 Character traits—bravery;
026.17 Character traits—kindness.

Wells, Peter. *Mr. Tootwhistle's Invention*. Illus. by author. Minneapolis: Winston Pr., 1942.
177.09 Toys—trains.

Wells, Rosemary. *Benjamin and Tulip*. Illus. by author. New York: Dial Pr., 1973.
008.47 Animals—raccoons;
016.10 Behavior—fighting, arguing;
016.32 Behavior—sibling rivalry.

Wells, Rosemary. *Don't Spill It Again, James*. Illus. by author. New York: Dial Pr., 1977.
008.18 Animals—foxes; 134 Poetry, rhyme; 179 Trains; 195.05 Weather—rain.

Wells, Rosemary. *Morris's Disappearing Bag; A Christmas Story*. Illus. by author. New York: Dial Pr., 1974.
008.46 Animals—rabbits;
083.03 Holidays—Christmas.

Wells, Rosemary. *Noisy Nora*. Illus. by author. New York: Dial Pr., 1973.
008.34 Animals—mice;
016.26 Behavior—needing someone;
134 Poetry, rhyme.

Wells, Rosemary. *A Song to Sing, O!* Illus. by author. From the Yeomen of the Guard by W. S. Gilbert and Arthur Sullivan. New York: Macmillan, 1968.
017 Birds; 116 Music; 164 Songs.

Wells, Rosemary. *Stanley and Rhoda*. Illus. by author. New York: Dial Pr., 1978.
002.01 Activities—babysitting;
008.34 Animals—mice;
016.32 Behavior—sibling rivalry.

Wells, Rosemary. *Unfortunately Harriet*. Illus. by author. New York: Dial Pr., 1972.
016.02 Behavior—bad day.

Wende, Philip. *Bird Boy*. Illus. by author. New York: Cowles, 1970.
002.05 Activities—flying; 047 Dreams.

Wenning, Elizabeth. *The Christmas Mouse*. Illus. by Barbara Remington. New York: Holt, 1959.
008.34 Animals—mice;
083.03 Holidays—Christmas; 116 Music;
164 Songs.

Werner, Jane. See Watson, Jane Werner.

Wersba, Barbara. *Do Tigers Ever Bite Kings?* Illus. by Mario Rivoli. New York: Atheneum, 1966.
008.10 Animals—cats, wild;
026.18 Character traits—kindness to animals; 134 Poetry, rhyme;
147 Royalty.

Werth, Kurt. *Lazy Jack*. Illus. by author. New York: Viking, 1970.
026.19 Character traits—laziness;
038 Cumulative tales; 062 Folk and fairy tales.

Westerberg, Christine. *The Cap That Mother Made*. Illus. by author. Englewood Cliffs, NJ: Prentice-Hall, 1977.
031 Clothing; 062 Folk and fairy tales;
064.35 Foreign lands—Sweden.

Weygant, Noemi. *It's Autumn!* Illus. by author. Philadelphia: Westminster Pr., 1968.
154.01 Seasons—fall.

Weygant, Noemi. *It's Spring!* Illus. by author. Philadelphia: Westminster Pr., 1969.
154.02 Seasons—spring.

Weygant, Noemi. *It's Summer!* Illus. by author. Philadelphia: Westminster Pr., 1970.
154.03 Seasons—summer.

Weygant, Noemi. *It's Winter!* Illus. by author. Philadelphia: Westminster Pr., 1969.
154.04 Seasons—winter.

Wezel, Peter. *The Good Bird.* Illus. by author. New York: Harper, 1964.
016.31 Behavior—sharing; 017 Birds; 060 Fish; 201 Wordless.

Wezel, Peter. *The Naughty Bird.* Illus. by author. Chicago: Follett, 1967.
008.09 Animals—cats; 017 Birds; 201 Wordless.

Wheeler, Opal. *Sing Mother Goose.* Illus. by Marjorie Torrey. Music by Opal Wheeler. New York: Dutton, 1945.
116 Music; 122 Nursery rhymes.

Wheeling, Lynn. *When You Fly.* Illus. by author. Boston: Little, 1967.
004 Airplanes; 134 Poetry, rhyme.

White, Florence M. *How to Lose Your Lunch Money.* Illus. by Chris Jenkyns. Pasadena, CA: Ritchie, 1970.
016.19 Behavior—losing things; 016.22 Behavior—misbehavior; 151 School.

White, Paul. *Janet at School.* Illus. by Jeremy Finlay. New York: Crowell, 1978.
077 Handicaps; 151 School.

Whitehead, Roberta. *Peter Opens the Door.* Illus. by Mildred Bronson. Boston: Houghton, 1946.
052.07 Emotions—loneliness.

Whitney, Alex. *Once a Bright Red Tiger.* Illus. by Charles Robinson. New York: Walck, 1973.
008.10 Animals—cats, wild; 026.27 Character traits—pride.

Whitney, Alma Marshak. *Just Awful.* Illus. by Lillian Hoban. Reading: Addison-Wesley, 1971.
023.19 Careers—nurses; 088 Illness; 151 School.

Whitney, Alma Marshak. *Leave Herbert Alone.* Illus. by David McPhail. Reading: Addison-Wesley, 1972.
008.09 Animals—cats; 026.18 Character traits—kindness to animals.

Whitney, Julie. *Bears Are Sleeping.* Illus. by Nonny Hogrogian. New York: Scribner's, 1967.
008.06 Animals—bears; 081 Hibernation; 116 Music; 162 Sleep; 164 Songs.

Widdecombe Fair; An Old English Folk Song. Illus. by Christine Price. New York: Warne, 1968.
056 Fairs; 062 Folk and fairy tales; 064.10 Foreign lands—England; 116 Music; 164 Songs.

Wiese, Kurt. *The Cunning Turtle.* Illus. by author. New York: Viking, 1956.
142.05 Reptiles—turtles.

Wiese, Kurt. *The Dog, the Fox and the Fleas.* Illus. by author. New York: McKay, 1953.
008.14 Animals—dogs; 008.18 Animals—foxes; 090 Insects and spiders.

Wiese, Kurt. *Fish in the Air.* Illus. by author. New York: Viking, 1948.
064.06 Foreign lands—China; 087 Humor; 094 Kites.

Wiese, Kurt, jt. author. *The Five Chinese Brothers.* By Claire Huchet Bishop, and Kurt Wiese.

Wiese, Kurt. *Happy Easter.* Illus. by author. New York: Viking, 1952.
008.46 Animals—rabbits; 083.04 Holidays—Easter.

Wiese, Kurt. *Rabbit Brothers Circus One Night Only.* Illus. by author. New York: Viking, 1963.
008.46 Animals—rabbits; 028 Circus, clowns.

Wiese, Kurt. *The Rabbit's Revenge.* Illus. by author. New York: Coward, 1940.
008.46 Animals—rabbits.

Wiese, Kurt, jt. author. *The Story about Ping.* By Marjorie Flack, and Kurt Wiese.

Wiese, Kurt. *The Thief in the Attic.* Illus. by author. New York: Viking, 1965.
008 Animals; 181 Trees.

Wiesenthal, Eleanor, and Wiesenthal, Ted. *Let's Find Out about Eskimos.* Illus. by Allan Eitzen. New York: Watts, 1969.
053.03 Ethnic groups in the U.S.—Eskimos.

Wiesenthal, Ted, jt. author. *Let's Find Out about Eskimos.* By Eleanor Wiesenthal, and Ted Wiesenthal.

Wiesner, William. *Happy-Go-Lucky.* Illus. by author. New York: Seabury Pr., 1970.
026.23 Character traits—optimism;
038 Cumulative tales; 058 Farms;
064.25 Foreign lands—Norway;
087 Humor.

Wiesner, William. *Noah's Ark.* Illus. by author. New York: Dutton, 1966.
141.01 Religion—Noah.

Wiesner, William. *Too Many Cooks.* Illus. by author. Philadelphia: Lippincott, 1961.
002.03 Activities—cooking; 087 Humor.

Wiesner, William. *Tops.* Illus. by author. New York: Viking, 1969.
068 Friendship; 072 Giants;
191 Violence, anti-violence.

Wiesner, William. *The Tower of Babel.* Illus. by author. New York: Viking, 1968.
096 Language; 141 Religion.

Wiesner, William. *Turnabout.* Illus. by author. New York: Seabury Pr., 1972.
016.09 Behavior—dissatisfaction;
064.25 Foreign lands—Norway;
087 Humor.

Wikland, Ilon, jt. author. *Christmas in Noisy Village.* By Astrid Ericsson Lindgren, and Ilon Wikland.

Wilcox, Daniel, jt. author. *The Sesame Street ABC Storybook.* By Jeffrey Moss; Norman Stiles; and Daniel Wilcox.

Wild, Jocelyn, jt. author. *Little Pig and the Big Bad Wolf.* By Robin Wild, and Jocelyn Wild.

Wild, Robin, and Wild, Jocelyn. *Little Pig and the Big Bad Wolf.* Illus. by authors. New York: Coward, 1972.
008.42 Animals—pigs;
008.61 Animals—wolves;
026.06 Character traits—cleverness;
083.03 Holidays—Christmas;
134 Poetry, rhyme.

Wilder, Alec. *Lullabies and Night Songs.* Illus. by Maurice Sendak. Music by Alec Wilder; edited by William Engvic. New York: Harper, 1965.
015 Bedtime; 116 Music; 164 Songs.

Wildsmith, Brian. *Brian Wildsmith's ABC.* Illus. by author. New York: Watts, 1963.
001 ABC Books.

Wildsmith, Brian. *Brian Wildsmith's Birds.* Illus. by author. New York: Watts, 1967.
017 Birds.

Wildsmith, Brian. *Brian Wildsmith's Circus.* Illus. by author. New York: Watts, 1970.
028 Circus, clowns.

Wildsmith, Brian. *Brian Wildsmith's Fishes.* Illus. by author. New York: Watts, 1968.
060 Fish.

Wildsmith, Brian. *Brian Wildsmith's 1, 2, 3's.* Illus. by author. New York: Watts, 1965.
033 Counting.

Wildsmith, Brian. *Brian Wildsmith's Puzzles.* Illus. by author. New York: Watts, 1970.
069 Games.

Wildsmith, Brian. *Brian Wildsmith's Wild Animals.* Illus. by author. New York: Watts, 1967.
008 Animals.

Wildsmith, Brian. *The Lazy Bear.* Illus. by author. New York: Watts, 1974.
008.06 Animals—bears;
026.19 Character traits—laziness;
068 Friendship.

Wildsmith, Brian. *The Little Wood Duck.* Illus. by author. New York: Watts, 1972.
017.08 Birds—ducks; 026.03 Character traits—being different.

Wildsmith, Brian. *The Owl and the Woodpecker.* Illus. by author. New York: Watts, 1971.
017.14 Birds—owls; 017.28 Birds—woodpeckers; 026.08 Character traits—compromising.

Wildsmith, Brian. *Python's Party.* Illus. by author. New York: Watts, 1975.
008 Animals; 016.36 Behavior—trickery; 142.04 Reptiles—snakes.

Wildsmith, Brian. *Squirrels.* Illus. by author. New York: Watts, 1974.
008.56 Animals—squirrels.

Wildsmith, Brian. *The True Cross.* Illus. by author. New York: Oxford Univ. Pr., 1977.
062 Folk and fairy tales.

Wildsmith, Brian. *What the Moon Saw.* Illus. by author. New York: Oxford Univ. Pr., 1978.
032.06 Concepts—opposites; 111 Moon;
169 Sun.

Wilkin, Eloise Burns. *Ladybug, Ladybug and Other Nursery Rhymes.* Illus. by author. New York: Random House, 1979.
067 Format, unusual; 122 Nursery rhymes.

Will (pseud.). See Lipkind, William.

Willard, Barbara. *To London! To London!* Illus. by Antony Maitland. New York: McKay, 1968.
064.10 Foreign lands—England.

Willard, Nancy. *Simple Pictures Are Best.* Illus. by Thomas Anthony de Paola. New York: Harcourt, 1977.
002.10 Activities—photographing; 087 Humor.

Williams, Barbara. *Albert's Toothache.* Illus. by Kay Chorao. New York: Dutton, 1974.
088 Illness; 142.05 Reptiles—turtles; 171 Teeth.

Williams, Barbara. *Chester Chipmunk's Thanksgiving.* Illus. by Kay Chorao. New York: Dutton, 1978.
008.11 Animals—chipmunks; 083.10 Holidays—Thanksgiving.

Williams, Barbara. *If He's My Brother.* Illus. by Thomas Anthony de Paola. New York: Harvey House, 1976.
026.28 Character traits—questioning; 057 Family life.

Williams, Barbara. *Jeremy Isn't Hungry.* Illus. by Martha G. Alexander. New York: Dutton, 1978.
002.01 Activities—babysitting; 013 Babies; 087 Humor.

Williams, Barbara. *Kevin's Grandma.* Illus. by Kay Chorao. New York: Dutton, 1975.
057.02 Family life—grandparents; great-grandparents; 068 Friendship.

Williams, Barbara. *Someday, Said Mitchell.* Illus. by Kay Chorao. New York: Dutton, 1976.
016.38 Behavior—wishing; 026.14 Character traits—helpfulness; 026.31 Character traits—smallness; 052.05 Emotions—happiness.

Williams, Barbara. *Whatever Happened to Beverly Bigler's Birthday?* Illus. by Emily Arnold McCully. New York: Harcourt, 1979.
016.22 Behavior—misbehavior; 018 Birthdays; 196 Weddings.

Williams, Garth Montgomery. *The Big Golden Animal ABC.* Illus. by author. New York: Simon & Schuster, 1957.
001 ABC Books; 008 Animals.

Williams, Garth Montgomery. *The Chicken Book.* Illus. by author. New York: Delacorte Pr., 1970.
017.04 Birds—chickens; 033 Counting; 134 Poetry, rhyme.

Williams, Garth Montgomery. *The Rabbits' Wedding.* Illus. by author. New York: Harper, 1958.
008.46 Animals—rabbits; 196 Weddings.

Williams, Gweneira Maureen. *Timid Timothy, the Kitten Who Learned to Be Brave.* Illus. by Leonard Weisgard. Reading: Addison-Wesley, 1944/1971.
008.09 Animals—cats; 026.04 Character traits—bravery; 052.04 Emotions—fear.

Williams, Jay. *Everyone Knows What a Dragon Looks Like.* Illus. by Mercer Mayer. New York: Four Winds Pr., 1976.
046 Dragons; 064.06 Foreign lands—China.

Williams, Jay. *Petronella.* Illus. by Frisco Henstra. New York: Parents, 1973.
062 Folk and fairy tales; 121 Non-sexist.

Williams, Jay. *The Practical Princess.* Illus. by Frisco Henstra. New York: Parents, 1969.
026.26 Character traits—practicality; 062 Folk and fairy tales; 121 Non-sexist; 147 Royalty.

Williams, Jay. *School for Sillies.* Illus. by Frisco Henstra. New York: Parents, 1969.
026.06 Character traits—cleverness; 087 Humor; 147 Royalty.

Williams, Jay, and Lubell, Winifred Milius. *I Wish I Had Another Name.* Illus. by authors. New York: Atheneum, 1962.
118 Names; 134 Poetry, rhyme.

Williams, Jenny, jt. author. *A Wet Monday.* By Dorothy Edwards, and Jenny Williams.

Williamson, Hamilton. *Lion Cub: A Jungle Tale.* Illus. by Berta Hoerner Hader, and Elmer Stanley Hader. Garden City, NY: Doubleday, 1931.
008.10 Animals—cats, wild.

Williamson, Hamilton. *Little Elephant.* Illus. by Berta Hoerner Hader, and Elmer Stanley Hader. Garden City, NY: Doubleday, 1930.
008.17 Animals—elephants.

Williamson, Hamilton. *Monkey Tale.* Illus. by Berta Hoerner Hader, and Elmer Stanley Hader. Garden City, NY: Doubleday, 1929.
008.37 Animals—monkeys.

Williamson, Mel, and Ford, George. *Walk On!* Illus. by authors. New York: Third Pr., 1972.
029 City; 053.01 Ethnic groups in the U.S.—Afro-Americans.

Williamson, Stan. *The No-Bark Dog.* Illus. by Tom O'Sullivan. Chicago: Follett, 1962.
008.14 Animals—dogs; 053.01 Ethnic groups in the U.S.—Afro-Americans.

Wilson, Charles Christopher, and others. *Our Good Health.* Illus. by Pauline Batchelder Adams, and Marvelle Landreth. Indianapolis: Bobbs-Merrill, 1942.
079 Health.

Wilson, Christopher B. *Hobnob.* Illus. by William Wiesner. New York: Viking, 1968.
016.31 Behavior—sharing.

Wilson, Joyce Lancaster. *Tobi.* Illus. by Anne Thiess. New York: Funk & Wagnells, 1968.
008.09 Animals—cats.

Wilson, Julia. *Becky.* Illus. by John Wilson. New York: Crowell, 1966.
026.15 Character traits—honesty; 053.01 Ethnic groups in the U.S.—Afro-Americans; 177.04 Toys—dolls.

Winn, Marie. *The Man Who Made Fine Tops.* Illus. by John E. Johnson. Educational consultant: Helen F. Robison. New York: Simon & Schuster, 1970.
023 Careers.

Winter, Paula. *The Bear and the Fly.* Illus. by author. New York: Crown, 1976.
008.06 Animals—bears; 090 Insects and spiders; 201 Wordless.

Winthrop, Elizabeth. *Bunk Beds.* Illus. by Ronald Norbert Himler. New York: Harper, 1972.
015 Bedtime; 057 Family life; 089 Imagination.

Winthrop, Elizabeth. *Potbellied Possums.* Illus. by Barbara McCluntock. New York: Holiday, 1977.
008.44 Animals—possums; 052.04 Emotions—fear; 063 Food; 119 Night.

Winthrop, Elizabeth. *That's Mine!* Illus. by Emily Arnold McCully. New York: Holiday, 1977.
002.12 Activities—playing; 016.10 Behavior—fighting, arguing; 016.13 Behavior—greed; 016.31 Behavior—sharing; 016.32 Behavior—sibling rivalry; 177.03 Toys—blocks.

Wisbeski, Dorothy. *Picaro, a Pet Otter.* Illus. by Edna Anita Miller. New York: Hawthorn, 1971.
008.40 Animals—otters; 131 Pets.

Wise, William. *The Cowboy Surprise.* Illus. by Paul Galdone. New York: Putnam's, 1961.
035 Cowboys; 073 Glasses.

Wise, William. *Nanette the Hungry Pelican.* Illus. by Winifred Milius Lubell. Skokie, IL: Rand McNally, 1969.
017.17 Birds—pelicans; 134 Poetry, rhyme.

Wiseman, Bernard. *Little New Kangaroo.* Illus. by Robert Martin Lopshire. New York: Macmillan, 1973.
008 Animals; 008.30 Animals—kangaroos; 064.30 Foreign lands—Russia; 134 Poetry, rhyme.

Withers, Carl. *Tale of a Black Cat.* Illus. by Alan E. Cober. New York: Holt, 1966.
069 Games.

Withers, Carl, adapter. *The Wild Ducks and the Goose.* Illus. by Alan E. Cober. New York: Holt, 1968.
069 Games.

Wittels, Harriet, and Greisman, Joan. *Things I Hate!* Illus. by Jerry McConnel. New York: Human Sci. Pr., 1973.
016 Behavior; 052 Emotions; 134 Poetry, rhyme.

Wittman, Sally Christensen. *Pelly and Peak.* Illus. by author. New York: Harper, 1978.
017.16 Birds—peacocks, peahens; 017.17 Birds—pelicans; 068 Friendship.

Wittman, Sally Christensen. *A Special Trade.* Illus. by Karen Gundersheimer. New York: Harper, 1978.
016.14 Behavior—growing up; 068 Friendship; 125 Old age.

Woerkom, Dorothy O. Van. See Van Woerkom, Dorothy O.

Wold, Jo Anne. *Tell Them My Name Is Amanda.* Illus. by author. Edited by Caroline Rubin. Chicago: Albert Whitman, 1977.
118 Names; 137 Problem solving.

Wold, Jo Anne. *Well! Why Didn't You Say So?* Illus. by Unada (pseud.). Chicago: Albert Whitman, 1975.
008.14 Animals—dogs; 016.20 Behavior—lost; 016.24 Behavior—misunderstanding; 029 City.

Wolde, Gunilla. *Betsy and Peter Are Different.* Illus. by author. New York: Random House, 1979.
057 Family life; 121 Non-sexist.

Wolde, Gunilla. *Betsy and the Chicken Pox*. Illus. by author. New York: Random House, 1976.
016.26 Behavior—needing someone; 016.32 Behavior—sibling rivalry; 088 Illness; 121 Non-sexist.

Wolde, Gunilla. *Betsy and the Doctor*. Illus. by author. New York: Random House, 1978.
023.09 Careers—doctors; 084 Hospitals; 088 Illness.

Wolde, Gunilla. *Betsy and the Vacuum Cleaner*. Illus. by author. New York: Random House, 1979.
057 Family life; 102 Machines.

Wolde, Gunilla. *Betsy's Baby Brother*. Illus. by author. New York: Random House, 1974.
013 Babies; 016.32 Behavior—sibling rivalry; 052.03 Emotions—envy, jealousy; 057 Family life.

Wolde, Gunilla. *Betsy's First Day at Nursery School*. Illus. by author. New York: Random House, 1976.
151 School.

Wolde, Gunilla. *Betsy's Fixing Day*. Illus. by author. New York: Random House, 1978.
026.14 Character traits—helpfulness; 057 Family life.

Wolde, Gunilla. *This Is Betsy*. Illus. by author. New York: Random House, 1975.
032.06 Concepts—opposites; 052 Emotions; 057 Family life.

Wolf, Ann. *The Rabbit and the Turtle*. Illus. by author. New York: Grosset, 1965.
008.46 Animals—rabbits; 062 Folk and fairy tales; 142.05 Reptiles—turtles.

Wolf, Bernard. *Adam Smith Goes to School*. Illus. by author. Philadelphia: Lippincott, 1978.
151 School.

Wolf, Bernard. *Anna's Silent World*. Illus. by author. Philadelphia: Lippincott, 1977.
077.02 Handicaps—deafness.

Wolf, Bernard. *Don't Feel Sorry for Paul*. Illus. by author. Philadelphia: Lippincott, 1974.
077 Handicaps.

Wolff, Robert Jay. *Feeling Blue*. Illus. by author. New York: Scribner's, 1968.
032.01 Concepts—color.

Wolff, Robert Jay. *Hello Yellow!* Illus. by author. New York: Scribner's, 1968.
032.01 Concepts—color.

Wolff, Robert Jay. *Seeing Red*. Illus. by author. New York: Scribner's, 1968.
032.01 Concepts—color.

Wolkstein, Diane. *The Cool Ride in the Sky*. Illus. by Paul Galdone. New York: Knopf, 1973.
002.05 Activities—flying; 008.37 Animals—monkeys; 017.02 Birds—buzzards; 017.27 Birds—vultures; 026.06 Character traits—cleverness.

Wolkstein, Diane, and Young, Ed. *The White Wave: A Chinese Tale*. Illus. by Ed Young. New York: Crowell, 1979.
062 Folk and fairy tales; 064.06 Foreign lands—China.

Wolo (pseud.). *Amanda*. Illus. by author. New York: Morrow, 1941.
142.04 Reptiles—snakes.

Wolo (pseud.). *The Secret of the Ancient Oak*. Illus. by author. New York: Morrow, 1942.
008 Animals; 017 Birds; 181 Trees.

Wolo (pseud.). *Tweedles Be Brave!* Illus. by author. New York: Morrow, 1943.
008.37 Animals—monkeys; 017.05 Birds—cockatoos.

Wondriska, William. *A Long Piece of String*. Illus. by author. New York: Holt, 1963.
001 ABC Books; 177.07 Toys—string; 201 Wordless.

Wondriska, William. *Mr. Brown and Mr. Gray*. Illus. by author. New York: Holt, 1968.
008.42 Animals—pigs; 052.05 Emotions—happiness; 109 Money.

Wondriska, William. *Puff*. Illus. by author. New York: Pantheon, 1960.
179 Trains.

Wondriska, William. *The Stop*. Illus. by author. New York: Holt, 1972.
041 Desert; 052.04 Emotions—fear; 053.04 Ethnic groups in the U.S.—Indians.

Wondriska, William. *The Tomato Patch*. Illus. by author. New York: Holt, 1964.
133 Plants; 191 Violence, anti-violence; 194 Weapons.

Wondriska, William. *Which Way to the Zoo?* Illus. by author. New York: Holt, 1961.
008 Animals; 204 Zoos.

Wong, Herbert H., and Vassel, Matthew F. *My Goldfish*. Illus. by Arvis L. Stewart. Reading: Addison-Wesley, 1969.
060 Fish; 131 Pets; 152 Science.

Wong, Herbert H., and Vassel, Matthew F. *My Ladybug*. Illus. by Marie Nonast Bohlen. Reading: Addison-Wesley, 1969.
090 Insects and spiders; 152 Science.

Wong, Herbert H., and Vassel, Matthew F. *My Plant*. Illus. by Richard Cuffari. Reading: Addison-Wesley, 1976.
131 Pets; 152 Science.

Wong, Herbert H., and Vassel, Matthew F. *Our Caterpillars*. Illus. by Arvis L. Stewart. Reading: Addison-Wesley, 1977.
090 Insects and spiders; 152 Science.

Wong, Herbert H., and Vassel, Matthew F. *Our Earthworms*. Illus. by Bill Davis. Reading: Addison-Wesley, 1977.
008.62 Animals—worms; 152 Science.

Wong, Herbert H., and Vassel, Matthew F. *Our Terrariums*. Illus. by Aldren A. Watson. Reading: Addison-Wesley, 1969.
133 Plants; 152 Science.

Wong, Herbert H., and Vassel, Matthew F. *Our Tree*. Illus. by Arvis L. Stewart. Reading: Addison-Wesley, 1969.
152 Science; 181 Trees.

Wood, Joyce. *Grandmother Lucy Goes on a Picnic*. Illus. by Frank Francis. Cleveland: Collins, 1976.
002.11 Activities—picnicking;
002.18 Activities—walking;
057.02 Family life—grandparents;
great-grandparents.

Wood, Joyce. *Grandmother Lucy in Her Garden*. Illus. by Frank Francis. Cleveland: Collins, 1975.
057.02 Family life—grandparents;
great-grandparents; 064.10 Foreign lands—England; 154 Seasons;
154.02 Seasons—spring.

Wood, Nancy. *Little Wrangler*. Illus. by Myron Wood. Garden City, NY: Doubleday, 1966.
035 Cowboys.

Wood, Ray. *The American Mother Goose*. Illus. by Ed Hargis. Philadelphia: Lippincott, 1940.
122 Nursery rhymes.

Wood, Ray. *Fun in American Folk Rhymes*. Illus. by Ed Hargis. Introduction by Carl Carmer. Philadelphia: Lippincott, 1952.
122 Nursery rhymes.

Woodcock, Louise Phinney. *Guess Who Lives Here*. Illus. by Eloise Wilkin. New York: Simon & Schuster, 1949.
069 Games.

Woodcock, Louise Phinney. *Hi Ho! Three in a Row*. Illus. by Eloise Wilkin. New York: Simon & Schuster, 1954.
008 Animals; 069 Games.

Woodcock, Louise Phinney, jt. author. *The Very Little Dog; and The Smart Little Kitty*. By Grace Marion Skaar, and Louise Phinney Woodcock.

Woods, Ruth Maurine. *Little Quack*. Illus. by Mel Pekarsky. Chicago: Follett, 1961.
017.08 Birds—ducks.

Wooley, Catherine. *Andy and His Fine Friends*. Illus. by Meg Wohlberg. New York: Morrow, 1960.
008 Animals; 089.01 Imagination—imaginary friends.

Wooley, Catherine. *Andy and the Runaway Horse*. Illus. by Meg Wohlberg. New York: Morrow, 1963.
008.28 Animals—horses; 178 Traffic signs.

Wooley, Catherine. *Andy and the Wild Worm*. Illus. by Beatrice Darwin. New York: Morrow, 1973.
008.62 Animals—worms;
089 Imagination.

Wooley, Catherine. *The Blueberry Pie Elf*. Illus. by Seymour Fleishman. New York: Morrow, 1959.
051 Elves and little people; 063 Food;
137 Problem solving.

Wooley, Catherine. *The Cat That Joined the Club*. Illus. by Seymour Fleishman. New York: Morrow, 1967.
008.09 Animals—cats.

Wooley, Catherine. *Charley and the New Car*. Illus. by Jay Hyde Barnum. New York: Morrow, 1957.
012 Automobiles.

Wooley, Catherine. *A Drink for Little Red Diker*. Illus. by Witold Tadeusz Mars, Jr. New York: Morrow, 1963.
008.02 Animals—antelopes;
016.14 Behavior—growing up.

Wooley, Catherine. *Gus and the Baby Ghost*. Illus. by Seymour Fleishman. New York: Morrow, 1972.
013 Babies; 071 Ghosts; 115 Museums.

Wooley, Catherine. *Gus Was a Christmas Ghost*. Illus. by Seymour Fleishman. New York: Morrow, 1970.
071 Ghosts; 083.03 Holidays—Christmas; 115 Museums.

Wooley, Catherine. *Gus Was a Friendly Ghost.* Illus. by Seymour Fleishman. New York: Morrow, 1962.
068 Friendship; 071 Ghosts.

Wooley, Catherine. *Gus Was a Gorgeous Ghost.* Illus. by Seymour Fleishman. New York: Morrow, 1978.
031 Clothing; 071 Ghosts; 083.07 Holidays—Halloween.

Wooley, Catherine. *The Horse with the Easter Bonnet.* Illus. by Jay Hyde Barnum. New York: Morrow, 1953.
008.28 Animals—horses; 031 Clothing; 083.04 Holidays—Easter.

Wooley, Catherine. *I Like Trains.* Illus. by George Fonseca. New York: Harper, 1965.
179 Trains.

Wooley, Catherine. *The Little House; A New Math Story-Game.* Illus. by Don Madden. New York: Morrow, 1972.
033 Counting; 069 Games.

Wooley, Catherine. *Mr. Turtle's Magic Glasses.* Illus. by Mamoru R. Funai. New York: Morrow, 1971.
016.04 Behavior—boredom; 073 Glasses; 103 Magic; 142.05 Reptiles—turtles.

Wooley, Catherine. *Part-Time Dog.* Illus. by Seymour Fleishman. New York: Morrow, 1954.
008.14 Animals—dogs; 016.26 Behavior—needing someone.

Wooley, Catherine. *The Popcorn Dragon.* Illus. by Seymour Fleishman. New York: Morrow, 1953.
046 Dragons; 063 Food; 068 Friendship.

Wooley, Catherine. *The Puppy Who Wanted a Boy.* Illus. by Seymour Fleishman. New York: Morrow, 1958.
008.14 Animals—dogs; 083.03 Holidays—Christmas.

Wooley, Catherine. *Quiet on Account of Dinosaur.* Illus. by Seymour Fleishman. New York: Morrow, 1964.
044 Dinosaurs; 120 Noise.

Wooley, Catherine. *Rockets Don't Go to Chicago, Andy.* Illus. by Meg Wohlberg. New York: Morrow, 1965.
002.16 Activities—traveling; 089 Imagination; 165 Space and space ships; 179 Trains.

Wooley, Catherine. *What's a Ghost Going to Do?* Illus. by Seymour Fleishman. New York: Morrow, 1966.

071 Ghosts; 086 Houses; 137 Problem solving.

Wooster, Mae. *My Busy Day.* Illus. by Ruth Griffin. Chicago: Melmont, 1954.
057 Family life; 134 Poetry, rhyme.

Wright, Betty Ren. *Teddy Bear's Book of 1, 2, 3.* Illus. by Gerry Swart. Racine, WI: Western Pub., 1969.
033 Counting; 177.08 Toys—teddy bears.

Wright, Dare. *The Doll and the Kitten.* Illus. by author. Garden City, NY: Doubleday, 1960.
008.09 Animals—cats; 177.04 Toys—dolls; 177.08 Toys—teddy bears.

Wright, Dare. *Edith and Big Bad Bill.* Illus. by author. New York: Random House, 1968.
177.04 Toys—dolls; 177.08 Toys—teddy bears.

Wright, Dare. *Edith and Little Bear Lend a Hand.* Illus. by author. New York: Random House, 1972.
049 Ecology; 177.04 Toys—dolls; 177.08 Toys—teddy bears.

Wright, Dare. *Edith and Midnight.* Illus. by author. Garden City, NY: Doubleday, 1978.
177.04 Toys—dolls; 177.08 Toys—teddy bears.

Wright, Dare. *Edith and Mr. Bear.* Illus. by author. New York: Random House, 1964.
016.27 Behavior—running away; 177.04 Toys—dolls; 177.08 Toys—teddy bears.

Wright, Dare. *A Gift from the Lonely Doll.* Illus. by author. New York: Random House, 1966.
177.04 Toys—dolls; 177.08 Toys—teddy bears.

Wright, Dare. *Holiday for Edith and the Bears.* Illus. by author. Garden City, NY: Doubleday, 1958.
002.17 Activities—vacationing; 153 Sea and seashore; 177.04 Toys—dolls; 177.08 Toys—teddy bears.

Wright, Dare. *The Little One.* Illus. by author. Garden City, NY: Doubleday, 1959.
177.04 Toys—dolls; 177.08 Toys—teddy bears.

Wright, Dare. *The Lonely Doll.* Illus. by author. Garden City, NY: Doubleday, 1957.
177.04 Toys—dolls; 177.08 Toys—teddy bears.

Wright, Dare. *The Lonely Doll Learns a Lesson.* Illus. by author. New York: Random House, 1961.
008.09 Animals—cats; 131 Pets; 177.04 Toys—dolls; 177.08 Toys—teddy bears.

Wright, Dare. *Look at a Calf.* Illus. by author. New York: Random House, 1974.
008.12 Animals—cows, bulls; 058 Farms.

Wright, Dare. *Look at a Colt.* Illus. by author. New York: Random House, 1969.
008.28 Animals—horses; 058 Farms.

Wright, Dare. *Look at a Kitten.* Illus. by author. New York: Random House, 1975.
008.09 Animals—cats.

Wright, Ethel. *Saturday Walk.* Illus. by Richard Rose. Reading: Addison-Wesley, 1941/1954.
002.18 Activities—walking; 029 City; 057.01 Family life—fathers.

Wright, Josephine. *Cotton Cat and Martha Mouse.* Illus. by John E. Johnson. New York: Dutton, 1966.
008.09 Animals—cats; 008.34 Animals—mice; 016.31 Behavior—sharing; 134 Poetry, rhyme.

Wright, Lula Esther. *Little Lost Dog.* Illus. by Winifred Bromhall. Lexington, MA: Heath, 1955.
008.14 Animals—dogs; 016.20 Behavior—lost.

Wyler, Rose. *Spooky Tricks.* Illus. by Talivaldis Stubis. New York: Harper, 1968.
103 Magic.

Wynants, Miche. *The Giraffe of King Charles X.* Illus. by author. New York: McGraw-Hill, 1961.
008.20 Animals—giraffes; 064.11 Foreign lands—France; 147 Royalty.

Wyse, Lois. *Two Guppies, a Turtle, and Aunt Edna:* Illus. by Roger Coast. Cleveland: Collins, 1966.
057 Family life; 060 Fish; 137 Problem solving; 142.05 Reptiles—turtles; 172 Telephone.

Yabuki, Seiji. *I Love the Morning.* Illus. by author. Cleveland: Collins, 1969.
052.05 Emotions—happiness; 112 Morning.

Yamaguchi, Marianne Illenberger. *Two Crabs and the Moonlight.* Illus. by author. New York: Holt, 1965.
037 Crustacea; 111 Moon.

Yashima, Taro (pseud.). See Iwamatsu, Jun.

Yeoman, John. *The Bears' Water Picnic.* Illus. by Quentin Blake. New York: Macmillan, 1970.
002.11 Activities—picnicking; 005 Amphibians; 008.06 Animals—bears; 008.26 Animals—hedgehogs; 008.42 Animals—pigs; 008.56 Animals—squirrels.

Yeoman, John. *Mouse Trouble.* Illus. by Quentin Blake. New York: Macmillan, 1972.
008.09 Animals—cats; 008.34 Animals—mice; 068 Friendship; 198 Windmills.

Yezback, Steven. *Pumpkinseeds.* Illus. by Mozelle Thompson. Indianapolis: Bobbs-Merrill, 1969.
016.33 Behavior—solitude; 029 City; 053.01 Ethnic groups in the U.S.—Afro-Americans.

Ylla (pseud.). See Koffler, Camilla.

Yolen, Jane. *The Emperor and the Kite.* Illus. by Ed Young. Cleveland: Collins, 1967.
026.31 Character traits—smallness; 064.06 Foreign lands—China; 094 Kites; 147 Royalty.

Yolen, Jane. *The Giants' Farm.* Illus. by Thomas Anthony de Paola. New York: Seabury Pr., 1977.
058 Farms; 072 Giants.

Yolen, Jane. *Greyling; A Picture Story for the Islands of Shetland.* Illus. by William Stobbs. Cleveland: Collins, 1968.
062 Folk and fairy tales; 064.31 Foreign lands—Scotland.

Yolen, Jane. *An Invitation to the Butterfly Ball; A Counting Rhyme.* Illus. by Jane Breskin Zalben. New York: Parents, 1976.
008 Animals; 033 Counting; 134 Poetry, rhyme.

Yolen, Jane. *Milkweed Days.* Illus. by Gabriel Amadeus. New York: Crowell, 1976.
154.03 Seasons—summer.

Yolen, Jane. *No Bath Tonight.* Illus. by Nancy Winslow Parker. New York: Crowell, 1978.

002.02 Activities—bathing; 039 Days of the week, months of the year;
057.02 Family life—grandparents; great-grandparents.

Yolen, Jane. *The Seeing Stick*. Illus. by Remy Charlip, and Demetra Maraslis. New York: Crowell, 1977.
064.06 Foreign lands—China;
077.01 Handicaps—blindness;
147 Royalty.

Youldon, Gillian. *Colors*. Illus. by author. New York: Watts, 1979.
032.01 Concepts—color; 067 Format, unusual.

Youldon, Gillian. *Numbers*. Illus. by author. New York: Watts, 1979.
033 Counting; 067 Format, unusual.

Youldon, Gillian. *Shapes*. Illus. by author. New York: Watts, 1979.
032.07 Concepts—shape; 067 Format, unusual.

Youldon, Gillian. *Sizes*. Illus. by author. New York: Watts, 1979.
032.08 Concepts—size; 067 Format, unusual.

Young, Ed, jt. author. *The White Wave: A Chinese Tale*. By Diane Wolkstein, and Ed Young.

Young, Evelyn. *Tale of Tai*. Illus. by author. New York: Oxford Univ. Pr., 1940.
016.20 Behavior—lost; 064.06 Foreign lands—China; 083.02 Holidays—Chinese New Year.

Young, Evelyn. *Wu and Lu and Li*. Illus. by author. New York: Oxford Univ. Pr., 1939.
057 Family life; 064.06 Foreign lands—China.

Young, Miriam Burt. *Beware the Polar Bear! Safety on Ice*. Illus. by Robert Mead Quackenbush. New York: Lothrop, 1970.
148 Safety; 166.09 Sports—ice skating;
195.02 Weather—cold.

Young, Miriam Burt. *If I Drove a Bus*. Illus. by Robert Mead Quackenbush. New York: Lothrop, 1973.
021 Buses.

Young, Miriam Burt. *If I Drove a Car*. Illus. by Robert Mead Quackenbush. New York: Lothrop, 1971.
012 Automobiles.

Young, Miriam Burt. *If I Drove a Tractor*. Illus. by Robert Mead Quackenbush. New York: Lothrop, 1973.
102 Machines.

Young, Miriam Burt. *If I Drove a Train*. Illus. by Robert Mead Quackenbush. New York: Lothrop, 1972.
179 Trains.

Young, Miriam Burt. *If I Drove a Truck*. Illus. by Robert Mead Quackenbush. New York: Lothrop, 1967.
184 Trucks.

Young, Miriam Burt. *If I Flew a Plane*. Illus. by Robert Mead Quackenbush. New York: Lothrop, 1970.
004 Airplanes.

Young, Miriam Burt. *If I Rode a Dinosaur*. Illus. by Robert Mead Quackenbush. New York: Lothrop, 1976.
044 Dinosaurs.

Young, Miriam Burt. *If I Rode a Horse*. Illus. by Robert Mead Quackenbush. New York: Lothrop, 1973.
008.28 Animals—horses.

Young, Miriam Burt. *If I Rode an Elephant*. Illus. by Robert Mead Quackenbush. New York: Lothrop, 1974.
008.17 Animals—elephants.

Young, Miriam Burt. *If I Sailed a Boat*. Illus. by Robert Mead Quackenbush. New York: Lothrop, 1971.
019 Boats, ships.

Young, Miriam Burt. *Jellybeans for Breakfast*. Illus. by Beverly Komoda. New York: Parents, 1968.
089 Imagination; 121 Non-sexist.

Young, Miriam Burt. *Miss Suzy's Easter Surprise*. Illus. by Arnold Stark Lobel. New York: Parents, 1972.
008.56 Animals—squirrels;
083.04 Holidays—Easter.

Young, Miriam Burt. *Please Don't Feed Horace*. Illus. by Abner Graboff. New York: Dial Pr., 1961.
008.27 Animals—hippopotami;
204 Zoos.

Young, Miriam Burt. *The Witch Mobile*. Illus. by Victoria Dickerson Chess. New York: Lothrop, 1969.
083.07 Holidays—Halloween;
199 Witches.

Yudell, Lynn Deena. *Make a Face*. Illus. by author. Boston: Little, 1970.
006 Anatomy; 052 Emotions;
069 Games; 129 Participation.

Yulya (pseud.). See Whitney, Julie.

Yurdin, Betty. *The Tiger in the Teapot.* Illus. by William Pène Du Bois. Minneapolis: Winston Pr., 1967.
008.10 Animals—cats, wild;
054 Etiquette.

Zacharis, Boris. *But Where Is the Green Parrot?* Illus. by Wanda Zacharis. New York: Delacorte Pr., 1968.
017.15 Birds—parrots, parakeets;
032.01 Concepts—color; 069 Games.

Zaffo, George J. *The Big Book of Real Airplanes.* Illus. by author. New York: Grosset, 1951.
004 Airplanes; 080 Helicopters.

Zaffo, George J. *The Big Book of Real Building and Wrecking Machines.* Illus. by author. New York: Grosset, 1951.
102 Machines.

Zaffo, George J. *The Big Book of Real Fire Engines.* Illus. by author. New York: Grosset, 1950.
023.10 Careers—firefighters.

Zaffo, George J. *The Big Book of Real Trucks.* Illus. by author. New York: Grosset, 1950.
184 Trucks.

Zaffo, George J. *The Giant Book of Things in Space.* Illus. by author. Garden City, NY: Doubleday, 1969.
165 Space and space ships.

Zaffo, George J. *The Giant Nursery Book of Things That Go.* Illus. by author. Garden City, NY: Doubleday, 1959.
004 Airplanes; 019 Boats, ships;
180 Transportation; 184 Trucks.

Zaffo, George J. *The Giant Nursery Book of Things That Work.* Illus. by author. Garden City, NY: Doubleday, 1967.
176 Tools; 180 Transportation.

Zagone, Theresa. *No Nap for Me.* Illus. by Lillian Hoban. New York: Dutton, 1978.
016.14 Behavior—growing up;
162 Sleep.

Zakhoder, Boris. *How a Piglet Crashed the Christmas Party.* Illus. by Kurt Werth. New York: Lothrop, 1971.
008.42 Animals—pigs;
083.03 Holidays—Christmas.

Zakhoder, Boris. *Rosachok.* Illus. by Yaroslava Surmach Mills. A Russian story translated by Marguerita Rudolph. New York: Lothrop, 1970.
005 Amphibians; 008 Animals;
016.09 Behavior—dissatisfaction;
026.23 Character traits—optimism.

Zalben, Jane Breskin. *Basil and Hillary.* Illus. by author. New York: Macmillan, 1975.
008 Animals; 008.42 Animals—pigs;
058 Farms.

Zallinger, Peter. *Dinosaurs.* Illus. by author. New York: Random House, 1977.
044 Dinosaurs; 152 Science.

Zemach, Harve. *Duffy and the Devil.* Illus. by Margot Zemach. New York: Farrar, 1973.
042 Devil; 062 Folk and fairy tales;
064.10 Foreign lands—England.

Zemach, Harve. *The Judge.* Illus. by Margot Zemach. New York: Farrar, 1969.
023.14 Careers—judges; 110 Monsters;
134 Poetry, rhyme.

Zemach, Harve. *Mommy Buy Me a China Doll.* Illus. by Margot Zemach. Adapted by Harve Zemach. Chicago: Follett, 1966.
038 Cumulative tales; 116 Music;
164 Songs; 177.04 Toys—dolls.

Zemach, Harve. *Nail Soup.* Illus. by Margot Zemach. Chicago: Follett, 1964.
026.06 Character traits—cleverness;
062 Folk and fairy tales; 064.35 Foreign lands—Sweden.

Zemach, Harve. *A Penny a Look.* Illus. by Margot Zemach. New York: Farrar, 1971.
087 Humor.

Zemach, Harve. *The Speckled Hen; A Russian Nursery Rhyme.* Illus. by Margot Zemach. New York: Holt, 1966.
017.04 Birds—chickens; 038 Cumulative tales; 050 Eggs; 064.30 Foreign lands—Russia; 122 Nursery rhymes.

Zemach, Harve. *The Tricks of Master Dabble.* Illus. by Margot Zemach. New York: Holt, 1965.
016.36 Behavior—trickery; 087 Humor;
147 Royalty.

Zemach, Margot. *Hush, Little Baby.* Illus. by author. New York: Dutton, 1976.
038 Cumulative tales; 064.10 Foreign lands—England; 087 Humor;
116 Music; 164 Songs.

Zemach, Margot. *It Could Always Be Worse.* Illus. by author. New York: Farrar, 1976.
062 Folk and fairy tales; 087 Humor;
093 Jewish culture; 137 Problem solving.

Zemach, Margot. *The Little Tiny Woman*. Illus. by author. Indianapolis: Bobbs-Merrill, 1965.
062 Folk and fairy tales; 071 Ghosts.

Zemach, Margot. *To Hilda for Helping*. Illus. by author. New York: Farrar, 1977.
026.14 Character traits—helpfulness;
052.03 Emotions—envy, jealousy;
057 Family life.

Ziegler, Ursina. *Squaps the Moonling*. Illus. by Sita Jucker. Translated by Barbara Kowal Gollob. New York: Atheneum, 1969.
111 Moon; 165 Space and space ships.

Zijlstra, Tjerk. *Benny and His Geese*. Illus. by Ivo de Weerd. New York: McGraw-Hill, 1975.
017.11 Birds—geese; 062 Folk and fairy tales; 200 Wizards.

Zimelman, Nathan. *Once When I Was Five*. Illus. by Carol Rogers. Austin: Steck-Vaughn, 1967.
018 Birthdays; 089 Imagination.

Zimelman, Nathan. *To Sing a Song as Big as Ireland*. Illus. by Joseph Low. Chicago: Follett, 1967.
016.38 Behavior—wishing;
064.17 Foreign lands—Ireland;
051 Elves and little people;
083.09 Holidays—St. Patrick's Day;
116 Music.

Zimelman, Nathan. *Walls Are to Be Walked On*. Illus. by Donald Carrick. New York: Dutton, 1977.
002.18 Activities—walking.

Zimmerman, Andrea Griffin. *Yetta the Trickster*. Illus. by Harold Berson. New York: Seabury Pr., 1978.
064.30 Foreign lands—Russia;
087 Humor.

Zimnik, Reiner. *The Bear on the Motorcycle*. Illus. by author. Translated by Cornelia Schaeffer. New York: Atheneum, 1963.
008.06 Animals—bears;
016.27 Behavior—running away;
028 Circus, clowns; 113 Motorcycles.

Zimnik, Reiner. *Little Owl*. Illus. by Hanne Axmann. New York: Atheneum, 1962.
017.14 Birds—owls.

Zimnik, Reiner. *The Proud Circus Horse*. Illus. by author. New York: Pantheon, 1957.
008.28 Animals—horses;
016.27 Behavior—running away;
026.27 Character traits—pride;
028 Circus, clowns.

Zindel, Paul. *I Love My Mother*. Illus. by John Melo. New York: Harper, 1975.
052.07 Emotions—loneliness;
052.08 Emotions—love; 057.03 Family life—mothers.

Ziner, Feenie. *Counting Carnival*. Illus. by Paul Galdone. New York: Coward, 1962.
002.12 Activities—playing;
033 Counting; 038 Cumulative tales;
053.01 Ethnic groups in the U.S. — Afro-Americans; 128 Parades;
134 Poetry, rhyme.

Ziner, Feenie, and Thompson, Elizabeth. *The True Book of Time*. Illus. by Katherine Evans. Chicago: Children's Pr., 1956.
174 Time.

Zion, Gene. *All Falling Down*. Illus. by Margaret Bloy Graham. New York: Harper, 1951.
032.10 Concepts—up and down.

Zion, Gene. *Dear Garbage Man*. Illus. by Margaret Bloy Graham. New York: Harper, 1957.
023.13 Careers—garbage collectors;
029 City.

Zion, Gene. *Harry and the Lady Next Door*. Illus. by Margaret Bloy Graham. New York: Harper, 1960.
008.14 Animals—dogs; 120 Noise;
137 Problem solving.

Zion, Gene. *Harry by the Sea*. Illus. by Margaret Bloy Graham. New York: Harper, 1965.
008.14 Animals—dogs; 153 Sea and seashore; 154.03 Seasons—summer.

Zion, Gene. *Harry the Dirty Dog*. Illus. by Margaret Bloy Graham. New York: Harper, 1956.
002.02 Activities—bathing;
008.14 Animals—dogs;
016.27 Behavior—running away.

Zion, Gene. *Hide and Seek Day*. Illus. by Margaret Bloy Graham. New York: Harper, 1954.
016.15 Behavior—hiding; 029 City;
069 Games.

Zion, Gene. *Jeffie's Party*. Illus. by Margaret Bloy Graham. New York: Harper, 1957.
069 Games; 130 Parties.

Zion, Gene. *The Meanest Squirrel I Ever Met*. Illus. by Margaret Bloy Graham. New York: Scribner's, 1962.
008.56 Animals—squirrels;
026.22 Character traits—meanness;
068 Friendship.

Zion, Gene. *No Roses for Harry!* Illus. by Margaret Bloy Graham. New York: Harper, 1958.
008.14 Animals—dogs; 031 Clothing.

Zion, Gene. *The Plant Sitter*. Illus. by Margaret Bloy Graham. New York: Harper, 1959.
133 Plants.

Zion, Gene. *Really Spring*. Illus. by Margaret Bloy Graham. New York: Harper, 1956.
154.02 Seasons—spring.

Zion, Gene. *The Sugar Mouse Cake*. Illus. by Margaret Bloy Graham. New York: Scribner's, 1964.
002.03 Activities—cooking;
008.34 Animals—mice;
023.03 Careers—bakers; 063 Food;
147 Royalty.

Zion, Gene. *The Summer Snowman*. Illus. by Margaret Bloy Graham. New York: Harper, 1955.
083.05 Holidays—Fourth of July;
154.03 Seasons—summer;
163 Snowmen; 195.07 Weather—snow.

Zirbes, Laura. *How Many Bears?* Illus. by E. Harper Johnson. New York: Putnam's, 1960.
008.06 Animals—bears; 033 Counting.

Zoll, Max Alfred. *Animal Babies*. Illus. by author. Translated by Violetta Castillo. Edited by Hanns Reich. New York: Hill & Wang, 1971.
008 Animals.

Zolotow, Charlotte Shapiro. *The Beautiful Christmas Tree*. Illus. by Ruth Robbins. Berkeley: Parnassus, 1972.
083.03 Holidays—Christmas; 181 Trees.

Zolotow, Charlotte Shapiro. *Big Brothers*. Illus. by Mary Eileen Chalmers. New York: Harper, 1960.
016.32 Behavior—sibling rivalry;
057 Family life.

Zolotow, Charlotte Shapiro. *Big Sister and Little Sister*. Illus. by Martha G. Alexander. New York: Harper, 1966.
016.27 Behavior—running away;
057 Family life.

Zolotow, Charlotte Shapiro. *The Bunny Who Found Easter*. Illus. by Betty F. Peterson. Berkeley: Parnassus, 1959.
008.46 Animals—rabbits;
083.04 Holidays—Easter.

Zolotow, Charlotte Shapiro. *Do You Know What I'll Do?* Illus. by Garth Montgomery Williams. New York: Harper, 1958.
013 Babies; 052.08 Emotions—love;
057 Family life.

Zolotow, Charlotte Shapiro. *A Father Like That*. Illus. by Ben Shecter. New York: Harper, 1971.
045 Divorce; 057 Family life;
057.01 Family life—fathers;
089 Imagination.

Zolotow, Charlotte Shapiro. *The Hating Book*. Illus. by Ben Shecter. New York: Harper, 1969.
016.12 Behavior—gossip;
052.06 Emotions—hate; 068 Friendship.

Zolotow, Charlotte Shapiro. *Hold My Hand*. Illus. by Thomas di Grazia. New York: Harper, 1972.
068 Friendship; 195.07 Weather—snow.

Zolotow, Charlotte Shapiro. *If It Weren't for You*. Illus. by Ben Shecter. New York: Harper, 1966.
016.32 Behavior—sibling rivalry;
057.04 Family life—the only child.

Zolotow, Charlotte Shapiro. *In My Garden*. Illus. by Roger Antoine Duvoisin. New York: Lothrop, 1960.
133 Plants; 154 Seasons.

Zolotow, Charlotte Shapiro. *It's Not Fair*. Illus. by William Pène Du Bois. New York: Harper, 1976.
016.09 Behavior—dissatisfaction;
052.03 Emotions—envy, jealousy;
057 Family life.

Zolotow, Charlotte Shapiro. *Janey*. Illus. by Ronald Norbert Himler. New York: Harper, 1973.
052.07 Emotions—loneliness;
068 Friendship; 114 Moving.

Zolotow, Charlotte Shapiro. *May I Visit?* Illus. by Erik Blegvad. New York: Harper, 1976.
016.14 Behavior—growing up;
057 Family life; 052.08 Emotions—love.

Zolotow, Charlotte Shapiro. *Mr. Rabbit and the Lovely Present*. Illus. by Maurice Sendak. New York: Harper, 1962.
008.46 Animals—rabbits; 018 Birthdays;
032.01 Concepts—color; 057.03 Family life—mothers; 083.04 Holidays—Easter.

Zolotow, Charlotte Shapiro. *My Friend John*. Illus. by Ben Shecter. New York: Harper, 1968.
068 Friendship.

Zolotow, Charlotte Shapiro. *My Grandson Lew*. Illus. by William Pène Du Bois. New York: Harper, 1974.
040 Death; 057 Family life;
057.02 Family life—grandparents;
great-grandparents.

Zolotow, Charlotte Shapiro. *One Step, Two*. Illus. by Roger Antoine Duvoisin. New York: Lothrop, 1955.
002.18 Activities—walking; 029 City;
033 Counting.

Zolotow, Charlotte Shapiro. *Over and Over*. Illus. by Garth Montgomery Williams. New York: Harper, 1957.
083 Holidays; 174 Time.

Zolotow, Charlotte Shapiro. *The Park Book*. Illus. by Hans Augusto Rey. New York: Harper, 1944.
002.12 Activities—playing; 029 City.

Zolotow, Charlotte Shapiro. *The Poodle Who Barked at the Wind*. Illus. by Roger Antoine Duvoisin. New York: Lothrop, 1964.
008.14 Animals—dogs; 120 Noise;
131 Pets.

Zolotow, Charlotte Shapiro. *The Quarreling Book*. Illus. by Arnold Stark Lobel. New York: Harper, 1963.
016.10 Behavior—fighting, arguing;
038 Cumulative tales;
052.01 Emotions—anger.

Zolotow, Charlotte Shapiro. *The Quiet Mother and the Noisy Little Boy*. Illus. by Kurt Werth. New York: Viking, 1953.
120 Noise.

Zolotow, Charlotte Shapiro. *A Rose, a Bridge and a Wild Black Horse*. Illus. by Uri Shulevitz. New York: Harper, 1964.
052.08 Emotions—love.

Zolotow, Charlotte Shapiro. *The Sky Was Blue*. Illus. by Garth Montgomery Williams. New York: Harper, 1963.
052.08 Emotions—love; 057 Family life.

Zolotow, Charlotte Shapiro. *The Sleepy Book*. Illus. by Vladimir Bobri. New York: Lothrop, 1958.
015 Bedtime; 162 Sleep.

Zolotow, Charlotte Shapiro. *Someday*. Illus. by Arnold Stark Lobel. New York: Harper, 1965.
016.38 Behavior—wishing; 047 Dreams.

Zolotow, Charlotte Shapiro. *Someone New*. Illus. by Erik Blegvad. New York: Harper, 1978.
016.14 Behavior—growing up;
057 Family life.

Zolotow, Charlotte Shapiro. *The Storm Book*. Illus. by Margaret Bloy Graham. New York: Harper, 1952.
052.04 Emotions—fear; 195 Weather;
195.05 Weather—rain;
195.06 Weather—rainbows.

Zolotow, Charlotte Shapiro. *The Summer Night*. Illus. by Ben Shecter. New York: Harper, 1974.
002.18 Activities—walking;
015 Bedtime; 057 Family life;
057.01 Family life—fathers.

Zolotow, Charlotte Shapiro. *The Three Funny Friends*. Illus. by Mary Eileen Chalmers. New York: Harper, 1961.
052.07 Emotions—loneliness;
068 Friendship; 089.01 Imagination—imaginary friends.

Zolotow, Charlotte Shapiro. *A Tiger Called Thomas*. Illus. by Kurt Werth. New York: Lothrop, 1963.
026.30 Character traits—shyness;
052.07 Emotions—loneliness;
083.07 Holidays—Halloween.

Zolotow, Charlotte Shapiro. *The Unfriendly Book*. Illus. by William Pène Du Bois. New York: Harper, 1975.
016.10 Behavior—fighting, arguing;
068 Friendship.

Zolotow, Charlotte Shapiro. *Wake Up and Good Night*. Illus. by Leonard Weisgard. New York: Harper, 1971.
015 Bedtime; 112 Morning; 119 Night.

Zolotow, Charlotte Shapiro. *When I Have a Little Girl*. Illus. by Hilary Knight. New York: Harper, 1955.
016.14 Behavior—growing up;
057 Family life; 089 Imagination.

Zolotow, Charlotte Shapiro. *When I Have a Son*. Illus. by Hilary Knight. New York: Harper, 1967.
016.14 Behavior—growing up;
057 Family life; 089 Imagination

Zolotow, Charlotte Shapiro. *When the Wind Stops*. Illus. by Howard Clayton Knotts. New York: Abelard-Schuman, 1962.
015 Bedtime; 119 Night;
195.08 Weather—wind.

Zolotow, Charlotte Shapiro. *The White Marble*. Illus. by Lilian Obligado. New York: Abelard-Schuman, 1963.
002.12 Activities—playing;
068 Friendship; 119 Night.

Zolotow, Charlotte Shapiro. *William's Doll.* Illus. by William Pène Du Bois. New York: Harper, 1972.
057 Family life; 057.02 Family life—grandparents; great-grandparents; 121 Non-sexist; 177.04 Toys—dolls.

Zweifel, Frances W. *Bony.* Illus. by Whitney Darrow, Jr. New York: Harper, 1977.
008.56 Animals—squirrels; 131 Pets.

Title Index

Animals in the Zoo (Feodor Stepanovich Rojankovsky)
Animals on the Ceiling (Richard Willard Armour)
Animals on the Farm (Feodor Stepanovich Rojankovsky)
Animals 'Round the Mulberry Bush (Tony Palazzo)
Animals That Live in the Sea (Joan Ann Straker)
Ann Can Fly (Frederick B. Phleger)
Anna and the Baby Buzzard (Helga Sandburg)
Anna, the Horse (Louise Fatio)
Annabelle (Ruth Bornstein)
Anna's Silent World (Bernard Wolf)
Annie's Spending Spree (Nancy Dingman Watson)
Anno's Alphabet (Mitsumasa Anno)
Anno's Counting Book (Mitsumasa Anno)
Anno's Journey (Mitsumasa Anno)
The Annotated Mother Goose (Mother Goose)
Another Day (Marie Hall Ets)
Another Story to Tell (Dick Bruna)
Answer Me That (Suzanne E. Dennis)
The Ant and the Elephant (Bill Peet)
An Anteater Named Arthur (Bernard Waber)
Ants Are Fun (Mildred Myrick)
The Ants Go Marching (Berniece Freschet)
Anybody at Home? (Hans Augusto Rey)
Apartment 3 (Ezra Jack Keats)
Ape in Cape (Fritz Eichenberg)
An Apple a Day (Judith Barrett)
Apple Pie (Anne Wellington)
Apples (Nonny Hogrogian)
Apples to Zippers (Patricia Ruben)
Appley Dapply's Nursery Rhymes (Beatrix Potter)
Apricot ABC (Miska Miles)
April Fools (Fernando Krahn)
April's Kittens (Clare Turlay Newberry)
Aranea (Jenny Wagner)
Are We Lost, Daddy? (Leonard P. Kessler)
Are You My Mother? (Philip Day Eastman)
Arm in Arm (Remy Charlip)
The Armadillo Who Had No Shell (Sidney B. Simon)
Around and Around...Love (Betty Miles)
Around the City (Bank Street College of Education)
Around the Year (Tasha Tudor)
Arrow to the Sun; A Pueblo Indian Tale (Gerald McDermott)
The Art Fair (Mary Villarejo)
Arthur's Christmas Cookies (Lillian Hoban)
Arthur's Eyes (Marc Tolon Brown)
Arthur's Honey Bear (Lillian Hoban)
Arthur's New Power (Russell Conwell Hoban)
Arthur's Pen Pal (Lillian Hoban)

Arthur's Prize Reader (Lillian Hoban)
As I Was Crossing Boston Common (Norma Farber)
As Right as Right Can Be (Anne K. Rose)
As the Leaves Fall Down (Aileen Lucia Fisher)
Ask Mr. Bear (Marjorie Flack)
At Home; A Visit in Four Languages (Esther Hautzig)
At Our House (Lois L. Lenski)
At the Beach (Tobi Tobias)
At the Zoo (Lillian Colonius, and Glen W. Schroeder)
August Explains (Phil Ressner)
Aunt Agatha, There's a Lion under the Couch! (Wende Devlin, and Harry Devlin)
Aunt Bella's Umbrella (William Cole)
The Authentic Mother Goose Fairy Tales and Nursery Rhymes (Jacques Barchilon, and Henry Pettit)
Authorized Autumn Charts of the Upper Red Canoe River Country (Peter Zachary Cohen)
Autumn Harvest (Alvin R. Tresselt)
Away in a Manger (Mares Nussbaumer, and Paul Nussbaumer)
Away Went Wolfgang (Virginia Caroline Kahl)

B

B Is for Bear; An ABC (Dick Bruna)
Babar and Father Christmas (Jean de Brunhoff)
Babar and His Children (Jean de Brunhoff)
Babar and the Willy-Wully (Laurent de Brunhoff)
Babar and Zephir (Jean de Brunhoff)
Babar Comes to America (Laurent de Brunhoff)
Babar Loses His Crown (Laurent de Brunhoff)
Babar the King (Jean de Brunhoff)
Babar Visits Another Planet (Laurent de Brunhoff)
Babar's Birthday Surprise (Laurent de Brunhoff)
Babar's Castle (Laurent de Brunhoff)
Babar's Cousin, That Rascal Arthur (Laurent de Brunhoff)
Babar's Fair Will Be Opened Next Sunday (Laurent de Brunhoff)
Babar's Mystery (Laurent de Brunhoff)
Baboushka and the Three Kings (Ruth Robbins)
Baby (Fran Manushkin)
The Baby Beebee Bird (Diane Redfield Massie)

Benjie on His Own (Joan M. Lexau)
Benjy and the Barking Bird (Margaret Bloy Graham)
Benjy's Blanket (Myra Berry Brown)
Benjy's Boat Trip (Margaret Bloy Graham)
Benjy's Dog House (Margaret Bloy Graham)
Bennett Cerf's Book of Animal Riddles (Bennett Alfred Cerf)
Bennett Cerf's Book of Laughs (Bennett Alfred Cerf)
Bennett Cerf's Book of Riddles (Bennett Alfred Cerf)
Benny and His Geese (Tjerk Zijlstra)
Benny and the Bear (Barbee Oliver Carleton)
Benny Rabbit and the Owl (Joseph Low)
Benny's Animals and How He Put Them in Order (Millicent Ellis Selsam)
Benny's Four Hats (Ruth Jaynes)
The Berenstain Bears and the Spooky Old Tree (Stanley Berenstain, and Janice Berenstain)
The Berenstain Bears' Counting Book (Stanley Berenstain, and Janice Berenstain)
The Berenstains' B Book (Stanley Berenstain, and Janice Berenstain)
Best Friends (Myra Berry Brown)
Best Friends (Miriam Cohen)
Best Friends for Frances (Russell Conwell Hoban)
Best Little House (Aileen Lucia Fisher)
The Best Mom in the World (Judy Delton, and Elaine Knox-Wagner)
The Best New Thing (Isaac Asimov)
The Best of Friends (Josephine Haskell Aldridge)
Best of Luck (Myra Berry Brown)
The Best of the Bargain (Janina Domanska)
The Best Train Set Ever (Pat Hutchins)
Betsy and Peter Are Different (Gunilla Wolde)
Betsy and the Chicken Pox (Gunilla Wolde)
Betsy and the Doctor (Gunilla Wolde)
Betsy and the Vacuum Cleaner (Gunilla Wolde)
Betsy's Baby Brother (Gunilla Wolde)
Betsy's First Day at Nursery School (Gunilla Wolde)
Betsy's Fixing Day (Gunilla Wolde)
Beware the Polar Bear! Safety on Ice (Miriam Burt Young)
Bhombal Dass, the Uncle of Lion (Ashraf Siddiqui)
Bianco and the New World (Tony Palazzo)
Biddy and the Ducks (Arensa Sondergaard, and Mary M. Reed)
Big Anthony and the Magic Ring (Thomas Anthony de Paola)
Big Bad Bruce (Bill Peet)

A Big Ball of String (Marion Holland)
The Big Book of Real Airplanes (George J. Zaffo)
The Big Book of Real Building and Wrecking Machines (George J. Zaffo)
The Big Book of Real Fire Engines (George J. Zaffo)
The Big Book of Real Trucks (George J. Zaffo)
Big Boss (Anne F. Rockwell)
Big Brother (Robert Kraus)
Big Brothers (Charlotte Shapiro Zolotow)
A Big City (Francine B. Grossbart)
Big Cowboy Western (Ann Herbert Scott)
A Big Fat Enormous Lie (Marjorie Weinman Sharmat)
The Big Golden Animal ABC (Garth Montgomery Williams)
The Big Hello (Janet Schulman)
The Big Jump and Other Stories (Benjamin Elkin)
Big Little Davy (Lois L. Lenski)
Big Max (Kin Platt)
Big Max in the Mystery of the Missing Moose (Kin Platt)
Big Ones, Little Ones (Tana Hoban)
Big Orange Splot (Manus Pinkwater)
Big Puppy and Little Puppy (Irma Simonton Black)
The Big Rain (Françoise Seignobosc)
Big Red Hen (Mary O'Neill)
Big Sister and Little Sister (Charlotte Shapiro Zolotow)
Big Sister Tells Me That I'm Black (Arnold Adoff)
The Big Snow (Berta Hoerner Hader, and Elmer Stanley Hader)
Big Store, Funny Door (Betty Russell)
The Big Yellow Balloon (Edward Fenton)
The Biggest Bear (Lynd Kendall Ward)
The Biggest Christmas Tree on Earth (Fernando Krahn)
The Biggest Family in the Town (Helen L. Hoke)
The Biggest Fish in the Sea (Dahlov Zorach Ipcar)
The Biggest House (Ruth Jaynes)
The Biggest House in the World (Leo Lionni)
Bikes (Dolores M. Baugh, and Marjorie P. Pulsifer)
Bill and Pete (Thomas Anthony de Paola)
Billions of Bugs (Haris Petie)
Billy and Blaze (Clarence William Anderson)
Billy and Our New Baby (Helen S. Arnstein)
Billy Boy (Illus. by Glen H. Rounds)
Billy Goat and His Well-Fed Friends (Nonny Hogrogian)
Billy the Barber (Dorothy Kunhardt)

C

Fresh Cider and Apple Pie (Franz Brandenberg)
Friday Night Is Papa Night (Ruth A. Sonneborn)
The Friend (John Mackintosh Burningham)
A Friend Is "Amie" (Charlotte Steiner)
A Friend Is Someone Who Likes You (Joan Walsh Anglund)
Friend of Miguel (Patricia Miles Martin)
Friendly Animals (Louis Slobodkin)
The Friendly Beasts and A Partridge in a Pear Tree (Illus. by Virginia Parsons)
Friendly Farm Animals (Esther K. Meeks)
The Friendly Wolf (Paul Goble)
Friends, Friends, Friends (Ruth Jaynes)
The Friends of Abu Ali (Dorothy O. Van Woerkom)
Frisky (Lydia Perera)
Frog and Toad All Year (Arnold Stark Lobel)
Frog and Toad Are Friends (Arnold Stark Lobel)
Frog and Toad Together (Arnold Stark Lobel)
The Frog Band and Durrington Dormouse (Jim Smith)
The Frog Band and the Onion Seller (Jim Smith)
Frog Fun (Clara Georgeanna Stratemeyer, and Henry Lee Smith, Jr.)
Frog Goes to Dinner (Mercer Mayer)
A Frog He Would A-Wooing Go (Illus. by William Stobbs)
The Frog in the Well (Alvin R. Tresselt)
Frog on His Own (Mercer Mayer)
The Frog Prince (Jane White Canfield)
Frog Went A-Courtin'. (Illus. by Feodor Stepanovich Rojankovsky)
Frog, Where Are You? (Mercer Mayer)
Frogs, Merry (Juliet Kepes)
From A to Z (Irene Coletta, and Hallie Coletta)
From King Boggen's Hall to Nothing at All (Blair Lent)
From Little to Big; A Parade of Animal Poems (Eleanor Graham Vance, comp.)
The Frowning Prince (David Johnson Leisk)
Fumio and the Dolphins (Chiyoko Nakatani)
Fun in American Folk Rhymes (Ray Wood)
Fun on Wheels (Joanna Cole)
The Funny Baby (Margaret Hillert)
The Funny Bunny Factory (Adam Green)
Funny Feet (Leatie Weiss)
A Funny Friend from Heaven (Fernando Krahn)
The Funny Little Woman (Arlene Mosel)
The Funny Thing (Wanda Gág)

G

A Gaggle of Geese (Eve Merriam)
Galumpf (Brenda Lansdown)
A Garland of Games and Other Diversions (Barbara Cooney)
Garth Pig and the Ice Cream Lady (Mary Rayner)
The Gay ABC (Françoise Seignobosc)
The Gay Mother Goose (Mother Goose)
The General (Janet Charters, and Michael Foreman)
George (Phyllis Rowand)
George and Martha (James Marshall)
George and Martha Encore (James Marshall)
George and Martha One Fine Day (James Marshall)
George and Martha Rise and Shine (James Marshall)
George Appleton (Mary Eileen Chalmers)
George Goes to Town (Phyllis Rowand)
George the Babysitter (Shirley Hughes)
George the Drummer Boy (Nathaniel Benchley)
Georgie (Robert Bright)
Georgie and the Noisy Ghost (Robert Bright)
Georgie and the Robbers (Robert Bright)
Georgie Goes West (Robert Bright)
Georgie to the Rescue (Robert Bright)
Georgie's Christmas Carol (Robert Bright)
Georgie's Halloween (Robert Bright)
Geraldine, the Music Mouse (Leo Lionni)
Gertie the Duck (Nicholas P. Georgiady)
Gertrude, the Goose Who Forgot (Joanna Galdone)
Ghost in a Four-Room Apartment (Ellen Raskin)
A Ghost Named Fred (Nathaniel Benchley)
The Ghost with the Halloween Hiccups (Stephen Mooser)
The Giant Alexander (Frank Herrmann)
The Giant Alexander and the Circus (Frank Herrmann)
The Giant Book of Things in Space (George J. Zaffo)
The Giant Devil-Dingo (Dick Roughsey)
Giant John (Arnold Stark Lobel)
The Giant Nursery Book of Things That Go (George J. Zaffo)
The Giant Nursery Book of Things That Work (George J. Zaffo)
The Giant of Grabbist (John D. Lawrence)
Giant Otto (William Pène Du Bois)
The Giant Story (Beatrice Schenk De Regniers)
The Giant's Birthday (Janet McNeill)
Giants Come in Different Sizes (Roger Bradfield)
The Giants' Farm (Jane Yolen)

Grandmother Lucy in Her Garden (Joyce Wood)

Grandpa, Me and Our House in the Tree (Barbara Kirk)

Grandparents around the World (Dorka Raynor)

Grandpa's Farm (James Flora)

Granny and the Desperadoes (Peggy Parish)

Granny and the Indians (Peggy Parish)

Granny, the Baby and the Big Gray Thing (Peggy Parish)

Grasshopper and Butterfly (Helen Piers)

Grasshopper on the Road (Arnold Stark Lobel)

The Great Ape (Fernando Krahn)

The Great Big Animal Book (Feodor Stepanovich Rojankovsky)

The Great Big Car and Truck Book (Richard McClure Scarry)

The Great Big Enormous Turnip (Alekesi Nikolaevich Tolstoy)

A Great Big Ugly Man Came Up and Tied His Horse to Me (Wallace Tripp)

The Great Big Wild Animal Book (Feodor Stepanovich Rojankovsky)

The Great Blueness and Other Predicaments (Arnold Stark Lobel)

The Great Cat Chase (Mercer Mayer)

The Great Custard Pie Panic (Scott Corbett)

A Great Day for Up (Theodor Seuss Geisel)

The Great Fish (Peter Parnall)

Great-Grandfather in the Honey Tree (Samuel F. Swayne, and Zoa Swayne)

The Great Picture Robbery (Leon A. Harris)

Green Eggs and Ham (Theodor Seuss Geisel)

The Green Grass Grows All Around (Illus. by Hilde Hoffman)

Green Light, Go (Bank Street College of Education)

Green Says Go (Edward Randolph Emberley)

The Greentail Mouse (Leo Lionni)

Gregory Griggs and Other Nursery Rhyme People (Arnold Stark Lobel)

Gregory, the Noisiest and Strongest Boy in Grangers Grove (Robert Bright)

Greg's Microscope (Millicent Ellis Selsam)

Greyling; A Picture Story for the Islands of Shetland (Jane Yolen)

Grimm Tom Thumb (Illus. by Svend Otto)

Grizzwold (Sydney Hoff)

The Groober (Betsy Cromer Byars)

The Grouchy Ladybug (Eric Carle)

The Growing Story (Ruth Krauss)

Growl Bear (Margot Austin)

Grumpus and the Venetian Cat (Rosalie Seidler)

The Guard Mouse (Don Freeman)

The Guess Book (Charles Green Shaw)

Guess Who Lives Here (Louise Phinney Woodcock)

Guess Who My Favorite Person Is (Byrd Baylor)

The Guest (James Marshall)

The Guinea Pigs That Went to School (Leonard Meshover, and Sally Feistel)

Gumdrop, the Adventures of a Vintage Car (Val Biro)

Gunhilde and the Halloween Spell (Virginia Caroline Kahl)

Gunhilde's Christmas Booke (Virginia Caroline Kahl)

The Gunniwolf (Wilhelmina Harper, reteller)

Gus and the Baby Ghost (Catherine Wooley)

Gus Was a Christmas Ghost (Catherine Wooley)

Gus Was a Friendly Ghost (Catherine Wooley)

Gus Was a Gorgeous Ghost (Catherine Wooley)

Gwendolyn and the Weathercock (Nancy Sherman)

Gwendolyn the Miracle Hen (Nancy Sherman)

Gyo Fujikawa's A to Z Picture Book (Gyo Fujikawa)

H

The Habits of Rabbits (Virginia Caroline Kahl)

Hair (Illus. by Christine Sharr)

Half for You (Meyer Azaad)

Halfway up the Mountain (Theo E. Gilchrist)

Halloween Party (Lonzo Anderson)

Hamilton (Robert Newton Peck)

Hand, Hand, Fingers, Thumb (Al Perkins)

Handella (Robert Tallon)

Hans and Peter (Heidrun Petrides)

Hans in Luck (Jakob Ludwig Karl Grimm, and Wilhelm Karl Grimm)

Hansi (Ludwig Bemelmans)

Happy Birthday, Sam (Pat Hutchins)

Happy Birthday to You (Theodor Seuss Geisel)

The Happy Day (Ruth Krauss)

Happy Easter (Kurt Wiese)

The Happy Egg (Ruth Krauss)

Happy-Go-Lucky (William Wiesner)

Happy Hunter (Roger Antoine Duvoisin)

Happy Jack (Malcolm Carrick)

The Happy Lion (Louise Fatio)

The Happy Lion and the Bear (Louise Fatio)

I

J

K

M

M Is for Moving (Velma Ilsley)
Ma nDa La (Arnold Adoff)
Mabel the Whale (Patricia King)
McElligot's Pool (Theodor Seuss Geisel)
Machines (Anne F. Rockwell, and Harlow Rockwell)
Madeline (Ludwig Bemelmans)
Madeline and the Bad Hat (Ludwig Bemelmans)
Madeline and the Gypsies (Ludwig Bemelmans)
Madeline in London (Ludwig Bemelmans)
Madeline's Rescue (Ludwig Bemelmans)
Madge's Magic Show (Mike Thaler)
The Maggie B (Irene Haas)
The Magic Auto (Horst Eckert)
The Magic Balloon (Iela Mari)
The Magic Beans (Margaret Hillert)
The Magic Convention (Sandra Hochman)
The Magic Feather Duster (William Lipkind, and Nicolas Mordvinoff)
Magic in the Mist (Margaret Mary Kimmel)
Magic Michael (Louis Slobodkin)
The Magic of Millicent Musgrave (Brinton Cassady Turkle)
The Magic Porridge Pot (Paul Galdone)
The Magic Pot (Patricia Coombs)
The Magic Pumpkin (Gloria Skurzynski)
The Magic Tree (James McCrea, and Ruth McCrea)
The Magic Tree; A Tale from the Congo (Gerald McDermott)
The Magic Wallpaper (Frank Francis)
The Magician (Uri Shulevitz)
The Magician of Cracow (Krystyna Turska)
The Maid and Her Pail of Milk (Katherine Evans)
Maila and the Flying Carpet (Denise Trez, and Alain Trez)
Make a Face (Lynn Deena Yudell)
Make Way for Ducklings (Robert John McCloskey)
Making Babies (Sara Bonnett Stein)
Mama, I Wish I Was Snow. Child, You'd Be Very Cold (Ruth Krauss)
The Man of the House (Joan Fassler)
The Man on the Flying Trapeze (Robert Mead Quackenbush)
The Man, the Boy, and the Donkey (Katherine Evans)
The Man Who Did Not Wash His Dishes (Phyllis Krasilovsky)
The Man Who Lost His Head (Claire Huchet Bishop)
The Man Who Made Fine Tops (Marie Winn)
The Man Who Was Going to Mind the House (David McKee)
The Mango Tooth (Charlotte Pomerantz)

The Mannerly Adventures of Little Mouse (Martha Keenan)
Manners Can Be Fun (Munro Leaf)
Manuela's Birthday in Old Mexico (Laura May Bannon)
The Many Lives of Chio and Goro (Betty Jean Lifton)
Many Moons (James Thurber)
Marc and Pixie and the Walls in Mrs. Jones's Garden (Louise Fatio, and Roger Antoine Duvoisin)
Marc the Magnificent (Sue Alexander)
The Marcel Marceau Counting Book (George Mendoza)
Marcella's Guardian Angel (Evaline Ness)
The March Wind (Inez Rice)
The Mare's Egg (Judy Varga)
Marie Louise's Heyday (Natalie Savage Carlson)
Marigold Garden (Kate Greenaway)
Marina (Ludwig Bemelmans)
Marshmallow (Clare Turlay Newberry)
The Marshmallow Ghosts (Priscilla Friedrich, and Otto Friedrich)
Martha Matilda O'Toole (Jim Copp)
Martha the Movie Mouse (Arnold Stark Lobel)
Martha's Mad Day (Miranda Hapgood)
Martin's Dinosaur (Reda Davis)
The Marvelous Merry-Go-Round (Jane Werner Watson)
Marvin K. Mooney, Will You Please Go Now! (Theodor Seuss Geisel)
Mary Alice, Operator Number 9 (Jeffrey Allen)
Mary Ann's Mud Day (Janice May Udry)
Mary Jo's Grandmother (Janice May Udry)
Master of All Masters (Joseph Jacobs)
Master of the Royal Cats (Jerzy Laskowski)
Matt's Mitt (Marilyn Sachs)
Max (Rachel Isadora)
Max and the Truffle Pig (Judith Gwyn Brown)
Max the Mouse (James Cressey)
Maxie (Virginia Caroline Kahl)
May I Bring a Friend? (Beatrice Schenk De Regniers)
May I Stay? (Harry Allard)
May I Visit? (Charlotte Shapiro Zolotow)
Maybelle, the Cable Car (Virginia Lee Burton)
Me and My Captain (Marilyn Brooks Goffstein)
Me and Nessie (Eloise Greenfield)
Me and the Bears (Robert Bright)
Me Day (Joan M. Lexau)
Mean Melissa (Michelle Price)
The Mean Mouse and Other Mean Stories (Janice May Udry)
The Mean Old Mean Hyena (Jack Prelutsky)

My Mama Says There Aren't Any:
Zombies, Ghosts, Vampires,
Creatures, Demons, Monsters,
Fiends, Goblins, or Things (Judith
Viorst)

My Mom Hates Me in January (Judy
Delton)

My Mother and I (Aileen Lucia Fisher)

My Mother the Mail Carrier: Mi Mama la
Cartera (Inez Maury)

My Noah's Ark (Marilyn Brooks Goffstein)

My Nursery School (Harlow Rockwell)

My Own Little House (Merriman B.
Kaune)

My Plant (Herbert H. Wong, and Matthew
F. Vassel)

My Red Umbrella (Robert Bright)

My Slippers Are Red (Charlotte Steiner)

My Special Best Words (John Steptoe)

My Teddy Bear (Chiyoko Nakatani)

My Uncle Podger (Wallace Tripp)

My Very Own Special Particular Private
and Personal Cat (Sandol Stoddard
Warburg)

My Zoo (Hermann Fay)

Mysteries in the Garden (Aileen Lucia
Fisher)

The Mysterious Tadpole (Steven Kellogg)

Mystery of the Gate Sign (Margaret
Friskey)

The Mystery of the Giant Footprints
(Fernando Krahn)

The Mystery of the Magic Green Ball
(Steven Kellogg)

The Mystery of the Missing Red Mitten
(Steven Kellogg)

N

N Is for Nursery School (Blossom Budney)

Nabob and the Geranium (Judith R.
Miller)

Nail Soup (Harve Zemach)

Nana Upstairs and Nana Downstairs
(Thomas Anthony de Paola)

Nancy's Backyard (Eros Keith)

Nanette the Hungry Pelican (William Wise)

Na-Ni (Alexis Deveaux)

Naptime (Gylbert Coker)

Natasha's New Doll (Frank Francis)

Nate the Great (Marjorie Weinman
Sharmat)

Nate the Great and the Lost List (Marjorie
Weinman Sharmat)

Nate the Great and the Phony Clue
(Marjorie Weinman Sharmat)

Nate the Great Goes Undercover (Marjorie
Weinman Sharmat)

The Naughty Bird (Peter Wezel)

Naughty Nancy (John Strickland Goodall)

A Near Thing for Captain Najork (Russell
Conwell Hoban)

The Neighbors (Marcia Brown)

A Nest of Wood Ducks (Evelyn S. Shaw)

Never Say Ugh to a Bug (Norma Farber)

Never Talk to Strangers (Irma Joyce)

New at the Zoo (Peter Lippman)

New Blue Shoes (Eve Rice)

New Boots for Salvador (Susan Gaston)

A New Day (Donald Alan Bolognese)

New Dog Next Door (Elizabeth P.
Bridgman)

The New Girl at School (Judy Delton)

A New Home for Snow Ball (Joan Chase
Bowden)

The New Pet (Marjorie Flack)

The New Teacher (Miriam Cohen)

New World for Nellie (Fredrick Rowland
Emmett)

Next Please (Robert E. Barry)

Nic of the Woods (Lynd Kendall Ward)

Nice Little Girls (Elizabeth Levy)

Nice New Neighbors (Franz Brandenberg)

The Nicest Gift (Leo Politi)

Nicholas' Favorite Pet (Inger Sandberg)

The Nickle Nackle Tree (Lynley Dodd)

Nicola Bayley's Book of Nursery Rhymes
(Nicola Bayley)

The Night Before Christmas (Clement
Clarke Moore) (Illus. by Gyo
Fujikawa)

The Night Before Christmas (Clement
Clarke Moore) (Illus. by Gustaf
Tenggren)

The Night Before Christmas (Clement
Clarke Moore) (Illus. by Tasha
Tudor)

The Night It Rained Toys (Dorothy
Stephenson)

The Night Ride (Aingelda Ardizzone)

The Night the Lights Went Out (Don
Freeman)

Night's Nice (Barbara Emberley, and
Edward Randolph Emberley)

Nikos and the Sea God (Hardie Gramatky)

Nils (Ingri Mortenson d'Aulaire, and
Edgar Parin d'Aulaire)

Nine Days to Christmas (Marie Hall Ets)

Nine Hundred Buckets of Paint (Edna
Becker)

Ninety-Nine Pockets (Jean Lockwood
Myrick)

The No-Bark Dog (Stan Williamson)

No Bath Tonight (Jane Yolen)

No Dogs Allowed, Jonathan! (Mary Blount
Christian)

No Ducks in Our Bathtub (Martha G.
Alexander)

No Fighting, No Biting! (Else Holmelund
Minarik)

No Funny Business (Edith Thacher Hurd)

No Kiss for Mother (Tomi Ungerer)

O

P

The Tale of Squirrel Nutkin (Beatrix Potter)

Tale of Tai (Evelyn Young)

The Tale of the Faithful Dove (Beatrix Potter)

The Tale of the Flopsy Bunnies (Beatrix Potter)

The Tale of the Turnip (Anita Hewett)

The Tale of Timmy Tiptoes (Beatrix Potter)

The Tale of Tuppenny (Beatrix Potter)

The Tale of Two Bad Mice (Beatrix Potter)

Talk to Me, Tiger (Dick Snyder)

The Talking Crocodile (M. Rudolph Campbell, adapter)

Talking Without Words; I Can. Can You? (Marie Hall Ets)

The Tall Book of Make-Believe (Jane Werner Watson)

The Tall Book of Mother Goose (Mother Goose)

The Tall Book of Nursery Rhymes (Illus. by Feodor Stepanovich Rojankovsky)

Tamarindo (Marcia Brown)

Taresh the Tea Planter (William Papas)

Taro and the Bamboo Shoot (Masako Matsuno)

Taro and the Tofu (Masako Matsuno)

Teach Us, Amelia Bedelia (Peggy Parish)

Teddy (Enid Warner Romanek)

Teddy Bear's Book of 1, 2, 3 (Betty Ren Wright)

Teddybears ABC (Susanna Gretz)

Teddybears One to Ten (Susanna Gretz)

The Teeny Tiny Woman (Barbara Seuling)

Teeny-Tiny and the Witch-Woman (Barbara K. Walker)

Teeth (Illus. by Michael Ricketts)

The Telephone (Kornei Chukovsky)

Telephones (Illus. by Christine Sharr)

Tell about the Cowbarn, Daddy (Jean Merrill)

Tell Me a Mitzi (Lore Groszmann Segal)

Tell Me a Trudy (Lore Groszmann Segal)

Tell Me, Mr. Owl (Doris Van Liew Foster)

Tell Me Please! What's That? (Ruth Jaynes)

Tell Me Some More (Crosby Newell Bonsall)

Tell Them My Name Is Amanda (Jo Anne Wold)

Ten Apples Up on Top! (Theodor Seuss Geisel)

Ten Bears in My Bed, a Goodnight Countdown (Stanley Mack)

Ten Big Farms (Dahlov Zorach Ipcar)

Ten Black Dots (Donald Crews)

Ten Brothers with Camels (Gladys Yessayan Cretan)

Ten Little Foxhounds (Christopher Gifford Ambler)

The Tent (Dorothy Z. Seymour)

The Tenth Good Thing about Barney (Judith Viorst)

The Terrible Terrier (Edith Battles)

Terrible Terrifying Toby (David Johnson Leisk)

The Terrible Thing That Happened at Our House (Marge Blaine)

The Terrible Tiger (Jack Prelutsky)

The Terrible Trick or Treat (Edith Battles)

Terrible Troll (Mercer Mayer)

The Terrible Troll-Bird (Ingri Mortenson d'Aulaire, and Edgar Parin d'Aulaire)

Terry and the Caterpillars (Millicent Ellis Selsam)

Thank You, Amelia Bedelia (Peggy Parish)

The Thank-You Book (Françoise Seignobosc)

Thank You—You're Welcome (Louis Slobodkin)

The Thanksgiving Story (Alice Dalgliesh)

That New Baby (Sara Bonnett Stein)

That New Boy (Mary Lystad)

That Pest Jonathan (William Cole)

That's Enough for One Day! (Susan Pearson)

That's Mine! (Elizabeth Winthrop)

That's Right Edie (Johanna Johnston)

That's What a Friend Is (Patrick K. Hallinan)

That's What It Is! (Ruth Jaynes)

Then What Did You Do? (Robert Pack)

Theodor Turtle (Ellen MacGregor)

Theodore (Edward Ormondroyd)

Theodore's Parents (Janice May Udry)

Theodore's Rival (Edward Ormondroyd)

There and Back Again (Harold Jones)

There Once Was a King (Gwain Sexton)

There Once Was a Woman Who Married a Man (Norma Farber)

There Was Timmy! (Sally Scott)

There'll Be a Hot Time in the Old Town Tonight (Robert Mead Quackenbush)

There's a Hippopotamus under My Bed (Mike Thaler)

There's a Nightmare in My Closet (Mercer Mayer)

There's a Wocket in My Pocket! (Theodor Seuss Geisel)

There's No Such Animal (Alf Evers)

There's No Such Thing as a Dragon (Jack Kent)

Thidwick, the Big Hearted Moose (Theodor Seuss Geisel)

The Thief in the Attic (Kurt Wiese)

The Thief Who Hugged a Moonbeam (Harold Berson)

The Thing in Dolores' Piano (Robert Tallon)

Things I Hate! (Harriet Wittels, and Joan Greisman)

The Things I Like (Françoise Seignobosc)

Things We Cut (Anthony Thomas)

The True Book of Time (Feenie Ziner, and Elizabeth Thompson)
The True Cross (Brian Wildsmith)
True or False? (Patricia Ruben)
The Truffle Pig (Claire Huchet Bishop)
Try and Catch Me (Nancy Jewell)
Try It Again, Sam (Judith Viorst)
Tubby and the Lantern (Al Perkins)
Tubby and the Poo-Bah (Al Perkins)
Tuggy (Clara Georgeanna Stratemeyer, and Henry Lee Smith, Jr.)
Tumble, the Story of a Mustang (Wesley Dennis)
Turnabout (William Wiesner)
The Turtle and the Dove (Don Freeman)
Turtle Pond (Berniece Freschet)
Turtle Spring (Lillian Hoban)
Tuttle's Shell (Salvatore Murdocca)
'Twas in the Moon of Wintertime (Roslyn Kroop Abisch)
Tweedles Be Brave! (Wolo [pseud.])
Twelve Bells for Santa (Crosby Newell Bonsall)
The Twelve Days of Christmas (Illus. by Ilonka Karasz)
Twenty Nursery Rhymes (Mother Goose)
Twenty Two Bears (Claire Huchet Bishop)
Twenty-One Children Plus Ten (Virginia H. Ormsby)
Two and Me Makes Three (Roberta Greene)
Two Can Toucan (David McKee)
Two Crabs and the Moonlight (Marianne Illenberger Yamaguchi)
Two Dog Biscuits (Beverly Cleary)
The Two Georges: Los Dos Jorges (Monica Gunning)
Two Greedy Bears (Mirra Ginsburg)
Two Guppies, a Turtle, and Aunt Edna (Lois Wyse)
Two Homes to Live In (Barbara Shook Hazen)
Two Hundred Rabbits (Lonzo Anderson, and Adrienne Adams)
Two Is a Team (Lorraine Levy Beim, and Jerrold Beim)
Two Little Bears (Camilla Koffler)
Two Lonely Ducks (Roger Antoine Duvoisin)
The Two Magicians (John Meredith Langstaff)
Two Moral Tales (Mercer Mayer)
The Two Reds (William Lipkind, and Nicolas Mordvinoff)
Two Roman Mice (Marilynne K. Roach)
Two Special Cards (Sonia O. Lisker, and Leigh Dean)
The Tyger Voyage (Richard George Adams)
Typewriter Town (William Jay Smith)
The Tyrannosaurus Game (Steven Kroll)

U

UFO Kidnap (Nancy Robison)
The Ugly Duckling (Hans Christian Andersen) (Illus. by Adrienne Adams)
The Ugly Duckling (Hans Christian Andersen) (Illus. by Johannes Larsen)
The Ugly Duckling (Hans Christian Andersen) (Illus. by Will Nickless)
The Ugly Duckling (Hans Christian Andersen) (Illus. by Josef Palecek)
Umbrella (Jun Iwamatsu)
Uncle Debunkel or Barely Believable Bear (Phoebe Erickson)
Uncle Eddie's Moustache (Bertolt Brecht)
Uncle Hugh, a Fishing Story (Rita Golden Gelman)
Under the Window (Kate Greenaway)
The Unexpected Grandchild (Jane Flory)
Unfortunately Harriet (Rosemary Wells)
The Unfriendly Book (Charlotte Shapiro Zolotow)
Up and Down and All Around (Marguerite Walters)
Up High and Down Low (Louis Slobodkin)
Up on a Hilltop (Kota Taniuchi)
Up the Alley with Jack and Joe (William Kotzwinkle)
Upside Down (David Johnson Leisk)
Upside-Downers (Mitsumasa Anno)
Uptown (John Steptoe)
Uptown, Downtown (Bank Street College of Education)

V

Veronica (Roger Antoine Duvoisin)
Veronica and the Birthday Present (Roger Antoine Duvoisin)
Veronica's Smile (Roger Antoine Duvoisin)
Very Far Away (Maurice Sendak)
The Very First Day (Ann Weil)
The Very First Story Ever Told (Lisl Weil)
The Very Hungry Caterpillar (Eric Carle)
The Very Little Boy (Phyllis Krasilovsky)
The Very Little Dog; and The Smart Little Kitty (Grace Marion Skaar, and Louise Phinney Woodcock)
The Very Little Girl (Phyllis Krasilovsky)
A Very Special House (Ruth Krauss)
The Very Tall Little Girl (Phyllis Krasilovsky)
Victoria's Castle (Felice Holman)
The Village Tree (Jun Iwamatsu)
Vim the Rag Mouse (Niki Daly)
The VIP's Mistake Book (Virgil Franklin Partch)

Y

Z

Illustrator Index

A

Adams, Adrienne. Bring a Torch, Jeannette, Isabella
Cabbage Moon (Jan Wahl)
The Christmas Party (Adrienne Adams)
The Day We Saw the Sun Come Up (Alice E. Goudey)
The Easter Bunny That Overslept (Priscilla Friedrich, and Otto Friedrich)
The Easter Egg Artists (Adrienne Adams)
Going Barefoot (Aileen Lucia Fisher)
Halloween Party (Lonzo Anderson)
Izzard (Lonzo Anderson)
The Littlest Witch (Jeanne Massey)
Mr. Biddle and the Birds (Lonzo Anderson)
Summer's Coming In (Natalie Maree Belting)
Theodore's Parents (Janice May Udry)
Thumbelina (Hans Christian Andersen)
Two Hundred Rabbits (Lonzo Anderson, and Adrienne Adams)
The Ugly Duckling (Hans Christian Andersen)
Where Does Everyone Go? (Aileen Lucia Fisher)
The White Rat's Tale (Barbara Schiller)
A Woggle of Witches (Adrienne Adams)
Adams, Pauline Batchelder. Picture Book Dictionary (Dilla Wittemore MacBean)
Adams, Pauline Batchelder, and Landreth, Marvelle. Our Good Health (Charles Christopher Wilson, and others)
Adams, Ruth Joyce. Fidelia (Ruth Joyce Adams)
Addams, Charles. The Charles Addams Mother Goose (Mother Goose)
Adler, David A. The House on the Roof (David A. Adler)
A Little at a Time (David A. Adler)

Agostinelli, Maria Enrica. I Know Something You Don't Know (Maria Enrica Agostinelli)
Agre, Patricia. Jeff's Hospital Book (Harriet L. Sobol)
My Brother Steven Is Retarded (Harriet L. Sobol)
Ahlberg, Allan, jt. illus. Burglar Bill (Janet Ahlberg, and Allan Ahlberg)
Each Peach Pear Plum; An "I Spy" Story (Janet Ahlberg, and Allan Ahlberg)
Ahlberg, Janet, and Ahlberg, Allan. Burglar Bill (Janet Ahlberg, and Allan Ahlberg)
Each Peach Pear Plum; An "I Spy" Story (Janet Ahlberg, and Allan Ahlberg)
Aichinger, Helga. I Never Saw (Judson Jerome)
Aitken, Amy. Ruby! (Amy Aitken)
Akino, Fuku. Sea Sums (Samuel French Morse)
Alajalov, Constantin. Timothy's Angels (William Rose Benét)
Albertson, Lee. The Day It Rained Watermelons (Mabel Watts)
Alexander, Martha G. And My Mean Old Mother Will Be Sorry, Blackboard Bear (Martha G. Alexander)
Big Sister and Little Sister (Charlotte Shapiro Zolotow)
Blackboard Bear (Martha G. Alexander)
Bobo's Dream (Martha G. Alexander)
Charles (Liesel Moak Skorpen)
Elizabeth (Liesel Moak Skorpen)
The Everyday Train (Amy Ehrlich)
I Sure Am Glad to See You, Blackboard Bear (Martha G. Alexander)
I'll Be the Horse If You'll Play with Me (Martha G. Alexander)
I'll Protect You from the Jungle Beasts (Martha G. Alexander)
Jeremy Isn't Hungry (Barbara Williams)
Mary Ann's Mud Day (Janice May Udry)

B

The Little House (Virginia Lee Burton)

Maybelle, the Cable Car (Virginia Lee Burton)

Mike Mulligan and His Steam Shovel (Virginia Lee Burton)

Byard, Carole. Africa Dream (Eloise Greenfield)

Byars, Betsy Cromer. The Groober (Betsy Cromer Byars)

Byfield, Barbara Ninde. The Haunted Churchbell (Barbara Ninde Byfield)

Byrd, Robert. Rebecca Hatpin (Robert Kraus)

C

Caldecott, Randolph. The Diverting History of John Gilpin (Randolph Caldecott)

Hey Diddle Diddle, and Baby Bunting (Randolph Caldecott)

Hey Diddle Diddle Picture Book (Randolph Caldecott)

Panjandrum Picture Book (Randolph Caldecott)

The Queen of Hearts (Randolph Caldecott)

Randolph Caldecott's John Gilpin and Other Stories (Randolph Caldecott)

Randolph Caldecott's Picture Book, No. 1 (Randolph Caldecott)

Randolph Caldecott's Picture Book, No. 2 (Randolph Caldecott)

Sing a Song for Sixpence (Randolph Caldecott)

The Three Jovial Huntsmen (Randolph Caldecott)

Cameron, Polly. The Cat Who Thought He Was a Tiger (Polly Cameron)

A Child's Book of Nonsense (Polly Cameron)

"I Can't," Said the Ant (Polly Cameron)

Campbell, Judy P. Big Red Hen (Mary O'Neill)

Cannon, Elizabeth. Why Worry? (Eric Kimmel)

Carigiet, Alois. A Bell for Ursli (Selina Chönz)

Florina and the Wild Bird (Selina Chönz)

The Pear Tree, the Birch Tree and the Barberry Bush (Alois Carigiet)

The Snowstorm (Selina Chönz)

Carle, Eric. All About Arthur (Eric Carle)

Do Bears Have Mothers Too? (Aileen Lucia Fisher)

Do You Want to Be My Friend? (Eric Carle)

The Grouchy Ladybug (Eric Carle)

Have You Seen My Cat? (Eric Carle)

The Hole in the Dike (Norma B. Green)

I See a Song (Eric Carle)

The Mixed-Up Chameleon (Eric Carle)

One, Two, Three to the Zoo (Eric Carle)

Pancakes, Pancakes (Eric Carle)

The Rooster Who Set Out to See the World (Eric Carle)

Secret Birthday Message (Eric Carle)

The Tiny Seed (Eric Carle)

The Very Hungry Caterpillar (Eric Carle)

Walter the Baker (Eric Carle)

Watch Out! A Giant! (Eric Carle)

Why Noah Chose the Dove (Isaac Bashevis Singer)

Carlos, Sanches M. Perez and Martina (Pura Belpré)

Carpentier, Ralph. Fish Out of School (Evelyn S. Shaw)

Octopus (Evelyn S. Shaw)

Carrick, Donald. The Accident (Carol Carrick)

Bear Mouse (Berniece Freschet)

A Clearing in the Forest (Carol Carrick, and Donald Carrick)

The Deer in the Pasture (Donald Carrick)

The Foundling (Carol Carrick)

The Highest Balloon on the Common (Carol Carrick, and Donald Carrick)

The Old Barn (Carol Carrick)

Old Mother Witch (Carol Carrick)

Peter and Mr. Brandon (Eleanor Schick)

A Rabbit for Easter (Carol Carrick)

Sleep Out (Carol Carrick)

Turtle Pond (Berniece Freschet)

Walls Are to Be Walked On (Nathan Zimelman)

The Washout (Carol Carrick)

A Wet and Sandy Day (Joanne Ryder)

Wind, Sand and Sky (Rebecca Caudill)

Carrick, Malcolm. Happy Jack (Malcolm Carrick)

Today Is Shrew's Day (Malcolm Carrick)

Carroll, Ruth Robinson. Pet Tale (Ruth Robinson Carroll, and Latrobe Carroll)

What Whiskers Did (Ruth Robinson Carroll)

Where's the Bunny? (Ruth Robinson Carroll)

Cartlidge, Michelle. Pippin and Pod (Michelle Cartlidge)

Carty, Leo. I Love Gram (Ruth A. Sonneborn)

Cassel, Lili. The Rainbow Mother Goose (Mother Goose)

Cassinelli, Attilio. Adam and the Wolf (Karen Gunthrop)

Cauley, Lorinda Bryan. Curley Cat Baby-Sits (Pauline Watson)

D

F

I

K

N

Nakàno, Hirotaka. Elephant Blue (Hirotaka Nakàno)

Nakatani, Chiyoko. The Brave Little Goat of Monsieur Seguin (Alphonse Daudet)

The Day Chiro Was Lost (Chiyoko Nakatani)

Fumio and the Dolphins (Chiyoko Nakatani)

The Hippo Boat (Eriko Kishida)

The Lion and the Bird's Nest (Eriko Kishida)

My Day on the Farm (Chiyoko Nakatani)

My Teddy Bear (Chiyoko Nakatani)

The Zoo in My Garden (Chiyoko Nakatani)

Napoli, Guillier. Adventure at Mont St. Michael (Guillier Napoli)

Nash, Linell. Custard the Dragon and the Wicked Knight (Ogden Nash)

Natti, Susanna. Midnight Moon (Clyde Watson)

Negri, Rocco. The Magic Pumpkin (Gloria Skurzynski)

The One Bad Thing About Father (Ferdinand N. Monjo)

Ness, Evaline. All in the Morning Early (Leclaire Alger)

Do You Have the Time, Lydia? (Evaline Ness)

Don't You Remember? (Lucille B. Clifton)

Everett Anderson's Christmas Coming (Lucille B. Clifton)

Exactly Alike (Evaline Ness)

The Girl and the Goatherd (Evaline Ness)

Joey and the Birthday Present (Maxine W. Kumin, and Anne Sexton)

Josefina February (Evaline Ness)

Josie and the Snow (Helen Elizabeth Buckley)

Josie's Buttercup (Helen Elizabeth Buckley)

Kellyburn Braes (Leclaire Alger)

Marcella's Guardian Angel (Evaline Ness)

Old Mother Hubbard and Her Dog (Sarah Catherine Martin)

Pavo and the Princess (Evaline Ness)

A Pocketful of Cricket (Rebecca Caudill)

Sam, Bangs and Moonshine (Evaline Ness)

Some of the Days of Everett Anderson (Lucille B. Clifton)

The Steamroller (Margaret Wise Brown)

Tom Tit Tot (Evaline Ness)

The Wizard's Tears (Maxine W. Kumin)

Neuhart, Marilyn. Nabob and the Geranium (Judith R. Miller)

Newberry, Clare Turley. April's Kittens (Clare Turlay Newberry)

Barkis (Clare Turlay Newberry)

Cousin Toby (Clare Turlay Newberry)

Herbert the Lion (Clare Turlay Newberry)

The Kittens' ABC (Clare Turlay Newberry)

Lambert's Bargain (Clare Turlay Newberry)

Marshmallow (Clare Turlay Newberry)

Mittens (Clare Turlay Newberry)

Pandora (Clare Turlay Newberry)

Percy, Polly and Pete (Clare Turlay Newberry)

Smudge (Clare Turlay Newberry)

T-Bone, the Baby-Sitter (Clare Turlay Newberry)

Widget (Clare Turlay Newberry)

Newell, Crosby. See Bonsall, Crosby Newell

Newell, Peter. Topsys and Turvys (Peter Newell)

Nichols, Marie C. Goomer (Dorothy Waldman)

Nicholson, William. Clever Bill (William Nicholson)

Nicklaus, Carol. Madge's Magic Show (Mike Thaler)

Nicklaus, Karol. Hey, Kid (Rita Golden Gelman)

Nickless, Will. The Ugly Duckling (Hans Christian Andersen)

Nicolas (pseud.). See Mordvinoff, Nicolas

Niland, Deborah. ABC of Monsters (Deborah Niland)

Niland, Deborah, jt. illus. Mulga Bill's Bicycle (Andrew Barton Paterson)

Niland, Kilmeny, and Niland, Deborah. Mulga Bill's Bicycle (Andrew Barton Paterson)

Ninon (pseud.). See MacKnight, Ninon

Nolan, Dennis. Wizard McBean and His Flying Machine (Dennis Nolan)

Nolden, Victor. The Fox and the Hare (Mirra Ginsburg)

Nook, Gerard. Have You Seen Roads? (Joanne Oppenheim)

Noonan, Julia. Peter's Pocket (Judith Barrett)

Puss in Boots (Charles Perrault)

Norman, Vera Stone. Christmas Time (Esther M. Schenk)

Numeroff, Laura Joffe. Amy for Short (Laura Joffe Numeroff)

Phoebe Dexter Has Harriet Peterson's Sniffles (Laura Joffe Numeroff)

You Can't Put Braces on Spaces (Alice Richter, and Laura Joffe Numeroff)

Q

T